DELPHI™
Developer's Guide

Xavier Pacheco
Steve Teixeira

SAMS
PUBLISHING

201 West 103rd Street
Indianapolis, Indiana 46290

With love, to my wonderful daughter, Amanda Nicole.—XP

For Skel, from Lou.—ST

Copyright © 1995 by Sams Publishing

FIRST EDITION

International Standard Book Number: 0-672-30704-9

Library of Congress Catalog Card Number: 94-074885

98 97 96 95   4 3 2 1

Interpretation of the printing code: the rightmost double-digit number is the year of the book's printing; the rightmost single-digit, the number of the book's printing. For example, a printing code of 95-1 shows that the first printing of the book occurred in 1995.

Composed in AGaramond and MCPdigital by Macmillan Computer Publishing

Printed in the United States of America

Publisher and President	*Richard K. Swadley*
Acquisitions Manager	*Greg Wiegand*
Development Manager	*Dean Miller*
Managing Editor	*Cindy Morrow*
Marketing Manager	*Gregg Bushyeager*
Assistant Marketing Manager	*Michelle Milner*
Aquisitions Editor	*Chris Denny*

Development Editor
Angelique Brittingham

Software Development Specialist
Tim Wilson

Production Editor
Kristi Hart

Copy Editors
Fran Blauw, Ryan Rader
Tonya Simpson

Technical Reviewers
Danny Thorpe, Pat Ritchey,
Jason Sprenger, Oktay Amiry
Rider Rishel

Editorial Coordinator
Bill Whitmer

Technical Edit Coordinator
Lynette Quinn

Formatter
Frank Sinclair

Editorial Assistant
Sharon Cox

Cover Designer
Tim Amrhein

Book Designer
Alyssa Yesh

Production Team Supervisor
Brad Chinn

Page Layout
Carol Bowers, Charlotte Clapp
Mary Ann Cosby, Terrie Deemer
Judy Everly, George Hanlin
Louisa Klucznik, Ayanna Lacey
Casey Price, Tina Trettin
Susan Van Ness, Mark Walchle
Dennis Wesner, Michelle Worthington

Proofreading
Georgiana Briggs, Michael Brumitt
Mike Dietsch, Donna Harbin
Mike Henry, Kevin Laseau
Paula Lowell, Donna Martin
Brian-Kent Proffitt, Erich Richter,
SA Springer

Indexer
Greg Eldred

Overview

Contents

II Real-World Building Blocks

III   Real-World Applications

Foreword

Delphi represents a small step in the evolution of development platforms yet a giant leap in the productivity of the developer. What makes Delphi, as a Rapid Application Development tool, unique is the fact that it was written by Delphi developers for Delphi developers. Because Delphi was written in itself, we had the opportunity to feel for ourselves what was right and what was wrong while developing the tool, and the end result is a programming environment not unlike a good book. Once you start using Delphi, it's difficult to put down.

Although Delphi provides an easy approach to Windows programming, real-world development with Delphi does require a good measure of application development know-how and an understanding of the underlying Windows API. Hence, the need for a book outlining these concepts written by Delphi developers for Delphi developers. I'm happy to say that Steve Teixeira and Xavier Pacheco have produced such a book in *Delphi Developer's Guide*.

Although Steve and Xavier's experience with Delphi dates back to the early days of the project, what makes this book special is the fact that Steve and Xavier hail from Borland's Technical Support department where they became intimately familiar with the issues important to you, the Delphi developer. That, combined with the fact that Danny Thorpe—one of the best and brightest in the business—handled the technical review for this work, leaves little doubt that *Delphi Developer's Guide* will be a valuable resource for all Delphi programmers.

I hope you get as much out of this book as Steve and Xavier have put into it, and I hope you have as much fun using Delphi as those of us on the Delphi development team had writing it.

Anders Hejlsberg, Delphi Chief Architect
Borland International, Inc.
Scotts Valley, California

Acknowledgments

If we knew how much work it was going to be before we started writing *Delphi Developer's Guide*, you might not be reading this right now. But here it is. We're proud of it, and we think we have created a unique work that developers will truly find useful.

We didn't do it alone, though, and we'd like to offer our sincere thanks to those who helped along the way. We want to point out, too, that any errors in this book are in spite of these folks' efforts and not because of them.

First and foremost, a big thank you goes to Danny Thorpe. Danny not only acted as technical reviewer for *Delphi Developer's Guide*, but it seems that every time we dipped into Danny's well of knowledge, we never came back thirsty. Much of the truly insightful portions of this book are Danny's own words—the sidebar on "DLL Voodoo" being only one example. With all the demands and pressures of getting Delphi shipped on schedule, we very much appreciate Danny's assistance, and we wonder if he ever sleeps.

Thanks to Pat Ritchey for handling portions of this book's technical review and also for some good code, including the `WinExecAndWait()` and the `Delay()` functions he contributed to Chapter 21, "Hard-Core Windows," and his techniques on making forms child windows.

Special thanks to Jeff Peters for his great work on Chapter 22, "Testing and Debugging," and for all his advice and tutelage along the way. Look up *guru* in the dictionary, and you'll see Jeff's smiling mug.

We want to thank Anders Hejlsberg for writing the foreword to *Delphi Developer's Guide*, and, of course, for playing a major role in making Delphi a reality.

Thanks to Kim Kokkonen and TurboPower Software for allowing us to write about Async Professional for Delphi. Also, thanks to Terry Hughes for the superb job on the APD Demo program.

Thanks to Scott Frolich for his Inventory Manager program shown in Chapter 29, "Inventory Manager—Preliminary Design Issues," and Chapter 30, "Inventory Manager—User Interface Development," and for the CD Player featured in the Chapter 13, "Multimedia Programming with Dephi." Scott not only shared his code, but also his advice and database expertise, and we really appreciate it.

Thank you, Charlie Calvert, for the nuggets of advice and technical insight. We also appreciate the patience of Matt Stave, our boss-man at Borland, for putting up with us.

Thank you to all our coworkers in Borland Delphi Technical Support who've offered their assistance along the way: particularly to Jason Sprenger, Ryder Rishel, and Oktay Amiry for doing an outstanding job on the Borland technical review, to Eric Uber and David Powell for their great work on the VCL poster, and to Todd Miller and Jim Allen for their advice on several chapters. Thanks, too, to all the Delphi users, particularly the field test group, whose questions and answers inspired much of the contents of this work.

We'd also like to thank the great staff at Sams Publishing, without whom this book wouldn't have been possible—Kristi Hart, Angelique Brittingham, Chris Denny, Fran Blauw, Greg Croy, and many others behind the scenes—for their hard work.

Special Thanks from Xavier

My first thanks goes to my mom, Martha—your strength and wisdom have been an inspiration. Thank you, Amanda, for making me an incredibly proud father. Many thanks to my cousin Monica, for being a good friend and an excellent listener. Finally, my deepest gratitude goes to my fiancée, Anne. Your patience, loving support, and encouraging words got me through many long hours of writing and coding. Mostly, thank you for saying, "Yes," and making me the happiest man in this world. I love you.

Special Thanks from Steve

I would first like to thank my mom, Debby—mostly for having the wisdom and trust to let me be me. Despite everything, things turned out just fine. I'd also like to thank my grandparents, Betty and Jerry, for always being there when the chips were down. Most of all, I extend my deepest thanks to my lovely wife, Helen. You're truly a special person, and I wouldn't have gotten through this book without your love, understanding, and support. I love you.

About the Authors

Xavier Pacheco is a Software Engineer at TurboPower Software Company. He previously was employed at Borland as a Consulting Engineer in Borland's Technical Support Department and currently writes articles for *The Delphi Magazine*. When not working, Xavier either is wrestling with his dog, finetuning his aim, or zooming down a snow-packed slope with a smile from ear to ear. Xavier lives in Colorado Springs, Colorado, with his soon-to-be wife, Anne, their German Shepherd, Sierra, and cat, Curry.

Steve Teixeira is a Senior Engineer in Borland International's Delphi Technical Support department. You'll find his articles published in several industry periodicals, including *The Delphi Magazine, Delphi Informant,* and *The Pascal Magazine.* When Steve is not sitting in front of a computer, you'll often find him on the basketball court or the firing range. Steve lives in Felton, California, with his wife, Helen, their two Labrador Retrievers, Dakota and Simba, and cat, Bob.

Introduction

Before we tell you what *Delphi Developer's Guide* is all about, we'd first like you to know what it is not. This book is not a regurgitation of the documentation that comes with Delphi. In fact, Delphi ships with some very detailed documentation, and, where appropriate, we point you to the proper place in the Delphi documentation or online help to obtain reference material. This book is not a users guide. Although we do demonstrate how to work within Delphi's Integrated Development Environment, that is by no means the focus of this work—this book provides you with a strong background in the fundamentals of programming Delphi and the Windows API. This book is not an encyclopedia. Although you will find that we discuss all the pertinent aspects of Delphi and the Windows API, we do so in the framework of applications development, where you learn by doing.

Simply stated, if you want to develop applications in Delphi, this is the book for you. Our goal is not just to show you how to develop applications using Delphi, but how to develop applications the right way. Delphi is a very unique tool that enables you to drastically reduce the time it takes to develop applications while still offering a level of performance that will please even the most cycle-stingy of developers. This book shows you how to get the best of these two worlds by demonstrating effective use of Delphi's design-time environment and proper techniques for code reuse and by showing you how to write good, clean, efficient code.

This book is divided into three parts. Part I, "Getting Started," is the largest part of the book. It provides you with strong foundations in all of the important aspects of Delphi programming. Part II, "Real-World Building Blocks," builds upon those foundations by helping you build small but useful utilities that take advantage of tip and tricks you learned in Part I. In Part III, "Real-World Applications," you use the techniques learned in the previous parts in building two large applications, from initial concept to production.

Who Should Read This Book

As the title of this book says, this book is for developers. So, if you're a developer, and you use Delphi, you should have this book. In particular, however, this book is aimed at three groups of people:

- Delphi developers who are looking to take their craft to the next level.
- Experienced Pascal, BASIC, or C/C++ programmers who are looking to hit the ground running with Delphi.
- Programmers who are looking to get the most out of Delphi by leveraging the Windows API and using some Delphi's less obvious features.

Conventions Used in This Book

The following typographic conventions are used in this book:

- Code lines, commands, statements, variables, program output, and any text you see on the screen appears in a `computer` typeface.
- Anything that you type appears in a **`bold computer`** typeface.
- Placeholders in syntax descriptions appear in an *`italic computer`* typeface. Replace the placeholder with the actual filename, parameter, or whatever element it represents.
- *Italics* highlight technical terms when they first appear in the text and sometimes are used to emphasize important points.
- Procedures and functions are indicated by open and close parentheses after the procedure or function name. Although this is not standard Pascal syntax, it helps to differentiate them from properties, variables, and types.

Within each chapter you will encounter several Note, Tips, and Cautions that help to highlight the important points and aid you in steering clear of the pitfalls.

You will find all the source code and project files on the CD-ROM accompanying this book, as well as source samples that we could not fit in the book itself. Also, take a look at the components and tools in the directory \THRDPRTY, where you'll find some powerful trial versions of third-party components.

Getting Started

Now it's time to relax and have some fun programming with Delphi. We'll start slow and gradually work into the more advanced topics at a comfortable pace. Before you know it, you'll have the knowledge and technique required to truly be called a Delphi guru.

I

Getting Started

1

Windows Programming in Delphi

This chapter explains how to use the Delphi Integrated Development Environment (IDE) and how programming Microsoft Windows with Delphi is different than with other languages and development environments. This chapter is intended for readers who have some Windows programming experience but are new to Delphi. If you have some experience programming in Delphi, it's okay to skip this chapter. You may, however, want to at least skim this chapter because it introduces many of the basic concepts you will use throughout the book.

A Little History

Delphi is, at heart, a Pascal compiler. Delphi is the next step in the evolution of the same Pascal compiler that Borland has been developing since Anders Hejlsberg wrote the first Turbo Pascal compiler more than 10 years ago. Pascal programmers throughout the years have enjoyed the stability, grace, and, of course, the compile speed that Turbo Pascal offers. Delphi is no exception. Anders still is responsible for Borland's Pascal compiler, and you will find the compiler that lies deep in the foundations of Delphi to be no less stable, graceful, and quick than any of its predecessors.

In the early days of DOS, programmers had a choice between productive-but-slow BASIC or efficient-but-complex assembly language. Turbo Pascal, which offered the simplicity of a structured language and the performance of a real compiler, bridged that gap. Windows programmers face a similar choice today—a choice primarily between a powerful yet unwieldy language such as C++, or a simple but limiting language such as Visual Basic. Delphi offers you a great deal: visual development and code generation, compiled executables, DLLs, databases, and the whole shebang.

What Is Delphi?

Delphi is a Rapid Application Development (sometimes called *RAD*) and database development tool for Microsoft Windows. Delphi is a visual, object-oriented, component-based development environment. What does all that mean? It's really not as imposing as it sounds.

The term *visual* refers to the fact that Delphi enables you to create applications by picking visual components from a Component palette and dropping them onto a window or form. The real beauty of this visual IDE, though, is that Delphi actually generates code for you as you drag and drop visual components onto your form. This approach to programming is similar to that of Microsoft's Visual Basic, but with one key difference: you can extend any of Delphi's components to suit your own needs. If you like everything about the functionality of a particular component but hate the way it is drawn on-screen, for example, you can create a descendant component that incorporates a new method for the component to draw itself. This is an object-oriented programming concept called *inheritance*. Inheritance is explained in more detail in Chapter 3, "The Object Pascal Language."

Database development refers to the fact that Delphi is an ideal tool to design database client applications that communicate with a variety of local or remote databases. The standard version of Delphi has the capability to connect to local Paradox, dBASE, and ODBC tables, and Delphi Client/Server comes with SQLLinks drivers for a variety of networked SQL server databases. If you're a database developer, this spells smooth scalability from local to remote databases. If you're a "regular programmer," this means you finally have a database engine built seamlessly into your development environments. Programmers don't have to rely on a third-party database library when they need the data-management capability of a true database in their applications.

Delphi's underlying language is a new and improved, object-oriented version of Pascal that Borland has dubbed *Object Pascal*. Object Pascal provides some excellent new additions to the Pascal language. *Exception handling* gives you the capability to detect and gracefully recover from errors. *Runtime Type Information* (RTTI) gives you the capability to determine the type of an object at runtime rather than compile time, as you previously only were capable of doing.

Visual Component Library, or VCL, is Delphi's object-oriented class framework. Similar to today's other major Windows frameworks, Object Windows Library (OWL) and Microsoft Foundation Classes (MFC), VCL provides an object-oriented cushion around the hairy Windows API. VCL's major advantage over these other frameworks is its close integration with the visual development environment. Each of the components that you drag and drop from the Component palette to a form is a VCL element or control.

The Delphi IDE

The Delphi IDE is divided into four main portions: the Code Editor, the form designer, the Object Inspector, and the main window. Figure 1.1 shows the main window.

FIGURE 1.1.
The main window in Delphi.

Think of the main window as the control center for the Delphi IDE. The main window has all the standard functionality of the main window of any other Windows program. It consists mainly of three parts: the main menu, the SpeedBar, and the Component palette. Like any Windows program, the main menu is where you go when you need to open, create, or save new projects, forms, units, or files. You also use the main menu when you need to cut, copy, paste, or bring up another programming tool such as Turbo Debugger or version control. The SpeedBar provides pushbutton access to some of the more commonly used main menu options.

Figure 1.2 shows Delphi's SpeedBar. The Component palette contains icons representing the Delphi components—such as buttons, listboxes, databases, and VBXs—that you can drop onto your forms. Because pictures on buttons often don't show what a particular button does, all the buttons on the SpeedBar and Component palette offer *Fly-by help hints*. These are little "bubbles" that contain a description of the function of a particular button. You activate the Fly-by help by leaving the mouse cursor on a button for more than a second or two.

FIGURE 1.2.
Delphi's SpeedBar.

> **TIP**
>
> Delphi's SpeedBar also is configurable! Right-click on Delphi's SpeedBar, and you will find options to add or remove buttons. For anything you can do with Delphi's pull-down menus, you can add a speed button to the SpeedBar to do it from there. Figure 1.3 illustrates a highly customized SpeedBar.

FIGURE 1.3.
A customized version of Delphi's SpeedBar.

The form designer begins as an empty window, ready for you to turn it into a Windows application. Consider the form designer your artist's canvas for creating Windows applications; here is where you determine how your applications will be represented visually to your users. You interact with the form designer by selecting components from the Component palette and dropping them onto your form. Once you have a particular component on the form, you can use the mouse to adjust the position or size of the component. You can control the appearance and behavior of these components by using the Object Inspector and Code Editor.

With the Object Inspector, you can modify a form's or component's properties or enable your form or component to respond to different events. *Properties* are data such as height, color, and font that determine how an object appears on-screen. *Events* are portions of code that are executed in response to occurrences within your application. A mouse click or a message to redraw itself are two examples of events. The Object Inspector window uses the *notebook tabs* metaphor for switching between component properties or events; just select the desired page from the tabs at the bottom of the window. The properties and events displayed in the Object Inspector reflect whichever form or component currently has focus in the form designer.

One of the most useful tidbits of knowledge that you, as a Delphi programmer, should know is that the help system is tightly integrated with the Object Inspector. If you ever get stuck on a particular property or event, just press the F1 key, and WinHelp comes to the rescue.

The Code Editor is where the actual programming—in the strictest sense—occurs. It is where you type the code that dictates how your program behaves, and where Delphi inserts the code that it generates based on the components in your application. The bottom of the Code Editor window contains notebook tabs, where each tab corresponds to a different source-code module in your program. Each time you add a new form to your application, a new unit is created and added to the set of tabs at the bottom of the Code Editor. You also can add units to your application that do not represent forms, and they will end up as a tab at the bottom of the Code Editor. The Code Editor also is tied closely to the help system, and pressing the F1 key while in the Code Editor casues Delphi to search its help files for the topic indicated by the token on which the cursor is located.

The Code Generator

The Delphi IDE generates code for you as you work with the visual components of the form designer. The most simplistic example of this capability is starting a new project. Select File | New Project in the main window to see a new form in the form designer and that form's source code skeleton in the Code Editor. The source code to the new form's unit is shown in Listing 1.1.

Listing 1.1. A program skeleton.

```
unit Unit1;

interface

uses
  SysUtils, WinTypes, WinProcs, Messages, Classes, Graphics, Controls,
  Forms, Dialogs;

type
  TForm1 = class(TForm)
  private
    { Private declarations }
  public
    { Public declarations }
  end;

var
  Form1: TForm1;

implementation

{$R *.DFM}

end.
```

It's important to note that the source code module associated with any form is stored in a unit. Although every form has a unit, not every unit has a form. If you're not familiar with how the Pascal language works and what exactly a unit is, you should pause right here and take a look at Chapter 2, "Moving to Pascal," which discusses the Pascal language for those of you who are new to Pascal from C, C++, Visual Basic, or another language.

The following construct:

```
TForm1 = class(TForm)
 private
  { Private declarations }
 public
  { Public declarations }
 end;
```

indicates that the form object itself is an object derived from TForm, and the space in which you can insert your own public and private variables is labeled clearly. Don't worry about what object, public, or private means right now. Chapter 3 discusses Object Pascal in more detail.

The following line is very important:

```
{$R *.DFM}
```

The $R directive in Pascal is used to load an external resource file. This line links the .DFM (which stands for *Delphi ForM*) file into the executable. The .DFM file contains a binary representation of the form you created in the form designer.

The application's project file is worth a glance, too. A project filename ends in .DPR (which stands for *Delphi PRoject*) and is really nothing more than a Pascal file with a funny extension. The project file is where the main portion of your program, in the Pascal sense, lives. Unlike in previous versions of Pascal, most of the "work" of your program is done in units rather than in the main module. Here is the project file from the sample application:

```
program Project1;

uses
  Forms,
  Unit1 in 'UNIT1.PAS' {Form1};

{$R *.RES}

begin
  Application.CreateForm(TForm1, Form1);
  Application.Run;
end.
```

As you add more forms and units to the application, they will appear in the uses clause of the project file. Notice, too, that after the name of a unit in the uses clause, the name of the related form appears in comments. If you ever get confused about which units go with which forms, you can regain your bearing by selecting View | Project manager to bring up the Project Manager window.

> **NOTE**
>
> Each form has exactly one unit associated with it, and you also can have other "code-only" units that are not associated with any form. In Delphi, you work mostly with units, and you rarely will edit the source code to your main program module, the .DPR file.

Creating a Small Application

The simple act of plopping a component such as a button onto a form causes code for that element to be generated and added to the Form object:

```
TForm1 = class(TForm)
  Button1: TButton;
private
  { Private declarations }
public
  { Public declarations }
end;
```

Now, as you can see, the button is an instance variable of the TForm1 class. When you refer to the button in other contexts later in your source code, you must remember to address it as part of TForm1's scope by saying Form1.Button1. Scoping is explained in more detail in Chapter 2, "Moving to Pascal."

When this button is selected in the form designer, you can change its behavior through the Object Inspector. Suppose that, at design-time, you want to change the width of the button to 100 pixels, and at runtime, you want to make the button respond to a press by doubling its own height. To change the button width, move over to the Object Browser window, find the Width property, and change the value associated with Width to 100. Note that the change doesn't take effect in the Form Designer until you press Enter or move off the Width property. To make the button respond to a mouse click, select the Events page on the Object Browser window to reveal the list of events to which the button can respond. Double-click in the column next to the OnClick event, and Delphi generates the a procedure skeleton for a mouse-click response and whisks you away to that spot in the source code. All that's left to do is insert the code to double the button's width between the begin..end of the event's response method:

```
Button1.Height := Button1.Height * 2;
```

To verify that the "application" compiles and runs, press the F9 key on your keyboard and watch it go!

> **NOTE**
>
> When you compile or save a source code module, Delphi scans your source code and removes all procedure skeletons for which you haven't entered any code between the begin and end.

After you have fun making the button really big on the form, terminate your program and go back to the Delphi IDE. Now is a good time to mention that you could have generated a response to a mouse click for your button just by double-clicking a control after dropping it onto the form. Double-clicking a component generates a response method for that component's default action. Each component has a different default action. A TButton's default response is to a mouse click, for example, but a TTimer's default response is to a Timer message.

What's So Great About Events, Anyway?

If you have ever developed Windows applications the traditional way, you without a doubt will find the ease of use of Delphi events a welcome alternative to manually catching Windows messages; cracking those messages; and testing for window handles, control IDs, wParams, lParams, and so on. If you don't know what all that means, that's okay; don't panic—Chapter 9, "Understanding Messages," covers messaging internals.

A Delphi event is often triggered by a Windows message. The OnClick response of a TButton, for example, is really just an encapsulation of Windows' wm_XButtonDown messages. Notice that the OnClick event method gives you information such as which button was pressed and the location of the mouse when it happened. A form's OnKeyDown event provides similar useful information. For example, here is the code Delphi generates for an OnKeyDown handler:

```
procedure TForm1.FormKeyDown(Sender: TObject; var Key: Word;
 Shift: TShiftState);
begin

end;
```

All the information you need about the key is right at your fingertips. If you're an experienced Windows programmer, you will appreciate that there aren't any lParams or wParams, inherited handlers, translates, or dispatches to worry about. This goes way beyond "message cracking" as you may know it, because one Delphi event can represent several different Windows messages as it does with OnMouseDown (which handles a veriety of mouse messages), and each of the message parameters are passed in as easy-to-understand parameters. Chapter 9 gets into the gory details of how Delphi's internal messaging system works.

Contract-Free Programming

Arguably the biggest benefit that Delphi's event system has over Windows' standard messaging system is that all events are contract-free. What *contract-free* means to you, the programmer, is that you never are *required* to do anything inside of your event handlers. Unlike standard Windows message-handling, you do not have to call an inherited handler or pass information back to Windows after handling an event.

Of course, the down side to the contract-free programming model that Delphi's event system provides is that it doesn't give you the power or flexibility that directly handling Windows messages gives you. You are at the mercy of those who designed the event in as far as what level of control you will have over your application's response to the event. For example, you can modify and kill keystrokes in an OnKeyPress handler, but an OnResize handler provides you only with a notification that the event occurred but no power to prevent the resize event from occuring.

Never fear, though. Delphi doesn't prevent you from working directly with Windows messages. It's not as straightforward as the event system because message handling assumes that the programmer has a greater level of knowledge of what Windows expects of every handled message. You have complete power to handle all Windows messages directly by using the message keyword. You find out much more about writing Windows message handlers in Chapter 9.

Part of the utility of the Delphi system is that you can use the high-level, easy stuff (such as events) when it suits you, and still have access to the low-level stuff whenever you need it.

Turbo Prototyping

After hacking Delphi for a little while, you probably will notice that the learning curve is especially mild. In fact, even if you're new to Delphi, you will find that writing your first project in Delphi pays immediate dividends in the forms of a short development cycle and a robust application. Delphi excels in the one facet of application development that has been the bane of many a Windows programmer: user-interface (UI) design.

Sometimes the designing of the UI and the general layout of a program is referred to as *prototyping*. In a nonvisual environment, prototyping an application often takes longer than writing the application's implementation, or what we call the *back end*. Of course, the back end of an application is the whole objective of the program in the first place, right? Sure, an intuitive and visually pleasing UI is a big part of the application, but what good would it be, for example, to have a communications program with pretty windows and dialog boxes but no capability to send data through a modem? As it is with people, it is with applications; a pretty face is nice to look at, but it has to have substance to be a regular part of our lives. Please, no comments about back ends.

Delphi enables you to use its custom controls to whip out nice-looking UIs in no time flat. In fact, you will find that after you become comfortable with Delphi's forms, controls, and event-response methods, you will cut huge chunks of time off the time you usually take to develop application prototypes. You also will find that the UIs you develop in Delphi are just as nice-looking, if not better, than those designed with traditional tools. Part II, "Real-World Building Blocks," and Part III, "Real-World Applications," give you more detail on application prototyping.

Extensible Components

Because of the object-oriented nature of Delphi, in addition to creating your own components from scratch, you also can create your own customized components based on stock Delphi components. Chapter 11, "Writing Custom Delphi Components," shows you how to take some existing Delphi components and extend their behavior create new components.

Summary

By now you should understand Delphi's IDE components and know enough about Delphi to create a small project. The next several chapters explore the specific elements of Delphi in greater detail. Before you continue, make sure that you have a grasp of elements of the Delphi IDE and how to navigate around that environment.

2

Moving to Pascal

If you're new to Pascal or perhaps haven't used Pascal since your school days way back (well, we won't say how long ago), don't touch that dial—this chapter is for you! It introduces you to some of the basics of the Object Pascal language. Because this isn't a beginner's book, it assumes that you have some experience with other high-level computer languages such as C, C++, or Visual Basic, and it compares Object Pascal language structure to that of other languages. By the time you're finished with this chapter, you will understand how typical programming concepts such as variables, types, operators, loops, cases, and objects work in Pascal as compared to C++ and Visual Basic.

Even if you have some recent experience with Pascal, you may want to dog-ear this chapter because this is really the only point in the book where you learn the nitty gritty of Pascal syntax and semantics.

Commentary

As a starting point, you should know how to make comments in your Pascal code. Delphi actually supports two types of Pascal comments: Turbo Pascal-style, using curly braces, and standard Pascal-style, using parentheses and asterisks. The two types of comments are virtually identical in behavior. Examples of each type of comment follow:

```
{ This is a Turbo Pascal-style comment }
(* This is a standard Pascal-style comment *)
```

> **NOTE**
>
> You cannot nest comments of the same type. It is okay to nest standard Pascal-style comments inside Turbo Pascal-style comments or vice versa, however:
>
> ```
> { (* This is good *) }
> (* { This is good } *)
> (* (* This is bad *) *)
> { { This is bad } }
> ```

As a point of style, most Pascal programmers today use the Turbo Pascal-style comments. You may want to take note, too, that there is no equivalent of C's single-line // comment; all Delphi comments must begin with an open-comment symbol and end with a close-comment symbol.

Variables

You might be used to declaring variables off the cuff—"I need another integer, so I'll just declare one right here in the middle of this block of code." If that has been your practice, you're going to have to retrain yourself a little in order to use variables in Pascal. Pascal requires you to declare all variables up front in their own section before you begin a procedure, function, or program. That means that free-wheeling code you used to write like this:

```c
void foo(void)
{
   int x = 1;
   x++;
   int y = 2;
   float f;
   ... etc ...
}
```

must be tidied up and structured a bit more to look like this:

```pascal
Procedure Foo;
var
  x, y: integer;
  f: double;
begin
  x := 1;
  inc(x);
  y := 2;
  ... etc ...
end;
```

> **NOTE**
>
> Object Pascal—like Visual Basic, but unlike C and C++—is not a case-sensitive language. Upper- and lowercase is used for clarity's sake, so use your best judgment, as the style used in this book indicates. If the variable or function name is several words mashed together, remember to capitalize for clarity. For example,
>
> ```pascal
> procedure thisprocedurenamemakesnosense;
> ```
>
> is unclear and difficult to read, whereas this is quite readable:
>
> ```pascal
> procedure ThisProcedureNameIsMoreClear;
> ```

You might be wondering what all this structure business is and why it's beneficial. You will find, however, that Pascal's structured style lends itself to code that is more readable, maintainable, and less buggy than the more scattered style of C++ or Visual Basic.

Notice how Pascal enables you to group more than one variable of the same type together on the same line with the following syntax:

```pascal
VarName1, VarName2 : SomeType;
```

Remember that when declaring a variable in Pascal, the variable name precedes the type, and there is a colon between the variables and types. Note that the variable initialization is always separate from the variable declaration.

Constants

Constants in Pascal are defined in a const clause similar to C's const keyword. Here is an example of three constant declarations in C:

```
const float ADecimalNumber = 3.14;
const int i = 10;
const char * ErrorString = "Danger, Danger, Danger!";
```

The major difference between C constants and Delphi constants is that in Object Pascal, as in Visual Basic, you do not have to declare the constant's type along with the value in the Pascal constant definition. The Delphi compiler automatically allocates proper space for the constant based on its value. In the case of scalar constants such as integers, space never is allocated, and the compiler keeps track of the values:

```
const
  ADecimalNumber = 3.14;
  i = 10;
  ErrorString = 'Danger, Danger, Danger!';
```

NOTE

Pascal uses a single-quote as a string delimiter rather than the double-quote that is common in other programming languages.

If you try to change the value of any of these constants, Delphi shows you a compiler error explaining that it's against the rules to change the value of a constant. Because constants are read-only, Object Pascal optimizes your data space by storing those constants that do merit storage in the application's code segments. If you're unclear as to what segments are or how code and data segments differ, see Chapter 3, "The Object Pascal Language."

NOTE

Object Pascal does not have a preprocessor as C and C++ do. There is no concept of a macro in Object Pascal and, therefore, no Object Pascal equivalent for C's #define macro. Although you may use Object Pascal's $DEFINE compiler directive for conditional compiles similar to C's #define, you cannot use it to define constants. Use const in Object Pascal where you would use #define in C.

Typed Constants

Here is where Object Pascal, frankly speaking, contradicts itself. You also can use the const clause to declare preinitialized variables, which commonly are referred to as *typed constants*. A common typed-constant declaration is identical to a constant declaration, except that it also includes a variable type, as in this example:

```
const
  i: integer = 2;
  d: double = 3.14;
```

You can change the value of typed constants in your program code just as you can change the value of regular variables. Of course, this makes *typed constant* a pretty grand misnomer—it's admittedly illogical to place identifiers that can be changed in a const clause. Typed constants are simply a convenient way of preinitializing variables before they are used. As a comparison, the method for accomplishing the same task in C is as follows:

```
static int i = 2;
static double d = 3.14;
```

Operators

Operators are the symbols in your code that enable you to manipulate all types of data. There are, for example, operators for adding, subtracting, multiplying, and dividing numeric data. There also are operators for addressing a particular element of an array. This section explains some of the Pascal operators and describes some of the differences between the C and Visual Basic counterparts.

Assignment Operator

If you're new to Pascal, Delphi's assignment operator is going to be one of the toughest things to get used to. To assign a value to a variable, use the := operator as you would C or Visual Basic's = operator. Pascal programmers often call this the *gets* operator, and the expression

```
Number1 := 5;
```

is pronounced "Number1 gets the value of 5."

Comparison Operators

If you've already programmed in Visual Basic, you should be very comfortable with Delphi's comparison operators because they are virtually identical. These operators are fairly standard throughout programming languages, so they are covered only briefly in this section.

Delphi uses the = operator to perform logical comparisons between two expressions or values. Delphi's = operator is analogous to C's == operator, so a C expression that would be written like this:

```
if (x == y)
```

would be written like this in Pascal:

```
if x = y
```

> **NOTE**
>
> Remember that in Pascal, the := operator is used to assign a value to a variable, and the = operator compares the values of two operands.

Delphi's not-equal-to operator is <>, and its purpose is identical to C's != operator. To determine whether two expressions are not equal, use this code:

```
if x <> y then DoSomething
```

Logical *and, or,* and *not* operators

Pascal uses the words *and* and *or* as logical and and or operators, whereas C uses the && and ¦¦ symbols, respectively, for these operators. The most common use of the and and or operators is as part of an if statement or loop, such as in the following two examples:

```
if (Condition1) and (Condition2) then
  DoSomething;

while (Condition1) or (Condition2) do
  Something;
```

Pascal's logical *not* operator is not, which is used to check a comparison for a false condition. It is analogous to C's ! operator. It often is used in if statements:

```
if not (condition) then (do something); { if condition is false then... }
```

Table 2.1 contains an easy reference of how Pascal operators map to corresponding C and Visual Basic operators.

Table 2.1. Assignment, comparison, and logical operators.

Operator	Pascal	C	Visual Basic
Assignment	:=	=	=
Comparison	=	==	=
Not equal to	<>	!=	<>
Less than	<	<	<
Greater than	>	>	>
Less than or equal to	<=	<=	<=
Greater than or equal to	>=	>=	>=
Logical and	and	&&	and
Logical or	or	¦¦	or
Logical not	not	!	not

Arithmetic Operators

You already should be familiar with most Pascal arithmetic operators because they generally are similar to those used in C, C++, and Visual Basic. Table 2.2 illustrates all the Pascal arithmetic operators and their C and Visual Basic counterparts.

Table 2.2. Arithmetic operators.

Operator	Pascal	C	Visual Basic
Addition	+	+	+
Subtraction	-	-	-
Multiplication	*	*	*
Floating-point division	/	/	/
Integer division	div	/	/
Modulus	mod	%	Mod

You may notice that the main difference between Pascal and other languages is that Pascal has different division operators for floating-point and integer math. The div operator automatically truncates any remainder when dividing two integer expressions.

CAUTION

Always use the correct division operator for the types of expressions with which you are working. The Object Pascal compiler gives you an error if you try to divide two floating-point numbers with the integer div operator or two integers with the floating-point / operator, as the following code illustrates:

```
var
  i: integer;
  r: real;
begin
  i := 4 / 3;        { This line will cause a compiler error }
  f := 3.4 div 2.3;  { This line also will cause an error    }
end;
```

Bitwise Operators

Bitwise operators are operators that enable you to modify individual bits of a given variable. Common bitwise operators enable you to shift the bits to the left or right or to perform bitwise and, not, or, and xor operations with two numbers. The shift-left and shift-right operators are shl and shr, respectively, and they are much like C's << and >> operators. The remainder of Pascal's bitwise operators are easy enough to remember: and, not, or, and xor. Table 2.3 lists the bitwise operators.

Table 2.3. Bitwise operators.

Operator	Pascal	C	Visual Basic
And	and	&	And
Not	not	~	Not
Or	or	¦	Or
Xor	xor	^	Xor
Shift left	shl	<<	*None*
Shift right	shr	>>	*None*

Increment and Decrement Operators

Increment and decrement operators generate optimized code for adding one or subtracting one from a given integral variable. Pascal doesn't really provide honest-to-gosh increment and decrement operators similar to C's ++ and -- operators, but Pascal's inc() and dec() procedures compile optimally to one line of assembly code.

You can call inc() or dec() with one or two parameters. For example, the following two lines of code:

```
inc(variable);
```

```
dec(variable);
```

increment and decrement *variable*, respectively, by one using the inc and dec assembly instructions, whereas, these two lines:

```
inc(variable, 3);
```

```
dec(variable, 3);
```

increment or decrement *variable* by 3 using the add and sub assembly instructions. Table 2.4 compares the increment and decrement operators of different languages.

> **TIP**
>
> Always use the inc() and dec() operators where possible to increment and decrement ordinal variables. These operators compile to more optimized code than using syntax such as *variable* := *variable* + 1 to increment a variable.

Table 2.4. Increment and decrement operators.

Operator	Pascal	C	Visual Basic
Increment	inc()	++	*None*
Decrement	dec()	--	*None*

Types

One of Object Pascal's greatest features is that it is strongly typed. *Typesafe* means that actual variables passed to procedures and functions must be of the same type as the formal parameters identified in the procedure or function definition. You will not see any of the famous suspicious pointer conversion compiler warnings that C programmers have grown to know and love because the Object Pascal compiler will not permit you to call a function with one type of pointer when another type is specified in the function's formal parameters (although functions that take untyped Pointer types accept any type of pointer). Basically, Pascal's strongly typed nature enables it to perform a sanity check of your code—to ensure you're not trying to put a square peg in a round hole.

Delphi's base types are similar to those of C and Visual Basic. Table 2.4 compares and contrasts the base types of Object Pascal versus those of C and Visual Basic. You probably will want to earmark this page because this table is an excellent reference for matching types when calling other-language Dynamic Link Libraries from Delphi or vice versa.

Table 2.5. A Pascal-to-C-to-Visual-Basic type comparison.

Type of Variable	Pascal	C (16-bit)	Visual Basic
8-bit signed integer	ShortInt	short	*None*
8-bit unsigned integer	Byte	BYTE, char, unsigned short	*None*
16-bit signed integer	Integer	int	Integer
16-bit unsigned integer	Word	unsigned int	*None*
32-bit signed integer	Longint	long	Long
32-bit unsigned integer	Comp	unsigned long	*None*
4-byte floating point	Single	float	Single
6-byte floating point	Real	*None*	*None*
8-byte floating point	Double	double	Double
8-byte currency	*None*	*None*	Currency
10-byte floating point	Extended	long double	*None*

continues

Table 2.5. continued

Type of Variable	Pascal	C (16-bit)	Visual Basic
1-byte character	`Char`	`char`	*None*
Length-byte string	`String`	*None*	`$`
Null-terminated string	`PChar`	`char far *`	*None*
Bool (1 = true / 0 = false)	`Bool,` `WordBool,` `LongBool`	`BOOL`	*None*
Boolean (true / false)	`Boolean`	`Any 1-byte type`	*None*

Strings

Strings are variable types used to represent groups of characters. Every language has its own spin on how string types are stored and used. Pascal has two different string types: `String`s, which are the general-purpose strings, and `PChar`s, which are null-terminated strings whose purpose is to be compatible with the Windows API and other languages.

Pascal Strings

Pascal's `String` type is somewhat similar to that of Visual Basic, but it still is a different sort of animal than what you may be used to. The `String` type sometimes is referred to as *Pascal strings* or *length-byte strings*. Three features set it apart from strings in other languages:

■ The first byte in the string contains the length of the string, and the string itself is contained in the following bytes.

■ The storage of a `String` is always 256 bytes. This means that you never can have more than 255 characters in the string (255 characters + 1 length byte = 256).

■ The compiler allocates string temps as needed, so you don't have to worry about allocating buffers for intermediate results or disposing of them as you do with C.

Figure 2.1 illustrates how a Pascal string is layed out in memory.

FIGURE 2.1.
A Pascal string in memory.

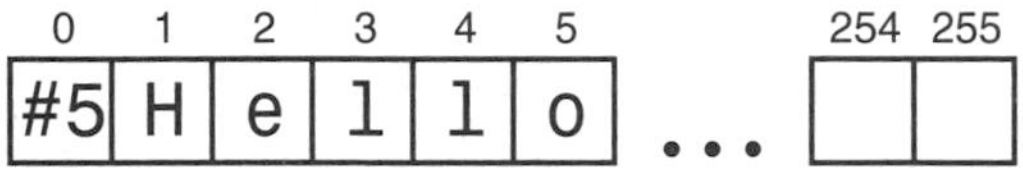

```
 0   1   2   3   4   5        254 255
#5   H   e   l   l   o   ...
```

A `String` variable is declared and initialized with the following syntax:

```
var
  S: String;
begin
  S := 'Bob the cat.';
end.
```

You can concatenate two Pascal strings by using the + operator or the Concat() function, as in the following examples:

```
{using + }
var
  S, S2: String
begin
  S:= 'Avtomat ':
  S2 := 'Kalashnikov';
  S := S + S2;    { Avtomat Kalashnikov }
end.

{ using Concat() }
var
  S, S2: String;
begin
  S:= 'Avtomat ';
  S2 := 'Kalashnikov';
  S := Concat(S, S2);    { Avtomat Kalashnikov}
end.
```

> **NOTE**
>
> Always use single quotation marks ('*string*') when working with strings in Pascal.

Optionally, you can allocate less than 256 bytes for a String, as in the following example:

```
var
  S: String[45];  { a 45-character string }
begin
  S := 'This string must be 45 or fewer characters.';
end.
```

Never store more characters to a string than you have allocated memory for. If you declare a variable as a String[8], for example, and try to assign '*a_pretty_darn_long_string*' to that variable, the string would be truncated to only eight characters, and you would lose data.

When using an array subscript to address a particular character in a String, you could get bogus results or corrupt memory if you attempt to use a subscript index that is greater than the declared value of the String. For example, if you declare a String variable as:

```
var
  Str: String[8];
```

and then attempt to write to the 10th element of the string as follows, you're likely to corrupt memory used by other variables:

```
Str[10] := 's';
```

You can have the compiler link in special logic to catch these types of errors at runtime by selecting Range Checking in the Options | Project dialog box.

Null-Terminated Strings

The PChar type in Delphi exists so that you can call functions in DLLs that require null-terminated strings—a good example is the Windows API. A PChar is defined as a pointer to a string followed by a null (zero) value (if you're unsure of exactly what a pointer is, read on; pointers are discussed in more detail later in this section). Because a PChar is actually a pointer, you usually will need to allocate memory for the string to which it points by using the GetMem() or StrNew() function. Although a bit more work is involved in using PChars, they are ideal for allocating strings longer than 256 characters. You can allocate PChar strings of up to 64 kilobytes. The layout of a PChar variable in memory is shown in Figure 2.2.

FIGURE 2.2.
A PChar in memory.

Because a PChar is a pointer type, you typically do not assign a string to a PChar using Pascal's := operator (although you may if you assign to a string constant), nor do you concatenate two PChars by using the + operator. Use StrPCopy() to assign a string value to a PChar, and use StrCat() to concatenate two PChar variables. The following illustrates working with PChar strings:

```
var
  P1, P2: PChar;
begin
  GetMem(P1, 64);    { Allocate memory for P1 and P2 }
  GetMem(P2, 64);
  StrPCopy(P1, 'Hello ');
  StrPCopy(P2, 'World');
  StrCat(P1, P2);    { P1 now points to 'Hello World'}
  { Use P1 and/or P2 here }
  FreeMem(P1, 64);
  FreeMem(P2, 64);   { Clean up when done }
end.
```

Notice that this example uses GetMem() to allocate memory for the PChar variables. You typically would do this if you didn't know what strings the variables would contain up-front. You also can allocate memory for PChar strings using the StrNew() function if you want to copy a string literal into a null-terminated string. Be careful when using this technique, though, so that you don't over-write memory because StrNew() allocates only enough memory to hold the string:

```
var
  P1, P2: PChar;
begin
  P1 := StrNew('Hello ');  {Allocate just enoughmemory for P1 and P2 }
  P2 := StrNew('World');
  StrCat(P1, P2);              { BEWARE: Corrupts memory! }
  .
  .
  .
end;
```

NOTE

Use StrDispose() to free memory allocated with StrNew(). Use FreeMem() to free memory allocated with GetMem().

CAUTION

The functions and procedures in the Windows API require PChar strings. Do not try to pass a String type to an API procedure because your program will not compile. Use the StrPas() and StrPCopy() functions to convert back and forth between String and PChar types.

Arrays

Delphi enables you to create arrays of any type of variable (except files). For example, a variable declared as an array of eight integers reads

```
var
  A: Array[1..8] of integer;
```

This statement is equivalent to the following C declaration:

```
int[8] A;
```

It also is equivalent to this Visual Basic statement:

```
Dim A(8) as Integer
```

Delphi arrays have a special property that differentiate them from C and Visual Basic arrays: they don't have to begin at a certain number. You therefore can declare a two-element array that starts at 28, as in the following example:

```
var
  A: Array[28..30] of Integer;
```

Although Delphi does allow this, this type of code often can be the programming equivalent of kamikaze. Whenever possible, you should start your arrays at 0 or 1 to preserve your sanity, and only begin arrays at another number when you're sure you have good reason.

> **TIP**
>
> Always begin character arrays at 0. Zero-based character arrays can be passed to functions that require PChar-type variables. This is a special-case allowance that the compiler provides.

User-Defined Types

Integers, strings, and floating-point numbers often are not enough to adequately represent variables in the real-world problems that programmers must try to solve. In cases like these, you must create your own types to better represent variables in the current problem. In Pascal, these user-defined types usually come in the form of records or objects; you declare these types using the Type keyword.

Records

A user-defined structure is referred to as a *record* in Pascal, and it is the equivalent of C's struct or Visual Basic's Type. As an example, here is a record definition in Pascal, and equivalent definitions in C and Visual Basic:

```
{ Pascal }
Type
  MyRec = record
    i: integer;
    d: double;
  end;

/* C */
typedef struct {
  int i;
  double d;
} MyRec;

'Visual Basic
Type MyRec
  i As Integer
  d As Double
End Type
```

When accessing these records, you use the dot symbol to access fields of the record. For example,

```
var
  N: MyRec;
begin
  N.i := 23;
  N.d := 3.4;
end;
```

Objects

Think of objects as records that also contain functions and procedures. Delphi's object model is discussed in much greater detail in Chapter 3, "The Object Pascal Language," so this chapter covers just the basic syntax of Object Pascal objects. An object is defined as follows:

```
Type
  TChildObject = class(TParentObject);
    SomeVar: Integer;
    procedure SomeProc;
  end;
```

Although Delphi objects are not identical to C++ objects, this declaration is roughly equivalent to the following C++ declaration:

```
class TChildObject : public TParentObject {
  int SomeVar;
  void SomeProc();
};
```

Methods are defined in the same way as normal procedures and functions (which are discussed later in this chapter), with the addition of the object name and the dot symbol operator:

```
procedure TChildObject.SomeProc;
begin
  { procedure code goes here }
end;
```

Pascal's . symbol is similar in functionality to Visual Basic's . operator and C++'s :: operator.

Pointers

A *pointer* is a variable that contains a memory location. You already saw an example of a pointer in the PChar type earlier in this chapter. Pascal's generic pointer type is called, aptly, Pointer. A Pointer is sometimes called an *untyped pointer* because it contains only a memory address and the compiler doesn't maintain any information on the data to which it points. That notion, however, goes against the grain of Pascal's typesafe nature, so pointers in your code will usually be typed pointers.

NOTE

Pointers are a somewhat advanced topic, and you definitely don't need to master them to write a Delphi application. As you become more experienced, pointers will become another valuable tool for your programmer's toolbox.

Typed pointers are declared by using the ^, or pointer, operator in the Type section of your program. Typed pointers help the compiler keep track of exactly what kind of type a particular pointer points to, enabling the compiler to keep track of what you're doing (and can do) with a pointer variable. Here are some typical declarations for pointers:

```
Type
  PInt = ^Integer; { PInt is now a pointer to an integer }
  Foo = record     { A record type }
    GobledyGook: String;
    Snarf: Real;
  end;
  PFoo = ^Foo;      { PFoo is a pointer to a foo type }
var
  P: Pointer;       { Untyped pointer }
  P2: PFoo;         { Instance of PFoo }
```

> **NOTE**
>
> C programmers will notice the similarity between Pascal's ^ operator and C's * operator. Pascal's Pointer type corresponds to C's void * type.

Remember that a pointer variable only stores a memory address. Allocating space for whatever the pointer points to is your job as a programmer. You can allocate space for a pointer by using Delphi's New() or GetMem() functions or the Windows API GlobalAlloc() series of functions.

> **NOTE**
>
> When a pointer that doesn't point to anything (its value is zero), its value is said to be *Nil*, and it is often called a *Nil pointer*.

If you want to access the data that a particular pointer points to, follow the pointer variable name with the ^ operator. This method is known as *dereferencing* the pointer. The following code illustrates working with pointers:

```
Program PtrTest;

Type
  MyRec = record
    I: integer;
    S: String;
    R: Real;
  end;
  PMyRec = ^MyRec;

var
  Rec : PMyRec;
begin
```

```
  New(Rec);  { allocate memory for Rec }
  Rec^.I := 10;  { Put stuff in Rec. Note the dereference }
  Rec^.S := 'And now for something completely different.';
  Rec^.R := 6.384;
  { Rec is now full }
  Dispose(Rec);  { Don't forget to free memory! }
end.
```

SHOULD YOU USE New() OR GetMem()?

You should use `GetMem()` to allocate memory for structures for which the compiler cannot know the size. The compiler cannot tell ahead of time how much memory you want to allocate for `PChar` or untyped `Pointer` types, for example, types because of their variable-length nature. Be careful not to try to manipulate more data than you have allocated through `GetMem` because this is one of the classic causes of the ubiquitous `General Protection Fault` error. You should use `FreeMem()` to clean up any memory you allocate with the `GetMem()` procedure.

Use the `New()` function to allocate memory for a pointer to a structure of a known size. `New()` basically calls `GetMem()` and passes the size of the structure to which the pointer points as a parameter, making it safer to use than `GetMem()`. Never allocate `Pointer` or `PChar` variables by using the `New()` function because the compiler cannot guess how many bytes you need for this allocation. Remember to use `Dispose()` to free any memory you allocate using the `New()` function.

When you know what strings you want to store in a `PChar`, allocate memory for them using the `StrNew()` function, and free memory using the `StrDispose()` function.

Typecasting

Typecasting is a technique by which you can force the compiler to view a variable of one type as another type. Because of Pascal's strongly typed nature, you will find that the compiler is very picky about types matching up in the formal and actual parameters of a function call. Hence, you occasionally will be required to cast a variable of one type to a variable of another type to make the compiler happy. Suppose that you need to assign the value of a character to a `byte` variable:

```
var
  c: char;
  b: byte;
begin
  c := 's';
  b := c;   { compiler complains on this line }
end.
```

In the following syntax, a typecast is required to convert c into byte. In effect, a typecast tells the compiler that you really know what you're doing and want to convert one type to another:

```
var
  c: char;
  b: byte;
begin
  c := 's';
  b := byte(c);    { compiler happy as clam on this line }
end.
```

> **NOTE**
>
> You can typecast a variable of one type to another type only if the data size of the two variables is the same. For example, you cannot typecast a real as an integer.

You learn about a special variety of typecasting using the as operator in Chapter 3.

Testing Conditions

This section compares if and case constructs in Pascal to similar constructs in C and Visual Basic. It assumes that you have used these types of programmatic constructs before, so it doesn't spend time explaining them to you.

The *if* Statement

An if statement enables you to determine whether certain conditions are met before executing a particular block of code. As an example, here is an if statement in Pascal, and equivalent definitions in C and Visual Basic:

```
{ Pascal }
if x = 4 then y := x;

/* C */
if (x == 4) then y = x;

'Visual Basic
If x = 4 Then y = x
```

> **NOTE**
>
> If you have an if statement that makes multiple comparisons, make sure you enclose each set of comparisons in parentheses for code clarity. Do this:
>
> ```
> if (x = 7) and (y = 8) then
> ```
>
> Don't do this:
>
> ```
> if x = 7 and y = 8 then
> ```

Use the begin and end keywords in Pascal almost as you would use { and } in C or C++. For example, use the following construct if you want to execute multiple lines of text when a given condition is true:

```
if x = 6 then begin
  DoSomething;
  DoSomethingElse;
  DoAnotherThing;
end;
```

You can combine multiple conditions using the if..else construct:

```
if x =100 do
  SomeFunction
else if x = 200 do
  SomeOtherFunction
else begin
  SomethingElse;
  Entirely;
end;
```

Using Case Statements

The case statement in Pascal works in much the same way as a switch statement in C or C++. A case statement provides a means for choosing one condition among many possibilities without a huge if..else if..else if construct. Here is an example of Pascal's case statement:

```
case SomeIntegerVariable of
  101 : DoSomething;
  202 : begin
          DoSomething;
          DoSomethingElse;
        end;
  303 : DoAnotherThing;
  else DoTheDefault;
end;
```

Here is the C switch statement equivalent to the preceding example:

```
switch (SomeIntegerVariable) {
  case 101: DoSomeThing; break;
  case 202: DoSomething;
            DoSomethingElse; break
  case 303: DoAnotherThing; break;
  default: DoTheDefault;
}
```

Looping Constructs

A *loop* is a construct that enables you to repeatedly perform some type of action. Pascal's loop constructs are very similar to what you should be familiar with from your experience with other languages, so this chapter doesn't spend any time teaching you about loops. This section describes the various loop constructs you can use in Pascal.

The *while* Loop

Use a while loop construct when you want some part of your code to repeat itself while some condition is true. A while loop's conditions are tested before the loop is executed, and a classic example for the use of a while loop is to repeatedly perform some action on a file as long as the end of the file is not encountered. Here is an example that demonstrates a loop that reads one line at a time from a file and writes it to the screen:

```
Program FileIt;

uses WinCRT;

var
  f: TextFile;  { a text file }
  s: String;
begin
  AssignFile(f, 'foo.txt');
  Reset(f);
  while not EOF(f) do begin
    readln(f, S);
    writeln(S);
  end;
  CloseFile(f);
end.
```

Pascal's while loop works basically the same as C's while loop or Visual Basic's Do While loop.

The *for* Loop

A for loop is ideal when you need to repeat an action a predetermined number of times. Here is an example, albeit not a very useful one, of a for loop that adds the loop index to a variable 10 times:

```
var
  I, X: integer;

begin
  X := 0;
  for I := 1 to 10 do
    inc(X, I);
end.
```

The C equivalent of the preceding example is as follows:

```
void main(void) {
  int X, I;
  X = 0;
  for(I=1; I<=10; I++)
    X = X + I;
}
```

Here is the Visual Basic equivalent of the same concept:

```
X = 0
For I = 1 to 10
  X := X + I
Next I
```

The *repeat..until* Loop

The repeat..until loop addresses the same type of problem as a while loop but from a different angle. It repeats a given block of code until a certain condition becomes True. Unlike a while loop, the loop code always is executed at least once because the condition is tested at the end of the loop. Repeat..until is roughly equivalent to C's do..while loop.

For example, here is a code snippet that repeats a statement that increments a counter until the value of the counter becomes greater than 100:

```
var
  x: integer;
begin
  repeat
    inc(x);
  until x > 100;
end.
```

The *Break* Procedure

Calling Break() from inside a while, for, or repeat loop causes the flow of your program to skip immediately to the end of the currently executing loop. This method is useful when you need to leave the loop immediately because of some circumstance that may arise within the loop. Pascal's Break() procedure is analogous to C's Break and Visual Basic's Exit statement.

The *Continue* Procedure

Call Continue() inside of a loop when you want to skip over a portion of code and the flow of control to continue with the next iteration of the loop. Note in the following example that the code after Continue() is executed only once:

```
var
  i: word;
begin
  for i := 1 to 3 do begin
    writeln(i, '. Before continue');
    if i = 1 then Continue;
    writeln(i, '. After continue');
  end;
end;
```

Procedures and Functions

As a programmer, you should already be familiar with the basics of procedures and functions. A *procedure* is a discrete program part that performs some particular task when it is called and then returns to the calling part of your code. A *function* works the same except that a function returns a value after its exit to the calling part of the program.

If you're familiar with C or C++, consider that a Pascal procedure is equivalent to a C or C++ function that returns void, whereas a function corresponds to a C or C++ function that returns some type of variable.

Listing 2.1 demonstrates a short Pascal program with a procedure and a function.

Listing 2.1. Example of functions and procedures.

```
Program FuncProc;

uses WinCRT;

procedure BiggerThanTen(i: integer);
{ writes something to the screen if I is greater than 10 }
begin
  if I > 10 then
    writeln('Funky.');
end;

function IsPositive(i: integer): Boolean;
{ Returns True if I is 0 or positive, False if I is negative }
begin
  Result := True;
  if I < 0 then
    Result := False;
end;

var
  Num: integer;
begin
  Num := 23;
  BiggerThanTen(Num);
  if IsPositive(Num) then
    writeln(Num, 'Is positive.')
  else
    writeln(Num, 'Is negative.');
end.
```

> **NOTE**
>
> The local variable Result in the IsPositive function deserves special attention. Every Object Pascal function has an implicit local variable called Result that contains the return value of the function. You also can return a value from a function by assigning the name of a function to a value inside the function's code. This is a change from previous versions of Pascal, which used only the function name as the return variable.

Passing Parameters

Pascal enables you to pass parameters by value or by reference to functions and procedures. The parameters you pass can be of any base or user-defined type, or open array (open arrays are discussed in the next chapter). Parameters also can be constant if their values will not change in the procedure or function.

Value Parameters

Value parameters are the default mode of parameter passing. When a parameter is passed by value, it means that a local copy of that variable is created, and the function or procedure operates on the copy. Consider the following example:

```
procedure Foo(s: string);
```

When you call a procedure in this way, a copy of string s will be made, and Foo() will operate on the local copy of s. This means that you can choose the value of s without having any effect on the variable passed into Foo().

Reference Parameters

Pascal enables you to pass variables to functions and procedures by reference; parameters passed by reference are also called *variable parameters*. *Passing by reference* means that the function or procedure receiving the variable can modify the value of that variable. To pass a variable by reference, use the keyword var in the procedure's or function's parameter list:

```
procedure ChangeMe(var x: longint);
begin
  x := 2;  { x is now changed in the calling procedure }
end;
```

Instead of making a copy of x, the var keyword causes the address of the parameter to be copied so that its value can be directly modified.

Using var parameters is equivalent to passing variables by reference in C++ using the & operator. Like C++'s & operator, the var keyword causes the address of the variable to be pushed onto the stack rather than the value of the variable.

Constant Parameters

If you don't want the value of a parameter passed into a function to change, you can declare it with the const keyword. The const keyword not only prevents you from modifying the value of the parameters, but it also generates more optimal code for strings and records passed into the procedure or function. Here is an example of a procedure that receives a constant string parameter:

```
procedure Goon(const s: string);
```

Scope

Scope refers to some part of your program in which a given function or variable is known to the compiler. A global constant is in scope at all points in your program, for example, whereas a variable local to some procedure only has scope within that procedure. Consider Listing 2.2.

Listing 2.2. An illustration of scope.

```
program Foo;

const
  SomeConstant = 100;

var
  SomeGlobal: Integer;

procedure SomeProc(var R: Real);
var
  LocalReal: Real;
begin
  LocalReal := 10.0;
  R := R - LocalReal;
end;

var
  R: Real;

begin
  SomeGlobal := SomeConstant;
  R := 4.593;
  SomeProc(R);
end.
```

SomeConstant and SomeGlobal have *global scope*—their values are known to the compiler at all points within the program. Procedure SomeProc has two variables in which the scope is local to that procedure: R and LocalReal. If you try to access either of these variables outside of SomeProc, the compiler displays an unknown identifier error. Notice, too, that a variable called R is defined outside of the SomeProc procedure. Because that R is defined after the procedure and because SomeProc's R doesn't have scope outside of the procedure, the two variables called R do not conflict with one another.

Units

Units are the individual source code modules that make up a Pascal program. A unit is a place for you to group functions and procedures that can be called from your main program. To be a unit, a source module must consist of at least three parts:

■ A unit *statement*. Every unit must have as its first line a statement saying that it is a unit and identifying the unit name. The name of the unit always must match the filename. For example, if you have a file named FooBar, the statement would be

```
unit FooBar;
```

■ The interface part. After the unit statement, a unit's next functional line of code should be the interface statement. Everything following this statement, up to the implementation statement, is information that can be shared with your program and with other units. The interface part of a unit is where you declare the types, constants, variables, procedures, and functions that you want to make available to your main program and to other units. Only declarations—never procedure bodies—can appear in the interface. The interface statement should be one word on one line:

```
interface
```

■ The implementation part. This follows the interface part of the unit. Although the implementation part of the unit contains primarily procedures and functions, it is also where you declare any types, constants, variables that you do not want to make available outside of this unit. The implementation part is where you define any functions or procedures that you declared in the interface part. The implemenation statement should be one word on one line:

```
implementation
```

The *uses* Clause

The uses clause is where you list the units that you want to include in a particular program or unit. For example, if you have a program named FooProg that uses functions and types in two units, UnitA and UnitB, the proper uses declaration is as follows:

```
Program FooProg;

uses UnitA, UnitB;
```

Keep in mind that units can have a uses clause. Actually, units can have two uses clauses: one in the interface section and one in the implementation section.

TIP

Move as many units as possible to the uses clause in the implementation part of a unit. This minimizes the number of files that the compiler must keep open while compiling, and it simplifies any debugging of your units that you might have to do later.

Circular Unit References

Occasionally, you will have a situation where UnitA uses UnitB and UnitB uses UnitA. This is called a *circular unit reference*. You should avoid structuring your program with a circular reference; however, as with most things, sometimes you just can't avoid it. In such a case, move one of the uses clauses to the implementation part of your unit and leave the other one in the interface part. This usually solves the problem.

Summary

In this chapter, you learned the basic syntax and semantics of the Pascal language including variables, operators, functions, procedures, types, constructs, and style. Now that you understand the core syntax of the Pascal language, it's time to move on to the next chapter, which tackles the topic of new additions to the Pascal language introduced in Delphi's Object Pascal. Chapter 3 focuses on Delphi's new object-oriented language features in preparation for learning about Delphi's object library in Chapter 4, "The Visual Component Library (VCL)."

3

The Object Pascal Language

This chapter sets aside the visual elements of Delphi and concentrates on the extremely powerful language and compiler found lurking deep within Delphi. Some fairly serious changes had to be made to Borland's Pascal language in order to bring to you the revolutionary interface, object model, and coding style that is Delphi. The new language features introduced in Object Pascal contribute to a renaissance for Pascal—it now contains powerful modern language features such as exception handling and runtime type information while retaining the long-time Pascal traditions of blindingly fast compile times and bug-free, readable code.

What Does Object-Oriented Mean?

Volumes have been written on the subject of object-oriented programming (OOP). Often, OOP seems more like a religion than a programming methodology, spawning arguments about its merits (or lack thereof) passionate and spirited enough to make the Crusades look like a slight disagreement. We're not orthodox OOPists, and we're not going to get involved in the relative merits of OOP; we just want to give you the low-down on a basic principle on which Delphi's Object Pascal Language is based.

OOP is a programming paradigm that uses discrete objects—containing both data and code— as application building blocks. Although the OOP paradigm doesn't necessarily lend itself to easier-to-write code, the result of using OOP traditionally has been easy-to-maintain code. Having objects' data and code together simplifies the process of hunting down bugs, fixing them with minimal effect on other object, and improving your program one part at a time. Traditionally, an OOP language contains implementations of at least three OOP concepts:

Encapsulation	Deals with combining related data fields and hiding the implementation details. The advantages of encapsulation include modularity and isolation of code from other code.
Inheritance	The capability to create new objects that maintain the properties and behavior of ancestor objects. This concept enables you to create object hierarchies like VCL—first creating generic objects, and then creating more specific descendants of those objects that have more narrow functionality.
	The advantage of inheritance is the sharing of common code. Figure 3.1 presents an example of inheritance—how one root object, fruit, is the ancestor object of all fruits, including the melon. The melon is ancestor of all melons including a watermelon. You get the picture.
Polymorphism	Literally, polymorphism means "many shapes." Calls to methods of an object variable will call code appropriate to whatever instance is actually in the variable.

FIGURE 3.1.
An illustration of inheritance.

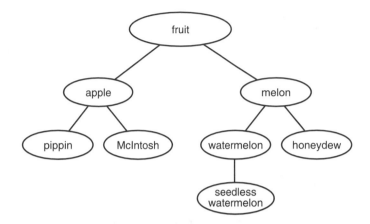

Object Pascal does not support multiple inheritance of objects like C++. *Multiple inheritance* is the concept of a given object being derived from two separate objects, creating an object that contains all the code and data of the two parent objects.

To expand on the analogy presented in Figure 3.1, multiple inheritance enables you to create a candy apple object by creating a new object that inherits from the apple class and some other class called candy. Although this functionality seems useful, it generally introduces more problems and inefficiencies into your code than it solves.

The Object Pascal approach to creating a candy apple object is to make the candy object a member of the apple object. This implementation of an object containing other objects rather than descending from multiple objects lends itself to more readable and more debuggable code. And after all, metaphorically speaking, a candy apple is still an apple—just with an extra layer of tasty skin.

Anatomy of an Object

You should understand the following three terms before you continue to explore the concept of objects:

Field	Also called *field definitions* or *instance variables*, fields are data variables contained within objects. A field in an object is just like a field in a Pascal record. In C++, fields sometimes are referred to as *data members*.
Method	The name for procedures and functions belonging to an object. Methods are called *member functions* in C++.
Property	A property is a an entity that acts as an accessor to the data and code contained within an object. Properties insulate the end user from the implementation details of an object.

> **NOTE**
>
> It generally is considered bad OOP style to access an object's fields directly. The reason for this is because the implementation details of the object may change. Instead use accessor properties, which allow a standard object interface without becoming embroiled in the details of how the objects are implemented. Properties are explained later in this chapter.

Object-Based Versus Object-Oriented

In some tools, you manipulate entities (objects), but you cannot create your own objects. VBX controls are a good example of this. You can use a VBX control in your Visual Basic application, but you cannot create one, and you cannot inherit one VBX control from another in Visual Basic. Environments such as these often are called *object-based environments*.

Delphi is a fully object-oriented environment. This means that you can create new objects in Delphi from scratch or based on existing components.

A New Class of Objects

If you've programmed in Borland Pascal before, the first thing you might notice about Object Pascal is that Borland Pascal's object-declaration keyword— object—has gone away and has been replaced by the class keyword. Well, perhaps gone away is a bad choice of words, because the Delphi compiler still will compile all your Borland Pascal 7.0 and Turbo Pascal for Windows 1.5 code, but the object keyword seems to be slated for retirement. The code change involved here is very small; instead of declaring an object like this:

```
TMyObject = Object(TParentObject)
```

you now declare it like this:

```
TMyObject = Class(TParentObject)
```

The first question that probably comes to mind about this change is, "Why?" There actually are several reasons. First and foremost, the object model was changed to provide a clean migration path between 16- and 32-bit environments. There were also some changes, such as the addition of properties, which help improve robustness and reduce code maintenance risks. Borland additionally couldn't easily add new functionality to objects such as exception handling and runtime type information (which are covered later in this chapter) while still maintaining backward-compatibility with object model programs such as Object Windows applications. Borland decided to add classes to Object Pascal rather than to break existing code by changing the behavior of objects.

Listings 3.1 and 3.2 illustrate the differences in object declaration, instantiation, and use between the old object model and the new class model. This section discusses some of the important differences between the two models.

Listing 3.1. The old object model.

```
Program OldObj;

Uses WinCRT;

Type
  PMyObject = ^TMyObject;  { pointer-to-object type }
  TMyObject = Object       { declaration of object }
    ANumber: Integer;
    constructor Init(Num: Integer);
  end;

constructor PMyObject.Init(Num);
begin
  ANumber := Num;
end;

Var
  PO: PMyObject;

Begin
  New(PO, Init(1));      { create an instance of the object }
  writeln(PO^.ANumber);  { note the dereference }
  Dispose(PO);           { get rid of the object }
End.
```

Listing 3.2. The new class model.

```
Program NewClass;

Uses WinCRT;

Type
  TMyClass := Class
    ANumber: Integer;
    constructor Create(Num: Integer);
  end;

constructor PMyClass.Create(Num);
begin
  ANumber := Num;
end;

Var
  MC: TMyClass;

Begin
  MC := TMyClass.Create(4);  { create an instance of the object }
```

continues

Listing 3.2. continued

```
    writeln(MC.ANumber);        { access an object field }
    MC.Free;                    { get rid of the object }
End.
```

The Differences Between Class and Object

EH and RTTI aside, there are a number of changes in the everyday use of the class model versus the object model. One of the more notable changes from the old object model is that you no longer have to declare pointer-to-object types for your objects. All class instances in Object Pascal are actually pointer-to-class types; when you try to access a class, the compiler performs a little bit of hocus-pocus that generates the code to de-reference that pointer for you.

> **CAUTION**
>
> When porting code from the object model to the class model, make sure that you remove declarations of pointers to objects and the use of pointer dereferences that access those objects. Remember that, as a rule, Object Pascal handles object pointers for you, so avoid using the ^ when dealing with classes.

Something else you might notice right away is how classes are instantiated by directly calling the constructor as opposed to using New() to allocate space for an object instance. Of course, in Listing 3.1, you could have avoided the use of New() altogether by changing the main portion of your program to this:

```
Var
  O: TMyObject;        { static instance of the object - no pointers! }

Begin
  O.Init(4);           { initialize the object }
  writeln(O.ANumber);  { access an object field }
End.
```

Making this change in your program, as you already might know, allocates space for object O in your application's data segment rather than in the global heap. The rub here, however, is that there is no corresponding way to allocate a class from an application's data segment rather than from the heap; all Object Pascal classes are allocated from global heap memory.

> **THANKS FOR THE MEMORIES!**
>
> If you're not familiar with the different regions of memory your application may occupy in RAM, here are some brief explanations of the memory regions for a Windows 3.1 application:

Data segment	A 64KB area of memory where a Windows application stores all its global data, stack, and local heap. Each executable or DLL written in Delphi gets only one code segment, so you should use this memory judiciously.
Code segment	An area of memory in which your application's code, or compiled procedures and functions, is kept. A code segment can be up to 64KB, and your application can be comprised of many individual code segments. Code segments are read-only, and writing to a code segment is one of the common causes of the ubiquitous General Protection Fault message. Because you never change the information in a code segment, the compiler is able to reduce the impact on the data segment by placing certain read-only information, such as constants, into code segments. Delphi applications also store pointers to each class's Virtual Method Table (VMT) and Dynamic Method Table (DMT) in code segments (VMTs and DMTs are explained later in this chapter).
Stack	An application's temporary storage area. Variables passed to procedures and functions are passed via the stack, and any variables declared within a procedure or function are stored on the stack. The stack is located in the data segment of an application (unlike DOS applications, where the stack has its own segment), and the default stack size of a Delphi program is 16KB. A DLL usually uses the stack of the executable from which it was called.
Local heap	Windows uses the local heap mainly to store information specific to your program, such as the contents and state of your application's controls. Because the local heap also resides in the data segment, it is available only to your application. The default size of 8KB generally is sufficient for the local heap because Windows expands the size of the local heap dynamically if necessary. You, as a Delphi programmer, typically do not make allocations from this area of memory.
Global heap	This often is referred to simply as *the heap*. The global heap includes basically all unallocated memory on the system, and there is no limit to the amount of heap that your application can use. Delphi classes are allocated automatically from the heap, but you must specifically allocate heap space in your application — usually by using GlobalAlloc(), New(), or GetMem() — for other types of structures.

You also might think it's unusual that the class in Listing 3.2 is disposed of by calling its `Free()` method, although no such method is declared in the class itself. The reason for this is because *all* classes are descendants of the `TObject` base class. The `Free()` method is inherited from `TObject`. Therefore, in Delphi, this declaration:

```
Type TFoo = Class;
```

is essentially equivalent to this declaration:

```
Type TFoo = Class(TObject);
```

> **NOTE**
>
> Because all Object Pascal classes are descendants of `TObject`, you must use special care when porting object model code to Delphi's class model. Borland and Turbo Pascal also have a basic object called `TObject`, but that `TObject`'s behavior is different than the Object Pascal class of the same name.

Properties

It may help to think of properties as special accessor fields that enable you to modify data and execute code contained within your class. For components, properties are those things that show up in the Object Inspector window. The following example illustrates a simplified Object with a property:

```
TMyObject = class
private
  SomeValue: Integer;
  procedure SetSomeValue(AValue: Integer);
public
  property Value: Integer read SomeValue write SetSomeValue;
end;

procedure TMyObject.SetSomeValue(AValue: Integer);
begin
  if SomeValue <> AValue then
    SomeValue := AValue;
end;
```

`TMyObject` is an object that contains the following: one field—an integer called `SomeValue`, one method—a procedure called `SetSomeValue`, and one property called `Value`. The sole purpose of the `SetSomeValue` procedure is to set the value of the `SomeValue` field. The `Value` property doesn't actually contain any data. `Value` is an accessor for the `SomeValue` field; when you ask `Value` what number it contains, it reads the value from `SomeValue`. When you attempt to set the value of the `Value` property, `Value` calls `SetSomeValue` to modify the value of `SomeValue`.

Methods

Methods are procedures and functions belonging to a given object. Methods are those things that give an object behavior rather than just data. Two important methods of the objects you create will be the constructor and the destructor methods.

The *constructor* is responsible for creating an instance of your object and allocating any memory or initializing any fields necessary so that the object is in a usable state when exiting the constructor. Remember that when creating an instance of an object, the syntax is

```
Instance := ObjectType.Create(Parameters);
```

> **NOTE**
>
> When an object instance is created using the constructor, the compiler will ensure that every field in your object is initialized. You can safely assume that all numbers will be initialized to 0, all pointers to nil, and all strings to ' '.

The *destructor*, of course, does the opposite of the constructor; it deallocates any allocated memory and performs any other housekeeping required in order for the object to be destroyed properly. Instead of directly calling the object's destructor, you should call the Free() method (inherited from TObject), which first checks for a valid object instance before attempting to dispose of your object.

> **CAUTION**
>
> Unlike in C++, your object's destructor will not be called automatically when your object leaves scope. Except when your object is owned by other objects (as described in Chapter 4, "The Visual Component Library"), you are responsible for destroying any objects that you create.

Defining Methods

Creating a method is a two-step process. You first must declare the method in the object type declaration, and then you must define the method in the code. The following code demonstrates the process of declaring and defining a method:

```
type
  TBoogieNights = class
    Dance: Boolean;
    procedure DoTheHustle;
  end;
```

```
procedure TBoogieNights.DoTheHustle;
begin
  Dance := True;
end;
```

Note that when defining the method body, you have to use the fully-qualified name, as we did when defining the DoTheHustle method. It's important also to note that the object's Dance field can be accessed directly from within the method.

Method Types

Object methods can be declared as static, virtual, dynamic, or message. Consider the following example object:

```
TFoo = class
  procedure IAmAStatic;
  procedure IAmAVirtual; virtual;
  procedure IAmADynamic; dynamic;
  procedure IAmAMessage(var M: TMessage); message wm_SomeMessage;
end;
```

IAmAStatic is a static method. *Static* methods are the default method type, and they work similarly to regular procedure or function calls. The compiler knows the address of these methods, and so, when you call a static method, it is able to link that information into the executable statically.

IAmAVirtual is a virtual method. *Virtual* methods are called in the same way as static methods, but because virtual methods can be overridden, the compiler does not know the address of a particular virtual function when you call it in your code. The compiler, therefore, builds a Virtual Method Table (VMT) that provides a means to look up function addresses at runtime. All virtual method calls are dispatched at runtime through the VMT. An object's VMT contains all of its ancestor's virtual methods as well as the ones it declares, so they tend to be a bit memory-hungry.

IAmADynamic is a dynamic method. *Dynamic* methods are basically virtual methods with a different dispatching system. The compiler assigns a unique number to each dynamic method and uses those numbers, along with method addresses, to build a Dynamic Method Table (DMT). Unlike the VMT, an object's DMT contains only the dynamic methods that it declares, and it relies on its ancestor's DMTs for the rest of its dynamic methods. Because of this, dynamic methods are less memory intensive than virtual methods, but they take longer to call because you may have to propagate through several ancestor DMTs before finding the address of a particular dynamic method. Unless speed is a critical necessity, you should use dynamic methods rather than virtual because they are more memory efficient.

IAmAMessage is a message-handling method. The value after the message keyword dictates what message the method will respond to. Message methods are used to create an automatic response to Windows messages, and you generally don't call them directly.

Overriding a Method

Overriding a method is Object Pascal's implementation of the OOP concept of polymorphism. It enables you to change the behavior of a method from descendant to descendant. Object Pascal methods can be overridden only if they are first declared as virtual or dynamic. To override a method, just use the override directive instead of virtual or dynamic in your descendant object type. As an example, override the IAmAVirtual and IAmADynamic methods in the following example:

```
TFooChild = class(TFoo)
  procedure IAmAVirtual; override;
  procedure IAmADynamic; override;
  procedure IAmAMessage(var M: TMessage); message wm_SomeMessage;
end;
```

If you had re-declared IAmAVirtual and IAmADynamic with the virtual or dynamic keyword instead of override, you would have created new methods rather than overriding the ancestor methods. Also, if you attempt to override a static method in a descendant type, the static method in the new object completely replaces the method in the ancestor type.

Self

An implicit variable called Self is available within all object methods. Self is a pointer to the class instance that was used to call the method. Self is passed by the compiler as a hidden parameter to all methods.

Class Visibility Specifiers

Delphi offers you further control over the behavior of your objects by enabling you to declare fields and methods with directives such as protected, private, public, and published. The syntax for using these keywords is as follows:

```
TSomeObject = class
private
  APrivateVariable: Integer;
  AnotherPrivateVariable: Boolean;
protected
  procedure AProtectedProcedure;
  function ProtectMe: Byte;
public
  constructor APublicContructor;
  destructor APublicKiller;
published
  property AProperty read APrivateVariable write APrivateVariable;
end;
```

You can place as many fields or methods as you want under each directive. Style dictates that you should indent the specifier the same as you indent the class name. The meanings of these directives follow:

private   These parts of your object are accessible only to code in the same unit
                   as your object's implementation. Use this directive to hide implementa-
                   tion details of your objects from users and to prevent users from
                   directly modifying sensitive members of your object.

protected   Your object's protected members can be accessed by descendants of
                   your object. This capability enables you to hide the implementation
                   details of your object from users while still allowing maximum flexibil-
                   ity to descendants of your object.

public   These fields and methods are accessible anywhere in your program.
                   Object constructors and destructors always should be public.

published   Runtime type information (RTTI) to be generated for the published
                   portion of your objects enables other parts of your application to get
                   information on your object's published parts. The Object Inspector
                   uses RTTI to build its list of properties.

Here, then, is code for the TMyObject class that was introduced earlier, with directives added to improve the integrity of the object:

```
TMyObject = class
private
  SomeValue: Integer;
  procedure SetSomeValue(AValue: Integer);
published
  property Value: Integer read SomeValue write SetSomeValue;
end;

procedure TMyObject.SetSomeValue(AValue: Integer);
begin
  if SomeValue <> AValue then
    SomeValue := AValue;
end;
```

Now, users of your object will not be able to modify the value of SomeValue directly, and they will have to go through the interface provided by the property Value to modify the object's data.

TObject: The Mother of Objects

Because everything descends from TObject, every class has some methods that it inherits from TObject, and you can make some special assumptions about the capabilities of an object. Every class has the capability, for example, to tell you its name, its type, or even whether it is inherited from a particular class. The beauty of this is that you, as an applications programmer, don't have to care what kind of magic the compiler does to makes this happen. You can just take advantage of the functionality it provides!

TObject is a special object because its definition comes from the SYSTEM unit, and it is written all in assembler. Unlike the old object model, the compiler is "aware" of TObject. The following code illustrates the definition of the TObject class:

```
Type
  TObject = class
    constructor Create;
    destructor Destroy; virtual;
    procedure Free;
    class function NewInstance: TObject; virtual;
    procedure FreeInstance; virtual;
    class procedure InitInstance(Instance: Pointer): TObject;
    function ClassType: TClass;
    class function ClassName: string;
    class function ClassParent: TClass;
    class function ClassInfo: Pointer;
    class function InstanceSize: Word;
    class function InheritsFrom(AClass: TClass): Boolean;
    procedure DefaultHandler(var Message); virtual;
    procedure Dispatch(var Message);
    class function MethodAddress(const Name: string): Pointer;
    class function MethodName(Address: Pointer): string;
    function FieldAddress(const Name: string): Pointer;
  end;
```

In particular, note the methods that are preceded by the keyword class. Prepending the class keyword to a method allows it to be called like a normal procedure or function without actually having an instance of the class of which the method is a member. This is a juicy bit of functionality that was borrowed from C++. Be careful, though, not to make a class method depend on any instance information or you'll get a compiler error.

CAN YOU FIND THE BUG IN THIS CODE?

The following code contains a bug. Can you find it?

```
Program Whoops;

Type
  TAnyOldClass = class
  public
    AField : Integer;
    class procedure SetAField(I: Integer);
    class function GetAField: Integer;
  end;

class procedure SetAField(I: Integer);
begin
  AField := I;
end;

class procedure GetAField: Integer;
begin
  Result := AField;
end;
```

```
begin
  TAnyOldClass.SetAField(4);
end.
```

The answer is that although SetAField is a class method, it tries to modify AField, which is an instance variable of the TAnyOldClass class. Of course, the Delphi compiler will flag you with an error in this case. You *must* ensure that your class methods do not reference instance data!

Getting a Handle on Exceptions

Exception handling (EH) is a method of error handling that enables your application to recover gracefully from otherwise fatal error conditions. The beauty of Object Pascal exceptions is that they are just classes that happen to contain information about the location and nature of a particular error. This makes exceptions as easy to implement and use in your applications as any other class.

Not only does Delphi enable you to use exception handling within your classes, but the Visual Component Library (which is discussed in more detail in the next chapter) also contains exceptions for common program-error conditions, such as out of memory, divide by zero, numerical overflow, numerical underflow, and file I/O errors. This is a far cry from the old days when such runtime error conditions had to be controlled through the use of compiler directives and checks on system variables. Listing 3.3 shows a small program that accesses a file with error checking the old way.

Listing 3.3. File I/O the old-fashioned way.

```
Program OldIO;

Uses WinCRT;

Var
  F: Text;
  S: String;
Begin
  Assign(F, 'FOO.TXT');
  {$I-}
  Reset(F);
  If IOResult <> 0 then
    writeln('Could not open file!')
  else begin
    ReadLn(F, S);
    If IOResult <> 0 then
      writeln('Could not read from file!');
    close(F);
    If IOResult <> 0 then
```

```
      writeln('Could not close file!');
  {$I+}
  end;
End.
```

This program uses a brute-force technique of checking for an I/O error after every operation. Admittedly, the program in Listing 3.3 does work, but the I/O checking makes the program less readable. Now take a look at Listing 3.4, which accesses the file in exactly the same manner but uses EH for error checking.

Listing 3.4. File I/O using exception handling.

```
Program NewIO;

uses Clesses, Dialogs;

Var
  F: TextFile;
  S: String;
Begin
  AssignFile(F, 'FOO.TXT');
  try
    Reset(F);
    try
      ReadLn(F, S);
    finally
      CloseFile(F);
    end;
  exception
    on EInOutError do
      ShowMessage('Error Accessing File!');
  end;
end.
```

In Listing 3.4, the inner try..finally block is used to detect any exceptions that may come down the pike. What this block means in English is "Hey, program, try to execute the statements between the try and the finally. If you finish them or run into an exception, execute the statements between the finally and the end, and then move on to the next exception-handling block."

> **NOTE**
>
> The statements after finally in a try..finally block execute regardless of whether or not an exception occurs. Make sure that the code in your finally block does not assume that an exception has occurred. Also, because the finally statement doesn't stop the migration of an exception, the flow of your program's execution will continue on to the next exception handler.

The outer `try..except` block is used to handle the exceptions as they occur in the program. After the file is closed in the `finally` block, the `except` block puts up a message informing the user that an I/O error occurred.

One of the key advantages that exception handling provides over the traditional method of error handling is the ability to distinctly separate the error-detection code from the error-correction code. This is a good thing primarily because it makes your code easier to read and maintain by enabling you to concentrate on one distinct aspect of the code at a time.

The fact that you cannot trap any specific exception by using the `try..finally` block is significant. When you use a `try..finally` block in your code, it means that you don't care what exceptions might occur. You just want to perform some tasks when they do occur to gracefully get out of a tight spot. The `finally` block is an ideal place to free any resources you've allocated (such as files or Windows resources), because it will always execute in the case of an error, but in many cases you need some type of error handling that is able to respond differently depending on the type of error that occurs. You can trap specific exceptions by using a `try..except` block, which is again illustrated in Listing 3.5.

Listing 3.5. A try..except exception-handling block.

```
Program HandleIt;

Uses WinCRT;

Var
  R1, R2: Real;
Begin
  while True do begin
    try
      Write('Enter a real number: ');
      ReadLn(R1);
      Write('Enter another real number: ');
      ReadLn(R2);
      Writeln('I will now divide the first number by the second...');
      Writeln('The answer is: ', (R1 / R2):5:2);
    except
      On EZeroDivide do
        Writeln('You cannot divide by zero!');
      On EInvalidInput do
        Writeln('That is not a valid number!');
    end;
  end;
End.
```

Although you can trap specific exceptions with the `try..except` block, you also can catch other exceptions by adding the catch-all `else` clause to this construct. The syntax of the `try..except..else` construct follows:

```
try
  Statements
except
  On ESomeException do Something;
```

```
else
  { do some default exception handling }
end;
```

> **CAUTION**
>
> When using the `try..except..else` construct, you should be aware that the `else` part will catch *all* exceptions—even exceptions you might not expect, such as out-of-memory or other runtime-library exceptions. Be careful when using the `else` clause, and use the clause sparingly. You always should re-raise the exception when you trap with unqualified exception handlers. This is explained later in this chapter.

You can achieve the same effect as a `try..except..else` construct also by not specifying the exception class in a `try..except` block, as shown in this example:

```
try
  Statements
except
  HandleException   { same as else statement }
end;
```

Exception Classes

Exceptions are merely special instances of objects. These objects are instantiated when an exception occurs and are destroyed when an exception is handled. The base exception object is called `Exception`, and that object is defined as in the following code:

```
type
  Exception = class(TObject)
  private
    MessagePtr: ^string;
  public
    constructor Create(const Msg: string);
    destructor Destroy; override;
    function Message: string;
  end;
```

The important element of the `Exception` object is the `Message` property, which is a string. `Message` provides more information or explanation on the exception. The information provided by `Message` depends on the type of exception that is raised.

> **CAUTION**
>
> If you define your own exception object, make sure that you derive it from a known exception object such as `Exception` or one of its descendants. The reason for this is so that generic exception handlers will be able to trap your exception.

When you handle a specific type of exception in an except block, that handler also will catch any exceptions that are descendants of the specified exception. For example, EMathError is the ancestor object for a variety of math-related exceptions, such as EZeroDivide and EOverflow. You can catch any of these exceptions by setting up a handler for EMathError as shown here:

```
try
  Statements
except
  on EMathError do  { will catch EMathError or any descendant }
    HandleException
end;
```

Any exceptions that you do not explicitly handle in your program eventually will flow to, and be handled by, the default handler located within the Delphi runtime library. The default handler will put up a message dialog informing the user that an exception occurred.

The Exception Object

When handling an exception, you sometimes needs to access the instance of the exception object in order to retrieve more information on the exception, such as that provided by its Message property. There are two ways to do this: use an optional identifier with the on ESomeException construct, or use the ExceptObject() function.

You can insert an optional identifier in the on ESomeException portion of an except block and have the identifier map to an instance of the currently raised exception. The syntax for this is to preface the exception type with an identifier and a colon, as follows:

```
try
  Something
except
  on E:ESomeException do
    ShowMessage(E.Message);
end;
```

In this case, the identifier E is the instance of the currently raised exception. This identifier is always of the same type as the exception it prefaces.

You also can use the ExceptObject() function, which returns an instance of the currently raised exception. The drawback to ExceptObject(), however, is that it returns a TObject that you must then typecast to the exception object of your choice. The following example shows the usage of this function:

```
try
  Something
except
  on ESomeException do
    ShowMessage(ESomeException(ExceptObject).Message);
end;
```

The ExceptObject() function will return Nil if there is no active exception.

Raising an Exception

The syntax for raising an exception is similar to the syntax for creating an object instance. To raise a user-defined exception called EBadStuff, for example, you would use this syntax:

```
Raise EBadStuff.Create('Some bad stuff happened.');
```

After an exception is raised, the flow of execution of your program propagates up to the next exception handler until the exception instance is finally handled and destroyed. This process is determined by the call stack and therefore works program wide (not just within one procedure or unit). Listing 3.6 illustrates the flow of execution of a program when an exception is raised. This listing is the main unit of a Delphi application that consists of one form with one button on the form. When the button is pressed, the Button1Click() method calls Proc1(), which calls Proc2(), which in turn calls Proc3(). An exception is raised in Proc3(), and you can witness the flow of execution propagating through each try..finally block until the exception is finally handled inside of Button1Click().

TIP

When you run this program from the Delphi IDE, you'll be able to see the flow of execution better if you disable the integrated debugger's handling of exceptions by unchecking Options | Environment | Preferences | Break on Exception.

Listing 3.6. **Main unit for the exception propagation project.**

```
unit Main;

interface

uses
  SysUtils, WinTypes, WinProcs, Messages, Classes, Graphics, Controls,
  Forms, Dialogs, StdCtrls;

type
  TForm1 = class(TForm)
    Button1: TButton;
    procedure Button1Click(Sender: TObject);
  private
    { Private declarations }
  public
    { Public declarations }
  end;

var
  Form1: TForm1;

implementation

{$R *.DFM}
```

continues

Listing 3.6. continued

```
type
  EBadStuff = class(Exception);

procedure Proc3;
begin
  try
    raise EBadStuff.Create('Up the stack we go!');
  finally
    ShowMessage('Proc3 sees the exception');
  end;
end;

procedure Proc2;
begin
  try
    Proc3;
  finally
    ShowMessage('Proc2 sees the exception');
  end;
end;

procedure Proc1;
begin
  try
    Proc2;
  finally
    ShowMessage('Proc1 sees the exception');
  end;
end;

procedure TForm1.Button1Click(Sender: TObject);
begin
  try
    Proc1;
  except
    on E:EBadStuff do
      ShowMessage('Back in calling procedure. Exception handled. ' +
                  'The message is "' + E.Message + '".');
  end;
end;

end.
```

Re-raising an Exception

When you need to perform special handling for a statement inside an existing try..except block and still allow the exception to flow to the block's outer default handler, use a technique called *re-raising the exception*. Listing 3.7 demonstrates an example of re-raising the exception.

Listing 3.7. Re-raising an exception.

```
try { this is outer block }
  { statements }
  { statements }
  ( statements }
  try { this is the special inner block }
    { some statement that may require special handling }
  except
    on ESomeException do
    begin
      { special handling for the inner block statement }
      Raise; { re-raise the exception to the outer block }
    end;
  end;
except
  on ESomeException do ...;    { outer block will always perform default handling }
end;
```

Runtime Type Information

Runtime Type Information (RTTI) is a language feature that gives a Delphi application the capability to retrieve information about its object at runtime. RTTI is also the key to links between Delphi components and their incorporation into the Delphi IDE, but it isn't just an academic process that occurs in the shadows of the IDE.

RTTI Methods

Objects, by virtue of being TObject descendants, contain a pointer to their RTTI and have several built-in methods that enable you to get some useful information out of the RTTI. The following table lists some of the TObject methods that use RTTI to retrieve information about a particular object instance.

Function	Return Type	Returns
ClassName()	String	The name of the object's class
ClassType()	TClass	The object's type
InheritsFrom()	Boolean	Boolean to indicate whether class descends from a given class
ClassParent()	TClass	The object ancestor's type
InstanceSize()	word	The size in bytes of an instance
ClassInfo()	Pointer	A pointer to the object's in-memory RTTI

RTTI Operators

Delphi provides two operators, is and as, that allow comparisons and typecasts of objects via RTTI.

The as keyword is a new form of typesafe typecast. It enables you to cast a low-level object to a descendent and will raise an exception if the typecast is invalid. Suppose that you have a procedure to which you want to be able to pass any type of object. This function definition could be defined as:

```
Procedure Foo(AnObject: TObject);
```

If you want to do something useful with AnObject later in this procedure, you probably will have to cast it to a descendent object. Suppose that you want to assume that AnObject is a TEdit descendant, and you want to change the text it contains. (A TEdit is a Delphi edit control; Delphi controls are discussed in the Chapter 4, "The Visual Component Library (VCL).") You can use the following code:

```
(Foo as TEdit).Text := 'Hello World.';
```

You can use the Boolean comparison operator is to check whether two objects are of compatible types. Use the is operator to compare an unknown object to a known type or instance to determine what properties and behavior you can assume about the unknown object. For example, you might want to check to see whether AnObject is pointer-compatible with TEdit before attempting to typecast it:

```
If (Foo is TEdit) then
  TEdit(Foo).Text := 'Hello World.';
```

Notice that we did not use the as operator to perform the typecast in this example. That's because a certain amount of overhead is involved in using RTTI, and because the first line has already determined that Foo is a TEdit, we can optimize by performing a pointer typecast in the second line.

Summary

Quite a bit of material was covered in this chapter. At this point, you should have a clear understanding of OOP, objects, fields, properties, methods, TObject, exception handling, and RTTI. Now that you have the big picture of how Delphi's object-oriented Object Pascal language works, you're ready to learn about Delphi's backbone: the Visual Component Library.

4

The Visual Component
Library (VCL)

When Borland first introduced the Object Windows Library (OWL) with Turbo Pascal for Windows, it ushered in a drastic simplification over traditional Windows programming. OWL objects automated and streamlined many of the tedious tasks that you otherwise were required to code yourself. No longer did you have to write huge case statements for capturing messages or big chunks of code to manage Windows classes; OWL did this for you. On the other hand, you had to learn a new programming methodology—object-oriented programming.

The Visual Component Library (VCL), OWL's successor, is based on an object model similar to OWL's in principle but is radically different in how it is implemented. The VCL is designed specifically to work within Delphi's visual environment. Instead of creating a window or dialog box with the traditional approach or creating a virtual method in OWL, for example, you can modify a component's behavioral and visual characteristics as you design your program visually.

To really understand the difference between the VCL and other Windows frameworks, you must realize that there are two types of Delphi developers: applications developers and visual component writers. *Applications developers* create complete applications by interacting with the Delphi visual environment (a concept nonexistent in many other frameworks), whereas *component writers* create the development tools for the applications developers.

Whether you plan to create applications with Delphi or to create Delphi components, your understanding of the Visual Component Library is essential. An applications developer should know which properties, events, and methods are available for each object; whereas a component writer must take this knowledge one step further to determine whether to write a new component or to extend an existing one.

This chapter introduces you to the Visual Component Library. It discusses the base objects from which components are derived and Delphi's most commonly used prebuilt components. In addition, you are introduced to the *Object Browser*—a powerful tool that enables you to explore VCL's object and component hierarchy.

Before reading this chapter, you should be familiar with the Delphi environment, using the Object Inspector, and creating simple applications in Delphi. You also should have a basic understanding of object-oriented programming concepts and the Object Pascal language. You might want to review Chapter 2, "Moving to Pascal," and Chapter 3, "The Object Pascal Language," if you think you need to brush up on these topics.

Types of Components

There are basically four types of components that you will use and create in Delphi: standard controls, custom controls, graphical controls, and nonvisual components. Figure 4.1 shows a simplified hierarchy of the Visual Component Library.

FIGURE 4.1.
*The Visual Component
Library hierarchy.*

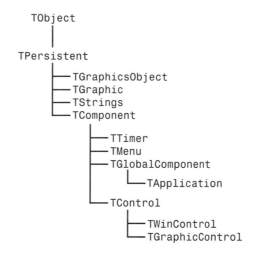

Most of the components you'll use in Delphi are accessible from the Component palette. You can manipulate the behavioral characteristics of a component by setting its properties and creating events from the Object Inspector. Programming with Delphi is different than using most other framework methods because changes in a component's color, size, shape, and other properties are made at design time. You still can modify a component's properties at runtime if you wish. Furthermore, if you are a component writer, you can dictate which component properties you want to make accessible to applications developers using your component.

TObject

You might remember from Chapter 3 that the abstract class TObject is the base class from which all classes descend. As a component writer, you wouldn't descend your components directly from TObject. The VCL already has TObject class descendants from which your new components may be derived. These existing classes provide much of the functionality that you would require for your own components. Only when creating non-component classes would your classes descend from TObject.

TObject's create-and-destroy methods are responsible for allocating and deallocating memory for an object instance. In fact, the TObject.Create constructor returns a reference to the object being created. TObject has several functions that return useful information about a specific object. Table 4.1 lists TObject's methods.

The VCL uses most of TObject's methods internally. You primarily will be using TObject's Create and Free methods, but you can obtain other useful information about an instance of a TObject or TObject descendant such as the instance's class type, classname, and ancestor classes.

Table 4.1. TObject's methods.

Method	Return Type
ClassInfo	Pointer
ClassParent	TClass
ClassType	TClass
Create	*object reference*
DefaultHandler(var)	*not applicable*
Destroy	*not applicable*
Dispatch(var)	*not applicable*
FieldAddress(const: string)	Pointer
Free	*not applicable*
FreeInstance	*not applicable*
InheritsFrom(TClass)	Boolean
InitInstance(Pointer)	TObject
InstanceSize	Word
MethodAddress(const String)	Pointer
MethodName(Pointer)	String
Name	String
NewInstance	TObject

CAUTION

Use TObject.Free instead of TObject.Destroy. The Free method calls destroy for you but first checks to see whether the object is nil before calling destroy. This method ensures that you will not generate an exception by attempting to destroy an invalid object.

To see how to use TObject's methods, create a new project. The main form has the components shown in Figure 4.2. Table 4.2 lists the components that should appear on the form and shows their event handlers as well.

Table 4.2. Object Inspector property settings.

Control	Event	Event Handler
Edit1	OnEnter	Edit1OnEnter
Button1	OnEnter	Edit1OnEnter
StringGrid1	OnEnter	Edit1OnEnter
BitBtn1	OnClick	BitBtn1OnClick
BitBtn2	OnClick	BitBtn2OnClick
ListBox1	*none*	*none*
Form1	OnActivate	FormActivate

If you wish, you can load the example project CLASINF.DPR from the \SOURCE\CH4 directory located on the CD in the back of this book.

FIGURE 4.2.
*Form1 from
CLASINF0.PAS.*

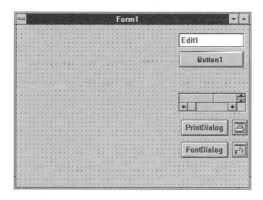

First, create a private procedure called `WriteClassInfo`. This procedure appears in the private section of your form's type definition as

```
private
    procedure WriteClassInfo(Sender: TObject);
```

The code for `WriteClassInfo` is shown in Listing 4.1.

Listing 4.1. The `WriteClassInfo` procedure.

```
procedure TForm1.WriteClassInfo(Sender: TObject);
var
  ParentClass: TClass;
begin
  with ListBox1.Items do begin
    Clear;                                    { Clear the listbox's strings }
```

continues

Listing 4.1. continued

```
    Add('Class Name: '+Sender.ClassName);  { Add Sender's class name to
➥Listbox1 }
    Add('Ancestry:');                       { Add the string, Ancestry: to
➥Listbox1 }
    PClass := Sender.ClassParent;           { Use ParentClass as a pointer to
➥Sender's parent }
    while PClass <> nil do begin            { Continue to point ParentClass to
➥the parent of itself }
      Add('    '+PClass.ClassName);         { until it's value is nil, and print
➥out the class name }
      PClass := PClass.ClassParent;         { When it is nil, the end of the
➥hierarchy is found }
    end;
  end;
end;
```

Inside WriteClassInfo, you will require the type definition TClass, which is defined in Delphi's typinfo unit. You therefore must add typinfo to your uses clause. See Listing 4.3 to see how this is done.

WriteClassInfo first clears all strings, if any, that are in ListBox1. Then it uses TObject's ClassName method to retrieve Sender's class name. The parameter Sender is of the type TObject. By declaring Sender as a TObject type, you can pass any descendant of TObject as a parameter to writeClassInfo, as we illustrate in this example. WriteClassInfo then assigns the return value of Sender's ClassParent method to the ParentClass local variable. ParentClass now points to Sender's Parent class. The while loop walks up Sender's hierarchy by continually assigning the return value of the object that ParentClass points to, back to ParentClass until ParentClass equals nil, or the end of the hierarchy.

Create an OnEnter event handler for Edit1 that contains the following code:

```
procedure TForm1.Edit1Enter(Sender: TObject);
begin
  WriteClassInfo(Sender);
end;
```

Here, Delphi created the variable Sender. Sender is associated with the object that caused the OnEnter method to be executed. Because the parameter is a TObject, and Delphi components are descendants of TObject, multiple controls can be linked to the same event handler. To illustrate this, link the OnEnter event handlers for the TStringGrid and TButton components to Edit1's OnEnter event handler. In the Object Inspector's events page, click the right side of either control's OnEnter event handler. A drop-down list contains the OnClick event handler for Edit1. Select it. Your control now is linked to the same OnClick event handler for Edit1.

BitBtn1's OnEnter event handler should contain the following code:

```
procedure TForm1.BitBtn1Click(Sender: TObject);
begin
  WriteClassInfo(PrintDialog1);
end;
```

Here, you pass the TPrintDialog object. You will see why you do this when you run the program. Remember, WriteClassInfo takes a TObject parameter. Because TPrintDialog is a TObject descendant, it is a valid parameter.

Do the same for the BitBtn2 object, except pass the FontDialog1 object instead of the PrintDialog1 object:

```
procedure TForm1.BitBtn2Click(Sender: TObject);
begin
  WriteClassInfo(FontDialog1);
end;
```

At this point, you should be able to compile and run the project. Listing 4.2 shows the project's project file CLASINF.DPR, and Figure 4.3 shows its output.

Listing 4.2. The source code for the CLASINF.DPR project file.

```
program Clasinfo;
uses
  Forms,
  Uclasinf in 'UCLASINF.PAS' {Form1};
{$R *.RES}

begin
  Application.Hun(Form1);
end.
```

FIGURE. 4.3.

Output from
CLASINF.DPR.

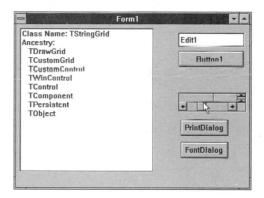

Listing 4.3 contains the complete source code for this project. When a component gets focus, its class name and ancestry are displayed on the form. Listing 4.3 is the unit for Form1, CLASINF0.PAS.

Listing 4.3. The source code for CLASINF0.PAS, Form1's unit.

```
unit Clasinf0;
interface

uses WinTypes, WinProcs, Classes, Graphics, Forms, Controls, StdCtrls,
     TypInfo, Buttons, Grids, Dialogs;

type
  TForm1 = class(TForm)
    Edit1: TEdit;
    Button1: TButton;
    StringGrid1: TStringGrid;
    BitBtn1: TBitBtn;
    PrintDialog1: TPrintDialog;
    FontDialog1: TFontDialog;
    BitBtn2: TBitBtn;
    ListBox1: TListBox;
    procedure Edit1Enter(Sender: TObject);
    procedure BitBtn1Click(Sender: TObject);
    procedure BitBtn2Click(Sender: TObject);
    procedure FormActivate(Sender: TObject);
  private
    procedure WriteClassInfo(Sender: TObject);
    { Private declarations }
  public
    { Public declarations }
  end;

var
  Form1: TForm1;

implementation

{$R *.DFM}

procedure TForm1.WriteClassInfo(Sender: TObject);
var
  ParentClass: TClass;
begin
  with ListBox1.Items do begin
    Clear;                                 { Clear the listbox's strings }
    Add('Class Name: '+Sender.ClassName); { Add Sender's class name to
➥Listbox1 }
    Add('Ancestry:');                      { Add the string, Ancestry: to
➥Listbox1 }
    ParentClass := Sender.ClassParent;     { Use ParentClass as a pointer to
➥Sender's parent }
    while ParentClass <> nil do begin      { Continue to point ParentClass to
➥the parent of itself }
      Add('   '+ParentClass.ClassName);    { until it's value is nil, and print
➥out the class name }
      ParentClass := ParentClass.ClassParent; { When it is nil, the end of the
➥hierarchy is found }
    end;
  end;
end;
```

```
procedure TForm1.Edit1Enter(Sender: TObject);
begin
  WriteClassInfo(Sender); { Call the WriteClassInfo() procedure }
end;

procedure TForm1.BitBtn1Click(Sender: TObject);
begin
  WriteClassInfo(PrintDialog1); { Call the WriteClassInfo() procedure but pass}
end;                            { the TPrintDialog to show its ancestry }

procedure TForm1.BitBtn2Click(Sender: TObject);
begin
  WriteClassInfo(FontDialog1); { Call the WriteClassInfo() procedure, but  }
end;                           { pass the TFontDialog to display its class
➡ancestry }

procedure TForm1.FormActivate(Sender: TObject);
begin
  WriteClassInfo(Edit1); { Call the WriteClassInfo() procedure }
end;

end.
```

TPersistent

TPersistent is an abstract class that descends directly from TObject. An *abstract* class is a class that defines an interface but does not implement it. The special characteristic of TPersistent is that objects descending from it can read/write their properties from/to a stream once they are created. A stream is basically a file in which information is stored. You'll hear more about streams later; for now, just know that TPersistent descendants can read/write their properties from/to a file after they are created. This is different from a TComponent, which has the capability to create oneself from a stream; a TPersistent can only read information about itself from a stream once it's created.

TComponent

The TComponent class descends directly from TPersistent. Almost all the components that you will use in Delphi descend from TComponent. TComponent's special purpose is its capability to own other components. When you work with Delphi, for example, you select components from the Component palette and drop them onto your form. The underlying code causes these components to be owned by the form onto which you dropped them.

As a component writer, your nonvisual component probably will descend from TComponent. A good example of a nonvisual TComponent descendant is the TTimer component. TTimers are not visual controls but still are available on the Component palette.

Examine some `TComponent` properties and methods in the following code:

```
Owner: TComponent
ComponentCount: integer
ComponentIndex: integer
Components[integer]: TComponent
Name: TComponentName
Tag: LongInt
```

`Owner` returns the component's owner, which also is a `TComponent` descendant. See the sidebar "Owner or Parent?" later in this chapter for a discussion on component ownership versus parenthood.

`ComponentCount` returns the number of components owned by the component. Somewhere deep down in the VCL hierarchy is a `TForm` class, for example. `TForm` is a descendant of `TComponent` and inherits all of `TComponent`'s properties. When you place controls from the Component palette onto your form, they are added to the form's component list. The form becomes the owner of those controls.

The `ComponentIndex` property returns its own position in its owner's component list. The first component in the component list has the index of zero.

The `Components` property is an array that returns a component specified by its index. For example, this line of code assigns the third component in `Form1`'s component list to `MyComponent`:

```
MyComponent := Form1.Components[2];
```

The `Tag` property is not used by Delphi. `Tag` is a `longint` type. Because the `longint` type is equal in size to a `pointer`, you can store any user-defined information with the `Tag` property as long as you typecast it as a `pointer` type if you're using it as a pointer.

The `Name` property returns the name of the component as displayed in the Object Inspector's drop-down combo box from which you select components.

To illustrate the use of some of these properties, create a new project. Table 4.3 contains the components and their properties for your new form. Listings 4.4 and 4.5 show the project's project file, EDITSHO.DPR, and the main form's unit, EDITSHO0.PAS, respectively. You also can load this project into Delphi from the \SOURCE\CH4\ directory on the CD.

Table 4.3. Object Inspector property settings and event handlers.

Control	Property	Value
		Property Settings
Edit1	Text	' '
Edit2	Text	' '
Edit3	Text	' '
Edit4	Text	' '
Edit5	Text	' '

Control	Property	Value
Edit6	Text	' '
Edit7	Text	' '
Button1	Caption	'Edit Mode'
Button2	Caption	'Add Edit'
Button3	Caption	'Delete Edit'
Label1	Caption	'Label1'

Control	Event	Event Handler
		Event Handlers
Button1	OnClick	Button1Click
Button2	OnClick	Button2Click
Button3	OnClick	Button3Click
Form1	OnShow	FormShow

Figure 4.4 shows what your form should look like.

FIGURE 4.4.

Form1 from EDITSHO0.PAS.

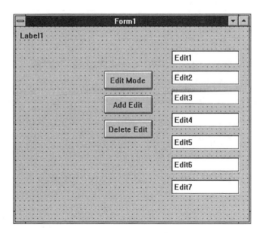

Create Form1's OnShow event handler, which sets Label1's Caption property to reflect the number of components it owns, by referring to its own ComponentCount property:

```
procedure TForm1.FormShow(Sender: TObject);
begin
  Label1.Caption := 'ComponentCount: '+IntToStr(ComponentCount);
end;
```

The Button1 OnClick event handler contains the for loop shown in following code:

```
procedure TForm1.Button1Click(Sender: TObject);
var
  i: integer;
begin
  for i := 0 to ComponentCount - 1 do  begin     { Look at each component on the
➥form }
    if Components[i] is TEdit then                { is the component a TEdit ? }
      with TEdit(Components[i]) do begin          { typecast and use the with
➥construct }
        if ReadOnly = false then                  { if the TEdit is readonly
➥then set its text }
          Text := 'Comp Index: '+ inttostr(ComponentIndex) { to display its
➥ComponentIndex value }
        else                                      { otherwise display its name }
          Text := Name;
        ReadOnly := not(ReadOnly);                { reverse the TEdit's readonly
➥flag }
      end; { with }

    if Components[i] is TButton then              { if the component is a TButton }
      with TButton(Components[i]) do              { typecast it as such and use the
➥with construct }
        if Caption = 'Edit Mode' then             { Check the button's caption and
➥change it depending }
          Caption := 'Read Only'                  { on its existing caption }
        else if Caption = 'Read Only' then
          Caption := 'Edit Mode';
  end; { for }
end;
```

The code here shows how one would iterate through the components a form owns with the for .. do construct:

```
for i := 0 to ComponentCount - 1 do
  begin
```

In this project, all TButton and TEdit components are owned by the Form1 because they appear on the Form1.

Inside the if..then block, you use RTTI to see whether Components[i] is an edit control. If it is an edit control, the code then reverses the TEdit control's read-only flag and modifies its contents.

The next if..then block changes the Button captions if the component is a TButton. Every TComponent descendent has the capability to iterate through its components. You can see that this is a powerful way to modify a components attributes at runtime without having to refer to the components by their individual instance variables, thus saving you lines of coding.

Button2's OnClick event handler demonstrates creating a control on the fly. Here, the variable MyEdit of type Tedit is declared. This line creates the Edit control:

```
MyEdit := TEdit.Create(Self);
```

By passing the Self parameter to the Create method, the form becomes the owner of the Edit control. You also make assignment to the Edit control's properties. All these properties, except for the parent property, affect this control's visual appearance. The parent property assigns the form as the parent for this control, again, using the Self parameter.

Notice that the FindComponent property also is used. This property returns the owned component with the name, which is passed as a parameter. This example uses FindComponent to determine whether the TEdit control already exists before creating another TEdit instance. Button3's OnClick event handler searches for the control named MyEdit before attempting to remove MyEdit from its component array. Figure 4.5 shows the output of the EDITSHO.DPR project after the control MyEdit is created. Listings 4.4 and 4.5 show the source code for the project file, EDITSHO.DPR, and the unit file, EDITSHO0.PAS, respectively.

FIGURE 4.5.

*Output of
EDITSHO.DPR with
added control.*

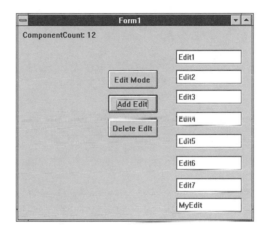

Listing 4.4. The source code for the EDITSHO.DPR project file.

```
program Editsho;

uses
  Forms,
  Editsho0 in 'EDITSHO0.PAS' {Form1};

{$R *.DFM}

begin
  Application.CreateForm(TForm1, Form1);
  Application.Run;
end.
```

Listing 4.5. The source code for EDITSHO0.PAS, Form1's unit file.

```
unit Editsho0;
interface

uses WinTypes, WinProcs, Classes, Forms, Controls, StdCtrls,
     TypInfo,  Buttons, sysutils, Dialogs, Graphics;

type
  TForm1 = class(TForm)
    Edit1: TEdit;
    Edit2: TEdit;
    Edit3: TEdit;
    Edit4: TEdit;
    Edit5: TEdit;
    Edit6: TEdit;
    Edit7: TEdit;
    Button1: TButton;
    Button2: TButton;
    Button3: TButton;
    Label1: TLabel;
    procedure Button1Click(Sender: TObject);
    procedure Button2Click(Sender: TObject);
    procedure Button3Click(Sender: TObject);
    procedure FormShow(Sender: TObject);
  private
    { Private declarations }
  public
    { Public declarations }
  end;

var
  Form1: TForm1;

implementation

{$R *.DFM}

procedure TForm1.Button1Click(Sender: TObject);
var
  i: integer;
begin
  for i := 0 to ComponentCount - 1 do  begin     { Look at each component on the
➥form }
    if Components[i] is TEdit then                { is the component a TEdit ? }
      with TEdit(Components[i]) do begin          { typecast and use the with
➥construct }
        if ReadOnly = false then                 { if the TEdit is readonly  then
➥set its text }
          Text := 'Comp Index: '+ IntToStr(ComponentIndex) { to display its
➥ComponentIndex value }
        else                                      { otherwise display its name }
          Text := Name;
        ReadOnly := not(ReadOnly);                { reverse the TEdit's readonly
➥flag }
      end; { with }
```

```
       if Components[i] is TButton then         { if the component is a TButton }
         with TButton(Components[i]) do          { typecast it as such and use the
➥with construct }
            if Caption = 'Edit Mode' then        { Check the button's caption and
➥change it depending }
               Caption := 'Read Only'            { on its existing caption }
            else if Caption = 'Read Only' then
               Caption := 'Edit Mode';
   end; { for }
end;

procedure TForm1.Button2Click(Sender: TObject);
begin
   if FindComponent('MyEdit') = nil then begin { if the component whose name is
➥'MyEdit' is not }
     with TEdit.Create(Self) do begin           { present, create a new one }
       Parent := Self;                           { Assign the new TEdit's parent
➥property to the form }
       Left := 288;                              { as reference by the implicit
➥self parameter. }
       Name := 'MyEdit';                         { Set MyEdit's name accordingly }
       Text := 'MyEdit';                         { Set MyEdit's text property to
➥show its name }
       Top := 312;                               { specify the coordinates. to place
➥the edit control }
       Width := 121;
       Height := 24;
       Visible := true;                          { Set the Visible property to true
➥so that it will display. }
     end;
   end;
   Label1.Caption := 'ComponentCount: '+IntToStr(ComponentCount); { Now show the
➥new component count }
end;

procedure TForm1.Button3Click(Sender: TObject);
begin
   FindComponent('MyEdit').Free; { Free the component named 'MyEdit' }
   { Show the new component count }
   Label1.Caption := 'ComponentCount: '+IntToStr(ComponentCount);
end;

procedure TForm1.FormShow(Sender: TObject);
begin
   { Show the new component count }
   Label1.Caption := 'ComponentCount: '+IntToStr(ComponentCount);
end;

end.
```

TControl

Earlier in this chapter, you learned that TComponent was the class from which components become known to Delphi. TControl is the class from which controls inherit the capability to display themselves and enable the user to interactively modify them in the Delphi environment. TControl provides the properties and methods common to all visible controls. Visible controls require properties to maintain their size and coordinates on the form, for example. TControl provides the Top and Left properties, as well as Width and Height properties, for holding the horizontal and vertical sizes, respectively.

TControl itself isn't very useful. Most of Delphi's controls are derived from TControl's descendants: TWinControl or TGraphicControl.

TWinControl

Standard Windows controls descend from the class TWinControl. As the name implies, standard controls are the interface objects you see in most Windows applications. Items such as edit controls, listboxes, combo boxes, and buttons are examples of these standard controls. Delphi encapsulates the behavior of these controls, so instead of using Windows API functions to manipulate them, you use the properties provided by each of the various control components.

The three basic characteristics of TWinControl objects are that they have a Windows handle, have the capability to receive input focus and can be parents to other controls.

HANDLES

Handles are 16-bit numbers issued by Windows that refer to individual window instances. This means that in the Windows environment, every window has a unique handle. Many Windows API functions require a handle to know on which window to perform the function. Delphi performs much of the Windows API for you, and also performs handle management. If you want to use a Windows API function that requires a window handle, use the Handle property of any TWinControl descendant.

Figure 4.6 illustrates TWinControl's descendant hierarchy. Each control has the same functionality of its equivalent Window's class.

You will use these controls extensively later in this book. Don't worry if you're not familiar with them yet. They'll be introduced as you use them in later examples. Some typical TWinControl descendants are

```
TButton
TCheckBox
TCustomComboBox
TCustomControl
TCustomEdit
TCustomListBox
TPage
TRadioButton
TScrollBar
TScrollingWinControl
TVBXControl
```

FIGURE 4.6.

TWinControl's descendant hierarchy.

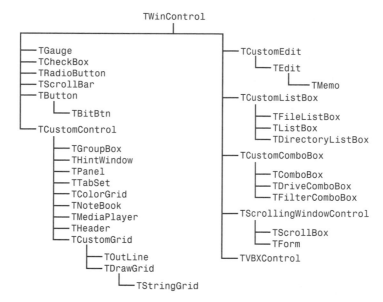

OWNER OR PARENT?

Don't confuse the parent and owner properties. An owner determines when an owned control is created and destroyed. A parent provides the visual display context for a control—no parent, no display. A parent also determines where the control is drawn. The top and left coordinates used for positioning a control are relative to the top-left corner of the parent.

Ownership

Every component has an owner property that specifies the control's owner. A component is responsible for freeing the components it owns when the component itself is destroyed. A component maintains a list of the components it owns, and the list is accessible from the TComponent.Components property. The TForm object owns all the components that appear on the form itself. TForm, in turn, is owned by the application. Therefore, when your application terminates, it destroys the form, which, in the process, causes the form to destroy the form's own components.

Parenthood

Parenthood refers specifically to windowed controls, meaning that only TWinControls can be parents. A control's parent property points to the actual parent component. When a control has a parent, it is considered a child of that parent. A TGroupBox object, for example, would be the parent to the TCheckBox objects that are placed into the groupbox. However, the form still owns the TCheckBox objects. When a parent control is destroyed, it is not responsible for freeing its children. Child controls are accessible from the TWinControl.Controls property.

An Applications developer primarily will use TWinControl descendants. A component writer will need to understand the TCustomControl descendant of TWinControl.

TCustomControl

You might have noticed that some TWinControl descendants' names began with TCustom. These included the following:

```
TCustomComboBox
TCustomControl
TCustomEdit
TCustomListBox
```

Custom controls have the same functionality of other TWinControl descendants, except for the capability to draw themselves. Because certain controls have very specialized visual and interactive characteristics, custom controls provide you with a base from which you can derive and create your own customized components.

Many components, however, will not receive input focus but still can interact with the user. The TGraphicControl class is used for this purpose.

TGraphicControl

Graphic controls have three characteristics that make them special: they don't contain a window handle, they don't receive the user input focus, and they cannot be parents to other components. Whenever a window is created, it requests a handle from Windows. These handles use up system resources. Controls that don't require user interaction would be better off not depleting Windows of its resources. Just how expensive can windowed controls be? Consider this: Delphi's Component palette is made of 67 speed buttons. That would require 67 separate windows handles, not to mention all the other windows handles Delphi needs. Additionally, not having a window handle means that TGraphicControls don't have to go through the convoluted Windows paint process. This makes their drawing much faster than their TWinControl equivalents. Following is a list of commonly used, noninteractive TGraphicControls that you'll find on Delphi's Component Palette and that you can use in your applications:

```
TBevel
TImage
TLabel
TShape
TSpeedButton
```

Other Components

There are many other components that are part of the VCL. Delphi provides you with an extremely useful set of tools you can use to build impressive applications; most of these components are discussed and used in sample programs in this book as the need arises. In the future, Delphi will evolve and grow richer as you continue to add to your library of components.

The Object Browser

The Object Browser is a tool that you can use to explore objects, units, and class hierarchies. By using the Browser, you can see not only the properties and methods of the object you are browsing but also all of its ancestors. You can access the Browser from the View I Browser menu. You first need to create a project, however, and compile it before this menu option is enabled. The reason for this is because the Browser looks at compiler symbol information which is generated only after compilation. Therefore, to see the Browser in action, you must create a very simple project: a form with a button will do. Compile this project. This will enable the Browser option.

Select View I Browser from Delphi's menu. Figure 4.7 shows the Object Browser window.

FIGURE 4.7.

The Object Browser window.

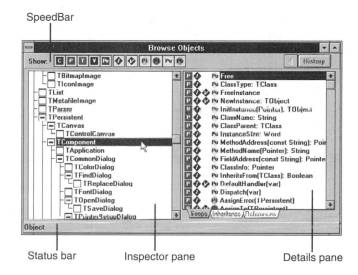

The Browser is made up of a SpeedBar, an Inspector pane, a Details pane, and a Status bar.

The *Inspector pane* is the large pane on the left side of the Browser. When you are browsing objects, the Inspector pane displays the object hierarchy in a collapsible tree. Nodes on the tree that are preceded by a plus sign (+) indicate they contain subnodes that represent descendant objects. You can expand the tree by clicking the + symbol. The minus sign (-) symbol indicates that the node is fully expanded. If no symbol is present, no objects descend from that particular node.

The Inspector pane displays the symbols that you can browse. You can bring up a local menu by right-clicking the mouse button while the mouse pointer is on the Inspector pane. You can browse objects, units, or globals from this menu.

If you are browsing units, the Inspector pane lists the units that have been compiled into your project. Finally, if you are browsing symbols, the Inspector pane displays all symbols declared in units that your project is using.

> **NOTE**
>
> The Object Browser shows all the symbols that are available in the units you use. The Delphi compiler's smart-linking will remove everything that is not actually used by the program.

The *Details pane,* which is on the right side of the Inspector pane, contains three pages: Scope, Inheritance, and Reference. The *Scope page* lists all the symbols that are declared in the unit or object being inspected in the Inspector pane. The *Inheritance page* shows a collapsible tree for item being inspected. The *Reference page* shows the unit's filenames and line numbers in which the selected item is declared or used in your source code.

You can limit or expand the various symbols you want the Object Browser to display based on symbol type and access level. To do so, select the buttons in the SpeedBar at the top of the Object Browser to specify which symbols you want to browse. Figure 4.8 shows you what each button on the SpeedBar represents.

FIGURE 4.8.
The Object Browser SpeedBar.

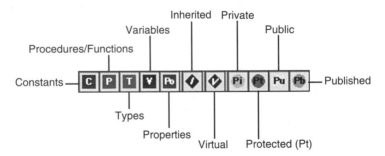

Experiment with the Browser to get a feel for how you can navigate through the object hierarchies. To see how you can use the Browser to locate symbols in your source code, create a new project—a form with two buttons. Double-click on the button labeled Button2. You now are in the editor for Button2's OnClick event handler. Place the following line between the begin..end statements:

```
Button1.Caption := 'hello';
```

Compile the project, and then select View|Browser from Delphi's menu. The Object Browser appears. With the mouse cursor in the Inspector pane, hold down the right mouse button and select the Symbol option. Type **Form1** in the edit control of the Browse Symbol dialog box, and click OK. The Object Browser's caption should change to Object Browser - [Form1], as shown in Figure 4.9.

FIGURE 4.9.

The Object Browser showing Form1 *symbols.*

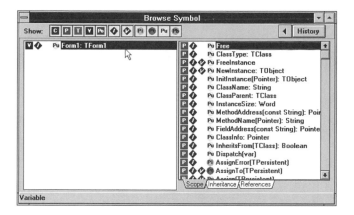

The items in the Inspector pane are the symbols belonging to your main form, Form1. Look at the list of symbols in the Inspector pane, and you will see the two buttons you placed on your form:

```
TForm1.Button1: TButton
TForm1.Button2.: TButton
```

Each of these lines is preceded by a symbol indicating its symbol type. Select Button1 in the list. Now select the References page on the Details pane. You will see two entries for your unit followed by a line number. Double-click the second entry. This takes you to the Code Editor where that symbol appears in the unit specified in the References page. You can see how, in a large program, you can use the Browser to locate symbols for you instead of having to search through thousands of lines of source code.

> **NOTE**
>
> Because the Object Browser uses compiler symbol information, you see only what the compiler sees. When searching for symbols using the Object Browser, you won't have to go through a multitude of "Button2" strings in comment blocks or in other forms, as is the case when using a text search.

Summary

This chapter introduced you to the Visual Component Library. You learned about the VCL Hierarchy and the special characteristics of components at different levels on the hierarchy. You also learned about using the Object Browser to navigate through VCL's hierarchy and to browse your application's symbols. The next chapter guides you through the objects that make up the framework on which all Delphi applications are built. For now, you might experiment with the various components and their properties before continuing on. You will learn from the experience and have fun doing it!

5

Basic Concepts in Delphi—*TForms, TScreen,* and *TApplication*

The previous four chapters gave you a hearty introduction to the basic language foundations with which you will build robust Delphi applications. This chapter gets you started by showing you how to use the Delphi environment to manipulate Delphi applications' basic objects, TForm, TScreen, and TApplication.

TForms are the foundation from which you build all Delphi application interfaces. TScreen is an object that encapsulates information and the behavior of your screen device. Finally, TApplication is the object encapsulating your project as a Windows application.

Before reading this chapter, you should be familiar with the Object Pascal language and have a working understanding of the Visual Component Library. You should know how to set component properties with the Object Inspector.

Strange New Life—Forms

In Chapter 1, "Windows Programming in Delphi," you were introduced to the Form Designer. You created a simple application consisting of a single form with a button. After compiling and running your project, your form executed just like a normal Windows application. You could have saved your form to retrieve later for another project, or you could have called it from another form. Forms, in Delphi, are your windows and dialog boxes for your Windows applications.

You gained a great deal of exposure to the Form Designer while creating the small sample projects in previous chapters. To further understand how you can use the Forms Designer to build complete applications, you must learn about more of TForm's properties and how to manipulate them at design and runtime.

Changing a Form's Icon Boxes and Borders

Create a new project with a blank form. In the Object Inspector, double-click on the left side of the BorderIcons property. The values side should expand to show you three possibilities: biSystemMenu, biMaximize, and biMinimize. By setting any or all of these to false, you can remove the system menu, the maximize box, or the minimize box from the form.

You also can change the non-client area of your form by changing the Border Style property. On the right side of the BorderStyle property, click the down arrow to display the four options:

NOTE

Changes to the BorderIcon and BorderStyle properties are not reflected at design-time. These changes happen at runtime only. This is the case with many other properties as well.

When you start a new project, bsSizable style is the default setting. This style causes your form to contain a thick, resizable border. The bsSingle style places a single line border on your form. The form will not be resizable. The bsDialog style gives your form the standard dialog box border, and makes it unable to be resized. The bsNone style creates a form with no border. To create a borderless, captionless form, set the BorderStyle property to bsNone and all BorderIcons to false.

STICKY CAPTIONS!

Creating captionless, resizable forms requires a little bit of trickery not yet covered. You must override the form's CreateParams() method and set the styles required for that window style. The following code snippet shows the code that does this:

```
unit Nocapu;

interface

uses
  SysUtils, WinTypes, WinProcs, Messages, Classes, Graphics, Controls,
  Forms, Dialogs;

type
  TForm1 = class(TForm)
  private
    { Private declarations }
  public
    { Public declarations }
    procedure CreateParams(var Params: TCreateParams); override;  { override
➥CreateParams method }
  end;

var
  Form1: TForm1;

implementation

{$R *.DFM}
procedure TForm1.CreateParams(var Params: TCreateParams);
begin
  inherited CreateParams(Params);  { Call the inherited Params }
  Params.Style := WS_THICKFRAME or WS_POPUP or WS_BORDER; { Set the style
➥accordingly }
end;

end.
```

This code is a look ahead to a topic covered in Chapter 11, "Writing Delphi Custom Components," about changing Window styles and the CreateParams() method.

Some properties in the Object Inspector affect the appearance of your form, while others define behavioral aspects for your form. You should experiment with each property that you are not familiar with. If you need to know more about a property, use Delphi's help system to find more information.

> **TIP**
>
> The Delphi Help system is without a doubt the most valuable and speedy reference that you have at your fingertips. It would be advantageous to learn how to use it to explore the thousands of Help screens available.
>
> Delphi contains help on everything from how to use the Delphi environment to details on complex Windows structures. You can get immediate help on a topic by typing the topic in the editor and, with the cursor still on the word you typed, press Ctrl+F1. The help screen will appear immediately. Otherwise, ask for help by selecting it from Delphi's menus.

You might remember that properties in the Object Inspector also can be modified with code at runtime along with even more properties that are not in the Object Inspector at design-time. We're going to illustrate how to give your users the capability to modify the appearance of the applications you create.

Create a new project. Change the name of Form1 from Form1 to MainForm in the Object Inspector.

> **CAUTION**
>
> Always change the form's Name property in the Object Inspector and not in the source code. Otherwise, Delphi will not be able to compile your projects.

Place a TButton control on MainForm. You'll learn what this button does later. Figure 5.1 shows this form.

FIGURE 5.1.
The main form for the sample project, MainForm.

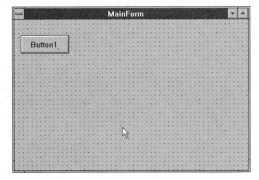

Now create another form by selecting File | New Form from the Main menu. Change this new form's name to OptionsForm. Figure 5.2 shows what OptionsForm should look like. It contains a TGroupBox component with four TRadioButtons, one TEdit, one TLabel, and two TBitBtn components. The Kind properties for the TBitBtn components are bkOK and bkCancel as shown in the figure.

FIGURE 5.2.

The OptionsForm specifies MainForm's property changes.

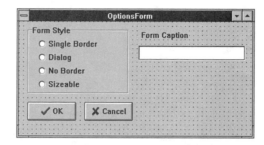

You do not have to code anything for OptionsForm. MainForm displays OptionsForm and then its component settings to modify its own styles. Go back to the MainForm and add the event handler shown in Listing 5.1 for Button1.

Listing 5.1. Button1's OnClick event handler.

```
procedure TMainForm.Button1Click(Sender: TObject);
begin
  { Initialize the Options forms selections with the current settings for }
  { TMainForm }
  case BorderStyle of
    bsSingle: OptionsForm.RadioButton1.Checked := true;
    bsDialog: OptionsForm.RadioButton2.Checked := true;
    bsNone: OptionsForm.RadioButton3.Checked := true;
    bsSizeable: OptionsForm.RadioButton4.Checked := true;
  end;
  { Set OptionsForm's edit control to reflect TMainForm's caption }
  OptionsForm.Edit1.Text := Caption;
  if OptionsForm.ShowModal = mrOK then  { Display OptionsForm }
  begin { Now set MainForm's styles to those specified by OptionsForm }
    if OptionsForm.RadioButton1.Checked then
      BorderStyle := bsSingle
    else if OptionsForm.RadioButton2.Checked then
      BorderStyle := bsDialog
    else if OptionsForm.RadioButton3.Checked then
      BorderStyle := bsNone
    else if OptionsForm.RadioButton4.Checked then
      BorderStyle := bsSizeable;
    if OptionsForm.Edit1.Text <> '' then
      Caption := OptionsForm.Edit1.Text;
  end
end;
```

This event handler first sets the appropriate RadioButtons on OptionsForm according to MainForm's BorderStyle property. It then sets Edit1's Text property to reflect MainForm's Caption. The line

```
if OptionsForm.ShowModal = mrOK then    { Display OptionsForm }
```

displays OptionsForm and checks its return value. ShowModal returns the form's modal result. The modal result is set when the user chooses one of the BitBtns on OptionsForm. You may recall that the Kind property for BitBtn1 and BitBtn2 is set to bkOk and bkCancel, respectively. This sets a pre-defined modal result value for each BitBtn. BitBtn1.ModalResult is mrOK and BitBtn2.ModalResult is mrCancel.

If the ShowModal returns mrOK, Form1's Borderstyle and Caption are set based on the component values in OptionsForm.

It's possible to extend OptionsForm's selections to enable you to fully configure the appearance of any application. Take a look at how Delphi does it by selecting Options | Environment from Delphi's menu. Listings 5.2, 5.3, and 5.4 show the code for CNGFORM.DPR, MAINCNGF.PAS, and OPTFORM.PAS, the source code for this project.

Listing 5.2. The source code for CHGFORM.DPR.

```
program Chgform;

uses
  Forms,
  Maincngf in 'MAINCNGF.PAS' {MainForm},
  Optform in 'OPTFORM.PAS' {OptionsForm};

{$R *.RES}

begin
  Application.CreateForm(TMainForm, MainForm);
  Application.CreateForm(TOptionsForm, OptionsForm);
  Application.Run;
end.
```

Listing 5.3. The source code for MAINCNGF.PAS.

```
unit Maincngf;
interface

uses WinTypes, WinProcs, Classes, Graphics, Forms, Controls,
StdCtrls, optform;

type
  TMainForm = class(TForm)
    Button1: TButton;
    procedure Button1Click(Sender: TObject);
  private
    { Private declarations }
```

```
  public
    { Public declarations }
  end;

var
  MainForm: TMainForm;

implementation

{$R *.DFM}

procedure TMainForm.Button1Click(Sender: TObject);
begin
  { Initialize the Options forms selections with the current settings for }
  { TMainForm }
  case BorderStyle of
    bsSingle: OptionsForm.RadioButton1.Checked := true;
    bsDialog: OptionsForm.RadioButton2.Checked := true;
    bsNone: OptionsForm.RadioButton3.Checked := true;
    bsSizeable: OptionsForm.RadioButton4.Checked := true;
  end;
  { Set OptionsForm's edit control to reflect TMainForm's caption }
  OptionsForm.Edit1.Text := Caption;
  if OptionsForm.ShowModal = IDOK then  { Display OptionsForm }
  begin { Now set MainForm's styles to those specified by OptionsForm }
    if OptionsForm.RadioButton1.Checked then
      BorderStyle := bsSingle
    else if OptionsForm.RadioButton2.Checked then
      BorderStyle := bsDialog
    else if OptionsForm.RadioButton3.Checked then
      BorderStyle := bsNone
    else if OptionsForm.RadioButton4.Checked then
      BorderStyle := bsSizeable;
    if OptionsForm.Edit1.Text <> '' then
      Caption := OptionsForm.Edit1.Text;
  end
end;

end.
```

Listing 5.4. The source code for OPTFORM.PAS.

```
unit Optform;
interface

uses WinTypes, WinProcs, Classes, Graphics, Forms, Controls, StdCtrls,
  Buttons;

type

  TOptionsForm = class(TForm)
    GroupBox1: TGroupBox;
    RadioButton1: TRadioButton;
    RadioButton2: TRadioButton;
    RadioButton3: TRadioButton;
```

continues

Listing 5.4. continued

```
   RadioButton4: TRadioButton;
   Edit1: TEdit;
   Label1: TLabel;
   BitBtn1: TBitBtn;
   BitBtn2: TBitBtn;
 private
   { Private declarations }
 public
   { Public declarations }
 end;

var
 OptionsForm: TOptionsForm;

implementation

{$R *.DFM}

end.
```

Making Forms Reusable

Delphi gives you the ability to reuse forms that you've already designed which saves you much needed time to work on other tasks. Two ways are demonstrated to make your forms reusable by making them templates and adding them as components to Delphi's Component Palette. Later, in Chapter 18, "Dynamic Link Libraries (DLLs)," you learn how to call forms from Dynamic Link Libraries.

Saving Your Form as a Template

Saving a form as a template is probably the simplest way to make it reusable. Templates are forms that act as starting points for your projects. To use templates, you first have to enable Delphi's Gallery so that the Gallery dialog box will appear when you create a new project or create a new form. The Gallery dialog box is like a repository for commonly used forms and pre-designed projects from which you can choose starting points for your applications.

To enable the Gallery dialog box, select Options | Environment from Delphi's menu bar. This displays the Options Environment dialog box. Now check the two Gallery checkboxes, Use on New Form and Use on New Project. Press the OK button. Now, every time you select File | New Project or File | New Form, you will be presented with the Browse Gallery dialog box. Here you learn how to add two new forms to the Gallery. The first is a context-sensitive help form which is used just to illustrate the process. The next form you add changes the default font for your forms and components to something more appealing than what Delphi chooses as the default font.

Adding a Context-Sensitive Help Form to the Template

Create a new project and select Blank Template from the Browse Gallery dialog box as shown in Figure 5.3.

FIGURE 5.3.
The Browse Gallery dialog box.

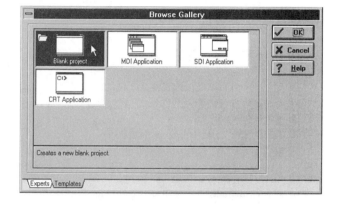

The project you create processes OnKeydown events to determine if the F1 key was pressed. If so, it displays the name of the active control at the time the key was pressed.

Listings 5.5 and 5.6 show the source for F1HELP.DRP and F1HELPU.PAS, respectively. Place three TEdit controls on the form as shown in Figure 5.4. Make sure to set the form's KeyPreview property to true. Also, you might give the form a more meaningful name like F1HelpForm.

FIGURE 5.4.
Project form for displaying F1 help.

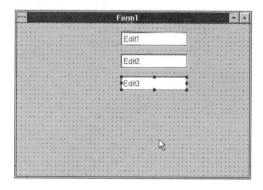

The KeyPreview property allows the form to process key-down events before the controls receive the events. Now create a way for the user to respond to F1 key-down events that could be expanded to provide context-sensitive help for the active control. First, create an OnKeyDown event handler for Form1. Examine the following code to see what this event handler does:

```
procedure TForm1.FormKeyDown(Sender: TObject; var Key: Word;
  Shift: TShiftState);
```

```
begin
  if Key = vk_F1 then
    MessageDlg('This Control is '+ ActiveControl.Name, mtInformation, [mbOk], 0)
end;
```

FormKeyDown() determines if the key pressed is an F1 key. If so, a message box tells the user which control generated the event. A more useful handler would bring up a simple help screen for the particular control.

NOTE

The technique described above is a simple method for displaying context-sensitive help. You can use the more elaborate method of providing a help file for your applications. Here, each control has context-sensitive help built in via the HelpContext property. When used, F1 invokes the Window's help system and loads the help file that you create and specify in the Project Options dialog box. This procedure is illustrated in Chapter 34, "Personal Information Manager—Finishing Touches," where you will add help to an existing application.

Now, to save this form as a template, select Options | Gallery from the main menu. Make sure that you still have the project loaded in Delphi. This brings up the Gallery Options dialog box as shown in Figure 5.5.

FIGURE 5.5.

The Gallery Options dialog box.

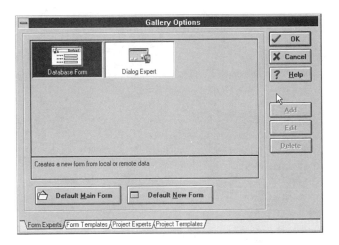

Now go to the Form Templates page shown in Figure 5.6.

FIGURE 5.6.

The Gallery Options dialog box with the Form Templates page displayed.

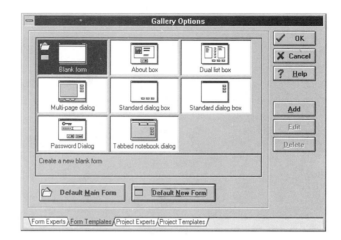

Press the Add button to bring up the Save Form Template dialog box shown in Figure 5.7.

FIGURE 5.7.

The Save Form Template dialog box.

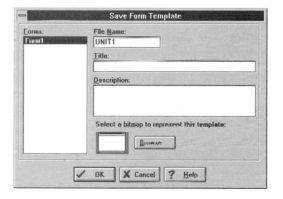

The form and file name that defines the form are already shown in the dialog box. Enter a descriptive title, such as Simple Help Form, in the Title edit control. You may enter a longer description in the Description memo control which will display on the Form Templates page. You may optionally add a bitmap to represent this form. When you have made your entries, press the OK button to add the form to the template. Your form will now show up in the Form Templates page of the Gallery Options dialog box as shown in Figure 5.8. The source code for this project is shown in Listings 5.5 and 5.6.

FIGURE 5.8.

The Gallery Options dialog box with new Simple Help Form highlighted.

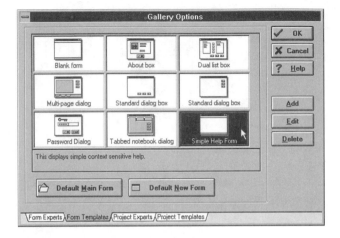

Listing 5.5. F1HELP.DPR is the project file for the F1 help example.

```
program F1help;

uses
  Forms,
  F1helpu1 in 'F1HELPU1.PAS' {Form1};

{$R *.RES}

begin
  Application.CreateForm(TForm1, Form1);
  Application.Run;
end.
```

Listing 5.6. F1HELPU1.PAS is the unit for the F1 help project form.

```
unit F1helpu1;

interface

uses
  SysUtils, WinTypes, WinProcs, Messages, Classes, Graphics, Controls,
  Forms, Dialogs, StdCtrls;

type
  TForm1 = class(TForm)
    Edit1: TEdit;
    Edit2: TEdit;
    Edit3: TEdit;
    procedure FormKeyDown(Sender: TObject; var Key: Word;
      Shift: TShiftState);
  private
    { Private declarations }
```

```
  public
    { Public declarations }
  end;

var
  Form1: TForm1;

implementation

{$R *.DFM}

procedure TForm1.FormKeyDown(Sender: TObject; var Key: Word;
  Shift: TShiftState);
begin
  if Key = vk_F1 then
    MessageDlg('This control is '+ActiveControl.Name, mtInformation, [mbok], 0);
end;

end.
```

Setting Default Main and New Form in the Gallery

We weren't satisfied with the default font that Delphi uses when creating a new form. You also might consider using a more appealing font. To avoid having to change the form's default font, System, to a more appealing font such as MS Sans Serif every time you create a new project or form, just add a form that already has that font set to the Form template. Just make that form the default main and new form by pressing the Default Main Form and Default New Form buttons in the Gallery Options dialog box (see Figure 5.8).

Your new, and more appealing, form will now be the default for any projects or forms you create. Such a form is used throughout the remaining chapters in the book so you might consider doing the same.

Templates are a handy way to free yourself of having to redo work. Another technique to re-using forms is to add them to the component palette.

Adding Forms to the Component Palette

You learned earlier that adding forms to the Gallery is a convenient way to give yourself a starting point. But what if you develop a form that you use quite a bit, yet doesn't require additional functionality or code to be added? Delphi provides a way that you can add your fully functional forms to Delphi's Component Palette, much like the TFontDialog, TOpenDialog and other dialogs on the Dialogs page of the Component Palette.

To add forms to the Component Palette, you must wrap your form with a component to make it a separate installable component. The process is described here using the simple password dialog box already available in the Gallery, except that our new dialog will verify your password automatically. Although this is a very simple project, the purpose of this discussion is not to show you how to install a complex dialog as a component, but rather to show you the general method for adding dialog boxes to the component palette. The same method applies to dialog boxes of any complexity.

Creating Your Form

Close any project you have open, then select File | New Form from the main menu. This should bring up the Browse Gallery dialog box, given that you set the Gallery options from the Environment Options dialog box. If not, do so by selecting Options | Environment, then request a new form. From the Browse Gallery dialog box, choose the Password dialog box by double-clicking on its icon. Delphi puts you in the Code Editor with PASSWORD.PAS loaded. By default, this file exists in the \DELPHI\GALLERY directory. Save this file to a different directory by choosing File | Save As from the main menu.

The next step is to remove the variable declaration for the Password form, PasswordDlg, which appears as shown in the following lines of code:

```
var
  PasswordDlg: TPasswordDlg;
```

After removing the lines, create a wrapper component to display the form. This is called a *wrapper* component because it wraps the form with a component that can be installed into Delphi's Component Palette. Following is the definition for this wrapper:

```
TPasswordDialog = class(TComponent)
  private
    PasswordDlg: TPasswordDlg;      { An instance of TPasswordDlg }
    FThePassWord: string;           { Place holder for the password }
  public
    function Execute: Boolean;       { method to display the dialog }
  published
    { A property to access FThePassWord }
    property ThePassword: string read FThePassWord write FThePassword;
  end;
```

You should know that we are jumping ahead to a topic that will be covered in depth in Chapter 11, "Writing Delphi Custom Components." For now, we'll just explain briefly what we've done to add the form to the palette. After reading Chapter 11, you'll have a complete understanding of what is actually happening here, so consider this a "heads up."

TPasswordDialog descends directly from TComponent. You may recall from Chapter 4, "The Visual Component Library (VCL)," that TComponent is the lowest level class that can be manipulated by the Form Designer in the IDE. This class has a two-private variable PasswordDlg of type TPasswordDlg and FThePassWord of type string. PasswordDlg is the TPasswordDlg instance that this wrapper component displays. FThePassWord is an *internal storage field* that will hold a password string.

FThePassWord gets its data at design-time or at runtime through the property ThePassWord. Thus, ThePassWord doesn't actually store data, but rather serves as an interface to the storage variable FThePassWord.

If you're totally confused, don't worry. All this becomes much clearer later. TPassWordDialog has an Execute() method that actually displays the dialog box. This method follows:

```
function TPasswordDialog.Execute: Boolean;
begin
  PasswordDlg := TPasswordDlg.Create(application); { Instantiate the dialog }
  try
    Result := false;                              { Set to false by default }
    with PasswordDlg do
    begin
      if ShowModal = mrOk then                    { Show the form }
        { Result get set to true if the password entered is correct. }
        Result := PasswordDlg.Password.Text = FThePassword;
    end;
  finally
    PasswordDlg.Free;  { Free the form }
  end;
end;
```

Execute() creates a TPasswordDlg instance and displays it as a modal dialog. When the dialog terminates, the string entered in the password TEdit control is compared against the string stored in FThePassword. How does FThePassword get its string? You see in a moment, when the component is added to the Component Palette.

The code here is contained within a try..finally construct. The finally portion ensures the TPasswordDlg is disposed of regardless of any error that might occur.

Before you can install the component to the Component Palette, you must create a Register() procedure in the unit's interface section. This procedure's implementation calls RegisterComponents() which tells Delphi on which Component Palette page to place the new component and its name. Register() follows:

```
procedure Register;
begin
  RegisterComponents('Dialogs', [TPasswordDialog]); { Register the new component }
end;
```

Finally, make sure to register the TPasswordDlg class in the unit's initialization block as follows:

```
initialization
  RegisterClasses([TPasswordDlg]);  { Register the TPasswordDlg class }
end.
```

Save PASSWORD.PAS before adding your component to the component palette. Select Options | Install components from the main menu. This brings up the Install Components dialog box (see Figure 5.9).

FIGURE 5.9.
The Install Components
Dialog box.

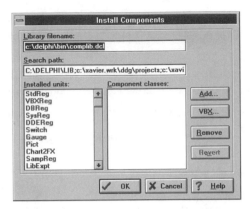

Now press the Add button. This brings up the Add Module dialog box as shown in Figure 5.10. You can either browse for the file PASSWORD.PAS or enter its full path as the module name. Now press the OK button. Delphi will start to compile and install TPasswordDialog to the component palette. When it is finished, you will see an additional icon on the Component Palette's Dialogs page.

FIGURE 5.10.
The Add Module
dialog box.

Using Your Component

Now that you have placed TPasswordDialog on the Component Palette, you can create a project that uses it. TPasswordDialog appears on the Dialogs page of the Component Palette with a default bitmap.

To use the TPasswordDialog new component, create a new project, then select and drop a TPasswordDialog component onto the form. TPasswordDialog shows up in the Object Inspector. It has three properties: Name, Tag, and ThePassWord, as shown in Figure 5.11.

Remember that through ThePassWord, FThePassword gets it value. Enter a value like coolness into the ThePassword property in the Object Inspector. Place a TButton on the form, and enter the following code for its OnClick event handler:

```
procedure TForm1.Button1Click(Sender: TObject);
begin
  if PasswordDialog1.Execute then
    ShowMessage('You Got It!')
  else
    ShowMessage('Sorry, wrong answer!');
end;
```

FIGURE 5.11.

The Object Inspector showing TPasswordDialog.

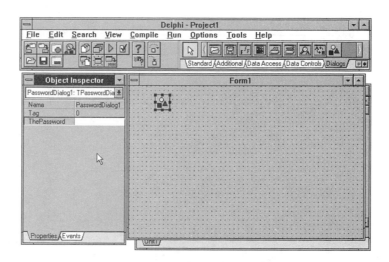

This code executes the dialog, and determines if the user correctly typed the value into the Password dialog box.

This is some pretty advanced stuff, so don't worry if you don't understand completely. You can always return to this chapter once you've gotten past Chapter 11, and when you have the knowledge to fully grasp what has only been skimmed through here. Listings 5.7, 5.8, and 5.9 show the source for PWTESTP.DPR, PWTESTU.PAS, and PASSWORD.PAS, respectively.

Listing 5.7. The source code for PWTESTP.DPR.

```
program Pwtestp;

uses
  Forms,
  Pwtestu in 'PWTESTU.PAS' {Form1};

{$R *.RES}

begin
  Application.CreateForm(TForm1, Form1);
  Application.Run;
end.
```

Listing 5.8. The source code for PWTESTU.PAS

```
unit Pwtestu;

interface

uses
  SysUtils, WinTypes, WinProcs, Messages, Classes, Graphics, Controls,
  Forms, Dialogs, StdCtrls, Password;
```

continues

Listing 5.8. continued

```
type
  TForm1 = class(TForm)
    PasswordDialog1: TPasswordDialog;
    Button1: TButton;
    procedure Button1Click(Sender: TObject);
  private
    { Private declarations }
  public
    { Public declarations }
  end;

var
  Form1: TForm1;

implementation

{$R *.DFM}

procedure TForm1.Button1Click(Sender: TObject);
begin
  if PasswordDialog1.Execute then
    ShowMessage('You Got It!')
  else
    ShowMessage('Sorry, wrong answer!');
end;

end.
```

Listing 5.9. The source code for PASSWORD.PAS.

```
unit Password;

interface

uses WinTypes, WinProcs, Classes, Graphics, Forms, Controls, StdCtrls, Buttons;

type

  TPasswordDlg = class(TForm)
    Label1: TLabel;
    Password: TEdit;
    OKBtn: TBitBtn;
    CancelBtn: TBitBtn;
  private
    { Private declarations }
  public
    { Public declarations }
  end;
```

```
  TPasswordDialog = class(TComponent)
  private
    PasswordDlg: TPasswordDlg;        { An instance of TPasswordDlg }
    FThePassWord: string;             { Place holder for the password }
  public
    function Execute: Boolean;        { method to display the dialog }
  published
    { A property to access FThePassWord }
    property ThePassword: string read FThePassWord write FThePassword;
  end;

procedure Register;   { Declare a Register procedure }

implementation

{$R *.DFM}

function TPasswordDialog.Execute: Boolean;
begin
  PasswordDlg := TPasswordDlg.Create(application); { Instantiate the dialog }
  try { Place code into a try..finally block }
    Result := false;                              { Set to false by default }
    with PasswordDlg do
    begin
      if ShowModal = mrOk then                    { Show the form }
        { Result get set to true if the password entered is correct. }
        Result := PasswordDlg.Password.Text = FThePassword;
    end;
  finally
    PasswordDlg.Free;  { Free the form }
  end;
end;

procedure Register;
begin
  RegisterComponents('Dialogs', [TPasswordDialog]); { Register the new component }
end;

initialization
  RegisterClasses([TPasswordDlg]);  { Register the TPasswordDlg class }
end.
```

The *TScreen* Component

The TScreen component simply encapsulates the state of the screen that your application runs on. This is not a component that you add to your Delphi forms nor do you need to create it dynamically during runtime. Delphi automatically creates a TScreen global variable called Screen which you can access from within your applications. The TScreen component contains several properties that you'll find useful. These are shown in Table 5.1.

Table 5.1. TScreen Properties.

Property	Meaning
ActiveForm	Indicates the form that has focus. This property is set when another form switches focus or when the Delphi application gains focus from another application.
Cursor	The cursor shape global to the application. This, by default, is set to crDefault. Each windowed component has its own Cursor property that may be modified. However, when the cursor is set to something other than crDefault, all other controls reflect that change until Screen.Cursor is set back to crDefault.
Cursors	A list of all available cursors to the Screen device.
FormCount	The number of available forms in the application.
Forms	A list of available forms to the application.
Fonts	A list of font names available to the Screen device.
Height	The height of the Screen device in device pixels.
PixelsPerInch	The number of pixels per inch on the Screen device.
Width	The width of the Screen device in device pixels.

Probably one of the most commonly used TScreen properties is the Cursor property that enables you to change the global cursor for the application. The code below, for example, changes the current cursor to that of an hourglass to indicate to users that they must wait while a lengthy process executes.

```
Screen.Cursor := crHourGlass
{ Do some lengthy process }
Screen.Cursor := crDefault;
```

crHourGlass is a pre-defined constant that indexes into the Cursors array. There are other cursor constants such as crBeam and crSize. The existing cursor values range from 0 - crDefault to -17 - crMultiDrag. Look in the online help for Cursors property to see a list of all available cursors. You may assign these values to Screen.Cursor when necessary.

You also may create your own cursors and add them to the Cursors property array. To do this, you must first define a constant with a value that does not conflict with the already available cursors, as shown in this example:

```
crCrossHair := 1;
```

Then, use any resource editor such as the Image Editor that ships with Delphi to create your custom cursor. You must save the cursor into an .RES (Resource) file. When you compile your project, make sure that the .RES file is in the same directory as your source files so that Delphi will link the cursor resource with your application. You tell Delphi to link in the .RES file by placing a statement such as the following into the application's .DPR file:

```
{$R CH5.RES}
```

Finally, you must add the following lines of code to load the cursor, add it to the Cursors property and then switch to that cursor:

```
procedure TForm1.Button2Click(Sender: TObject);
var
  HC: HCursor;
begin
  HC := LoadCursor (system.hInstance, 'CROSSHAIR');
  Screen.Cursors[crCrossHair] := HC;
  Screen.Cursor := crCrossHair;
end;
```

Here, the variable HC is of the type HCursor, a Windows handle to a cursor. First we use the LoadCursor() Windows API function to load the cursor. Load cursor takes two parameters: An instance handle to the module from which we want to get the cursor and the name of the cursor as specified in the .RES file in FULL CAPS!

System.hInstance refers to the application currently running. Next, assign the value returned from LoadCursor() to the Cursors property at the location specified by crCrossHair which was previously defined. Lastly, we assign the current cursor to Screen.Cursor.

To illustrate this, you find the project CRHAIR.DPR in the \SOURCE\CH5 directory. This project loads and changes to the crosshair cursor that we've created and placed in the file CH5.RES. Figure 5.12 shows this cursor.

FIGURE 5.12.

The crosshair cursor.

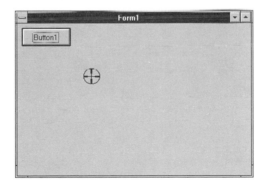

You might also want to invoke the Image Editor by selecting Tools | Image Editor and opening the CH5.RES file to see how we created the cursor.

TApplication

Every Delphi program you write contains a global variable called Application of the type TApplication. TApplication encapsulates your program and performs many behind-the-scenes functions that enable your applications to work correctly within the Windows environment. Some of these functions are creating your window class definition, creating the main window for your application, activating your application, processing messages, context-sensitive help, menu accelerator-key processing, and VCL exception handling.

As a Delphi developer, you won't be too concerned about the background tasks that TApplication does. A component writer might need to examine TApplication's internal workings, however. You'll examine some useful details of TApplication in later chapters where we actually use them in sample programs. You should, for now, be familiar with the more commonly used properties and methods.

TApplication does not appear in the Object Inspector; therefore, you cannot modify its properties there. You can choose Options | Project and choose the Application page in the Project Options dialog box where you can set some TApplication properties. Also, you must attach any event handler to TApplication at runtime. You learn later in the book how to add an event handler to all components at runtime.

TApplication is low in the VCL hierarchy and therefore inherits the properties and methods of its ancestors. Here is a summary of the common properties, methods, and events that you are likely to use in most applications that you create:

ExeName	Contains the full path and filename for your applications. This is a runtime, read-only property.
HelpFile	Contains the Windows help file name, enabling you to add online help to your application. Incorporating online help to your Delphi application is demonstrated later in this book.
MainForm	Points to the main form of your application that was set up in your project file. MainForm is a read-only property.
Title	The title that appears with a minimized application's icon. You can set this at runtime or from the Application page in the Project Options dialog box.
HandleException()	Enables you to handle exceptions at the Application level. ShowException() displays the exception that occurred in a message box.
HelpCommand() and HelpJump()	Methods that access the Windows help, WINHELP.EXE, for querying help information or displaying help screens.

Minimize()	Causes your application to minimize itself to an icon. Restore() restores your application to its previous size from a minimized or maximized state.
ProcessMessages()	Waits for Windows to process messages in the Windows message queue before continuing execution.
Run()	Starts your application with the Form parameter as the main window. Terminate() causes your application to end.
TApplication	Has several event handlers:

OnActivate	Occurs when the application becomes active and OnDeactivate occurs when your application stops being active such as when you switch to another application.
OnException	Occurs when an unhandled exception has occurred, enabling you to add default processing for unhandled exceptions.
OnHelp	Occurs when the user selects help. You would use the HelpCommand and HelpJump methods in this event handler.
OnMessage	Enables you to process messages before they are dispatched to their intended controls.
OnHint	Enables you to display hints associated with controls to the user when the mouse is positioned over the control.
OnIdle	Occurs whenever the application is in idle, that is, when the application is processing code or waiting for user input.

You'll work more with TApplication in later chapters. In fact, you'll find a simple animation example that illustrates it. For now, try changing some of the properties in the Project | Options dialog box, or create a small project and change various properties at run-time. The key is to become familiar with properties and methods of all the objects that you'll be using.

NOTE

TApplication's OnIdle event is a handy way to perform certain processing when no user interaction is occurring. One common use for the OnIdle event handler is to move an image on the screen for animation. You'll find a sample animation project that illustrates this process in the directory \SOURCE\OTHER\ANIMATE.

Summary

In this chapter, you learned more about various TForm properties. You learned how to make forms reusable by adding them to Delphi's Gallery or by making them components on your Component Palette. This chapter also discussed the TScreen and TApplication classes. In the next chapter, you learn how to make your forms more aesthetically pleasing and user friendly.

6

Sprucing Up Forms

This chapter teaches you how to design Delphi forms to create user-friendly interfaces for your applications. The concepts covered here are the stepping stones to learning many useful techniques that are much different than these concepts under a traditional Windows development environment. To begin with, the concepts here are faster and easier. Before you learn about form design, however, take a step back to get a Delphi perspective of the entities that forms have superseded: windows and dialog boxes.

Forms Versus Windows and Dialog Boxes

In Windows, the focal point for any user interface is usually a windows or a dialog box. In Delphi you really require little, if any, knowledge of window or dialog box behavior because forms have taken over the behavior of both. No longer do you have to know about window styles or subclassing windows. Delphi forms look and behave just like windows. Additionally, forms manage controls placed on them much like traditional dialog boxes manage controls.

Chapter 5, "Basic Concepts in Delphi—TForms, TScreen, and TApplication,"discussed many of the properties you can set to change a form's appearance. This chapter discusses in more depth how you can design forms that are more aesthetically pleasing and user friendly by using other properties.

Changing a Forms Appearance Through Its Properties

Forms contain several properties that enable you to dictate how they will appear to the user. In general, you can change attributes such as the form's color, size, and text fonts that it uses, and you also can specify whether the form has a two-dimensional or three-dimensional appearance.

A Form's Color and Size

You can change the form's background color through its Color property. The Object Inspector displays a list of available colors when you click on the value section of the Properties page for the Color property. The form's Width and Height properties enable you to specify the horizontal and vertical size of the form in pixels. These properties are accessible at runtime as well as at design-time, which means that you can change their values, and the form's appearance, on-the-fly—when the user is running the application.

Choosing Two- or Three-Dimensional Forms

The Ctl3D property gives your forms a three-dimensional appearance. This property is true by default. When Ctl3D is false, the form and its controls have a flat, two-dimensional appearance. You might consider giving your users a choice between Ctl3D and the standard two-dimensional look in your applications, especially if you're putting your form into a DLL for use with other applications. You cannot predict how the host application will look, so you want to be sure to give your users the flexibility of choosing between both styles.

> **NOTE**
>
> The Ctl3D capability is facilitated through Microsoft's CTL3D.DLL, which ships with Delphi and also is re-distributable with your applications. Be sure to include this DLL with any applications that use this feature.

The ParentCtl3D property determines whether the control assumes its parent's Ctl3D state. This property also is true by default.

Setting Fonts for Forms

Each form has its own font property that specifies the font used for text written on the form. Like the Ctl3D property, the ParentFont property determines whether a control gets its parent's font. To change a font for a form, for example, choose the small ellipsis button (...) on the value side of the form's Font property in the Object Inspector. This invokes the Font dialog box where you can select from fonts available on your system. You also can perform this process programmatically, as discussed in Chapter 8, "MDI Applications."

Adding Menus to a Project

Adding menus to projects is a straightforward process using the TMainMenu object from the Standard page on the Component Palette. The TMainMenu object contains a list of TMenuItems, each representing an item on a menu or submenu. Each TMenuItem has its own properties. Table 6.1 describes these properties.

Table 6.1. TMenuItem properties.

Property	*Description*
Caption	The menu item text. When creating menus, preceding a character with an ampersand (&) causes the following character to be an accelerator.
Checked	A Boolean property. When true, it places a checkmark in front of the menu item's text.
Enabled	A Boolean property that determines whether a menu item is enabled. When false, the menu item appears gray and cannot be selected.

continues

Table 6.1. continued

Property	Description
Handle	The handle to the menu item. This enables you to perform Windows API functions that require a menu handle. This property is available only at runtime.
Items	The array containing a list of TMenuItem objects representing menu items on the menu bar or in a drop-down menu. This property is available only at runtime.
ItemCount	The number of TMenuItems—only available at runtime.
Shortcut	Key sequence that causes an action to occur as if it were selected from the menu. Specify the key sequence by spelling out the shortcut property value. For example, put Alt+B as the ShortCut property value to invoke the menu command whenever user presses Alt plus the B key.

Creating a Main Menu

To create a main menu for your forms, select a TMainMenu component from the Component Palette's Standard page. Invoke the Menu Designer by double-clicking the TMainMenu icon on your form. The Object Inspector displays the properties for the menu items. You type a menu item's text in the caption property in the Object Inspector, and it appears in the Menu Designer after you press Enter. You can position menu items and submenus by dragging them with the mouse or by pressing standard editing keys, such as Ins and Del.

> **TIP**
>
> Right-click anywhere on the Menu Designer to bring up a local menu with useful menu-editing features. You can insert and delete menus, create submenus, save or retrieve menu templates, and even select menus residing in a *.MNU (menu) or *.RC (resource script) file, for example. Be sure to look at the available menu templates that Delphi already provides.

Create a new project and build its menu with the items listed in table 6.2. When you're done, exit the Menu Designer. Your menus then appear on the form.

Table 6.2. The main menu's `MenuItems`.

Menubar	Submenu	Shortcut
`"Menu &1"`	`"Item &1"`	Alt+A
	`"Item &2"`	Alt+B
	`"Item &3"`	Alt+C
`"Menu &2"`	`"Item &1"`	Alt+D
	`"Item &2"`	Alt+E
	`"Item &3"`	Alt+F
`"Menu &3"`	`"Item &1"`	Alt+G
	`"Item &2"`	Alt+H
	`"Item &3"`	Alt+I

To create an event hander for Menu 1 | Item 1, simply select the menu item Menu 1 | Item 1 in the Form Designer. Delphi generates the event handler for you and places you there in the Code Editor. The event handler for Menu 1|Item 1 would look like the following:

```
procedure TForm1.Item11Click(Sender: TObject);
begin

end;
```

You must enter the code that handles this event between the `begin..end` statements. For example, the following line tells the user which menu item was selected:

```
MessageDlg('Menu 1, Item 1', mtInformation, [mbOk], 0);
```

Create similar handlers for Menu 1|Item 2 and Menu1|Item 3. Listings 6.1 and 6.2 contain the source code for the XMENUS.DPR and XMENUS0.PAS. The next project shows you how to link speed buttons to the same event handlers.

Listing 6.1. XMENUS.DPR, the project file for the MENUS example.

```
program Xmenus;

uses
  Forms,
  Xmenus0 in 'XMENUS0.PAS' {Form1};

{$R *.RES}

begin
  Application.CreateForm(TForm1, Form1);
  Application.Run;
end.
```

Listing 6.2. XMENUS0.PAS, the unit for Form1.

```
unit Xmenus0;

interface

uses WinTypes, WinProcs, Classes, Graphics, Forms, Controls, Menus,
     dialogs;

type
  TForm1 = class(TForm)
    MainMenu1: TMainMenu;
    Menu11: TMenuItem;
    Item11: TMenuItem;
    Item21: TMenuItem;
    Item31: TMenuItem;
    Menu21: TMenuItem;
    Item12: TMenuItem;
    Item22: TMenuItem;
    Item32: TMenuItem;
    Menu31: TMenuItem;
    Item13: TMenuItem;
    Item23: TMenuItem;
    Item33: TMenuItem;
    procedure Item31Click(Sender: TObject);
    procedure Item11Click(Sender: TObject);
    procedure Item21Click(Sender: TObject);
  private
    { Private declarations }
  public
    { Public declarations }
  end;

var
  Form1: TForm1;

implementation

{$R *.DFM}

procedure TForm1.Item11Click(Sender: TObject);
begin
   MessageDlg('Menu 1, Item 1', mtInformation, [mbok], 0);
end;

procedure TForm1.Item21Click(Sender: TObject);
begin
   MessageDlg('Menu 1, Item 2', mtInformation, [mbok], 0);
end;

procedure TForm1.Item31Click(Sender: TObject);
begin
   MessageDlg('Menu 1, Item 3', mtInformation, [mbok], 0);
end;

end.
```

Creating SpeedBars and Floating Toolbars

SpeedBars provide an easy way for your users to execute common commands by just clicking a button. The next example shows you how to create a SpeedBar and a floating toolbar.

Using the project XMENUS.DPR, place two TPanel objects on your form and set their properties as shown in Table 6.3.

Table 6.3. Setting properties for TPanel objects.

Control	Property	Value
Panel1	Align	alTop
Panel1	Caption	<Blank>
Panel2	Caption	<Blank>

Add six TSpeedButton controls to each TPanel control so that they appear like those shown in Figure 6.1. You might have to resize the panel and the SpeedButtons to give your form a cleaner appearance.

FIGURE 6.1.
A form with
SpeedButtons.

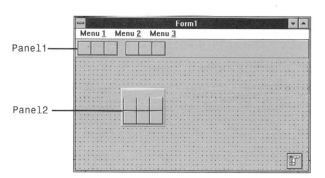

Attach the first group of three SpeedButtons on Panel1 to the first three menu items from the Object Inspector's Events page. Select a SpeedButton, press the down arrow next to the OnClick event, and select the appropriate menu event handler. Do the same for the top three SpeedButtons on Panel2.

Grouping controls makes them behave as a unit. To group the remaining three SpeedButtons on each panel, for example, set a common value to their GroupIndex properties. When grouped, only one SpeedButton in the group can be down at once. When GroupIndex is zero, the SpeedButtons behave independently of each other.

TIP

When you select multiple components on the Form Designer, the Object Inspector displays only shared properties. Changes in the Object Inspector affect all selected components. To select multiple components, hold down the Shift key and select each component individually, or hold down the Alt key while dragging the dotted rubberband rectangle over the components you want to select. If the components are on a `TGroupBox` or `TPanel`, use the Ctrl key instead.

This form will display only one panel at a time, with `Panel2` being movable on the form's surface. Add two variables to the form's `private` section, `Moving` and `MouseOrigin`. These variables are used in the logic for moving the Toolbar (`Panel2`):

```
private
    Moving: Boolean;
    MouseOrigin: TPoint;
```

Select the `MainMenu` on the form and bring up the Menu Designer. Change Menu2 | Item1's caption to Menu2 | Float Panel through the Object Inspector. Leave the Menu Designer and create an event handler for Menu2 | Float Panel. Listing 6.3 shows the event handler for Menu2 | Float Panel.

Listing 6.3. The event handler for Menu2 | Float Panel.

```
procedure TForm1.Item12Click(Sender: TObject);
begin
  with (Sender as TMenuItem) do begin
    if Checked then begin
      Panel2.Visible := false;
      Panel1.Visible := true;
    end
    else begin
      Panel2.Visible := true;
      Panel1.Visible := false;
    end;
    Checked := not Checked;
  end;
end;
```

TIP

When typecasting, take advantage of Delphi's RTTI to make your application more robust and easier to debug. For example, the following line typecasts the variable `Sender as a TMenuItem`:

```
with TMenuItem(Sender) do
```

However, it can lead to a fatal crash if Sender is not a TMenuItem. Instead, use this line:

`with (Sender as TMenuItem) do`

This line not only typecasts the variable accordingly; it also uses RTTI to ensure that these types are compatible. The actual test is performed at runtime and so RTTI will raise an exception as opposed to a program crash if the cast is invalid—the types are not compatible.

This event handler toggles the panel's visibility and places a checkmark next to the menu item if Panel2 is visible.

To make Panel2 movable, you need to create event handlers for Panel2's OnMouseDown, OnMouseMove, and OnMouseUp events. Listing 6.4 shows Panel2's OnMouseDown event handler.

Listing 6.4. Panel2's OnMouseDown event handler.

```
procedure TForm1.Panel2MouseDown(Sender: TObject; Button: TMouseButton;
  Shift: TShiftState; X, Y: Integer);
begin
  if Button = mbLeft then
  begin
    MouseOrigin := Point(X, Y);
    Moving := true;
  end
  else Moving := false;
end;
```

When an OnMouseDown event occurs, Panel2MouseDown() first checks for the left mouse button. It then sets the Boolean variable Moving to true and assigns the current mouse coordinates to the variable MouseOrigin.

Listing 6.5 shows Panel2's OnMouseMove event handler.

Listing 6.5. Panel2's OnMouseMove event handler.

```
procedure TForm1.Panel2MouseMove(Sender: TObject; Shift: TShiftState; X,
Shift: TShiftState; X, Y: Integer);
begin
  if Button = mbLeft then begin
    MouseOrigin := Point(X, Y);
    Moving := true;
  end
  else Moving := false;
end;
```

When the user moves the mouse, Panel2MouseMove() moves Panel2 to its new location. The location is determined by the difference between the new mouse position and the old mouse position stored in MouseOrigin.

Finally, Panel2's OnMouseUp event handler, Panel2MouseUp(), sets Moving to false, as shown in Listing 6.6.

Listing 6.6. Panel2's OnMouseUp event handler.

```
procedure TForm1.Panel2MouseUp(Sender: TObject; Button: TMouseButton;
  Shift: TShiftState; X, Y: Integer);
begin
  if Moving then
    Moving := false;
end;
```

Listings 6.7 and 6.8 show the source for SPEEDB.DPR and SPEEDB0.PAS, the project file and the main form's unit, respectively.

Listing 6.7. SPEEDB.DPR, the SpeedButton project file.

```
program Speedb;
program Speedb;

uses
  Forms,
  Speedb0 in 'SPEEDB0.PAS' {Form1};

{$R *.RES}

begin
  Application.CreateForm(TForm1, Form1);
  Application.Run;
end.
```

Listing 6.8. SPEEDB0.PAS, the main form's unit for the SpeedButton project.

```
unit Speedb0;
interface

uses WinTypes, WinProcs, Classes, Graphics, Forms, Controls, Menus,
     Dialogs, StdCtrls, Buttons, ExtCtrls;

type
  TForm1 = class(TForm)
    MainMenu1: TMainMenu;
    Menu11: TMenuItem;
    Item11: TMenuItem;
    Item21: TMenuItem;
    Item31: TMenuItem;
    Menu21: TMenuItem;
    Item12: TMenuItem;
    Item22: TMenuItem;
    Item32: TMenuItem;
    Menu31: TMenuItem;
```

```
      Item13: TMenuItem;
      Item23: TMenuItem;
      Item33: TMenuItem;
      Panel1: TPanel;
      SpeedButton1: TSpeedButton;
      SpeedButton2: TSpeedButton;
      SpeedButton3: TSpeedButton;
      SpeedButton4: TSpeedButton;
      SpeedButton5: TSpeedButton;
      SpeedButton6: TSpeedButton;
      Panel2: TPanel;
      SpeedButton7: TSpeedButton;
      SpeedButton8: TSpeedButton;
      SpeedButton9: TSpeedButton;
      SpeedButton10: TSpeedButton;
      SpeedButton11: TSpeedButton;
      SpeedButton12: TSpeedButton;
      procedure Item11Click(Sender: TObject);
      procedure Item21Click(Sender: TObject);
      procedure Item31Click(Sender: TObject);
      procedure Panel2MouseDown(Sender: TObject; Button: TMouseButton;
        Shift: TShiftState; X, Y: Integer);
      procedure Panel2MouseMove(Sender: TObject; Shift: TShiftState; X,
        Y: Integer);
      procedure Panel2MouseUp(Sender: TObject; Button: TMouseButton;
        Shift: TShiftState; X, Y: Integer);
      procedure Item12Click(Sender: TObject);
      procedure SpeedButton4Click(Sender: TObject);
      procedure FormCreate(Sender: TObject);
    private
      Moving: Boolean;
      MouseOrigin: TPoint;
      { Private declarations }
    public
      { Public declarations }
    end;

var
  Form1: TForm1;

implementation

{$R *.DFM}

procedure TForm1.Item11Click(Sender: TObject);
begin
   MessageDlg('Menu 1, Item 1', mtInformation, [mbok], 0);
end;

procedure TForm1.Item21Click(Sender: TObject);
begin
   MessageDlg('Menu 1, Item 2', mtInformation, [mbok], 0);
end;

procedure TForm1.Item31Click(Sender: TObject);
begin
   MessageDlg('Menu 1, Item 3', mtInformation, [mbok], 0);
end;
```

continues

Listing 6.8. continued

```
procedure TForm1.Panel2MouseDown(Sender: TObject; Button: TMouseButton;
  Shift: TShiftState; X, Y: Integer);
begin
  if Button = mbLeft then begin  { If the left mouse button is down }
    MouseOrigin := Point(X, Y);  { Save the mouse coordinates }
    Moving := true;              { Set the Moving varible to true }
  end
  else Moving := false;          { Otherwise set it to false }
end;

procedure TForm1.Panel2MouseMove(Sender: TObject; Shift: TShiftState; X,
  Y: Integer);
begin
  { If the mouse is moving, move the panel the same distance in the same  }
  { direction using MouseOrigin as the relative position }
  if Moving then begin
    Panel2.Left := Panel2.Left + (X - MouseOrigin.X);
    Panel2.Top := Panel2.Top + (Y - MouseOrigin.Y);
  end;
end;

procedure TForm1.Panel2MouseUp(Sender: TObject; Button: TMouseButton;
  Shift: TShiftState; X, Y: Integer);
begin
  if Moving then      { If Moving is true set it back to false }
    Moving := false;
end;

procedure TForm1.Item12Click(Sender: TObject);
begin
  with (Sender as TMenuItem) do begin  { View Sender as a TMenuItem and }
    if Checked then begin              { make the appropriate Panel's visible }
      Panel2.Visible := false;         { based on the checked menu options }
      Panel1.Visible := true;
    end
    else begin
      Panel2.Visible := true;
      Panel1.Visible := false;
    end;
    Checked := not Checked;
  end;
end;

procedure TForm1.SpeedButton4Click(Sender: TObject);
begin
  MessageDlg('Will it Dissappear?', mtinformation, [mbok], 0);
end;

procedure TForm1.FormCreate(Sender: TObject);
begin
  Panel2.Visible := false;
end;

end.
```

Creating Fancy Dialog Boxes

You've probably noticed the various notebooks and tabs in many of Delphi's dialogs. By using some simple yet powerful techniques, you can add the same look to your applications. Before you can use these helpful controls, however, you need to be familiar with the TStrings class. Many Delphi controls have one or more properties of the type TStrings.

Using *TStrings*

The abstract class TStrings defines the capability to manipulate strings maintained by common Windows controls. TStrings class instances don't actually maintain the memory for the strings—that is done by the native control that owns the TStrings class. Instead, TStrings classes define the methods and properties to access and manipulate the control's strings without having to use the control's set of specific Windows API messages.

To add a string to a TListBox using Windows API functions, for example, you would use the following code:

```
SendMessage(ListBox1.Handle, lb_addstring, 0, longint(StrPCopy(S, MyString)));
```

Here, you need the use ListBox1's handle and a specific listbox message lb_addstring. You also have to convert your Pascal-style string to a null-terminated string before passing it to SendMessage(). It would be much simpler to use TListBox.Item's Add() method. Items is a TStrings property, as shown in the following code:

```
ListBox1.Items.Add(MyString);
```

When you need to create your own list of strings, don't create a TStrings instance because it doesn't store data. Instead, use its general purpose descendant, TStringList.

TStringList maintains strings external to controls. The best part is that TStringList is totally compatible with TStrings. This means that you can directly assign a TStringList to a control's TStrings property. To create a TStringList, for example, use this code:

```
var
  MyStringList: TStringList;
begin
  MyStringList := TStringList.Create;
```

Now add strings to MyStringList:

```
MyStringList.Add('Mickey');
MyStringList.Add('Minnie');
MyStringList.Add('Goofy');
MyStringList.Add('Pluto');
```

Now, if you want to add these same strings to both a TMemo component and a TListBox1 component, all you have to do is take advantage of the compatiblity between the different components' TStrings properties and make the assignments in one line of code each:

```
Memo1.Lines.Assign(MyStrings);
ListBox1.Items.Assign(MyStrings);
```

Another advantage to using the Assign() method is that it actually copies the strings from one component to another. Therefore, each component maintains its own copy of the strings as opposed to having both TMemo and TListBox reference the same list of strings.

> **NOTE**
>
> What has TStrings as properties? TListBoxes and TComboBoxes have the property Items, and TMemos have Lines. TStrings are used for various other reasons by different controls, such as maintaining a list of fonts. It's a good idea to become familiar with TStrings because many Delphi components rely on their use.

Common methods you will use with TStrings are shown in Table 6.4.

Table 6.4. Common methods used with TStrings.

Method	Description
Add(const S: String): integer	Adds the string S to the string list.
AddStrings(Strings: TStrings)	Copies Strings from one TStringList to the end of another TStringList.
Assign(Strings: TStrings)	Clears out existing strings in the list, and copies in the new TStringList, Strings.
Clear	Removes the items from the list.
Delete(Index: integer)	Removes the string at the location specified by Index.
Exchange(Index1, Index2: integer)	Switches the location of the strings specified by the two index values.
IndexOf(const S: String): integer	Returns the position of the string S on the list.
Insert(Index: Integer; const S: String)	Inserts the string S into the position in the list specified by Index.
Move(CurIndex, NewIndex: integer)	Moves the string at the position CurIndex to the position NewIndex.

Method	*Description*
`LoadFromFile(const Filename: string)`	Reads the text file `Filename` and places its lines into the `string` list.
`SaveToFile(const Filename: string)`	Saves the string list to the text file `Filename`.

To illustrate using `TStringList` classes, here is an exercise in which you create a form containing a memo box and three buttons. The event handler for `Button1` loads your AUTOEXEC.BAT file into `Memo1`. `Button2`'s event handler loads your CONFIG.SYS into `Memo1`, and `Button3`'s event handler loads both files into `Memo1`.

First, create the form shown in Figure 6.2, and add a `TMemo` and three `TButtons` to the form. Set their properties as shown in Table 6.5.

FIGURE 6.2.
Form1—a StringList *example.*

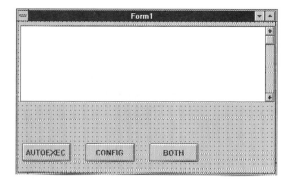

Table 6.5. Setting properties for `TMemo` and three `Tbuttons`.

Control	*Property*	*Value*
Memo1	Text	\<Blank\>
Memo1	ScrollBars	ssVertical
Button1	Caption	'AUTOEXEC'
Button2	Caption	'CONFIG'
Button3	Caption	'BOTH'

Next, add two private fields of type `TStringList` to the form:

```
TForm1 = class(TForm)
    Memo1: TMemo;
    Button1: TButton;
    Button2: TButton;
    Button3: TButton;
```

```
private
  { Private declarations }
    AutoExec: TStringList;
    Config: TStringList;
public
  { Public declarations }
end;
```

AutoExec will contain your AUTOEXEC.BAT file, and `Config` will contain your CONFIG.SYS file. In the form's OnCreate event, instantiate the two string lists and load the files accordingly:

```
procedure TForm1.FormCreate(Sender: TObject);
  AutoExec := TStringList.Create;                { Create two TStringList instances }
  Config := TStringList.Create;                  { Load the AUTOEXEC.BAT file into }
  AutoExec.LoadFromFile('c:\autoexec.bat');      { one instance and the CONFIG.SYS }
  Config.LoadFromFile('c:\config.sys');          { file into the other. }
end;
```

Here, TStringList's LoadFromFile method is called for both TStringList instances to load first the AUTOEXEC.BAT file and then the CONFIG.SYG file. Here is Button1's event handler:

```
procedure TForm1.Button1Click(Sender: TObject);
begin
  Memo1.Lines.Assign(AutoExec);
end;
```

AutoExec is passed to Memo1.Lines.Assign(), which copies the contents of AutoExec—TStringList—to Memo1.Lines—a TStrings type. Button2's event handler does the same thing, except that it passes Config to Assign():

```
procedure TForm1.Button2Click(Sender: TObject);
begin
  Memo1.Lines.Assign(Config);
end;
```

Button3's event handler clears the contents of the listbox and then adds both TStringLists by using the TStrings.Add() method. Unlike TStrings.Assign(), Add() doesn't remove the previous contents of Lines:

```
procedure TForm1.Button3Click(Sender: TObject);
begin
  Memo1.Lines.Clear;
  Memo1.Lines.Add('AUTOEXEC.BAT');
  Memo1.Lines.AddStrings(AutoExec);
  Memo1.Lines.Add('--------');
  Memo1.Lines.Add('CONFIG.SYS');
  Memo1.Lines.AddStrings(Config);
end;
```

Finally, when you shut down the application, the form must free the TStringList in its OnDestroy event handler:

```
Config.Free;                                     { Free both TStringList instances }
AutoExec.Free;
```

String lists are extremely useful and used quite a bit in Delphi. We use TStingLists quite a bit more in this book, so you'll have plenty of opportunity to learn them well. See Listings 6.9 and

6.10 for the complete source for LOADFIL.DPR and LOADFIL0.PAS, the example's project file and the main form's unit, respectively.

Listing 6.9. LOADFIL.DPR, the project file for the load-file example.

```
program Loadfil;

uses
  Forms,
  Loadfil0 in 'LOADFIL0.PAS' {Form1};

{$R *.RES}

begin
  Application.CreateForm(TForm1, Form1);
  Application.Run;
end.
```

Listing 6.10. LOADFIL0.PAS, the unit for Form1.

```
unit Loadfil0;
interface

uses WinTypes, WinProcs, Classes, Graphics, Forms, Controls, StdCtrls,
     Dialogs;

type
  TForm1 = class(TForm)
    Memo1: TMemo;
    Button1: TButton;
    Button2: TButton;
    Button3: TButton;
    procedure FormCreate(Sender: TObject);
    procedure Button1Click(Sender: TObject);
    procedure Button2Click(Sender: TObject);
    procedure Button3Click(Sender: TObject);
    procedure FormClose(Sender: TObject; var Action: TCloseAction);
  private
    AutoExec: TStringList;
    Config: TStringList;
    { Private declarations }
  public
    { Public declarations }
  end;

var
  Form1: TForm1;

implementation

{$R *.DFM}

procedure TForm1.FormCreate(Sender: TObject);
begin
```

continues

Listing 6.10. continued

```
  AutoExec := TStringList.Create;              { Create two TStringList instances }
  Config := TStringList.Create;                { Load the AUTOEXEC.BAT file into }
  AutoExec.LoadFromFile('c:\autoexec.bat');    { one instance and the CONFIG.SYS }
  Config.LoadFromFile('c:\config.sys');        { file into the other. }
end;

procedure TForm1.Button1Click(Sender: TObject);
begin
  Memo1.Lines.Assign(AutoExec);                { Copy AUTOEXEC.BAT to the TMemo }
end;

procedure TForm1.Button2Click(Sender: TObject);
begin
  Memo1.Lines.Assign(Config);                  { copy CONFIG.SYS to the TMemo }
end;

procedure TForm1.Button3Click(Sender: TObject);
begin
  Memo1.Lines.Clear;                           { Clear strings in the TMemo }
  Memo1.Lines.Add('AUTOEXEC.BAT');             { load the AUTOEXEC.BAT file to the }
  Memo1.Lines.AddStrings(AutoExec);            { TMemo and then also add the CONFIG.SYS }
  Memo1.Lines.Add('--------');                 { file to the TMemo }
  Memo1.Lines.Add('CONFIG.SYS');
  Memo1.Lines.AddStrings(Config);
end;

procedure TForm1.FormClose(Sender: TObject; var Action: TCloseAction);
begin
  Config.Free;                                 { Free both TStringList instances }
  AutoExec.Free;
end;

end.
```

Adding Tabs to Your Applications

The TTabSet component gives your application the look of having notebook tabs on your form as do many of Delphi's Options dialogs. To see how to use TTabSet, create a project in which its main form has a label, edit, and tabset, as shown in Figure 6.3.

Table 6.6 shows the property settings for this project.

Table 6.6. Property settings for the TTabSet project.

Component	Property	Value
Edit1	Text	\<Blank>
Label1	Caption	'Enter a Name'
TabSet1	*none*	*none*

FIGURE 6.3.
Using TTabSet.

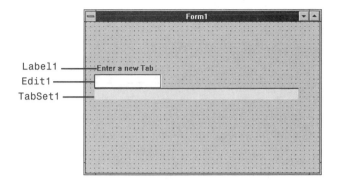

Create an event handler for Edit1's OnKeyPress event, as shown in Listing 6.11.

Listing 6.11. The event handler for Edit1.OnKeyPress.

```
procedure TForm1.Edit1KeyPress(Sender: TObject; var Key: Char);
begin
  if Key = chr(vk_Return) then        { Check for return key }
    if Edit1.Text <> '' then begin    { Check for no text }
      TabSet1.Tabs.Add(Edit1.Text);   { Add the tab with the text specified in }
      Edit1.Text := '';               { Edit1. Then set Edit1.Text back to }
    end;                              { empty. }
    ActiveControl := Edit1;           { Set the active control to Edit1 }
end;
```

This procedure checks for the Enter key and adds a new tab to TabSet1 based on Edit1.Text, demonstrating how you would add tabs to a TTabSet at runtime.

You also can enter tabs using the Property Editor on the Object Inspector by clicking the ellipsis (...) button that appears to the right of the value side of the Tabs property. This invokes the String List Editor, which you use to enter strings for your tabs at design-time.

Listings 6.12 and 6.13 show the example's project file and its form's unit, TABDEM.DPR and TABDEM0.PAS, respectively.

The next project shows you how to link TTabSets with a TNoteBook component to give your users a multi-page functionality without having to use multiple forms.

Listing 6.12. TABDEM.DPR project file for the TTabSet example.

```
program Tabdem;

uses
  Forms,
  Tabdem0 in 'TABDEM0.PAS' {Form1};

{$R *.RES}
```

continues

Listing 6.12. continued

```
begin
  Application.CreateForm(TForm1, Form1);
  Application.Run;
end.
```

Listing 6.13. TABDEMO.PAS, Form1's unit file for the TTabSet example.

```
unit Tabdem0;
interface

uses WinTypes, WinProcs, Classes, Graphics, Forms, Controls, StdCtrls, Tabs;

type
  TForm1 = class(TForm)
    Edit1: TEdit;
    TabSet1: TTabSet;
    Label1: TLabel;
    procedure Edit1KeyPress(Sender: TObject; var Key: Char);
  private
    { Private declarations }
  public
    { Public declarations }
  end;

var
  Form1: TForm1;

implementation

{$R *.DFM}

procedure TForm1.Edit1KeyPress(Sender: TObject; var Key: Char);
begin
  if Key = chr(vk_Return) then        { Check for return key }
    if Edit1.Text <> '' then begin    { Check for no text }
      TabSet1.Tabs.Add(Edit1.Text);   { Add the tab with the text specified in }
      Edit1.Text := '';               { Edit1. Then set Edit1.Text back to }
    end;                              { empty. }
    ActiveControl := Edit1;           { Set the active control to Edit1 }
end;

end.
```

Using Notebooks

By using a combination of tabs and notebooks, you can give your forms a multi-page appearance. The advantage of using notebooks is that you can put more functionality on one form, relieving your users of having to interact with multiple forms.

To illustrate using the TNoteBook component, create a new project and place a TNoteBook control on the main form. Set NoteBook1's align property to alTop, and adjust its size so that you can put controls on its surface, as shown in Figure 6.4.

FIGURE 6.4.

Page 1 of NoteBook1 *with* TMemo, TButton, *and* TLabel *components.*

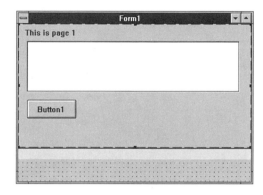

Set the properties for Page1 as shown in Table 6.7.

Table 6.7. Setting the properties for Page1.

Component	Property	Value
Label1	Caption	'This is page 1'
Memo1	Text	<Blank>
Button1	*none*	*none*

To create a second page, you must specify how many pages your notebook will have by using the Notebook Editor on the Object Inspector.

Select the Pages property from the Object Inspector and choose the ellipsis button to display the Notebook Editor. Change the name of the first page from Default to Page1 by choosing Edit. Add another page by choosing Add. Enter **Page2** for Page Name. Don't worry about the Help context. This is a feature you will learn about later. When you finish adding the second page, choose Done to close the Notebook Editor.

The pages you entered are strings that are stored in the TNoteBook property Pages—a TStrings property. Pages.Count contains the number of strings stored in Pages. You should have two items in Notebook1.Pages: Page1 and Page2.

Page1 is currently the visible page. To add controls to Page2, you first must make it the visible page on NoteBook1 by changing NoteBook1's PageIndex property from 0 to 1 in the Object Inspector.

`PageIndex`, a zero-based index, identifies the active page. When `PageIndex` has the value 0, for example, `Page1` is active. When its value is 1, `Page2` is active. With `Page2` active, `NoteBook1` appears blank. Place a `TGroupBox` (`GroupBox1`) component on `Page2`. Place three `TCheckBoxes` and three `TLabels` on `GroupBox1`, as shown in Figure 6.5.

FIGURE 6.5.

Page2 contains three
checkboxes and three labels.

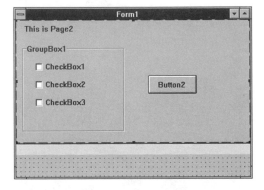

NOTE

Container components such as `TGroupBox` and `TPanel` cause components placed on them to behave as a unit. `TRadioButtons` are an example of controls that typically require grouping. When you place a component on a container, the container becomes the parent to the contained component. The form still owns all components, including those existing in a container. See the "Owner or Parent" sidebar in Chapter 4, "The Visual Component Library (VCL)," for a discussion of parent versus owner relationship.

Set the component's properties as shown in Table 6.8.

Table 6.8. Setting the properties for `Notebook1`.

Component	Property	Value
GroupBox1	*none*	*none*
CheckBox1	*none*	*none*
CheckBox2	*none*	*none*
CheckBox3	*none*	*none*
Label2	Caption	'This is page 2'
Button2	*none*	*none*

Change NoteBook1's PageIndex property back to 0 to make the first page the default active page when you start your application.

Place a TabSet control on your form below the NoteBook1, and set its Align property to alTop. This action positions the control directly below the notebook control.

Recall when we said that many components have properties that are actually TStrings? Both the TNoteBook and TTabSet have such properties. The TNoteBook has the Pages property, and the TTabSet has the Tabs property; both properties are of type TStrings. Form1's OnCreate event handler copies the strings from NoteBook1's Pages property to TabSet1's Tabs property. When you run the application, you will see that TabSet1's Tab strings are the same as NoteBook1's Pages strings. Here is the form's OnCreate event handler:

```
procedure TForm1.FormCreate(Sender: TObject);
begin
  TabSet1.Tabs.Assign(Notebook1.Pages); { Copy the Pages string into the
➡Tabset's Tabs TStringList }
end;
```

You cannot interactively hook TTabsets and TNotebooks at design-time. Instead, create the following event handler for TabSet1's OnChange property:

```
procedure TForm1.TabSet1Change(Sender: TObject; NewTab: Integer;
  var AllowChange: Boolean);
begin
  NoteBook1.PageIndex := NewTab;  { Change the Page }
end;
```

This event handler causes the notebook page to exactly match the TabIndex whenever the user changes it. The source code for this example's project file, NOTEBK.DPR, and Form1's unit, NOTEBK1.PAS, are shown in Listings 16.14 and 16.15, respectively.

Listing 6.14. NOTEBK.DPR, the project file for the NoteBook example.

```
program Notebk;

uses
  Forms,
  Notebk0 in 'NOTEBK0.PAS' {Form1};

{$R *.RES}

begin
  Application.CreateForm(TForm1, Form1);
  Application.Run;
end.
```

Listing 6.15. NOTEBK0.PAS, the unit for the main form in the NoteBook example.

```
unit Notebk0;

interface

uses WinTypes, WinProcs, Classes, Graphics, Forms, Controls, Tabs,
  StdCtrls, Buttons, ExtCtrls;

type
  TForm1 = class(TForm)
    Notebook1: TNotebook;
    TabSet1: TTabSet;
    Label1: TLabel;
    Memo1: TMemo;
    Button1: TButton;
    GroupBox1: TGroupBox;
    CheckBox1: TCheckBox;
    CheckBox2: TCheckBox;
    CheckBox3: TCheckBox;
    Label2: TLabel;
    Button2: TButton;
    procedure TabSet1Change(Sender: TObject; NewTab: Integer;
      var AllowChange: Boolean);
    procedure FormCreate(Sender: TObject);
  private
    { Private declarations }
  public
    { Public declarations }
  end;

var
  Form1: TForm1;

implementation

{$R *.DFM}

procedure TForm1.TabSet1Change(Sender: TObject; NewTab: Integer;
  var AllowChange: Boolean);
begin
  NoteBook1.PageIndex := NewTab;  { Change the Page }
end;

procedure TForm1.FormCreate(Sender: TObject);
begin
  TabSet1.Tabs.Assign(Notebook1.Pages); { Copy the Pages string into the
➥Tabset's Tabs TStringList }
end;

end.
```

Adding Drag-and-Drop Capabilities

Adding drag-and-drop capabilities to your applications gives your users an alternative method for manipulating controls. There are four tasks to using drag-and-drop capabilities: beginning, accepting, dropping, and ending the drag-and-drop operation.

There are two modes by which a dragging operation can begin: automatically or manually, as specified by a control's DragMode property. When DragMode is dmAutomatic, dragging begins when the user presses the left mouse button while the cursor is positioned on the control. When DragMode is set to dmManual, you must invoke dragging by calling the BeginDrag function.

Dragging an item over a control generates an OnDragOver event for that control. The control accepts the item by setting the Accept parameter to true. You normally test to see whether the *source parameter*—the item being dragged—is of a specific type before accepting the drag. A typical OnDragOver event handler might look like the following:

```
procedure TDrag.Item1DragOver(Sender, Source: TObject; X, Y: Integer;
  State: TDragState; var Accept: Boolean);
begin
  Accept := (source is TMyItem);
end;
```

By setting Accept to true, the control can accept the item being dragged.

An item is dropped when the user releases the mouse button, which generates an OnDragDrop event. A typical OnDragDrop event handler might look like the following:

```
procedure TDrag.Item1DragDrop(Sender, Source: TObject; X, Y: Integer);
begin
 if Source is TMyItem then
    Item1.Data := TMyItem(Source).Data
end;
```

Here, if Source is of type TMyItem, Item's Data property is assigned Source's Data property.

A drag operation ends when the user releases the mouse button. The OnEndDrag event handler that follows tells the user which control accepted the item:

```
procedure TDrag.Item1EndDrag(Sender, Target: TObject; X,Y,: Integer);
begin
  if Target <> nil then
    MessageDlg((Target as TMyItem).Name, mtInformation, [mbok], 0);
end.
```

The variable Target indicates which control accepted the item. If no control accepts the item, Target is nil. The values in X and Y contain the mouse coordinates when the event handler occurred.

NOTE

The `OnDragOver` and `OnDragDrop` events go to the receiver of the drag-and-drop operation. The `OnEndDrag` event goes to the control from which the dragging operation was initiated. This is a very important distinction that is often missed.

To illustrate the automatic method of drag-and-drop, create a project that contains the controls and property settings shown in Table 6.9. Figure 6.6 shows what your form should look like.

Table 6.9. Property settings for the drag-and-drop project.

Control	Property	Value
Shape1	Brush.Color	clWhite
Shape1	DragMode	dmAutomatic
Shape2	Brush.Color	clblue
Shape2	DragMode	dmAutomatic
Shape3	Brush.Color	clRed
Shape3	DragMode	dmAutomatic
Shape4	Brush.Color	clWhite
Shape4	DragMode	dmAutomatic
ListBox1	DragMode	dmManual

FIGURE 6.6.
The `DragDrop` *form.*

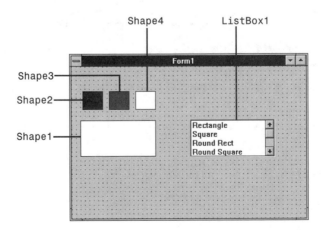

Set the DragMode property for Shape2, Shape3, and Shape4 to dmAutomatic. Create Shape1's OnDragOver event as shown in the following code:

```
procedure TDragIt.Shape1DragOver(Sender, Source: TObject; X, Y: Integer;
  State: TDragState; var Accept: Boolean);
begin
  Accept := (source is TShape);
end;
```

Here, Accept is set to true when Source is a TShape.

Create Shape1's OnDragDrop event handler, which uses RTTI to test whether Source is a TShape and sets Shape1's color to the same color as Source's color:

```
procedure TForm1.Shape1DragDrop(Sender, Source: TObject; X, Y: Integer);
begin
  if Source is TShape then
    Shape1.Brush.Color := TShape(Source).Brush.Color
end;
```

When you run the application, you should be able to change the color of Shape1 by dragging one of the other shapes over it.

To demonstrate manual drag-drop capability, add the following strings to ListBox1 in the Object Inspector. Be sure to enter these items in the same order as they are listed:

```
        Rectangle
        Square
        "Round Rect
        Round Square
        Ellipse
        Circle
```

The order of these items corresponds to the definition of the TShapeType enumerated type, as shown in the following code:

```
TShapeType = (stRectangle, stSquare, stRoundRect, stRoundSquare, stEllipse,
➥stCircle);
```

ListBox1 requires two event handlers: OnDblClick and OnMouseDown. OnMouseDown performs the task found in the following code:

```
procedure TDragIt.ListBox1MouseDown(Sender: TObject; Button: TMouseButton;
  Shift: TShiftState; X, Y: Integer);
begin
  if Button = mbLeft then
    TListBox(Sender).BeginDrag(false);
end;
```

When the user presses the left mouse button, BeginDrag() starts the dragging operation. Pass false to the BeginDrag() method to ensure that dragging does not start until the user moves the mouse; otherwise dragging begins immediately, which poses a problem for ListBox1 because it depends on mouse operations to scroll through its contents. The variable Shift enables you to test the mouse's shift state. X and Y contain the mouse position.

ListBox1's OnDblClick event is as follows. This procedure sets Shape1's shape to that specified by ListBox1's selected item.

```
procedure TDragIt.ListBox1DblClick(Sender: TObject);
begin
 if Sender is TListBox then
   Shape1.Shape := TShapeType(TListBox(Sender).ItemIndex)
end;
```

> **TIP**
>
> Earlier in this chapter, you learned to use RTTI to typecast objects. The preceding code uses the statement
>
> `TShapeType(TListBox(Sender).ItemIndex)`
>
> To clarify this statement, look at each typecast separately.
>
> Here, you use standard (non-RTTI) typecasting to typecast Sender as a TListBox:
>
> `TListBox(Sender).ItemIndex`
>
> The reason for not using RTTI is because you already tested for the TListBox type in the preceding statement. The next line of code does use RTTI:
>
> `if Sender is TListBox then`
>
> RTTI adds more overhead because it must traverse the inheritance tree to verify compatiblity. In this situation, there is no trade-off of robustness for performance. Don't use RTTI when you are absolutely certain of the type.
>
> The following outer typecast:
>
> `TShapeType(TListBox(Sender).ItemIndex)`
>
> takes the return value of the ListBox (Sender) and fakes it to be of type TShapeType. Again, RTTI is not necessary. The reason here is because RTTI applies only to class types, not data types. The TShapeType is just an enumerated type stored as a number 0..5. The typecast just enables us to look at the ItemIndex number as a TShapeType number.

Change Shape1's OnDragOver event to include logic to accept the TListBox object:

```
procedure TForm1.Shape1DragOver(Sender, Source: TObject; X, Y: Integer;
  State: TDragState; var Accept: Boolean);
begin
  Accept := (source is TShape) or (source is TListBox);
end;
```

You also must change Shape1's OnDragDrop event handler, as shown in the following code:

```
procedure TForm1.Shape1DragDrop(Sender, Source: TObject; X, Y: Integer);
begin
if Source is TShape then
    Shape1.Brush.Color := TShape(Source).Brush.Color
  else if Source is TListBox then
```

```
    Shape1.Shape := TShapeType(TListBox(Source).ItemIndex)
end;
```

The `else` statement in this procedure changes `Shape1`'s shape, as was done in `ListBox1`'s `OnDblClick` event handler.

The source code for the project file and the main form's unit are shown in Listings 6.16 and 6.17 as DRAGIT.DPR and DRAGIT0.PAS, respectively.

Listing 6.16. DRAGIT.DPR, the project file for the drag-and-drop example.

```
program Dragit;

uses
  Forms,
  Dragit0 in 'DRAGIT0.PAS' {Form1};

{$R *.RES}

begin
  Application.CreateForm(TForm1, Form1);
  Application.Run;
end.
```

Listing 6.17. DRAGIT0.PAS, the unit for the drag-and-drop example.

```
unit Dragit0;
interface

uses WinTypes, WinProcs, Classes, Graphics, Forms, Controls, StdCtrls,
     Dialogs, ExtCtrls;

type
  TForm1 = class(TForm)
    Shape1: TShape;
    Shape2: TShape;
    Shape3: TShape;
    Shape4: TShape;
    ListBox1: TListBox;
    procedure Shape1DragOver(Sender, Source: TObject; X, Y: Integer;
      State: TDragState; var Accept: Boolean);
    procedure Shape1DragDrop(Sender, Source: TObject; X, Y: Integer);
    procedure ListBox1MouseDown(Sender: TObject; Button: TMouseButton;
      Shift: TShiftState; X, Y: Integer);
    procedure ListBox1DblClick(Sender: TObject);
  private
    { Private declarations }
  public
    { Public declarations }
  end;

var
  Form1: TForm1;
```

continues

Listing 6.17. continued

```
implementation

{$R *.DFM}

procedure TForm1.Shape1DragOver(Sender, Source: TObject; X, Y: Integer;
  State: TDragState; var Accept: Boolean);
begin
{ Accept if the Source is a TShape or a TListBox }
  Accept := (source is TShape) or (source is TListBox);
end;

procedure TForm1.Shape1DragDrop(Sender, Source: TObject; X, Y: Integer);
begin
{ TShapeType = (stRectangle, stSquare, stRoundRect, stRoundSquare,
    stEllipse, stCircle);
}
  { change the color or shape depending ot Source's type }
  if Source is TShape then
    Shape1.Brush.Color := TShape(Source).Brush.Color
  else if Source is TListBox then
    Shape1.Shape := TShapeType(TListBox(Source).ItemIndex)
end;

procedure TForm1.ListBox1MouseDown(Sender: TObject; Button: TMouseButton;
  Shift: TShiftState; X, Y: Integer);
begin
  if Button = mbLeft then
    TListBox(Sender).BeginDrag(false);
end;

procedure TForm1.ListBox1DblClick(Sender: TObject);
begin
 if Sender is TListBox then
   Shape1.Shape := TShapeType(TListBox(Sender).ItemIndex)
end;

end.
```

Using Hints in Your Applications

Hints provide a way for you to tell your users what a control does. Hints commonly are used with SpeedBars because those small pictures often can be confusing at first and not very helpful when learning a new product. You certainly don't want your users pressing buttons at random just to see what they do.

To use hint captions, you must place your controls on a TPanel component. TPanel's ShowHints property enables hint captions for controls placed on it. Hint captions display when the user places or moves the mouse cursor over the control. Refer to the SpeedButton example, SPEEDB.DPR, in Listing 6.5. Set Panel1's ShowHints property to true. For each SpeedButton on Panel1, add a descriptive string to the Hint property. Save the project and run it. When you place the mouse over the button, you will see a hint caption, as shown in Figure 6.7.

FIGURE 6.7.

*A SpeedButton caption
from SPEEDB.DPR.*

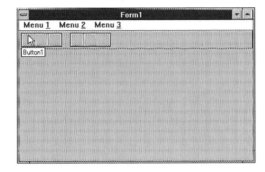

Summary

There are countless ways that you can spruce up your forms in Delphi. In this chapter you learned some of the more common methods. You learned about modifying your form's appearance by setting various properties. You learned about adding menus, SpeedBars and floating SpeedBars to your forms. You also learned about the TStrings class that you'll find yourself using quite often. You learned how to add tabs and notebooks to your applications. Finally, you used drag-and-drop capabilities in a sample project. You'll add more bells and whistles to applications later in this book. The next chapter shows you how to add even more user-interface tools by adding VBXs to Delphi's Component Palette.

7

Using VBX Controls with Delphi

Another great advantage that Delphi gives you is the capability to easily integrate Visual Basic VBX controls into your Delphi applications. This capability opens up a whole world of features and functionality available to you through VBX controls.

After you add a VBX to the Component palette, you can use it like any other Delphi control. This chapter discusses integrating VBXs into Delphi, shipping a VBX-equipped application, and using a VBX control in your application.

Understanding VBX Controls

VBX controls are stand-alone components, although they are similar to Delphi components. VBX controls originally were written for Microsoft's Visual Basic. Like Delphi components, Visual Basic controls have properties and events that you can modify and interact with while designing or running your application. VBX controls come in many shapes and sizes; a VBX can be something as simple as a pushbutton or as complex as a full-featured word processor.

Because of VBX controls' modularity and capability for providing instant productivity, support for them spread outside the Visual Basic environment into other major Windows development products like Microsoft Visual C++, Borland C++, and Borland's dBASE for Windows—just to name a few. This cross-product support for VBXs has fed on itself, and today VBX controlmakers are a whole industry within the industry of Windows development software.

The disadvantage of VBX controls is that, unlike their Delphi counterparts, they cannot be written in their native Visual Basic environment and generally are written in C, C++, or Pascal. The switch, chart, picture, and graph VBXs that come standard with Delphi are all written in Object Pascal. Despite any technological advantages that Delphi's visual components may have over VBXs, it would be foolhardy to ignore the vast numbers of VBX controls available on the market that offer "plug-and-play" productivity.

> **NOTE**
>
> The VBX control you choose to use with Delphi must be able to perform as a Level One VBX. VBXs of a higher level generally are intended for use only from within the Visual Basic environment. As a rule of thumb, if the VBX supports Visual C++ or Borland C++, it probably also will work within the Delphi environment.

Deciding When To Use a VBX

As a rule of thumb, you should use a VBX control only if there is no Delphi component available that fits the bill. Delphi controls offer you more flexibility, and they don't carry additional runtime baggage. VBX controls also come without any source code to benefit from, but many Delphi component authors share their source. Also, because VBX controls most often are written in C or C++, even having the source code to the control isn't always helpful for learning the control writer's secrets—whereas Delphi components are, well, written in Delphi.

Adding a VBX to the Component Palette

The first step toward using a particular VBX control in your Delphi application is adding that control to the Component palette in the Delphi IDE. This places an icon for the VBX control on the Component palette among your other Delphi and VBX controls. After you add a particular VBX control to the Component palette, you can drop it onto any form and use it as if it were any other Delphi control.

To add a VBX to the Component palette, follow these steps:

1. Choose Options|Install Components from the main menu. The Install Components dialog box appears, as shown in Figure 7.1.

FIGURE 7.1.

The Install Components dialog box.

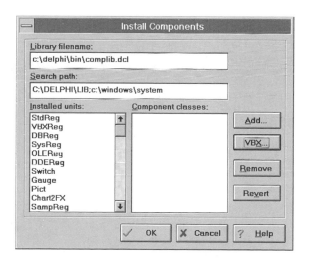

2. Click the VBX button. The Install VBX File dialog box appears, as shown in Figure 7.2.
3. Select and choose the name of the VBX file that represents the VBX control you want to use in the Delphi environment. Then choose OK. This will invoke the Install VBX dialog box as shown in Figure 7.3.

FIGURE 7.2.
The Install VBX File
dialog box.

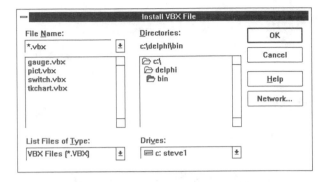

FIGURE 7.3.
The Install VBX
dialog box.

4. The Install VBX dialog box contains edit controls for the VBX file name, unit file name, and palette page, and a listbox containing the VBX classes contained within the VBX file. Edit the path name shown in the unit file name edit box. This is the path name of the unit that Delphi creates to interface with the VBX control. The file name defaults to the same as that of the VBX file, but with a PAS extension. Save this file in a subdirectory of the Delphi directory.

5. The Palette page edit control of the Install VBX dialog contains the name of the page on the Component palette where you want this control to reside. The default is the VBX page. You can choose another existing page or make up a new name, and a corresponding page is created on the Component palette.

6. The Class Names listbox of the Install VBX dialog contains the names of the new objects created in this control. You generally should leave these names set to the default.

7. Click the OK button in the Install VBX dialog. Delphi generates the source code for the interface unit for the VBX file and returns you to the Install Components dialog box.

8. If you have made an error, click the Revert button in the Install Components dialog to cancel the changes you made. If you feel confident of your changes, click the OK button.

Delphi compiles the source code to your VBX interface unit and links it in with the rest of the component library. (The component library is discussed in detail in Chapter 11, "Writing Delphi Custom Components.") Now your VBX is ready to roll.

NOTE

If an error occurs while Delphi is creating or compiling the source code to the VBX interface unit, you might be using a VBX control that does not support Level One VBX.

Using VBX Controls in Your Applications

After you've linked your VBX control wrapper into the component library, you've fought half the battle. Using a VBX on the Component palette is very much the same as using a regular Delphi component. This section shows you how to create a simple project that uses Delphi's BiSwitch VBX control.

To use the BiSwitch VBX control, follow these steps:

1. Create a new project and drop a BiSwitch control on the form so that your form resembles Figure 7.4.

FIGURE 7.4.
A simple VBX project.

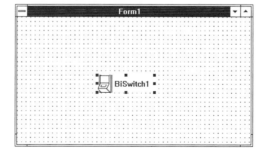

2. Choose File | Save Project from the main menu, and the Save Unit dialog will appear.
3. Save the unit as MAINVBX.PAS, and the Save Project dialog will appear. At this point, save the project as USEVBX.DPR.
4. Select BiSwitch1 on the form and flip the Object Inspector to the Events page.

5. Double-click OnOn to create an event handler for that event. In this event handler, display a dialog box informing the user of the selection by using the following code:

```
procedure TForm1.BiSwitch1On(Sender: TObject);
begin
  MessageDlg('The switch is turned on.', mtInformation, [mbOk], 0);
end;
```

6. Do the same for BiSwitch1's OnOff event:

```
procedure TForm1.BiSwitch1Off(Sender: TObject);
begin
  MessageDlg('The switch is turned off.', mtInformation, [mbOk], 0);
end;
```

7. Choose File|Save Project from the main menu to save your changes, and run the application by pressing the F9 key or selecting Run|Run.

Flip the switch by clicking the mouse on the switch to see a message dialog box—nothing too fancy, right? That's the point. VBXs, in most cases, should be as straightforward as native Delphi components.

Now make the project a little more interesting by adding one more VBX control. Follow these steps:

1. Select the BiPict object from the Component palette and place it on your form.

2. Place an OpenDialog and a Button on your form.

3. Set Button's caption to &Load File.

4. Change BiSwitch's caption to &Power.

5. Save this project. Your form now should look like Figure 7.5.

FIGURE 7.5.
The USEVBX project.

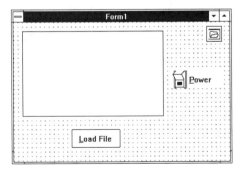

Now have some fun and make BiSwitch1 the power switch for the form. When the switch is on, the form appears as normal, and when the switch is off, the form is all black. Replace the code in the OnOn and OnOff event handlers with the code shown in Listing 7.1.

Listing 7.1. BiSwitch event handlers.

```
procedure TForm1.BiSwitch1On(Sender: TObject);
begin
  Color := clWindow;        { normal window color }
  BiPict1.Visible := True;  { make controls visible }
  Button1.Visible := True;
end;

procedure TForm1.BiSwitch1Off(Sender: TObject);
begin
  BiPict1.Visible := False;  { make controls invisible }
  Button1.Visible := False;
  Color := clBlack;          { make the window black }
end;
```

VBX Functions, Objects, and Types

One of the more challenging parts of using VBX controls with Delphi is using Delphi's VBX functions and Visual Basic types. The BIVBX and VBXCtrl units declare several new types and objects that are used with VBX controls. Additionally, you will find most of the functions and procedures used to interact with the data in VBX controls in the BIVBX and VBXCtrl units. In this section, you examine the functions and types relevant to using VBX controls in your Delphi projects.

VBX Graphics

Using the USEVBX project as a starting point, suppose that you want a picture from a graphics file to be loaded into BiPict1 at runtime. TBiPict's graphic is stored in its Picture property, which is of type TVBPic. Loading a picture into the TBiPict control is a two-step process: you first must call VBXGetPicFromFile() to obtain a TVBPicture from a graphics file, and then you must call VBXCreatePicture() to obtain a TVBPic from the TVBPicture. Listing 7.2 shows the code for Button1's OnClick event; this event opens OpenDialog1 and loads the picture from the file into BiPict.

Listing 7.2. Button1's OnClick event.

```
procedure TForm1.Button1Click(Sender: TObject);
var
  FName: PChar;
begin
  if OpenDialog1.Execute then begin
    FName := StrAlloc (Length(OpenDialog1.FileName));
    StrPCopy(FName, OpenDialog1.FileName);         { Copy String to PChar }
    VBXGetPicFromFile(Pic, FName);                 { Create TVBPicture }
    BiPict1.Picture := (VBXCreatePicture(Pic);     { Create TVBPic }
    StrDispose(FName);
  end;
end;
```

Notice that you must convert OpenDialog1's FileName string to a PChar type using the StrPCopy function because that is the type of string that VBXGetPicFromFile() accepts.

Listings 7.3 and 7.4 contain the complete source code for USEVBX.DPR, the project file, and MAINVBX.PAS, the unit.

Listing 7.3. The source code for USEVBX.DPR.

```
program Usevbx;

uses
  Forms,
  Mainvbx in 'MAINVBX.PAS' {Form1};

{$R *.RES}

begin
  Application.CreateForm(TForm1, Form1);
  Application.Run;
end.
```

Listing 7.4. The source code for MAINVBX.PAS.

```
unit MainVBX;

interface

uses
  SysUtils, WinTypes, WinProcs, Messages, Classes, Graphics, Controls,
  Forms, Dialogs, StdCtrls, Switch, VBXCtrl, Pict, BIVBX;

type
  TForm1 = class(TForm)
    BiPict1: TBiPict;
    BiSwitch1: TBiSwitch;
    Button1: TButton;
    OpenDialog1: TOpenDialog;
    procedure Button1Click(Sender: TObject);
    procedure FormCreate(Sender: TObject);
    procedure BiSwitch1On(Sender: TObject);
    procedure BiSwitch1Off(Sender: TObject);
  private
    Pic: TVBPicture;
  end;

var
  Form1: TForm1;

implementation

{$R *.DFM}

procedure TForm1.Button1Click(Sender: TObject);
```

```
var
  FName: PChar;
begin
  if OpenDialog1.Execute then begin
    FName := StrAlloc(Length(OpenDialog1.FileName));
    StrPCopy(FName, OpenDialog1.FileName);    { copy String to PChar }
    VBXGetPicFromFile(Pic, FName);            { Create TVBPicture }
    BiPict1.Picture := VBXCreatePicture(Pic); { Create TVBPic }
    StrDispose(FName);
  end;
end;

procedure TForm1.FormCreate(Sender: TObject);
begin
  { These could be set in Object Inspector, but we set them here for }
  { demonstration purposes. }
  with OpenDialog1 do
    Filter := 'All files (*.*)¦*.*¦Bitmap files (*.bmp)¦*.bmp¦'+
              'Meta files (*.wmf)¦*.wmf¦Icon files (*.ico)¦*.ico';
end;

procedure TForm1.BiSwitch1On(Sender: TObject);
begin
  Color := clWindow;        { normal window color }
  BiPict1.Visible := True;  { make controls visible }
  Button1.Visible := True;
end;

procedure TForm1.BiSwitch1Off(Sender: TObject);
begin
  BiPict1.Visible := False; { make controls invisible }
  Button1.Visible := False;
  Color := clBlack;         { make window black }
end;

end.
```

VBX Helper Functions

Occasionally, when working with VBX controls, you find functions that accept special VB types as parameters, or that return VB types. The VBXCTRL unit contains a number of functions that aid in conversion between Visual Basic types and Object Pascal variable types.

The VBXButtonShiftToShift() function converts VBX shift and button information (VBXShift and VBXButton types) into a variable of Delphi's TShiftState type. This function is defined as follows:

```
function VBXButtonShiftToShift(VBXShift, VBXButton: Integer): TShiftState;
```

The VBXButtonToButton() function converts a VBXButton type variable into a Delphi TMouseButton variable. This function is defined as follows:

```
function VBXButtonToButton(VBXButton: Integer): TMouseButton;
```

BStrPas() converts a TBasicString type into a Pascal String, and it is defined as follows:

```
function BStrPas(BasicStr: TBasicString): string;
```

BStrPCopy(), conversely, converts a Pascal String to a TBasicString usable by VBX controls. It is defined as follows:

```
function BStrPCopy(const Str: string): TBasicString;
```

The SetBStr() function enables you to set the value of a TBasicString variable to match the string contained in a String variable. This function is defined as follows:

```
procedure SetBStr(var BasicStr: TBasicString; const Str: string);
```

Some VBX functions return TCString null-terminated, string-type variables. Use the CStrPas() function to convert a TCString to a String.

```
function CStrPas(CStr: TCString): string;
```

Shipping VBX-Equipped Applications

Once you are ready to ship your VBX-equipped application, there are two or more files that you must ship in addition to the .EXE or .DLL file that makes up your Delphi application:

- You must ship the VBX files that contain the VBX controls you are using in your application. Delphi does not link the VBX file into your executable, and the .VBX file must be installed in the \WINDOWS\SYSTEM directory. However, there are some third-party products on the market that will attach VBX files to an executable so that you can avoid shipping separate files.

- The BIVBX11.DLL that comes with Delphi provides Borland's runtime support for VBX controls. This file is redistributable, and it must be installed in the \WINDOWS\SYSTEM directory of the machine that will run your VBX-enabled Delphi application.

- Many VBX controls also come with a license file that is required in order to use the control at design-time. This file is available from the VBX vendor, and it prevents your end-users from designing their applications with VBXs that you ship with your applications.

- Some VBX controls require external DLLs or other files in order to operate. You should check with the VBX vendor to determine if any external files are required by your VBX control.

Summary

By now, you're familiar with VBX controls and how to effectively use them in the Delphi environment and in your applications. Because of their market presence, VBX controls often can offer you a blast of instant productivity, but remember to look first for a Delphi control before jumping into a VBX.

8

MDI Applications

The Multiple Document Interface, otherwise known as MDI, was introduced to Windows version 2.0 in Microsoft Excel's spreadsheet. MDI gave Excel users the ability to work on more than one spreadsheet at a time. Today, MDI is used with just about any application that uses documents such as Program Manager, File Manager, Microsoft Word, and Borland Pascal. Figure 8.1 shows the MDI application Borland Pascal 7.0 with several files open.

FIGURE 8.1.

Borland Pascal 7.0, an MDI application.

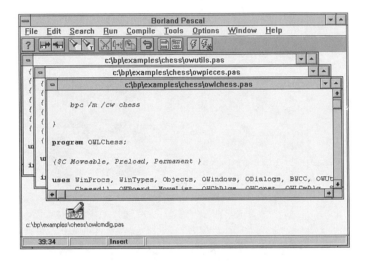

Until now, the sample applications you have created use one form, or at least one modal form, at a time. MDI enables you to manipulate multiple forms concurrently.

Handling events between multiple forms simultaneously may seem difficult. In traditional Windows programming, you had to have knowledge of the Windows class MDICLIENT, MDI data structures, and the additional functions and messages specific to MDI. With Delphi, creating MDI applications has been greatly simplified. When you finish this chapter, you will have a solid foundation for building MDI applications with which you easily can expand to more advanced techniques.

Creating the MDI Application

To create MDI applications, you only need familiarity with the form styles fsMDIForm and fsMDIChild, and a bit of MDI programming methodology. We present some basic concepts regarding MDI and show how MDI works with special MDI child forms in the sections to follow.

Understanding MDI Basics

To understand MDI applications, you first must understand how they are constructed. Figure 8.2 shows an MDI application similar to one that you will build in this chapter.

FIGURE 8.2.

The structure of an MDI application.

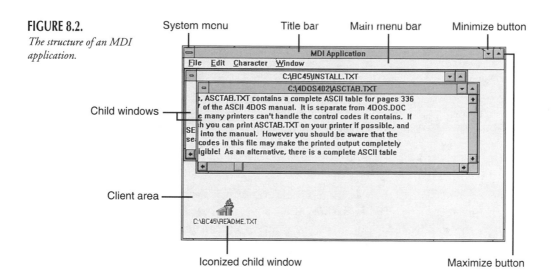

The windows involved with an MDI application follow:

Frame window   The application's main window. It has a caption, menu bar, and system menu. A Minimize and Maximize button appear in its upper-left corner. The blank space inside the frame window is known as its *client area* and is actually the *client window.*

Client window   The manager for MDI applications. The client window handles all MDI-specific commands and manages the child windows that reside on its surface. The client is created automatically when you create a frame window.

Child windows   These contain your actual documents—text files, spreadsheets, bitmaps, and other document types. Child windows, like frame windows, have a caption, system menu, Minimize button, Maximize button, and possibly a menu. A child window's menu is combined with the frame window's menu. Child windows never move outside the client area.

Delphi does not require you to be familiar with the special MDI window's messages. The client window is responsible for handling all MDI routines, such as cascading and tiling child windows. To cascade child windows using the traditional method, for example, use the Windows API function SendMessage() to send a WM_MDICASCADE message to the client window:

```
procedure TFrameForm.Cascade1Click(Sender: TObject);
begin
  SendMessage(ClientHandle, WM_MDICASCADE, 0, 0);
end;
```

In Delphi, just call the cascade method:

```
procedure TFrameForm.Cascade1Click(Sender: TObject);
begin
  cascade;
end;
```

In the following section, you will create a complete MDI editor and bitmap file viewer without using any MDI messages; Delphi will perform the calls for you.

Using the Child Forms

Earlier we said that MDI applications enable you to work with multiple documents. These documents, text files, spreadsheets, images and so forth, are loaded into child windows of the MDI parent window. In Delphi, these child windows are actually forms that have an fsMDIChild FormStyle. You'll create two MDI child forms here: one to edit text and one to view bitmapped images.

The Text Editor Form

The Text Editor Form will enable you to load any text file and edit it. In this section, you'll create just the framework for the form. Later you'll add complete functionality to it.

Create a new form and place a TMemo on it. Set the properties shown in Table 8.1.

Table 8.1. Setting properties for TMemo objects.

Control	Property	Value
EditForm	Name	'EditForm'
EditForm	FormStyle	fsMDIChild
Memo1	Align	alClient
Memo1	BorderStyle	bsNone
Memo1	Cursor	crBeam
Memo1	ScrollBars	ssBoth
Memo1	Text	' '

Setting Memo1's align property to alClient causes Memo1 to cover EditForm's entire client area. Also, remove the declaration of the TEditForm variable:

```
var
  EditForm: TEditForm;
```

You'll declare and create this form instance elsewhere so it doesn't need to be declared here. Make sure that EditForm is not automatically created by removing it from the list of Auto-Create

Forms in the Project Options dialog, which you access by selecting Options | Project from Delphi's main menu. Save this unit as MDIEDIT.PAS, and save the project as MDIAPP.DPR. You will create event handlers later when you add menus to the form.

The Bitmap Viewer

The Bitmap Viewer Form will enable you to load a bitmap file for viewing. Again, you'll create just the framework now for the form and add functionality to it later.

Create another form and place a TImage on it. Set the properties shown in Table 8.2.

Table 8.2. Setting properties for TImage objects.

Control	Property	Value
BMPForm	Name	'BMPForm'
BMPForm	Caption	' '
BMPForm	FormStyle	fsMDIChild
Image1	Align	alLeft
Image1	AutoSize	true

Exclude this Form as an Auto-Create form from the Options|Projects dialog box, and delete the following BMPForm variable declaration. Save this unit as MDIBMP.PAS.

```
var
  BMPForm: TBMPForm;
```

Creating the MDI Frame Form

Here, you'll create the MDI Frame Form, the parent to the Text Editor Form and Bitmap Viewer Form. You'll add its functionality later.

Create a new form and set the properties shown in Table 8.3.

Table 8.3. Setting properties for the MDI Frame Form.

Control	Property	Value
FrameForm	Name	'FrameForm'
FrameForm	Caption	'MDI Application'
FrameForm	FormStyle	fsMDIForm

Save this unit as MDIFRAME.PAS. Select FrameForm as the main form from the Project Options dialog box.

You now can run the application, although it doesn't do anything useful except bring up an MDI client form. You must add menus to FrameForm so that you can create child forms.

Adding Menus to MDI Applications

Adding menus to MDI applications is no different than what you've done in previous examples. There are a few differences in how menus work in MDI applications, however. This section shows how an MDI application allows its child forms to share the same menu bar using a method called *menu merging*.

Creating the Menus

This section explains how to add a menu to FrameForm by placing a TMainMenu object on it. Follow these steps:

1. Place a TMainMenu component on your frame form and bring up the Menu Designer by double-clicking on the TMainMenu icon. Add the common File menu items listed in Table 8.4.

Table 8.4. FrameForm's File menu items.

Menubar	Submenu	Shortcut
"&File"	"&New"	Ctrl+N
	"&Open"	Ctrl+O
	"&Close"	*none*
	"-"	
	"&Save"	Ctrl+S
	"Save &As"	*none*
	"-"	
	"&Print"	Ctrl+P
	"Prin&t Setup"	*none*
	"-"	
	"E&xit"	

Figure 8.3 shows the File menu items.

Notice the use of the – character in the Menu Designer to create a separator bar on the menu.

The File menu has common commands that you probably will want to add to other applications. Therefore, it's a good idea to save your menu as a template for later use.

FIGURE 8.3.

The File menu items.

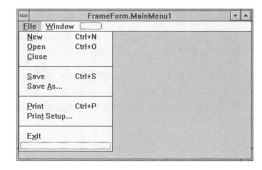

2. Right-click on the Menu Designer to bring up a local menu. Choose Save As Template to display the Save Template dialog box. Type **File Menu** to describe your menu and choose OK to close the dialog box and save your menu. You now can reuse this menu with other forms.

3. You will need a menu with window commands, so create another template by first deleting the File menu from the Menu Editor; otherwise, it will be added to your new menu template. To delete the File Menu just press the delete key with the File Menu highlighted in the Menu Designer.

4. Create the menu items listed in Table 8.5 in the Menu Editor. Figure 8.4 shows the Window menu items.

Table 8.5. Frame Form's Window menu items.

Menubar	Submenu	Shortcut
"&Window"	"&Tile"	*none*
	"&Cascade"	*none*
	"&Arrange Icons"	*none*
	"C&lose All"	*none*

FIGURE 8.4.

The Window menu items.

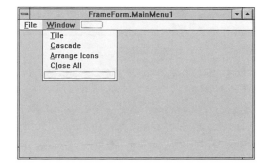

5. Save this template as a menu template named Window Menu using the same technique that you used to save the File menu. Just name it something different, such as "Window Menu." Now you can reinsert the File menu by choosing Insert From Template from the Menu Designer's local menu.

6. Select the Windows menu bar and change its GroupIndex property to 9 in the Object Inspector. The reason for this procedure is explained in the following section, "Merging Menus."

7. Select the EditForm and add a TMainMenu object to it. Select Insert From Template from the Menu Designer's SpeedBar. Choose File menu and choose OK. The menu that you previously designed appears in your new menu.

8. Create the additional menu and submenu items listed in Table 8.6 to add to the EditForm.

Table 8.6. Additional EditForm menu items.

Menubar	*Submenu*	*Shortcut*
"&Edit"	"&Cut"	Ctrl+X
	"Co&py"	Ctrl+C
	"&Paste"	Ctrl+V
	"&Delete"	Ctrl+D
	"-"	
	"Select &All"	*none*
"&Character"	"&Left"	*none*
	"&Right"	*none*
	"&Center"	*none*
	"-"	
	"&Word Wrap"	*none*
	"-"	
	"Font"	*none*

9. Before leaving the Menu Designer, set the GroupIndex property for the Edit and Character menu bar items to the value 1.

10. Leave the Menu Designer, and set MainMenu1's AutoMerge property to true from the Object Inspector. (For more information about setting the AutoMerge property, see the following section.)

11. Bring up the BMPForm and add a TMainMenu to it.

12. Bring up the Menu Designer, and select Insert From Template from the SpeedBar. Select the File menu. Remove the menu items Save, Save As, and one of the separators. These items do not apply to the BMPForm.

13. Add the menu and submenu items listed in Table 8.7 to BMPForm's menu:

Table 8.7. BMPForm's main menu.

Menubar	*Submenu*	*Shortcut*
"&Edit"	"Co&py"	Ctrl+C
	"&Paste"	Ctrl+V

14. Now change MainMenu1's AutoMerge property to true in the Object Inspector.

You've just completed all that is required to add menus to your MDI application. The only new feature that you used is the AutoMerge property, which allows a child form's menu to merge with the parent form's menu; this is called menu merging.

Merging Menus

The AutoMerge property specifies how a form's menu is merged with other menus. If true, it can be merged into the frame form's menu bar. The only menu that can receive merges is the main menu of the MDIForm.

In this chapter, both the EditForm's and BMPForm's MainMenus have an AutoMerge set to true so that their menus will be merged into FrameForm's MainMenu.

The GroupIndex property determines the order in which menu bar items appear on the form's menu bar when its menus are merged with menus from a child form. When the child form's GroupIndex property equals the GroupIndex property for one of the menu items on the frame form's menu bar, the child's menu replaces the frame form's menu item. If there's no match for GroupIndex, the child's menu is inserted in the frame's menu in GroupIndex order. Only whole menus are merged/replaced—merging occurs at the main menu-bar level, not at the submenu level.

In our example, the File menu's GroupIndex property equals 0 for each form. EditForm's Window menu's GroupIndex property equals 9, and both Edit and Character menu items equal 1. When no child form is present, only FrameForm's menus appear. When an EditForm is open, it replaces FrameForm's File menu and inserts its Edit and Character menus between the File menu and Window menus. BMPForm's menus behave much like EditForm's menus.

Working with Child Windows

At this point you have a working shell for your MDI application. Now, we'll show you how to approach adding the functionality to an MDI application. Additionally, we'll show you the common methods and techniques used when writing MDI code. You'll see how to create your MDI children at runtime when requested by the user. You'll learn about common MDI child window commands. You'll also learn some other techniques that, although not MDI specific, illustrate how MDI children can have completely different functionality from one another.

Creating a Child Edit Form at Runtime

To create a new `EditForm`, create the method `TFrameForm.OpenTextFile()`, which creates an instance of a `TEditForm`. This method is called from the `FrameForm`'s File | New `OnClick` event handler. Both the menu event handler and the method `OpenTextFile()` are shown in Listing 8.1. The complete source code for MDIAPP.DPR, MDIFRAME.PAS, MDIEDIT.PAS, and MDIBMP.PAS is shown in Listings 8.2, 8.3, 8.4, and 8.5, respectively.

Listing 8.1. The File | New event handler and `OpenTextFile` method.

```
procedure TFrameForm.New1Click(Sender: TObject);
begin
  OpenTextFile('');
end;

procedure TFrameForm.OpenTextFile(FileName: string);
begin
  with TEditForm.Create(self) do
  begin
    if FileName <> '' then
    begin
      OpenFile(FileName);
    end;
    Parent := self;
    Visible := true;
  end;
end;
```

Listing 8.2. The source code for MDIAPP.DPR.

```
program Mdiapp;

uses
  Forms,
  Mdiframe in 'MDIFRAME.PAS' {FrameForm},
  Mdiedit in 'MDIEDIT.PAS' {EditForm},
  Mdibmp in 'MDIBMP.PAS' {BMPForm};

{$R *.DFM}
```

```
begin
  Application.CreateForm(TFrameForm, FrameForm);
  Application.Run;
end.
```

Listing 8.3. The source code for MDIFRAME.PAS.

```
unit Mdiframe;

interface

uses WinTypes, WinProcs, Classes, Graphics, Forms, Controls, Menus,
     MDIEdit, MDIBMP, StdCtrls, WinDos, Messages, Dialogs, SysUtils;

type
  TFrameForm = class(TForm)
    MainMenu1: TMainMenu;
    OpenDialog1: TOpenDialog;
    File1: TMenuItem;
    Exit1: TMenuItem;
    N1: TMenuItem;
    PrintSetup1: TMenuItem;
    Print1: TMenuItem;
    N2: TMenuItem;
    SaveAs1: TMenuItem;
    Save1: TMenuItem;
    N3: TMenuItem;
    Close1: TMenuItem;
    Open1: TMenuItem;
    New1: TMenuItem;
    Window1: TMenuItem;
    ArrangeIcons1: TMenuItem;
    Cascade1: TMenuItem;
    Tile1: TMenuItem;
    PrinterSetupDialog1: TPrinterSetupDialog;
    CloseAll1: TMenuItem;
    procedure OpenTextFile(Filename: string);
    procedure Tile1Click(Sender: TObject);
    procedure ArrangeIcons1Click(Sender: TObject);
    procedure Cascade1Click(Sender: TObject);
    procedure New1Click(Sender: TObject);
    procedure OpenBMPFile(FileName: String);
    procedure Open1Click(Sender: TObject);
    procedure Exit1Click(Sender: TObject);
    procedure Close1Click(Sender: TObject);
    procedure PrintSetup1Click(Sender: TObject);
end;

procedure TFrameForm.Exit1Click(Sender: TObject);
begin
  Close;
end;

procedure TFrameForm.Close1Click(Sender: TObject);
```

continues

Listing 8.3. continued

```
begin
    procedure CloseAll1Click(Sender: TObject);
    procedure Close1Click(Sender: TObject);
  protected
  private
    { Private declarations }
  public
    { Public declarations }
    procedure OpenTextFile(Filename: string);
    procedure OpenBMPFile(FileName: String);
  end;

var
  FrameForm: TFrameForm;

implementation

const
  BMPExt: PChar = '.BMP';
  TextExt: PChar = '.TXT';

{$R *.DFM}

procedure TFrameForm.OpenTextFile(FileName: string);
var
  EditForm: TEditForm;
begin
  Editform := TEditForm.Create(self);
  if FileName <> '' then
  begin
    EditForm.OpenFile(FileName);
  end;
  Editform.Visible := true;begin
  with TEditForm.Create(self) do       { Create a TEditForm instance }
    if FileName <> '' then             { If FileName contains a name then call }
      OpenFile(FileName);              { OpenFile() passing the file name. }
end;

procedure TFrameForm.OpenBMPFile(FileName: String);
var
  BMPForm: TBMPForm;
begin
  BMPform := TBMPForm.Create(self);
  BMPForm.OpenFile(FileName);
  BMPForm.Visible := true;
end;begin
  with TBmpForm.Create(self) do        { Create a TBMPForm instance }
    OpenFile(FileName);                { Call OpenFile, passing the valid BMP file}
end;                                   { name }

procedure TFrameForm.Tile1Click(Sender: TObject);
begin
  Tile;    { Call the Tile method to tile forms }
end;

procedure TFrameForm.ArrangeIcons1Click(Sender: TObject);
```

```
begin
   ArrangeIcons;   { Call the ArrangeIcons method to arrange icons in the
➡client area }
end;

procedure TFrameForm.Cascade1Click(Sender: TObject);
begin
   Cascade;        { Call the Cascade method to cascade forms }
end;

procedure TFrameForm.New1Click(Sender: TObject);
begin
   OpenTextFile('');   { This is a new Form, no filename is given so pass a
➡blank string }
end;

procedure TFrameForm.Open1Click(Sender: TObject);
var
   FName, Dir,Name,
   Ext: array[0..79] of char;
begin
   OpenDialog1 := TOpenDialog.Create(self);Ext: string[4];
begin
   OpenDialog1.Filter := 'Text File¦*.txt¦Bitmap File¦*.bmp'; { Set the
➡OpenDialog Filters. }
   OpenDialog1.DefaultExt := 'txt';                    { Set the default
➡extension }
   if OpenDialog1.Execute then
 begin                           { Execute OpenDialog }
     beginExt := ExtractFileExt(OpenDialog1.FileName);      { Get the
➡extension }
     StrPCopy(FName, OpenDialog1.FileName);
if CompareStr(UpperCase(Ext), TextExt) = 0 then      { Compare with extension
➡constants }
     FileSplit(FName, Dir, Name, Ext);OpenTextFile(OpenDialog1.FileName) { Open
➡a text file if EXT is TextExt }
     if strcomp(StrUpper(Ext), TextExt) = 0 then
     else if CompareStr(UpperCase(Ext), BMPExt) = 0 then       { Open a BMP file
➡if EXT is BMPExt }
OpenTextFile(OpenDialog1.FileName)
     else if strcomp(StrUpper(Ext), BMPExt) = 0 then
        OpenBMPFile(OpenDialog1.FileName);
   end;
OpenDialog1.Free;
end;
   Close;
end;

procedure TFrameForm.PrintSetup1Click(Sender: TObject);
begin
   PrinterSetupDialog1.Execute;
end;

begin
   RegisterClasses([TFrameForm, TMainMenu, TMenuItem, TMemo, TOpenDialog,
     TSaveDialog]);
end.procedure TFrameForm.CloseAll1Click(Sender: TObject);
var
```

continues

Listing 8.3. continued

```
  i: integer;
begin
  for i := 0 to MDIChildCount -1 do    { For the total number of child windows }
    MDIChildren[0].Close                { always close window at position 0.
►Windows at }
end;                                    { position 1, will then move position 0 }

procedure TFrameForm.Close1Click(Sender: TObject);
begin
  Close;  { Close all forms and the main form }
end;

end.
```

Listing 8.4. Source code for MDIEDIT.PAS.

```
unit Mdiedit;

interface

uses WinTypes, WinProcs, Classes, Graphics, Forms, Controls, Menus,
  StdCtrls, Dialogs, SysUtils, Printers;

type
  TEditForm = class(TForm)
    MainMenu1: TMainMenu;
    Edit1: TMenuItem;
    Cut1: TMenuItem;
    Copy1: TMenuItem;
    Paste1: TMenuItem;
    Delete1: TMenuItem;
    N4: TMenuItem;
    SelectAll1: TMenuItem;
    Character1: TMenuItem;
    Left1: TMenuItem;
    Right1: TMenuItem;
    Center1: TMenuItem;
    N5: TMenuItem;
    WordWrap1: TMenuItem;
    N6: TMenuItem;
    Font1: TMenuItem;
    Memo1: TMemo;
    File1: TMenuItem;
    Exit1: TMenuItem;
    N1: TMenuItem;
    PrintSetup1: TMenuItem;
    Print1: TMenuItem;
    N2: TMenuItem;
    SaveAs1: TMenuItem;
    Save1: TMenuItem;
    N3: TMenuItem;
    Close1: TMenuItem;
    Open1: TMenuItem;
    New1: TMenuItem;
```

```
    SaveDialog1: TSaveDialog;
    FontDialog1: TFontDialog;
    PrintDialog1: TPrintDialog;
    procedure New1Click(Sender: TObject);
    procedure Left1Click(Sender: TObject);
    procedure WordWrap1Click(Sender: TObject);
    procedure Open1Click(Sender: TObject);
    procedure OpenFile(FileName: string);
    procedure Save1Click(Sender: TObject);
    procedure Exit1Click(Sender: TObject);
    procedure Close1Click(Sender: TObject);
    procedure FormCloseQuery(Sender: TObject; var CanClose: Boolean);
    procedure Cut1Click(Sender: TObject);
    procedure Copy1Click(Sender: TObject);
    procedure Paste1Click(Sender: TObject);
    procedure Delete1Click(Sender: TObject);
    procedure SelectAll1Click(Sender: TObject);
    procedure SaveAs1Click(Sender: TObject);
    procedure Font1Click(Sender: TObject);
    procedure PrintSetup1Click(Sender: TObject);
    procedure Print1Click(Sender: TObject);
    procedure FormClose(Sender: TObject; var Action: TCloseAction);
  private
    { Private declarations }
  public
    { Public declarations }
  end;

implementation
uses MDIFrame;

{$R *.DFM}

procedure TEditForm.New1Click(Sender: TObject);
begin
  FrameForm.OpenTextFile('');  { Create an empty window }
end;

procedure TEditForm.Left1Click(Sender: TObject);
begin
  { Initialize text options }
  Left1.Checked := false;
  Right1.Checked := false;
  Center1.Checked := false;
  with Sender as TMenuItem do TMenuItem(Sender).Checked := true;
  With Memo1 do
    if Left1.Checked then
      Alignment := taLeftJustify
    else if Right1.Checked then
      Alignment := taRightJustify
    else if Center1.Checked then
      Alignment := taCenter;
end;

procedure TEditForm.WordWrap1Click(Sender: TObject);
begin
  with Memo1 do
```

continues

Listing 8.4. continued

```
begin
    beginWordWrap := not WordWrap;  { Reverse the value of the WordWrap
➥property and }
    WordWrap := not WordWrap;
if WordWrap then                { if wordwrapping is then enabled, get rid of the }
        if WordWrap then
  ScrollBars := ssVertical { scrollbars since they're not necessary }
    ScrollBars := ssVertical
    else                        { otherwise, bring 'em back. }
else
      ScrollBars := ssBoth;
    WordWrap1.Checked := WordWrap;  { Check the menu item accordingly. }
  end;
end;

procedure TEditForm.OpenFile(FileName: string);
begin
  Memo1.Lines.LoadFromFile(FileName);
  Caption := FileName; { Load the text file from disk and set the }
  Caption := FileName;              { caption to the filename }
end;

procedure TEditForm.Open1Click(Sender: TObject);
begin
  FrameForm.Open1Click(Sender); { Call frame form's event handler here }
end;

procedure TEditForm.Save1Click(Sender: TObject);
begin
    if Caption = '' then                { If no caption (no filename) then call }
      SaveAs1Click(Sender)             { SaveAs.. since it gets a filename }
    else
 begin
    beginMemo1.Lines.SaveToFile(Caption);    { Otherwise, call SaveToFile with
➥the filename }
    Memo1.Lines.SaveToFile(Caption);
    Modified := false;         { specified by the form's caption and set
➥modified }
  Memo1.Modified := false;
 end;                                   { to false since it's just been saved }
  end;
end;

procedure TEditForm.SaveAs1Click(Sender: TObject);
begin
  SaveDialog1.FileName := Caption;   { Set the SaveDialog's FileName property
➥to that }
  if SaveDialog1.Execute then
 begin { of the Caption. Then execute and assign the }
    beginCaption := SaveDialog1.FileName; { SaveDialogs FileName back to the
➥caption since it }
    Caption := SaveDialog1.FileName;
  Save1Click(Sender);                { may have changed by the user }
  Save1Click(Sender);
 end;
  end;
end;
```

```
procedure TEditForm.Exit1Click(Sender: TObject);
begin
  FrameForm.Exit1Click(Sender);Close1Click(Sender); { Call Frameform's OnClose
➥procedure }
end;

procedure TEditForm.Close1Click(Sender: TObject);
begin
  Close; { Close the edit form }
end;

procedure TEditForm.FormCloseQuery(Sender: TObject; var CanClose: Boolean);
const
  CloseMsg = '''%s'' has been modified, Save?';
var
  MsgVal: integer;
  FileName: string;
begin
  FileName := Caption;   { Set FileName to whatever's in the Caption property }
  if Memo1.Modified then
  begin { Only if the memo is modified ...}
begin
    MsgVal := MessageDlg(Format(CloseMsg, [@FileName]),FileName]), { Display an
➥are you sure message }
              mtConfirmation, [mbYes,mbNo,mbCancel], 0);
    case MsgVal of
      id_yes: Save1Click(Self);
      id_Cancel: CanClose := false;  { If yes, save the memo back to disk
➥otherwise cancel the }
      id_Cancel: CanClose := false; { close request }
    end;
  end;
end;

procedure TEditForm.Cut1Click(Sender: TObject);
begin
  Memo1.CutToClipBoard; { Cut the text to the clipboard }
end;

procedure TEditForm.Copy1Click(Sender: TObject);
begin
  Memo1.CopyToClipBoard; { Copy the text in the memo to the clipboard }
end;

procedure TEditForm.Paste1Click(Sender: TObject);
begin
  Memo1.PasteFromClipBoard; { Paste the text from the clipboard }
end;

procedure TEditForm.Delete1Click(Sender: TObject);
begin
  Memo1.ClearSelection; { Clear the selected text }
end;

procedure TEditForm.SelectAll1Click(Sender: TObject);
begin
  Memo1.SelectAll; { Select all the text in the memo }
end;
```

continues

Listing 8.4. continued

```pascal
procedure TEditForm.Font1Click(Sender: TObject);
begin
  FontDialog1.Font := Memo1.Font;    { Set the FontDialog's Font to that of the
➡Memo }
  if FontDialog1.Execute then        { Execute the FontDialog and if specified,
➡change }
    Memo1.Font := FontDialog1.Font; { The font for the memo }
end;

procedure TEditForm.PrintSetup1Click(Sender: TObject);
begin
  FrameForm.PrintSetup1Click(Sender); { Invoke the PrinterSetupDialog }
end;

procedure TEditForm.Print1Click(Sender: TObject);
var
  i: integer;
  ptext: system.textPText: TextFile;
begin
  if PrintDialog1.Execute then
 begin
    AssignPrn(PText);
    Rewrite(PText);
    try
      Printer.Canvas.Font := Memo1.Font;
      for i := 0 to Memo1.Lines.Count [ms]-1 do
        writeln(PText, Memo1.Lines[i]);
    System.Close(PText);
  end;finally
      CloseFile(PText);
    end;
  end;
end;

procedure TEditForm.FormClose(Sender: TObject; var Action: TCloseAction);
begin
  Action := caFree; { Allow the form to be free'd when closed }
end;

end.
```

Listing 8.5. The source code for MDIBMP.PAS.

```pascal
unit Mdibmp;

interface

uses WinTypes, WinProcs, Classes, Graphics, Forms, Controls, Menus,
  StdCtrls, Dialogs, printers, sysutils;

type
  TBMPForm = class(TForm)
    MainMenu1: TMainMenu;
    File1: TMenuItem;
    Exit1: TMenuItem;
```

```
    N1: TMenuItem;
    PrintSetup1: TMenuItem;
    Print1: TMenuItem;
    N3: TMenuItem;
    Close1: TMenuItem;
    Open1: TMenuItem;
    Image1: TImage;
    New2: TMenuItem;
    procedure New2Click(Sender: TObject);
    procedure Open1Click(Sender: TObject);
    procedure Save1Click(Sender: TObject);
    procedure Exit1Click(Sender: TObject);
    procedure Close1Click(Sender: TObject);
    procedure Print1Click(Sender: TObject);
  private
    { Private declarations }
  public
    procedure OpenFile(FileName: string);
    { Public declarations }
  end;

implementation
uses MDIFrame;

{$R *.DFM}
procedure TBMPForm.OpenFile(FileName: String);
begin
  Image1.Picture.LoadFromFile(FileName);
  Caption := FileName;
  VertScrollBar.Range := Image1.Height;
  HorzScrollBar.Range := Image1.Width;
  ClientWidth := Image1.Picture.Width;
end;

procedure TBMPForm.New2Click(Sender: TObject);
begin
  FrameForm.OpenTextFile('');
end;

procedure TBMPForm.Open1Click(Sender: TObject);
begin
  FrameForm.Open1Click(Sender);
end;

procedure TBMPForm.Save1Click(Sender: TObject);
begin
  MessageDLG('TBMPFormSave', mtInformation, [mbok], 0);
end;

procedure TBMPForm.Exit1Click(Sender: TObject);
begin
  FrameForm.Exit1Click(Sender);
end;

procedure TBMPForm.Close1Click(Sender: TObject);
begin
  Close;
end;
```

continues

Listing 8.5. continued

```
procedure TBMPForm.Print1Click(Sender: TObject);
var
  GRect: TRect;
  ISizeDif: real;
begin
  ISizeDif := Image1.Picture.Height / Image1.Picture.Width;

  GRect.Left := GetDeviceCaps(Printer.Handle, LOGPIXELSY);
  GRect.Top := GetDeviceCaps(Printer.Handle, LOGPIXELSX);
  GRect.Right := Printer.PageWidth - GetDeviceCaps(Printer.Handle, LOGPIXELSY);
  GRect.Bottom := trunc(Printer.PageHeight * ISizeDif) -
                  GetDeviceCaps(Printer.Handle, LOGPIXELSX);
  with Printer do
  begin
    BeginDoc;
    Canvas.StretchDraw(GRect, Image1.Picture.Graphic);
    EndDoc;
  end;
end;

end.
```

Declare `OpenTextFile()` as a public `TFrameForm` method, as shown in the following code:

```
type
  TFrameForm = class(TForm)
{ . . . }
  private
  public
    procedure OpenTextFile(FileName: string);
  end;
```

`OpenTextFile()` first creates a new `EditForm` and calls `EditForm.OpenFile()` if a filename is passed to it. `OpenFile()` reads a text file from disk.

Place `MDIEDIT` and `MDIBMP` in MDIFrame's uses clause because you will make references to `TBMPForm` and `TEditForm`. Create `TEditForm.OpenFile()` as shown in the following code:

```
procedure TEditForm.OpenFile(FileName: string);
begin
  Memo1.Lines.LoadFromFile(FileName);
  Caption := FileName;
end;
```

This code calls `Memo1.Lines.LoadFromFile()`, which reads in a text file to a `TMemo`'s `TStrings` component. It also sets `EditForm`'s caption to `FileName`.

Create an event handler for `TEditForm`'s File|New menu item that calls `FrameForm`'s File|New event handler:

```
procedure TEditForm.New1Click(Sender: TObject);
begin
  FrameForm.OpenTextFile('');
end;
```

This may seem like a bunch of skipping around, but you actually avoid rewriting a lot of code. By calling FrameForm's OpenTextFile() method from EditForm's File | New event handler, you execute the same code.

Add MDIFRAME to MDIEDIT's uses clause. Otherwise, you will get the Unknown Identifier compiler error when compiling the project. Add MDIFRAME to the implementation section to avoid a circular unit reference.

You now can open your application and create a new EditForm.

Closing Child Forms

MDI child form's don't close automatically when you call their Close() method. You must specify, in their OnClose event handler, what you want done with the child form when its Close() method is called. The child form's OnClose event handler passes in a variable Action, of type TCloseAction, to which you must assign one of four possible values:

caNone	Do nothing.
caHide	Hide the form but don't destroy it.
caFree	Free the form.
caMinimize	Minimize the form (this is the default).

TCloseAction is just an enumerated type. The following OnClose event handler would cause the child form to be freed when its Close() method is called:

```
procedure TBMPForm.FormClose(Sender: TObject; var Action: TCloseAction);
begin
  Action := caFree;  { Allow form to be freed when closed. }
end;
```

Add this OnClose event handler to each MDI child form.

Now, to close a child form while it is active, create event handlers for EditForm's and BMPForm's File | Close menu items:

```
procedure TEditForm.Close1Click(Sender: TObject);
begin
  Close;
end;

procedure TBMPForm.Close1Click(Sender: TObject);
begin
  Close;
end;
```

Do the same for FrameForm's File | Close menu item:

```
procedure TFrameForm.Close1Click(Sender: TObject);
begin
  Close;
end;
```

The child's close event closes only the active child, whereas TFrameForm's event closes the application after closing all children. To exit the application gracefully without having to close each individual child form, simply connect the frame form's `OnExit` event handler with the frame form's File | Close menu event handler through the Object Inspector. Then set `TEditForm`'s and `TBMPForm`'s `OnExit` event handers to call `FrameForms`'s `OnClose` event handler.

```
procedure TEditForm.Exit1Click(Sender: TObject);
begin
  FrameForm.Close1Click(Sender); { Call FrameForm's OnClose event handler }
end;

procedure TBMPForm.Exit1Click(Sender: TObject);
begin
  FrameForm.Close1Click(Sender); { Call FrameForm's OnClose event handler }
end;
```

To close all child forms at once without leaving the application, create the event handler that follows for `FrameForm`'s Window | Close All menu item:

```
procedure TFrameForm.CloseAll1Click(Sender: TObject);
var
  i: integer;
begin
  for i := 0 to MDIChildCount -1 do    { For the total number of child windows }
    MDIChildren[0].Close               { always close window at postion 0. Windows
at }
end;                                   { position 1, will then move  position 0 }
```

`MDIChildCount` maintains the number of open MDI child windows on `FrameForm`'s client area. `MDIChildren` is an array of MDI children that you can access by the index.

Using Window Commands

The MDI client window can arrange MDI children cascaded (see Figure 8.5) or tiled (see Figure 8.6) on the client area. The Window | Tile and Window | Cascade `OnClick` event handlers call the methods to do this. Additionally, Window | Arrange neatly positions child window icons on `FrameForm`'s client area. Each event handler calls the appropriate `TForm` method.

FIGURE 8.5.

Cascaded child windows.

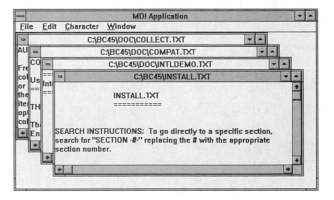

FIGURE 8.6.
Tiled child windows.

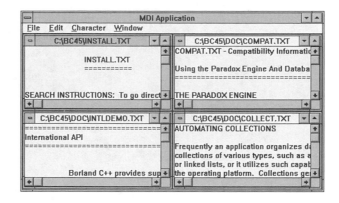

Listing 8.6 shows the methods for the Window event handlers.

Listing 8.6. The Window event handlers.

```
procedure TFrameForm.Tile1Click(Sender: TObject);
begin
  Tile;            { Call the Tile method to tile forms }
end;

procedure TFrameForm.ArrangeIcons1Click(Sender: TObject);
begin
   ArrangeIcons;  { Call the ArrangeIcons method to arrange icons in the client
➥area }
end;

procedure TFrameForm.Cascade1Click(Sender: TObject);
begin
  Cascade;         { Call the Cascade method to cascade forms }
end;
```

Adding a List of Open Documents to the Menu

To add a list of open documents to the Window menu, as shown in Figure 8.7, select FrameForm's Property page on the Objects Inspector. In the WindowMenu property, choose Window from the drop-down list. This selection must be a menu that appears on the menu bar—not a submenu. The application displays a list of open documents in the Window menu.

Using Text Editor Commands

You can left-justify, right-justify, or center-justify Memo1's text in the EditForm and specify whether to apply word wrapping. Listing 8.7 shows the event handler for the Character | Left, Character | Right, and Character | Center menus, which all hook to the Character | Left event handler.

FIGURE 8.7.

*Adding a document list to
the menu.*

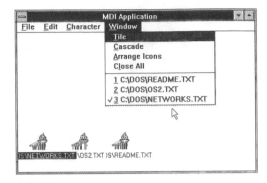

Listing 8.7. The Character I Left event handler.

```
procedure TEditForm.Left1Click(Sender: TObject);
begin
  Left1.Checked := false;
  Right1.Checked := false;
  Center1.Checked := false;
  TMenuItem(Sender).Checked := true;
  With Memo1 do
    if Left1.Checked then
      Alignment := taLeftJustify
    else if Right1.Checked then
      Alignment := taRightJustify
    else if Center1.Checked then
      Alignment := taCenter;
end;
```

`Sender` is the menu item that invoked the event. After setting `Checked` to `true`, a test determines exactly which menu item caused the event to occur and sets `Memo1.Alignment` accordingly. Listing 8.8 shows how to set word wrapping for `Memo1`.

Listing 8.8. The Character I WordWrap event handler.

```
procedure TEditForm.WordWrap1Click(Sender: TObject);
begin
  with Memo1 do
  begin
    WordWrap := not WordWrap;
    if WordWrap then
      ScrollBars := ssVertical
    else
      ScrollBars := ssBoth;
    WordWrap1.Checked := WordWrap;
  end;
end;
```

After toggling the `WordWrap` property, if it is `true`, the appropriate scrollbars are assigned to `Memo1`. The event handler also checks the WordWrap menu item accordingly.

Adding Common Dialog Boxes to Your MDI Application

Windows 3.1 provides common dialog boxes to help maintain a consistent look—and feel—for operations common to all Windows applications. The advantages are twofold: Users don't have to learn a different method to perform standard operations such as opening a file, and developers spend less time programming these operations. You can select Delphi's common dialog boxes from the Component Palette's Dialogs page.

Opening Files

The TOpenDialog component gives users a common interface for selecting files (see Figure 8.8). Place a TOpenDialog component onto the FrameForm and set its properties to the following:

Table 8.7. OpenDialog1 property settings.

Control	Property	Value
OpenDialog1	Filter	"Text File ¦ *.txt ¦ Bitmap File ¦ *.bmp"
OpenDialog1	DefaultExt	"txt"

FIGURE 8.8.
The TOpenDialog component.

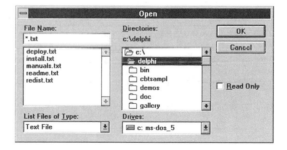

The Filter property specifies the file type to display in OpenDialog1's file list. It contains one or more descriptive name/filename pairs. To set a Filter, invoke the Filter Editor by clicking on the ellipsis button on the value side of the Filter property in the Object Inspector.

The filter for OpenDialog1 contains the strings Text File and Bitmap File as descriptive names and *.txt and *.bmp as filters. Set the Filter property by typing it directly into the Object Inspector or by accessing the Filter Editor dialog box by clicking the . . . button on the value side of the Filter property.

The DefaultExt property enables you to specify an extension to add to the filename returned from OpenDialog1 if the user doesn't include one. If DefaultExt is txt, for example, and the user types **myfile** in OpenDialog1, the filename will be MYFILE.TXT.

The File | Open OnClick event handler for FrameForm is shown in Listing 8.9. Both TEditForm and TBMPForm's File | Open event handlers call TFrameForm's File | Open event handler, as shown in Listing 8.10.

Listing 8.9. The TFrameForm File | Open OnClick event handler.

```
procedure TFrameForm.Open1Click(Sender: TObject);
var
  Ext: string[4];
begin
  OpenDialog1.Filter := 'Text File¦*.txt¦Bitmap File¦*.bmp'; { Set the OpenDialog
➥Filters. }
  OpenDialog1.DefaultExt := 'txt';                           { Set the default
➥extension }
    if OpenDialog1.Execute then begin                        { Execute OpenDialog }
      Ext := ExtractFileExt(OpenDialog1.FileName);           { Get the extension }
      if CompareStr(UpperCase(Ext), TextExt) = 0 then        { Compare with
➥extension constants }
        OpenTextFile(OpenDialog1.FileName)                   { Open a text file if
➥EXT is TextExt }
      else if CompareStr(UpperCase(Ext), BMPExt) = 0 then    { Open a BMP file if
➥EXT is BMPExt }
        OpenBMPFile(OpenDialog1.FileName);
    end;
end;
```

Listing 8.10. The TEditForm and TBMPForm File | Open event handlers.

```
procedure TEditForm.Open1Click(Sender: TObject);
begin
  FrameForm.Open1Click(Sender);
end;
procedure TBMPForm.Open1Click(Sender: TObject);
begin
  FrameForm.Open1Click(Sender);
end;
```

TFrameForm.Open1Click first executes OpenDialog1 and calls OpenTextFile() if the file extension matches the constant TextExt, or calls OpenBMPFile if the file extension matches BMPExt.

TFrameForm.OpenBMPFile() is defined in MDIFRAME.PAS:

```
procedure TFrameForm.OpenBMPFile(FileName: String);
begin
  with TBmpForm.Create(self) do   { Create a TBMPForm instance }
    OpenFile(FileName);           { Call OpenFile, passing the valid BMP file}
end;                              { name }
```

`TFrameForm.OpenBMPFile()` calls `BMPForm.OpenFile()`, which is defined in BMPFORM.PAS:

```
procedure TBMPForm.OpenFile(FileName: String);
begin
  Image1.Picture.LoadFromFile(FileName);        { Load the image from disk }
  Caption := FileName;                          { Set the form's caption }
  ClientWidth := Image1.Picture.Width;          { Set the clientWidth property
➡to the }
  VertScrollBar.Range := Image1.Picture.Height; { width of the image and set the
➡horizontal }
  HorzScrollBar.Range := Image1.Picture.Width;  { scroll range accordingly. }
end;
```

`TImage`'s picture property, of type `TPicture`, encapsulates a bitmap, icon, or metafile, as specified by the `TPicture.Graphic` property. `TPicture`'s methods `LoadFromFile()` and `SaveToFile()` take a filename as a parameter and load or save the image. `TBMPForm.OpenFile()` calls `LoadFromFile()` and sets the horizontal and vertical scrollbar ranges according to the bitmapped image's size.

You now can open any text or bitmapped image into your `EditForm` or `BMPForm` children as shown in Figure 8.9.

FIGURE 8.9.

MDI application displaying bitmaps and text.

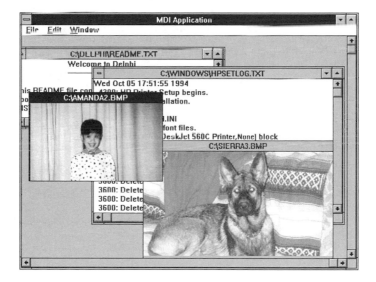

Saving Your Files with the Text Editor

Use the `TSaveDialog` to specify a filename to which `EditForm` will save its contents. Drop a `TSaveDialog` component onto the `EditForm` and set the properties listed in Table 8.8.

Table 8.8. `SaveDialog` **property settings.**

Control	Property	Value
SaveDialog1	Filter	Text File ¦ *.txt ¦ All Files ¦ *.*
SaveDialog1	Options	[ofHideReadOnly,ofNoReadOnlyReturn, ofOverWritePrompt]
SaveDialog1	DefaultExt	"txt"

Again, set the `Filter` and `DefaultExt` properties as you did with the `OpenDialog1`. Additionally, use the `Options` property, which contains a set of predefined values that affect the dialog box's appearance and behavior. The three values you have used do the following:

`ofHideReadOnly`	When `true`, hides the read-only checkbox that normally appears in the `OpenDialog1`.
`ofNoReadOnlyReturn`	When `true`, no read-only files are displayed in the listbox of selectable files.
`ofOverWritePrompt`	When `true`, prompts the user for verification to save the file to an already existing filename.

You can examine the many values that you can assign to the `Options` property in the online help.

A `TSaveDialog1` component is used in response to `EditForm`'s File | Save As menu item. Its event handler follows:

```
procedure TEditForm.SaveAs1Click(Sender: TObject);
begin
  SaveDialog1.FileName := Caption;    { Set the SaveDialog's FileName property to
➥that }
  if SaveDialog1.Execute then begin   { of the Caption. Then execute and assign
➥the }
    Caption := SaveDialog1.FileName; { SaveDialogs FileName back to the caption
➥since it }
    Save1Click(Sender);                { may have changed by the user }
  end;
end;
```

`SaveDialog1.FileName` gets `TEditForm`'s caption, which contains a valid filename. If `SaveDialog1.Execute` returns `true`, `Caption` gets `SaveDialog1.FileName` because the user might have changed the original filename. `EditForm`'s File | Save event handler follows:

```
procedure TEditForm.Save1Click(Sender: TObject);
begin
  if Caption = '' then                   { If no caption (no filename) then call }
    SaveAs1Click(Sender)                 { SaveAs.. since it gets a filename }
  else begin
    Memo1.Lines.SaveToFile(Caption);     { Otherwise, call SaveToFile with the
➥filename }
    Memo1.Modified := false;             { specified by the form's caption and set
➥modified }
  end;                                   { to false since it's just been saved }
end;
```

When the user creates a new file with File | New, EditForm.Caption doesn't have a valid filename. Therefore, if Caption equals '', File | Save calls the event handler for File | Save As to get a valid filename from SaveDialog1. Then Memo1.Lines.SaveToFile() saves Memo1.Lines to the filename specified by Caption.

The TMemo.Modified property automatically indicates when the user has made changes to TMemo's contents. Set Modified to false, because after Memo1 is saved, it no longer is in a modified state.

Earlier in this chapter, you learned how to close your forms by calling the close method. If your users forget to save changes before closing the EditForm, however, their changes will be lost. Use TForm's OnCloseQuery event handler to ask your users whether they want to save changes before closing the form. OnCloseQuery takes a Boolean variable CanClose to determine whether to close the form. The OnCloseQuery event handler is shown in Listing 8.11.

Listing 8.11. The `EditForm.OnCloseQuery` event handler.

```
procedure TEditForm.FormCloseQuery(Sender: TObject; var CanClose: Boolean);
const
  CloseMsg = '''%s'' has been modified, Save?';
var
  MsgVal: integer;
  FileName: string;
begin
  FileName := Caption;   { Set FileName to whatever's in the Caption property }
  if Memo1.Modified then begin { Only if the memo is modified ...}
    MsgVal := MessageDlg(Format(CloseMsg, [FileName]), { Display an are you
➥sure message }
              mtConfirmation, [mbYes,mbNo,mbCancel], 0);
    case MsgVal of
      id_Yes: Save1Click(Self);  { If yes, save the memo back to disk otherwise
➥cancel the }
      id_Cancel: CanClose := false; { close request }
    end;
  end;
end;
```

If Memo1.Modified is true, a MessageDlg asks the users whether they would like to save the file. If they select Yes, the File | Save event handler gets called. If they select Cancel, the form remains open because CanClose is assigned false. If users select No, the form closes without saving the text.

Using the Font Dialog Box

You can allow your users to select different fonts for components like EditForm's TMemo component by using the TFontDialog component shown in Figure 8.10. TFontDialog encapsulates the Windows common Font dialog box. Place a TFontDialog on EditForm and set the properties listed in Table 8.9.

Table 8.9. TFontDialog property settings.

Control	Property	Value
FontDialog1	Device	fdBoth
FontDialog1	Options	[fdEffects,fdForceFontExist]

FIGURE 8.10.

The TFontDialog component.

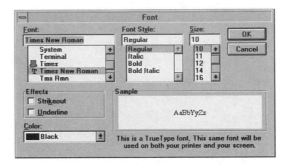

The Device property causes the TFontDialog to display the fonts available on the device speci-fied: fdScreen shows the fonts available for the screen, fdPrinter shows fonts available for the printer, and fdBoth show the fonts available to both the screen and the printer. The Options property affects the appearance and behavior of the Font dialog box, much like the Options property for the Open and Save dialog boxes does. The two options you have set do the follow-ing:

fdEffects	When true, an Effects checkbox and Color listbox appear in the dialog box. The user can select strikeout and underlining with the Effects checkbox, and specify the font color with the Color listbox.
fdForceFontExists	When true, informs the user of an invalid entry in the Font combo box that appears in the Font dialog box.

You can experiment with many other options. Look through the online help for a description of these options.

The event handler for TEditForm's Character | Font menu item follows:

```
procedure TEditForm.Font1Click(Sender: TObject);
begin
  FontDialog1.Font := Memo1.Font;    { Set the FontDialog's Font to that of the
➡Memo }
  if FontDialog1.Execute then        { Execute the FontDialog and if specified,
➡change }
    Memo1.Font := FontDialog1.Font; { The font for the memo }
end;
```

This method sets FontDialog1's font to Memo1's font so that its initial selection will match the current font in Memo1. If the user selects a new font, Memo1's font is set to match the font se-lected.

Using the Print Dialog Boxes

Printing, the bane of many a Windows programmer, is simplified with Delphi when you use the functions and printer objects defined in the printers unit. This section does not cover all aspects of printing; the other aspects are discussed in Chapter 12, "Printing in Delphi." This section shows you how to perform simple text printing from EditForm and how to print graphics images from BMPForm.

FIGURE 8.11.

The PrintDialog1 component.

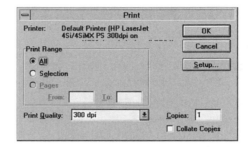

Using the *TPrinter* Object

The TPrinter object encapsulates the Windows printing interface, making most of the printing management invisible to you. The global variable printer of type TPrinter is defined in the printers unit. TPrinter contains the properties that TPrintDialog and TPrintSetupDialog use.

TPrinter.Canvas is similar to the canvas for your form because it represents the drawing surface on which text or graphics are drawn. The difference is that TPrinter's canvas represents the drawing surface for your printed output as opposed to your screen's output.

Using the *TPrintDialog* Component

The TPrintDialog, shown in Figure 8.11, enables the user to specify printing options like choosing a printer to print to, specifying the number of copies to print, and selecting a page range. TPrintDialog's Options property enables you to change the TPrintDialog's behavior.

The following list explains some of the settings for the Options property:

poPrintToFile	When true, a Print to File checkbox option is available from the dialog box. This doesn't cause anything to print to a file, however. Your code must handle that.
poPageNums	Enables the user to select the pages to print. The FromPage and ToPage properties may contain the pages to print. MaxPages specifies the maximum number that can be entered for ToPage.
poSelection	When true, gives the user the option of printing only the selected text.

| poWarning | When `true`, gives the user a warning when no printer is installed and the user chooses OK. |
| poHelp | When `true`, places a Help button in the `TPrinterDialog`. |

Place a `TPrintDialog` on `EditForm`, and set the properties listed in Table 8.10.

Table 8.10. `TPrintDialog` property settings.

Control	Property	Value
PrintDialog1	PrintRange	prAllPages
PrintDialog1	Options	[poSelection, poWarning]

The `PrintRange` property selects the All checkbox in the dialog box. Create an event handler for the File | Print menu shown in Listing 8.12.

Listing 8.12. The File | Print event handler for `EditForm`.

```
procedure TEditForm.Print1Click(Sender: TObject);
var
  i: integer;
  PText: TextFile;
begin
  if PrintDialog1.Execute then begin
    try
      AssignPrn(PText);
      Rewrite(PText);
      Printer.Canvas.Font := Memo1.Font;
      for i := 0 to Memo1.Lines.Count -1 do
        writeln(PText, Memo1.Lines[i]);
    finally
      CloseFile(PText);
    end;
  end;
end;
```

If `PrintDialog1.Execute` returns `true`, `AssignPrn()` assigns a text file variable to the printer device. `Rewrite()` opens the device for output. Write text to the file variable as you would any text file. It doesn't matter that the device is a printer; the output goes to the printer using `TPrinter.Canvas`'s font and pen. Listing 8.12 prints `Memo1`'s contents. `CloseFile(PText)` closes the device when printing is finished. That's all there is to printing text from a `TMemo` component.

Using the *TPrinterSetupDialog*

Invoking the `TPrinterSetupDialog` requires only one line of code for the event handler `TEditForm.PrintSetup1Click`:

```
procedure TEditForm.PrintSetup1Click(Sender: TObject);
begin
  FrameForm.PrintSetup1Click(Sender);
end;
```

The TPrinterSetupDialog enables users to select and configure the various printers installed on your system and invoke other dialog boxes specific to the selected printer driver. The TPrinterSetupDialog dialog box gets information about various printers from the WIN.INI file. You should rarely, if ever, have to write additional code for TPrinterSetupDialog. This topic is explored further in Chapter 12. Figure 8.12 shows TPrinterSetupDialog.

FIGURE 8.12.

The
TPrinterSetupDialog
component.

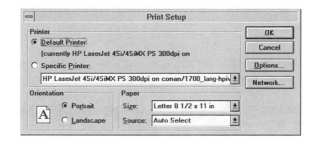

Printing Bitmaps

Printing bitmaps is also very easy to implement. BMPForm's File | Print menu's event handler is shown in Listing 8.13.

Listing 8.13. The File | Print event handler for BMPForm.

```
procedure TBMPForm.Print1Click(Sender: TObject);
var
  GRect: TRect;
  ISizeDif: real;
begin
  { Execute the PrintDialog }
  if PrintDialog1.Execute then begin
    { Calculate a ratio of the images height to its width }
    ISizeDif := Image1.Picture.Height / Image1.Picture.Width;
    { Get the various sizes for the printers canvas }
    GRect.Left := GetDeviceCaps(Printer.Handle, LOGPIXELSX);
    GRect.Top := GetDeviceCaps(Printer.Handle, LOGPIXELSY);
    GRect.Right := Printer.PageWidth - GetDeviceCaps(Printer.Handle, LOGPIXELSX);
    { Set the bottom of the rect to a size based on the ratio of the actual image }
    GRect.Bottom := trunc(Printer.PageHeight * ISizeDif) -
                    GetDeviceCaps(Printer.Handle, LOGPIXELSY);

    with Printer do begin
      BeginDoc;  { Start the print job }
      { StretchDraw expands the image to the size specified by GRect }
      Canvas.StretchDraw(GRect, Image1.Picture.Graphic)
      EndDoc;    { Stop the print job }
    end;
  end;
end;
```

A bit of explanation is in order for `TBMPForm`'s File | Print event handler. The main part of the code that performs the printing consists of the following three lines:

```
BeginDoc;
Canvas.StretchDraw(GRect, Image1.Picture.Graphic);
EndDoc;
```

The procedure `BeginDoc` starts a print job. When `BeginDoc` is used, you should call `EndDoc` to end the print job. The line

```
Canvas.StretchDraw(GRect, Image1.Picture.Graphic);
```

draws a graphic with the size specified by the first parameter, `GRect`. Why use `TCanvas`'s `StretchDraw()` method instead of the `Draw()` method? `Draw()` prints an image based on its original size in pixels, whereas `StretchDraw()` enables you to expand or compress the images to a size specified by `GRect`. This capability is useful when printing graphics, because display resolution for a screen and printer are very different.

CAUTION

Different devices have different capabilities. Some printers may not support stretching of bitmaps using the Windows API function `StretchBlt()` (`Canvas.StetchDraw` calls `StetchBlt`). Use the `GetDeviceCaps()` Windows API function to test the capabilities of your printer. Look up `GetDeviceCaps()` in the Windows API help for a detailed list of what you can test for.

`TImage`'s `picture` property encapsulates a bitmapped image, and its `Height` and `Width` properties represent the image's size in pixels. On a printer with a 300-dots-per-inch (dpi) resolution, an $8^1/_2 \times 11$-inch paper has 2550×3300 pixels. A 640×480 bitmap would print on a 2.1× 1.6-inch area of paper. On a 600-dpi printer, that would be a 1×0.8-inch area—not a pretty picture! `StretchDraw` enables you to expand the image to a size to better represent its appearance on-screen. The following line of code calculates the image's height in relation to its width:

```
ISizeDif := Image1.Picture.Height / Image1.Picture.Width;
```

You use this value to determine a size to print your image on the printer.

The Windows API function `GetDeviceCaps()` returns specific information about an output device based on the value of the second parameter. Passing `LOGPIXELSX`, for example, returns the number of pixels per inch along the device's horizontal axis. Passing `LOGPIXELSY` returns the number of pixels per inch along the device's vertical axis. The following line of code assigns the number of pixels per inch for a printer device to `GRect.Left`.

```
GRect.Left := GetDeviceCaps(Printer.Handle, LOGPIXELSX);
```

You do the same for the `GRect.Top` to obtain the vertical pixels per inch:

```
GRect.Top := GetDeviceCaps(Printer.Handle, LOGPIXELSY);
```

This effectively sets up your image to be printed with one-inch left and top margins. This line sets up a one-inch right margin:

```
GRect.Right := Printer.PageWidth - GetDeviceCaps(Printer.Handle, LOGPIXELSX);
```

Finally, this line sets up the bottom of your image relative to the size of the original images as dictated by ISizeDif:

```
GRect.Bottom := trunc(Printer.PageHeight * ISizeDif) -
GetDeviceCaps(Printer.Handle, LOGPIXELSY);
```

You make the assumption that the graphic's height does not exceed that of a printed page. If this were the case, the output would be clipped. You would have to add the logic to test for this condition.

Although these are simple printing examples, they actually accomplish quite a bit. Printing certainly has been one of the more painful aspects of writing Windows applications. After reading Chapter 12, you should be well on your way to writing elaborate windows-printing routines— minus the agony.

Using the Clipboard

What good is a text editor without being able to make use of the Windows Clipboard? You will want to be able to cut, copy, and paste your text to and from other applications. Listing 8.14 shows the event handlers for performing these edit commands from EditForm's Edit | Cut, Edit | Copy, Edit | Paste, Edit | Delete, and Edit | Select All menu items.

Listing 8.14. EditForm's Edit event handlers.

```
procedure TEditForm.Cut1Click(Sender: TObject);
begin
  Memo1.CutToClipBoard;
end;

procedure TEditForm.Copy1Click(Sender: TObject);
begin
  Memo1.CopyToClipBoard;
end;

procedure TEditForm.Paste1Click(Sender: TObject);
begin
  Memo1.PasteFromClipBoard;
end;

procedure TEditForm.Delete1Click(Sender: TObject);
begin
  Memo1.ClearSelection;
end;

procedure TEditForm.SelectAll1Click(Sender: TObject);
```

continues

Listing 8.14. continued

```
begin
  Memo1.SelectAll;
end;
```

THE WINDOWS CLIPBOARD

The Clipboard is the easiest way for two applications to share information with each other. It is nothing more than a global memory block that Windows maintains for any application to access through a specific set of Windows functions.

The Clipboard supports several standard formats such as text, OEM text, bitmaps, metafiles, and other specialized formats. Additionally, you can extend the Clipboard to support application-specific formats.

Delphi encapsulates the Windows Clipboard with the global variable clipboard of type TClipBoard, making it much easier for you to use. The TClipBoard class is covered in more detail in Chapter 14, "Sharing Information with the Clipboard and DDE."

To use the Clipboard to copy and paste bitmaps, use the global TClipBoard object—ClipBoard. Include the CLIPBRD unit in MDIBMP.PAS's uses clause. Listing 8.15 shows BMPForm's Edit | Copy and Edit | Paste menus items.

Listing 8.15. BMPForm's Edit | Copy and Edit | Paste event handlers.

```
procedure TBMPForm.Copy1Click(Sender: TObject);
begin
  ClipBoard.Assign(Image1.Picture); { Copy image to the clipboard }
end;

procedure TBMPForm.Paste1Click(Sender: TObject);
begin
  if ClipBoard.HasFormat(CF_BITMAP) or { Check for the correct clipboard format }
     Clipboard.HasFormat(CF_PICTURE) then begin
    Image1.Picture.Assign(ClipBoard);  { Copy contents of clipboard to Image1 }
    ClientWidth := Image1.Picture.Width; { Adjust clientwidth to match }
    VertScrollBar.Range := Image1.Picture.Height; { Adjust the scrollbars }
    HorzScrollBar.Range := Image1.Picture.Width;
  end;
end;
```

Edit | Copy assigns Image1's picture property to the Clipboard by passing Image1.Picture to the ClipBoard's Assign() method. You then paste your image into another Windows application that supports this format, such as Windows Paintbrush (PBRUSH.EXE).

`Edit1.Paste` determines whether the Clipboard has a supported image. If so, it assigns the contents of the `ClipBoard` to `Image1.Picture` by passing `ClipBoard` to `Image1.Picture`'s `Assign()` method and readjusts the scrollbars accordingly.

Changing Child Styles

By default, child windows in MDI applications have certain styles set and changing a child form's style in a MDI application isn't as easy as just modifying properties in the Object Inspector. You first must set a special style, `MDIS_ALLCHILDSTYLES`, to the frame form's client window because Windows assumes that all MDI children want the MDI—including styles that Windows sets for you by default, such as a system menu, Maximize/Minimize buttons, and sizable borders. By performing an OR operation against the client window's default style and the constant `MDIS_ALLCHILDSTYLES`, your changes in the Object Inspector will take effect.

To add the special style to `FrameForm`'s client window, override `FrameForm`'s `CreateWnd` procedure where it creates the client window. The following code shows you how to declare this procedure in the `FrameForm`'s declaration:

```
  TFrameForm = class(TForm)
...
  protected
    procedure CreateWnd; override;
...
  end;
```

You can see how `TFrameForm.CreateWnd` is defined by examining the following code:

```
procedure TFrameForm.CreateWnd;
var
  Sty: Longint;
begin
  inherited CreateWnd;
  Sty := GetWindowLong(ClientHandle, GWL_STYLE);
  SetWindowLong(ClientHandle, GWL_STYLE, Sty or MDIS_ALLCHILDSTYLES);
end;
```

First, call the original `CreateWnd` procedure to make sure that the client window is created. Then, get its style using `GetWindowLong()`, which retrieves the window's style by passing the `GWL_STYLE` constant and calling `SetWindowLong()` to set a new style of

```
Sty or MDIS_ALLCHILDSTYLES
```

GetWindowLong() AND SetWindowLong()

The Windows API function

`GetWindowLong(Wnd: HWnd; Index: Integer): LongInt;`

retrieves a 4MB value from a window's extra memory pool, as specified by `Index` (a zero-based offset into the extra memory location). The possible values that can be retrieved follow:

GWL_EXSTYLE	Extended window style
GWL_STYLE	Window style
GWL_WNDPROC	Long pointer to the window procedure

The API function

`function SetWindowLong(Wnd: HWnd; Index: Integer; NewLong: LongInt): LongInt;`

sets the window's extra memory specified by `Index` to the value in `NewLong`.

`GetWindowLong()` and `SetWindowLong()` often are used to subclass windows—a powerful technique for changing windows behavior, much of which is already done by Delphi.

Summary

This chapter showed you how to build MDI applications in Delphi. With this foundation, you should be well on your way to creating MDI applications to meet a very specific and advanced need. You will be able to combine your knowledge of MDI with topics that you will learn in the upcoming chapters to build full-blown, user-friendly applications.

9

Understanding Messages

Although Delphi encapsulates some Windows messages in its event system, it is still essential that you, as a Windows programmer, understand how Windows' message system works.

As a Delphi applications programmer, you will find that Delphi's event system will suit most of your needs, and you only occasionally will need to handle messages directly. As a Delphi component developer, however, you and messages will become very good friends, because you will need to directly handle many Windows messages and then invoke events corresponding to those messages.

What Is a Message?

A *message* is a notification of some occurrence sent by Windows to an application. Clicking a mouse button, resizing a window, or pressing a key on the keyboard, for example, cause Windows to send a message to an application notifying the program of what occurred.

A message manifests itself as a *record* that is passed to an application by Windows. That record contains information such as what type of event occurred and additional information specific to the message. For a mouse-button click message, for example, the message record contains the mouse coordinates at the time the button was pressed. The record type that is passed from Windows to the application is called a *TMsg*. TMsg is defined in the following code:

```
TMsg = record
   hwnd: HWnd;        { the handle of the Window the message is intended for }
   message: Word;     { the message constant identifier }
   wParam: Word;      { 16 bits of additional message-specific information }
   lParam: LongInt;   { 32 bits of additional message-specific information }
   time: Longint;     { the time that the message was created }
   pt: TPoint;        { the position of the mouse cursor when message was created }
   end;
```

WHAT'S IN A MESSAGE?

Does the information in a message record look like Greek to you? If so, here's a little insight to what's what:

Window handle   The 16-bit window handle of the window for which the message is intended. This handle can represent a window, dialog box, or control, because Windows maintains a handle for each one of those objects.

Message   A constant value that represents some message. These constants can be defined by Windows in the WINTYPES unit, or by you through user-defined messages.

wParam   This field often contains a constant value associated with the message, or a windows handle or identification number of some window or control associated with the message.

lParam	This field often holds a pointer to some data in memory. Because a Longint is the same size as a pointer, you often will typecast lParam.

Types of Messages

Windows predefines a constant for each Windows message. These constants are the values kept in the message field of the TMsg record. All these constants are defined in Delphi's MESSAGES unit, and most are described in the online help. Notice that each of these constants begin with the letters *wm*, which stand for *Windows Message*. Table 9.1 shows you some of the common Windows messages, along with their meanings and values.

Table 9.1. Common Windows messages.

Message identifier	Value	Tells a window that
wm_Activate	$0006	It is being activated or deactivated.
wm_Char	$0102	wm_KeyDown and wm_KeyUp messages have been sent for one key.
wm_Close	$0010	It should terminate.
wm_KeyDown	$0100	A keyboard key is being pressed.
wm_KeyUp	$0101	A keyboard key has been released.
wm_LButtonDown	$0201	The user is pressing the left mouse button.
wm_MouseMove	$0200	The mouse is being moved.
wm_Paint	$000F	It needs to repaint its client area.
wm_Timer	$0113	A timer event has occurred.
wm_Quit	$0012	The program is about to stop running.

How the Windows Message System Works

A Windows application's message system has three key components:

Message queue   Windows maintains a message queue for each application. A Windows application must get messages from this queue and dispatch them to the proper windows.

Message loop	The loop mechanism in a Windows program that fetches a message from the application queue and dispatches it to the appropriate window, fetches the next message, dispatches it to the appropriate window, and so on.
Window procedure	Each window in your application has a window procedure that receives each of the messages passed to it by the message loop. The window procedure's job is to take in each window message and respond to it accordingly. A window procedure is a callback function, and a window procedure usually returns a value to windows after processing a message.

NOTE

A *callback function* is a function in your program that is called by Windows or some other external module.

Getting a message from point A (some event occurs, creating a message) to point B (a window in your application responds to the message) is a five-step process:

1. Some event occurs in the system.
2. Windows translates this event into a message and places it into the message queue for your application.
3. Your application retrieves this message from the queue and places it into a TMsg record.
4. Your application passes this message on to the window procedure of the appropriate window in your application.
5. The window procedure now can perform some action in response to the message.

Steps 3 and 4 make up the application's message loop. The message loop often is considered the heart of a Windows program, because it is the facility that enables your program to respond to external events. The message loop spends its whole life fetching messages from the application queue and passing them along to the appropriate windows in your application. If there are no messages in your application's queue, then Windows will allow other applications to process their messages. Figure 9.1 illustrates these steps.

FIGURE 9.1.

The Windows message system.

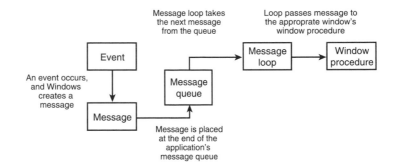

Delphi's Message System

Delphi handles many of the details of Windows' message system for you. The message loop is built into VCL, for example, so you don't have to worry about fetching messages from the queue or dispatching them to a window procedure. Delphi also places the information located in Windows' TMsg record into a generic TMessage record:

```
TMessage = record
    Msg: Word;
    case Integer of
      0: (
        WParam: Word;
        LParam: Longint;
        Result: Longint);
      1: (
        WParamLo: Byte;
        WParamHi: Byte;
        LParamLo: Word;
        LParamHi: Word;
        ResultLo: Word;
        ResultHi: Word);
  end;
```

Notice that TMessage record has a little bit less information than TMsg. That is because Delphi internalizes the other TMsg fields, and TMessage contains just the essential information that you need to be able to handle a message.

It's important to note that the TMessage record also contains a Result field. As mentioned earlier, some messages require a window procedure to return some value after processing a message. With Delphi, you accomplish this process in a much more straightforward fashion by placing the return value in the Result field of TMessage. This process is explained in more detail later in this chapter in the "Assigning Message Result Values" section.

Message-Specific Records

In addition to the generic TMessage record, Delphi defines a message-specific record for every Windows message. The purpose of these message-specific records is to give you all the information that the message offers without having to decipher the wParam and lParam fields of a record. All the message-specific records can be found in the MESSAGES unit. As an example, here is the message record used to hold most mouse messages:

```
TWMMouse = record
    Msg: TMsgParam;
    Keys: Word;
    case Integer of
      0: (
        XPos: Integer;
        YPos: Integer);
      1: (
        Pos: TPoint;
        Result: Longint);
  end;
```

All the record types for specific mouse message (wm_LButtonDown and wm_RButtonUp, for example) simply are defined as equal to TWMMouse, as in the following example:

```
TWMRButtonUp = TWMMouse;
TWMLButtonDown = TWMMouse;
```

> **NOTE**
>
> There is a message record defined for every standard Windows message. The naming convention dictates that the name of the record is the same as the name of the message with a *T* prepended and without the underscore. The name of the message record type for a wm_SetFont message therefore is TWMSetFont. By the way, TMessage will work with all messages in all situations, but it is not as convenient as message-specific records.

Handling Messages

Handling, or *processing,* a message means to cause your application to respond in some manner to a Windows message. In a standard Windows application, message handling is performed in each window procedure. By internalizing the window procedure, however, Delphi makes it much easier to handle individual messages; instead of having one procedure that handles all messages, each message has its own procedure. There are three requirements in order for a procedure to be a message-handling procedure:

- The procedure must be a method of an object.
- The procedure must take one var parameter of a TMessage or other message-specific record type.

■ The procedure must use the message directive followed by the constant value of the message you want to process.

Here is an example of a procedure that handles wm_Paint messages:

```
procedure WMPaint(var Msg: TWMPaint); message wm_Paint;
```

NOTE

When naming message-handling procedures, the convention is to give them the same name as the message itself without the underscore.

As an example, write a simple message-handling procedure for wm_Paint that processes the message simply by beeping. Start by creating a new, blank project. Then access the Code Editor window for this project, and add the header for your WMPaint function to the private section of the TForm1 object:

```
procedure WMPaint(var Msg: TWMPaint); message wm_Paint;
```

Now add the function definition to the implementation part of this unit. Remember to use the dot operator to scope this procedure as a method of TForm1. Don't use the message directive as part of the function implementation:

```
procedure TForm1.WMPaint(var Msg: TWMPaint);
begin
  MessageBeep(0);
  inherited;
end;
```

Notice the new keyword, inherited. Call inherited when you want to pass the message on to the ancestor object's handler. By calling inherited in this example, you are passing the message on to TForm's wm_Paint handler.

NOTE

Unlike normal calls to inherited methods, here you do not give the name of the inherited method. That's because the name of the method is unimported when it is dispatched. Delphi knows what method to call based on the *message* directive in the class interface.

Listing 9.1 shows a simple example of a form that processes the wm_Paint message. Creating this project is easy: Just create a new project and add the code for the WMPaint procedure to the TForm object.

Listing 9.1. GetMess: **a message-handling example.**

```
program GetMess;

uses
  Forms,
  GMMain in 'GMMAIN.PAS' {Form1};

{$R *.RES}

begin
  Application.CreateForm(TForm1, Form1);
  Application.Run;
end.

unit GMMain;

interface

uses
  SysUtils, WinTypes, WinProcs, Messages, Classes, Graphics, Controls,
  Forms, Dialogs;

type
  TForm1 = class(TForm)
  private
    procedure WMPaint(var Msg: TWMPaint); message wm_Paint;
  end;

var
  Form1: TForm1;

implementation

{$R *.DFM}

procedure TForm1.WMPaint(var Msg: TWMPaint);
begin
  MessageBeep(0);
  Inherited;
end;

end.
```

Whenever a wm_Paint message comes down the pike, it is passed to the WMPaint procedure. The WMPaint procedure simply informs you of the wm_Paint message by making some noise with the MessageBeep() procedure, and then it passes the message on to the inherited handler.

MessageBeep( ): THE POOR-MAN'S DEBUGGER

The MessageBeep() procedure is one of the most straightforward yet useful elements in the Windows API. Its use is simple: Call MessageBeep() and pass a predefined constant, and Windows beeps the PC's speaker; or, if you have a sound card, it plays a WAV file.

Big deal, you say? On the surface it might not seem like much, but MessageBeep() really shines as an aid in debugging your programs.

If you're looking for a quick-and-dirty way to tell whether your program is reaching a certain place in your code—without having to bother with the debugger and breakpoints—then MessageBeep() is for you. Because it doesn't require a handle or some other Windows resource, it can be used practically anywhere in your code. If you have a sound card, you can pass it one of several predefined constants in order to have it play a wider variety of sounds—these constants are defined under MessageBeep in the Delphi Windows API Help file.

Message Handling: Not Contract-Free

Unlike responding to Delphi events, handling Windows messages is not contract-free. Often, when you decide to handle a message yourself, Windows expects you to perform some action when processing the message. Most of the time, VCL has much of this basic message processing built in, and all you have to do is call inherited to get to it. Think of it this way: you write a message handler so that your application will do the things that you expect, and you call inherited so that your application will do the additional things that Windows expects.

As a demonstration of these inherited elements, try running the program in Listing 9.1 without calling inherited in the WMPaint method. Just remove the line that calls inherited so that the procedure looks like this:

```
{ Warning! you should save all files currently open and close all other Windows }
{ programs before you try this. }

procedure TForm1.WMPaint(var Msg: TWMPaint);
begin
  MessageBeep(0);
end;
```

Because you never give Windows a chance to perform basic handling of the wm_Paint message, this procedure almost certainly will crash and burn your program, and it even may take Windows along for the ride—a lesson you don't want to learn the hard way.

Sometimes there are circumstances where you don't want to call the inherited message handler. An example of this is handling the wm_SysCommand messages to prevent a window from being minimized or maximized.

Assigning Message Result Values

When you handle some Windows messages, Windows expects you to return a result value. The classic example is the wm_CtlColor message. When you handle this message, Windows expects you to return a handle to a brush with which you want Windows to paint a dialog or control (Delphi provides a `Color` property for components that does this for you, so that example is just for illustration purposes). You can do this easily with a message-handling procedure by assigning a value to the `Result` field of `TMessage` (or other message record) before calling `inherited`. For example, if you were handling `wm_CtlColor`, you could return a brush handle value to Windows with the following code:

```
procedure TForm1.WMCtlColor(var Msg: TWMCtlColor);
var
  BrushHand: hBrush;
begin
  { Create a brush handle and place into BrushHand variable }
  Msg.Result := BrushHand;
end;
```

TApplication's OnMessage Event

Another technique for handling messages is to use `TApplication`'s `OnMessage` event. When you assign a procedure to `OnMessage`, it will be called whenever a message is pulled from the queue and about to be processed. This event handler is called before Windows itself has a chance to process the message. The `Application.OnMessage` event handler is of `TMessageEvent` type and must be defined with a parameter list as shown here:

```
procedure SomeObject.AppMessageHandler(var Msg: TMsg; var Handled: Boolean);
```

All the message parameters are passed to the `OnMessage` event handler in the `Msg` parameter. (Note that this parameter is of the Windows `TMsg` record type described earlier in this chapter.) The `Handled` field requires you to assign a `Boolean` value indicating whether or not you have handled the message.

The first step in creating an `OnMessage` event handler is to create a method that accepts the same parameter list as a `TMessageEvent`; for example, here is a method that keeps a running count of how many messages your application receives:

```
procedure Form1.AppMessageHandler(var Msg: TMsg; var Handled: Boolean);
const
  NumMessages: Longint = 0;
begin
  inc(NumMessages);
  Handled := False;
end;
```

The second and final step is to assign a procedure to `Application.OnMessage` somewhere in your code. Typically, this is done in the DPR file prior to creating your project's forms:

```
Application.OnMessage := AppMessageHandler;
```

One limitation of `OnMessage` is that it is executed only for messages that are pulled out of the queue and not for messages that are sent directly to a window procedure. Chapter 21, "Hard-Core Windows," shows a technique for working around this limitation by subclassing the application window procedure.

Sending Your Own Messages

Just as Windows sends messages to your application's windows, you too will occasionally need to send messages between windows and controls within your application. Delphi provides several ways to send messages within your application: the `Perform()` method, which works independently of the Windows API, and the `SendMessage()` and `PostMessage()` API functions.

Perform()

VCL provides a method for all `TControl` descendants called `Perform()` which enables you to send a message to any form or control given an object instance. The `Perform()` method takes three parameters—a message and its corresponding `lParam` and `wParam`—and is defined in the following code:

```
function Perform(Msg, WParam: Word; LParam: Longint): Longint;
```

To send a message to a form or control, use the following syntax:

```
RetVal := ObjectName.Perform(MessageID, wParam, lParam);
```

After you call `Perform()`, it does not return until the message has been handled. The `Perform()` procedure packages up its parameters into a `TMessage` record and then calls the object's `Dispatch()` method to send the message—bypassing Windows API's messaging system. The `Dispatch()` method is described later in this chapter.

Send and Post

Sometimes you need to send a message to a window for which you don't have a Delphi object instance. Perhaps, for example, you want to send a message to a non-Delphi window, but you only have a handle to that window. Fortunately, the Windows API offers two functions that fit this bill: `SendMessage()` and `PostMessage()`. These two functions essentially are identical, except for one key difference: `SendMessage()`, similar to `Perform()`, sends a message directly to the window procedure of the intended window and waits until the message is processed before returning, whereas `PostMessage()` posts a message to Windows' message queue and returns immediately.

`SendMessage()` and `PostMessage()` are called with exactly the same parameters, which are shown in Table 9.2.

Table 9.2. Parameters for `SendMessage()` and `PostMessage()`.

Parameter	Type	Description
1	hWnd	Handle of the window for which this message is intended
2	word	Message identifier
3	word	The message-specific wParam
4	Longint	The message-specific lParam

`SendMessage()` and `PostMessage()` are particularly useful with user-defined messages, which are described later in this chapter.

> **NOTE**
>
> Although `SendMessage()` and `PostMessage()` are used similarly, their respective return values are very different. `SendMessage()` returns the result value of the message being processed, but `PostMessage()` only returns a Bool that indicates whether or not the message was placed in the target window's queue.

Non-Standard Messages

Up to now, discussion has centered around regular Windows messages (those that begin with wm_*xxx*). However, there are two other major categories of messages that merit some discussion: notification messages and user-defined messages.

Notification Messages

Notification messages are messages that are sent to a parent window when something happens in one of its child controls that may require the parent's attention. Notification messages occur only with the standard Windows controls: button, listbox, combobox, and edit control. As an example, clicking or double-clicking a control, selecting some text in a control, or moving the scrollbar in a control generates notification messages.

You will find all the notification messages enumerated in Delphi's online API help under the topic "Notification Messages (3.1)." Notification messages are an artifact of traditional Windows programming wherein you usually created a window procedure only for a dialog, but not for each of its controls. Because of VCL's robust event system for controls, you probably will not have much need to directly handle notification messages, but it's nice to know that they're there if you need them.

Internal VCL Messages

VCL has an extensive collection of its own internal messages and notification messages. Although you won't commonly use these in your Delphi applications, Delphi component writers will find them useful. These messages deal with component states such as focus, color, and visibility. You'll find a complete list of these messages in the Component Writer's online help (CWG.HLP) under the topic "Component Messages."

User-Defined Messages

At some point, you will come across a situation where you need one of your own applications to send a message to itself, or you need to send messages between two of your own applications.

Messages Within Your Application

Having an application send a message to itself is easy. Just use the `Perform()`, `SendMessage()`, or `PostMessage()` function, and use a message value in the range of `wm_User` through `$7FFF` (this is the value that Windows reserves for user-defined messages):

```
const
 sx_MyMessage = wm_User;

begin
  SomeForm.Perform(sx_MyMessage, 0, 0);
  { or }
  SendMessage(SomeForm.Handle, sx_MyMessage, 0, 0);
  { or }
  PostMessage(SomeForm.Handle, sx_MyMessage, 0, 0);
  .
  .
  .
end;
```

Then create a normal message-handling procedure for this message in the form in which you want to handle this message:

```
TForm1 = class(TForm)
  .
  .
  .
private
  procedure SXMyMessage(var Msg: TMessage); message sx_MyMessage;
end;

procedure TForm1.SXMyMessage(var Msg: TMessage);
begin
  MessageDlg('She turned me into a newt!', mtInformation, [mbOk], 0);
end;
```

As you can see, there is little difference between using a user-defined message in your application and handling any old Windows message. The real key here is to start at `wm_User` + 100 for interapplication messages, and to give each message a name that has something to do with its purpose. The values of wm_User through wm_User + 99 are used by Windows for control messages.

> **CAUTION**
>
> Never send messages with values of wm_User through $7FFF a window unless you are sure that the intended recipient is equipped to handle the message. Because each window can define these values independently, the potential for bad things to happen is great unless you keep careful tabs on to whom you send wm_User through $7FFF messages.

Messaging Between Applications

When you want to send messages between two or more applications, it's usually best to use the RegisterWindowMessage() API function in each application. This method ensures that every application uses the same message number for a given message.

RegisterWindowMessage() accepts a null-terminated string as a parameter, and it returns a new message constant in the range of $C000 through $FFFF. This means that all you have to do is call RegisterWindowMessage() with the same string in each application between which you want to send messages, and Windows returns the same message value for each application. The true benefit of RegisterWindowMessage() is that, because a message value for any given string is guaranteed to be unique throughout the system, you safely can broadcast such messages to all windows with fewer harmful side-effects. This technique is demonstrated in Chapter 21.

> **NOTE**
>
> The number returned by RegisterWindowMessage() will vary between Windows sessions, and it cannot be determined until runtime.

Broadcasting Messages

TWinControl descendants have the capability to broadcast a message record to each of its owned controls—thanks to the Broadcast() method. This technique is useful when you need to send the same message to a whole group of components. For example, to send a user-defined message called um_Foo to all of Panel1's owned controls, you would use the following code:

```
var
  M: TMessage;
begin
  with M do begin
    Message := um_Foo;
    wParam := 0;
```

```
    lParam := 0;
    Result := 0;
  end;
  Panel1.Broadcase(M);
end;
```

Anatomy of a Message System: VCL

There is much more to VCL's message system than handling messages with the message direc-tive. After a message is issued by Windows, it makes a couple of stops before reaching your message-handling procedure, and then it even may make a few more stops afterward. All along the way, you have the power to act on the message.

The first stop for a Windows message in VCL is the StdWndProc() function. StdWndProc() is an assembler function that accepts the message from Windows and routes it to the object for which the message is destined.

The object method that receives the message is called DefWndProc(). Beginning with DefWndProc(), you can begin to perform any special handling of the message that your pro-gram may require. Generally, you would handle a message here only if you didn't want a mes-sage to go through VCL's normal dispatching.

After leaving the DefWndProc() method, the message is routed to the object's dispatch mecha-nism. The dispatch mechanism, found in the object's Dispatch() method, routes the message to any specific message-handling procedure that you have defined or that already exists within VCL.

At this point, the message finally reaches your message-specific handling procedure. After flowing through your handler and the inherited handlers you may have invoked via the inherited key-word, the message goes to the object's DefaultHandler() method. DefaultHandler() performs any final message processing and then passes the message to Windows' DefWindowProc() func-tion or other default window procedure (such as DefMDIProc) for any Windows-default pro-cessing. Figure 9.2 shows an illustration of VCL's message-processing mechanism.

> **NOTE**
>
> You always should call inherited when handling messages unless you are absolutely certain that you want to prevent normal message processing.

> **TIP**
>
> Because all unhandled messages flow to DefaultHandler(), it is usually the best place to handle interapplication messages in which the values were obtained by way of the RegisterWindowMessage() procedure.

FIGURE 9.2.

VCL's message system.

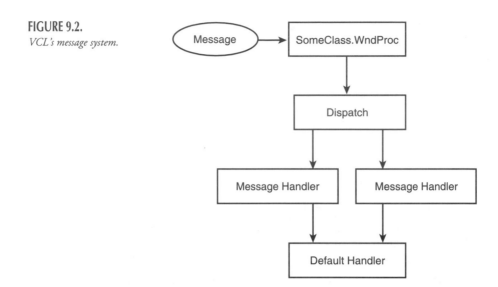

To better illustrate VCL's message system, create a small program that is able to handle a message at the `DefWndProc()`, message procedure, or `DefaultHandler()` stage.

Start with a blank form, and add two group boxes with three checkboxes each. Also add two buttons at the bottom of the form. Save this project as CATCHIT.DPR. You may wish to change the names and captions of the components in this project as shown by the CATCHIT project main window in Figure 9.3.

FIGURE 9.3.

The CatchIt! message example.

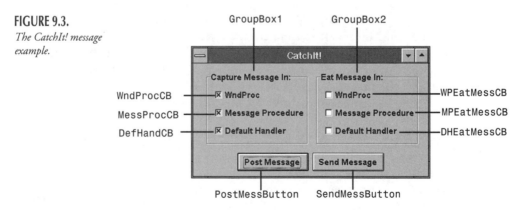

The `OnClick` event handlers for `PostMessButton` and `SendMessButton` are shown in the following code. The former uses `PostMessage()` to post a user-defined message to the form, and the latter uses `SendMessage()` to send a user-defined message to the form. Note that the value one is passed in the `wParam` of the `PostMessage()`—whereas zero is passed for `SendMessage()`—in order to differentiate between post and send.

```
procedure TMainForm.PostMessButtonClick(Sender: TObject);
begin
  PostMessage(Handle, sx_MyMessage, 1, 0);
end;

procedure TMainForm.SendMessButtonClick(Sender: TObject);
begin
  SendMessage(Handle, sx_MyMessage, 0, 0);
end;
```

In the `WndProc()`, message-handling procedure, and `DefaultHandler()`, you should perform some action when the user-defined message comes down the pike. Listings 9.2 and 9.3 show the completed source code for this project, demonstrating the flow of messages in a Delphi application.

Listing 9.2. The source code for CATCHIT.DPR.

```
program Catchit;

uses
  Forms,
  Cimain in 'CIMAIN.PAS' {MainForm};

{$R *.RES}

begin
  Application.CreateForm(TMainForm, MainForm);
  Application.Run;
end.
```

Listing 9.3. The source code for CIMAIN.PAS

```
unit Cimain;

interface

uses
  SysUtils, WinTypes, WinProcs, Messages, Classes, Graphics, Controls,
  Forms, Dialogs, StdCtrls;

const
  { this will be the user-defined message value }
  sx_MyMessage = wm_User + 100;
  { string used by MessageDlg() }
  MessString = '%s message now in %s';

type
  TMainForm = class(TForm)
    GroupBox1: TGroupBox;
    PostMessButton: TButton;
    WndProcCB: TCheckBox;
    MessProcCB: TCheckBox;
    DefHandCB: TCheckBox;
```

continues

Listing 9.3. continued

```
  GroupBox2: TGroupBox;
  WPEatMessCB: TCheckBox;
  MPEatMessCB: TCheckBox;
  DHEatMessCB: TCheckBox;
  SendMessButton: TButton;
  procedure PostMessButtonClick(Sender: TObject);
  procedure WndProcCBClick(Sender: TObject);
  procedure MessProcCBClick(Sender: TObject);
  procedure DefHandCBClick(Sender: TObject);
  procedure SendMessButtonClick(Sender: TObject);
private
  { Handles messages at WndProc level }
  procedure WndProc(var Msg: TMessage); override;
  { Handles message after dispatch }
  procedure SXMyMessage(var Msg: TMessage); message sx_MyMessage;
  { Default message handler }
  procedure DefaultHandler(var Msg); override;
end;

var
  MainForm: TMainForm;

implementation

{$R *.DFM}

procedure TMainForm.WndProc(var Msg: TMessage);
{ WndProc procedure of form }
begin
  if Msg.Msg = sx_MyMessage then begin
    if WndProcCB.Checked then begin      { is WndProc checked? }
      if Msg.wParam = 1 then             { check for post or send }
        MessageDlg(Format(MessString, ['Posted', 'WndProc.']), mtInformation,
                  [mbOk], 0)
      else
        MessageDlg(Format(MessString, ['Sent', 'WndProc.']), mtInformation,
                  [mbOk], 0);
      if not WPEatMessCB.Checked then
        inherited WndProc(Msg);          { eat message if directed }
    end
    else
      inherited WndProc(Msg);
  end
  else
    inherited WndProc(Msg);
end;

procedure TMainForm.SXMyMessage(var Msg: TMessage);
{ Message procedure for user-defined message }
begin
  if MessProcCB.Checked then begin       { is Message Procedure checked? }
    if Msg.wParam = 1 then               { check for post or send }
      MessageDlg(Format(MessString, ['Posted', 'Message Procedure.']),
                mtInformation, [mbOk], 0)
    else
      MessageDlg(Format(MessString, ['Sent', 'Message Procedure.']),
```

```
                    mtInformation, [mbOk], 0);
    if not MPEatMessCB.Checked then      { eat message if directed }
       inherited;
  end
  else
    inherited;
end;

procedure TMainForm.DefaultHandler(var Msg);
{ Default message handler for form }
begin
  if TMessage(Msg).Msg = sx_MyMessage then begin
    if DefHandCB.Checked then begin      { is Message Procedure checked? }
      if TMessage(Msg).wParam = 1 then   { check for post or send }
        MessageDlg(Format(MessString, ['Posted', 'DefaultHandler.']),
                   mtInformation, [mbOk], 0)
      else
        MessageDlg(Format(MessString, ['Sent', 'DefaultHandler.']),
                   mtInformation, [mbOk], 0);
      if not DHEatMessCB.Checked then
        inherited DefaultHandler(Msg);   { eat message if directed }
    end
    else
      inherited DefaultHandler(Msg);
  end
  else
    inherited DefaultHandler(Msg);
end;

procedure TMainForm.PostMessButtonClick(Sender: TObject);
{ posts message to form }
begin
  PostMessage(Handle, sx_MyMessage, 1, 0);
end;

procedure TMainForm.SendMessButtonClick(Sender: TObject);
{ sends message to form }
begin
  SendMessage(Handle, sx_MyMessage, 0, 0); { send message to form }
end;

procedure TMainForm.WndProcCBClick(Sender: TObject);
{ enables proper checkboxes for WndProc }
begin
  if WndProcCB.Checked then
    WPEatMessCB.Enabled := True
  else
    WPEatMessCB.Enabled := False;
end;

procedure TMainForm.MessProcCBClick(Sender: TObject);
{ enables proper checkboxes for Message Procedure }
begin
  if MessProcCB.Checked then
    MPEatMessCB.Enabled := True
  else
    MPEatMessCB.Enabled := False;
end;
```

continues

Listing 9.3. continued

```
procedure TMainForm.DefHandCBClick(Sender: TObject);
{ enables proper checkboxes for Default Handler }
begin
  if DefHandCB.Checked then
    DHEatMessCB.Enabled := True
  else
    DHEatMessCB.Enabled := False;
end;

end.
```

CAUTION

Although it is okay to just use the `inherited` keyword to send the message on to an inherited handler in message-handler procedures, that technique does not work in `DefWndProc()` or `DefaultHandler()`. In those procedures, you also must provide the name of the inherited procedure or function, as in this example,

`inherited DefWndProc(Msg);`

You may have noticed that the `DefaultHandler()` procedure is somewhat unusual in that it takes one *untyped* var parameter. That's because `DefaultHandler()` assumes that the first word in the parameter is the message number, and it isn't concerned with the rest of the information being passed. Because of this, you typecast the parameter as a `TMessage` in order to access the message parameters.

The Relationship Between Messages and Events

Now that you know all the ins and outs of messages, recall that this chapter began by stating that VCL encapsulates many Windows messages in its event system. Delphi's event system is designed to be an easy interface into windows messages, and many VCL events have a direct correlation with a `wm_xxx` Windows message. Table 9.3 shows some common VCL events and the Windows message responsible for the event.

Table 9.3. VCL events and corresponding Windows messages.

VCL Event	Windows Message
OnActivate	wm_Activate
OnClick	wm_XButtonDown
OnCreate	wm_Create

VCL Event	Windows Message
OnDblClick	wm_XButtonDblClick
OnKeyDown	wm_KeyDown
OnKeyPress	wm_Char
OnKeyUp	wm_KeyUp
OnPaint	wm_Paint
OnResize	wm_Size
OnTimer	wm_Timer

Although events generally behave a bit differently than their Windows message counterparts, Table 9.3 is a good rule-of-thumb reference when looking for events that correspond directly to messages.

> **TIP**
>
> Never write a message handler when you can use a predefined event to do the same thing. Because of their contract-free nature, you will have many fewer problems handling events rather than messages.

Summary

By now, you should have the gist of how Windows' messaging system works and how VCL encapsulates that messaging system. Although Delphi's event system is great, knowing how messages work is essential for any serious Windows programmer.

If you're eager to learn more about handling Windows messages, read Chapter 11, "Creating Delphi Custom Components." In that chapter, you'll see practical application of the knowledge gained in this chapter.

10

GDI and Graphics Programming

In previous chapters, you worked with a property called Canvas. Appropriately dubbed, because you can think of a window as an artist's blank canvas on which you paint various Windows objects. Each button, window, cursor, and so on is nothing more than a collection of pixels in which the colors have been set to give it some useful appearance. In fact, think of each individual window as a separate surface on which its separate components are painted. To take this analogy a bit further, imagine that you are an artist who will require various tools in order to accomplish your task. You will need a palette from which to pick different colors. You probably will make use of different styles of brushes, drawing tools, and special artist's techniques as well. Windows makes use of similar tools and techniques, in the programming sense, to paint the various objects with which users interact. These tools are made available through the Graphics Device Interface, otherwise known as the GDI.

Windows makes use of the GDI to paint or draw the images you see on your computer screen. In traditional Windows programming, programmers worked directly with the GDI functions and tools. In Delphi, however, the TCanvas object encapsulates and simplifies using these functions, tools, and techniques. This chapter teaches you how to make use of TCanvas to perform useful graphics functions as well as shows you a few advanced techniques working with the Windows API.

Drawing with the Canvas

Higher level classes like TForm and other TWinControls descendants have a Canvas property. The canvas serves as the painting surface for your forms and some components. The tools that Canvas uses to do the drawing are pens, brushes, and fonts.

Using Pens

Pens enable you to draw lines on the canvas and are accessed from Canvas's Pen property. You can change how lines are drawn by modifying the Pen's properties: Color, Width, Style, and Mode.

The Color property specifies a pen's color. Delphi provides predefined color constants that match many common colors. There are the constants clRed and clYellow, for example, which correspond to red and yellow. There also are constants that correspond to Windows' Control Panel settings like clActiveCaption, which is the color of Windows' active captions. The following line assigns the color blue to the canvas's pen:

```
Canvas.Pen.color := clblue;
```

This line shows you how to assign a random color to Canvas's Pen property:

```
Pen.Color := TColor(RGB(Random(255),Random(255), Random(255)));
```

The pen also can draw lines with a different drawing style, as specified by its Style property. Table 10.1 shows the different styles that you can set for Pen.Style.

RGB() AND TColor

Windows represents colors as long integers in which the lowest three bytes each signify a red, green, and blue intensity level. The combination of the three values makes up a valid Windows color. The RGB(R, G, B) function takes three parameters for the red, green, and blue intensity levels. It returns a Windows color as a long integer value. There are 255 possible values for each intensity level and approximately 16 million colors that can be returned from the RGB() function. RGB(0, 0, 0), for example, returns the color value for black, whereas RGB(255, 255, 255) returns the color value for white. RGB(255, 0 ,0), RGB(0, 255, 0), and RGB(0, 0, 255) return the color values for red, green, and blue, respectively. By varying the values passed to RGB(), you can obtain a color anywhere within the Windows palette of available colors.

Delphi defines TColor as

```
TColor = -(COLOR_ENDCOLORS + 1)..$02FFFFFF;
```

TColor is basically a superset of RGB colors. In addition to including the full range of positive long integer color values, it includes a few negative values to represent Windows' system constants. Therefore, TColors may not be within the range for an RGB color, but RGB will always be within the range for a TColor.

TIP

Use the ColorToRGB function to convert Windows system colors like clWindow to a valid RGB color. The function is described in Delphi's online help.

Table 10.1. Pen styles.

Style	Draws
psClear	Invisible lines
psDash	A line made up of a series of dashes
psDashDot	A line made up of alternating dashes and dots
psDashDotDot	A line made up of a series of dash-dot-dot combinations
psDot	A line made up of a series of dots
psInsideFrame	Lines within the frame of closed shapes that specify a bounding rectangle
psSolid	A solid line

The pen's Width property enables you to specify the width in pixels that the pen uses for drawing. When this property is set to a larger width, the pen draws with thicker lines.

You can change the pen's drawing style, as shown in the following line. Figure 10.1 shows how the different pen styles appear when drawn on the form's canvas.

```
Canvas.Pen.Style := psDashDot;
```

FIGURE 10.1.

Different pen styles.

Three factors determine how Windows draws pixels or lines to a canvas surface: the pen's color, the surface or destination color, and the bitwise operation that Windows performs on the two color values. This operation is known as a *raster operation* (ROP). The pen's Mode property specifies the ROP to be used for a given canvas. There are 16 predefined modes defined in Windows, as shown in Table 10.2.

Table 10.2. Windows pen modes on source Pen.Color (S) and Destination (D) color.

Mode	Result Pixel Color	Boolean Operation
pmBlack	Always black	0
pmWhite	Always white	1
pmNOP	Unchanged	D
pmNOT	Inverse of D color	not D
pmCopy	Color specified by S	S
pmNotCopy	Inverse of S	not S
pmMergePenNot	Combination P and inverse of D	S or not D
pmMaskPenNot	Combination of colors common to S and inverse of D	S and not D
pmMergeNotPen	Combination of D and inverse of S	not S or D
pmMaskNotPen	Combination of colors common to D and inverse of S	not S and D

Mode	Result Pixel Color	Boolean Operation
pmMerge	Combination of S and D	S or D
pmNotMerge	Inverse of pmMerge operation on P and D	not (S or D)
pmMask	Combination of colors common to S and D	S and D
pmNotMask	Inverse of pmMask operation on S and D	not (S and D)
pmXor	Combination of colors in either S or D but not both	S XOR D
pmNotXor	Inverse of pmXOR operation on S and D	not (S XOR D)

Pen.mode is pmCopy by default. This means that the pen draws with the color specified by its Color property. Suppose that you want to draw black lines on a white background. If a line crosses over a previously drawn line, it should draw white instead of black.

One way to do this would be to check the color of the area you're going to draw to—if it is white, set pen.Color to black; if it is black, set pen.Color to white. Although this approach works, it would be cumbersome and slow. A better approach would be to set Pen.Color to clBlack and Pen.Mode to pmNotMerge. This would result in the pen drawing the inverse of the merging operation with the pen and surface color. The output shown in Figure 10.2 shows you the result of this operation when drawing with a black pen in a crisscross fashion.

FIGURE 10.2.

The output of a pmNotMerge operation.

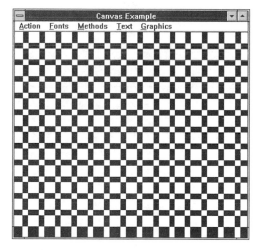

Using Brushes

A canvas's brush fills in areas and shapes drawn on the canvas using various colors and patterns. Canvas's TBrush object has three important properties: Color, Style, and Bitmap. Color specifies the brush's color, Style specifies the pattern of the brush background, and Bitmap specifies a bitmap that you can use to create custom patterns for the brush's background.

There are eight brush options specified by the `Style` property: `bsSolid`, `bsClear`, `bsHorizontal`, `bsVertical`, `bsFDiagonal`, `bsBDiagonal`, `bsCross`, or `bsDiagCross`. By default, the brush color is `clWhite` with a `bsSolid` style and no bitmap. You can change the color and style to fill an area with different patterns. Figure 10.3 shows the output using different brush patterns.

FIGURE 10.3.

Brush patterns.

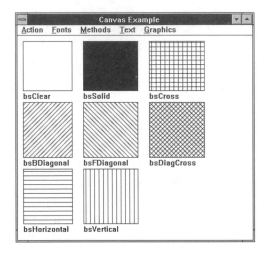

Using Fonts

The `Canvas`'s `Font` property enables you to draw text to the form's surface using any of the available Windows fonts. You can change the appearance of text written to the canvas by modifying the font's `Color`, `Name`, `Size`, `Height`, or `Style` property.

You can assign any of Delphi's predefined colors to `Font.Color`. The following code, for example, assigns the color red to the canvas's font:

```
Canvas.Font.Color := clRed;
```

The `Name` property specifies the Window's font name. For example,

```
Canvas.Font.Name := 'New Times Roman';
```

and

```
Canvas.Font.Name := 'Courier';
```

assign different typefaces to `Canvas`'s font.

`Canvas.Font.Size` specifies the font's size in points.

`Canvas.Font.Style` is a set composed of one style or a combination of the styles shown in Table 10.3.

Table 10.3. Font styles.

Value	*Style*
fsBold	Boldface
fsItalic	Italic
fsUnderline	Underlined
fsStrikeOut	A horizontal line through the font, giving it a strikethrough appearance

To combine two styles, use the syntax for combining multiple set values:

```
Canvas.Font.Style := [fsBold, fsItalic];
```

In Chapter 8, "MDI Applications," you used the TFontDialog to obtain a Windows font and assigned that font to TMemo's Font property:

```
if FontDialog1.Execute then
  Memo1.Font.Assign(FontDialog1.Font);
```

The same can be done to assign the font selected in the TFontDialog to the Canvas's font:

```
Canvas.Font.Assign(FontDialog1.Font);
```

> **CAUTION**
>
> Make sure to use the Assign() method when copying TBitMap, TBrush, TIcon, TMetaFile, TPen, and TPicture classes. A statement such as
> ```
> MyBrush1 := MyBrush2
> ```
> might seem valid, but it performs a direct pointer copy so that both instances point to the same brush resource which can result in a loss of GDI memory. By using Assign(), you ensure that previous resources are freed.
>
> This is not so when assigning between two TFont properties. Therefore, a statement such as
> ```
> Form1.Font := Form2.Font
> ```
> is a valid statement. Be careful, however, this is only valid with when assigning TFont properties and not TFont variables. As a general rule, use the Assign() method, always.

Additionally, you can assign individual attributes from the selected font in the TFontDialog to the Canvas's font:

```
Canvas.Font.Name := Font.Dialog1.Font.Name;
Canvas.Font.Size := Font.Dialog1.Font.Size;
```

We've brushed over fonts here. A more advanced discussion on fonts appears at the end of the this chapter.

Using *Canvas's* Drawing Methods

The `Canvas` class encapsulates many GDI drawing functions. With `Canvas`'s methods, you can draw lines and shapes, write text, copy areas from one canvas to another, and even stretch an area on the canvas to fill a larger area—all of which are demonstrated in this chapter.

Drawing Lines

`Canvas`'s `MoveTo()` method changes `Canvas.Pen`'s drawing position on the `Canvas`'s surface. The following code, for example, moves the drawing position to the upper-left corner of the canvas:

```
Canvas.MoveTo(0, 0);
```

`Canvas`'s `LineTo()` method draws a line on the canvas from its current position to the position specified by the parameters passed to `LineTo()`. Use `MoveTo()` with `LineTo()` to draw lines anywhere on the canvas. The following code draws a line from the upper-left position of the form's client area to the form's lower-right corner:

```
Canvas.MoveTo(0, 0);
Canvas.LineTo(ClientWidth, ClientHeight);
```

Drawing Shapes

`TCanvas` offers various methods for rendering shapes to the canvas: `Arc()`, `Chord()`, `Ellipse()`, `Pie()`, `Polygon()`, `PolyLine()`, `Rectangle()`, and `RoundRect()`. To draw an ellipse in the form's client area, you would use `Canvas`'s `Ellipse()` method, as in the following code:

```
Canvas.Ellipse(0, 0, ClientWidth, ClientHeight);
```

You also can fill an area on the canvas with a brush pattern specified in the `Canvas.Brush.Style` property. The following code draws an ellipse and fills the ellipse interior with the brush pattern specified by `Canvas.Brush.Style`:

```
Canvas.Brush.Style := bsCross;
Canvas.Ellipse(0, 0, ClientWidth, ClientHeight);
```

You will see an example of a brush pattern later in this chapter in the section "The Canvas Sample Project."

Some of `Canvas`' other methods take additional or different parameters to describe the shape being drawn. The `PolyLine()` method, for example, takes an array of `TPoint` records that specify positions on the canvas to be connected by a line—sort of like connect the dots. A `TPoint` is a record in Delphi that signifies an X,Y coordinate. A `TPoint` is defined as

```
TPoint = record
  X: Integer;
  Y: Integer;
end;
```

The following code illustrates the `PolyLine()` methods and results in the output shown in Figure 10.4:

```
Canvas.PolyLine([Point(0,0), Point(120,30), Point(250,120),Point(140,200),
➥Point(80,100), Point(0,0)]);
```

FIGURE 10.4.

Output of the
Canvas.PolyLine()
method.

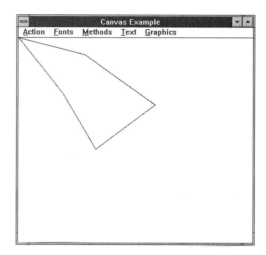

Displaying Text with the Canvas

You used Canvas's TextOut() function to output text to the form's client area in previous chapters. Canvas has some other useful methods for determining the size in pixels of text contained in a string using Canvas's rendered font. These functions are TextWidth() and TextHeight(). The following code determines the width and height for the string "Delphi - Yes!":

```
var
  S: String;
begin
  S := 'Delphi - Yes!';
  w := Canvas.TextWidth(S);
  h := Canvas.TextHeight(S);
end.
```

The TextRect() method also writes text to the form, but only within a rectangle specified by a TRect structure. A TRect is defined as

```
TRect = record
  case Integer of
    0: (Left, Top, Right, Bottom: Integer);
    1: (TopLeft, BottomRight: TPoint);
  end;
```

The text not contained within the TRect boundaries is clipped. In the line:

```
Canvas.TextRect(R,0,0,'Delphi Yes!');
```

The string `"Delphi Yes!"` is written to the canvas at location 0,0. However, the portion of the string that falls outside of the coordinates specified by R, a TRect structure, gets clipped. Figure 10.11, later in this chapter, illustrates what this output looks like.

The canvas also has the methods `Draw()`, `Copy()`, `CopyRect()`, and `StretchDraw()`, which enable you to draw, copy, expand, or shrink an image or a portion of an image to another canvas.

Using *Canvas's* Pixels

`Canvas`'s `Pixels` property is a two-dimensional array where each element represents a pixel's `TColor` value on the form's surface or client area. The upper-left corner of your form's painting surface is given by

```
Canvas.Pixels[0,0]
```

and the lower-right corner is

```
Canvas.Pixels[clientwidth, clientheight];
```

It's rare that you will ever have to access individual pixels on your form; however, it's nice to know you can when you need to. To set the color of a specific pixel location, use this code:

```
Canvas.Pixels[10, 10] := clBlue;
```

Delphi's Representation of Pictures: *TImage*

The `TImage` component represents a graphical image that can be displayed anywhere on a form and is available from Delphi's Component palette. With `TImage`, you can load and display a bitmap file (BMP), a metafile (WMF), or an icon file (ICO). The image data actually is stored by `TImage`'s `Picture` property, which is of the type `TPicture`.

GRAPHIC IMAGES: BITMAPS, METAFILES, AND ICONS

Bitmaps

Windows *bitmaps* are binary information arranged in a pattern of bits that represent a graphical image. The binary data is stored in a file with a BMP extension. If the file also contains color-palette information, it is referred to as *a device-independent bitmap* (DIB). DIBs are really no different from bitmaps, except that they provide their own color palette, whereas BMP files use the system palette. In essence, a BMP is the same as a DIB when the DIB is stored in memory. This is assuming that the BMP was created with the currently installed video driver. BMP pixel information varies with video hardware, whereas DIB pixel information doesn't.

Metafiles

Metafiles are files in which a series of GDI routines are stored, enabling you to save GDI function calls to disk so that you can redisplay the image later. This also enables you to share your drawing routines with other programs without having to call the specific GDI functions in each program. Metafiles usually contain a WMF file extension.

Icons

Icons are Windows resources that usually are stored in an icon file with an ICO extension. Icons typically consist of two 32×32 pixel bitmaps, although other, less common, formats exist. One bitmap, referred to as the *image*, is the actual icon images as it is displayed. The other bitmap, referred to as the *mask*, makes it possible to achieve transparency when the icon is displayed. Icons are used for a variety of purposes—such as showing that an application is minimized; or as attention grabbers like the question mark, exclamation point, or stop sign shown in message boxes.

TPicture is a container class for the TGraphic abstract class. A *container* class, means that TPicture can store the image types TBitMap, TMetaFile, and TIcon. Use TImage.Picture's properties and methods to load a bitmap, meta file or icon files into a TImage component, for example, use the following statement:

```
MyImage.Picture.LoadFromFile('FileName.bmp');
```

Use a similar statement to load icon files or metafiles. For example, the following code loads a Windows metafile:

```
MyImage.Picture.LoadFromFile('FileName.wmf');
```

and this code loads a Windows icon file:

```
MyImage.Picture.LoadFromFile('FileName.ico');
```

To save an image, use the SaveToFile() method, which automatically determines the file type that it should save:

```
MyImage.Picture.SaveToFile('FileName.bmp');
```

The TBitMap class encapsulates the Windows HBITMAP and HPALETTE, and provides the methods to load, store, display, save, and copy the bitmapped images. TBitMap also manages palette realization automatically. This means that the tedious task of managing bitmaps has been simplified substantially with Delphi's TBitMap class, enabling you to focus on using the bitmap and not having to worry about all the underlying implementation details. To create an instance of a TBitMap class and load a bitmap file, for example, you use the following commands:

```
MyBitMap := TBitMap.Create;
MyBitMap.LoadFromFile('MyBMP.BMP');
```

To copy one bitmap to another, you use the canvas's `Assign()` method, as in this example:

```
BitMap1.Assign(BitMap2);
```

You also can copy a portion of a bitmap from one `TBitMap` instance to another `TBitMap` instance or even to the form's canvas by using the `CopyRect()` method:

```
var
 R1: TRect;
begin
  with R1 do begin
    Top := 0; Left := 0; Right := MyBitMap.Width;
    Bottom := MyBitMap.Height;
  end;
  Canvas.CopyRect(ClientRect, MyBitMap.Canvas, R1);
end;
```

First, calculate the appropriate values in a `TRect` record and then use the `Canvas`'s `CopyRect()` method to copy a portion of the bitmap. To copy the entire bitmap to the form's canvas so that it shrinks or expands to fit inside the canvas's boundaries, replace the call to `CopyRect()` with the `StretchDraw()` method:

```
Canvas.StretchDraw(R1, MyBitMap);
```

Using GDI Functions

Delphi's encapsulation of Windows GDI through the `TCanvas` class doesn't prevent you from making use of the abundant Window GDI functions. Instead, `TCanvas` really just simplifies using the more common routines while still enabling you to call any Windows GDI function that you might need.

If you look at the various GDI functions such as `BitBlt()` or `DrawText()`, you will find that one of the required parameters is a DC, or device context. The device context is accessible through the canvas's `Handle` property. `TCanvas.Handle` is the DC for that canvas.

DEVICE CONTEXTS

Device contexts (DCs) are handles that are provided by Windows to identify a Windows application's connection to an output device such as a monitor, printer, or plotter through a device driver. In traditional Windows programming, you, the programmer, were responsible for requesting a DC whenever you needed to paint to a window's surface; and, when done, you had to return the DC back to Windows. Delphi simplifies the management of DCs by encapsulating DC management in the `TCanvas` class. In fact, `TCanvas` even caches your DC, saving it for later so that requests to Windows occur less often—thus, speeding up your program's overall execution.

To see how to use TCanvas with a Windows GDI function, use the GDI routine DrawText() to output text with advanced formatting capabilities. DrawText is one of the routines that is not available through the TCanvas class. DrawText takes the following five parameters:

Parameter	*Description*
DC	Device context of the drawing surface.
Str	Pointer to a buffer containing the text to be drawn. This must be a null-terminated string if the Count parameter is -1.
Count	Number of bytes in Str. If this value is -1, then Str is a pointer to a null-terminated string.
Rect	Pointer to a TRect structure containing the coordinates of the rectangle in which the text is formatted.
Format	A bit field that contains flags specifying the various formatting options for Str.

The following code shows how you can format text output to appear as shown in Figure 10.5:

```
Canvas.Rectangle(8, 8, 82, 102);
R := Rect(10, 10, 80, 100);
MyOutText := StrNew('Delphi, It''s going to change our lives');
DrawText(Canvas.Handle, MyOutText, -1, R, dt_WordBreak or dt_Center);
StrDispose(MyOutText);
```

FIGURE 10.5.

Formatting text output with the DrawText() function.

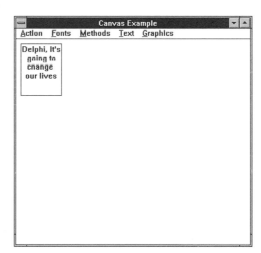

First, the Rect() function assigns values to the TRect record, R. Then, the dt_WordBreak and dt_Center formatting flags are passed to the DrawText() function. dt_WordBreak causes the text to break lines between words and span multiple lines if the line exceeds R's width. dt_Center centers each line in R's rectangular region.

Coordinate Systems and Mapping Modes

Most GDI drawing routines require a set of coordinates that specify the location where drawing is to occur. These coordinates are based on a unit of measure, such as the pixel. Additionally, GDI routines assume an orientation for the vertical and horizontal axis—that is, how increasing or decreasing the values of the X,Y coordinates moves the position at which drawing occurs. Windows relies on two factors to perform drawing routines. These are the Windows coordinates system and the mapping mode of the area being drawn to.

Coordinate Systems

Windows coordinates systems are, in a general sense, no different that any other coordinate system. You define a coordinate for an X,Y axis, and Windows plots that location to a point on your drawing surface based on a given orientation. Windows uses two coordinates systems to plot areas on drawing surfaces called the *device* and *logical* coordinates. Device coordinates, as the name implies, refer to the device on which Windows is running. Its measurements are in pixels and the orientation is such that the horizontal and vertical axis increase from left to right and top to bottom. For example, if you are running Windows on a 640×480 pixel display, the coordinates at the top-left corner on your device are (0,0) whereas the bottom-right coordinates are (639,479). You'll rarely need to use device coordinates since you typically don't draw directly to the device, per se. Instead, you draw to a window with a DC like a TForm or a TPanel using logical coordinates.

Logical coordinates refer to the coordinates system used by any area in windows that has a device context or DC like a screen, a form, or a form's client area. The difference between device and logical coordinates are explained in a moment. The screen, form window, and form client-area coordinates are explained first.

Screen coordinates refer to the display device and therefore, its logical coordinates are based on pixel measurements. On a 650×480 display, Screen.Width and Screen.Height are also 640 and 480 pixels, respectively. To obtain a device context for the screen, use the Windows API function GetDC(). Remember that you must match any function that retrieves a device context with a call to ReleaseDC(). The following code illustrates this:

```
var
 ScreenDC: HDC;
begin
  Screen DC := GetDC(0);
  { Do whatever you need to do with ScreenDC }
  ReleaseDC(0, ScreenDC);
end;
```

Form coordinates are synonymous with the term *window coordinates* and refer to an entire form or window, including the caption bar and borders. Delphi doesn't provide a DC to the form's drawing area through a form's property, but you can obtain one by using the Windows API function GetWindowDC() as follows:

```
MyDC := GetWindowDC(Form1.Handle);
```

This function returns the DC for the window handle passed to it.

A form's *client-area coordinates* refer to a form's client area whose DC is the Handle property of the form's Canvas and whose measurements are obtained from Canvas.ClientWidth and Canvas.ClientHeight.

So why not just use device coordinates instead of logical coordinates when doing drawing routines? Examine the following line of code:

```
Form1.Canvas.TextOut(0, 0, 'Upper Left Corner of Form');
```

This line places the string at the upper-left corner of the form. The coordinates (0,0) map to the position (0,0) in the form's device context—logical coordinates. However, the position (0,0) for the form is completely different in device coordinates and depends on where the form is located on your screen. If the form just happens to be located at the upper left corner of your screen, the form's coordinates (0,0) may in fact map to (0,0) in device coordinates. However, as you move the form to another location, (0,0) will no longer map to (0,0) in device coordinates.

TIP

You can obtain the device coordinates from logical coordinates and vice versa using the Windows API functions ClientToScreen() and ScreenToClient(), respectively.

Underneath the call to Canvas.TextOut(), Windows does actually use device coordinates. In order for Windows to do this, it must "map" the logical coordinates of the DC being drawn to, to device coordinates. It does this via the mapping mode associated with the DC.

Another reason for using logical coordinates is that you might not want to use pixels to perform drawing routines. Perhaps you want to draw using inches or millimeters. Windows enables you to change the unit with which you perform your drawing routines by changing its mapping mode, as you'll see in a moment.

Mapping modes define two attributes for the DC: the translation that Windows uses to convert logical units to device units, and the orientation of the X,Y axis for the DC.

> **NOTE**
>
> It might not seem apparent that drawing routines, mapping modes, orientation, and so on, are associated with a DC because, in Delphi, you use the canvas to draw. Remember, that `TCanvas` is a wrapper for a DC. This becomes obvious when comparing Windows GDI routines to their equivalent `Canvas` routines such as:
>
> **Canvas routine:** `Canvas.Rectangle(0, 0, 50, 50));`
>
> **GDI routine:**   `Rectangle(ADC, 0, 0, 50, 50);`
>
> When using the GDI routine, a DC is passed to the function, whereas the canvas's routine uses the DC that it encapsulates.

Mapping Modes

Windows enables to you define the mapping mode for a DC or `Canvas.Handle`. In fact, Windows defines eight mapping modes you can use. These mapping modes, along with their attributes, are shown in Table 10.4. The sample project in the next section illustrates more about mapping modes.

Table 10.4. Windows mapping modes.

Mapping Mode	Logical Unit size	Orientation (X,Y)
MM_ANISOTROPIC	arbitrary (x <> y) or (x = y)	definable/definable
MM_HIENGLISH	0.001 inch	Right/Up
MM_HIMETRIC	0.01 mm	Right/Up
MM_ISOTROPIC	arbitrary (x = y)	definable/definable
MM_LOENGLISH	0.01 inch	Right/Up
MM_LOMETRIC	0.1 mm	Right/Up
MM_TEXT	1 pixel	Right/Down
MM_TWIPS	1/1440 inch	Right/Up

Windows defines a few functions that enable you to change or retrieve information about the mapping modes for a given DC. Here is a summary of these functions:

`SetMapMode()`	Sets the mapping mode for a given device context.
`GetMapMode()`	Gets the mapping mode for a given device context.
`SetWindowOrg()`	Defines an window origin (point 0,0) for a given DC.
`SetViewPortOrg()`	Defines a viewport origin (point 0,0) for a given DC.

| `SetWindowExt()` | Defines the X,Y extents for a given window DC. These values are used in conjunction with the viewport X,Y extents to perform translation from logical to device units. |
| `SetViewPortExt()` | Defines the X,Y extents for a given viewport DC. These values are used in conjunction with the window X,Y extents to perform translation from logical to device units. |

Notice that these functions contain either the word *Window* or *ViewPort*. The window and viewport are simply a means by which Windows GDI can perform the translation from logical to device units. The functions with *Window* are referring to the logical coordinate system, whereas those with *ViewPort* refer to the device coordinates system. With the exception of the `MM_ANISOTROPIC` and `MM_ISOTROPIC` mapping modes, you don't have to worry about this much. In fact, Windows uses the `MM_TEXT` mapping mode by default.

NOTE

There's a logical reason behind `MM_TEXT` being the default mapping mode. When reading/writing text we do so from left to right, and from top to bottom. This matches `MM_TEXT`'s orientation.

You will notice that each mapping mode uses a different logical unit size. In some cases, it may be convenient to use a different mapping mode for that reason. For example, you may wish to display a line two inches wide, regardless of the resolution of your output device. In this instance, `MM_LOENGLISH` would be a good candidate for a mapping mode to use.

As an example of drawing a one-inch rectangle to the form, you first change the mapping mode to for `Form1.Canvas.Handle` to `MM_HIENGLISH` or `MM_LOENGLISH`. We'll use `MM_LOENGLISH`:

```
SetMapMode(Canvas.Handle, MM_LOENGLISH);
```

Then, you draw the rectangle using the appropriate units of measure for a one-inch rectangle. Because `MM_LOENGLISH` uses 1/100 inch, you simply pass the value 100, as follows. This will be illustrated further in a later example.

```
Canvas.Rectangle(0, 0, 200, 200);
```

NOTE

Because `MM_TEXT` uses pixels as its unit of measurement, you can use the Windows API function `GetDeviceCaps()` to retrieve the information you need to perform translation from pixels to inches or millimeters. Then, you can do your own calculations if you wish. We demonstrate this in Chapter 12, "Printing in Delphi." Mapping modes are simply a convenient way to let Windows do the work for you.

The `SetWindowExt()` and `SetViewPortExt()` functions enable to you define how Windows translates logical to device units. So, the following lines of code mean that one logical unit requires two device units (pixels):

```
SetWindowExt(Canvas.Handle, 1, 1)
SetViewportExt(Canvas.Handle, 2, 2);
```

Likewise, these lines of code mean that five logical units require 10 device units:

```
SetWindowExt(Canvas.Handle, 5, 5)
SetViewportExt(Canvas.Handle, 10, 10);
```

Notice that this is exactly the same as the previous example. Both, have the same effect of having a 1:2 ratio of logical to device units. An example of how this may be used to change the units for a form is

```
SetWindowExt(Canvas.Handle, 500, 500)
SetViewportExt(Canvas.Handle, ClientWidth, ClientHeight);
```

This enables to you work with a form who's client width and height are 500×500 units (not pixels) despite any re-sizing of the form.

The `SetWindowOrg()` and `SetViewPortOrg()` functions enable you to relocate the origin or position (0,0) which, by default, is at the upper-left corner of a form's client area in the MM_TEXT mapping mode. Typically, you just modify the viewport origin. For example, the following line sets up a four-quadrant coordinate system like that shown in Figure 10.6.

```
SetViewportOrg(Canvas.Handle, ClientWidth div 2, ClientHeight div 2);
```

FIGURE 10.6.
*A four-quadrant
coordinate system.*

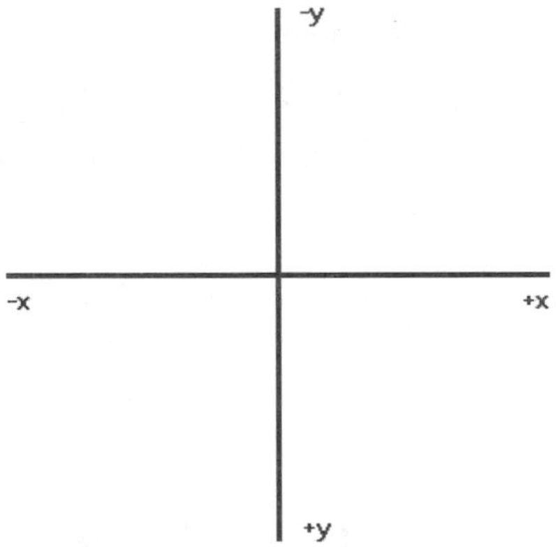

The Canvas Sample Project

The canvas sample project demonstrates `TCanvas`'s many useful properties and methods discussed in this chapter. Listings 10.1, 10.2, and 10.3 show the source code for CANVRTNS.DPR, CR1.PAS, and CR2.PAS, respectively.

Listing 10.1. CANVRTNS.DPR.

```
program canvrtns;

uses
  Forms,
  Cr1 in 'CR1.PAS' {Form1},
  Cr2 in 'CR2.PAS' {Form2};

{$R *.RES}

begin
  Application.CreateForm(TForm1, Form1);
  Application.CreateForm(TForm2, Form2);
  Application.Run;
end.
```

Listing 10.2. CR1.PAS.

```
unit Cr1;

interface

uses WinTypes, WinProcs, Classes, Graphics, Forms, Controls, StdCtrls,
  Menus, Dialogs, SysUtils;

type
  TForm1 = class(TForm)
    MainMenu1: TMainMenu;
    Action1: TMenuItem;
    Sticks1: TMenuItem;
    Pens1: TMenuItem;
    dmNotMergeOperation1: TMenuItem;
    BrushPatterns1: TMenuItem;
    BrushBitmap1: TMenuItem;
    Fonts1: TMenuItem;
    Functions1: TMenuItem;
    Arc1: TMenuItem;
    Chord1: TMenuItem;
    Ellipse1: TMenuItem;
    Pie1: TMenuItem;
    Polygon1: TMenuItem;
    Polyline1: TMenuItem;
    Rectangle1: TMenuItem;
    RoundRect1: TMenuItem;
    Fill1: TMenuItem;
    N1: TMenuItem;
    Text1: TMenuItem;
    TextRect1: TMenuItem;
    TextSize1: TMenuItem;
    Graphics1: TMenuItem;
    ShowBitMap1: TMenuItem;
    MMISOTROPIC1: TMenuItem;
    MMANSITROPIC1: TMenuItem;
    DrawText1: TMenuItem;
    ScreenFonts1: TMenuItem;
```

continues

Listing 10.2. continued

```
    PrinterFonts1: TMenuItem;
    MMLOENGLISH1: TMenuItem;
    MMHIINGLISH1: TMenuItem;
    procedure FormCreate(Sender: TObject);
    procedure FormDestroy(Sender: TObject);

    procedure Sticks1Click(Sender: TObject);
    procedure Pens1Click(Sender: TObject);
    procedure dmNotMergeOperation1Click(Sender: TObject);
    procedure BrushPatterns1Click(Sender: TObject);
    procedure BrushBitmap1Click(Sender: TObject);

    procedure ScreenFonts1Click(Sender: TObject);
    procedure PrinterFonts1Click(Sender: TObject);

    procedure Arc1Click(Sender: TObject);
    procedure Chord1Click(Sender: TObject);
    procedure Ellipse1Click(Sender: TObject);
    procedure Pie1Click(Sender: TObject);
    procedure Polygon1Click(Sender: TObject);
    procedure Polyline1Click(Sender: TObject);
    procedure Rectangle1Click(Sender: TObject);
    procedure RoundRect1Click(Sender: TObject);
    procedure Fill1Click(Sender: TObject);

    procedure TextRect1Click(Sender: TObject);
    procedure TextSize1Click(Sender: TObject);
    procedure DrawText1Click(Sender: TObject);

    procedure ShowBitMap1Click(Sender: TObject);
    procedure MMLOENGLISH1Click(Sender: TObject);
    procedure MMHIINGLISH1Click(Sender: TObject);
    procedure MMISOTROPIC1Click(Sender: TObject);
    procedure MMANSITROPIC1Click(Sender: TObject);

  private
    OldBrush: TBrush;
    OldPen: TPen;
    OldFont: TFont;
    procedure ClearCanvas;
    procedure FillIt;
    { Private declarations }
  public
    { Public declarations }
  end;

var
  Form1: TForm1;

implementation
uses cr2, printers;

{$R *.DFM}

procedure TForm1.ClearCanvas;
begin
```

```pascal
  Canvas.Brush.Assign(OldBrush);    { Copy Brush in OldBrush to Canvas.Brush }
  Canvas.Pen.Assign(OldPen);        { Copy Pen in OldPen to Canvas.Pen }
  Canvas.Font.Assign(OldFont);      { Copy Font in OldFont to Canvas.Font }
  Refresh;                          { Repaint the canvas }
end;

procedure TForm1.FillIt;
begin
  Canvas.Brush.Color := clBlue;   { Assign clBlue to Canvas's brush color }
  Canvas.Brush.Style := bsCross;  { Specify a brush style with which to draw }
end;

procedure TForm1.FormCreate(Sender: TObject);
begin
  OldBrush := TBrush.Create;      { Create a TBrush class instance }
  OldPen := TPen.Create;          { Create a TPen class instance }
  OldFont := TFont.Create;        { Create a TFont class instance }
  OldBrush.Assign(Canvas.Brush);  { Copy the canvas's Brush, Pen, and Font to }
  OldPen.Assign(Canvas.Pen);      {   the newly created class instances }
  OldFont.Assign(Canvas.Font);
end;

procedure TForm1.FormDestroy(Sender: TObject);
begin
  OldBrush.Free;                  { Free up the Brush, Pen and Font created in }
  OldPen.Free;                    { The form's OnCreate event handler. }
  OldFont.Free;
end;

procedure TForm1.Sticks1Click(Sender: TObject);
var
  i: integer;
begin
 ClearCanvas;               { Clear the Canvas }
 for i := 1 to 100 do begin
   with Canvas do begin
     { Get a random pen color draw a line using that color }
     Pen.Color := RGB(Random(255),Random(255), Random(255));
     MoveTo(random(ClientWidth), Random(ClientHeight));
     LineTo(random(ClientWidth), Random(ClientHeight));
   end
 end;
end;

procedure TForm1.Pens1Click(Sender: TObject);
var
  i: integer;
  PenStyle: TPenStyle;
begin
 ClearCanvas;              { Clear the canvas }
 PenStyle := psSolid; { Change the pen style to a solid style }

 i := 20;              { initialize i }
 with Canvas do begin
   while i <= 140 do begin
     Pen.Style := PenStyle;   { Set Pen style  }
     MoveTo(100, i);          { Set drawing location }
     LineTo(ClientWidth, i);  { Draw a line }
```

continues

Listing 10.2. continued

```
    inc(i, 20);                { Increment i }
    inc(PenStyle);             { Increment Penstyle to new pen style }
  end;

  { Write out titles for the various pen styles }
  TextOut(1, 10, ' psSolid ');
  TextOut(1, 30, ' psDash ');
  TextOut(1, 50, ' psDot ');
  TextOut(1, 70, ' psDashDot ');
  TextOut(1, 90, ' psDashDotDot ');
  TextOut(1, 110, ' psClear ');
  TextOut(1, 130, ' psInsideFrame ');
  end;
end;

procedure TForm1.dmNotMergeOperation1Click(Sender: TObject);
var
  x,y: integer;
begin
  ClearCanvas;                         { Clear the canvas }
  y := 10;                             { set Y to 10 }
  canvas.Pen.Width := 20;              { Set the pen width }
  canvas.Pen.Color := clBlack;         { Set the pen color }
  while y < ClientHeight do begin
    canvas.MoveTo(0, y);               { Draw a line and increment the vertical }
    canvas.LineTo(ClientWidth, y);     { position }
    inc(y, 30);
  end;
  x := 5;
  canvas.pen.Mode := pmNotMerge;       { Set the pen style to pmNotMerge }
  while x < ClientWidth do begin
    Canvas.MoveTo(x, 0);               { Draw a line and increment the horizontal }
    canvas.LineTo(x, ClientHeight);    { position }
    inc(x, 30);
  end;
end;

procedure TForm1.BrushPatterns1Click(Sender: TObject);
begin
 ClearCanvas;                          { clear the canvas }
 with Canvas do begin
   { Write out titles for the various brush styles }
   TextOut(120, 101, 'bsSolid');
   TextOut(10, 101, 'bsClear');
   TextOut(240, 101, 'bsCross');
   TextOut(10, 221, 'bsBDiagonal');
   TextOut(120, 221, 'bsFDiagonal');
   TextOut(240, 221, 'bsDiagCross');
   TextOut(10, 341, 'bsHorizontal');
   TextOut(120, 341, 'bsVertical');

   { Now draw a rectangle with the various brush styles }
   Rectangle(10, 10, 100, 100);
   Brush.Color := clBlack;

   Brush.Style := bsSolid;
```

```
   Rectangle(120, 10, 220, 100);

   Brush.Style := bsCross;
   Rectangle(240, 10, 340, 100);

   Brush.Style := bsBDiagonal;
   Rectangle(10, 120, 100, 220);

   Brush.Style := bsFDiagonal;
   Rectangle(120, 120, 220, 220);

   Brush.Style := bsDiagCross;
   Rectangle(240, 120, 340, 220);

   Brush.Style := bsHorizontal;
   Rectangle(10, 240, 100, 340);

   Brush.Style := bsVertical;
   Rectangle(120, 240, 220, 340);

 end;
end;

procedure TForm1.BrushBitmap1Click(Sender: TObject);
var
  NewBrush: TBrush;
begin
  ClearCanvas;                   { Clear the canvas }
  NewBrush := TBrush.Create; { Create a new TBrush object }
  try
    { Allocate the Brush's bitmap property }
    NewBrush.Bitmap := TBitMap.Create;
    NewBrush.Bitmap.LoadFromFile('Pattern.bmp'); { Load a bitmap from the file }
    Canvas.Brush.Assign(NewBrush);            { Assign the new brush to the
➥bitmap }
    Canvas.Rectangle(0, 0, ClientWidth, ClientHeight);   { Draw a rectangle
➥using }
  finally
    NewBrush.Free; { Free the bitmap }
  end;
end;

procedure TForm1.ScreenFonts1Click(Sender: TObject);
var
  i: integer;
begin
  ClearCanvas;                            { Clear the canvas }
  Form2.ListBox1.Items := Screen.Fonts;   { Copy the Screen.Fonts TStrings to
➥the listbox }
  Form2.Caption := 'Screen Fonts';        { Set the caption to indicate Screen
➥fonts }
  Form2.ShowModal;                        { Display the form as modal }
end;

procedure TForm1.PrinterFonts1Click(Sender: TObject);
var
  i: integer;
begin
```

continues

Listing 10.2. continued

```
  ClearCanvas;                            { Clear the canvas }
  Form2.ListBox1.Items := Printer.Fonts;  { Copy the Printer.Fonts TStrings
➥to the listbox }
  Form2.Caption := 'Printer Fonts';       { Set caption to indicate Printer
➥fonts }
  Form2.ShowModal;                        { show the form as modal }
end;

procedure TForm1.Arc1Click(Sender: TObject);
begin
  ClearCanvas;                  { Clear the canvas }
  with ClientRect do            { Draw an arc to the canvas }
    Canvas.Arc(Left, Top, Right, Bottom, Right, Top, Left, Top);
end;

procedure TForm1.Chord1Click(Sender: TObject);
begin
  ClearCanvas;                          { Clear the canvas }
  with ClientRect do begin              { Fill the area if Fill1.Checked }
    if Fill1.Checked then
      FillIt;
    { Draw the shape }
    Canvas.Chord(Left, Top, Right, Bottom, Right, Top, Left, Top);
  end;
end;

procedure TForm1.Ellipse1Click(Sender: TObject);
begin
  ClearCanvas;                  { Clear the canvas }
  if Fill1.Checked then         { Fill the area if Fill1.Checked }
    FillIt;
  { Draw the shape }
  Canvas.Ellipse(0, 0, ClientWidth, ClientHeight);
end;

procedure TForm1.Pie1Click(Sender: TObject);
begin
  ClearCanvas;                  { Clear the canvas }
  if Fill1.Checked then         { Fill the area if Fill1.Check then draw the }
    FillIt;                     { shape }
  Canvas.Pie(0, 0, ClientWidth, ClientHeight, 50, 5, 300, 50);
end;

procedure TForm1.Polygon1Click(Sender: TObject);
begin
  ClearCanvas;                  { Clear the canvas }
  if Fill1.Checked then         { Fill the area if Fill1.Checked then }
    FillIt;                     { draw the shape }
  Canvas.Polygon([Point(0, 0), Point(150, 20), Point(230, 130),
                Point(40, 120)]);
end;

procedure TForm1.Polyline1Click(Sender: TObject);
begin
  ClearCanvas;                    { Clear the canvas }
  if Fill1.Checked then           { Fill the area if Fill1.Checked then }
```

```
    FillIt;                                   { Draw the shape }
  { Draw the shape }
  Canvas.PolyLine([Point(0, 0), Point(120, 30), Point(250, 120),
    Point(140, 200), Point(80, 100), Point(0, 0)]);
  Canvas.FloodFill(20, 20, clBlack, fsBorder);    { Fill the shape }
end;

procedure TForm1.Rectangle1Click(Sender: TObject);
begin
  ClearCanvas;                          { Clear the canvas }
  if Fill1.Checked then                 { Fill the area if Fill1.Checked }
    FillIt;                             { and draw the shape }
  Canvas.Rectangle(10 , 10, 125, 240);
end;

procedure TForm1.RoundRect1Click(Sender: TObject);
begin
  ClearCanvas;                          { Clear the canvas }
  if Fill1.Checked then                 { Fill the area if Fill1.Checked }
    FillIt;                             { and draw the shape }
  Canvas.RoundRect(15, 15, 150, 200, 50, 50);
end;

procedure TForm1.Fill1Click(Sender: TObject);
begin
  Fill1.Checked := not Fill1.Checked;   { Perform a not operation to set or
➥not set }
end;

procedure TForm1.TextRect1Click(Sender: TObject);
var
  R: TRect;
  TWidth, THeight: integer;
begin
  ClearCanvas;                                { Clear the canvas }
  Canvas.Font.Size := 18;                     { Specify a font size }
  TWidth := Canvas.TextWidth('Delphi Yes!');  { Calculate the text size }
  THeight := Canvas.TextHeight('Delphi Yes!'); { Calculate the font height }
  { Initialize a TRect structure with values based on the text height/width }
  R := Rect(1, THeight div 2, TWidth + 1, THeight+(THeight div 2));
  { Draw a rectangle based on the text sizes }
  Canvas.Rectangle(R.Left-1, R.Top-1, R.Right+1, R.Bottom+1);
  Canvas.TextRect(R,0,0,'Delphi Yes!');       { Draw the text }
end;

procedure TForm1.TextSize1Click(Sender: TObject);
var
  TextStr: string;
begin
  TextStr := 'Delphi - YES!';     { Initialize the string }
  ClearCanvas;                    { Clear the canvas }
  with Canvas do begin
    Font.Size := 18;              { Specify a font size }
    TextOut(10, 10, TextStr);     { Draw the text and its sizes }
    TextOut(50, 50, 'TextWidth = '+IntToStr(TextWidth(TextStr)));
    TextOut(100, 100, 'TextHeight = '+IntToStr(TextHeight(TextStr)));
  end;
end;
```

continues

Listing 10.2. continued

```
procedure TForm1.DrawText1Click(Sender: TObject);
var
 R: TRect;
 MyOutText: PChar;
begin
  ClearCanvas;                         { Clear the canvas }
  Canvas.Rectangle(8, 8, 82, 102);     { Draw a rectangle }
  R := Rect(10, 10, 80, 100);          { Initialize the TRect structure }
  { Create the output text }
  MyOutText := StrNew('Delphi, It''s going to change our lives');
  { Draw the text inside rectangle with the specified formatting options}
  DrawText(Canvas.Handle, MyOutText, -1, R, dt_WordBreak or dt_Center);
  StrDispose(MyOutText);               { Free the string }
end;

procedure TForm1.ShowBitMap1Click(Sender: TObject);
var
  MyBitMap: TBitMap;
begin
  ClearCanvas;                              { Clear the canvas }
  MyBitMap := TBitMap.Create;
  try                                    { Create a bitmap object }
    MyBitMap.LoadFromFile('MyBmp.bmp');    { Load the bitmap from a file }
    Canvas.StretchDraw(ClientRect, MyBitMap); { expand the bitmap when
➥displaying }
  finally
    MyBitMap.Free;                         { Free the bitmap object }
  end;
end;

procedure TForm1.MMISOTROPIC1Click(Sender: TObject);
begin
  ClearCanvas;                                { Clear the canvas }
  SetMapMode(Canvas.Handle, MM_ISOTROPIC);    { Set mapping mode to
➥MM_ISOTROPIC }
  SetWindowExt(Canvas.Handle, 500, 500);      { Set the window extent
➥to 500 x 500 }
  SetViewportExt(Canvas.Handle, ClientWidth, ClientHeight); { Set the Viewport
➥extent to }
                                            { that of the Window's
➥client area }
  { Set the ViewPortorg to the center of the client area }
  SetViewportOrg(Canvas.Handle, ClientWidth div 2, ClientHeight div 2);
  Canvas.Rectangle(0, 0, 250, 250);        { Draw a rectangle based on current
➥settings }

  { Set the viewport extent to a different value, continue to do this three more
➥times }
  SetViewportExt(Canvas.Handle, ClientWidth, -ClientHeight);
  Canvas.Rectangle(0, 0, 250, 250);

  SetViewportExt(Canvas.Handle, -ClientWidth, -ClientHeight);
  Canvas.Rectangle(0, 0, 250, 250);

  SetViewportExt(Canvas.Handle, -ClientWidth, ClientHeight);
```

```
    Canvas.Rectangle(0, 0, 250, 250);
    { Now draw an ellipse in the center of the client area }
    Canvas.Ellipse(-50, -50, 50, 50);
    SetMapMode(Canvas.Handle, MM_TEXT); { Reset the mapping mode to MM_TEXT }
end;

procedure TForm1.MMANSITROPIC1Click(Sender: TObject);
begin
    ClearCanvas;                                    { Clear the canvas }
    SetMapMode(Canvas.Handle, MM_ANISOTROPIC);  { Set the mapping mode to
➥MM_ANISOTROPIC }
    SetWindowExt(Canvas.Handle, 500, 500);        { Set the window extent to
➥500 x 500 }

    {Set the Viewport extent to that of the Window's client area }
    SetViewportExt(Canvas.Handle, ClientWidth, ClientHeight);

    { Set the ViewPortorg to the center of the client area }
    SetViewportOrg(Canvas.Handle, ClientWidth div 2, ClientHeight div 2);
    Canvas.Rectangle(0, 0, 250, 250); { Draw a rectangle based on current
➥settings }

    { Set the viewport extent to a different value, continue to do this three
➥more times }
    SetViewportExt(Canvas.Handle, ClientWidth, -ClientHeight);
    Canvas.Rectangle(0, 0, 250, 250);

    SetViewportExt(Canvas.Handle, -ClientWidth, -ClientHeight);
    Canvas.Rectangle(0, 0, 250, 250);

    SetViewportExt(Canvas.Handle, -ClientWidth, ClientHeight);
    Canvas.Rectangle(0, 0, 250, 250);

    Canvas.Ellipse(-50, -50, 50, 50);   { Draw an ellipse in the center of the
➥client area }
    SetMapMode(Canvas.Handle, MM_TEXT);{ Reset the mapping mode to MM_TEXT }
end;

procedure TForm1.MMLOENGLISH1Click(Sender: TObject);
begin
    ClearCanvas;                                    { Clear the canvas }
    SetMapMode(Canvas.Handle, MM_LOENGLISH);       { Set mapping mode to
➥MM_LOENGLISH }
    SetViewPortOrg(Canvas.Handle, 0, ClientHeight); { Set the viewport org to
➥left, bottom }
    Canvas.Rectangle(0, 0, 200, 200);              { Draw a 2-inch rectangle }
    SetMapMode(Canvas.Handle, MM_TEXT);            { Reset mapping mode to
➥MM_TEXT }
end;

procedure TForm1.MMHIINGLISH1Click(Sender: TObject);
begin
    ClearCanvas;                                    { Clear the canvas }
    SetMapMode(Canvas.Handle, MM_HIENGLISH);        { Set the mapping mode to
➥MM_HIENGLISH }
    SetViewPortOrg(Canvas.Handle, 0, ClientHeight);  { Set the viewport org to
➥left bottom }
    Canvas.Rectangle(0, 0, 200, 200);                { Draw a 2/10th inch
```

continues

Listing 10.2. continued

```
➥rectangle }
  SetMapMode(Canvas.Handle, MM_TEXT);              { Reset mapping mode
➥to MM_TEXT }
end;

end.
```

Listing 10.3. CR2.PAS.

```
unit Cr2;

interface

uses
  SysUtils, WinTypes, WinProcs, Messages, Classes, Graphics, Controls,
  Forms, Dialogs, StdCtrls;

type
  TForm2 = class(TForm)
    ListBox1: TListBox;
  private
    { Private declarations }
  public
    { Public declarations }
  end;

var
  Form2: TForm2;

implementation

{$R *.DFM}

end.
```

Change the main form's caption to `"Canvas Example"` and its `Color` property to `clWhite`. Also place a `TMenuItem` to the form. `TMainMenu1` has the following menu options:

Menubar	*Submenu*
`"&Action"`	`"Sticks"`
	`"Pens"`
	`"dmNotMerge Operation"`
	`"Brush Patterns"`
	`"Brush BitMap"`
`&Fonts"`	`"Screen Fonts"`
	`"Printer Fonts"`

```
"&Methods"      "Arc"
                "Chord"
                "Ellipse"
                "Pie"
                "Polygon"
                "Polyline"
                "Rectangle"
                "RoundRect"
                "-"
                "Fill"
"&Text"         "TextRect"
                "TextSize"
                "DrawText"
"&Graphics"     "Show Bitmap"
                "MM_ISOTROPIC"
                "MM_ANISOTROPIC"
                "MM_LOENGLISH"
                "MM_HIENGLISH"
```

Create another form which contains a TListBox component whose Align property is set to alClient. Rename UNIT1.PAS to CR1.PAS, and rename UNIT2.PAS to CR2.PAS. Be sure to add CR2 to CR1's uses clause.

TForm1's OnCreate event handler, TForm1.FormCreate(), creates a TBrush, TFont, and TPen, which then are assigned a copy of the canvas's brush, font, and pen by using their Assign() methods. OldBrush, OldFont, and OldPen are private members of the TForm1 class. TForm1.FormDestroy() frees OldPen, OldFont, and OldBrush.

Copies of the canvas's original contents are required because you modify the original canvas throughout the application. By having a copy of the Canvas properties, you can create a method to reassign the original properties to the canvas. This method is TForm1.ClearCanvas().

The event handler TForm1.Sticks1Click() uses the Canvas's Pen property to draw lines on the canvas surface, as Figure 10.7 shows. Here, a color is assigned to Canvas.pen.color using the Windows GDI routine RGB(). The variable PenStyle is used to hold the value of a pen-style constant:

```
Canvas.Pen.Style := PenStyle;
Canvas.MoveTo(100, i);
Canvas.LineTo(ClientWidth, I);
```

Then Canvas.MoveTo() and Canvas.LineTo() are used to draw lines at random locations on the canvas's surface.

The event handler TForm1.Pens1Click() demonstrates the appearance of the different pen styles shown earlier in Figure 10.1.

FIGURE 10.7.

Sticks drawn to the canvas.

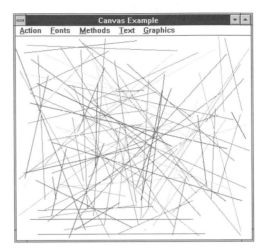

The event handler `TForm1.dmNotMergeOperation1Click()` demonstrates drawing using one of the raster operation codes, `dmNotMerge`, to produce the effect shown earlier in Figure 10.2.

`TForm1.BrushPatterns1Click()` demonstrates the different brush styles as shown earlier in Figure 10.3. Here, you assign the different brush styles to `Canvas.Brush.Style` and draw a rectangle to display each style.

The event handler `TForm1.BrushBitMap1Click()` first creates a `TBrush` instance and then creates and loads a bitmap to the new `TBrush`'s `BitMap` property. The actual bitmap is an 8×8, 16-color bitmap that the canvas's brush uses to paint to the canvas surface. Later in this chapter, you learn how to stretch this bitmap to fill the entire canvas surface.

Calling `Canvas.Rectangle()` with the bitmap loaded results in the pattern shown in Figure 10.8.

FIGURE 10.8.

A bitmap pattern.

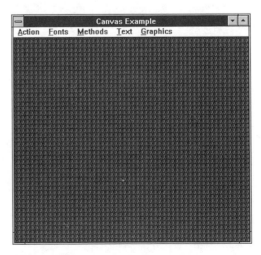

TForm1.ScreenFonts1Click() copies the font names from the global Screen variable to the listbox's Items and then calls Form2.ShowModal() to display them to the user.

TForm1.Printer1Fonts.Click() does the same, except that it copies the font names from the printer's fonts by using the global Printer variable. Fonts is a read-only property that returns a list of the available fonts for the selected device.

The event handler for the methods under the Methods menu items illustrate how to use the various canvas drawing methods. TForm1.Arc1Click() calls Canvas.Arc(), for example, to display an arc (see Figure 10.9):

```
ClearCanvas;
  with ClientRect do
    Canvas.Arc(Left, Top, Right, Bottom, Right, Top, Left, Top);
```

FIGURE 10.9.

Output of the
Canvas.Arc() method.

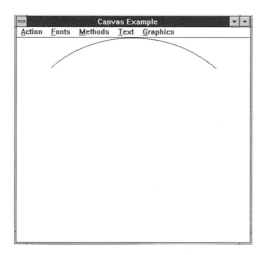

The other event handler under the Method menu item illustrate similar Canvas drawing routines.

Most of the drawing event handlers contain the following lines:

```
if Fill1.Checked then
  FillIt;
```

Fill1 is the TMenuItem for Methods | Fill1. If it is checked, the procedure FillIt() is called, which contains the following code:

```
Canvas.Brush.Color := clBlue;
Canvas.Brush.Style := bsCross;
```

This code changes the Canvas.Brush.Color to blue. It also changes the Canvas.Brush.Style so that it fills shapes that it draws with a bsCross style as shown in Figure 10.10.

FIGURE 10.10.

TForm1.Ellipse1Click()
with a brush pattern.

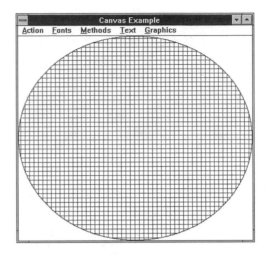

TForm1.TextRect1Click() uses the Canvas.TextRect() method to draw text inside a clipping rectangle. The clipping rectangle is passed as the first parameter to Canvas.TextRect(). In this event handler, the line

```
Canvas.TextRect(R,0,0,'Delphi Yes!');
```

passes R as the clipping rectangle. The text Delphi Yes! is drawn at location 0,0, as specified by the X and Y parameters to TextRect(). The output produced is shown in Figure 10.11.

FIGURE 10.11.

Output of the
Canvas.TextRect().

TForm1.TextSize1Click() illustrates the use of the Canvas.TextWidth() and Canvas.TextHeight() methods, both which take a string as a parameter and return the appropriate value in pixels based on the currently rendered font.

`TForm1.DrawText1Click()` contains the same code used earlier in this chapter to describe the use of Windows GDI functions. Its output is shown in Figure 10.5 (earlier in this chapter).

`TForm1.ShowBitmap1Click()` illustrates how to instantiate a `TBitMap` object and to copy its image to another canvas—in this case, the `Form1`'s canvas. This is done using `Canvas`'s `StretchDraw()` method.

The `MMISOTROPIC1Click()` method illustrates drawing with the form's canvas in the `MM_ISOTROPIC` mode. After setting the mode, we set the canvas's viewport extent to that of the form's client area with the line:

```
SetViewportExt(Canvas.Handle, ClientWidth, ClientHeight); { Set the Viewport
➥extent to }
```

We then set the origin to the center of `Form`'s client area with the call to `SetViewPortOrg()`:

```
SetViewportOrg(Canvas.Handle, ClientWidth div 2, ClientHeight div 2);
```

Now, all four quadrants of our coordinate system can be viewed. We then draw a rectangle in each plane and lastly an ellipse in the center of the client area. Notice how we can use the same values in the parameters passed to `Canvas.Rectangle()` yet draw to different areas of the canvas. This is accomplished by passing negative values to the X parameter, the Y parameter, or both parameters passed to `SetViewPortExt()`.

The `MMANISOTROPICClick()` method performs the same operations except it uses the `MM_ANISOTROPIC` mode. The purpose of showing both is to illustrate the principle difference between the `MM_ISOTROPIC` and `MM_ANISOTROPIC` mapping modes.

Using the `MM_ISOTROPIC` mode, Windows ensures that the two axes use the same physical size and makes the necessary adjustments to see this is the case. The `MM_ANISOTROPIC` mode, however, uses physical dimensions that may not be equal. Figures 10.12 and 10.13 illustrate this more clearly. You can see that the `MM_ISOTROPIC` mode ensures equality with the two axes, whereas the same code using the `MM_ANISOTROPIC` mode does not ensure equality.

FIGURE 10.12.

Example using the
MM_ISOTROPIC mode.

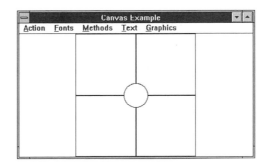

FIGURE 10.13.

Example using the
MM_ANISOTROPIC
mode.

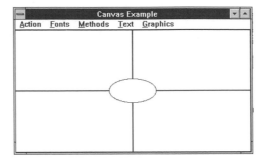

The MMLOENGLISH1Click() and MMHIENGLISH1Click() methods also perform the same code but use different mapping modes. Both result in a different size of rectangle being drawn, as shown in Figures 10.14 and 10.15. This illustrates how GDI uses different units of measurement based on the mapping mode of the Device Context.

FIGURE 10.14.

Example using the
MM_LOENGLISH mode.

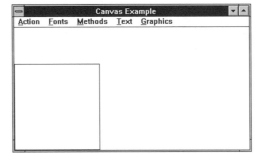

FIGURE 10.15.

Example using the
MM_HIENGLISH mode.

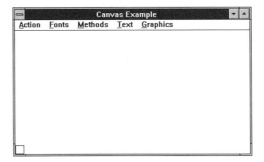

Advanced Fonts

Although the VCL enables you to manipulate fonts with relative ease, it doesn't provide the vast font-rendering capabilities provided by the Windows API. This section goes beyond the Font property and TFontDialog just presented (and also demonstrated back in Chapter 8, "MDI Applications.") It gives you a background on Windows fonts and shows you how to create your own custom fonts.

Types of Windows Fonts

There are basically two types of fonts in Windows: GDI fonts and device fonts. GDI fonts are stored in font resource files and have an extension of FON (for raster and vector fonts), or TOT and TTF (for True Type fonts). Device fonts are specific to a particular device such as a printer. Unlike with the GDI fonts, when Windows uses a device font for printing text, it only needs to send the ASCII character to the device, and the device takes care of printing the character in the specified font. Otherwise, Windows converts the font to a bitmap or performs the GDI function to draw the font. Drawing the font using bitmaps or GDI functions generally takes longer, as is the case with GDI fonts. Although device fonts are faster, they are device specific and often very limiting in what fonts a particular device supports.

Basic Font Elements

Before you learn how to use the various fonts in Windows, you should know the various terms and elements associated with Windows fonts.

A Font's Typeface, Family, and Measurements

Think of a font as just a picture or *glyph* representing a character. This character has two characteristics, a typeface and a size.

In Windows, a font's *typeface* refers to the font's style and its size. Probably the best definition of typeface and how it relates to a font is in the Windows help file. This definition says, "A typeface is a collection of characters that share design characteristics; for example, Courier is a common typeface. A font is a collection of characters that have the same typeface and size."

Windows categorizes these different typefaces into five font families: Decorative, Modern, Roman, Script, and Swiss. The distinguishing font features in these families are the font's *serifs* and *stroke widths*.

A serif is a small line at the beginning or end of a font's main strokes that give the font a finished appearance. A stroke is the primary line that makes up the font. Figure 10.16 illustrates these two features.

FIGURE 10.16.
Serifs and strokes.

Some of the typical fonts you'll find in the different font families are listed in Table 10.5.

Table 10.5. Font families and typical fonts.

Font Family	Typical Fonts
Decorative	Novelty fonts: Old English
Modern	Fonts with constant strike widths which may or may not have serifs: Pica, Elite, Courier New
Roman	Fonts with variable stroke widths and serifs: Times New Roman, New Century SchoolBook
Script	Fonts that look like handwriting: Script, Cursive
Swiss	Fonts with variable stroke widths without serifs: Arial, Helvetica

A font's size is represented in points, which are 1/72 of an inch. A font's height consists of its *ascender and descender.* The ascender and descender are represented by the tmAscent and tmDecent values as shown in Figure 10.17. Figure 10.17 shows other values essential to the character measurement as well.

FIGURE 10.17.
Character measurement values.

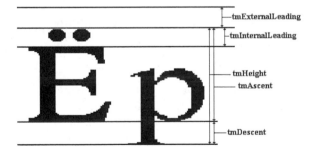

Characters reside in a character *cell,* an area surrounding the character that consists of whitespace. When referring to character measurements, keep in mind that the measurement may include both the character glyph (the character's visible portion) and the character cell. Others may refer to only one or the other.

Table 10.6 explains the meaning of the various character measurements.

Table 10.6. Character measurements.

Measurement	Meaning
external leading	The space between text lines.
internal leading	The difference between the character's glyph height and the font's cell height.
ascent	Measurement from the baseline to the top of the character cell.
descent	Measurement from the baseline to the bottom of the character cell.
point size	Character height minus the tmInternalLeading.
height	Sum on ascent, descent, and internal leading.
baseline	Line on which characters sit.

GDI Font Categories

There are essentially three separate categories of GDI fonts. These are raster fonts, vector fonts (also referred to as stroke fonts), and True Type fonts. The first two existed in previous versions of Windows, whereas the latter was introduced in Windows 3.1.

Raster Fonts Explained

Raster fonts are basically bitmaps that are provided for a specific resolution or *aspect ratio* (ratio of the pixel height and width on a given device) and font size. Because these fonts are provided in specific sizes, Windows can synthesize the font to generate a new font in the requested size, but it can do so only to produce a larger font from a smaller font. The reverse is not possible because the technique Windows uses to synthesize the fonts is to duplicate the rows and columns that make up the original font bitmap. Raster fonts are convenient when the size requested is available. They're fast to display and look good when used at the intended size. The disadvantage is that they tend to look a bit sloppy when scaled to larger sizes, as shown in Figure 10.18, which displays the Windows System font.

FIGURE 10.18.
A raster font.

Vector Fonts Explained

Vector fonts are generated by Windows with a series of lines created by GDI functions as opposed to bitmaps. These fonts offer better scalability then do raster fonts, but they have a much lower density when displayed, which may or may not be desired. Also, the performance of vector fonts is slow compared to raster fonts. Vector fonts lend themselves best to use with plotters but aren't recommended for designing appealing user interfaces. Figure 10.19 shows a typical vector font.

FIGURE 10.19.
A vector font.

True Type Fonts Explained

True Type fonts are probably the most preferred of the three font types. The advantage to True Type fonts is that they can represent virtually any style of font in any size and look pleasing to the eye. Windows displays True Type fonts by using a collection of points and hints that describe the font outline. *Hints* are simply algorithms to distort a scaled font's outline in order to improve its appearance at different resolutions. Figure 10.20 shows a True Type font.

FIGURE 10.20.
A True Type font.

Creating Your Own Fonts

So far, we've given you the general concepts surrounding Window's font technology. If your interested in getting to the many nuts and bolts about fonts, take a look at the Windows online help file on "Fonts Overview," which provides you with a vast amount of information on the topic. Now, you'll learn how to use the Windows API and Windows structures to create and display fonts of any shape and size.

Creating the Font

To illustrate the process of creating a font, we've provided the project FONTPROJ.DPR. This project's main form enables you to choose the various attributes for the font you wish to create. You then can draw the font to a TPaintBox component. You also can bring up another form that displays information about the font in that component. Figure 10.21 shows the main form for this project. Listings 10.4 and 10.5 show the code for FONTPROJ.DPR, the main form, and FONTSU.PAS, the main form's unit.

FIGURE 10.21.

FontStuffForm.

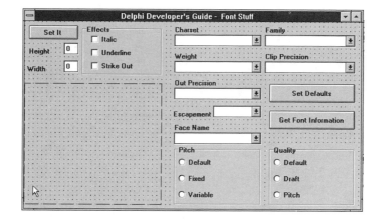

Listing 10.4. The source code for FONTPROJ.DPR.

```
program Fontproj;

uses
  Forms,
  Fontsu in 'FONTSU.PAS' {FontStuffForm},
  Fontinfu in 'FONTINFU.PAS' {FontInfoForm};

{$R *.RES}

begin
  Application.CreateForm(TFontStuffForm, FontStuffForm);
  Application.CreateForm(TFontInfoForm, FontInfoForm);
  Application.Run;
end.
```

Listing 10.5. The source code for FONTSU.PAS.

```
unit Fontsu;

interface

uses
  SysUtils, WinTypes, WinProcs, Messages, Classes, Graphics, Controls,
  Forms, Dialogs, StdCtrls, ExtCtrls, Mask;

const

{ Array to represent the TLOGFONT.lfCharSet values }
CharSetArray: array[0..4] of byte = (ANSI_CHARSET, DEFAULT_CHARSET,
  SYMBOL_CHARSET, SHIFTJIS_CHARSET, OEM_CHARSET);

{ Array to represent the TLOGFONT.lfWeight values }
WeightArray: array[0..9] of integer =
  (FW_DONTCARE, FW_THIN, FW_EXTRALIGHT, FW_LIGHT, FW_NORMAL, FW_MEDIUM,
```

continues

Listing 10.5. continued

```
  FW_SEMIBOLD, FW_BOLD, FW_EXTRABOLD, FW_HEAVY);

{ Array to represent the TLOGFONT.lfOutPrecision values }
OutPrecArray: array[0..7] of byte = (OUT_DEFAULT_PRECIS, OUT_STRING_PRECIS,
  OUT_CHARACTER_PRECIS, OUT_STROKE_PRECIS, OUT_TT_PRECIS, OUT_DEVICE_PRECIS,
  OUT_RASTER_PRECIS, OUT_TT_ONLY_PRECIS);

{ Array to represent the TLOGFONT.lfPitchAndFamily higher four-bit values }
FamilyArray: array[0..5] of byte = (FF_DONTCARE, FF_ROMAN, FF_SWISS, FF_MODERN,
  FF_SCRIPT, FF_DECORATIVE);

{ Array to represent the TLOGFONT.lfPitchAndFamily lower two-bit values }
PitchArray: array[0..2] of byte = (DEFAULT_PITCH, FIXED_PITCH, VARIABLE_PITCH);

{ Array to represent the TLOGFONT.lfClipPrecision values }
ClipPrecArray: array[0..6] of byte = (CLIP_DEFAULT_PRECIS, CLIP_CHARACTER_PRECIS,
  CLIP_STROKE_PRECIS, CLIP_MASK, CLIP_LH_ANGLES, CLIP_TT_ALWAYS, CLIP_EMBEDDED);

{ Array to represent the TLOGFONT.lfQuality values }
QualityArray: array[0..2] of byte = (DEFAULT_QUALITY, DRAFT_QUALITY,
  PROOF_QUALITY);

type
  TFontStuffForm = class(TForm)
    Button1: TButton;
    MaskEdit1: TMaskEdit;
    MaskEdit2: TMaskEdit;
    Label1: TLabel;
    Label2: TLabel;
    GroupBox1: TGroupBox;
    CBItalic: TCheckBox;
    CBUnderline: TCheckBox;
    CBStrikeOut: TCheckBox;
    CBWeight: TComboBox;
    Label3: TLabel;
    Label4: TLabel;
    CBEscapement: TComboBox;
    PaintBox1: TPaintBox;
    CBCharSet: TComboBox;
    Label5: TLabel;
    CBOutPrec: TComboBox;
    Label6: TLabel;
    CBFontFace: TComboBox;
    Pitch: TRadioGroup;
    CBFamily: TComboBox;
    Label7: TLabel;
    Label8: TLabel;
    CBClipPrec: TComboBox;
    Quality: TRadioGroup;
    Button2: TButton;
    Button3: TButton;
    Label9: TLabel;
    procedure Button1Click(Sender: TObject);
    procedure PaintBox1Paint(Sender: TObject);
    procedure Button2Click(Sender: TObject);
    procedure FormActivate(Sender: TObject);
```

```
      procedure Button3Click(Sender: TObject);
    private
      { Private declarations }
      ALogFont: TLogFont;
      AHFont: HFont;
      procedure MakeFont;
      procedure SetDefaults;
    public
      { Public declarations }
    end;

var
  FontStuffForm: TFontStuffForm;

implementation
uses fontinfu;

{$R *.DFM}

procedure TFontStuffForm.MakeFont;
begin
  fillChar(ALogFont, sizeof(TLogFont), 0);  { Clear the contents of ALogFont }
  { Set the TLOGFONT's fields }
  with ALogFont do begin
    lfHeight          := StrToInt(MaskEdit1.Text);
    lfWidth           := StrToInt(MaskEdit2.Text);
    { Heads UP! These lfEscapement and lfOrientation get set to the same value }
    { As this is significant for Win32 }
    lfEscapement      := StrToInt(CBEscapement.Items[CBEscapement.ItemIndex]);
    lfOrientation     := StrToInt(CBEscapement.Items[CBEscapement.ItemIndex]);
    lfWeight          := WeightArray[CBWeight.ItemIndex];
    lfItalic          := ord(CBItalic.Checked);
    lfUnderline       := ord(CBUnderLine.Checked);
    lfStrikeOut       := ord(CBStrikeOut.Checked);
    lfCharSet         := CharSetArray[CBCharset.ItemIndex];
    lfOutPrecision    := OutPrecArray[CBOutPrec.ItemIndex];
    lfClipPrecision   := ClipPrecArray[CBClipPrec.ItemIndex];
    lfQuality         := QualityArray[Quality.ItemIndex];
    lfPitchAndFamily  := PitchArray[Pitch.ItemIndex] or
                              FamilyArray[CBFamily.ItemIndex];
    StrPCopy(lfFaceName, CBFontFace.Items[CBFontFace.ItemIndex]);
  end;
  AHFont := CreateFontIndirect(ALogFont); { Retrieve the requested font }
  PaintBox1.Font.Handle := AHFont;        { Assign to the Font.Handle }
  PaintBox.Refresh
end;

procedure TFontStuffForm.SetDefaults;
var
 i: integer;
begin
  { Set the various conrols to default values for ALogFont }
  MaskEdit1.Text := '0';
  MaskEdit2.Text := '0';
  CBItalic.Checked := false;
  CBStrikeOut.Checked := false;
  CBUnderline.Checked := false;
  CBWeight.ItemIndex := 0;
```

continues

Listing 10.5. continued

```
  CBEscapement.ItemIndex := 0;
  CBCharset.ItemIndex := 1;
  CBOutPrec.Itemindex := 0;
  CBFamily.ItemIndex := 0;
  CBClipPrec.ItemIndex := 0;
  Pitch.ItemIndex := 0;
  Quality.ItemIndex := 0;
  { Fill CBFontFace TComboBox with the screen's fonts }
  for i := 0 to Screen.Fonts.Count -1 do
    CBFontFace.Items.Add(Screen.Fonts[i]);
  CBFontFace.ItemIndex := CBFontFace.Items.IndexOf(Font.Name);
end;

procedure TFontStuffForm.Button1Click(Sender: TObject);
begin
  MakeFont;  { Create the new font }
end;

procedure TFontStuffForm.PaintBox1Paint(Sender: TObject);
begin
  with PaintBox1 do begin
    Canvas.Rectangle(2, 2, Width-2, Height-2);                    { Draw a
➥rectangle }
    Canvas.TextOut(Width div 2, Height div 2, CBFontFace.Text);  { Write the
➥font's name }
  end;
end;

procedure TFontStuffForm.FormActivate(Sender: TObject);
begin
  SetDefaults; { Set the font's default values }
  MakeFont;    { Make the new font }
end;

procedure TFontStuffForm.Button3Click(Sender: TObject);
begin
  FontInfoForm.ShowModal;  { Show the font information form }
end;

procedure TFontStuffForm.Button2Click(Sender: TObject):
begin
  SetDefaults; { Set the font's default values }
  MakeFont;    { Make the new font }
end;

end.
```

In FONTSU.PAS, you'll see several array definitions, which are explained shortly. Notice that the form has two private variables: ALogFont and AHFont. ALogFont is of type TLOGFONT, a record structure used to describe the font to create. AHFont is the handle to the font that gets created. The private method MakeFont() is where we create the font by first filling the ALogFont structure with values specified from FontStuffForm's components, and then passing that structure to CreateFontIndirect(), which returns a font handle to the new font. Before we go on, however, you need to understand the TLOGFONT structure.

The *TLOGFONT* Structure

As stated earlier, you use the TLOGFONT structure to define the font you wish to create. This structure is defined in the WinTypes unit as follows:

```
TLogFont = record
    lfHeight: Integer;
    lfWidth: Integer;
    lfEscapement: Integer;
    lfOrientation: Integer;
    lfWeight: Integer;
    lfItalic: Byte;
    lfUnderline: Byte;
    lfStrikeOut: Byte;
    lfCharSet: Byte;
    lfOutPrecision: Byte;
    lfClipPrecision: Byte;
    lfQuality: Byte;
    lfPitchAndFamily: Byte;
    lfFaceName: array[0..lf_FaceSize - 1] of Char;
  end;
```

You place values in the TLOGFONT's fields that specify the attributes you want your font to have. Each field represents a different type of attribute. By default, most of the fields can be set to zero, which is what the Set Defaults button on the FontStuffForm does. In this instance, Windows chooses the attributes for the font and returns whatever it pleases. The general rule is this: The more fields you fill in, the more you can fine tune your font style. The following list explains what each TLOGFONT field represents. Some of the fields may be assigned constant values that are pre-defined in the WINTYPES unit. Refer to Windows help for a detailed description of these values; we show you only the most commonly used ones here:

Field Value	Description
lfHeight	The font height. A value greater than zero indicates a cell height. A value less than zero indicates the glyph height (the cell height minus the internal leading). Set to zero to let Windows decide a height for you.
lfWidth	The average font width. Set to zero to let Windows choose a font width for you.
lfEscapement	The angle (in tenths of degrees) with which to draw the font. A zero value draws the font normally—from left to right. Increasing this value draws the font in a counter-clockwise manner. The value 900 draws the font straight up, whereas 1800 draws it upside down, from right to left. This is available only with true type fonts.

Field Value	Description
lfOrientation	Enables you to specify an angle at which to draw individual characters. This value is ignored with the current version of Windows; however, it will be used in later versions. Make sure to specify the same value as set for lfEscapement because this is significant in Win32.
lfWeight	This affects the font density. WINTYPES defines several constants for this field such as FW_BOLD and FW_NORMAL. Set to FW_DONTCARE to let Windows choose a weight for you.
lfItalic	Non-zero means italic, and zero means non-italic.
lfUnderline	Non-zero means underlined, and zero means not underlined.
lfStrikeOut	Non-zero means that a line gets drawn through the font, whereas zero does not draw a line through the font.
lfCharSet	Windows defines the character sets: ANSI_CHARSET=0, DEFAULT_CHARSET=1, SYMBOL_CHARSET=2, SHIFTJIS_CHARSET=128, and OEM_CHARSET = 255. Use the ANSI_CHARSET by default.
lfOutPrecision	Specifies how Windows should match the requested font's size and characteristics to an actual font. Use TT_ONLY_PRECIS to specify only true type fonts. Other types are defined in the WINTYPES unit.
lfClipPrecision	Specifies how windows clips characters outside of a clipping region. Use CLIP_DEFAULT_PRECIS to let Windows choose.
lfQuality	Defines the font's output quality as GDI will draw it. Use DEFAULT_QUALITY to let Windows decide or you may specify PROOF_QUALITY of DRAFT_QUALITY.
lfPitchAndFamily	Defines the font's pitch in the two low-order bits. Specifies the family in the higher four high-order bits. Table 10.5 displays these families.
lfFaceName	The typeface name of the font.

The MakeFont() procedure uses the values defined in the constant section of the FONTU.PAS unit. These array constants contain the various pre-defined constant values for the TLOGFONT structure. These values are placed in the same order as the order of the choices in FontStuffForm's TComboBoxes. For example, the choices for the font family in the CBFamily TComboBox shown in Figure 10.22 are in the same order as the values in the FamilyArray. We used this technique to reduce the code required to set the TLOGFONT structure.

FIGURE 10.22.

CBFamily TComboBox.

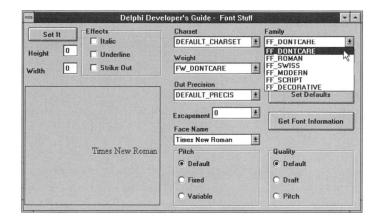

Examine the first line in MakeFont():

```
fillChar(ALogFont, sizeof(TLogFont), 0);
```

This clears the ALogFont before we set any values. When ALogFont has been set, the line:

```
AHFont := CreateFontIndirect(ALogFont);
```

calls the Windows API function CreateFontIndirect(), which accepts the TLOGFONT structure as a parameter and returns a handle to the requested font. This handle is then set to the TPaintBox.Font's handle property. Delphi takes care of destroying the TPaintBox's previous font before making the assignment. Once the assignment is made, we redraw PaintBox1 by calling its Invalidate() method.

The SetDefaults() method initializes the TLOGFONT structure with default values. This method is called when FontStuffForm first comes up and whenever the user presses the Set Defaults button. You might experiment with the FONTPROJ project a bit to see the different effects you can get with font, as shown in Figure 10.23.

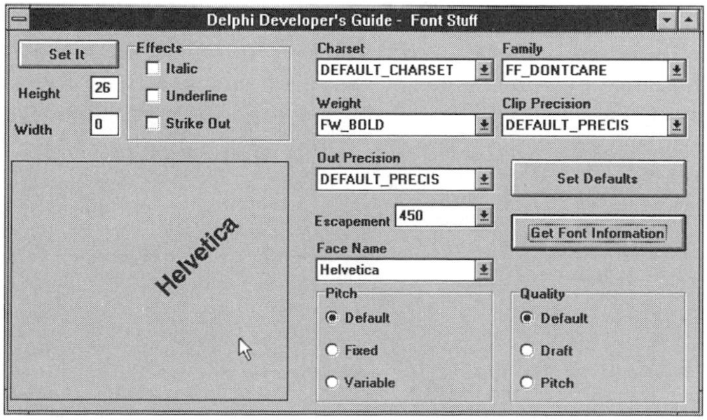

FIGURE 10.23.

FONTPROJ running with a rotated font.

Displaying Font Information

FontStuffForm's Get Font Information button invokes the FontInfoForm, which displays information about the font in FontStuffForm.PaintBox1. When you specify font attributes in the TLOGFONT structure, Windows attempts to provide you with a font that best resembles your requested font. It's entirely possible that the font you get back from the CreateFontIndirect() function has completely different attributes than what you requested. FontInfoForm lets you inspect your selected font's attributes. It uses the Windows API function GetTextMetrics() to retrieve the font information.

GetTextMetrics() takes two parameters, the handle to the device context whose font you want to examine, and a reference to another Windows structure, TTEXTMETRIC. GetTextMetrics() then updates the TTEXTMETRIC structure with information about the given font. The WINTYPES unit defines the TTEXTMETRIC record as follows:

```
TTextMetric = record
    tmHeight: Integer;
    tmAscent: Integer;
    tmDescent: Integer;
    tmInternalLeading: Integer;
    tmExternalLeading: Integer;
    tmAveCharWidth: Integer;
    tmMaxCharWidth: Integer;
    tmWeight: Integer;
    tmItalic: Byte;
    tmUnderlined: Byte;
    tmStruckOut: Byte;
    tmFirstChar: Byte;
    tmLastChar: Byte;
    tmDefaultChar: Byte;
    tmBreakChar: Byte;
    tmPitchAndFamily: Byte;
    tmCharSet: Byte;
    tmOverhang: Integer;
    tmDigitizedAspectX: Integer;
    tmDigitizedAspectY: Integer;
end;
```

The TTEXTMETRIC record's fields contain much of the information about a font that we've already discussed. For example, it shows the font's height, average character width, and whether or not the font is underlined, italicized, or struck out, just to name a few. Refer to the Windows API online help for detailed information on the TTEXTMETRIC structure. Listing 10.6 shows the code for FONTINFU.PAS, the font information form.

Listing 10.6. The source code for FONTINFU.PAS.

```
unit Fontinfu;

interface

uses
  SysUtils, WinTypes, WinProcs, Messages, Classes, Graphics, Controls,
  Forms, Dialogs, ExtCtrls, StdCtrls;
```

```
type

  FontInfoRec = record
    Characteristic,
    Value: string;
  end;

  TFontInfoForm = class(TForm)
    ListBox1: TListBox;
    procedure FormActivate(Sender: TObject);
  private
    { Private declarations }
  public
    { Public declarations }
  end;

var
  FontInfoForm: TFontInfoForm;

implementation
uses Fontsu; { Make sure to add fontsu to the uses statement }

{$R *.DFM}

procedure TFontInfoForm.FormActivate(Sender: TObject);
const
  PITCH_MASK: byte = $0F;  { Set the lower order four bits }
  FAMILY_MASK: byte = $F0; { Set to higher order four bits }
var
  TxMetric: TTextMetric;
  FaceName: array[0..lf_FaceSize - 1] of Char;
  PitchTest, FamilyTest: byte;
begin
    { First get the font information }
    with FontStuffForm.PaintBox1.Canvas do begin
      GetTextFace(Handle, strlen(FaceName), FaceName); { Get the font's name }
      GetTextMetrics(Handle, TxMetric);                { Fill the TEXTMETRIC }
    end;                                               { structure }

  { Now add the font information to the listbox }
  with ListBox1.Items, TxMetric do begin
    Clear;  { Clear the listbox from previous entries }
    { Add the elements from the TTEXTMETRIC structure }
    Add('Font face name:    '+StrPas(FaceName));
    Add('tmHeight:      '+IntToStr(tmHeight));
    Add('tmAscent:      '+IntToStr(tmAscent));
    Add('tmDescent:      '+IntToStr(tmDescent));
    Add('tmInternalLeading:    '+IntToStr(tmInternalLeading));
    Add('tmExternalLeading:    '+IntToStr(tmExternalLeading));
    Add('tmAveCharWidth:    '+IntToStr(tmAveCharWidth));
    Add('tmMaxCharWidth:    '+IntToStr(tmMaxCharWidth));
    Add('tmWeight:      '+IntToStr(tmWeight));

    if tmItalic <> 0  then Add('tmItalic:    '+'YES')
    else Add('tmItalic:    '+'NO');
```

continues

Listing 10.6. continued

```
      if tmUnderlined <> 0 then Add('tmUnderlined:       '+'YES')
      else Add('tmUnderlined:       '+'NO');

      if tmStruckOut <> 0 then Add('tmStruckOut:       '+'YES')
      else Add('tmStruckOut:       '+'NO');

      { Check the font's pitch type }
      PitchTest := tmPitchAndFamily and PITCH_MASK;
      if (PitchTest and TMPF_FIXED_PITCH) <> 0 then
        Add('tmPitchAndFamily-Pitch: '+'Fixed Pitch');
      if (PitchTest and TMPF_VECTOR) <> 0 then
        Add('tmPitchAndFamily-Pitch: '+'Vector');
      if (PitchTest and TMPF_TRUETYPE) <> 0 then
        Add('tmPitchAndFamily-Pitch: '+'True type');
      if (PitchTest and TMPF_DEVICE) <> 0 then
        Add('tmPitchAndFamily-Pitch: '+'Device');
      if PitchTest = 0 then
        Add('tmPitchAndFamily-Pitch: '+'Unknown');


      { Check the fonts family type }
      FamilyTest := tmPitchAndFamily and FAMILY_MASK;
      if (FamilyTest and FF_ROMAN) <> 0 then
        Add('tmPitchAndFamily-Family: '+'FF_ROMAN');
      if (FamilyTest and FF_SWISS) <> 0 then
        Add('tmPitchAndFamily-Family: '+'FF_SWISS');
      if (FamilyTest and FF_MODERN) <> 0 then
        Add('tmPitchAndFamily-Family: '+'FF_MODERN');
      if (FamilyTest and FF_SCRIPT) <> 0 then
        Add('tmPitchAndFamily-Family: '+'FF_SCRIPT');
      if (FamilyTest and FF_DECORATIVE) <> 0 then
        Add('tmPitchAndFamily-Family: '+'FF_DECORATIVE');
      if FamilyTest = 0 then
        Add('tmPitchAndFamily-Family: '+'Unknown');

      Add('tmCharSet:       '+IntToStr(tmCharSet));
      Add('tmOverhang:      '+IntToStr(tmOverhang));
      Add('tmDigitizedAspectX:      '+IntToStr(tmDigitizedAspectX));
      Add('tmDigitizedAspectY:      '+IntToStr(tmDigitizedAspectY));
    end;
end;

end.
```

FontInfoForm's OnActivate event handler first retrieves the font's name with the Windows API function GetTextFace(), which takes a device context, a buffer size, and a Pchar buffer as parameters. FormActivate() then uses GetTextMetrics() to fill TxMetric, a TTEXTMETRIC record structure, for FontStuffForm.PaintBox1's rendered font. The event handler then adds the values in TxMetric to the listbox as strings. For tmPitchAndFamily value, we mask out the high- or low-order bit depending on the value we're testing for and add the appropriate values to the listbox. Figure 10.24 shows the FontInfoForm displaying information about a font.

FIGURE 10.24.

FontInfoForm.

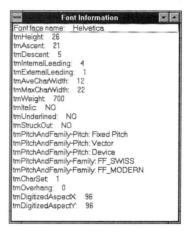

Summary

This chapter presented you with a lot of information about the Windows Graphics Device Interface. You learned about Delphi's TCanvas and about Canvas's properties and drawing methods. You also learned about Delphi's representation of images with its TImage component, and you learned about mapping modes and Windows coordinate systems. Finally, you learned about fonts—how to create them and how to display information about them. One of the nice things about the GDI is that working with it can be a lot of fun. Take some time to experiment with the drawing routines, create your own fonts, or just fool around with the mapping modes to see what type of effects you can get. The next chapter presents you with one of the most exciting aspects of Delphi, writing custom components.

11

Writing Delphi Custom Components

The capability to easily write custom components in Delphi is a chief productivity advantage that you wield over other programmers. In most other environments, folks are stuck using the standard controls available through Windows or using complex-to-write VBX controls that someone else created. Being able to incorporate your custom components into your Delphi applications means that you have complete control over the application's user interface. Custom controls give you the final say in your application's look and feel.

If your forte is component design, you will appreciate all the information this chapter has to offer. You will learn about all aspects of component design from concept to integration into the Delphi environment. You also will learn about the pitfalls of component design, as well as some tips and tricks to developing highly functional and extensible components.

Even if your primary interest is application development and not component design, you will get a great deal out of this chapter. Incorporating a custom component or two into your programs is an ideal way to spice up and enhance the productivity of your applications. Invariably, you will get caught in a situation while writing your application where, of all the components at your disposal, none is quite right for some particular task. That's where component design comes in. You are able to tailor a component to meet your exact needs, and hopefully design it smart enough to use again and again in subsequent applications.

Deciding Whether to Write a Custom Component

Why go through the trouble of writing a custom control in the first place when it's probably less work to make do with an existing component or hack together something quick and dirty that "will do?" There are a number of reasons to write your own custom control:

- You want to design a new user-interface element that can be used in more than one application.

- You want to make your application more robust by separating its elements into logical object-oriented classes.

- You cannot find an existing Delphi component or VBX control that suits your needs for a particular situation.

- You recognize a market for a particular component, and you want to create a component to share with other Delphi developers for fun or profit.

- You want to increase your knowledge of Delphi, VCL internals, and the Windows API.

One of the best ways to learn how to create custom components is from the people who invented them. Delphi's VCL source code is an invaluable resource for component writers, and it is highly recommended for anyone who is serious about creating custom components. If you don't have Delphi's VCL source code, get it.

Writing Custom Components

Writing custom components can seem like a pretty daunting task, but don't believe the hype. Writing a custom component is only as hard or as easy as you make it. Components can be tough to write, of course, but you also can create very useful components fairly easily.

Creating a *TRunButton*

As an illustration of the ease with which you can create custom components, you'll jump in and write a special descendant of a button that enables you to execute a program. Start by choosing File | New Component. This brings up the Component Expert dialog box. As the class name of this component, you will use TRunButton. From the drop-down list, select TSpeedButton as the Ancestor Type. You will put the new component on a palette page called DDG. The completed Component Expert dialog box is shown in Figure 11.1.

FIGURE 11.1.

The Component Expert dialog box for TRunButton.

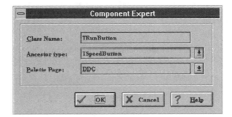

Delphi will create a component skeleton unit, as shown in Listing 11.1.

Listing 11.1. The TRunButton component skeleton unit.

```
unit Unit2;

interface

uses
  SysUtils, WinTypes, WinProcs, Messages, Classes, Graphics, Controls,
  Forms, Dialogs, Buttons;

type
  TRunButton = class(TSpeedButton)
  private
    { Private declarations }
  protected
    { Protected declarations }
  public
    { Public declarations }
  published
    { Published declarations }
  end;
```

continues

Listing 11.1. continued

```
procedure Register;

implementation

procedure Register;
begin
  RegisterComponents('DDG', [TRunButton]);
end;

end.
```

Adding Code to the Skeleton

First, save the unit as BUTTRUN.PAS. Then add a private string field called FCommandLine to this component. FCommandLine will hold the command line of the program you want to execute. In order to be able to modify that field in the Object Inspector, you need to add a published property to access FCommandLine. This property will be called CommandLine, and it will read from and write to the FCommandLine field.

Finally, when the button is clicked, you need to be able to execute the program given in FCommandLine. For that, you will override the Click() method of TSpeedButton. The Click() method is called every time the button is clicked with the left mouse button.

Based on the description of TRunButton thus far, the following code shows the class definition.

```
type
  TRunButton = class(TSpeedButton)
  private
    FCommandLine: String;
  public
    procedure Click; override;
  published
    property CommandLine: String read FCommandLine write FCommandLine;
  end;
```

Now you just have to define the overridden Click() method. The overridden method is shown with the rest of the completed component in Listing 11.2.

NOTE

When writing components, the convention is to make private field names begin with the letter *F*. For components and types in general, give the object or type a name starting with the letter *T*. Your code will be much more clear if you follow these simple conventions.

Listing 11.2. The BUTTRUN unit.

```
unit ButtRun;

interface

uses
  SysUtils, WinTypes, WinProcs, Classes, Buttons;

type
  ERunError = class(Exception);

  TRunButton = class(TSpeedButton)
  private
    FCommandLine: String;
  public
    procedure Click; override;
  published
    property CommandLine: String read FCommandLine write FCommandLine;
  end;

procedure Register;

implementation

procedure TRunButton.Click;
var
  WERetVal: word;
begin
  { do the default behavior }
  inherited Click;
  { if string is at maximum, then reduce size by one.  This shouldn't hurt }
  { anything, since 255 is larger than the maximum DOS command line.  This }
  { is mainly a safety precaution. }
  if FCommandLine[0] = #255 then
    FCommandLine[0] := #254;
  { Add a null terminator to the end of the string so we can emulate a PChar }
  FCommandLine[Length(FCommandLine) + 1] := #0;
  { Call the WinExec() API function. Passing the address of element 1 makes }
  { this string look like a PChar }
  WERetVal := WinExec(@FCommandLine[1], sw_ShowNormal);
  { a return value of less than 32 indicates error.  Raise exception on error }
  if WERetVal < 32 then
    raise ERunError.Create('Error executing program.  Code: ' +
                            IntToStr(WERetVal));  inherited Click;
end;

procedure Register;
begin
  RegisterComponents('DDG', [TRunButton]);
end;
```

The Windows API WinExec() function is used to execute another program. Because the first parameter to WinExec() is a PChar-type string, you "trick" the compiler into thinking a string is a PChar by appending a #0 character to the end of the string and passing the address of the first element (remember, the 0th element is the size of the string).

Notice, too, that an exception type for this component is created. Because none of the exception classes already provided by VCL seem to fit the bill, it's common to create your own exception types as was done for the TRunButton component.

The TRunButton component now is ready to add to the Component palette. This component is discussed later as a part of the PIM shown in Part III, "Real-World Applications." The important thing is that you now see how easy it can be to create Delphi custom components.

Developing a Component

This section will walk you through the steps involved in developing a custom component. You'll find that a logical approach to Delphi custom component development will save you time and code in the long run.

Step One: Come Up with an Idea

Often, the most difficult part about creating a custom Delphi component is coming up with an idea of what kind of component to create. The best way to come up with ideas for custom components is to sit down and write Delphi applications. At some point while developing the application, you may think, "Hey, it would be great to have a component that does this," or, "It seems like there's a better approach to this problem." Without actually getting your hands dirty, it's difficult to come up with ideas for new components.

Step Two: Create a Game Plan

Now that you have an idea, you need a game plan for implementing the idea. Developing the game plan is a two-step process. When formulating the game plan, you first must determine how the component will be implemented and what other components or other elements you will need to help make your component come to life. Questions such as, "Will the component be visual or nonvisual?" and "Will the component be used at design time or only in code?" need to be addressed at this time.

After you know what you need to do in order to make the component, you can determine the exact implementation of the component. This includes issues such as what component you will descend from and how to create any supporting components or elements. Table 11.1 offers a bit of guidance in choosing the right descendant for your custom component.

Table 11.1. VCL classes as custom component base classes.

VCL Class	Types of Custom Controls
TObject	Although classes descending directly from TObject are not components, strictly speaking, they do merit mention. You will use TObject as a base class for many things that you don't need to work with at design time. A good example is the TIniFile object.
TComponent	A starting point for many nonvisual components. Its forte is that it offers built in streaming capability to load and save itself in the IDE at design time.
TGraphicControl	Use this class when you want to create a custom component that has no Window handle. TGraphicControl descendants are drawn on their parent's client surface, so they are easier on resources.
TWinControl	This is the base class for all components that require a window handle. It provides you with common properties and events you need to access Window concepts.
TCustomControl	This class descends from TWinControl. It introduces the concepts of a canvas and a Paint() method to give you greater control over the component's appearance. Use this class for most of your window-handled custom component needs.
TCustomXxx, a "custom" version of an existing class	Use these classes when you want to "unpublish" properties found in the regular version of each component. The custom classes do not publish all their properties, but leave it up to descendant classes.
TXxx, an existing class such as TEdit, Tpanel, or TScrollBox	Use an already established component as a base class for your custom components when you want to extend the behavior of an existing control rather than create a new one from scratch. Most of your custom components will fall into this category.

Step Three: Write the Code

After you have formulated a solid game plan for writing a component, you should put the plan into effect by writing code for your component and any collateral elements. You will find the coding much easier when you follow through completely with steps one and two, rather than jumping right to the coding.

Extending the *TListbox* Component

VCL's TListbox component is merely an Object Pascal wrapper around the standard Windows API listbox control. Although it does do a fair job encapsulating most of that functionality, there is a little bit of room for improvement. This section will take you through the steps in creating a custom component based on TListbox.

The Idea and Game Plan

The idea for this component, like most, was borne out of necessity. A listbox was needed with the capability to use tab stops (which is supported in the Windows API, but not in a TListbox), and a horizontal scrollbar was needed to view strings that were longer than the listbox width (also supported by the API but not a TListbox). This component will be called a TTabListbox.

The game plan for the TTabListbox component isn't terribly complex; you just have to descend from a TListbox, create the correct field properties, and override and introduce the correct methods to achieve the behavior for which you're searching.

The Code

The first step in creating a scrollable listbox with tab stops is to include those window styles in the TTabListbox's style when the listbox window is created. The window styles you need to use are lbs_UseTabStops for tabs and ws_HScroll to allow a horizontal scrollbar. When you need to add window styles to a descendant of TWinControl, you do so by overriding the CreateParams() method, as shown in the following code:

```
procedure TTabListbox.CreateParams(var Params: TCreateParams);
begin
  inherited CreateParams(Params);
  Params.Style := Params.Style or lbs_UseTabStops or ws_HScroll;
end;
```

CREATEPARAMS()

Whenever you need to modify any of the parameters—such as style or window class—that are passed to the CreateWindowEx() API function, you should do so in the CreateParams() method. CreateWindowEx() is the function used to create the window handle associated with a `TWinControl` descendant. By overriding `CreateParams()`, you can control the creation of a window on the API level.

CreateParams accepts one parameter of type `TCreateParams`, which follows:

```
type
  TCreateParams = record
    Caption: PChar;
    Style: Longint;
    ExStyle: Longint;
    X, Y: Integer;
    Width, Height: Integer;
    WndParent: HWND;
    Param: Pointer
    WindowClass: TWndClass;
    WinClassName: array[0..63] of Char;
  end;
```

As a component writer, you will override `CreateParams()` frequently—whenever you need to control the creation of a component on the API level. Make sure that you call the inherited `CreateParams()` first in order to fill up the `Params` record for you.

To set the tab stops, you can have the `TTabListbox` perform an `lb_SetTabStops` message, passing the number of tab stops and a pointer to an array of tabs as the `wParam` and `lParam` (these two variables will be stored in the class as `FNumTabStops` and `FTabStops`). The only catch is that listbox tab stops are handled in a unit of measure called *dialog box units*. Because dialog box units don't make sense for the Delphi programmer, you will surface tabs only in pixels. With the help of the `PixDlg` unit shown in Listing 11.3, you can convert back and forth between dialog box units and screen pixels in both the X and Y planes.

Listing 11.3. The source code for PIXDLG.PAS.

```
unit Pixdlg;

interface

function DialogUnitsToPixelsX(DlgUnits: word): word;
function DialogUnitsToPixelsY(DlgUnits: word): word;
function PixelsToDialogUnitsX(PixUnits: word): word;
function PixelsToDialogUnitsY(PixUnits: word): word;

implementation

uses WinProcs;

function DialogUnitsToPixelsX(DlgUnits: word): word;
begin
  Result := (DlgUnits * LoWord(GetDialogBaseUnits)) div 4;
end;

function DialogUnitsToPixelsY(DlgUnits: word): word;
```

continues

Listing 11.3. continued

```
begin
  Result := (DlgUnits * HiWord(GetDialogBaseUnits)) div 8;
end;

function PixelsToDialogUnitsX(PixUnits: word): word;
begin
  Result := PixUnits * 4 div LoWord(GetDialogBaseUnits);
end;

function PixelsToDialogUnitsY(PixUnits: word): word;
begin
  Result := PixUnits * 8 div HiWord(GetDialogBaseUnits);
end;

end.
```

After you know the tab stops, you can know the extent of the horizontal scrollbar. The scrollbar should extend at least to the end of the longest string in the listbox. Luckily, the Windows API provides a function called `GetTabbedTextExtent()` that retrieves just the information you need. After you know the length of the longest string, you can set the scrollbar range by performing the `lb_SetHorizontalExtent` message, passing the desired extent as the `wParam`.

You also need to write message handlers for some special Windows' messages. In particular, you need to handle the messages that control inserting and deleting, because you need to be able to measure the length of any new string or know when a long string has been deleted. The messages you're concerned with are `lb_AddString`, `lb_InsertString`, and `lb_DeleteString`. Listing 11.4 contains the source code for the `LBTAB` unit, which contains the `TTabListbox` component.

Listing 11.4. The source code for LBTAB.PAS.

```
unit Lbtab;

interface

uses
  SysUtils, WinTypes, WinProcs, Messages, Classes, Controls, StdCtrls;

type
  ETabListboxError = class(Exception);

  TTabListbox = class(TListBox)
  private
    FLongestString: Word;
    FNumTabStops: Word;
    FTabStops: PWord;
    FSizeAfterDel: Boolean;
    function GetLBStringLength(P: PChar): word;
    procedure FindLongestString;
    procedure SetScrollLength(P: PChar);
    procedure LBAddString(var Msg: TMessage); message lb_AddString;
```

```pascal
    procedure LBInsertString(var Msg: TMessage); message lb_InsertString;
    procedure LBDeleteString(var Msg: TMessage); message lb_DeleteString;
  protected
    procedure CreateParams(var Params: TCreateParams); override;
  public
    constructor Create(AOwner: TComponent); override;
    procedure SetTabStops(A: array of word);
  published
    property SizeAfterDel: Boolean read FSizeAfterDel write FSizeAfterDel
              default True;
  end;

procedure Register;

implementation

uses PixDlg;

constructor TTabListbox.Create(AOwner: TComponent);
begin
  inherited Create(AOwner);
  FSizeAfterDel := True;
  { set tab stops to Windows defaults... }
  FNumTabStops := 1;
  GetMem(FTabStops, SizeOf(Word) * FNumTabStops);
  FTabStops^ := DialogUnitsToPixelsX(32);
end;

procedure TTabListbox.SetTabStops(A: array of word);
{ This procedure sets the listbox's tabstops to those specified in the open }
{ array of word, A.  New tabstops are in pixels, and must be in ascending   }
{ order.  An exception will be raised if new tabs fail to set.              }
var
  i: word;
  TempTab: word;
  TempBuf: PWord;
begin
  { Store new values in temps in case exception occurs in setting tabs }
  TempTab := High(A) + 1;                   { Figure number of tabstops }
  GetMem(TempBuf, SizeOf(A));               { Allocate new tabstops }
  Move(A, TempBuf^, SizeOf(A));             { copy new tabstops }
  { convert from pixels to dialog units, and... }
  for i := 0 to TempTab - 1 do
    A[i] := PixelsToDialogUnitsX(A[i]);
  { Send new tabstops to listbox.  Note that we must use dialog units. }
  if Perform(lb_SetTabStops, TempTab, Longint(@A)) = 0 then begin
    { if zero, then failed to set new tabstops }
    FreeMem(TempBuf, SizeOf(Word) * TempTab);  { Free temp tabstop buffer }
    raise ETabListboxError.Create('Failed to set tabs.') { raise exception }
  end
  else begin
    { if nonzero, then new tabstops set okay, so... }
    FreeMem(FTabStops, SizeOf(Word) * FNumTabStops); { Free previous tabstops }
    { copy values from temps... }
    FNumTabStops := TempTab;                 { set number of tabstops }
    FTabStops := TempBuf;                     { set tabstop buffer }
    FindLongestString;                        { reset scrollbar }
```

continues

Listing 11.4. continued

```
    Invalidate;                                  { repaint }
  end;
end;

procedure TTabListbox.CreateParams(var Params: TCreateParams);
{ We must OR in the styles necessary for tabs and horizontal scrolling }
{ These styles will be used by the API CreateWindowEx() function.      }
begin
  inherited CreateParams(Params);
  { lbs_UseTabStops style allows tabs in listbox }
  { ws_HScroll style allows horizontal scrollbar in listbox }
  Params.Style := Params.Style or lbs_UseTabStops or ws_HScroll;
end;

function TTabListbox.GetLBStringLength(P: PChar): word;
{ This function returns the length of the listbox string P in pixels }
begin
  { Get the length of the text string }
  Result := LoWord(GetTabbedTextExtent(Canvas.Handle, P, StrLen(P),
                   FNumTabStops, FTabStops^));
  { Add a little bit of space to the end of the scrollbar extent for looks }
  Inc(Result, GetTextExtent(Canvas.Handle, 'x', 1));
end;

procedure TTabListbox.SetScrollLength(P: PChar);
{ This procedure resets the scrollbar extent if P is longer than the }
{ previous longest string                                           }
var
  Extent: Word;
begin
  Extent := GetLBStringLength(P);
  { If this turns out to be the longest string... }
  if Extent > FLongestString then begin
    FLongestString := Extent;                    { reset longest string }
    Perform(lb_SetHorizontalExtent, Extent, 0);  { reset scrollbar extent }
  end;
end;

procedure TTabListbox.LBInsertString(var Msg: TMessage);
{ This procedure is called in response to a lb_InsertString message.  This   }
{ message is sent to the listbox everytime a string is inserted.  Msg.lParam }
{ holds a pointer to the null-terminated string being inserted.  This        }
{ will cause the scrollbar length to be adjusted if the new string is        }
{ longer than any of the existing strings.                                   }
begin
  inherited;
  SetScrollLength(PChar(Msg.lParam));
end;

procedure TTabListbox.LBAddString(var Msg: TMessage);
{ This procedure is called in response to a lb_AddString message.  This   }
{ message is sent to the listbox everytime a string is added.  Msg.lParam }
{ holds a pointer to the null-terminated string being added.  This        }
{ will cause the scrollbar length to be adjusted if the new string is     }
{ longer than any of the existing strings.                                }
begin
```

```
  inherited;
  SetScrollLength(PChar(Msg.lParam));
end;

procedure TTabListbox.FindLongestString;
var
  i: word;
  Strg: String;
begin
  FLongestString := 0;
  { iterate through strings and look for new longest string }
  for i := 0 to Items.Count - 1 do begin
    Strg := Items[i];
    { truncate if string is 255 chars, and add null }
    if Strg[0] = #255 then Strg[0] := #254; { Str[0] for speed }
    Strg[Ord(Strg[0]) + 1] := #0;           { Str[0] for speed }
    SetScrollLength(@Strg[1]);
  end;
end;

procedure TTabListbox.LBDeleteString(var Msg: TMessage);
{ This procedure is called in response to a lb_DeleteString message.  This   }
{ message is sent to the listbox everytime a string is deleted.  Msg.wParam  }
{ holds the index of the item being deleted.  Note that by setting the       }
{ SizeAfterDel property to False, you can cause the scrollbar update to not   }
{ occur.  This will improve performance if you're doing a lot of deletes.    }
var
  Str: String;
begin
  if FSizeAfterDel then begin
    Str := Items[Msg.wParam] + #0;                { Get string to be deleted }
    inherited;                                    { Delete string }
    { Is deleted string the longest? }
    if GetLBStringLength(@Str[1]) = FLongestString then
      FindLongestString;
  end
  else
    inherited;
end;

procedure Register;
begin
  RegisterComponents('DDG', [TTabListbox]);
end;

end.
```

CAUTION

Don't try to override existing constructors with new ones that take different parameters. It's okay to have more than one constructor that takes different parameters—just make sure that you give each constructor a unique name.

One particular point of interest in this component is the `SetTabStops()` method, which accepts an open array of `word` as a parameter. This enables users to pass in as many tab stops as they want. For example,

```
TabListboxInstance.SetTabStops([50, 75, 150, 300]);
```

If the text in the listbox extends beyond the viewable window, then the horizontal scrollbar will appear automatically.

Creating a Marquee

Once upon a time, while writing a Delphi application, we thought to ourselves, "This is a really cool application, but our About dialog box is kind of boring. We need something to spice it up a little." The light bulb came on, and the idea for a new component was born: We would create a scrolling credits marquee window to incorporate into our About dialog boxes.

Analyzing How Your Component Will Work

Take a moment to analyze how the `Marquee` component will work. The marquee control should be able to take a bunch of strings and scroll them across the component on command like a real-life marquee. You will use `TCustomPanel` as the base class for the `TMarquee` component, because it already has the basic built-in functionality you need, including a pretty 3D, beveled border.

`TMarquee` will paint some text strings to a bitmap residing in memory, and then copy portions of the memory bitmap to its own canvas to simulate a scrolling effect. It will do this using the `BitBlt()` API function to copy a component-sized portion of the memory canvas to the component starting at the top. Then it will move down a couple of pixels on the memory canvas and copy that image to the control, move down again, copy again, and repeat the process over and over so that the entire contents of the memory canvas appear to scroll through the component. This logic is illustrated in Figure 11.2.

Now is the time to identify any additional classes you might need to integrate into the `TMarquee` component in order to bring it to life. There are really only two such classes. First, you need a `TStringList` class to hold all the strings you want to scroll. Also, you must have a memory bitmap on which you can render all the text strings. VCL's own `TBitmap` component will do nicely for that.

Now it's time to put the game plan into effect. Start a new Delphi component project, and in the Component Expert dialog box, type `TMarquee` for the Class Name, select `TCustomControl` as the Ancestor Type, and select Samples as the Palette page. Click the OK button, and Delphi creates a new unit that contains a skeleton class definition for `TMarquee`. Save this file as MARQUEE.PAS.

FIGURE 11.2.

How the TMarquee *component works.*

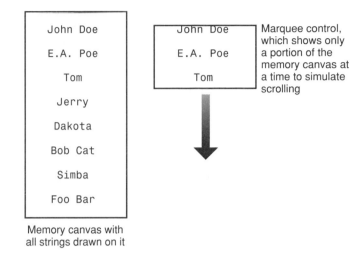

Memory canvas with
all strings drawn on it

Marquee control,
which shows only
a portion of the
memory canvas at
a time to simulate
scrolling

Writing the Component

As with the previous components in this chapter, the code for TMarquee should be approached with a logical plan of attack. In this case, break up the code work into reasonable parts. The TMarquee component can be divided into five major parts as shown here:

1. The mechanism that renders the text onto the memory canvas.
2. The mechanism that copies the text from the memory canvas to the marquee window.
3. The timer that keeps track of when and how to scroll the window.
4. The class constructor, destructor, and associated methods.
5. The finishing touches: various helper properties and methods.

Using the Memory Canvas

When creating an instance of TBitmap, you need to know how big it needs to be so that it has room to hold the entire list of strings in memory. Do this first by figuring out how high each line of text will be, and then multiplying by the number of lines. To find the height and spacing of a line of text in a particular font, use the GetTextMetrics() API function by passing in the canvas's handle and a TTextMetric record to be filled in by the function:

```
var
  Metrics: TTextMetric;
begin
  GetTextMetrics(Canvas.Handle, Metrics);
```

> **NOTE**
>
> The GetTextMetrics() API function modifies a TTextMetric record that contains a great deal of quantitative information about a device context's currently selected font. This function gives you information not only on font height and width, but also on whether the font is in boldface, italicized, or struck out, or what the character set name is.
>
> The TextHeight() method of TCanvas wouldn't work here, because that method only determines the height of a specific line of text, rather than general spacing for a font.

The height of a character cell in canvas's current font is given by the tmHeight field of the Metric record. If you add to that value the tmInternalLeading field—to allow for some space between lines—you get the height for each line of text to be drawn on the memory canvas:

```
LineHi := Metrics.tmHeight + Metrics.tmInternalLeading;
```

The height necessary for the memory canvas then can be determined by multiplying LineHi by the number of lines of text and adding that value to two times the height of the TMarquee control (to create the blank space at the beginning and end of the marquee). Suppose that the TStringList in which all the strings live is called FItems; now place the memory canvas dimensions in a TRect structure:

```
var
  VRect: TRect;
begin
  with VRect do begin          { rectangle represents entire memory canvas }
    Top := 0;
    Left := 0;
    Right := Width;
    Bottom := LineHi * FItems.Count + Height * 2;
  end;
end;
```

After being instantiated and sized, the memory bitmap is initialized further by setting the font to match that of TMarquee's Font property, filling the background with a color determined by TMarquee's Color property, and setting the Brush's Style property to bsClear.

> **TIP**
>
> When you render text on a TCanvas, the text background is filled with TCanvas.Brush's current color. To cause the text background to be invisible, set TCanvas.Brush.Style to bsClear.

Most of the preliminaries are now in place, so it's time to render text on the memory bitmap. As you learned in Chapter 10, "GDI and Graphics Programming," there are a couple of ways to output text onto a canvas. The most straightforward way is using TCanvas's TextOut() method, but you have more control over the formatting of the text using the more complex DrawText() API function. Because it requires control over justification, TMarquee will use the DrawText() function. An enumerated type is ideal to represent the text justification:

```
type
  TJustification = (tjCenter, tjLeft, tjRight);
```

The listing below shows TMarquee's PaintLine() method, which makes use of DrawText() to render text onto the memory bitmap. In this method, FJust represents an instance variable of type TJustification.

```
procedure TMarquee.PaintLine(R: TRect; LineNum: integer);
{ this method is called to paint each line of text onto MemBitmap }
const
  Flags: array[TJustification] of Longint = (dt_Center, dt_Left, dt_Right);
var
  p: array[0..255]of char;
begin
  StrPCopy(p, FItems.Strings[LineNum]);
  if DrawText(MemBitmap.Canvas.Handle, p, StrLen(p), R,
          Flags[FJust] or dt_SingleLine or dt_Top) <= 0 then
    raise EMarqueeError.Create('Failed to render text');
end;
```

Now that you know how to create the memory bitmap and paint text on it, the next step is learning how to copy that text to TMarquee's canvas.

Using the Paint Method

The Paint() method of a component is invoked in response to a Windows wm_Paint message. The Paint() method is what gives your component life; you use the Paint() method to paint, draw, and fill to determine the graphical appearance of your components.

It is TMarquee.Paint()'s job to copy the strings from the memory canvas to TMarquee's canvas. This feat will be accomplished by the BitBlt() API function which, as discussed in Chapter 10, copies the bits from one device context to another.

In order to determine whether TMarquee currently is running, it will maintain a Boolean instance variable called FActive that reveals whether the marquee's scrolling capability has been activated. Therefore, in the Paint() method, you will paint differently, depending on whether the component is active:

```
procedure TMarquee.Paint;
{ this virtual method is called in response to a Windows paint message }
begin
  if FActive then
    BitBlt(Canvas.Handle, 0, 0, InsideRect.Right, InsideRect.Bottom,
          MemBitmap.Canvas.Handle, 0, CurrLine, srcCopy)
  else
    inherited Paint;
end;
```

If the marquee is active, the component instead is painted by BitBlting a portion of the memory canvas onto TMarquee's canvas. Notice the CurrLine variable, which is passed as the next-to-last parameter to BitBlt(). The value of this parameter determines which portion of the memory canvas to transfer onto the screen. By continuously incrementing or decrementing the value of CurrLine, you can give TMarquee the appearance that the text is scrolling up or down.

TMarquee's Timer

The visual aspects of the TMarquee component now are in place, so the rest of the work involved in getting the component working is hooking up the plumbing, so to speak. At this point, TMarquee requires some mechanism to change the value of CurrLine every so often and repaint the component. This trick can be accomplished fairly easily using Delphi's TTimer component.

Before you can use a TTimer, of course, you must create and initialize the class instance. The TMarquee will have a TTimer instance called FTimer, and you will initialize it in a procedure called DoTimer:

```
procedure DoTimer;
  { procedure sets up TMarquee's timer }
  begin
    FTimer := TTimer.Create(Self);
    with FTimer do begin
      Enabled := False;
      Interval := TimerInterval;
      OnTimer := FTimerOnTimer;
    end;
  end;
```

In this procedure, FTimer is created, and it is disabled initially. Its Interval property then is assigned to the value of a constant called TimerInterval. Finally, FTimer's OnTimer event is assigned to a method of TMarquee called FTimerOnTimer. This is the method that will be called when an OnTimer event occurs.

NOTE

When assigning values to events in your code, there are two rules to follow:

■ The procedure that you assign to the event must be a method of some object instance. It cannot be a stand-alone procedure or function.

■ The method that you assign to the event must accept the same parameter list as the event type. TTimer's OnTimer event, for example, is of type TNotifyEvent. Because a TNotifyEvent accepts one parameter, Sender, of type TObject, any method that you assign to OnTimer also must take one parameter of type TObject.

The `FTimerOnTimer()` method is defined as the following:

```
procedure TMarquee.FTimerOnTimer(Sender: TObject);
{ This procedure is executed in response to a timer event }
begin
  IncLine;
  InvalidateRect(Handle, @InsideRect, False);   { only repaint within borders }
end;
```

In this method, a procedure named `IncLine()` first is called; this procedure increments or decrements the value of `CurrLine` as necessary. Then, the `InvalidateRect()` API function is called to "invalidate" or repaint the interior portion of the component. `InvalidateRect()` was chosen rather than `TCanvas`'s `Invalidate()` method because `Invalidate()` causes the entire canvas to repaint, rather than just the portion within a defined rectangle, as with `InvalidateRect()`. This method, rather than continuously repainting the whole component, eliminates much of the flicker that otherwise would occur. Remember: Flicker is bad.

This `IncLine()` method, which updates the value of `CurrLine` and detects whether scrolling has completed, is defined as the following:

```
procedure TMarquee.IncLine;
{ this method is called to increment a line }
begin
  if not FScrollDown then           { if Marquee is scrolling upward }
  begin
    { Check to see if marquee has scrolled to end yet }
    if FItems.Count * LineHi + ClientRect.Bottom - ScrollPixels >= CurrLine then
      inc(CurrLine, ScrollPixels) { not at end, so increment current line }
    else Deactivate;
  end
  else begin                        { if Marquee is scrolling downward }
    { Check to see if marquee has scrolled to end yet }
    if CurrLine >= ScrollPixels then
      dec(CurrLine, ScrollPixels) { not at end, so decrement current line }
    else Deactivate;
  end;
end;
```

Construction Ahead

The constructor for `TMarquee` is actually quite simple. You just call the inherited `Create()` method, create a `TStringList` instance, set up the `FTimer`, and then set all the default values for the instance variables. It's very important that you remember to call the inherited `Create` in your components. Failure to do so means that your component will miss out on all the important and useful functionality such as handle and canvas creation, streaming, and Windows message-response. The following code shows `TMarquee`'s constructor, `Create()`:

```
constructor TMarquee.Create(AOwner: TComponent);
{ constructor for TMarquee class }
begin
  inherited Create(AOwner);
  FItems := TStringList.Create;   { instantiate string list }
```

```
    DoTimer;                         { set up timer }

    { set instance variable default values }
    Width := 100;
    Height := 75;
    FActive := False;
    FScrollDown := False;
    FJust := tjCenter;
    BevelWidth := 3;
end;
```

TMarquee's destructor is even simpler. In that method, you deactivate the component by calling Deactivate(), free the timer and the string list, and then call the inherited Destroy:

```
destructor TMarquee.Destroy;
{ destructor for TMarquee class }
begin
  Deactivate(False);
  FTimer.Free;                     { free allocated classes }
  FItems.Free;
  inherited Destroy;
end;
```

> **TIP**
>
> As a rule of thumb, when you override constructors, you usually call the inherited first, and when you override destructors, you usually call the inherited last. This ensures that the class has been set up before you modify it and that all dependent resources have been cleaned up before you dispose of a class.
>
> There are exceptions to this rule, but you generally should stick with it unless you have good reason not to.

The Deactivate() method, which is called by both the IncLine() method and the destructor, serves as a vehicle to stop the marquee from scrolling and cleans up the canvas:

```
procedure TMarquee.Deactivate;
begin
  if FActive then begin
    FTimer.Enabled := False;                    { disable timer, }
    if Assigned(FOnDone) then FOnDone(Self);    { fire OnDone event, }
    FActive := False;                           { set FActive to False }
    MemBitmap.Free;                             { free memory bitmap }
    Invalidate;                                 { clear control window }
  end;
end;
```

Creating Events

An important feature that TMarquee is lacking is a method by which to tell the user that it is done scrolling. Never fear, though, this feature is very straightforward to add by way of an event.

The first step to adding an event to your component is to declare an instance variable of some event type in the private portion of the class definition. You will use the TNotifyEvent type for your FOnDone event,

```
FOnDone: TNotifyEvent;
```

Then the event should be declared in the published part of the class as a property:

```
property OnDone: TNotifyEvent read FOnDone write FOnDone;
```

Recall that the read and write directives specify from which function or variables a given property should get or set its value.

Taking just these two small steps will cause an entry for OnDone to be displayed on the Events page of the Object Inspector at design time. The only other thing that needs to be done is to call the user's handler for OnDone (if a method is assigned to OnDone), as TMarquee demonstrates with this line of code in the Deactivate() method:

```
if Assigned(FOnDone) then FOnDone(Self); { fire OnDone event, }
```

This line basically reads, *If the component user has assigned a method to the* OnDone *event, call that method and pass the* TMarquee *class instance (*Self*) as a parameter.*

Listing 11.5 shows the completed source code for the Marquee unit. Notice that because you are descending from a custom class, you need to publish many of those properties provided by TCustomPanel.

Listing 11.5. The source code for MARQUEE.PAS.

```
unit Marquee;

interface

uses
  SysUtils, WinTypes, WinProcs, Classes, Forms, Controls, Graphics,
  Messages, ExtCtrls, Dialogs;

const
  ScrollPixels = 2;
  TimerInterval = 50;

type
  TJustification = (tjCenter, tjLeft, tjRight);

  EMarqueeError = class(Exception);

  TMarquee = class(TCustomPanel)
  private
    MemBitmap: TBitmap;
    InsideRect: TRect;
    FItems: TStringList;
    FJust: TJustification;
    FScrollDown: Boolean;
```

continues

Listing 11.5. continued

```
    LineHi : integer;
    CurrLine : integer;
    VRect: TRect;
    FTimer: TTimer;
    FActive: Boolean;
    FOnDone: TNotifyEvent;
    procedure SetItems(Value: TStringList);
    procedure FTimerOnTimer(Sender: TObject);
    procedure MakeRects;
    procedure PaintLine(R: TRect; LineNum: integer);
    procedure SetLineHeight;
    procedure SetStartLine;
    procedure IncLine;
  protected
    procedure Paint; override;
    procedure FillBitmap; virtual;
  public
    property Active: Boolean read FActive;
    constructor Create(AOwner: TComponent); override;
    destructor Destroy; override;
    procedure Activate;
    procedure Deactivate; virtual;
  published
    property ScrollDown: Boolean read FScrollDown write FScrollDown;
    property Justify: TJustification read FJust write FJust default tjCenter;
    property Items: TStringList read FItems write SetItems;
    property OnDone: TNotifyEvent read FOnDone write FOnDone;
    property Align;
    property Alignment;
    property BevelInner;
    property BevelOuter;
    property BevelWidth;
    property BorderWidth;
    property BorderStyle;
    property Color;
    property Ctl3D;
    property Font;
    property Locked;
    property ParentColor;
    property ParentCtl3D;
    property ParentFont;
    property Visible;
    property OnClick;
    property OnDblClick;
    property OnMouseDown;
    property OnMouseMove;
    property OnMouseUp;
    property OnResize;
  end;

procedure Register;

implementation

procedure TMarquee.FTimerOnTimer(Sender: TObject);
{ This method is executed in response to a timer event }
```

```
var
  R: TRect;
begin
  IncLine;
  InvalidateRect(Handle, @InsideRect, False);   { only repaint within borders }
end;

procedure TMarquee.IncLine;
{ this method is called to increment a line }
begin
  if not FScrollDown then          { if Marquee is scrolling upward }
  begin
    { Check to see if marquee has scrolled to end yet }
    if FItems.Count * LineHi + ClientRect.Bottom - ScrollPixels >= CurrLine then
      inc(CurrLine, ScrollPixels) { not at end, so increment current line }
    else Deactivate;
  end
  else begin                       { if Marquee is scrolling downward }
    { Check to see if marquee has scrolled to end yet }
    if CurrLine >= ScrollPixels then
      dec(CurrLine, ScrollPixels) { not at end, so decrement current line }
    else Deactivate;
  end;
end;

constructor TMarquee.Create(AOwner: TComponent);
{ constructor for TMarquee class }

  procedure DoTimer;
  { procedure sets up TMarquee's timer }
  begin
    FTimer := TTimer.Create(Self);
    with FTimer do begin
      Enabled := False;
      Interval := TimerInterval;
      OnTimer := FTimerOnTimer;
    end;
  end;

begin
  inherited Create(AOwner);
  FItems := TStringList.Create;  { instantiate string list }
  DoTimer;                       { set up timer }

  { set instance variable default values }
  Width := 100;
  Height := 75;
  FActive := False;
  FScrollDown := False;
  FJust := tjCenter;
  BevelWidth := 3;
end;

destructor TMarquee.Destroy;
{ destructor for TMarquee class }
begin
  Deactivate;
  FTimer.Free;                   { free allocated classes }
```

continues

Listing 11.5. continued

```
  FItems.Free;
  inherited Destroy;
end;

procedure TMarquee.SetItems(Value: TStringList);
begin
  if FItems <> Value then
    FItems.Assign(Value);
end;

procedure TMarquee.SetLineHeight;
{ this virtual method sets the LineHi instance variable }
var
  Metrics : TTextMetric;
begin
  GetTextMetrics(Canvas.Handle, Metrics);  { get metric info for font }
  LineHi := Metrics.tmHeight + Metrics.tmInternalLeading; { adjust line height }
end;

procedure TMarquee.SetStartLine;
{ this virtual method initializes the CurrLine instance variable }
begin
  if not FScrollDown then                   { initialize current line to... }
    CurrLine := 0                           { top if scrolling up, or }
  else
    CurrLine := VRect.Bottom - Height;      { bottom if scrolling down }
end;

procedure TMarquee.PaintLine(R: TRect; LineNum: integer);
{ this method is called to paint each line of text onto MemBitmap }
const
  Flags: array[TJustification] of Longint = (dt_Center, dt_Left, dt_Right);
var
  p: array[0..255]of char;
begin
  StrPCopy(p, FItems.Strings[LineNum]);
  if DrawText(MemBitmap.Canvas.Handle, p, StrLen(p), R,
          Flags[FJust] or dt_SingleLine or dt_Top) <= 0 then
    raise EMarqueeError.Create('Failed to render text');
end;

procedure TMarquee.MakeRects;
{ procedure sets up VRect and InsideRect TRects }
begin
  { VRect rectangle represents entire memory bitmap }
  with VRect do begin
    Top := 0;
    Left := 0;
    Right := Width;
    Bottom := LineHi * FItems.Count + Height * 2;
  end;
  { InsideRect rectangle represents interior of beveled border }
  with InsideRect do begin
    Top := BevelWidth;
    Left := BevelWidth;
```

```
    Right := Width - (2 * BevelWidth);
    Bottom := Height - (2 * BevelWidth);
  end;
end;

procedure TMarquee.FillBitmap;
var
  y, i : integer;
  Rect: TRect;
begin
  SetLineHeight;                        { set height of each line }
  MakeRects;                            { make rectangles }
  with Rect do begin
    Left := InsideRect.Left;
    Bottom := VRect.Bottom ;
    Right := InsideRect.Right;
  end;
  SetStartLine;
  MemBitmap.Width := Width;
  with MemBitmap do begin
    Height := VRect.Bottom;
    with Canvas do begin
      Font := Self.Font;
      Brush.Color := Color;
      FillRect(VRect);
      Brush.Style := bsClear;
    end;
  end;
  y := Height;
  i := 0;
  repeat
    Rect.Top := y;
    PaintLine(Rect, i);
    inc(y, LineHi);  { increment y by the height (in pixels) of a line }
    inc(i);
  until i >= FItems.Count;              { repeat for all lines }
end;

procedure TMarquee.Activate;
{ this method is called to activate the marquee }
begin
  if (not FActive) and (FItems.Count > 0) then begin
    FActive := True;                    { set active flag }
    MemBitmap := TBitmap.Create;
    FillBitmap;                         { Paint Image on bitmap }
    FTimer.Enabled := True;             { start timer }
  end;
end;

procedure TMarquee.Deactivate;
begin
  if FActive then begin
    FTimer.Enabled := False;                { disable timer, }
    if Assigned(FOnDone) then FOnDone(Self); { fire OnDone event, }
    FActive := False;                       { set FActive to False }
    MemBitmap.Free;                         { free memory bitmap }
    Invalidate;                             { clear control window }
  end;
```

continues

Listing 11.5. continued

```
end;

procedure TMarquee.Paint;
{ this virtual method is called in response to a Windows paint message }
begin
  if FActive then
    BitBlt(Canvas.Handle, 0, 0, InsideRect.Right, InsideRect.Bottom,
           MemBitmap.Canvas.Handle, 0, CurrLine, srcCopy)
  else
    inherited Paint;
end;


procedure Register;
{ procedure registers component for Component palette }
begin
  RegisterComponents('DDG', [TMarquee]);
end;

end.
```

TIP

Note that the `default` directive was used, followed by a value for some of `TMarquee`'s properties. This use of default optimizes streaming of your component, which improves your component's design time performance. You can give default values to properties of any ordinal type (integer, word, longint, and enumerated type, for example), but you cannot give them to nonordinal property types such as strings, floating-point numbers, arrays, records, and classes.

You still will need to initialize the default values for the properties in your constructor as well. Failure to do so could result in streaming problems.

NOTE

Don't forget to create a `Register()` procedure that makes a call to `RegisterComponents()` inside of your unit. Failure to do this means that you will not be able to place your components on the Component Palette.

The Four P's: Private, Protected, Public, and Published

Part of designing a component is to know what to make private, public, protected, and published. Keep in mind not only users of your component, but also those who may use your component as an ancestor for yet another custom component. Table 11.2 will help you decide what goes where in your custom component.

Table 11.2. Private, protected, public, or published?

Directive	What Goes There?
Private	Instance variables and methods that you do not want the descendent type to be able to access or modify. Typically, you will give access to some private instance variables through properties that have read and write directives set in such a way as to help prevent the users from shooting themselves in the foot.
Protected	Instance variables, methods, and properties that you want descendant classes to be able to access and modify—but not users of your class. It is a common practice to place properties in the protected section of a base class for descendant classes to publish at their discretion.
Public	Methods and properties that you want to be accessible to any user of your class. If you have properties that you want to be accessible at runtime, but not at design time, then this is the place to put them.
Published	Properties that you want to be placed on the Object Inspector at design time. Runtime Type Information is generated for all properties in this section.

Virtual or Nonvirtual?

Don't make the mistake of not making enough functions virtual so that no useful descendants of your component can be created. Remember: only virtual and dynamic methods can be over-ridden.

Construct your component with the thought that someone might want to create a descendant of it, and you should leave that someone enough room to modify the appearance and behavior of your component without going against the "spirit" of your component. In the TMarquee component, for example, the most was made of the painting and output procedure virtual so that new components will be able to extend the behavior of TMarquee by modifying how it appears and functions.

Testing the Component

Although it's very exciting to finally have your component written and in the testing stages, don't get carried away by trying to add your component to the Component Palette before it has been debugged sufficiently. You should do all preliminary testing with your component by creating a project that creates and uses a dynamic instance of the component. Listings 11.6 and 11.7 depict a unit for testing the TMarquee component—a simple form that contains two buttons.

Listing 11.6. The source code for TESTMARQ.DPR.

```
program Testmarq;

uses
  Forms,
  Testu in 'TESTU.PAS' {Form1};

{$R *.RES}

begin
  Application.CreateForm(TForm1, Form1);
  Application.Run;
end.
```

Listing 11.7. The source code for TESTU.PAS.

```
unit TestU;

interface

uses
  SysUtils, WinTypes, WinProcs, Messages, Classes, Graphics, Controls,
  Forms, Dialogs, Marquee, StdCtrls;

type
  TForm1 = class(TForm)
    Button1: TButton;
    Button2: TButton;
    procedure FormCreate(Sender: TObject);
    procedure Button1Click(Sender: TObject);
    procedure Button2Click(Sender: TObject);
  private
    Marquee1: TMarquee;
    procedure MDone(Sender: TObject);
  public
    { Public declarations }
  end;

var
  Form1: TForm1;

implementation

{$R *.DFM}
```

```
procedure TForm1.MDone(Sender: TObject);
begin
  MessageBeep(0);
end;

procedure TForm1.FormCreate(Sender: TObject);
begin
  Marquee1 := TMarquee.Create(Self);
  with Marquee1 do begin
    Parent := Self;
    Top := 10;
    Left := 10;
    Height := 200;
    Width := 150;
    OnDone := MDone;
    Show;
    with Items do begin
      Add('One');
      Add('Two');
      Add('Three');
      Add('Four');
      Add('Five');
    end;
  end;
end;

procedure TForm1.Button1Click(Sender: TObject);
begin
  Marquee1.Activate;
end;

procedure TForm1.Button2Click(Sender: TObject);
begin
  Marquee1.Deactivate(True);
end;

end.
```

> **TIP**
>
> *Always* create a test project for your new components. *Never* try to do initial testing on a component by adding it to the Component Palette. Not only will you spend a great deal of time recompiling the Component Palette, but you are much more likely to crash Delphi (and possibly Windows!) during your testing.

Figure 11.3 shows the TestMarq project in action.

FIGURE 11.3.

Testing the TMarquee component.

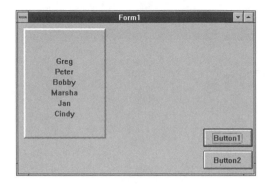

Using the Component

After you squash all the bugs you find in your program, it's time to add it to the Component Palette. Doing so is easy: simply choose Options | Install Components from the main menu, and then click the Add button in the Install Components dialog box. Now just type the full path name of the unit containing your component, or choose Browse to search for it. After your component is found, choose OK from the Install Components dialog box, and Delphi rebuilds the component library.

THE COMPONENT LIBRARY: COMPLIB.DCL

The *component library* is the file in which Delphi stores all components for design time usage. It is from the component library that the Component Palette gets all its components and their associated icons.

By default, the name of the component library is COMPLIB.DCL. Think of this file as really nothing more than a large DLL that contains a whole bunch of components, Property Editor, experts, and so on that all help make up the Delphi IDE. It's important to note that COMPLIB.DCL is used only at design time by the Delphi IDE. At runtime, your applications will have the component units linked into the executable file, so COMPLIB.DCL is not used.

Whenever you change the source code to a custom component that you already have installed into the Component palette, remember to rebuild the COMPLIB.DCL so that your changes are built into the Delphi IDE.

Helpful hint: before rebuilding the component library, Delphi makes a backup of the file and calls it COMPLIB.~DC. If your installation of COMPLIB becomes corrupted, you can just rename the backup to COMPLIB.DCL, or if things have gotten really hosed, copy COMPLIB.DCL from the \RUNIMAGE\DELPHI\BIN directory on the Delphi CD-ROM.

Creating a Component Palette Icon

No custom component would be complete without its own icon for the Component Palette. To create one of these icons, use Delphi's Image Editor (or your favorite bitmap editor) to create a bitmap of up to 32×32 pixels—24×24 is a good size—on which you will draw the component's icon. This bitmap must be stored within a DCR file (or an RES file renamed to DCR).

> **TIP**
>
> Even if you have a 256 or higher color driver, save your Component Palette icon as a 16-color bitmap if you plan on releasing the component to others. 256 colors might look nice on your machine, but you should take pity on the poor stiffs (and there are many of them) who still use 16-color drivers. Your 256-color bitmaps most likely will look awful on their machines.

You optionally can create a double-wide bitmap that shows the icon's pressed and unpressed appearances, but Delphi does a good job with creating a pressed appearance for your normal bitmaps if you would rather not grapple with these artsy concepts.

After you create the bitmap in the DCR file, give the bitmap the same name as the class name of your component—in ALL CAPS. Save the resource file as the same name as your component's unit with a DCR extension. In the case of the TMarquee component, the bitmap name is TMARQUEE and the file name is MARQUEE.DCR. Place this file in the same directory as the unit, and when you recompile the unit, the bitmap automatically is linked into the component library.

Summary

By now, you should have a solid understanding of how to build custom Delphi components. Here are the important points in creating a component—from concept to COMPLIB:

- First, you need an idea for a useful and hopefully unique component.
- Then sit down and map out the algorithm for how the component will work.
- Start with the preliminaries, and don't jump right into the component. Ask yourself, "What do I need up front to make this component work?"
- Try to break up the construction of your component into logical portions. This will not only modularize and simplify the creation of the component, but it also will help you to write cleaner, more organized code. Design your component with the thought that someone else might try to create a descendant component.

■ Test your component in a test project first. You will be sorry if you immediately add it to the Component Palette.

■ Finally, add the component and an optional bitmap to the Component Palette. After a little fine tuning, it will be ready for you to drop into your Delphi applications.

Knowing how components work is fundamental to understanding Delphi, and you work with many more custom components later in the book. Now that you can see what happens behind the scenes, components no longer will seem like just a black box.

12

Printing in Delphi

Printing in Windows has been the bane of many a Windows programmer. What was once a cakewalk under DOS is now a minefield in Windows. Don't be discouraged, however; Delphi simplifies most of what you need to know for printing. Simple printing routines to output text or bitmapped images can be written with little effort. For more complex printing, all you really need are a few concepts and techniques under your belt to enable you to perform any type of custom printing. Once you have that, printing isn't so difficult.

> **NOTE**
>
> Delphi ships with a TReport component that enables you to view and print database reports by using the runtime version of *ReportSmith*—a subset of a powerful reporting tool that you can deploy with your applications. Although ReportSmith is suitable for applications that generate complex reports, many developers are frustrated with this option because it requires you to deploy your application with ReportSmith runtime (which is quite large), and it limits you from getting to the nuts and bolts of printing at the source code level where you have more control over what gets printed. ReportSmith, therefore, is not covered in this chapter; instead, you learn how to create your own reports in Delphi.

Delphi's TPrinter object, which encapsulates Windows' printing engine, does a great deal for you that you otherwise would have to handle yourself.

This chapter teaches you how to perform a whole range of printing operations by using TPrinter. You will learn the simple tasks that Delphi has made much easier for generating printouts. You also will learn the techniques for creating advanced printing routines that should lead you on your way to becoming a printing guru.

The *TPrinter* Object

The TPrinter object encapsulates the Windows printing interface, making most of the printing management invisible to you. TPrinter's methods and properties enable you to print onto its canvas as though you were drawing your output to a form's surface. You don't have to worry about initializing the printer because this is done in the initialization section of the printers unit. The global variable printer, of type TPrinter, is defined in the printers unit. TPrinter's properties and methods are listed in Tables 12.1 and 12.2.

Table 12.1. TPrinter's properties.

Property	Purpose
Aborted	Boolean variable that determines whether the user has aborted the print job.
Canvas	The printing surface for the current page.
Fonts	Contains a list of fonts supported by the printer.
Handle	A unique number representing the printer's device context. See the sidebar "Handles" in Chapter 4, "The Visual Component Library (VCL)."
Orientation	Determines horizontal (poLandScape) or vertical (poPortrait) printing.
PageHeight	Height, in pixels, of the printed page's surface.
PageNumber	Indicates the page being printed. This is incremented with each subsequent call to TPrinter.NewPage().
PageWidth	Width, in pixels, of the printed page's surface.
PrinterIndex	Indicates the selected printer from the available printers on the user's system.
Printers	A list of the available printers on the system.
Printing	Determines whether a print job is printing.
Title	Text appearing on the Print Manager and on networked pages.

Table 12.2. TPrinter's methods.

Method	Purpose
Abort	Terminates a print job.
BeginDoc	Begins a print job.
EndDoc	Ends a print job. (EndDoc ends a print job when printing is finished; Abort can terminate the job before printing is complete.)
GetPrinter	Retrieves the current printer (rarely used).
NewPage	Forces the printer to start printing on a new page and increments the PageCount property.
SetPrinter	Specifies a printer as a current printer.

TPrinter.Canvas

TPrinter.Canvas is much like the canvas for your form; it represents the drawing surface on which text or graphics are drawn. The difference is that TPrinter's canvas represents the drawing surface for your printed output as opposed to your screen. Most of the routines that you use to draw text, to draw shapes, and to display images are used in the same manner for printed output. There are differences that you must take into account when printing, however:

- Drawing to the screen is *dynamic*—you can erase what you have placed on the screen's output. Drawing to the printer is not so flexible. What is drawn to the TPrinter's canvas is printed to the printer.

- Drawing text or graphics to the screen is nearly instantaneous, whereas drawing to the printer is slow, even on some high-performance laser printers. You therefore must allow users to abort a print job either by using an Abort dialog box or by some other method that allows them to terminate the print job.

- Because your users are running Windows, you can assume that their display supports graphics output. However, you cannot assume the same for their printers. Different printers have different capabilities. Some printers may be high-resolution printers; other printers may be very low-resolution, and may not support graphics printing at all. You must take this into account in your printing routines.

- You never will see an error message like Display ran out of screen space, please insert more screen space into your display. You can bet that you will see an error telling you that the printer ran out of paper, however. You will have to provide error handling in your printing routines to deal with any number of mechanical errors that might pop up.

- Text and graphics on your screen don't look the same on hard copy. Printers and displays have very different resolutions. That 300×300 bitmap might look spectacular on a 640×480 display, but it is a mere 1×1-inch square blob on your 300dpi laser printer. You're responsible for making adjustments to your drawing routines so that your users will not need a magnifying glass to read their printed output.

Simple Printing

In many cases, you want to send a stream of text to your printer without any regard for special formatting or placement of the text. Delphi facilitates simple printing, as the following subsections illustrate.

Printing a *TMemo* Component

Printing lines of text is actually quite simple using the AssignPrn() procedure. The AssignPrn() procedure enables you to assign a text file variable to the current printer. It is used with the Rewrite() and CloseFile() procedures. The following lines of code illustrate this syntax:

```
var
  f: TextFile;                { Declare a text file variable }
begin
  AssignPrn(f);              { Assign the text file variable f to the printer }
  Rewrite(f);               { Open the file for output }
  { do your printing here }  { Perform your printing }
  CloseFile(f);             { Close the text file }
end;
```

Printing a line of text to the printer is the same as printing a line of text to a file. You use this syntax:

```
writeln(f, 'This is my line of text');
```

Remember from Chapter 8, "MDI Applications," that you put in the event handler for printing the contents of the EditForm form. Listing 12.1 shows you how to print the contents from TEditForm's File | Print event handler.

Listing 12.1. `TEditForm.Print1.Click()` **from MDIAPP.DPR.**

```
procedure TEditForm.Print1Click(Sender: TObject);
var
  i: integer;
  MemoText: TextFile;                       { Declare a text file variable }
begin
  if PrintDialog1.Execute then              { Execute the print dialog }
    AssignPrn(MemoText);                    { Assign the file variable to the
➥printer }
  try
    Rewrite(MemoText);                      { Open the file for output }
      Printer.Canvas.Font.Assign(Memo1.Font); { Assign the memo's font to the
➥printer's canvas }
      for i := 0 to Memo1.Lines.Count -1 do { Print each line in the memo
➥control }
        writeln(MemoText, Memo1.Lines[i]);  { by using the writeln()
➥procedure. }
    finally
      CloseFile(MemoText);                  { Close the printer file }
    end;
end;
```

Notice that the Memo's font also was assigned to the Printer's font, causing the output to print with the same font as Memo1.

CAUTION

Be aware that the printer will print with the font specified by Printer.Font only if the printer supports that font. Otherwise, the printer will use a font that approximates the characteristics of the specified font.

Using *BeginDoc()* and *EndDoc()*—Printing a Bitmap

Printing a bitmap also is quite simple. These lines of code show what is required:

```
with Printer do begin
  BeginDoc;
  Canvas.Draw(0,0, Image1.Picture.Graphic);
  EndDoc;
end;
```

Here, the `BeginDoc()` procedure is used to start a print job. The `Printer.Canvas.Draw()` proce-dure draws a graphic to the canvas—in this case, the printed surface. Finally, the `EndDoc()` procedure is called to stop the print job.

To illustrate this further, modify the MDIAPP project from Chapter 8 to print the contents of a bitmap in the `BMPForm` MDI child form. Again, in Chapter 8, you only invoked `PrintDialog1` in the `TEditForm.Print1Click()` event handler. Now insert the code shown in Listing 12.2.

Listing 12.2. The `TBMPForm.Print1Click()` event handler from MDIAPP.

```
procedure TBMPForm.Print1Click(Sender: TObject);
var
  GRect: TRect;
  SizeRatio: Double;
begin
  if PrintDialog1.Execute then begin
    SizeRatio := Image1.Picture.Height / Image1.Picture.Width;  { Get a ratio
➥of height to width }
    GRect := Rect(0, 0, Printer.PageWidth, trunc(Printer.PageHeight *
➥SizeRatio) - GetDeviceCaps(Printer.Handle, LOGPIXELSX));
    with Printer do begin
      BeginDoc;        { Start the print job }
      { Draw a rectangle to show the margins }
      Canvas.Rectangle(GRect.Left, GRect.Top, GRect.Right, GRect.Bottom);
      { Decrease the size of the rectangle so the image doesn't draw over it }
      GRect := Rect(GRect.Left+10, GRect.Top+10, GRect.Right-10,
➥GRect.Bottom-10);
      { Draw the graphic }
      Canvas.StretchDraw(GRect, Image1.Picture.Graphic);
      EndDoc;          { End the print job }
    end;
  end;
end;
```

`SizeRatio` is a ratio of the image's height to its width. `Print1Click()` uses `SizeRatio` to calcu-late the values for a `TRect` structure that will have the same width and height ratio, but for which the values are based on `TPrinter.Canvas`'s height and width. This enables you to stretch the image so that it is not a small blob on the printed page, while still maintaining its original shape. `TPrinter.Canvas`'s `StretchDraw()` procedure is used to stretch the image.

NOTE

One of the keys to printing is to be able to print images as they appear on-screen at approximately the same size. A 3×3-inch image on a 640×480 pixel screen uses less pixels than it would on a 300dpi printer, for example. Therefore, you must calculate how many pixels on TPrinter's canvas are required to achieve the same 3×3-inch size. After that information is received, you can stretch the image to TPrinter's canvas. Another technique is to draw the image using a different mapping mode, as described in Chapter 10, "GDI and Graphics Programming." Keep in mind that some older printers may not support the stretching of images. You can obtain valuable information about the printer's capabilities by using the Windows API function GetDeviceCaps().

Print1Click() uses GetDeviceCaps() to determine how many pixels make up an inch along TPrinter.Canvas's X- and Y-axis. GetDeviceCaps() is used to retrieve specifics about a device context, and TPrinter.Handle is a device context. See the sidebar "Device Contexts" in Chapter 10. The second parameter passed to GetDeviceCaps() determines what information it returns. In this case, passing the LOGPIXELSX constant returns the pixels per inch along the X-axis. Passing LOGPIXELSY returns the pixels per inch along the Y-axis. A great deal of information can be returned from GetDeviceCaps(). It might be worthwhile to read about GetDeviceCaps() in the online API help, which covers this function in depth. This function is used again in later examples.

Finally, Print1Click() calls Printer.BeginDoc() to start the print job, to print the image along with a rectangle, and to stop the printing with Printer.EndDoc().

Printing a Form

Conceptually, printing a form can be one of the more difficult tasks to perform. However, this task has been simplified greatly thanks to VCL's Print() method of TForm. The following one-line procedure prints your form's client areas, as well as all components residing on the client area:

```
procedure TForm1.PrintMyForm(Sender: TObject);
begin
  Print;
end;
```

NOTE

Printing your form is a quick-and-dirty way to print graphical output. However, only what is visible on-screen will be printed due to Windows' clipping. You must use more elaborate techniques to print complex graphics; these techniques are discussed in this and other chapters.

Advanced Printing

Often you need to print something very specific that isn't facilitated by the development tool you're using, nor is it provided by a third-party reporting tool. In this case, you need to perform the low-level printing tasks yourself. In the next several sections, we'll show you how to write such printing routines, and we'll present a methodology that you can apply to all your printing tasks.

Printing a Columnar Report

Many applications, particularly those using databases, print some type of report. One common report style is the columnar report. A *columnar report* prints data in columns across the printed page, as shown in Figure 12.1.

FIGURE 12.1.
A columnar report.

Address Listing

LAST NAME	FIRST NAME	ADDRESS	CITY	STATE	ZIP
	Jennifer	100 Cranberry St.	Wellesley	MA	02181
Jones	Arthur	10 Hunnewell St.	Los Altos	CA	94024
Parker	Debra	74 South St.	Atherton	CA	98765
Sawyer	Dave	101 Oakland St.	Los Altos	CA	94022
White	Cindy	1 Wentworth Dr.	Los Altos	CA	94022

The next project prints a columnar report from one of the tables in Delphi's demo directories. Each page contains a header, column titles, and then the record list. Each subsequent page also has the header and column titles preceding the record list. Figure 12.1 is actually a printout from this project.

Create a new project, name the form ColReportForm, and save the project's files as PRNPAGEU.PAS and PRNPAGE.DPR. Set the properties shown in Table 12.3. Set other properties so that the form looks like that shown in Figure 12.2.

Table 12.3. ColReportForm's properties.

Component	Property	Value
Table1	DataBaseName	DBDEMOS
	TableName	CLIENTS.DBF
DataSource1	DataSet	Table1
DBGrid1	Align	alBottom
	DataSource	DataSource1
SpinEdit1—6	MinValue	10
	MaxValue	20
	Value	10

FIGURE 12.2.
ColReportForm.

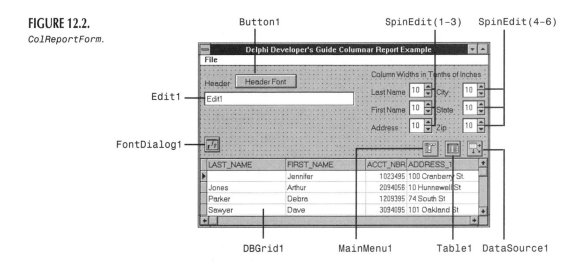

The spin-edit control enables the user to specify the column widths in tenths of inches. These controls are convenient because they enable you to specify minimum and maximum values. Edit1 contains a header that can be printed using a different font than the rest of the report. Add a TMainMenu object that contains one menu item, Print, to the main form.

The TColReportForm.Print1Click() event handler basically performs the following steps:

1. Initiates a print job
2. Prints a header
3. Prints column names
4. Prints a page
5. Continues steps 2, 3, and 4 until printing finishes
6. Ends the print job

Listings 12.3 and 12.4 show the source code for PRNPAGE.DPR and PRNPG0.PAS, respectively.

Listing 12.3. The source code for PRNPAGE.DPR.

```
program Prnpage;

uses
  Forms,
  Prnpg2 in 'PRNPG2.PAS' {ColReportForm},
  Stabox in 'STABOX.PAS' {StatusForm};

{$R *.RES}

begin
  Application.CreateForm(TColReportForm, ColReportForm);
```

continues

Listing 12.3. continued

```
  Application.CreateForm(TStatusForm, StatusForm);
  Application.Run;
end.
```

Listing 12.4. The source code for PRNPG0.PAS.

```
unit Prnpg0;
interface

uses
  SysUtils, WinTypes, WinProcs, Messages, Classes, Graphics, Controls,
  Forms, Dialogs, Grids, DBGrids, DB, DBTables, Menus, StdCtrls, Spin,
  Gauges, ExtCtrls;

type
  TColReportForm = class(TForm)
    Table1: TTable;
    DataSource1: TDataSource;
    DBGrid1: TDBGrid;
    MainMenu1: TMainMenu;
    File1: TMenuItem;
    Print1: TMenuItem;
    SpinEdit1: TSpinEdit;
    Label1: TLabel;
    Label2: TLabel;
    SpinEdit2: TSpinEdit;
    SpinEdit3: TSpinEdit;
    SpinEdit4: TSpinEdit;
    Label3: TLabel;
    Label4: TLabel;
    Label5: TLabel;
    SpinEdit5: TSpinEdit;
    Label6: TLabel;
    SpinEdit6: TSpinEdit;
    Label7: TLabel;
    Edit1: TEdit;
    Label8: TLabel;
    Button1: TButton;
    FontDialog1: TFontDialog;
    procedure Print1Click(Sender: TObject);
    procedure Button1Click(Sender: TObject);
  private
    { Private declarations }
    PixelsInInchx: integer;        { Stores Pixels per inch }
    LineHeight: Integer;           { Stores the line height }
    AmountPrinted: integer;        { Stores amount, in pixels, printed on
➥a page }
    TenthsOfInchPixelsY: integer; { Pixels in 1/10 of an inch used for
➥line spacing }
    procedure PrintLine(Items: TStringList);
    procedure PrintHeader;
    procedure PrintColumnNames;
  end;
```

```
var
  ColReportForm: TColReportForm;
  a: Boolean;

implementation
uses printers, abortbx;

{$R *.DFM}

procedure TColReportForm.PrintLine(Items: TStringList);
var
  OutRect: TRect;
  Inches: double;
  i: integer;
begin
  OutRect.Left := 0;                          { left position is zero }
  OutRect.Top := AmountPrinted;               { Set Top to Amount printed }
  OutRect.Bottom := OutRect.Top + LineHeight; { Set bottom position }
  With Printer.Canvas do
    for i := 0 to Items.Count - 1 do begin
      Inches := longint(Items.Objects[i]) * 0.1;               { Get
➥inches }
      OutRect.Right := OutRect.Left + round(PixelsInInchx*Inches);   { Determine
➥Right position }
      if not Printer.Aborted then
        TextRect(OutRect, OutRect.Left, OutRect.Top, Items[i]);    { Print the
➥line }
      OutRect.Left := OutRect.Right;                           { Set left
➥to Right }
    end;
  { Increment the amount printed }
  AmountPrinted := AmountPrinted + TenthsOfInchPixelsY*2;
end;

procedure TColReportForm.PrintHeader;
var
  SaveFont: TFont;
begin
  { Save the current printer's font and assign Edit1's font to Printer }
  SaveFont := TFont.Create;
  Savefont.Assign(Printer.Canvas.Font);
  Printer.Canvas.Font.Assign(Edit1.Font);
  { Print out the Header }
  with Printer do begin
    if not Printer.Aborted then
      Canvas.TextOut((PageWidth div 2)-(Canvas.TextWidth(Edit1.Text) div 2),
                     0, Edit1.Text);
    { Increment AmountPrinted by the LineHeight }
    AmountPrinted := AmountPrinted + LineHeight+TenthsOfInchPixelsY;
  end;
  Printer.Canvas.Font.Assign(SaveFont);   { Re-assign the old font }
  SaveFont.Free;                          { Free the saved font }
end;

procedure TColReportForm.PrintColumnNames;
var
  ColNames: TStringList;
```

continues

Listing 12.4. continued

```
begin
  ColNames := TStringList.Create;                        { Create the string list }
  Printer.Canvas.Font.Style := [fsBold, fsUnderline]; { Use a Bold/underline
➥style }
  with ColNames do begin
    { Create the column headers }
    AddObject('LAST NAME',  pointer(SpinEdit1.Value));
    AddObject('FIRST NAME', pointer(SpinEdit2.Value));
    AddObject('ADDRESS',    pointer(SpinEdit3.Value));
    AddObject('CITY',       pointer(SpinEdit4.Value));
    AddObject('STATE',      pointer(SpinEdit5.Value));
    AddObject('ZIP',        pointer(SpinEdit6.Value));
  end;
  PrintLine(ColNames);                     { Print the line }
  Printer.Canvas.Font.Style := [];         { Set to normal style }
  ColNames.Free;                           { Free the string list }
end;

procedure TColReportForm.Print1Click(Sender: TObject);
var
  Items: TStringList;
begin
  Items := TStringList.Create;             { Create a new TStringList }
  PixelsInInchx := GetDeviceCaps(Printer.Handle, LOGPIXELSX); { Get Pixels per
➥inch horizonally}
  TenthsOfInchPixelsY := GetDeviceCaps(Printer.Handle, LOGPIXELSY) div 10;

  AmountPrinted := 0;                      { Set to zero }
  try
    ColReportForm.Enabled := false;        { Disable the parent Form }
    Printer.BeginDoc;                      { Initiate a print job }
➥AbortForm.Show;
    Application.ProcessMessages;           { Allow Drawing of abort  box }
    { Calculate an arbitrary line height }
    LineHeight := Printer.Canvas.TextHeight('X')+TenthsOfInchPixelsY;
    if Edit1.Text <> '' then
      PrintHeader;                         { Print the header }
    PrintColumnNames;                      { Print the column Names }
    Table1.First;                          { Go to the first record }
    { Add the data in the fields into a TStringList in the order that they are }
    { Going to be printed }
    while (not Table1.Eof) or Printer.Aborted do begin
      Application.ProcessMessages;
      with Items do begin
        AddObject(Table1.FieldByName('LAST_NAME').AsString,
                        pointer(SpinEdit1.Value));
        AddObject(Table1.FieldByName('FIRST_NAME').AsString,
                        pointer(SpinEdit2.Value));
        AddObject(Table1.FieldByName('ADDRESS_1').AsString,
                        pointer(SpinEdit3.Value));
        AddObject(Table1.FieldByName('CITY').AsString,
                        pointer(SpinEdit4.Value));
        AddObject(Table1.FieldByName('STATE').AsString,
                        pointer(SpinEdit5.Value));
        AddObject(Table1.FieldByName('ZIP').AsString,
                        pointer(SpinEdit6.Value));
      end;
```

```
      PrintLine(Items);    { Print the line }
      { Force printjob to begin a new page if printed output has exceeded the }
      { Page height }
      if AmountPrinted + LineHeight > Printer.PageHeight then
      begin
        AmountPrinted := 0;              { Reset to zero }
        if not Printer.Aborted then
          Printer.NewPage;              { Force page eject }
        PrintHeader;                     { Print the header again }
        PrintColumnNames;                { Print the column names again }
      end;
      Items.Clear;                       { Clear this record from the TStringList }
      Table1.Next;                       { Go to the next record }
    end;
    AbortForm.Hide;                      { Hide the abort form, no longer needed }
    if not Printer.Aborted then
      Printer.EndDoc;                    { End the print job }
    ColReportForm.Enabled := true;
  except
    on E: Exception do MessageDlg(E.Message, mtError, [mbok], 0);
  end;
  Items.Free;                            { Free the TStringList }
end;

procedure TColReportForm.Button1Click(Sender: TObject);
begin
{ Assign a new font to Edit1 }
  FontDialog1.Font.Assign(Edit1.Font);
  if FontDialog1.Execute then
    Edit1.Font.Assign(FontDialog1.Font);
end;

end.
```

In `TColReportForm.Print1Click()`, a `TStringList` first is instantiated to hold the strings for a line to be printed. Then the number of pixels per inch along the vertical axis is determined in `PixelsPerInchX`, which is used to calculate column widths. `TenthsOfInchPixelsY` is used to space each line by $1/10$ inch. `AmountPrinted` holds the total amount of pixels along the printed surface's vertical axis for each line printed. This is required to determine whether to start a new page when `AmountPrinted` exceeds `Printer.PageHeight`.

If a header exists in `Edit1.Text`, it is printed in `PrintHeader()`. `PrintColumnNames()` prints the names of the columns for each field to be printed. (These two procedures are discussed later in this section.) Finally, the table's records are printed.

The following loop increments through `Table1`'s records and prints selected fields within each of `Table1`'s records:

```
while (not Table1.Eof) or Printer.Aborted do begin
```

It appends the fields to the `Items` `TStringList` using the `AddObject()` method. Notice that it stores both the string and the column width in `Items`. The column width is added to `Items`'

Objects array property. Items then is passed to the PrintLine() procedure, which prints the strings in a columnar format.

In much of the previous code, you saw references to Printer.Aborted. This is a test to determine if the user has aborted the print job, which is covered in the next section.

> **TIP**
>
> The TStrings and TStringList's Objects array property is a convenient place to store integer values. Using AddObject() or InsertObject(), you can hold any number up to MaxLongInt. Because AddObject() expects a TObject reference as its second parameter, you must typecast that parameter as a pointer, as shown in the following code:
>
> MyList.AddObject('SomeString', pointer(SomeInteger));
>
> To retrieve the value, use a Longint typecast:
>
> MyInteger := Longint(MyList.Objects[Index]);

The event handler then determines whether printing a new line will exceed the page height:

```
if AmountPrinted + LineHeight > Printer.PageHeight then
```

If this evaluates to true, AmountPrinted is set back to 0, Printer.NewPage is invoked to print a new page, and the header and column names are printed again. Printer.EndDoc is called to end the print job after Table1's records have printed.

The PrintHeader() procedure prints the header centered at the top of the report using Edit1.Text and Edit1's rendered font. AmountPrinted then is incremented and Printer's font is restored to its original style.

As the name implies, PrintColumnNames() prints the column names of the report. In this method, names are added to a TStringList object, ColNames, which then is passed to PrintLine(). Notice that the column names are printed in a bold and underlined font. This is done by setting Printer.Canvas's font accordingly.

The PrintLine() procedure takes a TStringList argument called Items and prints each string in Items on a single line in a columnar manner. The variable OutRect holds values for a binding rectangle at a location on Printer's canvas to which the text is drawn. OutRect is passed to TextRect(), along with the text to draw. By multiplying Items.Object[i] by 0.1, OutRect.Right's value is obtained because Items.Objects[i] is in tenths of inches. Inside the for loop, OutRect is recalculated along the same X-axis to position it to the next column and draw the next text value. Finally, AmountPrinted is incremented by LineHeight + TenthsOfInchPixelsY.

Although this report is fully functional, you might consider extending it to include a footer, page numbers, or even margin settings.

Aborting the Printing Process

Earlier in this chapter, you learned that your users need a way to terminate printing after they already have initiated it. Thanks to TPrinter's Abort() procedure and Aborted property, the code above contains such logic. To add abort logic to your printing routines, your code must meet the three conditions:

■ You must establish an event that, when activated, calls Printer.Abort, thus aborting the printing process.

■ You must check for TPrinter.Aborted = true before calling any of TPrinter's print functions such as TextOut(), NewPage(), and EndDoc().

■ You must end your printing logic by checking the value of TPrinter.Aborted for true.

A simple Abort dialog box can satisfy the first condition. The unit ABORTBX.PAS defines an abort dialog. This unit is added to PRNPG0.PAS's uses clause. AbortForm is shown in Figure 12.3.

FIGURE 12.3.
AbortForm.

The event handler to the BitBtn on AbortForm simply calls TPrinter.Abort, which terminates the print job and cancels any printing requests made to TPrinter. Listing 12.5 shows ABORTBX.PAS.

Listing 12.5. ABORTBX.PAS

```
unit Abortbx;

interface

uses
  SysUtils, WinTypes, WinProcs, Messages, Classes, Graphics, Controls,
  Forms, Dialogs, Gauges, StdCtrls, Buttons;

type

  TAbortForm = class(TForm)
    BitBtn1: TBitBtn;
    procedure BitBtn1Click(Sender: TObject);
  private
    { Private declarations }
  public
    { Public declarations }
  end;

var
  AbortForm: TAbortForm;
```

continues

Listing 12.5. continued

```
implementation
uses Printers;

{$R *.DFM}
procedure TAbortForm.BitBtn1Click(Sender: TObject);
begin
  AbortDoc(Printer.Handle);   { This line will disappear when the bug is fixed. }
  Printer.Abort;              { This procedure is supposed to call the above }
  Close;
end;

end.
```

In the unit PRNPG0.PAS, examine the code to show AbortForm shortly after calling TPrinter.Begindoc():

```
Printer.BeginDoc;                  { Initiate a print job }
AbortForm.Show;                    { Display the AbortForm }
Application.ProcessMessages;       { Allow Drawing of abort box }
```

Because AbortForm is shown as a nonmodal dialog box, call Application.ProcessMessages to make sure that it has drawn properly before any processing of the printing logic continues. You must add ABORTBX to PRNPG0.PAS's uses clause.

To satisfy the second condition, make sure to test for Printer.Aborted = true before calling any TPrinter methods. The Aborted property is set to true when the Abort() method is called from AbortForm. As an example, before calling Printer.TextRect, check for Aborted = true:

```
if not Printer.Aborted then
    TextRect(OutRect, OutRect.Left, OutRect.Top, Items[i]); { Print the line }
```

Also, don't call EndDoc() or any of TPrinter.Canvas's drawing routines because the printer has been effectively closed by previously calling Abort().

To satisfy the third condition in this example, the while not Table.Eof also checks whether the value of Printer.Aborted is true, which causes execution to jump out of the loop where the print logic is executed.

Printing Envelopes

The previous example showed you a method for printing a columnar report. Although this technique was somewhat more complicated than doing a series of writeln()s to the printer, it is still, for the most part, a line-by-line print. Printing envelopes introduces a few factors that complicate things a bit further and are common to most printing you'll do in Windows. First, the objects, or items, you must print probably need to be positioned at some specific location on the printed surface. Second, the item's metrics, or units of measurement, can be completely different than those of the printer canvas's metrics. Taking these two factors into account, printing becomes much more than just printing a line and keeping track of how much print space you have used.

This envelope-printing example shows you a step-by-step process that you can use to print just about anything. Keep in mind that everything drawn on the printer's canvas is drawn within some bounding rectangle on the canvas or to specific points on the printer canvas.

Printing in Abstract

Think of the printing task in a more abstract sense for a moment. In all cases, two things are certain: you have a surface on which to print, and you have one or more elements to plot onto that surface. Take a look at Figure 12.4.

FIGURE 12.4.
Three planes.

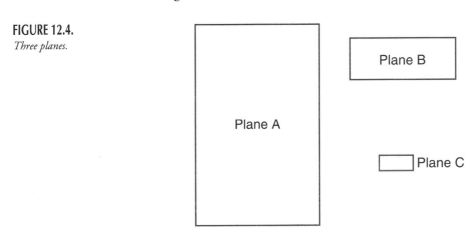

Here, Plane A is your destination surface. Planes B and C are the elements that you want to superimpose or print onto plane A. Assume a coordinate system for each plane where the unit of measurement increases as you travel east along the X-axis and south along the Y-axis—that is, unless you live in Australia. Figure 12.5 depicts this coordinate system. The result of combining the planes is shown in Figure 12.6.

FIGURE 12.5.
The Plane A, B, and C coordinate system.

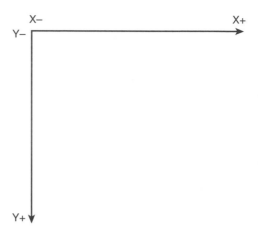

FIGURE 12.6.
Planes B and C superimposed on Plane A.

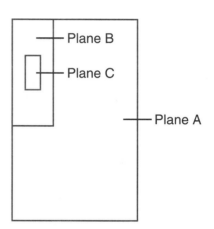

Notice that Planes B and C were rotated by 90 degrees to achieve the final result. So far, this doesn't appear to be too bad. Given that your planes are measured using the same unit of measurement, you easily can draw out these rectangles to achieve the final result with some simple geometry. But what if they're not the same unit of measurement?

Suppose that Plane A represents a surface for which the measurements are given in pixels. Its dimensions are 2550×3000 pixels. Plane B is measured in inches: $6^1/_2×3^3/_4$ inches. Suppose that you don't know the dimensions for Plane C; you do know, however, that it is measured in pixels, and that you will know its measurements later. These measurements are illustrated in Figure 12.7.

FIGURE 12.7.

Plane measurements.

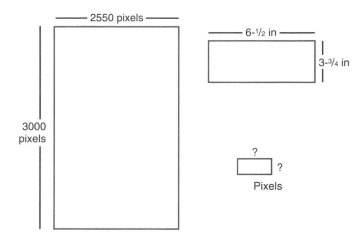

This abstraction illustrates the problem associated with printing. In fact, it illustrates the very task of printing an envelope. Plane A represents a printer's page size on a 300-dots-per-inch (dpi) printer (at 300dpi, 8¹/₂×11 inches equals 2550×3000 pixels). Plane B represents the envelope's size in inches, and Plane C represents the bounding rectangle for the text making up the address. Keep in mind, however, that this abstraction isn't tied to just envelopes. Planes B and C might represent TImage components measured in millimeters.

By looking at this task in its abstraction, you have achieved the first three steps to printing in Windows: identify each element to print, identify the unit of measurement for the destination surface, and identify the units of measurement for each individual element to be plotted onto the destination surface.

Now consider another twist—literally. When printing an envelope in a vertical fashion, the text must rotate vertically, as shown in Figure 12.8.

FIGURE 12.8.

Text rotated vertically.

A Step-by-Step Process to Printing

The following list summarizes the process you should follow when laying out your printed output in code:

1. Identify each element to be printed to the destination surface.
2. Identify the unit of measurement for the destination surface, or printer canvas.
3. Identify the unit of measurement for each individual element to be plotted onto the destination surface.
4. Decide on the common unit of measurement with which to perform all drawing routines. Almost always, this will be the printer canvas's units—pixels.
5. Write the translation routines to convert the other units of measurement to that of the common unit of measurement.
6. Write the routines to calculate the size for each element to print in the common unit of measurement. In Object Pascal, this can be represented by a TPoint structure. Keep in mind dependencies on other values. For example, the address rect values are dependent on the envelope's position. Therefore, the envelope's data must be calculated first.
7. Write the routines to calculate the position of each element as it will appear on the printer canvas based on the printer canvas's coordinate system and the sizes obtained from step 6. In Object Pascal, this can be represented by a TRect structure. Again, keep in mind dependencies.
8. Write your printing function using the data gathered from the previous steps to position items on the printed surface.

Getting Down to Business

Given the step-by-step process, your task of printing an envelope should be much clearer. You will use this process in developing the envelope printing project. The first step is to identify the elements to print or represent. The elements for the envelope example are the envelope itself and the address.

> **NOTE**
>
> In this example, you will not print a return address because the purpose is to show you how to follow a printing process to print in Windows. That doesn't mean, however, that you are restricted from enhancing these routines; be ambitious!

In this example, you learn how to print two standard envelope sizes: a size 10 and a size $6^3/_4$.

Start by declaring an array constant to hold records containing your envelope sizes:

```
TEnvelope = record
  Kind: string;            { Stores the envelope type's name }
  Width: double;           { Width of the envelope }
  Height: double;          { Height of the envelope }
end;

const
  { An array constant of envelope types }
  EnvArray: array[1..2] of TEnvelope =
  ((Kind:'Size 10';Width:9.5;Height:4.125),        { 9-1/2 x 4-1/8 }
   (Kind:'Size 6-3/4';Width:6.5;Height:3.625));     { 6-1/2 x 3-3/4 }
```

Steps 2 and 3 are covered: you know that the destination surface is the TPrinter.Canvas, which is represented in pixels. The envelopes are represented in inches and the address is represented in pixels. Step 4 requires you to select a common unit of measurement. For this project, there is no need to use any other unit of measurement, so it is best to use pixels as your common unit of measurement.

For step 5, the only units you need to convert are from inches to pixels. The GetDeviceCaps() function can return the amount of pixels per one inch along the horizontal and vertical axis for Printer.Canvas:

```
PixPerInX := GetDeviceCaps(Printer.Handle, LOGPIXELSX);  { Pixels per inch
➥horizontally }
PixPerInY := GetDeviceCaps(Printer.Handle, LOGPIXELSY);  { Pixels per inch
➥vertically }
```

Now, to convert the envelope's size to pixels, just multiply the number of inches by PixPerInX or PixPerInY to get its horizontal and vertical measurement in pixels:

```
EnvelopeWidthInPixels := trunc(EnvelopeWidthValue * PixPerInX);
EnvelopeHeightInPixels := trunc(EnvelopeHeightValue * PixPerInY);
```

Because the envelope width or height can be a fractional value, you use the Trunc() function to return the real type value as an integer value rounded toward zero.

Steps 6 and 7 are covered in the implementation of the project. Create a new project and change Form1's Name property to EnvPrintForm. Change its border style to bsSingle. Save the project as ENVLOPE.DPR and ENVLOPEU.PAS. Add the components listed in Table 12.4.

Table 12.4. EnvPrintForm's components.

Component	Property	Value
GroupBox1	Caption	Envelope Size
GroupBox2	Caption	Envelope Out
Edit1	Text	' '
Edit2	Text	' '
Edit3	Text	' '

Also, add six TRadioButtons to the group box so that they appear as shown in Figure 12.9.

FIGURE 12.9.
EnvPrintForm.

GroupBox1

GroupBox2

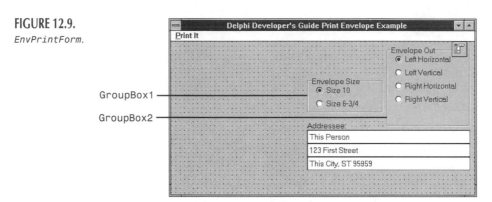

When the user clicks one of the radio buttons in GroupBox1 or GroupBox2, an event-handler is called. This event handler calls the routines to calculate the envelope's size and position based on the radio button choices. The address rectangle's size and position also are calculated based on the longest width of the three edit controls and their combined height. All calculations are based on Printer.Canvas's pixels. The PrintIt menu event handler contains the logic to print the envelope based on the choices selected. Additional logic to handle font rotation when the envelope is positioned vertically is provided. Additionally, a pseudo-print preview is created in the form's OnCreate event handler. This print preview is updated as the user selects the radio buttons. Listings 12.6 and 12.7 show the source code for ENVLOPE.DPR and ENVLOPEU.PAS, respectively.

Listing 12.6. The source code for ENVLOPE.DPR.

```
program Envlope;

uses
  Forms,
  Envlopeu in 'ENVLOPEU.PAS' {EnvPrintForm};

{$R *.RES}

begin
  Application.CreateForm(TEnvPrintForm, EnvPrintForm);
  Application.Run;
end.
```

Listing 12.7. The source code for ENVLOPEU.PAS.

```
unit Envlopeu;

interface
```

```
uses
  SysUtils, WinTypes, WinProcs, Messages, Classes, Graphics, Controls,
  Forms, Dialogs, printers, StdCtrls, ExtCtrls, Menus;

type

  TEnvelope = record
    Kind: string;              { Stores the envelope type's name }
    Width: double;             { Width of the envelope }
    Height: double;            { Height of the envelope }
  end;

const
  { An array constant of envelope types }
  EnvArray: array[1..2] of TEnvelope =
  ((Kind:'Size 10';Width:9.5;Height:4.125),       { 9-1/2 x 4-1/8 }
   (Kind:'Size 6-3/4';Width:6.5;Height:3.625));    { 6-1/2 x 3-3/4 }

type

  TFeedType = (epLHorz, epLVert, epRHorz, epRVert); { Enumerated type of }
                                                    { printing positions }
  TPrintPrevPanel = class(TPanel)
  public
    property Canvas; { Publicize this property }
  end;

  TEnvPrintForm = class(TForm)
    GroupBox1: TGroupBox;
    RBSize10: TRadioButton;
    RBSize6: TRadioButton;
    GroupBox2: TGroupBox;
    RBLHorz: TRadioButton;
    RBLVert: TRadioButton;
    RBRHorz: TRadioButton;
    RBRVert: TRadioButton;
    MainMenu1: TMainMenu;
    PrintIt1: TMenuItem;
    Label1: TLabel;
    Edit1: TEdit;
    Edit2: TEdit;
    Edit3: TEdit;
    procedure FormCreate(Sender: TObject);
    procedure RBLHorzClick(Sender: TObject);
    procedure PrintIt1Click(Sender: TObject);
  private
    { Private declarations }
    PrintPrev: TPrintPrevPanel; { Print  preview panel }
    EnvSize: TPoint;            { Stores the envelopes size }
    EnvPos: TRect;             { Stores the envelope's position }
    ToAddrSize: TPoint;        { Stores the address's bounding rectangle size }
    ToAddrPos: TRect;          { Stores the address's position }
    FeedType: TFeedType;       { Stores the feed type from TEnvPosition }
    function GetEnvelopeSize: TPoint;
    function GetEnvelopePos: TRect;
    function GetToAddrSize: TPoint;
    function GetToAddrPos: TRect;
```

continues

Listing 12.7. continued

```pascal
  procedure DrawIt;
  procedure RotatePrintFont;
public
  { Public declarations }
end;

var
  EnvPrintForm: TEnvPrintForm;

implementation

{$R *.DFM}

function TEnvPrintForm.GetEnvelopeSize: TPoint;
{ Gets the envelope's size represented by a TPoint }
var
  EnvW, EnvH: integer;
  PixPerInX,
  PixPerInY: integer;
begin
  PixPerInX := GetDeviceCaps(Printer.Handle, LOGPIXELSX);  { Pixels per inch
➥horizontally }
  PixPerInY := GetDeviceCaps(Printer.Handle, LOGPIXELSY);  { Pixels per inch
➥vertically }

  { Envelope size differs depending on the selection }
  if RBSize10.Checked then begin
    EnvW := trunc(EnvArray[1].Width * PixPerInX);    { Set size to Size 10
➥envelope Width }
    EnvH := trunc(EnvArray[1].Height * PixPerInY);   { Set size to Size 10
➥envelope Height }
  end
  else begin
    EnvW := trunc(EnvArray[2].Width * PixPerInX);    { set size to size 6
➥envelope Width }
    EnvH := trunc(EnvArray[2].Height * PixPerInY);   { set size to size 6
➥envelope Height }
  end;
  Result := Point(EnvW, EnvH)                        { Pass back the result
➥TPoint }
end;

function TEnvPrintForm.GetEnvelopePos: TRect;
{ Returns the envelope's position relative to its feed type }
var
 i: integer;
begin
  { Get the feed type from the radio buttons. }
  for i := 0 to GroupBox2.ControlCount -1 do
    if TRadioButton(GroupBox2.Controls[i]).Checked then
      FeedType := TFeedType(i);

  { Return the TRect structure representing the envelopes position as it is }
  { ejected from the printer. }
  case FeedType of
   epLHorz:
     Result := Rect(0, 0, EnvSize.X, EnvSize.Y);
```

```
  epLVert:
     Result := Rect(0, 0, EnvSize.Y, EnvSize.X);
  epRHorz:
     Result := Rect(Printer.PageWidth - EnvSize.X, 0,
                            Printer.PageWidth, EnvSize.Y);
  epRVert:
     Result := Rect(Printer.PageWidth - EnvSize.Y, 0,
                            Printer.PageWidth, EnvSize.X);
  end; { Case }
end;

function MaxLn(V1, V2: Integer): Integer;
{ Returns the larger of the two. If equal, returns the first }
begin
  Result := V1;      { Default result to V1 }
  if V1 < V2 then    { Return V2, only if it is }
    Result := V2     { larger than V1 }
end;

function TEnvPrintForm.GetToAddrSize: TPoint;
var
  TempPoint: TPoint;
begin
  { Calculate the size of the longest line using the above MaxLn() function }
  TempPoint.x := Printer.Canvas.TextWidth(Edit1.Text);
  TempPoint.x := MaxLn(TempPoint.x, Printer.Canvas.TextWidth(Edit2.Text));
  TempPoint.x := MaxLn(TempPoint.x, Printer.Canvas.TextWidth(Edit3.Text))+10;
  { Calculate the height of all the address lines }
  TempPoint.y := Printer.Canvas.TextHeight(Edit1.Text)+
                 Printer.Canvas.TextHeight(Edit2.Text)+
                 Printer.Canvas.TextHeight(Edit3.Text)+10;
  Result := TempPoint; { Return the Result TRect }
end;

function TEnvPrintForm.GetToAddrPos: TRect;
{ This function requires that EnvSize, and EnvPos be initialized }
Var
  TempSize: TPoint;
  LT, RB: TPoint;
begin
  TempSize := GetToAddrSize;  { Get the Address size }
  { Calculate two points, one representing the Left Top (LT) position and one
    representing the Right Bottom (RB) position of the address's bounding rect
    This depends on the FeedType }
  case FeedType of
    epLHorz: begin
      LT := Point((EnvSize.x div 2) - (TempSize.x div 2),
                  ((EnvSize.y div 2) - (TempSize.y div 2)));
      RB := Point(LT.x + TempSize.x, LT.y + TempSize.Y);
    end;
    epLVert: begin
      LT := Point((EnvSize.y div 2) - (TempSize.y div 2),
                  ((EnvSize.x div 2) - (TempSize.x div 2)));
      RB := Point(LT.x + TempSize.y, LT.y + TempSize.x);
    end;
    epRHorz: begin
      LT := Point((EnvSize.x div 2) - (TempSize.x div 2) + EnvPos.Left,
                  ((EnvSize.y div 2) - (TempSize.y div 2)));
```

continues

Listing 12.7. continued

```
    RB := Point(LT.x + TempSize.x, LT.y + TempSize.Y);
  end;
  epRVert:begin
    LT := Point((EnvSize.y div 2) - (TempSize.y div 2) + EnvPos.Left,
              ((EnvSize.x div 2) - (TempSize.x div 2)));
    RB := Point(LT.x + TempSize.y, LT.y + TempSize.x);
  end;
  end; { End Case }
 Result := Rect(LT.x, LT.y, RB.x, RB.y);  { Return the result TRect }
end;

procedure TEnvPrintForm.DrawIt;
{ This procedure assumes that EnvPos and EnvSize have been initialized }
begin
  PrintPrev.Invalidate;            { Erase what was previously on the Panel }
  Application.ProcessMessages;      { Ensure the wm_Paint message gets through }
  SetMapMode(PrintPrev.Canvas.Handle, MM_ISOTROPIC); { Set appropriate map mode }
  SetWindowExt(PrintPrev.Canvas.Handle,          { Set the panel's extent to }
     Printer.PageWidth, Printer.PageHeight);   { that of the printer }
  SetViewPortExt(PrintPrev.Canvas.Handle,        { Set the Viewport's extent }
     PrintPrev.Width, PrintPrev.Height);         { To that of the panel's size }
  SetViewportOrg(PrintPrev.Canvas.Handle, 0, 0);{ Set the origin to 0, 0       }
  PrintPrev.Brush.Style := bsSolid;              { Give the brush a solid color }
  with EnvPos do
   { Draw a rectangle that represents the envelope }
   PrintPrev.Canvas.Rectangle(Left, Top, Right, Bottom);
  with ToAddrPos do
    case FeedType of
    epLHorz, epRHorz: begin
      PrintPrev.Canvas.Rectangle(Left, Top, Right, Top+2);
      PrintPrev.Canvas.Rectangle(Left, Top+(Bottom-Top) div 2, Right,
                                 Top+(Bottom-Top) div 2+2);
      PrintPrev.Canvas.Rectangle(Left, Bottom, Right, Bottom+2);
    end;
    epLVert, epRVert: begin
      PrintPrev.Canvas.Rectangle(Left, Top, Left+2, Bottom);
      PrintPrev.Canvas.Rectangle(Left + (Right-Left)div 2, Top,
                                 Left + (Right-Left)div 2+2, Bottom);
      PrintPrev.Canvas.Rectangle(Right, Top, Right+2, Bottom);
    end;
    end ;
end;

procedure TEnvPrintForm.FormCreate(Sender: TObject);
var
  Ratio: double;
begin
  Ratio := Printer.PageHeight / Printer.PageWidth; { Calculate a ratio of
➥PageWidth to }
                                                   { Page height }
  with TPanel.Create(self) do begin              { Create a new TPanel
➥component }
    Parent := self;                              { Set parent to self }
    SetBounds(15, 15, 203, trunc(203*Ratio));    { Set Panel's bounds,
➥use ratio }
    Color := clBlack;                            { Set its color to black }
```

```
      BevelInner := bvNone;                        { Set its BevelInner
➡property to bvNone }
      BevelOuter := bvNone;                        { Set its BevelOuter
➡property to bvNone }
    end;

  PrintPrev := TPrintPrevPanel.Create(self);       { Create a Print preview
➡panel }

  with PrintPrev do begin
    Parent := self;                                { Set parent to the form }
    SetBounds(10, 10, 200, trunc(200*Ratio));      { Ser PrintPrev's bounds }
    BevelInner := bvNone;                          { Set BevelInner to bvNone }
    BevelOuter := bvNone;                          { Set BevelOuter to bvNone }
    Color := clWhite;                              { Set the color to white }
    BorderStyle := bsSingle;                       { Set to a single border }
  end;

end;

procedure TEnvPrintForm.RBLHorzClick(Sender: TObject);
begin
  EnvSize := GetEnvelopeSize;
  EnvPos := GetEnvelopePos;
  ToAddrPos := GetToAddrPos;
  DrawIt;
end;

procedure TEnvPrintForm.PrintIt1Click(Sender: TObject);
var
  TempHeight: integer;
  SaveFont: TFont;
begin
  Printer.BeginDoc;                        { Start a print job }
  TempHeight := Printer.Canvas.TextHeight(Edit1.Text); { Calculate a temporary
➡Line Height }
  with ToAddrPos do begin
    if (FeedType = eplVert) or (FeedType = epRVert) then begin { Only with
➡vertical feeds }
      SaveFont := TFont.Create;                            { Create a new TFont
➡class instance }
      SaveFont.Assign(Printer.Canvas.Font);                { Save the printer's
➡current font }
      RotatePrintFont;                                     { Call to rotate the
➡font 90 degrees }
      Printer.Canvas.TextOut(Left, Bottom, Edit1.Text);  { Output the address
➡lines of text }
      Printer.Canvas.TextOut(Left+TempHeight+2, Bottom, Edit2.Text);
      { Make note of the precedence of these math routines. }
      Printer.Canvas.TextOut(Left+TempHeight*2+2, Bottom, Edit3.Text);
      Printer.Canvas.Font.Assign(SaveFont);                { Get back the
➡saved font }
      SaveFont.Free;                                       { Free the created
➡font }
    end
    else begin
      { If not vertical just output the lines of text as they are }
      Printer.Canvas.TextOut(Left, Top, Edit1.Text);
```

continues

Listing 12.7. continued

```
      Printer.Canvas.TextOut(Left, Top+TempHeight+2, Edit2.Text);
      Printer.Canvas.TextOut(Left, Top+TempHeight*2+2, Edit3.Text);
    end;
  end;
  Printer.EndDoc;
end;

procedure TEnvPrintForm.RotatePrintFont;
var
  LogFont: TLogFont;
begin
  with Printer.Canvas do begin
    with LogFont do begin
      lfHeight := Font.Height;          { Set to Printer.Canvas.font.height }
      lfWidth := 0;                     { let font mapper choose width}
      lfEscapement := 900;              { tenths of degrees so 900 = 90 degrees }
      lfOrientation := 0;               { ignored by Windows }
      lfWeight := FW_NORMAL;            { default }
      lfItalic := 0;                    { no italics }
      lfUnderline := 0;                 { no underline }
      lfStrikeOut := 0;                 { no strikeout }
      lfCharSet := ANSI_CHARSET;        { default }
      StrPCopy(lfFaceName, Font.Name);  { Printer.Canvas's font's name }
      lfQuality := PROOF_QUALITY;       { Windows gets a better one if avail }
      lfOutPrecision := OUT_TT_ONLY_PRECIS;   { force True type fonts }
      lfClipPrecision := CLIP_DEFAULT_PRECIS; { default }
      lfPitchAndFamily := Variable_Pitch;     { default }
    end;
  end;
  Printer.Canvas.Font.Handle := CreateFontIndirect(LogFont);
end;
end.
```

Notice the definition of the TFeedType enumerated type:

```
TFeedType = (epLHorz, epLVert, epRHorz, epRVert);
```

This represents each position of the envelope as it may feed out of the printer.

TEnvPrintForm contains variables to hold the envelope's size and position, the address's TRect size and position, and the current TFeedType value:

```
EnvSize: TPoint;           { Stores the envelope's size }
EnvPos: TRect;             { Stores the envelope's position }
ToAddrSize: TPoint;        { Stores the address's bounding rectangle size }
ToAddrPos: TRect;          { Stores the address's position }
FeedType: TFeedType;       { Stores the feed type from TEnvPosition }
```

TEnvPrintForm declares the methods GetEnvelopeSize() GetEnvelopePos(), GetToAddrSize(), and GetToAddrPos() to determine the various measurements for elements to be printed as specified in steps 6 and 7 of this chapter's model.

In GetEnvelopeSize(), the GetDeviceCaps() function is used to convert the envelope size in inches to pixels based on the selection from GroupBox1. GetEnvelopPos() determines the position of the envelope on TPrinter.Canvas based on Printer.Canvas's coordinate system.

GetToAddrSize() calculates the size of the address's bounding rectangle based on the measurements of text contained in the edit controls. Here, Printer.Canvas's TextHeight() and TextWidth() methods are used to determine these sizes. The function MaxLn() is a helper function used to determine the longest text line of the three TEdits, which is used as the rectangle's width.

GetToAddrPos() calls GetToAddrSize() and uses the returned value to calculate the address's bounding rectangle's position on Printer.Canvas. Note that the envelope's size and placement are needed in order for this function to properly position the address rect.

The PrintIt1Click() event handler performs the actual printing logic. First, it initializes printing with the BeginDoc() method. Then, it calculates a temporary line height used for text positioning. It determines the TFeedType, and if it is one of the vertical types, it saves the printer's font and calls the method RotatePrintFont(), which rotates the font 90 degrees. When it returns form RotatePrintFont(), it restores Printer.Canvas's original font. If the TFeedType is one of the horizontal types, it performs the TextOut() calls to print the address. Finally, PrintIt1Click() ends printing with the EndDoc() method.

RotatePrintFont() creates a TLogFont structure and initializes its various values obtained from Printer.Canvas and other default values. Notice the assignment to its lfEscapement member. Remember from Chapter 10 that lfEscapement specifies an angle in tenths of degrees at which the font is to be drawn. Here, you specify to print the font at a 90-degree angle by assigning 900 to lfEscapement. One thing to note here is that only TrueType fonts can be rotated. Read about fonts in Chapter 10, "GDI and Graphics Programming."

A Simple Print Preview

Often, a good way to help your users not make a mistake by choosing the wrong selection is to enable them to view what the printed output would look like before actually printing. The project in this section contains a print preview panel. To construct this, you need to create a descendant class of TPanel and publicize its Canvas property, as was done in the ENVLOPEU.PAS's interface section:

```
TPrintPrevPanel = class(TPanel)
  public
    property Canvas; { Publicize this property }
  end;
```

The TEnvPrintForm.FormCreate() event handler performs the logic to instantiate a TPrintPrevPanel. The line

```
Ratio := Printer.PageHeight / Printer.PageWidth; { Calculate a ratio of PageWidth
to }
```

determines a ratio of the printer's width to its height. This is used to calculate the width and height for the `TPrintPrevPanel` instance.

Before the `TPrintPrevPanel` is created, however, a regular `TPanel` with a black color is created to serve as a shadow to the `TPrintPrevPanel` instance, `PrintPrev`. Its boundaries are adjusted so that they are slightly to the right and below the `PrintPrev`'s boundaries. The effect is that it gives `PrintPrev` a three-dimensional look with a shadow behind it. `PrintPrev` is used primarily to show how the envelope would be printed. The routine `DrawIt()` performs this logic.

`TEnvPrintForm.DrawIt()` calls `PrintPrev.Invalidate` to erase its previous contents. Then it calls `Application.ProcessMessages` to ensure that the paint message is processed before executing the remaining code. It then sets `PrintPrev`'s mapping mode to `MM_ISOTROPIC` to allow it to accept arbitrary extents along the X- and Y-axes. `SetWindowExt()` sets `PrintPrev`'s windows' extents to that of `Printer.Canvas`'s extents, and `SetViewPortExt()` sets `PrintPrev`'s viewport extents to that of its own height and width (see Chapter 10 for a discussion on mapping modes).

This enables `DrawIt()` to use the same metric values used for the `Printer.Canvas`, the envelope, the address rectangle, and the `PrintPrev` panel. This routine also uses rectangles to represent text lines. The effect is shown in Figure 12.10.

FIGURE 12.10.
An envelope printing form
with print preview.

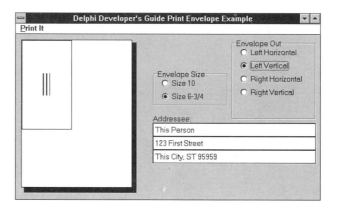

Summary

This chapter taught you the techniques you need to know in order to program any type of custom printing, from simple printing to more advanced techniques. You also learned a methodology that you can apply to any printing task. You'll use more of this knowledge in upcoming chapters where you build even more powerful printing methods. For now, take what you have learned and expand on the existing code you already have written.

13

Multimedia Programming with Delphi

Delphi's `TMediaPlayer` component is proof that good things come in small packages. In the guise of this little component, Delphi encapsulates a great deal of the functionality of Windows' *Media Control Interface* (MCI)—the portion of the Windows API that provides control for multimedia devices.

Delphi makes multimedia programming so easy that the traditional and boring "Hello World" program may be a thing of the past. Why write `Hello World` to the screen when it is almost as easy to play a sound or video file that offers its greetings?

In this chapter, you will learn how to write a simple yet powerful media player, and you will even construct a fully functional audio CD player. This chapter explains the uses and nuances of the `TMediaPlayer`. Of course, your computer must be equipped with multimedia devices such as a sound card and CD-ROM in order for this chapter to be of real use to you.

Creating a Simple Media Player

The best way to learn is by doing, so start by creating a media player project. Create a new project and drop a button, `MediaPlayer`, and `OpenDialog` onto the main form. The main form is shown in Figure 13.1.

FIGURE 13.1.

The DDG Media Player.

The DDG Media Player works like this: After you click `Button1`, the `OpenDialog` box appears, and you choose a file from it. The Media Player prepares itself to play the file you chose in the `OpenDialog`. You then can click the Play button on the Media Player to play the file. The following code belongs to the button's `OnClick` method, and it opens the Media Player with the file you chose:

```
procedure TForm1.Button1Click(Sender: TObject);
begin
  if OpenDialog1.Execute then begin
    MediaPlayer1.Filename := OpenDialog1.Filename;
    MediaPlayer1.Open;
  end;
end;
```

This code executes the `OpenDialog` dialog box, and if a filename is chosen, the `OpenDialog`'s `FileName` property is copied to the `MediaPlayer`'s `FileName`. The `MediaPlayer`'s `Open` method then is called to prepare it to play the file.

You also may want to limit the files to browse through with the `OpenDialog` to only multimedia files. `TMediaPlayer` supports a whole gaggle of multimedia device types, but for now, you will just browse WAVE, AVI, and MIDI files. You can add this capability to the OpenDialog by selecting OpenDialog1 in the Object Inspector, choosing the Mask property, and clicking the ellipsis to the right of this item to invoke the Filter Editor. Fill in the WAV, AVI, and MID extensions, as shown in Figure 13.2.

FIGURE 13.2.

The Filter Editor.

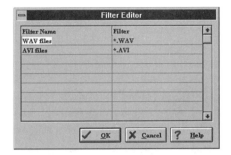

Save this project as DDGMPLAY.DPR, and save the main unit as MPMAIN.PAS. The Media Player now is ready to run. Run the program, and if you're not sure whether you have any multimedia files to try it out on, you can use TADA.WAV, which is placed in the \WIN-DOWS directory when you install Windows 3.1 (your installation may differ). Others may have convinced you—or perhaps you had convinced yourself—that multimedia programming is difficult, but now you have firsthand proof that this just isn't true.

Using WAV Files in Your Applications

WAV (pronounced *"wave,"* which is short for *waveform*) files have become the *de facto* standard file format for sharing audio in Windows. As the name implies, WAV files store sounds in a binary format that resembles a mathematical wave. The great thing about WAV files is that they have gained industry acceptance, and you can find them everywhere. The bad thing about WAV files is that they tend to be bulky, and just a few of those Homer Simpson WAV files can take up a hefty chunk of hard disk space.

The TMediaPlayer component enables you to easily integrate WAV sounds into your applications. As just illustrated, playing WAV files in your program is no sweat—just feed a TMediaPlayer a filename, open it, and play it. A little audio capability can be just the thing your applications need to go from neat to way cool.

If playing WAV files is all you want to do, you may not need the overhead of a TMediaPlayer component. Instead, you can use the sndPlaySound() API function found in the MMSystem unit. sndPlaySound() is defined in the following code:

```
function sndPlaySound(lpszSoundName: PChar; uFlags: Word): Bool;
```

sndPlaySound() has the capability to play a WAV sound from a file, from memory, or from a resource file linked into the application. sndPlaySound() takes two parameters. The first parameter, lpszSoundName, is a PChar variable that represents a filename or entry from the [sounds] section of your WIN.INI file; or, it is a pointer to a WAV sound located somewhere in memory. The second parameter, uFlags, contains flags that describe how the sound should be played. The flag values follow:

Flag	Description
snd_Async	Plays the sound asynchronously, and returns the function almost immediately. This achieves a background music effect.
snd_Loop	Plays the sound over and over again until you go crazy. snd_Async also must be specified when using this flag.
snd_Memory	Plays the WAV sound in the memory area pointed to by the first parameter to sndPlaySound.
snd_NoDefault	If the sound cannot be found, sndPlaySound() returns immediately without playing the default sound as specified in WIN.INI.
snd_NoStop	Plays the sound only if it is not already playing. sndPlaySound() returns True if the sound is played, and False if the sound is not played.
snd_Sync	Plays the sound synchronously, and doesn't return the function until the sound finishes playing.

NOTE

To terminate a sound currently playing asynchronously, call sndPlaySound() and pass Nil in the lpszSoundName parameter.

Playing Video

AVI, or Audio-Video Interleave, is one of most common file formats used to exchange audio and video information simultaneously. In fact, you will find two AVI files on the CD-ROM that contain your copy of Delphi; they are located in the \VIDEOS subdirectory, and they are called BORLAND.AVI and DELPHI.AVI.

TIP

Windows 3.1 does not come with the files needed to support AVI playback, but these files are available for you to use and redistribute with your application. You can obtain these drivers from Microsoft's Windows multimedia forum on CompuServe (GO WINMM).

You can use the simple multimedia player program that you have written to display AVI files. Simply select an AVI file in the OpenDialog, and click the Play button. Note that the AVI file plays in its own window.

Showing the First Frame

You may want to display the first frame of an AVI file in a window before you actually play the file. This achieves something like a freeze-frame effect. To do this after opening the TMediaPlayer, just set the Frames property of the TMediaPlayer to 1 and then call the Step() method. The Frames property tells the TMediaPlayer how many frames to move when Step() or Back() methods are called. Step() advances the TMediaPlayer frames and displays the current frame. The code for this follows:

```
procedure TForm1.Button1Click(Sender: TObject);
begin
  if OpenDialog1.Execute then
    with MediaPlayer1 do begin
      Filename := OpenDialog1.Filename;
      Open;
      Frames := 1;
      Step;
      Notify := True;
    end;
end;
```

Using the *Display* Property

You can assign a value to TMediaPlayer's Display property in order to cause the AVI file to play to a specific window, instead of creating its own window. To do this, you add a TPanel component to your media player, as shown in Figure 13.3. After adding the panel, save the project as EASYMM.DPR, and save the unit as EASYMAIN.PAS.

FIGURE 13.3.
The EASYMM.DPR main window.

Click the drop-down arrow for MediaPlayer1's Display property, and note that all the components in this project appear in the listbox. Select Panel1 into the Display property.

Now notice that when you run the program and select and play an AVI file, the AVI file output appears in the panel. Also note that the AVI file doesn't take up the whole area of the panel; the AVI file has a certain default size programmed into it.

Using the *DisplayRect* Property

DisplayRect is a property of type TRect that determines the size of the AVI file output window. You can use the DisplayRect property to cause your AVI file's output to stretch or shrink to a certain size. If you want the AVI file to take up the whole area of Panel1, for example, you can assign DisplayRect to the size of the panel:

```
MediaPlayer1.DisplayRect := Rect(0, 0, Panel1.Width, Panel1.Height);
```

You can add this line of code to the OnClick handler for Button1:

```
procedure TForm1.Button1Click(Sender: TObject);
begin
  if OpenDialog1.Execute then begin
    MediaPlayer1.Filename := OpenDialog1.Filename;
    MediaPlayer1.Open;
    MediaPlayer1.DisplayRect := Rect(0, 0, Panel1.Width, Panel1.Height);
  end;
end;
```

Understanding *TMediaPlayer* Events

TMediaPlayer has two unique events: OnPostClick and OnNotify.

The OnPostClick event is very similar to OnClick, except that, whereas OnClick occurs as soon as the component is clicked, OnPostClick executes only after some action occurs that was caused by a click. If you click the Play button on the TMediaPlayer at runtime, for example, an OnClick event is generated, but an OnPostClick event is generated only after the media device is done playing.

The OnNotify event is a little more interesting. The OnNotify event executes whenever the TMediaPlayer completes a media-control method (such as Back, Close, Eject, Next, Open, Pause, PauseOnly, Play, Previous, Resume, Rewind, StartRecording, Step, or Stop) and only when TMediaPlayer's Notify property is set to True. To illustrate OnNotify, add a handler for this event to the EasyMM project. In the event handler method, you cause a message dialog box to appear after a command executes:

```
procedure TForm1.MediaPlayer1Notify(Sender: TObject);
begin
  MessageDlg('Media control method executed', mtInformation, [mbOk], 0);
end;
```

Don't forget to also set the `Notify` property to `True` in `Button1`'s `OnClick` handler after opening the Media Player:

```
procedure TForm1.Button1Click(Sender: TObject);
begin
  if OpenDialog1.Execute then
    with MediaPlayer1 do begin
      Filename := OpenDialog1.Filename;
      Open;
      DisplayRect := Rect(0, 0, Panel1.Width, Panel1.Height);
      Notify := True;
    end;
end;
```

Viewing the Source Code for EasyMM

By now, you should know the basics of how to play WAV and AVI files. Listings 13.1 and 13.2 show the complete source code for the EasyMM project.

Listing 13.1. The source code for EASYMM.DPR.

```
program Easymm;

uses
  Forms,
  Easymain in 'EASYMAIN.PAS' {Form1};

{$R *.RES}

begin
  Application.CreateForm(TForm1, Form1);
  Application.Run;
end.
```

Listing 13.2. The source code for EASYMAIN.PAS.

```
unit Easymain;

interface

uses
  SysUtils, WinTypes, WinProcs, Messages, Classes, Graphics, Controls,
```

Listing 13.2. continued

```
  Forms, Dialogs, StdCtrls, MPlayer, ExtCtrls;

type
  TForm1 = class(TForm)
    MediaPlayer1: TMediaPlayer;
    OpenDialog1: TOpenDialog;
    Button1: TButton;
    Panel1: TPanel;
    procedure Button1Click(Sender: TObject);
    procedure MediaPlayer1Notify(Sender: TObject);
  private
    { Private declarations }
  public
    { Public declarations }
  end;

var
  Form1: TForm1;

implementation

{$R *.DFM}

procedure TForm1.Button1Click(Sender: TObject);
begin
  if OpenDialog1.Execute then
    with MediaPlayer1 do begin
      Filename := OpenDialog1.Filename;
      Open;
      DisplayRect := Rect(0, 0, Panel1.Width, Panel1.Height);
      Notify := True;
    end;
end;

procedure TForm1.MediaPlayer1Notify(Sender: TObject);
begin
  MessageDlg('Media control method executed', mtInformation, [mbOk], 0);
end;

end.
```

Examining Device Support

TMediaPlayer supports the vast array of media devices supported by MCI. The type of device that a TMediaPlayer controls is determined by its DeviceType property. Table 13.1 describes the different values of the DeviceType property.

Table 13.1. Values of `TMediaPlayer`'s `DeviceType` property.

`DeviceType` *Value*	*Media Device*
`dtAutoSelect`	The `TMediaPlayer` automatically should select the correct device type based on the filename to be played.
`dtAVIVideo`	AVI, or Audio-Video Interleave file. These files have the AVI extension and contain both sound and full-motion video.
`dtCDAudio`	An audio CD played from your computer's CD-ROM drive.
`dtDAT`	A digital audio tape (DAT) player connected to your PC.
`dtDigitalVideo`	A digital video.
`dtMMMovie`	Multimedia movie format.
`dtOther`	An unspecified multimedia format.
`dtOverlay`	A video overlay device.
`dtScanner`	A scanner connected to your PC.
`dtSequencer`	A sequencer device capable of playing MIDI files. MIDI files typically end in a MID or RMI extension.
`dtVCR`	A video cassette recorder (VCR) connected to your PC.
`dtVideodisc`	A video disc player connected to your PC.
`dtWaveAudio`	A WAV audio file. These files end in the WAV extension.

TIP

You can control which file extensions map to which MCI devices by editing the `[MCI Extensions]` section of your WIN.INI file.

This chapter focuses primarily on the WAV, AVI, and CD Audio formats because those are the most common under Windows.

Creating an Audio CD Player

You will learn about the finer points of the `TMediaPlayer` component by creating a full-featured audio CD player. Start with a form containing the components arranged as shown in Figure 13.4. Save the project as MPLYR.DPR, and save the main unit as MPLYMAIN.PAS.

FIGURE 13.4.

The audio CD player's main form.

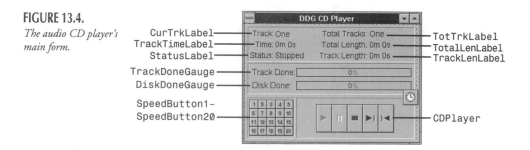

Table 13.2 shows the important properties to be set for the components contained on the CD player's main form.

Table 13.2. Important properties for the CD player's components.

Component	Property	Value
CDPlayer	DeviceType	dtAudioCD
SpeedButton1–SpeedButton20	Caption	'1' – '20'
SpeedButton1–SpeedButton20	Tag	1 – 20

Displaying a Splash Screen

When the CD player is run, it takes a couple of seconds for it to load, and it may take several more seconds for the TMediaPlayer to initialize after calling its Open method. This delay from the time the user clicks the icon in Program Manager to the time he or she actually sees the program often gives the user an *is my program gonna start, or isn't it?* feeling. This delay is caused by the time Windows takes to load its multimedia subsystem, which occurs when the TMediaPlayer is opened. To avoid this problem, give the CD player program a splash screen that displays as the program starts. The splash screen will tell users that, *yes, the program will eventually start—it's just taking a moment to load, so enjoy this little screen.*

The first step in creating a splash screen is to create a form that you want to use as the splash screen. Generally, you want this form to contain a panel, but not to have a border or title bar; this gives a 3D, floating-panel appearance. On the panel, place one or more TLabel components and perhaps a TImage component that displays a bitmap or icon.

The splash screen form for the CD player is shown in Figure 13.5, and the unit, SPLASH.PAS, is shown in Listing 13.3.

FIGURE 13.5.

The CD player's splash screen form.

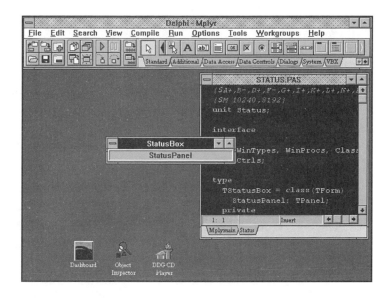

Listing 13.3. The source code for SPLASH.PAS.

```
unit Splash;

interface

uses WinTypes, WinProcs, Classes, Graphics, Forms, Controls, StdCtrls,
  ExtCtrls;

type
  TSplashScreen = class(TForm)
    StatusPanel: TPanel;
end;

var
  SplashScreen: TSplashScreen;

implementation

{$R *.DFM}

begin
  { Since the splash screen is displayed before the main screen is created,
    it must be created before the main screen. }
  SplashScreen := TSplashScreen.Create(Application);
  SplashScreen.Show;
  SplashScreen.Update;
end.
```

Unlike a normal form, the splash screen is created and shown in the initialization section of its unit. Because the initialization section for all units is executed before the main program block in the DPR file, this form is displayed before the main portion of the program runs.

CAUTION

Do not use `Application.CreateForm()` to create your splash screen form instance. The first time `Application.CreateForm()` is called in an application, Delphi makes that form the main application form. It would be a Bad Thing to make your splash screen the main form.

Beginning the CD Player

Create an event handler for the form's `OnCreate` method. In this method, you open and initialize the CD player program. First, call `CDPlayer`'s `Open()` method. `Open()` checks to make sure that the system is capable of playing audio CDs, and then initializes the device. If `Open()` fails, it raises an exception of type `EMCIDeviceError`. In the event of an exception opening the device, you should terminate the application:

```
try
  CDPlayer.Open; { Open the CD Player device. }
except
  { If a error occured, the system may be incapable of playing CDs. }
  on EMCIDeviceError do begin
    MessageDlg('Error Initializing CD Player.  Program will now exit.',
              mtError, [mbOk], 0);
    Application.Terminate;   { bail out }
  end;
end;
```

NOTE

The preferred way to end a Delphi application is by calling the main form's `Close()` method or, if you are not in a method of the main form, by calling `Application.Terminate`.

After opening `CDPlayer`, you should set its `EnabledButtons` property to ensure that the proper buttons are enabled for the device. Which buttons to enable, however, depends on the current state of the CD device. If a CD already is playing when you call `Open()`, for example, you obviously don't want to enable the Play button. To perform a check on the current status of the CD device, you can inspect `CDPlayer`'s `Mode` property. The `Mode` property, which has all its possible values laid out nicely in the online help, provides information on whether a CD device currently is playing, stopped, paused, seeking, and so on. In this case, your concern is only whether the device is stopped, paused, or playing. The following code enables the proper buttons:

```
case CDPlayer.Mode of
   mpPlaying : CDPlayer.EnabledButtons := [btPause, btStop, btNext, btPrev];
   mpStopped,          { show default buttons if stopped }
   mpPaused  : CDPlayer.EnabledButtons := [btPlay, btNext, btPrev];
   end;
```

The following code shows the completed source code for the TCDPlayerForm.FormCreate() method. Notice in this listing that you make calls to several methods after successfully opening CDPlayer. The purpose of these methods is to update various aspects of the CD player application, such as the number of tracks on the current CD or current track position. These methods are described in more detail later in this chapter.

```
procedure TCDPlayerForm.FormCreate(Sender: TObject);
{ This method is called when the form is created. It opens and initializes the
  player }
begin
  try
    CDPlayer.Open; { Open the CD Player device. }
    { If a CD is already playing at startup, show playing status. }
    if CDPlayer.Mode = mpPlaying then
      StatusLabel.Caption := 'Playing';
    GetCDTotals;      { Show total time and tracks on current CD }
    ShowTrackNumber;  { Show current track }
    ShowTrackTime;    { Show the minutes and seconds for the current track }
    ShowCurrentTime;  { Show the current position of the CD }
    ShowPlayerStatus; { Update the CD Player's status }
  except
    { If an error occured, the system may be incapable of playing CDs. }
    on EMCIDeviceError do begin
      MessageDlg('Error initializing CD Player.  Program will now exit.',
                 mtError, [mbOk], 0);
      Application.Terminate;    { bail out }
    end;
  end;
  { Check the current mode of the CD-ROM and enable the
    appropriate buttons. }
  case CDPlayer.Mode of
    mpPlaying : CDPlayer.EnabledButtons := [btPause, btStop, btNext, btPrev];
    mpStopped,           { show default buttons if stopped }
    mpPaused  : CDPlayer.EnabledButtons := [btPlay, btNext, btPrev];
  end;
  SplashScreen.Release;  { Close and free the splash screen. }
end;
```

Notice that the last line of code in this method closes the splash screen form. The OnCreate event of the main form is generally the best place to do this.

Updating the CD Player Information

As the CD device plays, you can keep the information on CDPlayerForm up to date by using a TTimer component. Every time a timer event occurs you can call the necessary updating methods, as shown in the form's OnCreate method to ensure that the display stays current. Double-click Timer1 to generate a method skeleton for its OnTimer event. The following shows the source code that you should use for this event.

```
procedure TCDPlayerForm.UpdateTimerTimer(Sender: TObject);
{ This method is the heart of the CD Player.  It updates all information at
  every timer interval. }
begin
  if CDPlayer.EnabledButtons = [btPause, btStop, btNext, btPrev] then begin
    CDPlayer.TimeFormat := tfMSF;
```

```
      DiskDoneGauge.Progress := (mci_msf_Minute(CDPlayer.Position) * 60 +
                          mci_msf_Second(CDPlayer.Position));
    CDPlayer.TimeFormat := tfTMSF;
    ShowTrackNumber; { Show track number the CD player is currently on }
    ShowTrackTime;   { Show total time for the current track }
    ShowCurrentTime; { Show elapsed time for the current track }
  end;
end;
```

Notice that, in addition to calling the various updating methods, this method also updates the DiskDoneGauge for the amount of time elapsed on the current CD. To get the elapsed time, the method changes CDPlayer's TimeFormat property to tfMSF and gets the minute and second value from the Position property using the mci_msf_Minute() and mci_msf_Second() functions. This merits a bit more explanation.

TimeFormat

The TimeFormat property of a TMediaPlayer component determines how the values of the StartPos, Length, Position, Start, and EndPos properties should be interpreted. Table 13.3 lists the possible values for TimeFormat. These values represent information packed into a longint type variable.

Table 13.3. Values for the TMediaPlayer.TimeFormat property.

Value	Time Storage Format
tfBytes	Number of bytes
tfFrames	Frames
tfHMS	Hours, minutes, and seconds
tfMilliseconds	Time in milliseconds
tfMSF	Minutes, seconds, and frames
tfSamples	Number of samples
tfSMPTE24	Hours, minutes, seconds, and frames based on 24 frames per second
tfSMPTE25	Hours, minutes, seconds, and frames based on 25 frames per second
tfSMPTE30	Hours, minutes, seconds, and frames based on 30 frames per second
tfSMPTE30Drop	Hours, minutes, seconds, and frames based on 30 drop frames per second
tfTMSF	Tracks, minutes, seconds, and frames

Time-Conversion Routines

The Windows API provides routines to retrieve the time information from the different packed formats shown in Table 13.4. *Packed format* means that multiple data values are packed, or encoded, into one Longint value. These functions are located in MMSYSTEM.DLL, so be sure to have MMSystem in your uses clause when using them.

Table 13.4. Functions to unpack multimedia time formats.

Function	Works With	Returns
mci_HMS_Hour()	tfHMS	Hours
mci_HMS_Minute()	tfHMS	Minutes
mci_HMS_Second()	tfHMS	Seconds
mci_MSF_Frame()	tfMSF	Frames
mci_MSF_Minute()	tfMSF	Minutes
mci_MSF_Second()	tfMSF	Seconds
mci_TMSF_Frame()	tfTMSF	Frames
mci_TMSF_Minute()	tfTMSF	Minutes
mci_TMSF_Second()	tfTMSF	Seconds
mci_TMSF_Track()	tfTMSF	Tracks

Methods for Updating the CD Player

As you learned earlier in this chapter, you use several methods to help keep the information displayed by the CD player up to date. The primary purpose of each of these methods is to update the labels in the top portion of the CD player form and to update the gauges in the middle portion of that form.

GetCDTotals()

The purpose of the GetCDTotals() method shown in the following code is to retrieve the length and total number of tracks on the current CD. This information then is used to update several labels and the DiskDoneGauge. This code also calls the AdjustSpeedButtons() method, which enables the same number of SpeedButtons as tracks. Note that this method also makes use of the TimeFormat and time-conversion routines that were discussed earlier.

```
procedure TCDPlayerForm.GetCDTotals;
{ This method gets the total time and tracks of the CD and displays them. }
var
  l: longint;
begin
  CDPlayer.TimeFormat := tfTMSF;                     { set time format }
  l := CDPlayer.Length;                              { get CD length }
  TotalTracks := mci_Tmsf_Track(CDPlayer.Tracks);   { get total tracks }
  TotalLengthM := mci_msf_Minute(l);                 { get total length in mins }
  TotalLengthS := mci_msf_Second(l);                 { get total length in secs }
  { set caption of Total Tracks label }
  TotTrkLabel.Caption := TrackNumToString(TotalTracks);
  { set caption of Total Time label }
  TotalLenLabel.Caption := IntToStr(TotalLengthM) + 'm' + ' ' +
                           IntToSTr(TotalLengthS) + 's';
  { intitialize gauge }
  DiskDoneGauge.MaxValue := (TotalLengthM * 60) + TotalLengthS;
  { enable the correct number of speedbuttons }
  AdjustSpeedButtons;
end;
```

ShowCurrentTime()

The ShowCurrentTime() method is shown in the following code. This method is designed to obtain the elapsed minutes and seconds for the currently playing track, and to update the necessary controls. Here, you also use the time-conversion routines provided by MMSystem.

```
procedure TCDPlayerForm.ShowCurrentTime;
{ This method displays the current time of the current track }
begin
  { Minutes for this track }
  m := mci_Tmsf_Minute(CDPlayer.Position);
  { Seconds for this track }
  s := mci_Tmsf_Second(CDPlayer.Position);
  { update track time label }
  TrackTimeLabel.Caption := IntToStr(m)+ 'm' + ' ' + IntToStr(s) + 's';
  { update track gauge }
  TrackDoneGauge.Progress := (60 * m) + s;
end;
```

ShowTrackTime()

The ShowTrackTime() method shown in the following code obtains the total length of the current track in minutes and seconds, and updates a label control. Again, you make use of the time-conversion routines. Also note that you check to make sure that the track isn't the same as when this function was last called. This comparison ensures that you don't make unnecessary function calls or repaint components unnecessarily.

```
procedure TCDPlayerForm.ShowTrackTime;
{ This method changes the track time to display the total length of the
  currently selected track. }
var
  Min, Sec: Byte;
begin
  { Don't update the information if player is still on the same track }
```

```
if CurrentTrack <> OldTrack then begin
  Min := mci_msf_Minute(CDPlayer.TrackLength[mci_Tmsf_Track
                                      (CDPlayer.Position)]);
  Sec := mci_msf_Second(CDPlayer.TrackLength[mci_Tmsf_Track
                                      (CDPlayer.Position)]);
  TrackDoneGauge.MaxValue := (60 * Min) + Sec;
  TrackLenLabel.Caption := IntToStr(Min) + 'm' + ' ' + IntToStr(Sec) + 's';
end;
OldTrack := CurrentTrack;
end;
```

CD Player Source

You now have seen all aspects of the CD player as they relate to multimedia. Listings 13.4 and 13.5 show complete source code for the MPLYR.DPR and MPLYMAIN.PAS modules, respectively. MPLYMAIN.PAS also shows some of the techniques you use to manipulate the speed buttons using their Tag property and other techniques for updating the controls.

Listing 13.4 The source code for MPLYR.DPR.

```
program MPlyr;

uses
  Forms,
  Mplymain in 'MPLYMAIN.PAS' {CDPlayerForm},
  Status in 'STATUS.PAS' {StatusBox};

begin
  Application.CreateForm(TCDPlayerForm, CDPlayerForm);
  Application.Run;
end.
```

Listing 13.5 The source code for MPLYMAIN.PAS.

```
unit Mplymain;

interface

uses
  WinTypes, WinProcs, Classes, Graphics, Forms, Controls,
  MPlayer, StdCtrls, Menus, MMSystem, Gauges, SysUtils,
  Messages, Buttons, Dialogs, ExtCtrls, Splash;

type
  TCDPlayerForm = class(TForm)
    UpdateTimer: TTimer;
    MainScreenPanel: TPanel;
    StatusLabel: TLabel;
    Label2: TLabel;
    CurTrkLabel: TLabel;
    Label4: TLabel;
```

continues

Listing 13.5. continued

```
    TrackTimeLabel: TLabel;
    Label7: TLabel;
    Label8: TLabel;
    TotTrkLabel: TLabel;
    TotalLenLabel: TLabel;
    Label12: TLabel;
    TrackLenLabel: TLabel;
    Label15: TLabel;
    CDInfo: TPanel;
    Panel2: TPanel;
    Panel1: TPanel;
    CDPlayer: TMediaPlayer;
    SpeedButton1: TSpeedButton;
    SpeedButton2: TSpeedButton;
    SpeedButton3: TSpeedButton;
    SpeedButton4: TSpeedButton;
    SpeedButton5: TSpeedButton;
    SpeedButton6: TSpeedButton;
    SpeedButton7: TSpeedButton;
    SpeedButton8: TSpeedButton;
    SpeedButton9: TSpeedButton;
    SpeedButton10: TSpeedButton;
    SpeedButton11: TSpeedButton;
    SpeedButton12: TSpeedButton;
    SpeedButton13: TSpeedButton;
    SpeedButton14: TSpeedButton;
    SpeedButton15: TSpeedButton;
    SpeedButton16: TSpeedButton;
    SpeedButton17: TSpeedButton;
    SpeedButton18: TSpeedButton;
    SpeedButton19: TSpeedButton;
    SpeedButton20: TSpeedButton;
    TrackDoneGauge: TGauge;
    DiskDoneGauge: TGauge;
    Label1: TLabel;
    Label3: TLabel;
    procedure UpdateTimerTimer(Sender: TObject);
    procedure CDPlayerPostClick(Sender: TObject; Button: TMPBtnType);
    procedure FormCreate(Sender: TObject);
    procedure SpeedButton1Click(Sender: TObject);
    procedure FormClose(Sender: TObject; var Action: TCloseAction);
  private
    OldTrack, CurrentTrack: Byte;
    TestStatus: Boolean;
    m, s: Byte;
    TotalTracks: Byte;
    TotalLengthM: Byte;
    TotalLengthS: Byte;
    procedure GetCDTotals;
    procedure ShowTrackNumber;
    procedure ShowTrackTime;
    procedure ShowCurrentTime;
    procedure ShowPlayerStatus;
    procedure AdjustSpeedButtons;
    procedure HighlightTrackButton;
    function TrackNumToString(InNum: Byte): String;
end;
```

```pascal
var
  CDPlayerForm: TCDPlayerForm;

implementation

{$R *.DFM}

const
  { Array of strings representing numbers from one to twenty: }
  NumStrings: array[1..20] of String[10] =
      ('One', 'Two', 'Three', 'Four', 'Five', 'Six', 'Seven', 'Eight', 'Nine',
       'Ten', 'Eleven', 'Twelve', 'Thirteen', 'Fourteen', 'Fifteen', 'Sixteen',
       'Seventeen', 'Eighteen', 'Nineteen', 'Twenty');

function TCDPlayerForm.TrackNumToString(InNum: Byte): String;
{ This function returns a string corresponding to an integer between 1 and 20.
  If the number is greater than 20, then the integer is returned as a string. }
begin
  if (InNum > High(NumStrings)) or (InNum < Low(NumStrings)) then
    Result := IntToStr(InNum)    { if not in array, then just return number }
  else
    Result := NumStrings[InNum]; { return the string from NumStrings array }
end;

procedure TCDPlayerForm.AdjustSpeedButtons;
{ This method enables the proper number of speed buttons }
var
  i: integer;
begin
  { iterate through form's Components array... }
  for i := 0 to ComponentCount - 1 do
    if Components[i] is TSpeedButton then begin  { is it a speed button? }
      { disable buttons higher than number of tracks on CD }
      if TSpeedButton(Components[i]).Tag <= TotalTracks then
        TSpeedButton(Components[i]).Enabled := True
      else
        TSpeedButton(Components[i]).Enabled := False;
    end;
end;


procedure TCDPlayerForm.GetCDTotals;
{ This method gets the total time and tracks of the CD and displays them. }
var
  TimeValue: longint;
begin
  CDPlayer.TimeFormat := tfTMSF;                     { set time format }
  TimeValue := CDPlayer.Length;                      { get CD length }
  TotalTracks := mci_Tmsf_Track(CDPlayer.Tracks);    { get total tracks }
  TotalLengthM := mci_msf_Minute(TimeValue);         { get total length in mins }
  TotalLengthS := mci_msf_Second(TimeValue);         { get total length in secs }
  { set caption of Total Tracks label }
  TotTrkLabel.Caption := TrackNumToString(TotalTracks);
  { set caption of Total Time label }
  TotalLenLabel.Caption := IntToStr(TotalLengthM) + 'm' + ' ' +
                           IntToStr(TotalLengthS) + 's';
```

continues

Listing 13.5. continued

```
  { initialize gauge }
  DiskDoneGauge.MaxValue := (TotalLengthM * 60) + TotalLengthS;
  { enable the correct number of speedbuttons }
  AdjustSpeedButtons;
end;

procedure TCDPlayerForm.ShowPlayerStatus;
{ This method displays the status of the CD Player the CD is currently
  being played. }
begin
  if CDPlayer.EnabledButtons = [btPause, btStop, btNext, btPrev] then
    with StatusLabel do begin
      case CDPlayer.Mode of
        mpNotReady: Caption := 'Not Ready';
        mpStopped:  Caption := 'Stopped';
        mpSeeking:  Caption := 'Seeking';
        mpPaused:   Caption := 'Paused';
        mpPlaying:  Caption := 'Playing';
      end;
    end
  { If these buttons are displayed the CD Player must be stopped... }
  else if CDPlayer.EnabledButtons = [btPlay, btNext, btPrev] then
    StatusLabel.Caption := 'Stopped';
end;

procedure TCDPlayerForm.ShowCurrentTime;
{ This method displays the current time of the current track }
begin
  { Minutes for this track }
  m := mci_Tmsf_Minute(CDPlayer.Position);
  { Seconds for this track }
  s := mci_Tmsf_Second(CDPlayer.Position);
  { update track time label }
  TrackTimeLabel.Caption := IntToStr(m)+ 'm' + ' ' + IntToStr(s) + 's';
  { update track gauge }
  TrackDoneGauge.Progress := (60 * m) + s;
end;

procedure TCDPlayerForm.ShowTrackTime;
{ This method changes the track time to display the total length of the
  currently selected track. }
var
  Min, Sec: Byte;
begin
  { Don't update the information if player is still on the same track }
  if CurrentTrack <> OldTrack then begin
    Min := mci_msf_Minute(CDPlayer.TrackLength[mci_Tmsf_Track
                                      (CDPlayer.Position)]);
    Sec := mci_msf_Second(CDPlayer.TrackLength[mci_Tmsf_Track
                                      (CDPlayer.Position)]);
    TrackDoneGauge.MaxValue := (60 * Min) + Sec;
    TrackLenLabel.Caption := IntToStr(Min) + 'm' + ' ' + IntToStr(Sec) + 's';
  end;
  OldTrack := CurrentTrack;
end;
```

```
procedure TCDPlayerForm.HighlightTrackButton;
{ This procedure changes the color of the speedbutton font for the current
  track to red, while changing other speedbuttons to navy blue. }
var
  i: longint;
begin
  { iterate through form's components }
  for i := 0 to ComponentCount - 1 do
    { is it a speedbutton? }
    if Components[i] is TSpeedButton then
      if TSpeedButton(Components[i]).Tag = CurrentTrack then
        { turn red if current track }
        TSpeedButton(Components[i]).Font.Color := clRed
      else
        { turn blue if not current track }
        TSpeedButton(Components[i]).Font.Color := clNavy;
end;

procedure TCDPlayerForm.ShowTrackNumber;
{ This method displays the currenty playing track number. }
var
  t: byte;
begin
  t := mci_Tmsf_Track(CDPlayer.Position);      { get current track }
  CurrentTrack := t;                           { set instance variable }
  CurTrkLabel.Caption := TrackNumToString(t); { set Curr Track label caption }
  HighlightTrackButton;                        { Highlight current speedbutton }
end;

procedure TCDPlayerForm.UpdateTimerTimer(Sender: TObject);
{ This method is the heart of the CD Player.  It updates all information at
  every timer interval. }
var
  CurTrack: Byte;
begin
  if CDPlayer.EnabledButtons = [btPause, btStop, btNext, btPrev] then begin
    CDPlayer.TimeFormat := tfMSF;
    DiskDoneGauge.Progress := (mci_msf_minute(CDPlayer.Position) * 60 +
                               mci_msf_second(CDPlayer.Position));
    CDPlayer.TimeFormat := tfTMSF;
    ShowTrackNumber; { Show track number the CD player is currently on }
    ShowTrackTime;   { Show total time for the current track }
    ShowCurrentTime; { Show elapsed time for the current track }
  end;
end;

procedure TCDPlayerForm.CDPlayerPostClick(Sender: TObject;
  Button: TMPBtnType);
{ This method displays the correct CD Player buttons when one of the buttons
  is clicked. }
begin
  Case Button of
    btPlay : begin
      CDPlayer.EnabledButtons := [btPause, btStop, btNext, btPrev];
      StatusLabel.Caption := 'Playing';
    end;
    btPause : begin
      CDPlayer.EnabledButtons := [btPlay, btNext, btPrev];
```

continues

Listing 13.5. continued

```
      StatusLabel.Caption := 'Paused';
    end;
    btStop : begin
      CDPlayer.Rewind;
      CDPlayer.EnabledButtons := [btPlay, btNext, btPrev];
      CurTrkLabel.Caption := 'One';
      TrackTimeLabel.Caption := '0m 0s';
      TrackDoneGauge.Progress := 0;
      DiskDoneGauge.Progress := 0;
      StatusLabel.Caption := 'Stopped';
    end;
    btPrev, btNext : begin
      CDPlayer.Play;
      CDPlayer.EnabledButtons := [btPause, btStop, btNext, btPrev];
      StatusLabel.Caption := 'Playing';
    end;
  end;
end;

procedure TCDPlayerForm.FormCreate(Sender: TObject);
{ This method is called when the form is created. It opens and initializes the
  player }
var
  buf: array[0..15] of char;
begin
  try
    CDPlayer.Open; { Open the CD Player device. }
    { If a CD is already playing at startup, show playing status. }
    if CDPlayer.Mode = mpPlaying then
      StatusLabel.Caption := 'Playing';
    GetCDTotals;      { Show total time and tracks on current CD }
    ShowTrackNumber;  { Show current track }
    ShowTrackTime;    { Show the minutes and seconds for the current track }
    ShowCurrentTime;  { Show the current position of the CD }
    ShowPlayerStatus; { Update the CD Player's status }
  except
    { If a error occured, the system may be incapable of playing CDs. }
    on EMCIDeviceError do begin
      MessageDlg('Error Initializing CD Player.  Program will now exit.',
                 mtError, [mbOk], 0);
      Application.Terminate;   { bail out }
    end;
  end;
  { Check the current mode of the CD-ROM and enable the
    appropriate buttons. }
  case CDPlayer.Mode of
    mpPlaying : CDPlayer.EnabledButtons := [btPause, btStop, btNext, btPrev];
    mpStopped,
    mpPaused  : CDPlayer.EnabledButtons := [btPlay, btNext, btPrev];
  end;
  SplashScreen.Release;  { Close and free the splash screen. }
end;

procedure TCDPlayerForm.SpeedButton1Click(Sender: TObject);
{ This method sets the current track when the user presses one of the track
  speed buttons. This method works with all 20 speed buttons, so by looking at
```

```
  the 'Sender' it can tell which button was pressed by the button's tag. }
begin
  CDPlayer.Stop;
  { Set the start position on the CD to the start of the newly selected track }
  CDPlayer.StartPos := CDPlayer.TrackPosition[(Sender as TSpeedButton).Tag];
  { Start playing CD at new position }
  CDPlayer.Play;
  CDPlayer.EnabledButtons := [btPause, btStop, btNext, btPrev];
  StatusLabel.Caption := 'Playing';
end;

procedure TCDPlayerForm.FormClose(Sender: TObject;
  var Action: TCloseAction);
begin
  CDPlayer.Close;
end;

end.
```

Summary

That about wraps up the basic concepts of Delphi's TMediaPlayer component. This chapter demonstrated through a couple of examples the power and simplicity of this component. In particular, you have learned about the common multimedia formats of WAVE audio, AVI audio/video, and CD audio. In Part III, "Real-World Applications," you learn how to incorporate these multimedia concepts into larger, commercial-quality applications.

14

Sharing Information with the Clipboard and DDE

Once upon a time, mankind struggled just to survive. People lived in dark caves, hunted for food with spears and rocks, and communicated with gruntlike sounds and hand motions. They worshiped fire because it gave them light under which they would work on their very slow computers. Computers back then could run only one application at a time due to hardware and software limitations. The only way to share information was to save it on disk and to pass the disk along for others to copy to their machines.

Nowadays, at least the equipment and software have improved. Under operating systems such as Windows, multiple applications can be run simultaneously, making life much easier and more productive for the computer user. One of the advantages gained from Windows is that information can be shared between applications on the same machine. By using the Windows Clipboard or Dynamic Data Exchange (DDE), you can make it possible for your users to copy information from one application to another application with little effort. In fact, you even can have a change in one application automatically show up in another running application without any user interaction.

This chapter teaches you how to maximize on Delphi's encapsulation of both the Windows Clipboard and DDE capabilities. Later, in Chapter 15, "Object Linking and Embedding with OLE," you will learn how to link and embed objects, another powerful form of data exchange.

In the Beginning, There Was the Clipboard

If you are an experienced Windows programmer, you may already be familiar with the Windows Clipboard, at least in functionality. If you are new to Windows programming, but have been using Windows, you probably have been using the Clipboard all along but never really understood how it was implemented.

Almost any application that has an Edit menu option makes use of the Clipboard. So what exactly is the Clipboard? It simply is an area of memory and a set of Windows API functions that enables applications to store and retrieve information to and from that area in memory. You can copy a portion of your source code from the Delphi editor, for example, and paste that same code into the Windows notebook or any other editor.

Why does Windows require a special set of functions and messages in order to use the Clipboard? Copying data to the Clipboard is more than just allocating an area of memory and placing data in that area. Other applications have to know how to retrieve that data, and whether the data is in a format that the application supports. Windows takes care of the memory management and enables you to copy, paste, and query about the information on the Clipboard.

CLIPBOARD FORMATS

Windows supports 16 predefined formats that applications can copy to or paste from the Clipboard. The most common formats are as follows:

CF_BITMAP	Specifies bitmap data.
CF_DIB	Specifies bitmap data along with the bitmap's palette information.
CF_PALETTE	Specifies a color palette.
CF_TEXT	Specifies a character array where each line ends with a carriage return/linefeed. This is the most commonly used format.

You can refer to the online API help if you are curious about less common formats. Additionally, Windows enables you to define your own private Clipboard format, which is illustrated later in this chapter.

Before Delphi, you, the programmer, called the various Clipboard functions directly and were responsible for ensuring that your application didn't do anything ill-advised with the Clipboard's contents. Now, in Delphi, you just use the global variable ClipBoard. ClipBoard is a Delphi class that encapsulates the Windows Clipboard.

Using the Clipboard with Text

To see how to use the Clipboard from a text editor, look at the source code for the MDI application in Chapter 8, "MDI Applications." The source files are MDIAPP.DPR, MDIFRAME.PAS, MDIEDIT.PAS, and MDIBMP.PAS.

In Chapter 8, you created menu items for cutting, copying, pasting, deleting, and selecting text as shown in Figure 14.1.

FIGURE 14.1.

The MDI application's Edit menu.

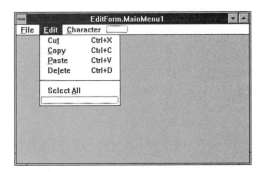

Here, the editor is actually a TMemo component that covers the client area of the form. The TMemo component has its own functions that interact with the global Clipboard. These functions are CutToClipBoard(), CopyToClipBoard(), and PasteFromClipBoard(). The methods ClearSelection() and SelectAll() aren't necessarily Clipboard interface routines, but they enable you to select the text that you want to copy to the Clipboard. Listing 14.1 shows the event handlers for the Edit menu items.

Listing 14.1. `EditForm`'s `Edit` event handlers.

```
procedure TEditForm.Cut1Click(Sender: TObject);
begin
  Memo1.CutToClipBoard;
end;

procedure TEditForm.Copy1Click(Sender: TObject);
begin
  Memo1.CopyToClipBoard;
end;

procedure TEditForm.Paste1Click(Sender: TObject);
begin
  Memo1.PasteFromClipBoard;
end;

procedure TEditForm.Delete1Click(Sender: TObject);
begin
  Memo1.ClearSelection;
end;

procedure TEditForm.SelectAll1Click(Sender: TObject);
begin
  Memo1.SelectAll;
end;
```

Again, all you're doing is calling the memo component's appropriate methods that perform the Clipboard functions for you. You also can place text on the Clipboard manually by using the Clipboard's `AsText` property if the text is 255 characters or less; otherwise, use the Clipboard's `SetTextBuf()` and `GetTextBuf()` methods to retrieve text larger than 255 characters. The following line shows you how to use the `AsText` property:

```
Clipboard.AsText := 'Delphi Rules';
```

> **NOTE**
>
> The Clipboard's `GetTextBuf()` and `SetTextBuf()` methods use Pascal `PChar` types as buffers to pass and retrieve data from the Clipboard. It is best to use a component's own methods for working with the Clipboard; otherwise, you might get caught having to convert strings to `PChar`s.

Using the Clipboard with Images

Earlier in this chapter, you learned that the Clipboard also can copy and paste images. Using the same MDI example program, you can add the event handlers shown in Listing 14.2 for `TBMPForm`'s Edit menu items: Copy and Paste.

Listing 14.2. TBMPForm's Edit menu event handlers.

```
procedure TBMPForm.Copy1Click(Sender: TObject);
begin
  ClipBoard.Assign(Image1.Picture); { Copy image to the clipboard }
end;

procedure TBMPForm.Paste1Click(Sender: TObject);
begin
  if ClipBoard.HasFormat(CF_BITMAP) or { Check for the correct clipboard format }
     ClipBoard.HasFormat(CF_PICTURE) then
  begin
    Image1.Picture.Assign(ClipBoard);  { Copy contents of clipboard to Image1 }
    ClientWidth := Image1.Picture.Width; { Adjust clientwidth to match }
    VertScrollBar.Range := Image1.Picture.Height; { Adjust the scrollbars }
    HorzScrollBar.Range := Image1.Picture.Width;
  end;
end;
```

TIP

In order to access the ClipBoard global variable, you must include CLIPBRD in the uses clause of the unit that will be using ClipBoard.

In Listing 14.2, TBMPForm.Copy1Click() uses the Clipboard's Assign() to copy the image to the Clipboard. By doing this, you can paste the image into another Windows application that supports the CF_BITMAP format, such as Window's Paintbrush (PBRUSH.EXE).

TBMPForm.Paste1Click() determines whether the Clipboard has a supported format: CF_BITMAP or CF_PICTURE. If so, it uses the Image's Assign() method to copy the image from the Clipboard and readjusts the scrollbars accordingly.

NOTE

CF_PICTURE is not a standard Windows Clipboard format. Instead, it is a private format used by Delphi applications for supporting VCL's TImage and TPicture classes. CF_PICTURE is basically a catchall for bitmaps and DIBs. When a CF_PICTURE is copied to the Clipboard, it simply means that there is a CF_BITMAP or CF_DIB on the Clipboard, and the application that pastes the data is free to use the type it prefers.

Creating Your Own Clipboard Format

Imagine working with an address entry box like that shown in Figure 14.2. Suppose that the current record you're entering has only a different name from the preceding record. It would be nice to be able to copy the contents from the preceding record and paste them to the current one, instead of having to enter each field individually. You might want to use the same information in other applications as well. The next example shows you how to create an object that knows about the Clipboard and can save its special formatted data to the Clipboard. You also learn how to store your information as CF_TEXT format so that you can retrieve the same data in other applications.

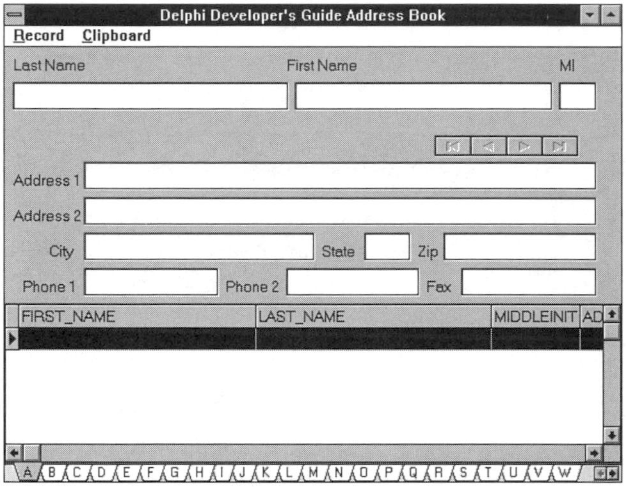

FIGURE 14.2.

The entry screen.

The main form has three TEdit controls and two TButtons controls, as shown in Figure 14.3. Listings 14.3 and 14.4 show the source code for DDGCBP.DPR and DDGCBU.PAS, respectively.

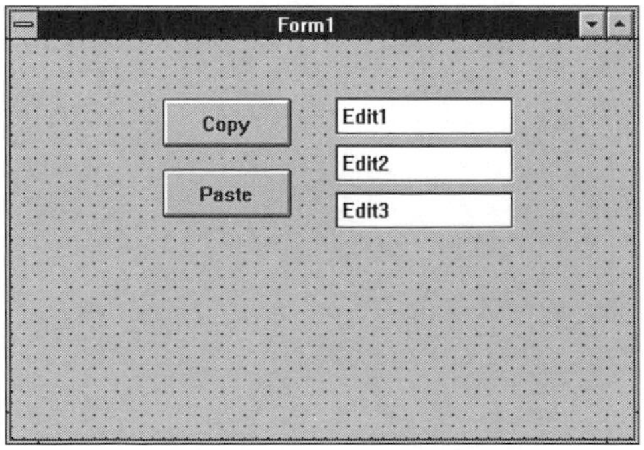

FIGURE 14.3.

The Clipboard format form.

Listing 14.3. The source code for DDGCBP.DPR.

```
program Ddgcbp;

uses
  Forms,
  Ddgcbu in 'DDGCBU.PAS' {Form1};

{$R *.RES}

begin
  Application.CreateForm(TForm1, Form1);
  Application.Run;
end.
```

Listing 14.4. The source code for DDGCBU.PAS.

```
unit Ddgcbu;

interface

uses
  SysUtils, WinTypes, WinProcs, Messages, Classes, Graphics, Controls,
  Forms, Dialogs, StdCtrls, clipbrd;
var
  CF_DDGDATA: word;
type

  TForm1 = class(TForm)
    Button1: TButton;
    Button2: TButton;
    Edit1: TEdit;
    Edit2: TEdit;
    Edit3: TEdit;
    procedure Button1Click(Sender: TObject);
    procedure Button2Click(Sender: TObject);
  private
    { Private declarations }
  public
    { Public declarations }
  end;

  PDDGRec = ^TDDGRec;
  TDDGRec = record
    LName: string;
    FName: string;
    MI: String;
  end;

  TDDGObject = class(TObject)
   private
     Rec: TDDGRec;
```

continues

Listing 14.4. continued

```
  protected
    procedure CopyToClipBoard;
    procedure GetFromClipBoard;
  end;

var
  Form1: TForm1;

implementation

{$R *.DFM}

procedure TDDGObject.CopyToClipBoard;
const
  CRLF = #13#10;  { Carriage return linefeed }
var
  Data: THandle;
  DataPtr: Pointer;
  Len: Integer;
  TempStr: string;
begin
  { Allocate memory from global heap }
  Data := GlobalAlloc(GMEM_MOVEABLE, SizeOf(Rec));
  try
    DataPtr := GlobalLock(Data);         { Get a pointer to the lock memory area }
    try
      Move(Rec, DataPtr^, SizeOf(Rec)); { Move the data in Buffer to DataPtr    }
      ClipBoard.Open; { This is only required if multiple clipboard formats are }
                      { being saved at once. Otherwise, if only one format is }
                      { being sent to the clipboard, don't call it. }
      ClipBoard.SetAsHandle(CF_DDGDATA, Data);
      { Now copy also in the CF_TEXT format }
      TempStr := Rec.FName+CRLF+Rec.LName+CRLF+Rec.MI+CRLF;
      ClipBoard.AsText := TempStr;
      Clipboard.Close; { Only call this if you previously called Clipboard.Open() }
    finally
      GlobalUnlock(Data);                     { Unlock the globally allocated memory  }
    end;
  except
    GlobalFree(Data);                    { Free the memory allocated, only if     }
    raise;                               { an exception occurs as this memory is }
  end;                                   { managed by the clipboard.              }
end;

procedure TDDGObject.GetFromClipBoard;
var
  Data: THandle;
  DataPtr: Pointer;
  C: Char;
  Size: Integer;
begin
  Data := ClipBoard.GetAsHandle(CF_DDGDATA); { Get the data on the clipboard }
  try
    if Data = 0 then Exit;                  { Exit is unsuccessful }
    DataPtr := GlobalLock(Data);            { Lock the Global memory object }
    try
```

```
      if SizeOf(Rec) > GlobalSize(Data) then Size := GlobalSize(Data);
      Move(DataPtr^, Rec, SizeOf(Rec));   { Copy contents of DataPtr to Buffer }
    finally
      GlobalUnlock(Data);                 { Unlock the global memory object }
    end;
  except
    GlobalFree(Data);               { Free the memory allocated, only if   }
    raise;                          { an exception occurs as this memory is }
  end;
end;

procedure TForm1.Button1Click(Sender: TObject);
var
  DDGObj: TDDGObject;
begin

  DDGObj := TDDGObject.Create; { Instantiate a TDDGObj }
  With DDGObj do
  begin
    Rec.FName := Edit1.Text;    { Copy the TEdit contents to the DDGObj.Rec }
    Rec.LName := Edit2.Text;
    Rec.MI := Edit3.Text;
    CopyToClipBoard;            { Copy contents of DDGObj to Clipboard }
  end;
  DDGObj.Free;                  { Free DDGObj }
end;

procedure TForm1.Button2Click(Sender: TObject);
var
  DDGObj: TDDGObject;
begin
  DDGObj := TDDGObject.Create;             { Instantiate a TDDGObj           }
  if ClipBoard.HasFormat(CF_DDGDATA) then { Check if format is available }
  with DDGObj do
  begin
    GetFromClipBoard;           { Copy contents of clipboard into DDGObj.Rec }
    Edit1.Text := Rec.FName;    { Update edit controls with the contents of  }
    Edit2.Text := Rec.LName;    { the clipboard                              }
    Edit3.Text := Rec.MI;
  end;
  DDGObj.Free;                  { Free DDGObj                                }
end;

initialization
  CF_DDGDATA := RegisterClipBoardFormat('CF_DDG'); { Register our clipboard }
end.
```

DDGDBU.PAS defines a record that has three data fields. This record will hold the data to be
sent to the Clipboard:

```
PDDGRec = ^TDDGRec;
  TDDGRec = record
    LName: string;
    FName: string;
    MI: String;
  end;
```

You also will see the TDDGObject class that has one data member of the TDDRec type. This object has two methods: one to send data to the Clipboard and one to retrieve data back from the Clipboard. The object's definition follows:

```
TDDGObject = class(TObject)
  private
     Rec: TDDGRec;
  protected
   procedure CopyToClipBoard;
   procedure GetFromClipBoard;
  end;
```

The unit DDGDBU.PAS contains initialization code that registers our new Clipboard format:

```
CF_DDGDATA := RegisterClipBoardFormat('CF_DDG');
```

The call to RegisterClipBoardFormat('CF_DDG') is a Windows API function that registers a Clipboard format. The new format then is available on the Clipboard's list of formats, which can be accessed by using the Clipboard's Formats property.

Copying Data to the Clipboard

The event handler for the Copy button TForm1.Button1Click() creates an instance of TDDGObject, initializes its data with the contents of the edit controls, and calls DDGObj's CopyToClipBoard() method before freeing the object's instance.

The TDDGObject.CopyToClipBoard() method illustrates how you would make your objects copy themselves to the Clipboard by using ClipBoard's SetAsHandle() method. SetAsHandle() places a given handle onto the Clipboard in the format specified by its parameter. In this case, the parameter is the newly defined Clipboard format CF_DDGDATA.

```
ClipBoard.SetAsHandle(CF_DDGDATA, Data);
```

Before calling SetAsHandle(), however, the method prepares a valid THandle that it must pass to SetAsHandle(). This handle will represent the block of memory that contains the data being sent to the Clipboard. See the sidebar entitled "Working with Global Memory: THandles" later in this chapter. The line

```
Data := GlobalAlloc(GMEM_MOVEABLE, SizeOf(Rec));
```

tells Windows to allocate Sizeof(Rec) bytes of memory on the global heap, which may be moved if necessary, and to return a handle to that memory to the variable Data. You then get a pointer to that memory area with the following line:

```
DataPtr := GlobalLock(Data);
```

The data then is moved to the memory block with the Move() function. Examine the following five lines of code:

```
ClipBoard.Open;
ClipBoard.SetAsHandle(CF_DDGDATA, Data);
TempStr := Rec.FName+CRLF+Rec.LName+CRLF+Rec.MI+CRLF;
ClipBoard.AsText := TempStr;
Clipboard.Close;
```

ClipBoard.Open() opens the Clipboard and prevents other applications from using it. Typically, it's not necessary to call Open() unless you're sending multiple formats to the Clipboard, as we're doing here. This is because each assignment to the Clipboard using one of its methods, such as ClipBoard.SetTextBuf(), or properties, such as ClipBoard.AsText, causes the Clipboard to erase its previous contents because they call Open() and Close() internally. By calling ClipBoard.Open() first, you prevent this from happening and therefore can assign multiple formats simultaneously. Had we not called the Open() method, only the CF_TEXT format would be available on the Clipboard. The lines after the call to Open() simply assign the data to the Clipboard and then call the ClipBoard.Close() method accordingly.

At this point, Windows is responsible for managing that data as Clipboard data. The remaining lines unlock the memory with the Windows API function GlobalUnlock(), enabling Windows to relocate it, if necessary, and to call GlobalFree() only if an exception occurred during this process. You don't call GlobalFree() if successful because Windows has taken over that memory for the Clipboard.

With both CF_DDGDATA and CF_DDGTEXT available on the Clipboard, you can paste the data back into either this sample program, as we'll illustrate momentarily, or into other applications that can receive Clipboard data in text format, as shown in Figure 14.4.

FIGURE 14.4.

Pasting custom Clipboard formats as text.

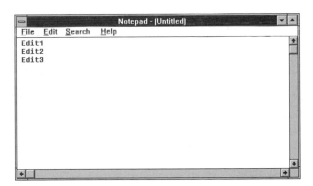

WORKING WITH GLOBAL MEMORY: THandles

A THandle is nothing more than a 16-bit variable representing an index into a table in Windows that contains information about a memory block. There are many types of THandles, and Delphi encapsulates most of them with TIcons, TBitmaps, Canvases, and so on.

Windows functions like the various Clipboard functions use the global heap to manipulate Clipboard data. To get access to the global heap, you make use of the memory allocation function shown in the following list. Note that there are similar functions for working with the local heap, but these are used mostly by Windows internally:

GlobalAlloc()	Allocates the number of bytes specified on the global heap and returns a THandle to that memory object.
GlobalFree()	Frees the memory allocated with GlobalAlloc().
GlobalLock()	Returns a pointer to a global memory object received from GlobalAlloc().
GlobalUnlock()	Unlocks memory previously locked with GlobalLock().

Pasting Data from the Clipboard

The TForm1.Button2Click() event handler instantiates a TDDGObject instance, and calls its GetFromClipBoard() method if the format CF_DDGDATA is available from the Clipboard. It then updates the edit controls with the new data.

The TDDGObject.GetFromClipBoard performs the opposite of the CopyToClipBoard() method. It calls the Clipboard's GetAsHandle(), which returns a Handle to the data in the specified format. It then gets a pointer to the memory referenced by the handle by calling GlobalLock() and copies the data to a buffer.

CAUTION

Do not free the handle returned from GetAsHandle() because it does not belong to your application. It belongs to the Clipboard. Therefore, the data that the handle references should be copied.

Flexible Applications

Adding the capability for your application to share information with other applications makes it more usable and appealing, especially in the multitasking environment of Windows. In some cases, however, just being able to copy and paste data is not quite enough. You might need to get data from another application without having to depend on the data being copied to the Clipboard by that application. Or, you might even need to change another application's data or have it perform some action. This is where Dynamic Data Exchange comes into play.

Dynamic Data Exchange

Dynamic Data Exchange gives your applications even more powerful data-sharing capabilities. With DDE, your application can be updated continually by another application with current data. You also can make your application provide other programs with important information. Additionally, your application can control another application's actions. This section teaches you how to create DDE server and client applications with Delphi to perform these intricate yet useful techniques.

Communication Among Applications

Applications that communicate with each other do so by one application invoking a "conversation" with another application. The term *conversation* is appropriate because applications actually engage in sending information back and forth between each other. This conversation, or *link*, usually involves two applications: one is called a *client* (the application requesting the link) and the other is the *server* (the application sending the requested data to the client). A server application cannot be a client application in the same conversation, and a client application cannot be a server application in the same conversation. However, an application can be both a server and a client, as long as it carries on two separate conversations. Delphi encapsulates DDE by use of its TDDEServerConv, TDDEServerItem, TDDEClientConv, and TDDEClientItem classes. The following list explains their purposes:

TDDEClientConv	Establishes the link with DDE server applications. This is used with a TDDEClientItem class.
TDDEClientItem	Establishes a link to the item of a DDE client application. This is used with a TDDEClientConv class.
TDDEServerConv	Establishes a link with DDE client applications. This is used with TDDEServerItem.
TDDEServerItem	Establishes a link to the item of a DDE server application. This component is used alone or with a TDDEServerConv class.

The linkage between two applications engaged in a DDE conversation happens by means of their service, topic, and item.

DDE Services

A DDE *service* refers to the DDE server application's name. Usually, this is the name of the executable filename minus the EXE file extension, but it is not guaranteed to be such.

Delphi servers obtain the name of the project file minus the EXE or DPR file extension. Therefore, a Delphi application named PROJECT.DPR would have a service name of PROJECT.

DDE Topics

A DDE *topic* is an identifier that refers to a data unit containing the linked information, such as file in a word processor or a worksheet in a spreadsheet.

In Delphi server applications, the topic refers to the form's caption. There may instances in which a form's caption may change; in such a case, it would not be wise to use the caption as the topic identifier. The TServerConv, which you learn about later in this chapter, takes care of this problem.

DDE Items

The DDE *item* refers to the actual piece of data to be sent to a DDE client application. This data is sent in the form of a null-terminated string. The actual name that for a DDE item is specific to the server application. Usually, with spreadsheet applications, the item contains a cell location; whereas in a database application, the item might be a field name. The returned information would be the data contained in those data elements, whether it be a number from a spreadsheet or a last name from a database.

In a Delphi application, you might use a TEdit or TMemo control for the DdeItem property. You would write the code to copy the contents of the control to the DDE link.

Breaking the Ice

Earlier in this chapter, you learned that a client application invokes the conversation with a server application. To fully illustrate this process, you will build both a server application and a client application with Delphi. Finally, you will learn how to use DDE to control another Windows application—the Program Manager.

Creating a DDE Server Project

To create a Delphi DDE server, create a new project and save it as DDESERV.DPR. Save the main form as DDESERVU.PAS. From the System page on the Component palette, place a TDDEServerItem on the form. Also, place a TEdit component on the form.

The data that this application will share with client applications is contained in the DDEServerItem.Text property. Because you want to provide the text contained in Edit1.Text, place the following line of code in Edit1's OnChange event handler, TForm1.Edit1Change():

```
DDEServerItem1.Text := Edit1.Text;
```

If your DdeItem is linked to a TMemo component, use the following syntax:

```
DdeServerItem1.Lines.Assign(Memo1.Lines);
```

At this point, you pretty much have a DDE server application in place. Your server name is DDESERV and the topic is FORM1. The form's caption and the item is `DDEServerItem1.Text`, which contains `Edit.Text`.

Making the Data Available from a DDE Server

Normally, the DDE server application doesn't go out of its way to make its data available to client applications. Clients must establish a link with the server before communication is enabled. However, `TDDEServerItem` does have the method `CopyToClipBoard()`, which places the data and DDE link information in the Clipboard for server applications to retrieve. After the information is received, clients can use that information to establish a continual link.

Place a `TButton` component on your form and enter the following code for its `OnClick` event handler:

```
DDEServerItem1.CopyToClipBoard;
```

This code provides one method for DDE clients to link to the server application. Now that you have a DDE server application, you must create a client to talk to it. Run your DDE server, and minimize it for now. You will return to it later.

Creating a DDE Client Project

Create a new project and save it to DDECLNT.DPR. Save the main form to DDECLNTU.PAS. From the System page on the Component palette, place a `TDDEClientItem` and a `TDDEClientConv` on your form. Also place a `TEdit` component on the form.

Now set the `DDEClientItem`'s `DDEConv` property to `DDEClientConv1`. Because `DDEClientConv1` establishes the link with a DDE server, `DDEClientItem1` must be connected to it through this property.

You now are set up to establish a connection to a DDE server. First, however, you need a way to view the data from the server. You've guessed it! `Edit1.Text` will serve this purpose. For `DDEClientItem`'s `OnChange` event handler, enter the following line of code:

```
Edit1.Text := DDEClientItem1.Text;
```

Establishing Links with a DDE Server

There are two ways for a DDE client application to establish a link with a DDE server: automatically or manually, as specified by the `DDEClientConv1.ConnectMode` property.

Connecting Automatically with DDE Using the *ddeAutomatic* Connect Mode

When DDEClientConv's ConnectMode property is set to ddeAutomatic, the connection is attempted when the application is run or when the form containing the DDEClientConv component is activated. Before making the connection, however, you must specify the DDEService and DDETopic properties for DDEClientConv. You can enter the data by hand, or, better, paste the data and link information from the Clipboard after the DDE server application has copied it there.

You probably have been itching to press that little Copy to Clipboard button in your server application, if you haven't already. Now you can go ahead and bring up the server application and press away; this copies the server data and link information to the Clipboard.

Now that you have pasted the data and link information to the Clipboard, it will be easy to link the data to your client components. Minimize the server again and bring up your DDE client form in Delphi. Select the DDEClientConv component and, from the DDEService or DDETopic property in the Object Inspector, choose the ellipsis button (...). You will see the DDE Info dialog box. The Paste Link button should be enabled, so click it now. You are magically presented with the appropriate DDETopic and DDEService names in the entry fields, as shown in Figure 14.5. Even better, you will actually understand what just happened because you read the section in this chapter on the Windows Clipboard.

FIGURE 14.5.

The DDE Info dialog box with pasted data.

Choose OK. Now select DdeServerItem1 for DdeClientItem1's DdeItem property in the Object Inspector. The DDEClientItem's text property in the Object Inspector should now contain the information in the server application's edit component. When you run the client application, the edit control also will contain that information. Now, bring up the server application and resize both applications so that you can watch both of them simultaneously. From the server application, modify the contents of the Edit component and watch the same change being made in the client application as shown in Figure 14.6—WOW!

FIGURE 14.6.

The server updating the client automatically.

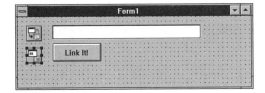

The example you just ran showed you how to connect to the DDE server application at design time. To connect to the server at runtime is just as easy, as long as you know the server's service and topic name. To illustrate this, place a TButton and two TEdit components on the DDE client's form, as shown in Figure 14.7.

FIGURE 14.7.

The DDE client form.

Add the following lines of code to TButton1's OnClick event handler:

```
DDEClientConv1.SetLink('DDESERV', 'Form1'); { Set a link with the server }
DDEClientItem1.DDEItem := 'DdeServerItem1'; { Establish link to item }
```

First, you call the SetLink() method, which takes two parameters: the DDEService name and the DDETopic name. Next, you assign the server's Item name to DDEClientItem1's DDEItem property to establish a link.

TIP

The DDE functions are case sensitive to the DdeService, DdeTopic, and DdeItem names passed to them. Pay careful attention, or you won't be able to establish a link.

Make sure that the properties DdeService and DdeTopic for TDDEClientConv in the Object Inspector have been cleared to illustrate this example correctly before running it. Figure 14.8 shows the results of clicking the Link It! button.

FIGURE 14.8.
The client linked to the
server.

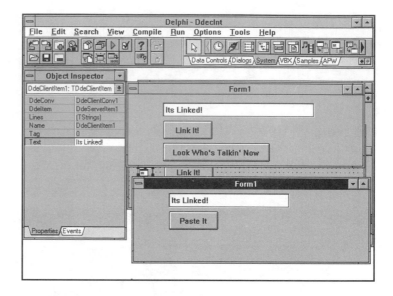

Connecting Manually with DDE Using the *ddeManual* Connect Mode

When DDEClientConv1's ConnectMode property is set to ddeManual, the call to SetLink does not automatically establish a link. You must call DDEClientConv1.OpenLink() to open a link to the server. Likewise, the link can be separated by calling DDEClientConv1.CloseLink.

Using the *TDDEServerConv* Component

There are two cases in which you will want to use a TDDEServerConv component with your server application:

■ The server application's caption may change, as is the case with a word processor.

■ The server can be sent macro commands from client applications, in which case the TDDEServerConv.OnMacroExecute method is invoked.

In the first case, the topic name for the server application becomes the name of the TDDEServerConv component, such as DDEServerConv1. Therefore, the change in the server application's caption doesn't affect the linkage to client applications.

In the second case, you would define a macro language with your applications and provide documentation on how to use this language so that other DDE-compliant applications can communicate with yours.

Poking Data

You also can send data from the client application to the server application with DDEClientConv1's PokeData() or PokeDataLines() method. PokeData() sends a PChar to the server applications, whereas PokeDataLines() sends TStrings. To see how to use PokeData(), add a new button to the form, as shown in Figure 14.9.

FIGURE 14.9.

A client form with a Poke button.

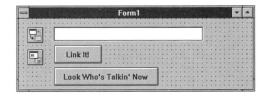

Add the following event handler for the new TButton class:

```
procedure TForm1.Button2Click(Sender: TObject)
var
  PokeText: array[0..255] of Char;
begin
  StrPCopy(PokeText, Button2.Caption);              { Copy text to poke         }
  DDEClientConv1.PokeData(DDEClientItem1 DDEItem, PokeText); { Poke
➥servers item     }
end;
```

Here, the variable PokeData, an array of char, is passed as the second parameter to PokeData(). PokeData's first parameter is the name of the server's DdeItem. You also must modify the server application a bit. If you have the DDE client application loaded at this time, save it and load the DDE server application. Add the Boolean variable Fpoking to the main form as shown in Listing 14.6. Then, modifying Edit1's OnChange event handler to contain the following code:

```
procedure TForm1.Edit1Change(Sender: TObject);
begin
  if not FPoking then
    DDEServerItem1.Text :=Edit1.Text; {Link text in edit to DDEServerItem.Text}
end;
```

Next, add the OnPokeData event handler to DDEServerItem1:

```
procedure TForm1.DdeServerItem1PokeData (Sender: TObject);
begin
  FPoking := true;
  Edit1.Text :=DDEServerItem1.Text;
  FPolking := false;
end;
```

Here, the variable Fpoking serves to keep the DDEServerItem's text from being modified by the user when data is being poked from the client.

The source code for the client and server applications is shown in Listings 14.5, 14.6, 14.7, and 14.8.

Listing 14.5. The source code for DDESERV.DPR.

```
program Ddeserv;

uses
  Forms,
  Ddeservu in 'DDESERVU.PAS' {Form1};

{$R *.RES}

begin
  Application.CreateForm(TForm1, Form1);
  Application.Run;
end.
```

Listing 14.6. The source code for DDESERVU.PAS.

```
unit Ddeservu;

interface

uses
  SysUtils, WinTypes, WinProcs, Messages, Classes, Graphics, Controls,
  Forms, Dialogs, StdCtrls, DdeMan;

type
  TForm1 = class(TForm)
    DdeServerItem1: TDdeServerItem;
    Edit1: TEdit;
    Button1: TButton;
    procedure Edit1Change(Sender: TObject);
    procedure Button1Click(Sender: TObject);
  procedure DdeServerItem1PokeData(Sender: TObject);
  private
    { Private declarations }
    FPoking: Boolean;
  public
    { Public declarations }
  end;

var
  Form1: TForm1;

implementation

{$R *.DFM}

procedure TForm1.Edit1Change(Sender: TObject);
begin
  if not FPoking then
    DDEServerItem1.Text := Edit1.Text; { Link text in edit to DDEServerItem.Text }
end;

procedure TForm1.Button1Click(Sender: TObject);
begin
  DDEServerItem1.CopyToClipBoard; { Copy data/link information to clipboard }
end;
```

```
procedure TForm1.DdeServerItem1PokeData(Sender: TObject);
begin
  FPoking := true;
  Edit1.Text := DDEServerItem1.Text;
  FPoking :+ false;
end;

end.
```

Listing 14.7. The source code for DDECLNT.DPR.

```
program Ddeclnt;

uses
  Forms,
  Ddeclntu in 'DDECLNTU.PAS' {Form1};

{$R *.RES}

begin
  Application.CreateForm(TForm1, Form1);
  Application.Run;
end.
```

Listing 14.8. The source code for DDECLNTU.PAS.

```
unit Ddeclntu;

interface

uses
  SysUtils, WinTypes, WinProcs, Messages, Classes, Graphics, Controls,
  Forms, Dialogs, DdeMan, StdCtrls;

type
  TForm1 = class(TForm)
    Edit1: TEdit;
    DdeClientConv1: TDdeClientConv;
    DdeClientItem1: TDdeClientItem;
    Button1: TButton;
    Button2: TButton;
    procedure DdeClientItem1Change(Sender: TObject);
    procedure Button1Click(Sender: TObject);
    procedure Button2Click(Sender: TObject);
  private
    { Private declarations }
  public
    { Public declarations }
  end;

var
  Form1: TForm1;
```

continues

Listing 14.8. continued

```
implementation

{$R *.DFM}

procedure TForm1.DdeClientItem1Change(Sender: TObject);
begin
  Edit1.Text := DDEClientItem1.Text; { Establish link with Edit.text }
end;

procedure TForm1.Button1Click(Sender: TObject);
begin
  DDEClientConv1.SetLink('DDESERV', 'Form1'); { Set a link with the server }
  DDEClientItem1.DDEItem := 'DdeServerItem1'; { Establish link to item }
end;

procedure TForm1.Button2Click(Sender: TObject);
var
  PokeText: array[0..255] of char;
begin
  StrPCopy(PokeText, Button2.Caption);              { Copy text to poke          }
  DDEClientConv1.PokeData(DDEClientItem1.DDEItem, PokeText); { Poke
➥servers item    }
end;

end.
```

Executing Macros

One of the more powerful methods of controlling another application from a client application is to use DdeClientConv's ExecuteMacro() or ExecuteMacroLines() method. Macros are really commands that a client can send to a server to process. The actual commands sent are server specific, and you need to refer to the documentation for that particular server to see which commands are available. One of the more popular applications to process commands is the Program Manager.

This section shows you how to send commands to another application by creating a group in the Program Manager and adding items to that group. This functionality is useful for developing custom install programs.

Creating the Project

The main form is simple: just add a TListBox, two TButtons, a TDDEClientConv component, and a TOpenDialog. For the form's OnCreate event handler, add the following line of code to specify a filter for OpenDialog1:

```
OpenDialog1.Filter := 'Executable *.EXE¦*.exe';
```

Enter the following in the Add Item button's event hander:

```
if OpenDialog1.Execute then
    ListBox1.Items.Add(OpenDialog1.FileName);
```

This code adds paths to the executable program to your ListBox1's items.

The event handler for the Create Group button contains the code shown in Listing 14.9.

Listing 14.9. The Create Group button event handler.

```
var
  i: integer;
begin
  with DDEClientConv1 do
  begin
    SetLink('PROGMAN', 'PROGMAN');  { Establish a link with the server }
    ExecuteMacro(DDECreateGroup, False);    { Create a group }
    ExecuteMacro(DDEShowGroup, False);      { Show the group      }
    with ListBox1 do
    for i := 0 to Items.Count - 1 do  { For each item in the listbox, call }
      AddItem(Items[i]);              { AddItem() method.                  }
    CloseLink;                        { Close the link to the DDE server   }
  end;
end;
```

First, you establish a link with the Program Manager by invoking the SetLink() method.

> **NOTE**
>
> If you are using a shell program other than the Windows Program Manager, this example may not work. To illustrate it, change the shell= entry in your SYSTEM.INI file to read shell=PROGMAN.EXE and restart Windows.

You call the ExecuteMacro() method twice: once to create a group window, and another to display it. This is done by passing a string macro to Program Manager that actually performs these actions. The string constants passed are defined as the following:

```
DDECreateGroup = '[CreateGroup(DDG)]';
DDEShowGroup   = '[ShowGroup(DDG,1)]';
```

The syntax for these macros is specific to Program Manager. Here, Program Manager macro commands are contained in square brackets. The CreateGroup commands tell Program Manager to create a group named DDG. The ShowGroup command tells Program Manager to display the group.

Next, iterate through each entry in ListBox1 and pass that item to the AddItem() method. Finally, close the link. Listing 14.10 shows the AddItem() method.

Listing 14.10. The `TForm1.AddItem()` method.

```
procedure TForm1.AddItem(ItemToAdd: string);
var
  Temp1 : String;
  Temp2: array[0..255] of char;
begin
  with DdeClientConv1 do
  begin
    { Execute the ProgMan macro to add an item to the group }
    Temp1 := Format(DDEAddItem, [ItemToAdd, ItemToAdd]);
    StrPCopy(Temp2, Temp1);          { Copy contents of string to Pchar }
    { Add Item to group }
    if not ExecuteMacro(Temp2, False) then
      MessageDlg('Item could not be created', mtWarning, [mbok], 0);
  end;
end;
```

Here, you use the `Format()` function to format the string `DDEAddItem`, which is defined as

```
DDEAddItem       = '[AddItem(%s,"DDGITEM",%s)]';
```

If the parameter passed to `AddItem()` is `c:\delphi\bin\delphi.exe`, the resulting string becomes

```
'[AddItem(c:\delphi\bin\delphi.exe, "DDGITEM", c:\delphi\bin\delphi.exe]'
```

This creates a group with the path `c:\delphi...`; the name that appears under the icon in the group box is `DDGITEM`, and the working directory is the same as the path. The source code for this project is shown in Listings 14.11 and 14.12 as DDEP.DPR and DDEU.PAS, respectively. To learn about the Program Manager macro, you can look in the online API help for *shell* or *progman*, which contains complete instructions for communicating with Program Manager.

Listing 14.11. The source code for DDEP.DPR.

```
program Ddep;

uses
  Forms,
  Ddeu in 'DDEU.PAS' {Form1};

{$R *.RES}

begin
  Application.CreateForm(TForm1, Form1);
  Application.Run;
end.
```

Listing 14.12. The source code for DDEU.PAS.

```
unit Ddeu;

interface

uses
  SysUtils, WinTypes, WinProcs, Messages, Classes, Graphics, Controls,
  Forms, Dialogs, StdCtrls, DdeMan;

const
  DDECreateGroup = '[CreateGroup(DDG)]'; { Macro command to Create a group }
  DDEShowGroup   = '[ShowGroup(DDG,1)]'; { Macro command to show the group }
  DDEAddItem     = '[AddItem(%s,"DDGITEM",%s)]'; { Macro command to add an }
                                                 { item to the group.      }

type

  TForm1 = class(TForm)
    DdeClientConv1: TDdeClientConv;
    OpenDialog1: TOpenDialog;
    ListBox1: TListBox;
    Label2: TLabel;
    Button1: TButton;
    Button2: TButton;
    procedure Button1Click(Sender: TObject);
    procedure Button2Click(Sender: TObject);
    procedure FormCreate(Sender: TObject);
  private
    procedure AddItem(ItemToAdd: string);
    { Private declarations }
  public
    { Public declarations }
  end;

var
  Form1: TForm1;

implementation

{$R *.DFM}

procedure TForm1.Button1Click(Sender: TObject);
begin
  { Get an executable filename and add its path to listbox1.items. }
  if OpenDialog1.Execute then
    ListBox1.Items.Add(OpenDialog1.FileName);
end;

procedure TForm1.AddItem(ItemToAdd: string);
var
  Temp1 : String;
  Temp2: array[0..255] of char;
begin
  with DdeClientConv1 do
  begin
    { Execute the ProgMan macro to add an item to the group }
    Temp1 := Format(DDEAddItem, [ItemToAdd, ItemToAdd]);
```

continues

Listing 14.12. continued

```
    StrPCopy(Temp2, Temp1);            { Copy contents of string to Pchar }
    { Add Item to group }
    if not ExecuteMacro(Temp2, False) then
      MessageDlg('Item could not be created', mtWarning, [mbok], 0);
  end;
end;

procedure TForm1.Button2Click(Sender: TObject);
var
  i: integer;
  PMHand: hWnd;
begin
  with DDEClientConv1 do
  begin
    { Get a handle to the Program Manager's main window }
    PMHand := FindWindow('Progman', 'Program Manager');
    SetLink('PROGMAN', 'PROGMAN');  { Establish a link with the server }
    ExecuteMacro(DDECreateGroup, False);    { Create a group }
    ExecuteMacro(DDEShowGroup, False);      { Show the group    }
    with ListBox1 do
    for i := 0 to Items.Count - 1 do   { For each item in the listbox, call }
      AddItem(Items[i]);               { AddItem() method.                  }
    CloseLink;                         { Close the link to the DDE server   }
  end;
end;

procedure TForm1.FormCreate(Sender: TObject);
begin
  OpenDialog1.Filter := 'Executable *.EXE¦*.exe'; { Set the filter for the }
end;                                              { OpenDialog.            }

end.
```

Summary

The capability to share data with other applications is a powerful and extremely useful technique. By making your application capable of being used with other applications, your application becomes more usable and your users become more productive. In this chapter, you learned how to use the Clipboard's built-in functions to work with Delphi controls. You also saw how to create your own custom Clipboard formats. You'll get an opportunity in a later chapter to implement that knowledge in a useful application. Finally, you learned how to use Delphi's Dynamic Data Exchange components. The next chapter teaches you yet another very powerful method for communicating with other Windows applications called *Object Linking and Embedding* otherwise known as *OLE*.

15

Object Linking and Embedding with OLE

Object linking and embedding (OLE—pronounced *Olé,* like at a bullfight) is a method for sharing data among different applications. OLE deals primarily with linking or embedding data associated with one type of application to data associated with another application—for example, embedding a Quattro Pro spreadsheet into a Word for Windows document.

In this chapter, you get a solid background in the basics of OLE in general, some advanced OLE 2 topics, and then some more specific information on VCL's TOleContainer class, which encapsulates OLE containers. This chapter will not teach you everything there is to know about OLE—that could take volumes—but it covers all the important features of OLE, particularly as they apply to Delphi.

OLE Basics

Before we jump into OLE, it's important that you understand the terminology and basic concepts associated with the technology. This section will introduce you to basic terms and ideas behind OLE.

OLE Terminology

OLE brings with it a great deal of new terminology, so some terms are presented here before you go any deeper into the guts of OLE.

The data shared between applications is referred to as an *OLE object.* Applications having the capability to contain OLE objects are referred to as *OLE containers.* Applications having the capability to have their data contained within an OLE container are called *OLE servers.*

A program such as a word processor that serves as an OLE container would have the capability to embed a graphic, an audio clip, or a video clip within the document text. Such a document, containing multiple OLE objects, sometimes is referred to as a *compound document.*

As the name implies, an OLE object can be *linked* or *embedded* into a compound document. Linked objects are stored in a disk file. With object linking, multiple containers, or even the server application, can link to the same OLE object on disk. When one application modifies the linked object, it is reflected to all the other applications maintaining a link to that object. Embedded objects are stored by the OLE container application. Only the container application is able to edit the OLE object. Embedding prevents other applications from accessing (and therefore modifying or corrupting) your data, but it does put the burden of managing the data on the container.

Another facet of OLE that is worth mentioning, although it is not covered in detail in this chapter, is called *OLE automation.* OLE automation is a means by which you can allow applications (called *OLE automation controllers*) to execute code associated with OLE objects native to another application (called an *OLE automation server*). Automation enables you to manipulate another application through a standard macro-style interface.

What's So Great About OLE?

The coolest thing about OLE is that it enables you to easily build the capability to manipulate many types of data into your applications. You might snicker at the word *easily*, but it's true. It is much easier, for example, to give your application the capability to contain OLE objects than it is to build word processor, or spreadsheet, or graphics-manipulation capabilities into your application.

OLE fits very well with Delphi's tradition of maximum code reuse. You don't have to write code to manipulate a particular kind of data if you already have an OLE server application that does the job. As complicated as OLE can be, it often makes more sense than the alternatives.

It also is no secret that Microsoft has big plans for OLE technology, and serious developers for Windows 95 and other upcoming operating systems will have to become familiar with using OLE in their applications. So, like it or not, OLE probably is here for a while, and it behooves you, as a developer, to become comfortable with it.

OLE 1 Versus OLE 2

One of the primary differences between OLE objects associated with OLE version 1 servers and those associated with OLE version 2 servers is in how they activate themselves. When you activate an object created with an OLE 1 server, the server application starts up, receives focus, and the OLE object appears in the server application ready for editing. When you activate an OLE 2 object, the OLE 2 server application becomes active "inside" your container application. This is known as *in-place activation* or *visual editing*.

When an OLE 2 object is activated, the menus and SpeedBars of the server application replace or merge with those of the client application, and a portion of the client application's window essentially becomes the window of the server application. This process is demonstrated in the sample application shown later in this chapter.

OLE 2 Behind the Scenes

Now that you understand the basic concepts and terms behind OLE, you're ready to be introduced to OLE's underlying technologies. This section gives you a look at what's under the hood of OLE.

Component Object Model

The *component object model* is an API specification that provides a standard interface for component objects (special Windows objects) and their programming language-independent implementation. Component objects are similar to the VCL objects you are familiar with, except that they only have code associated with them, not properties or data fields.

The component object model API is provided by a DLL called COMPOBJ.DLL. When you use this API function to create an instance of a component object, you receive a pointer to the table of functions associated with that object. You then can use these functions as if they were methods of any type of object.

The component objects that you use can be implemented from any EXE or DLL, although the implementation is transparent to you as a use of the object because of a process provided by OLE 2 called *marshalling*. OLE 2's marshalling mechanism handles all the intricacies of calling functions across process boundaries, so it is safe to use a 32-bit component object from a 16-bit application, for example.

Structured Storage

OLE 2 defines a new system for storing information on disk known as *structured storage*. This system basically does on a file level what DOS does on a disk level. A storage object is one physical file on a disk, but it equates with the DOS concept of a directory, and it is made up of multiple storages and streams. A storage equates to a subdirectory and a stream equates to a DOS file. You often will hear this implementation referred to as *compound files*.

The API for navigating storage objects is provided by OLE 2's STORAGE.DLL. The interface for STORAGE.DLL is found in Delphi's OLE2 unit.

Uniform Data Transfer

OLE 2 also has the concept of a data object, which is the basic object used to exchange data under the rules of uniform data transfer. *Uniform data transfer* governs data transfers through the Clipboard, drag-and-drop, DDE, and OLE. Data objects allow for a greater degree of description about the kind of data they contain than previously was practical given the limitations of those transfer media. A data object can be aware of its important properties like size, color, or even what device it is designed to be rendered on, for example. Try doing that on the Windows Clipboard!

TOleContainer

Now that you have some OLE background under your belt, take a look at Delphi's TOleContainer class. TOleContainer is found in the TOCTRL unit, and it encapsulates the complexities of an OLE container into an easily digestible VCL component.

A Small Sample Application

Now jump right in and create an OLE container application. Create a new project and drop a `TOleContainer` on the form. Click the ellipses next to the `ObjClass` or `ObjDoc` property in the Object Inspector, and Delphi invokes the Insert Object dialog box, as shown in Figure 15.1.

FIGURE 15.1.

The Insert Object dialog box.

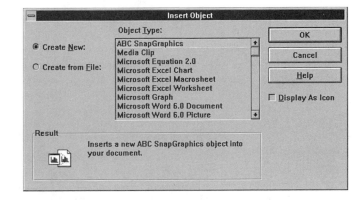

Embedding a New OLE Object

By default, the Insert Object dialog box contains the names of OLE server applications registered with Windows. To embed a new OLE object, you can select a server application from the Object Type listbox. This causes the OLE server to execute in order to create a new OLE object to be inserted into the `TOleContainer`. When you close the server application, the `TOleContainer` object is updated with the embedded object. For this example, you will create a new Word for Windows 6 document, as shown in Figure 15.2.

FIGURE 15.2.

An embedded Word for Windows 6 document.

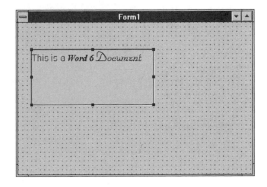

> **NOTE**
>
> An OLE object will not activate in place at design-time. You will only be able to take advantage of the in-place activation capability of TOleContainer at runtime.

Embedding or Linking an Existing OLE File

To embed an existing OLE file into the TOleContainer, select the Create From File radio button on the Insert Object dialog box. This enables you to pick an existing file, as shown in Figure 15.3. After you choose the file, it behaves in much the same way as with a new OLE object.

FIGURE 15.3.
Insert Object from file.

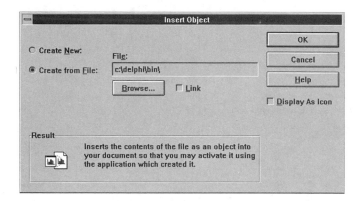

To link (rather than embed) the OLE object, simply check the **L**ink checkbox in the Insert Object dialog box shown in Figure 15.3. As described earlier, this creates a link from your application to the OLE file so that you can edit and view the same linked object from multiple applications.

A Bigger Sample Application

Now that you have the basics of OLE and the TOleContainer class behind you, you will create a more sizable application that truly reflects the usage of OLE in realistic applications.

Start by creating a new project based on the MDI application template. The main form makes only a couple of modifications to the standard MDI template, as shown in Figure 15.4.

The MDI child form is shown in Figure 15.5. It is simply a normal fsMDIChild style form with a TOleContainer component aligned to alClient.

FIGURE 15.4.
The MDIOLE application main window.

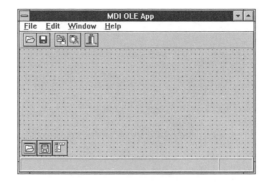

FIGURE 15.5.
The MDIOLE application child window.

Listing 15.1 shows CHILDWIN.PAS, the source code unit for the MDI child form. Note that this unit is fairly standard except for the addition of the OLEFileName property and the associated method and private instance variable. This property stores the path and filename of the OLE file, and the property accessor sets the child form's caption to the filename.

Listing 15.1. The source code for CHILDWIN.PAS.

```
unit Childwin;

interface

uses WinTypes, WinProcs, Classes, Graphics, Forms, Controls, ToCtrl;

type
  TMDIChild = class(TForm)
    OleContainer1: TOleContainer;
    procedure FormClose(Sender: TObject; var Action: TCloseAction);
    procedure FormCreate(Sender: TObject);
  private
    FOLEFilename: String;
    procedure SetOLEFileName(Value: String);
  public
    property OLEFileName: String read FOLEFileName write SetOLEFileName;
  end;

implementation
```

continues

Listing 15.1. continued

```
{$R *.DFM}

uses Main, SysUtils;

procedure TMDIChild.SetOLEFileName(Value: String);
begin
  if Value <> FOLEFileName then begin
    FOLEFileName := Value;
    Caption := ExtractFileName(FOLEFileName);
  end;
end;

procedure TMDIChild.FormClose(Sender: TObject; var Action: TCloseAction);
begin
  Action := caFree;
end;

procedure TMDIChild.FormCreate(Sender: TObject);
begin
  OleContainer1.OnStatusLineEvent := MainForm.StatusLineEvent; ( from the
➥main form )
end;

end.
```

Preparing for Clipboard Usage

The first order of business for the main form is to register OLE link and embed formats with the Windows Clipboard. Do this by using the `RegisterClipboardFormat()` API function (you used this function in Chapter 14, "Sharing Information with the Clipboard and DDE"). These functions return a Clipboard format value that should be saved away in instance variables. You will do this in the constructor for the main form, as follows:

```
constructor TMainForm.Create(AOwner: TComponent);
begin
  inherited Create(AOwner);
  { Register OLE formats for clipboard use }
  OLELinkClipFormat := RegisterClipboardFormat('Link Source');
  OLEEmbedClipFormat := RegisterClipboardFormat('Embedded Object');
end;
```

> **NOTE**
>
> Registering Clipboard formats for OLE objects enables you to use the Clipboard for OLE data transfers and to use OLE drag-and-drop capability in your applications.

Creating a Child Form

When an MDI child form is created, the Insert Object dialog box (the same one you grew to know and love in Design mode) automatically is invoked using the `InsertOLEObjectDlg()` function. This function takes three parameters:

- A `TForm` instance that will act as the owner of the dialog box. In an MDI situation, be sure to pass the MDI child form rather than the MDI parent.

- A variable of type `THelpContext` that indicates the help context of the dialog box. If the variable is zero, then no Help button is shown in the dialog box.

- A pointer that contains OLE initialization information after the dialog box terminates. Assign this pointer to `TOleContainer`'s `PInitInfo` property to insert the OLE object into the container.

> **NOTE**
>
> Be sure to free the OLE Init Info pointer immediately after assigning it to `TOleContainer.PInitInfo` by using the `ReleaseOLEInitInfo()` method.

The following code shows the main form's `CreateMDIChild()` method:

```
procedure TMainForm.CreateMDIChild(const Name: string);
var
  InitInfo: Pointer;
  ChildForm: TMDIChild;
begin
  InitInfo := Nil;
  { create a new MDI child window }
  ChildForm := TMDIChild.Create(Application);
  with ChildForm do begin
    Caption := Name;
    { bring up insert OLE object dialog and insert into child }
    if InsertOLEObjectDlg(ChildForm, 0, InitInfo) then begin
      OleContainer1.PInitInfo := InitInfo;
      ReleaseOLEInitInfo(InitInfo);
    end;
  end;
end;
```

Saving to and Reading from Streams

As discussed earlier in this chapter, OLE objects lend themselves to the capability of being written to and read from streams. The `TOleContainer` component has `SaveToStream()` and

LoadFromStream() methods that make this a fairly easy chore, as TMainForm's SaveOLEFile() and FileOpenItemClick() methods show in the following code:

```
procedure TMainForm.SaveOLEFile(const FileName: String);
var
  Stream: TFileStream;
begin
  { open stream }
  Stream := TFileStream.Create(FileName, fmCreate);
  try
    { save OLE object in active child to stream }
    (ActiveMDIChild as TMDIChild).OleContainer1.SaveToStream(Stream);
  finally
    Stream.Free;
  end;
end;

procedure TMainForm.FileOpenItemClick(Sender: TObject);
var
  Stream: TFileStream;
  ChildForm: TMDIChild;
begin
  if OpenDialog.Execute then begin
    { Open file stream }
    Stream := TFileStream.Create(OpenDialog.FileName, fmOpenRead);
    { create child }
    ChildForm := TMDIChild.Create(Application);
    ChildForm.OLEFileName := OpenDialog.FileName;
    try
      { load OLE object from file stream }
      ChildForm.OleContainer1.LoadFromStream(Stream);
    finally
      Stream.Free;
    end;
    ChildForm.Show;  { make sure form is visible }
  end;
end;
```

TIP

Note our use of exception handling when working with streams. Nesting the stream access functions in a Try..Finally block ensures that the stream is freed properly, even in the case of an exception.

Using the Clipboard to Copy and Paste

Thanks to the universal data-transfer mechanism described earlier, it also is possible to use the Windows Clipboard to transfer OLE objects. Once again, the TOleContainer component automates these tasks to a great degree.

Copying an OLE object from a `TOleContainer` to the Clipboard, in particular, is a trivial task: Simply call the `CopyToClipboard()` method:

```
procedure TMainForm.CopyItemClick(Sender: TObject);
begin
  if ActiveMDIChild <> Nil then
    TMDIChild(ActiveMDIChild).OleContainer1.CopyToClipboard(True);
end;
```

After you think that you have an OLE object on the Clipboard, though, it requires a little bit more work to read it out into a `TOleContainer` component. The first step is to use the `PasteSpecialEnabled()` function to determine whether there is an OLE object on the Clipboard. The `PasteSpecialEnabled` function returns `True` if there are any OLE objects on the Clipboard—meaning that it's okay to call the `PasteSpecialDlg()` function to bring up the Paste Special dialog box. The Paste Special dialog box is shown in Figure 15.6.

FIGURE 15.6.

The Paste Special dialog box.

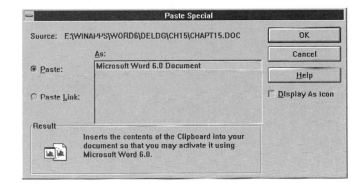

Both `PasteSpecialEnabled()` and `PasteSpecialDlg()` take an open array of `BOleFormat` records as a parameter. The formats in this array determine which types of objects meet the search criteria. `BOleFormat` records can be created dynamically using the `OleFormat()` function. The `OleFormat` function is defined as the following:

```
function OleFormat(AFmtId: Word; AName, AResultName: String;
                   AIsLinkable: Bool): BOleFormat;
```

In this code,

■ `AFmtId` is the Clipboard format of the object. This value was obtained from the `RegisterClipboardFormat()` function.

■ `AName` and `AResultName` are the object and result name. These values will be obtained from the OLE server if you pass the `"%s"` string for these parameters.

■ `AIsLinkable` should be set to `true` if the OLE object is linkable or `false` if embedded.

After obtaining the `BOleFormat` records, you can pass them to `PasteSpecialEnabled()` and `PasteSpecialDlg()`. The last parameter to `PasteSpecialDlg()` is the pointer to the OLE Init information that you need to initialize the `PInitInfo` property of `TOleContainer`. The following listing shows the source code for `TMainForm`'s `PasteItem()` method. This method uses all the functions discussed in this section to pull an OLE object from the Clipboard and paste it into the active MDI child's `TOleContainer`.

```
procedure TMainForm.PasteItemClick(Sender: TObject);
var
  InitInfo : Pointer;
  Fmt, Hdl: word;
begin
  if ActiveMDIChild <> Nil then
    { check to be sure that there are valid OLE objects on the clipboard }
    if PasteSpecialEnabled(ActiveMDIChild,
                    [OleFormat(OLEEmbedClipFormat, '%s', '%s', FALSE),
                     OleFormat(OLELinkClipFormat,  '%s', '%s', TRUE)]) then
      { bring up Paste Special dialog, insert into active child's OLE object }
      if PasteSpecialDlg(ActiveMDIChild,
                    [OleFormat(OLEEmbedClipFormat, '%s', '%s', FALSE),
                     OleFormat(OLELinkClipFormat,  '%s', '%s', TRUE)], 0,
                    Fmt, Hdl, InitInfo) then begin
        { initialize ole container with init info pointer }
        TMDIChild(ActiveMDIChild).OleContainer1.PInitInfo := InitInfo;
        { free init info pointer }
        ReleaseOleInitInfo(InitInfo);
      end;
end;
```

When run, the server controlling the OLE object in the active MDI child merges with or takes control of the application's menu and SpeedBar. Figures 15.7 and 15.8 show OLE 2's in-place activation feature—the MDI OLE application is controlled by two different OLE 2 servers.

FIGURE 15.7.

OLE 2: Editing a Word for Windows 6 document.

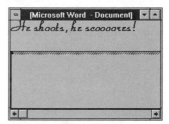

FIGURE 15.8.

OLE 2: A WordArt graphic.

Figure 15.9 shows the OLE object being edited by an OLE 1 server, which is not capable of in-place activation. The complete listing for MAIN.PAS, the MDI OLE application's main unit, is shown in Listing 15.2.

FIGURE 15.9.

OLE 1: A Paintbrush graphic.

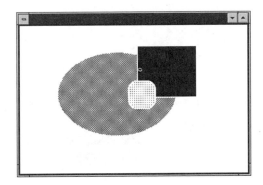

Listing 15.2. The source code for MAIN.PAS.

```
unit Main;

interface

uses WinTypes, WinProcs, SysUtils, Classes, Graphics, Forms, Controls, Menus,
  StdCtrls, Dialogs, Buttons, Messages, ExtCtrls, ChildWin;

type
  TMainForm = class(TForm)
    MainMenu1: TMainMenu;
    Panel1: TPanel;
    StatusLine: TPanel;
    File1: TMenuItem;
    FileNewItem: TMenuItem;
    FileOpenItem: TMenuItem;
    Panel2: TPanel;
    FileCloseItem: TMenuItem;
    Window1: TMenuItem;
    Help1: TMenuItem;
    N1: TMenuItem;
    FileExitItem: TMenuItem;
    WindowCascadeItem: TMenuItem;
    WindowTileItem: TMenuItem;
    WindowArrangeItem: TMenuItem;
    HelpAboutItem: TMenuItem;
    OpenDialog: TOpenDialog;
    FileSaveItem: TMenuItem;
    FileSaveAsItem: TMenuItem;
    Edit1: TMenuItem;
    PasteItem: TMenuItem;
    WindowMinimizeItem: TMenuItem;
    SpeedPanel: TPanel;
    OpenBtn: TSpeedButton;
```

continues

Listing 15.2. continued

```
      SaveBtn: TSpeedButton;
      ExitBtn: TSpeedButton;
      SaveDialog: TSaveDialog;
      PasteBtn: TSpeedButton;
      CopyItem: TMenuItem;
      CopyBtn: TSpeedButton;
      CloseAll1: TMenuItem;
      procedure FormCreate(Sender: TObject);
      procedure FileNewItemClick(Sender: TObject);
      procedure WindowCascadeItemClick(Sender: TObject);
      procedure UpdateMenuItems(Sender: TObject);
      procedure WindowTileItemClick(Sender: TObject);
      procedure WindowArrangeItemClick(Sender: TObject);
      procedure FileCloseItemClick(Sender: TObject);
      procedure FileOpenItemClick(Sender: TObject);
      procedure FileExitItemClick(Sender: TObject);
      procedure FileSaveItemClick(Sender: TObject);
      procedure FileSaveAsItemClick(Sender: TObject);
      procedure PasteItemClick(Sender: TObject);
      procedure WindowMinimizeItemClick(Sender: TObject);
      procedure FormDestroy(Sender: TObject);
      procedure HelpAboutItemClick(Sender: TObject);
      procedure CopyItemClick(Sender: TObject);
      procedure CloseAll1Click(Sender: TObject);
    private
      procedure CreateMDIChild(const Name: string);
      procedure ShowHint(Sender: TObject);
      procedure SaveOLEFile(const FileName: String);
    public
      OLELinkClipFormat: word;
      OLEEmbedClipFormat: word;
      constructor Create(AOwner: TComponent); override;
      procedure StatusLineEvent(Sender: TObject; Msg: String);
    end;

var
  MainForm: TMainForm;

implementation

{$R *.DFM}

uses TOCtrl, BoleDefs, About;

constructor TMainForm.Create(AOwner: TComponent);
begin
  inherited Create(AOwner);
  { Register OLE formats for clipboard use }
  OLELinkClipFormat := RegisterClipboardFormat('Link Source');
  OLEEmbedClipFormat := RegisterClipboardFormat('Embedded Object');
end;

procedure TMainForm.FormCreate(Sender: TObject);
begin
  Application.OnHint := ShowHint;
  Screen.OnActiveFormChange := UpdateMenuItems;
end;
```

```
procedure TMainForm.ShowHint(Sender: TObject);
begin
  { Change status line when hints change }
  StatusLine.Caption := Application.Hint;
end;

procedure TMainForm.CreateMDIChild(const Name: string);
var
  InitInfo: Pointer;
  ChildForm: TMDIChild;
begin
  InitInfo := Nil;
  { create a new MDI child window }
  ChildForm := TMDIChild.Create(Application);
  with ChildForm do begin
    Caption := Name;
    { bring up insert OLE object dialog and insert into child }
    if InsertOLEObjectDlg(ChildForm, 0, InitInfo) then begin
      OleContainer1.PInitInfo := InitInfo;
      ReleaseOLEInitInfo(InitInfo);
    end;
  end;
end;

procedure TMainForm.FileNewItemClick(Sender: TObject);
begin
  CreateMDIChild('Untitled ' + IntToStr(MDIChildCount + 1));
end;

procedure TMainForm.FileOpenItemClick(Sender: TObject);
var
  Stream: TFileStream;
  ChildForm: TMDIChild;
begin
  if OpenDialog.Execute then begin
    { Open file stream }
    Stream := TFileStream.Create(OpenDialog.FileName, fmOpenRead);
    { create child }
    ChildForm := TMDIChild.Create(Application);
    ChildForm.OLEFileName := OpenDialog.FileName;
    try
      { load OLE object from file stream }
      ChildForm.OleContainer1.LoadFromStream(Stream);
    finally
      Stream.Free;
    end;
    ChildForm.Show;  { make sure form is visible }
  end;
end;

procedure TMainForm.FileCloseItemClick(Sender: TObject);
begin
  if ActiveMDIChild <> nil then
    ActiveMDIChild.Close;
end;
```

continues

Listing 15.2. continued

```
procedure TMainForm.SaveOLEFile(const FileName: String);
var
  Stream: TFileStream;
begin
  { open stream }
  Stream := TFileStream.Create(FileName, fmCreate);
  try
    { save OLE object in active child to stream }
    (ActiveMDIChild as TMDIChild).OleContainer1.SaveToStream(Stream);
  finally
    Stream.Free;
  end;
end;

procedure TMainForm.FileSaveItemClick(Sender: TObject);
begin
  if ActiveMDIChild <> Nil then
    { if no name is assigned, then do a "save as" }
    if (ActiveMDIChild as TMDIChild).OLEFileName = '' then
      FileSaveAsItemClick(Sender)
    else
      { otherwise save under current name }
      SaveOLEFile((ActiveMDIChild as TMDIChild).OLEFileName);
end;

procedure TMainForm.FileSaveAsItemClick(Sender: TObject);
begin
  if ActiveMDIChild <> Nil then
    if SaveDialog.Execute then begin
      (ActiveMDIChild as TMDIChild).OLEFileName := SaveDialog.FileName;
      SaveOLEFile(SaveDialog.FileName);
    end;
end;

procedure TMainForm.FileExitItemClick(Sender: TObject);
begin
  Close;
end;

procedure TMainForm.PasteItemClick(Sender: TObject);
var
  InitInfo : Pointer;
  Fmt, Hdl: word;
begin
  if ActiveMDIChild <> Nil then
    { check to be sure that there are valid OLE objects on the clipboard }
    if PasteSpecialEnabled(ActiveMDIChild,
                   [OleFormat(OLEEmbedClipFormat, '%s', '%s', FALSE),
                    OleFormat(OLELinkClipFormat,  '%s', '%s', TRUE)]) then
      { bring up Paste Special dialog, insert into active child's OLE object }
      if PasteSpecialDlg(ActiveMDIChild,
                   [OleFormat(OLEEmbedClipFormat, '%s', '%s', FALSE),
                    OleFormat(OLELinkClipFormat,  '%s', '%s', TRUE)], 0,
                    Fmt, Hdl, InitInfo) then begin
        { initialize ole container with init info pointer }
        TMDIChild(ActiveMDIChild).OleContainer1.PInitInfo := InitInfo;
```

```
        { free init info pointer }
        ReleaseOleInitInfo(InitInfo);
      end;
  end;

procedure TMainForm.WindowCascadeItemClick(Sender: TObject);
begin
  Cascade;
end;

procedure TMainForm.WindowTileItemClick(Sender: TObject);
begin
  Tile;
end;

procedure TMainForm.WindowArrangeItemClick(Sender: TObject);
begin
  ArrangeIcons;
end;

procedure TMainForm.WindowMinimizeItemClick(Sender: TObject);
var
  I: Integer;
begin
  { Must be done backward through the MDIChildren array }
  for I := MDIChildCount - 1 downto 0 do
    MDIChildren[I].WindowState := wsMinimized;
end;

procedure TMainForm.UpdateMenuItems(Sender: TObject);
begin
  { only enable options if there are active children }
  FileCloseItem.Enabled := MDIChildCount > 0;
  FileSaveItem.Enabled := MDIChildCount > 0;
  FileSaveAsItem.Enabled := MDIChildCount > 0;
  CopyItem.Enabled := MDIChildCount > 0;
  PasteItem.Enabled := MDIChildCount > 0;
  CopyBtn.Enabled := MDIChildCount > 0;
  SaveBtn.Enabled := MDIChildCount > 0;
  PasteBtn.Enabled := MDIChildCount > 0;
  WindowCascadeItem.Enabled := MDIChildCount > 0;
  WindowTileItem.Enabled := MDIChildCount > 0;
  WindowArrangeItem.Enabled := MDIChildCount > 0;
  WindowMinimizeItem.Enabled := MDIChildCount > 0;
end;

procedure TMainForm.FormDestroy(Sender: TObject);
begin
  Screen.OnActiveFormChange := nil;
end;

procedure TMainForm.HelpAboutItemClick(Sender: TObject);
begin
  AboutBox.ShowModal;
end;
```

continues

Listing 15.2. continued

```
procedure TMainForm.CopyItemClick(Sender: TObject);
begin
  if ActiveMDIChild <> Nil then
    TMDIChild(ActiveMDIChild).OleContainer1.CopyToClipboard(True);
end;

procedure TMainForm.StatusLineEvent(Sender: TObject; Msg: String);
begin
  StatusLine.Caption := Msg;
end;

procedure TMainForm.CloseAll1Click(Sender: TObject);
begin
  while ActiveMDIChild <> Nil do begin
    ActiveMDIChild.Release;              { use Release(), not Free()! }
    Application.ProcessMessages;         { let Windows take care of business }
  end;
end;

end.
```

Summary

That wraps up this lesson on object linking and embedding. This chapter gave you a firm introduction to OLE terminology and basics and also a description of how it all happens behind the scenes. By now, you should be familiar with the basic workings of the OLE system in general and how to use VCL's TOleContainer component. Now that you know how to use OLE, you'll probably have a whole hard drive full of OLE server applications that you're dying to try out in your applications! The next chapter introduces you to working with databases in your Delphi applications.

16

Writing Database Applications

In this chapter you'll learn the art and science of accessing external database files from your Delphi applications. If you're new to database programming, this chapter will get you started on the road to creating high-quality database applications. If database applications are old hat to you, then you'll benefit from the chapter's demonstration of Delphi's spin on database programming.

The Borland Database Engine

Delphi VCL's database-access capability is facilitated through the Borland Database Engine, or BDE. The BDE, formerly called IDAPI, is the same engine used by products such as Borland's Paradox for Windows and dBASE for Windows and Novell's Quattro Pro. Being able to imbed such an industrial-strength data-access engine into your applications has obvious advantages: large feature set, proven reliability, and scalability. The primary disadvantage, however, is that you have to tote the entire engine around with your application, which can be cumbersome when you are deploying applications.

> **NOTE**
>
> One of the big, but less obvious, benefits of the BDE is that it allows navigable SQL tables and queries. SQL data generally is not navigable—you can move forward through the rows of a query but not backward. Unlike ODBC, BDE makes SQL data navigable.

The BDE offers you the capability to communicate with Paradox, dBASE, ODBC, and SQL server databases, all in much the same manner. The standard desktop version of Delphi contains the Paradox, dBASE, and ODBC functionality, whereas Delphi Client/Server adds the high-performance SQL server connections.

TDataset

`TDataset` is an abstraction of a set of data rows and columns of data—a column being a certain type of data, and a row being a set of data of one of each column data type. It is in `TDataset` that most of the properties and methods exist for manipulating and navigating your data.

VCL represents datasets with three components: `TTable`, `TQuery`, and `TStoredProc`. These components all descend directly from the `TDBDataset` component, which, in turn, descends from `TDataset`. As their names imply, `TTable` is a component that represents the structure and data contained within a database table, and `TQuery` is a component representing the set of data returned from a SQL query operation. `TStoredProc` encapsulates a stored procedure on a SQL server. Figure 16.1 shows the `TQuery` and `TTable` components on the Data Access page of the Component Palette.

FIGURE 16.1.

TTable and TQuery on the Component Palette.

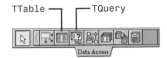

To help keep the nomenclature clear, and to cover some of the basics, the following list explains some of the common database terms that are used in this and the next chapter:

- A *dataset* is a collection of discrete data records. Each record is made up of multiple fields. Each field can contain a different type of data (integer number, string, decimal number, graphic, and so on). Datasets are represented by VCL's abstract TDataset class.

- A *table* is a special type of dataset. A table is generally a file containing records that are physically stored on a disk somewhere. VCL's TTable class encapsulates this functionality.

- A *query* is also a special type of dataset. Think of queries as "memory tables" that are generated by special commands which manipulate some physical table or set of tables. VCL has a TQuery class to handle queries.

- A *database* refers to a directory on a disk (when dealing with non-server data such as Paradox and dBASE files) or a database file (when dealing with SQL servers). A database can contain multiple tables. As you may have guessed, Delphi also has a TDatabase class.

- An *index* defines rules by which a table is ordered. To have an index on a particular field in a table means to sort its records based on the value that field holds for each record. And, no, there is no TIndex class in VCL—you find properties and methods in the TTable class to help you manipulate indexes.

In this chapter, you first learn techniques for manipulating data from datasets in general, and later you will learn how to work with tables in particular. The next chapter focuses on the TQuery class.

Navigating Datasets

Think of a dataset as a collection of rows and columns, or, more properly, records and fields. Of course, these collections of records and fields can be massive, so you will usually only work with them one record or field at a time. Because of this, you'll need to know how to move around from one record or field to the next. Handily enough, the methods to do this are built right into the TDataset component.

Opening a *TDataset*

Before you can do any nifty manipulation of your dataset you must first open it. To open a dataset, simply call its Open() method, as in this example:

```
Table1.Open;
```

This is equivalent, by the way, to setting a dataset's `Active` property to `true`:

```
Table1.Active := true;
```

There is slightly less overhead in the latter because the `Open()` method ends up setting the `Active` property to `true`, but the overhead is so minimal that it's not worth worrying about.

Once the dataset has been opened you're free to manipulate it, as you'll see in just a moment. When you finish using the dataset, you should close it by calling its `Close()` method, like this:

```
Table1.Close;
```

or by setting its `Active` property to `false`, like this:

```
Table1.Active := false;
```

> **TIP**
>
> When you are communicating with SQL servers, a connection to the database must be established when you first open a dataset in that database. When you close the last dataset in a database, your connection is terminated. Opening and closing these connections imparts a certain amount of overhead, so if you find that you often open and close the connection to the database, instead use a `TDatabase` component to maintain a connection to a SQL server's database throughout many open and close operations. The `TDatabase` component is explained in more detail in the next chapter.

Navigating Records

`TDataset` provides some simple methods for basic record navigation. The `First()` and `Last()` methods move you to the first and last records in the dataset, respectively, and the `Next()` and `Prior()` methods move you either one record forward or back in the dataset. Additionally, the `MoveBy()` method, which accepts an `Integer` parameter, moves you a specified number of records forward or back.

The `BOF` and `EOF` properties of `TDataset` reveal if the current record is the first or last record in the dataset.

Bookmarks

Bookmarks enable you to save your place in a dataset so that you can come back to the same spot in the dataset at a later time. It is very easy to use bookmarks because you only have three functions to remember.

First, the `GetBookmark()` method returns an instance of a `TBookmark` class that describes your current position in a dataset. When you find a particularly interesting place in a dataset that you'd like to be able to easily get back to, the syntax you should use to call this method is

```
var
  BM: TBookmark;
begin
  BM := Table1.GetBookmark;
```

When you want to get back to the place in the dataset that you marked with `GetBookmark()`, just call the `GotoBookmark()` method and pass it the `TBookmark` that was returned to you by `GetBookmark()`:

```
Table1.GotoBookmark(BM);
```

Keep in mind that the `GetBookmark()` method allocates some memory, so when you're done using the bookmark you should free the `TBookmark` instance by calling the `FreeBookmark()` method:

```
Table1.FreeBookmark(BM);
```

Navigational Example

Create a small project that illustrates these navigational methods and properties. The main form of the project contains a `TTable`, a `TDataSource`, a `TDBGrid`, a `TEdit`, a couple of labels, and several `TButtons`, as shown in Figure 16.2. Save this project as NAVIG8.DPR.

FIGURE 16.2.

The NAVIG8 project's main form.

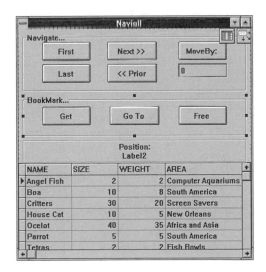

To set up the `TTable` and "wire" the `TDBGrid` to the `TTable`, you must do the following:

1. Set `Table1`'s `DatabaseName` property to an existing alias or directory. Use the `DBDEMOS` alias if you installed Delphi's example programs.
2. Choose a table from the list presented in `Table1`'s `TableName` property.
3. Wire the `TDataSource` to the `TTable` by setting `DataSource1`'s `DataSet` property to `Table1`.
4. Wire the `TDBGrid` to the `TDataSource` by setting `DBGrid1`'s `DataSource` property to `DataSource1`.
5. Open the table by setting `Table1`'s `Active` property to True.
6. Poof! You now have data in the grid control.

TIP

A shortcut to picking components from the drop-down list provided for the `DataSet` and `DataSource` properties is to double-click the area to the right of the property name in the Object Inspector. This will make the first item in the drop-down list the property value.

The source code to NAVIG8's main unit, NAV.PAS, is shown in Listing 16.1.

Listing 16.1. The source code for NAV.PAS.

```
unit Nav;

interface

uses
  SysUtils, WinTypes, WinProcs, Messages, Classes, Graphics, Controls,
  Forms, Dialogs, StdCtrls, Grids, DBGrids, DB, DBTables, ExtCtrls;

type
  TForm1 = class(TForm)
    Table1: TTable;
    DataSource1: TDataSource;
    DBGrid1: TDBGrid;
    GroupBox1: TGroupBox;
    GetButton: TButton;
    GotoButton: TButton;
    FreeButton: TButton;
    GroupBox2: TGroupBox;
    FirstButton: TButton;
    LastButton: TButton;
    NextButton: TButton;
    PriorButton: TButton;
    MoveByButton: TButton;
    Edit1: TEdit;
    Panel1: TPanel;
```

```
    Label2: TLabel;
    Label1: TLabel;
    procedure FirstButtonClick(Sender: TObject);
    procedure LastButtonClick(Sender: TObject);
    procedure NextButtonClick(Sender: TObject);
    procedure PriorButtonClick(Sender: TObject);
    procedure MoveByButtonClick(Sender: TObject);
    procedure DataSource1DataChange(Sender: TObject; Field: TField);
    procedure GetButtonClick(Sender: TObject);
    procedure GotoButtonClick(Sender: TObject);
    procedure FreeButtonClick(Sender: TObject);
  private
    BM: TBookmark;
  public
    { Public declarations }
  end;

var
  Form1: TForm1;

implementation

{$R *.DFM}

procedure TForm1.FirstButtonClick(Sender: TObject);
begin
  Table1.First;
end;

procedure TForm1.LastButtonClick(Sender: TObject);
begin
  Table1.Last;          { Go to last record in table }
end;

procedure TForm1.NextButtonClick(Sender: TObject);
begin
  Table1.Next;          { Go to next record in table }
end;

procedure TForm1.PriorButtonClick(Sender: TObject);
begin
  Table1.Prior;         { Go to last record in table }
end;

procedure TForm1.MoveByButtonClick(Sender: TObject);
begin
  { Move a specified number of record foward or back in the table }
  Table1.MoveBy(StrToInt(Edit1.Text));
end;

procedure TForm1.DataSource1DataChange(Sender: TObject; Field: TField);
begin
  { Set caption appropriately, depending on status of Table1 BOF/EOF }
  if Table1.BOF then Label2.Caption := 'Beginning'
  else if Table1.EOF then Label2.Caption := 'End'
  else Label2.Caption := 'Somewheres in between';
end;
```

continues

Listing 16.1. continued

```
procedure TForm1.GetButtonClick(Sender: TObject);
begin
  BM := Table1.GetBookmark;        { Get a bookmark }
  GotoButton.Enabled := True;      { Enable/disable proper buttons }
  GetButton.Enabled := False;
  FreeButton.Enabled := True;
end;

procedure TForm1.GotoButtonClick(Sender: TObject);
begin
  Table1.GotoBookmark(BM);         { Go to the bookmark position }
end;

procedure TForm1.FreeButtonClick(Sender: TObject);
begin
  Table1.FreeBookmark(BM);         { Free the bookmark instance }
  GotoButton.Enabled := False;     { Enable/disable appropriate buttons }
  GetButton.Enabled := True;
  FreeButton.Enabled := False;
end;

end.
```

This example illustrates quite well the fact that you can use Delphi's database classes to do quite a lot of database manipulation in your programs with very little code.

Note that you should initially set the Enabled property of the GotoButton and FreeButton to false, because you can't use them until a bookmark is allocated. The FreeButtonClick() and GetButtonClick() methods ensure that the proper buttons are enabled depending on whether or not a bookmark has been set.

Most of the other procedures in this example are one-liners, although one method that does require some explanation is TForm1.DataSource1DataChange(). This method is wired to DataSource1's OnDataChange event, which fires every time you move from one record to another. This event checks to see if you're at the beginning, in the middle, or at the end of a dataset, and changes a label's caption appropriately. You'll learn more about the TTable and TDataSource events a bit later in this chapter.

BOF AND EOF

You may notice that when you run the NAVIG8 project, Label2's caption indicates that you're at the beginning of the dataset, which makes sense. However, if you move to the next record and back again, Label2's caption isn't aware that you're at the first record. Notice, however, that Label2.Caption does indicate BOF if you click the Prior button once more. Note that the same holds true for EOF if you try this at the end of the dataset. Why?

The reason is because the BDE cannot be sure you are at the beginning or end of the dataset anymore because another user of the table (if it is a networked table), or even another process within your program, could have added a record to the beginning or end of the table in the time it took you to move from the first to the second record and back again.

With that in mind, BOF can only be true under one of the following circumstances:

■ You just opened the dataset.

■ You just called the dataset's First() method.

■ A call to TDataset.Prior() failed, indicating that there are no prior records.

Likewise, EOF can only be true under the following circumstances:

■ You opened an empty dataset.

■ You just called the dataset's Last() method.

■ A call to TDataset.Next() failed, indicating that there are no more records.

Loop Navigation

If you need to perform an action for every record in a dataset, the most common method is a while-not-EOF loop:

```
while not Table1.EOF do begin
  DoSomeStuff;
  Table1.Next;
end;
```

CAUTION

Be sure to call the Next() method inside of your while-not-EOF loop or you'll get caught in an endless loop that only a three-finger-salute (Ctrl+Alt+Del) can get you out of.

Avoid using a repeat..until loop to perform actions on a dataset. The following code may look OK on the surface, but bad things may happen if you try to use it on an empty dataset because the DoSomeStuff() procedure will always execute at least once, regardless of whether or not the dataset contains records.

```
repeat
  DoSomeStuff;
  Table1.Next;
until Table1.EOF;
```

Because the while-not-EOF loop performs the check up front you won't have such a problem with the while-not-EOF construct.

Fields

You can use TDataset's Fields[] array property or FieldsByName() function to access individual fields of the current record. Each of these returns a component of type TField that gives information about a specific field. Fields[] is a zero-based array of fields, so Fields[0] returns a TField component representing the first field in the record. FieldsByName() accepts a string parameter that corresponds to a given field name in the table, so FieldsByName('OrderNo') would return a TField component representing the value of the OrderNo field in the current record of the dataset.

Field Names and Numbers

To find the name of a specified field use TField's FieldName property. For example, the following code places the name of the first field in the current table in the string S:

```
var
  S: String;
begin
  S := Table1.Fields[0].FieldName;
end;
```

Likewise, you can obtain the number of a field that you know only by name by using the FieldNo property, so the following code stores the number of the OrderNo field in the integer variable I:

```
var
  I: integer;
begin
  I := Table1.FieldsByName('OrderNo').FieldNo;
end;
```

> **NOTE**
>
> To determine how many fields a dataset contains, use TDataset's FieldCount property.

Field Values

Depending on the data type of the field in question, you can retrieve or assign the field's value using one of the TField properties shown in Table 16.1.

Table 16.1. Properties to access `TField` values.

Property	*Return Type*
AsBoolean	Boolean
AsFloat	Double
AsInteger	Longint
AsString	String
AsDateTime	TDateTime

If the first field in the current dataset is a string, you can view its value in a `TEdit` like this:

```
Edit1.Text := Table1.Fields[0].AsString;
```

The following code sets the integral variable `I` to contain the value of the `'OrderNo'` field in the current record of the table:

```
I := Table1.FieldsByName('OrderNo').AsInteger;
```

If you wish to know the type of a field, look at `TField`'s `DataType` property, which indicates the data type with respect to the database table, irrespective of a corresponding Object Pascal type. The `DataType` property is of `TFieldType`, and `TFieldType` is defined as

```
TFieldType = (ftUnknown, ftString, ftSmallint, ftInteger, ftWord, ftBoolean,
              ftFloat, ftCurrency, ftBCD, ftDate, ftTime, ftDateTime, ftBytes,
              ftVarBytes, ftBlob, ftMemo, ftGraphic);
```

Modifying and Adding Data

There is a three-step process to edit one or more fields in the current record.

1. Call the dataset's `Edit()` method to put the dataset into edit mode.
2. Assign new values to the fields of your choice.
3. Post the changes to the dataset either by calling the `Post()` method or by moving to a new record, which will automatically post the edit.

For instance, a typical record edit looks like the following:

```
with Table1 do begin
  Edit;
  FieldsByName('Age').AsInteger := 23;
  Post;
end;
```

> **TIP**
>
> If there's a chance that the data source that you're trying to modify is not editable (that is, the ReadOnly property on a TTable or TQuery is set to true), you can determine that before you try to modify the dataset by checking the value of the CanModify property. If CanModify is true, you have the green light to edit the dataset.

Along the same lines as editing data, you can insert or append records to a dataset in much the same way.

1. Call the dataset's Insert() or Append() methods to put the dataset into insert or append mode.
2. Assign values to the dataset's fields.
3. Post the new record to the dataset either by calling Post() or by moving to a new record, which forces a post to occur.

> **NOTE**
>
> When you are in edit, insert, or append mode, keep in mind that your changes will always post when you move off the current record. Therefore, be careful when you use the Next(), Prior(), First(), Last(), and MoveBy() methods while in edit mode.

If, at some point before your additions or modifications to the dataset are posted, you wish to abandon your changes, you can do so by calling the Cancel() method. For instance, the following code cancels the edit before changes are posted to the table:

```
with Table1 do begin
  Edit;
  FieldsByName('Age').AsInteger := 23;
  Cancel;
end;
```

Cancel() undoes changes to the dataset, takes the dataset out of edit, append, or insert mode, and puts it back into browse mode.

To round out the set of TDataset's record manipulation method, the Delete() method removes the current record from the dataset. For example, the following code deletes the last record in the table:

```
Table1.Last;
Table1.Delete;
```

Refreshing the Dataset

If there's one thing you can count on when you create database applications it's that data contained in a dataset is in a constant state of flux. Records will constantly be added to, removed from, and modified in your dataset, particularly in a networked environment. Because of this, you may occasionally need to re-read the dataset information from disk or memory to update the contents of your dataset.

You can update your dataset using TDataset's Refresh() method. It functionally does about the same thing as doing a Close() and then Open() on the dataset, but Refresh() is a bit faster.

SQL tables and queries must have a unique index before the BDE will attempt a Refresh() operation. This is because Refresh() tries to preserve the current record, if possible. This means that the BDE has to Seek() to the current record at some point, which is practical only on a SQL dataset if a unique index is available.

CAUTION

When you call Refresh(), it can create some unexpected side effects for the users of your program. For example, if a user is viewing a record that has been deleted, and a call is made to Refresh(), it will appear to the user that the record suddenly went away for no apparent reason. The fact that data could be changing beneath the user is something you need to keep in mind when you call this function.

Altered States

At some point you may need to know whether a table is in edit mode or append mode, or even if it is active. You can obtain this information by inspecting TDataset's State property. The State property can have any one of the values shown in Table 16.2.

Table 16.2. Values for TDataset.State.

Value	Meaning
dsBrowse	The dataset is in browse (normal) mode.
dsCalcFields	The OnCalcFields event has been called.
dsEdit	The dataset is in edit mode. This means the Edit() method has been called, but the edited record has not yet been posted.
dsInactive	The dataset is closed.
dsInsert	The dataset is in insert mode. This typically means that Insert() has been called, but changes haven't been posted.
dsSetKey	The dataset is in SetKey mode, meaning SetKey() has been called, but GotoKey() hasn't yet been called.

Using *TTable*

This section describes the common properties and methods of the TTable component and how to use them. In particular, you learn how to search for records, filter records using ranges, and create tables. This section also contains a discussion of TTable events.

Searching

When you need to search for records in a table, VCL provides several methods to help you out. When you are working with dBASE and Paradox tables, Delphi assumes that the field(s) on which you search are indexed.

Say, for example, that you have a table that is keyed on field one, which is numeric, and on field two, which is alphanumeric. You can search for a specific record based on those two criteria in one of two ways: using the FindKey() technique or the SetKey()..GotoKey() technique.

FindKey()

TTable's FindKey() method enables you to search for a record matching one or more keyed fields in one function call. FindKey() accepts an array of const (the search criteria) as a parameter, and returns true when it is successful. For example, the following code causes the dataset to move to the record in which the first field in the index has the value 123, and the second field in the index contains the string Hello:

```
if not Table1.FindKey([123, 'Hello']) then MessageBeep(0);
```

If a match is not found, FindKey() returns false and the computer beeps.

SetKey()..GotoKey()

Calling TTable's SetKey() method puts the table in a mode that prepares its fields to be loaded with values representing search criteria. Once the search criteria have been established, use the GotoKey() method to do a top-down search for a matching record. The previous example can be rewritten with SetKey()..GotoKey() as follows:

```
with Table1 do begin
  SetKey;
  Fields[0].AsInteger := 123;
  Fields[1].AsString := 'Hello';
  if not GotoKey then MessageBeep(0);
end;
```

The Closest Match

Similarly, you can use FindNearest() or the SetKey..GotoNearest methods to search for a value in the table that is the closest match to the search criteria. To search for the first record in which the value of the first indexed field is closest to (greater than or equal to) 123, use the following code:

```
Table1.FindNearest([123]);
```

Once again, `FindNearest()` accepts an `array of const` as a parameter that contains the field values for which you wish to search.

To search using the longhand technique provided by `SetKey()..GotoNearest()`, you can use this code:

```
with Table1 do begin
  SetKey;
  Fields[0].AsInteger := 123;
  GotoNearest;
end;
```

If the search is successful and the table's `KeyExclusive` property is set to `false`, the record pointer will be on the first matching record. If `KeyExclusive` is `true`, the current record will be the one immediately following the match.

> **TIP**
>
> Use `FindKey()` and `FindNearest()` whenever possible to search for records because you type less code and leave less room for human error.

Which Index?

All of these searching methods assume that you are searching under the table's primary index. If you wish to search using a secondary index you need to set the table's `IndexName` parameter to the desired index. For instance, if your table had a secondary index on the fourth field and that index was called `LastName`, the following code would enable you to search for Smith:

```
with Table1 do begin
  IndexName := 'LastName';
  SetKey;
  Fields[3].AsString := 'Smith';
  GotoKey;
end;
```

> **NOTE**
>
> Be sure that the table is unopened (its `Active` property is set to `false`) before attempting to change an index; otherwise, an exception will be raised explaining that you can't change the index of an active dataset.

Ranges

Ranges enable you to filter a table so that it contains only records with field values that fall within a certain range that you define. Ranges work similar to key searches, and like searches there are a couple of ways to apply a range to a given table—either using the SetRange() method, or the manual SetRangeStart(), SetRangeEnd(), and ApplyRange() methods.

> **CAUTION**
>
> If you are working with dBASE or Paradox tables, ranges only work with indexed fields. If you're working with SQL data, performance will suffer greatly if you don't have an index on the ranged field.

SetRange()

Like FindKey() and FindNearest(), SetRange() enables you to perform a fairly complex action on a table in one function call. SetRange() accepts two array of const variables as parameters: the first represents the field values for the start of the range, and the second for the end of the range. As an example, the following code filters through only those records in which the value of the first field is greater than or equal to 10, but less than or equal to 15:

```
Table1.SetRange([10], [15]);
```

ApplyRange()

To use the ApplyRange() method of setting a range, follow these steps:

1. Call the SetRangeStart() method and then modify the Fields[] array property of the table to establish the starting value of the keyed field(s).

2. Call the SetRangeEnd() method and modify the Fields[] array property once again to establish the ending value of the keyed field(s).

3. Call ApplyRange() to establish the new range filter.

The preceding range example could be rewritten using this technique as follows:

```
with Table1 do begin
  SetRangeStart;
  Fields[0].AsInteger := 10;        { range starts at 10 }
  SetRangeEnd;
  Fields[0].AsInteger := 15;        { range ends at 15 }
  ApplyRange;
end;
```

Use `SetRange()` whenever possible to filter records—your code will be less prone to error when doing so.

Removing a Range Filter

To remove a range filter from a table and restore the table to the state it was in before you called `ApplyRange()` or `SetRange()`, just call `TTable`'s `CancelRange()` method.

`Table1.CancelRange;`

Search and Range Demo

To help further illustrate how to implement key searches and range filters in your applications, you will write a small sample program. This project is called SrchRng, and the main form is shown in Figure 16.3.

FIGURE 16.3.
SrchRng project's main form.

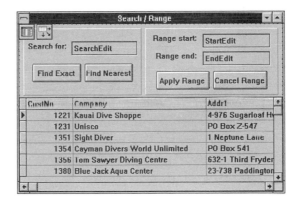

`Table1` uses the CUSTOMER.DB table found in the `DBDEMOS` database alias. Hook `Table1` to `DataSource1` to `DBGrid1`, as demonstrated earlier in this chapter. This program enables you to search for exact or nearest matches using the edit component and buttons on the left side of the form, and set range filters using the edit components and buttons on the right side of the form.

This sample application enables you to search for exact or nearest matches on the keyed field (the first field, in this case), and it enables you to filter your view of the table by applying ranges.

The source code to the form's unit, MAIN.PAS, is shown in Listing 16.2. As you can see, this code looks a lot like the small code examples in this chapter.

Listing 16.2. MAIN.PAS unit for the SrchRng project.

```pascal
unit Main;

interface

uses
  SysUtils, WinTypes, WinProcs, Messages, Classes, Graphics, Controls,
  Forms, Dialogs, StdCtrls, ExtCtrls, Grids, DBGrids, DB, DBTables;

type
  TForm1 = class(TForm)
    Table1: TTable;
    DataSource1: TDataSource;
    DBGrid1: TDBGrid;
    Panel1: TPanel;
    SearchEdit: TEdit;
    ExactButton: TButton;
    Label3: TLabel;
    NearestButton: TButton;
    Panel2: TPanel;
    StartEdit: TEdit;
    EndEdit: TEdit;
    Label1: TLabel;
    Label2: TLabel;
    ApplyButton: TButton;
    CancelButton: TButton;
    procedure ExactButtonClick(Sender: TObject);
    procedure NearestButtonClick(Sender: TObject);
    procedure ApplyButtonClick(Sender: TObject);
    procedure CancelButtonClick(Sender: TObject);
  private
    { Private declarations }
  public
    { Public declarations }
  end;

var
  Form1: TForm1;

implementation

{$R *.DFM}

procedure TForm1.ExactButtonClick(Sender: TObject);
begin
  if not Table1.FindKey([SearchEdit.Text]) then
    MessageDlg('Match for "' + SearchEdit.Text + '" not found.', mtInformation,
               [mbOk], 0);
end;

procedure TForm1.NearestButtonClick(Sender: TObject);
begin
  Table1.FindNearest([SearchEdit.Text]);
end;

procedure TForm1.ApplyButtonClick(Sender: TObject);
begin
  Table1.SetRange([StartEdit.Text], [EndEdit.Text]);
end;
```

```
procedure TForm1.CancelButtonClick(Sender: TObject);
begin
  Table1.CancelRange;
end;

end.
```

NOTE

Pay close attention to the following line of code in the sample program:

```
if not Table1.FindKey([SearchEdit.Text]) then
```

You might notice that although the keyed field is of numeric type, FindKey() enables you to pass it a string representation of the number. This is because FindKey(), FindNearest(), and SetRange() will perform the conversion from String to integer automatically.

TTable Events

TTable provides you with events that occur before and after a record in the table is deleted, edited, and inserted, whenever a modification is posted or canceled, and whenever the table is opened or closed. This is so you have full control of your database application. The nomenclature for these events is Before*XXX* and After*XXX*, where *XXX* stands for Delete, Edit, Insert, Open, and so on. These events are fairly self-explanatory, and you will use them in the database applications in Parts II and III of this book.

TTable's OnNewRecord event fires every time a new record is posted to the table. It's ideal to do various housekeeping tasks in a handler for this event. An example of this would be to keep a running total of records added to a table.

The OnCalcFields event occurs whenever the table cursor is moved off the current record or the current record changes. Adding a handler for the OnCalcFields event enables you to keep a calculated field current whenever the table is modified.

NOTE

A *calculated field* is a field that is not necessarily a physical member of a table, but is associated with the logical TTable. A calculated field enables you to display some value that is based on the contents of one or more fields in the current record. An example of this is a table that keeps track of how much time you spend working for different clients and how much you charge them per hour; a calculated field in this table would multiply the hours worked by the charge per hour to determine your take. The sample application in Chapter 28, "Building a Time-Tracker Application," shows how to use calculated fields.

Creating a Table

Instead of creating all of your database tables up front (using the Database Desktop) and deploying them with your application, a time will come when you'll need your program to have the capability to create tables for you. When this need arises, once again VCL has you covered. TTable contains a CreateTable() method that enables you to create tables on disk. Simply follow these steps to create a table:

1. Create an instance of a TTable.

2. Set the DatabaseName property of the table to a directory or existing alias.

3. Give the table a unique name in the TableName property.

4. Set the TableType property to indicate what type of table you wish to create. If you set this property to ttDefault, the table type will correspond to the extension of the name provided in the TableName property (for example, .DB stands for Paradox, and .DBF stands for dBASE).

5. Use TTable.FieldDefs' Add() method to add fields to the table. The Add() method takes four parameters:

   ■ A string indicating the field name.

   ■ A TFieldType variable indicating the field type.

   ■ A word parameter that represents the size of the field. Note that this parameter is only valid for types such as String and Memo, where the size may vary. Fields such as integer and date are always the same size, so this parameter doesn't apply to them.

   ■ A Boolean that dictates whether or not this is a required field. All required fields must have a value before a record can be posted to a table.

6. If you want the table to have an index, use the Add() method of TTable.IndexDefs to add indexed fields. IndexDefs.Add() takes the following three parameters:

   ■ A string that identifies the index.

   ■ A string that matches the field name to be indexed. Composite-key indexes (indexes on multiple fields) can be specified as a semicolon-delimited list of field names.

   ■ A set of TIndexOptions that determines the index type.

7. Call TTable.CreateTable().

The code in the following code creates a table with integer, string, and float fields with an index on the integer field. The table is called FOO.DB, and it will live in the C:\TEMP directory.

```
with TTable.Create(Self) do begin
    DatabaseName := 'c:\temp';                { point to directory or alias }
    TableName := 'FOO';                       { give table a name }
    TableType := ttParadox;                   { set table type }
    with FieldDefs do begin
      Add('Age', ftInteger, 0, True);         { add an integer field }
      Add('Name', ftString, 25, False);       { add a string field }
      Add('Weight', ftFloat, 0, False);       { add a floating-point field }
    end;
    { create an index on the integer field... }
    IndexDefs.Add('MainIndex', 'IntField', [ixPrimary, ixUnique]);
    CreateTable;                              { create the table }
  end;
```

TDataSource

TDataSource is the conduit that enables data access components such as TTables to connect to data controls such as TDBEdit and TDBLookupCombo components. In addition to being the interface between datasets and data-aware controls, TDataSource contains a couple of handy properties and events that make your life easier when manipulating data.

The State property of TDataSource reveals the current state of the underlying dataset. The value of State will tell you whether the dataset is currently inactive or in insert, edit, SetKey, or CalcFields mode. The OnStateChange event fires whenever the value of this property changes.

The OnDataChange event of TDataset, which was used in an example earlier in this chapter, is executed whenever the dataset becomes active or a data-aware control informs the dataset that something has changed.

The OnUpdateData event occurs whenever a record is posted or updated. This is the event that causes data-aware controls to change their value based on the contents of the table. You can respond to the event yourself to keep track of such changes within your application.

Calling the BDE

Occasionally, the capabilities of VCL aren't enough to achieve some end result, and you need to call directly to the BDE. Fortunately, this is not very difficult—the hardest part is figuring out which BDE function you need to call. For that, we recommend you obtain the Borland Database Engine reference manual from Borland. The .INT files found in the \DELPHI\DOC directory may be of little help; although they do document how to call each BDE function, they unfortunately do not document the purpose of each function.

When calling a BDE function, you should first make sure to have dbiProcs, dbiTypes, and dbiErrs in the Uses clause of the unit that will be calling the BDE. Next, call the BDE function with the required parameter list. Two parameter types that the BDE makes extensive use of that may not be obvious are Handle and Cursor.

Handle refers to a database handle, and for functions wherein a handle is required, you can pass the DBHandle property of any TDataset descendant or the Handle property of a TDatabase.

Cursor is a special handle that represents a unique data session. For functions requiring a cursor, you can pass the Handle property of any TDataset descendant.

To demonstrate, the function in the following code calls the dbiGetRecordCount() BDE function to obtain the number of records in the current dataset. This is just for demonstration purposes; this particular function works only with Paradox tables. Notice the way the return result of the function is examined for errors.

```
uses dbiTypes, dbiProcs;

function GetNumRecords(T: TTable): longint;
var
  Count: longint;
begin
  { call BDE to get number of records in Paradox table.
  Check(dbiGetRecordCount (T.Handle,Count));
  Result := Count;
end;
```

> **CAUTION**
>
> After calling any BDE function that modifies the current record or record position, make sure to call the TDataset's CursorPosChanged() function to keep the VCL wrapper in sync with the underlying BDE.

Deploying Database Applications

When you deploy applications that use Delphi's built-in database components you must be aware that you have to deploy more than just your program's .EXE file. For even the most basic of database programs, you must also deploy the Borland Database Engine with your application. The BDE takes the form of two disk images that you'll find in the \REDIST\BDEINST subdirectory of your Delphi CD-ROM. The most convenient way to redistribute these files is to copy the \DISK1 and \DISK2 subdirectories onto separate disks to be deployed along with your application.

If you're a shareware author and redistributing the BDE is very cumbersome for you, you can also have your clients download the BDE from CompuServe's DELPHI forum, Borland's Download Bulletin Board System, or Borland's `ftp.borland.com` FTP site. The filename is BDEDEMO.ZIP.

Summary

This chapter gave you all of the basic concepts you need to manipulate database tables in your application. You learned the ins and outs of Delphi's `TDataset` component, which is the ancestor of the `TTable`, `TQuery`, and `TStoredProc` components. You also learned techniques for manipulating `TTable` objects, and on using the BDE. As you've seen, VCL offers a pretty tight object-oriented wrapper around the procedural BDE. The next chapter focuses a bit more on client/server technology and using related VCL classes such as `TQuerys` and `TStoredProcs`.

17

Working with SQL and the *TQuery* Component

In the preceding chapter, you learned how to use powerful database components to connect to record-oriented databases and then to manipulate the data contained in them. Delphi also gives you the capability to access data existing on set-oriented databases on servers such as Oracle, Sybase, Informix, and InterBase by using Structured Query Language (SQL). By using SQL, you can perform operations that otherwise couldn't be done on record-oriented databases.

This chapter teaches you how to incorporate the SQL command set into your Delphi applications by using the TQuery component. It assumes that you have properly installed Delphi, SQL-Links, and InterBase. You also will need to refer to the Delphi section titled "Using the BDE Configuration Utility," which is part of the *Database Application Developer's Guide* in the Delphi documentation set. This manual teaches you how to set up aliases for your data-access components. *Aliases* are shorthand names for the location of databases to which your components refer. By setting up an alias, you can specify a database for your database components without having to type long directory names.

Because it would be impossible for this chapter to teach the SQL command set, it shows you, instead, how to use some common SQL commands that will take you well on your way to developing powerful database applications. In the Part III of this book, "Real-World Applications," you will learn how to create a completely functional inventory manager program that uses the more complex features of the SQL command set.

What Is SQL?

SQL is an industry standard database-manipulation command set that is used with applications programming environments such as Delphi. SQL gained great acceptance as a database query language throughout the '80s and '90s, and today it has become the standard for working with databases across networked environments. Delphi enables you to use SQL through its TQuery component. SQL gives you the advantage of viewing your data in the way that only SQL commands will generate, which also gives you much more flexibility than its record-oriented counterpart.

Set-Oriented Versus Record-Oriented Databases

So, what's the difference between record-oriented databases and set-oriented databases? Probably the key difference is in how the tables in the databases are managed. In record-oriented databases such as Paradox and dBASE, the tools for navigating, retrieving, and saving data, as well as other database operations, are designed to work directly with the table itself. In set-oriented databases, you really are working with a subset of the table's records. So as a user, when you access server-based tables through SQL, you really are sending a request to the server to process your SQL statement and return to you a portion of the data based on the conditions in your SQL statement. You don't directly access data in those tables as you do with record-oriented tables. Instead, you access a subset of those tables, a *data set*, which may differ in structure than actual tables on the server. The TQuery component gives you the capability to work with SQL-based databases by using SQL. An added benefit is that you can use TQuery to perform the same SQL statements on the record-oriented databases you previously worked with, giving you much more flexibility in designing any database application. Additionally, because only the data matching your query is sent across the network, SQL greatly reduces network traffic when dealing with large databases, as compared to record-oriented databases.

Using the *TQuery* Component

The TQuery component connects to data-aware components such as TDBEdits, TDBComboBoxes, and so on by way of a TDataSource component—as does TTable. To connect to a database with TQuery, enter an alias in the DataBaseName property in the Object Inspector. You also can enter a local or remote path where the tables exist, or a filename for a database on a server. In this chapter, you use a TQuery component to connect to different databases.

To get started, create a new project and place a TQuery component on the form. Also, place a TDataSource and a TDBGrid component on the form. Set the properties specified in Table 17.1. If you set up Delphi correctly, you already will have the alias DBDEMOS available in the Object Inspector. Select this alias for Query1's Alias property.

Your form should look like that shown in Figure 17.1. The source code for this project is in Listings 17.1 and 17.2, QUERY.DPR and QUERY0.PAS, respectively.

FIGURE 17.1.

Main form for
QUERY.DPR example.

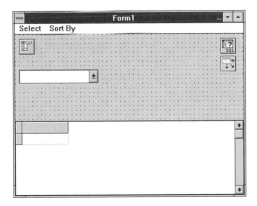

Table 17.1. Form1's component property settings.

Control	Property	Value
Query1	DataBaseName	DBDEMOS
DataSource1	DataSet	Query1
DBGrid1	Align	alBottom
DBGrid1	DataSource	DataSource1

Listing 17.1. The source code for QUERY.DPR.

```
program Query;

uses
  Forms,
  Query0 in 'QUERY0.PAS' {Form1};

{$R *.RES}

begin
  Application.CreateForm(TForm1, Form1);
  Application.Run;
end.
```

Listing 17.2. The source code for QUERY0.PAS.

```
unit Query0;

interface

uses
  SysUtils, WinTypes, WinProcs, Messages, Classes, Graphics, Controls,
  Forms, Dialogs, Grids, DBGrids, DB, DBTables, StdCtrls, Mask, Menus;

type
  TForm1 = class(TForm)
    Query1: TQuery;
    DataSource1: TDataSource;
    DBGrid1: TDBGrid;
    MainMenu1: TMainMenu;
    SortBy1: TMenuItem;
    VendorNo1: TMenuItem;
    Description1: TMenuItem;
    Select1: TMenuItem;
    Params1: TMenuItem;
    All1: TMenuItem;
    ParamByName1: TMenuItem;
    ComboBox1: TComboBox;
    procedure VendorNo1Click(Sender: TObject);
    procedure Description1Click(Sender: TObject);
    procedure Params1Click(Sender: TObject);
    procedure All1Click(Sender: TObject);
    procedure ParamByName1Click(Sender: TObject);
```

```
    procedure ComboBox1Change(Sender: TObject);
  private
    { Private declarations }
  public
    { Public declarations }
  end;

var
  Form1: TForm1;

implementation

{$R *.DFM}

procedure TForm1.VendorNo1Click(Sender: TObject);
begin
  with Query1 do
  begin
    Close;              { Close TQuery }
    SQL.Clear;          { Clear contents of SQL property }
    SQL.ADD('SELECT * FROM PARTS ORDER BY VENDORNO'); { Add SQL statement }
    Open;               { Open and run the query }
  end;
end;

procedure TForm1.Description1Click(Sender: TObject);
begin
  with Query1 do
  begin
    Close;     { Close TQuery }
    SQL.Clear; { Clear contents of SQL property  and add next Query statement }
    SQL.ADD('SELECT * FROM PARTS ORDER BY DESCRIPTION');
    Open;      { Open and run the query }
  end;
end;

procedure TForm1.Params1Click(Sender: TObject);
var
  Input: string;
  Ival: integer;
begin
  { Prompt the user for an order number }
  Input := InputBox('Order No', 'Enter the Vendor Number', '');
  if Input <> '' then
  begin
  try
    IVal := StrToInt(Input);  { Convert the string to an integer }
    with Query1 do
    begin
      Close;     { Close TQuery }
      SQL.Clear; { Clear contents of SQL property and add next SQL statement }
      SQL.Add('SELECT * FROM PARTS WHERE VENDORNO = :SomeValue');
      Prepare;   { Prepare the Params property }
      Params[0].AsInteger := IVal; { Assign a value to first item in Params }
      Open;      { Open and run the query }
    end;
  except
    on EConvertError do MessageDlg('Entry must be a number', mtWarning, [mbok], 0)
```

continues

Listing 17.2. continued

```
    end;
    end;
end;

procedure TForm1.All1Click(Sender: TObject);
begin
  with Query1 do
  begin
    Close; { Close the Query }
    SQL.Clear; { Clear the contents of SQL property and add new SQL statement }
    SQL.Add('SELECT * FROM PARTS');
    Open; { Open and run the query }
  end;
end;

procedure TForm1.ParamByName1Click(Sender: TObject);
var
  Input: string;
  Ival: integer;
begin
  { Prompt the user for a part number }
  Input := InputBox('Part No', 'Enter an Part Number', '');
  if Input <> '' then
  begin
  try
    IVal := StrToInt(Input); { convert the string to an integer }
    with Query1 do
    begin
      Close;       { Close the query }
      SQL.Clear;   { Clear the contents of SQL propery, add next SQL statement }
      SQL.Add('SELECT * FROM PARTS WHERE PARTNO = :SomeValue');
      Prepare;        { Prepare the Params property }
      ParamByName('SomeValue').AsInteger := IVal; { Initialize Params }
      Open;         { Open and run the query }
    end;
  except
    on EConvertError do MessageDlg('Entry must be a number', mtWarning, [mbok], 0)
  end;
  end;
end;

procedure TForm1.ComboBox1Change(Sender: TObject);
var
  SQLStr: string;
begin
  SQLStr := 'SELECT * FROM PARTS ORDER BY %s'; { Create a dynamic SQL statement }
  with Query1 do
  begin
    Close;  { close query }
    SQL.Clear; { Clear contents of SQL statement }
    { Add to SQL propery the result of the format function and SQL string }
    SQL.ADD(Format(SQLStr, [ComboBox1.Text]));
    Open; { Open and run the query }
  end;
end;

end.
```

Using *TQuery's* SQL Property

The SQL property is the key to using the TQuery component. SQL is where you place the SQL commands to be sent to the server to process. SQL is a TString class. There are two types of SQL statements: static and dynamic.

Static SQL Statements

Static SQL statements are created at design time from within the Object Inspector by invoking the String Editor from the Object Inspector for the SQL property. An example of a static SQL statement follows:

```
SELECT * FROM PARTS
```

This statement is a simple example of the SQL language. In plain English, the statement says *Select all records, columns, and rows from the table named PARTS.* Descriptions of the code follow:

SELECT	A SQL command that retrieves data from one or more tables in the database.
*	Indicates to retrieve all rows for the specified tables. You may specify only certain rows.
FROM	Indicates that the table name(s) to select from will follow.
PARTS	The table name.

To create a static SQL statement, bring up the String List Editor for the SQL property in the Object Inspector. Enter the preceding SQL statement, as shown in Figure 17.2.

FIGURE 17.2.

Entering the SQL statement.

By setting Query1.Active to true, the DBGrid component will be populated with a set of data, as shown in Figure 17.3.

FIGURE 17.3.
The query, when activated.

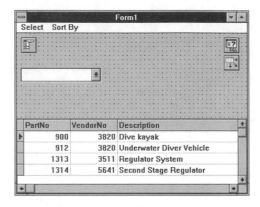

You also can embed static SQL statements into your source code. Add statements to the project you're already working on. First, add a TMainMenu to your form and add the items shown in Table 17.2 to the menu.

Table 17.2. TForm1's main menu.

Menubar	*Submenu*
"Select"	"All"
	"Params"
	"ParamByName"
"SortBy"	"VendorNo"
	"Description"

Now add the following code to TForm1's event handler TForm1.All1Click():

```
with Query1 do
  begin
    Close;                          { Close the TQuery Component }
    SQL.Clear;                      { Clear previous contents of SQL }
    SQL.Add('SELECT * FROM PARTS');  { Add the SQL statement       }
    Open;                           { Open the TQuery Component }
  end;
```

The first statement closes the TQuery object. This is necessary to force any pending updates to occur before executing the SQL statement. SQL.Clear clears any strings currently contained in the SQL property. The new query statement then is added to the SQL property and the TQuery object is reopened, causing it to execute the statement against the database.

Dynamic SQL Statements

Dynamic SQL statements are statements that are not bound at design-time, but instead are bound when executed by using parameterized SQL statements.

Parameterized queries give you more flexibility in varying the conditions on which you base your SQL statements. Look at the following static SQL statement, for example:

```
SELECT * FROM PARTS WHERE PARTNO = 1313;
```

Here, you extract all records from the table in which the PARTNO field has the value 1313. Suppose that you want all records in which the PARTNO field is 1314. You would have to modify your source code every time you wanted to query on another value. It would be better to use values that are set up in the Params property along with placeholders in the actual query statement.

Using the *Params* Property

An example of a parameterized SQL statement follows:

```
SELECT * FROM PARTS WHERE PARTNO = :SomeValue
```

This statement performs basically the same function as the previous static statement with one exception: the variable SomeValue, preceded by a colon, serves as a placeholder for the value on which to perform a query. The value of SomeValue is unknown at design-time. Instead, it is resolved in your code when you run your application. The value it contains is provided through TQuery's Params property.

To illustrate this point, look at the code for TForm1.Order1Click() in Listing 17.3. The code selects items based on a parameter value passed as part of the SQL statement.

Listing 17.3. The source code for TForm1.Order1Click().

```
var
  Input: string;
  Ival: integer;
begin
{ Get a value from the user }
  Input := InputBox('Order No', 'Enter the Vendor Number', '');
  if Input <> '' then
  begin
  try
    IVal := StrToInt(Input);            { Convert the value to a string }
    with Query1 do
    begin
      Close;                            { Close the Query }
      SQL.Clear;                        { Clear the SQL property and add another SQL
statement}
      SQL.Add('SELECT * FROM PARTS WHERE VENDORNO = :SomeValue');
      Prepare;                          { Prepare the Params property }
      Params[0].AsInteger := Ival;      { Place the value in the Params array }
      Open;                             { Open and run the query }
    end;
  except
    on EConvertError do MessageDlg('Entry must be a number', mtWarning, [mbok], 0)
  end;
end;

end.
```

TIP

Use an input box as a quick way to prompt the user for information when all that is required is a prompt to the user for one entry line.

The first few lines of code prompt the user for a value on which to base the SELECT statement. When a value is obtained, the TQuery class is closed again, and the SQL property is cleared. Here, you use the placeholder SomeValue to specify a value for the SQL statement to use.

Query1's Prepare() method sets up the Params property to take the parameters specified in the SQL statement. It does so by parsing the SQL statement and determining the number and types of parameters used. Prepare() only needs to be called once so that the server can pre-process the SQL statement. Although we call Prepare() in each method in our example, we do this for illustration purposes only (see the following Note).

CAUTION

The SQL property must be set before you call Prepare(). Otherwise, the server will not know to expect parameters when you call Query1.Open. Additionally, you will not be able to use the Params property until you call Prepare().

Query1.Params is a zero-based, indexed property that refers to the parameters passed via the SQL statement. You substitute values for the Params before calling Query1.Open, which tells the server to process the SQL statement with the parameters specified by Params.

NOTE

Our examples of parameterized queries are designed for illustration purposes only and do not represent an ideal way of building query statements. By re-creating and re-preparing the query as was done here, you lose the performance advantage of using SQL. Typically, the query statement is predetermined, and you call Prepare() once. Then you fill in the Params based on some variable data from elsewhere and call Open(). You will see this in action in later chapters.

If you had used two placeholders, you would have set up the Params property with two values. Suppose that you used the following SQL statement:

```
SELECT * FROM PARTS WHERE PARTNO = :SomeValue and VENDORNO = :SomeOtherValue
```

Here, you're using the variables SomeValue and SomeOtherValue as placeholders. You initialize your Params property as such:

```
Params[0].AsInteger := Val1;
Params[1].AsInteger := Val2;
```

Using the *ParamByName* Method

Instead of assigning values to the SQL parameters with index numbers, you can use the `ParamByName()` method to assign values to the SQL parameters by passing the name used in the SQL statement to the `ParamByName` method. For example, given the following SQL statement:

```
SELECT * FROM PARTS WHERE PARTNO = :SomeValue and VENDOR = :SomeOtherValue
```

you would use the `ParamByName()` method, as in the following code:

```
Query1.ParamByName('SomeValue').AsInteger := Val1;
Query1.ParamByName('SomeOtherValue').AsInteger.Val2;
```

This is just another way to use parameters for creating dynamic SQL statements that make your source code more readable. However, searching for a name match is slower than hard-coding an index. Another method is by using the `Query`'s `DataSource` property, which is discussed later in this chapter in the section "Joining Multiple Tables."

Sorting the Data

One of SQL's major advantages over accessing data from record/index-based tables is that it is relatively simple to sort and display tables in any manner without regard to indexes. Look at the event handler for `TForm1.VendorNo1Click()`:

```
with Query1 do
begin
  Close;                { Close the Query }
  SQL.Clear;            { Clear contents of SQL and add a new statement }
  SQL.ADD('SELECT * FROM PARTS ORDER BY VENDORNO');
  Open;                 { Open and run the query }
end;
```

Here, you set the `ORDER BY` clause to specify a field by which to sort the data. The `TForm1.Description1Click()` contains the same code, except that it requires that you change the last item in the SQL string to `DESCRIPTION` to sort on the Description field.

Using the *Format()* Function to Create SQL Strings

Using parameterized queries, it might seem that the following code would work as a valid query:

```
SQL.ADD('SELECT * FROM PARTS ORDER BY :SortVal');
Prepare;
Params[0].AsString := 'VENDORNO';
```

Unfortunately, you cannot use placeholders such as `SortVal` to replace field names in a query statement. However, you still can get around this by using the `Format()` function. The `SQL.Add()` property takes a string as a parameter, and you can build that string any way you want, as long as the result is valid SQL syntax. `Format()` provides this capability.

Look at the preceding situation, where you want to vary the field name on which to sort your data. Use the Format() function to build the string to pass to SQL.ADD(). To illustrate this, add a TComboBox to your form. Change its Text property to a blank string and its Style property to csDropDownList. Then add the following strings to its Items property: "VENDORNO", "DESCRIPTION", and "ONHAND". Now add the following event handler to the combo box's OnChange event, TForm1.ComboBox1Change():

```
var
  SQLStr: string;
begin
  SQLStr := 'SELECT * FROM PARTS ORDER BY %s';  { Build an initial string }
  with Query1 do
  begin
    Close;                     { Close the Query }
    SQL.Clear;                 { Clear the contents of SQL }
    SQL.ADD(Format(SQLStr, [ComboBox1.Text])); { Use the Format function to build
the Query string }
    Open;                      { Open and run the query }
  end;
end;
```

This event handler takes the string assigned to SQLStr and uses the Format function to place the selection into its argument specified by the %s sequence. By running the project and selecting VENDORNO from the combo box, for example, the resulting string would follow:

```
'SELECT * FROM ITEMS ORDER BY PARTNO';
```

FORMAT STRINGS

You can use the Format() function to format strings containing format specifiers. A *format specifier* consists of a percent symbol (%) and at least a type specifier. The type specifiers follow:

- c Specifies a char type
- d Specifies an integer type
- f Specifies a float type
- p Specifies a pointer type
- s Specifies a string type

For example, the sequence "%s" indicates a string, and "%d" indicates an integer. Format specifiers may contain additional arguments to give you more flexibility in formatting the resulting string.

Format() replaces format specifiers with arguments contained in the argument list passed to Format(). See Delphi's online help for detailed information on format specifiers.

This is an extremely powerful technique that enables your projects to be as flexible as Object Pascal will allow, without concern about the limitation imposed by the SQL language. You might try as an exercise to use the following string as SQLStr:

```
"SELECT * FROM %s WHERE %s = %d ORDER BY %s"
```

Using *TQuery's DataSource* Property

TQuery's DataSource property enables you to link your TQuery class instance to other TDataSet descendants (TTable and TQuery, for example) by way of a TDataSource instance. This is one way that you can create a one-to-many relationship with multiple tables. To illustrate this, create a new project. Save the project file as ONE2MANY.DPR and the main form's unit as ONE2MANU.PAS.

Place two of each of the following components on your main form: TQuery, TDataSource, TDBGrid, and TLabel. Then set the components' property values as shown in Table 17.3, and arrange them on the form so that they appear like those shown in Figure 17.4. Note that Query1 and Query2 both use the DBDEMOS alias for their Alias properties.

Table 17.3. TForm1's main menu.

Control	*Property*	*Value*
Query1	DataBaseName	DBDEMOS
DataSource1	DataSet	Query1
Query2	DataBaseName	DBDEMOS
	DataSource	DataSource1
DataSource2	DataSet	Query2
DBGrid1	Align	alBottom
	DataSource	DataSource1
Label1	Align	alBottom
	Caption	"Orders"
DBGrid2	Align	
	DataSource	DataSource2
Label2	Align	alBottom
	Caption	"Customer"

FIGURE 17.4.
*The main form for
ONE2MANU.DPR.*

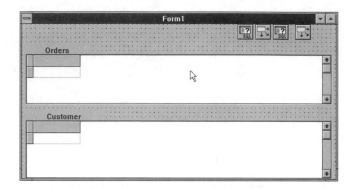

Creating the link between the Customer table and the Order table is simple. First, invoke the String List Editor for Query2's SQL property, and enter the following SQL statement to select all records from the Customer table:

```
SELECT * FROM CUSTOMER
```

Now bring up the String List Editor for Query2's SQL property, and enter the following SQL statement:

```
SELECT * FROM ORDERS WHERE CUSTNO = :CUSTNO
```

Notice the parameterized syntax used for this statement. The first reference to CUSTNO refers to the CUSTNO field in the data set that Query2 references. The second reference to CUSTNO preceded by the colon refers to the field, CUSTNO, in the data set referenced by Query1. This is valid because Query2's DataSource property is set to DataSource1, which is linked to Query1. Query2 obtains the data it requires through Query1's DataSource.

You also might notice that the query was executed at design-time. Delphi binds parameterized queries by looking to a TQuery's data source before looking to the Param's array. To analyze this a bit further, :CUSTNO refers to the CUSTNO field in the Customer table. This match with the CUSTNO field in the Orders table gives you the one-to-many relationship with the two tables. Set the Active property for both Query1 and Query2 to true in the Object Inspector, or simply run the project. You will see the query result as shown in Figure. 17.5. There were no source code changes to this project, so we didn't list the project's source here. Nevertheless, you'll find the project in the \SOURCE\CH17\ directory on the accompanying CD-ROM as ONE2MANY.DPR.

FIGURE 17.5.

A one-to-many relationship between two tables.

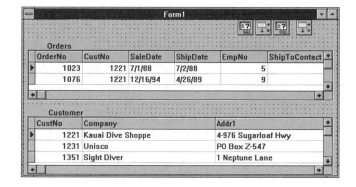

Inserting, Deleting, and Updating Records

It makes sense to provide the capability to insert and delete data from the databases that your applications access. In order to do this, you must know how to use TQuery's ExecSQL() function.

Create a new form with the properties specified in Table 17.4. Also place eight TEdits, eight TLabels, and two TButtons on the form, and then set their properties so they appear as shown in Figure 17.6. Save this project as INSDEL.DPR and the main form's unit as INSDEL0.PAS. You'll find several files in the \SOURCE\DATA\ directory on the accompanying CD-ROM. You'll need to copy these files to your hard disk. You might create a directory where you can store data files provided with this book while you are learning these techniques. You can name your directories to whatever you wish; just be sure to set up the alias DDGLOCAL in the BDE configuration utility so that it points to those data files.

Table 17.4. TForm1's main menu.

Control	Property	Value
Query1	DataBaseName	DDGLOCAL
	Name	GridQuery
DataSource1	DataSet	GridQuery
Query2	DataBaseName	DDGLOCAL
	Name	DeleteQuery
Query3	DataBaseName	DDGLOCAL
	Name	InsertQuery
DBGrid1	Align	alBottom
	DataSource	DataSource1

FIGURE 17.6.

*The main form for
INSDEL.DPR.*

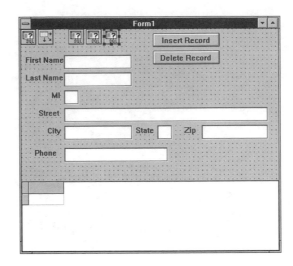

Listings 17.4 and 17.5 show the source code for INSDEL.DPR and INSDEL0.PAS.

Listing 17.4. The source code for INSDEL.DPR.

```
program Insdel;

uses
  Forms,
  Insdel0 in 'INSDEL0.PAS' {Form1};

{$R *.RES}

begin
  Application.CreateForm(TForm1, Form1);
  Application.Run;
end.
```

Listing 17.5. The source code for INSDEL0.PAS.

```
unit Insdel0;

interface

uses
  SysUtils, WinTypes, WinProcs, Messages, Classes, Graphics, Controls,
  Forms, Dialogs, StdCtrls, DB, DBTables, Grids, DBGrids;

type
  TForm1 = class(TForm)
    DBGrid1: TDBGrid;
    InsRecord: TButton;
    DelRecord: TButton;
    GridQuery: TQuery;
    DataSource1: TDataSource;
    Label1: TLabel;
```

```
      Label2: TLabel;
      Label3: TLabel;
      DeleteQuery: TQuery;
      InsertQuery: TQuery;
      Edit1: TEdit;
      Edit2: TEdit;
      Edit3: TEdit;
      Edit4: TEdit;
      Edit5: TEdit;
      Edit6: TEdit;
      Edit7: TEdit;
      Edit8: TEdit;
      Label4: TLabel;
      Label5: TLabel;
      Label6: TLabel;
      Label7: TLabel;
      Label8: TLabel;
      UpdateQuery: TQuery;
      UpdRecord: TButton;
      GetRecord: TButton;
      procedure InsRecordClick(Sender: TObject);
      procedure DelRecordClick(Sender: TObject);
      procedure GetRecordClick(Sender: TObject);
      procedure UpdRecordClick(Sender: TObject);
    private
      { Private declarations }
      procedure ClearFields;
    public
      { Public declarations }
    end;

var
  Form1: TForm1;

implementation

{$R *.DFM}

procedure TForm1.ClearFields;
var
 i: integer;
begin
  for i := 0 to ControlCount - 1 do
    if Controls[i] is TEdit then
      TEdit(Controls[i]).Text := '';
end;

procedure TForm1.InsRecordClick(Sender: TObject);
begin
  Screen.Cursor := crHourGlass;
  try
    with InsertQuery do
    begin
      try
      Close;
      Prepare;
      Params[0].AsString := Edit1.Text;
      Params[1].AsString := Edit2.Text;
```

continues

Listing 17.5. continued

```
      Params[2].AsString := Edit3.Text;
      Params[3].AsString := Edit4.Text;
      Params[4].AsString := Edit5.Text;
      Params[5].AsString := Edit6.Text;
      Params[6].AsString := Edit7.Text;
      Params[7].AsString := Edit8.Text;
      ExecSQL;
      GridQuery.Close;
      GridQuery.Open;
    except
      on E: EDataBaseError do
        MessageDlg(E.Message, mtInformation, [mbok], 0);
    end;
  end;
  ClearFields;
end;
  finally
    Screen.Cursor := crDefault;
    Clearfields;
  end;
end;

procedure TForm1.DelRecordClick(Sender: TObject);
var
  FName: string;
  LName: string;
  MI: string;
begin
  FName := GridQuery.Fields[0].AsString;
  LName := GridQuery.Fields[1].AsString;
  MI := GridQuery.Fields[2].AsString;
  if MessageDlg(Format('Delete "%s %s"?', [FName, LName]),
    mtConfirmation, mbOKCancel, 0) = mrOK then
  begin
    Screen.Cursor := crHourGlass;
    try
      with DeleteQuery do
      begin
        Prepare;
        Params[0].AsString := FName;
        Params[1].AsString := LName;
        Params[2].AsString := MI;
        ExecSQL;
      end;
      GridQuery.Close;
      GridQuery.Open;
    finally
      Screen.Cursor := crDefault;
    end;
  end;
end;

procedure TForm1.GetRecordClick(Sender: TObject);
var
  i: integer;
begin
  for i := 0 to ControlCount - 1 do
  begin
```

```
    if Controls[i] is TEdit then
      with TEdit(Controls[i]) do
        Text := GridQuery.Fields[Tag].AsString;
  end;
  UpdRecord.Enabled := true;
end;

procedure TForm1.UpdRecordClick(Sender: TObject);
var
  i: integer;
begin
  Screen.Cursor := crHourGlass;
  try
    UpdateQuery.Prepare;
    for i := 0 to ControlCount - 1 do
    begin
     if Controls[i] is TEdit then
        with TEdit(Controls[i]) do
          UpdateQuery.Params[Tag].AsString := Text;
    end;
    UpdateQuery.Params[8].AsString := Edit8.Text;  { Based on the last name }
    UpdateQuery.ExecSQL;
    GridQuery.Close;
    GridQuery.Open;
    UpdRecord.Enabled := false;
  finally
    Screen.Cursor := crDefault;
  end;
end.
```

Enter the following SQL statement for GridQuery's SQL property:

```
SELECT * FROM ADDRESS
```

For DeleteQuery's SQL property, enter this code:

```
DELETE FROM ADDRESS WHERE FIRST_NAME = :FIRSTNAME and
    LAST_NAME = :LASTNAME and MI = :MI
```

Finally, for InsertQuery's SQL property, enter this code:

```
INSERT INTO ADDRESS (FIRST_NAME, LAST_NAME, MI, STREET, CITY, STATE, ZIP, PHONE)
VALUES (:FIRSTNAME, :LASTNAME, :MI, :STREET, :CITY, :STATE, :ZIP, :PHONE)
```

Notice that these two statements use parameterized queries. The SQL DELETE command, when not followed by a WHERE clause, deletes all rows and columns from a table. The WHERE clause used with the DELETE command ensures that only the selected record is deleted by including all the table's fields.

The INSERT INTO ADDRESSES command specifies the fields in which to insert data. The VALUES command is used to construct your parameter list.

Inserting Records

Examine the event handler for the Insert Record button, TForm1.InsRecordClick(), in Listing 17.7 to see how you would use the INSERT SQL statement with your Object Pascal code. Here, once again, you set the parameters for TQuery's SQL statement with values in the Params property. Notice that you call InsertQuery's Close() and Prepare() methods as before. This time, however, instead of calling Open(), you call ExecSQL(). ExecSQL() does not open the DataSet—in this case, InsertQuery. ExecSQL() simply passes to the SQL statement to the server to process. Finally, the following lines ensure that Grid1 is updated with the latest changes to the table:

```
GridQuery.Close;
GridQuery.Open;
```

This is an example of how a client can modify the data on a server that is not seen by other clients unless they explicitly refresh the data set originally retrieved from the server. You can think of InsertQuery and GridQuery as different clients for illustration purposes.

TQuery.Open OR TQuery.ExecSQL?

Use TQuery's Open method when the remote SQL server returns a set or subset of its data as a result of the SQL statement sent to it. Use TQuery's ExecSQL method when the remote SQL server does not return a subset of its data based on the SQL statement. The SQL command SELECT, for example, requests data from the server, whereas INSERT tells the server to insert a given record in the data set. A subset is not returned by the INSERT action. UPDATE and DELETE are other examples of commands that return no subset.

Deleting Records

The event handler for Delete Record, TForm1.DelRecordClick(), gets the first fields from the active record in the GridQuery and uses their contents for the parameters in DeleteQuery's SQL statement:

```
FName := GridQuery.Fields[0].AsString;
LName := GridQuery.Fields[1].AsString;
MI := GridQuery.Fields[2].AsString;
```

Like the Insert operation, DeleteQuery calls ExecSQL instead of Open, because no result set is returned. Refresh the GridQuery with the new data by executing the following lines:

```
GridQuery.Close;
GridQuery.Open;
```

Updating Records

To update or modify an existing record with new data, you will need two additional TButtons on your form, as shown in Figure 17.7.

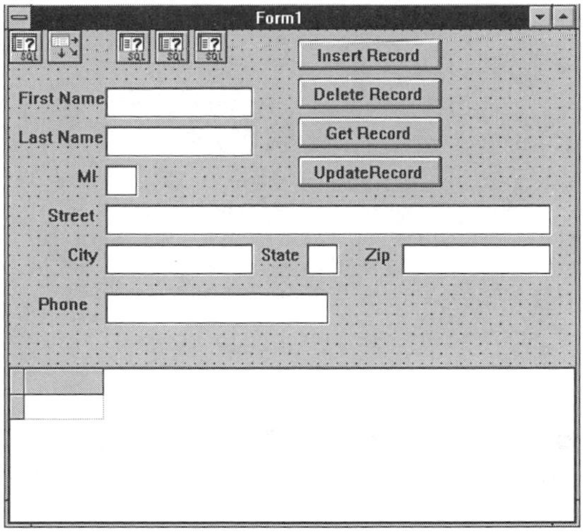

FIGURE 17.7.

*The main form with the
Get Record and
UpdateRecord buttons.*

Change the caption of one button to Get Record and the other to UpdateRecord. Now change their names to GetRecord and UpdateRecord. Set the Enabled property for the Update Record button to false.

Additionally, because you're not using "data aware" edit controls, you must associate your edit controls with the fields in your data set. This is simple: Just change the Tag property in each edit control to match the Fields array for the GridQuery control. GridQuery.Fields[0] is the First_Name, for example, so Edit1.Tag should be 0, and so on. Figure 17.8 shows the main form when the application is running.

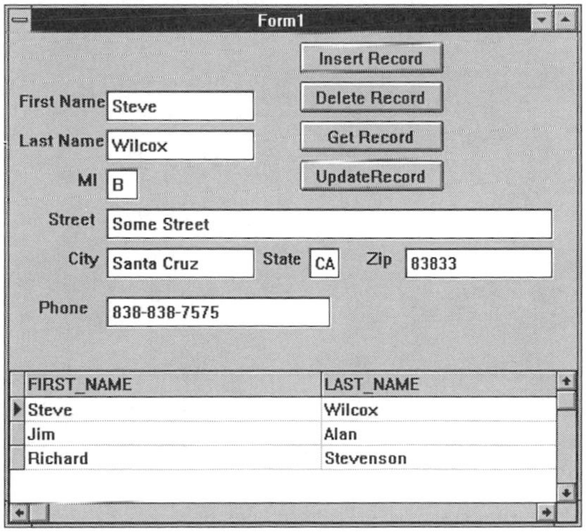

FIGURE 17.8.

*The main form with
additional buttons.*

To retrieve a record into the edit controls, create an event handler for the Get Record button, `TForm1.GetRecordClick()`:

```
var
  i: integer;
begin
  for i := 0 to ControlCount - 1 do
  begin
   if Controls[i] is TEdit then        { Only if the conrol is a TEdit descendant }
      with TEdit(Controls[i]) do
        Text := GridQuery.Fields[Tag].AsString;      { Access Data by the Fields
array }
  end;
  UpdRecord.Enabled := true;
```

> **NOTE**
>
> Use `TQuery`'s `Fields` array to access individual fields in the data set. `Fields` represents the columns in the data set for the active record. `Fields[0]` represents the first column, for example. Use the type conversion methods `AsString()` and `AsInteger` to convert the result value from `Fields`.

The event handler loops through all controls and, if the current control is a `TEdit` class, its text property is assigned the `GridQuery`'s respective field value. The UpdateRecord button then is enabled.

Now that you can edit the contents of the edit controls, you need a way to replace the record in the table with their new contents. To do this, add yet another `TQuery` component to the form, set its `DataBaseName` property to `DDGLOCAL`, set its `Name` to `UpdateQuery`, and set its `SQL` property to the following:

```
UPDATE ADDRESS
SET FIRST_NAME = :FIRSTNAME,
LAST_NAME = :LASTNAME,
MI = :M,
STREET = :ST,
CITY = :CT,
STATE = :STA,
ZIP = :ZP,
PHONE = :PHN
WHERE PHONE = :PNO
```

Here, every field in the record is assigned a value based on the parameter passed to it. When this SQL statement is sent to the server, the server has no way of knowing which record to update. The WHERE clause ensures that the correct record is updated. In this example, the PHONE field is probably the most unique field in the table, so it serves the need here for illustration. Realistically, you'll probably have a field specifically used to maintain unique values for each record. You'll see how to create such fields in a later chapter. The event handler Update Record, `TForm1.UpdRecordClick()`, also makes use of the edit control's `Tag` property:

```
var
  i: integer;
begin
  Screen.Cursor := crHourGlass;
  try
    UpdateQuery.Prepare;
    for i := 0 to ControlCount - 1 do
    begin
     if Controls[i] is TEdit then
        with TEdit(Controls[i]) do
           UpdateQuery.Params[Tag].AsString := Text;
    end;
    UpdateQuery.Params[8].AsString := Edit8.Text;  { Based on the last name }
    UpdateQuery.ExecSQL;
    GridQuery.Close;
    GridQuery.Open;
    UpdRecord.Enabled := false;
  finally
    Screen.Cursor := crDefault;
  end
```

This event handler uses the edit control values to set up the Params property for UpdateQuery based on their tag values. Remember that it is essential that the tags exactly match the fields specified in the SQL statement. Also, you set UpdateQuery.Params[8] to the value of the Edit8, which holds the phone number. This value is used for the WHERE clause in the SQL statement. Finally, the same sequence of commands to process the query and refresh the GridQuery are executed.

Joining Multiple Tables

Joining tables is another method that you can use to view data from two or more tables in a single data set.

Suppose that you have three tables: PARTS, ORDERS, and ITEMS. ORDERS is related to ITEMS on a one-to-many basis, linked by an ORDERNO field. ITEMS contains records that refer to line-item entries in a given order. For each entry in ORDERS, there are multiple entries in ITEMS. ITEMS contains information such as part number, date of purchase, and discount (if any).

PARTS also is related to ITEMS on a one-to-many basis, linked by the PARTNO field. PARTS contains specific information about a part such as a vendor number and part description, number on hand, and so on.

In this illustration, you will join the PARTS and ITEMS tables so that fields from each table appear in one data set.

Create a new project. Place a TQuery, TDataSource, and TDBGrid on the form. Set Query1's DataBaseName to IBDDG, DataSource1's DataSet property to Query1, and DBGrid1's DataSource property to DataSource1. Add the following SQL statement to Query1's SQL property:

```
SELECT P.PARTNO, P.DESCRIPTION, P.VENDORNO, I.ORDERNO, I.QTY, I.DISCOUNT
FROM PARTS  P, ITEMS I
WHERE P.PARTNO = I.PARTNO
```

Examine the FROM clause. FROM specifies the tables from which the SELECT statement will extract its data. By following each table name with an identifier, you can create an alias or correlation name that you can use in the SELECT clause, as done here. The WHERE clause establishes a link between the tables that are being joined.

Change the Active property for Query1 in the Object Inspector to true. Your data set should contain the information from both tables, as shown in Figure 17.9. Because no modifications were made to this project's source code, the source isn't listed here. However, you'll find the project under in the \SOURCE\CH17\ directory on the accompanying CD-ROM as JOIN.DPR.

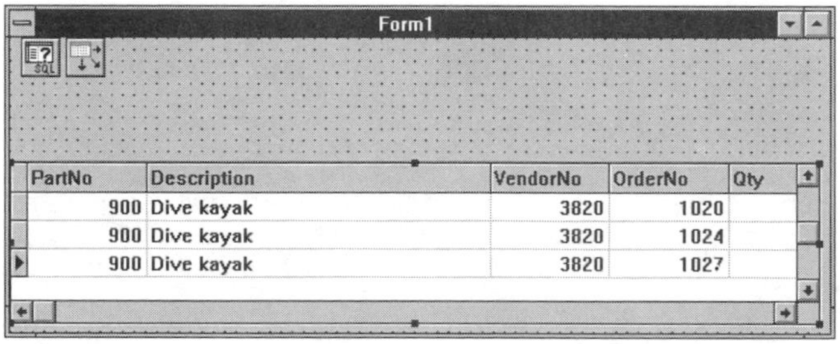

FIGURE 17.9.
A joined table data set.

PartNo	Description	VendorNo	OrderNo	Qty
900	Dive kayak	3820	1020	
900	Dive kayak	3820	1024	
900	Dive kayak	3820	1027	

Using Heterogeneous Queries

Delphi supports *heterogeneous queries*—queries that perform join operations on tables existing on different servers. In order to execute this type of query, the SQL syntax must adhere to the local SQL specifications. You should refer the documentation provided with local SQL if you are unsure whether your syntax is correct.

Before you can perform a heterogeneous query, you must set up an alias for each server from which you will request data. For example, the following statement selects on two tables that exist on different servers:

```
SELECT PARTS.DESCRIPTION,   ITEMS.ORDERNO
FROM :SOMEALIAS:PARTS,  :SOMEOTHERALIAS:ITEMS
```

The PARTS table would exist on some server pointed to by the SOMEALIAS alias, whereas the ITEMS table is pointed to by the SOMEOTHERALIAS alias. On other servers such as Sybase and Informix, the statement might read as follows:

```
SELECT PARTS.DESCRIPTION,   ITEMS.ORDERNO
FROM :SYBASE:PARTS,  :INFORMIX:ITEMS
```

In this example, :SYBASE and :INFORMIX are really aliases and not server names.

Creating and Altering Tables

Creating a table requires using SQL's ALTER TABLE clause. For example, look at the following SQL statement:

```
CREATE TABLE "TESTTBL.DB"
(
FIELD_1 CHAR[20],
FIELD_2 NUMERIC(5, 2),
FIELD_3 SMALLINT,
FIELD_4 CHAR(2)
)
```

This statement creates a table named TESTTBL.DB, whose fields are FIELD_1, FIELD_2, FIELD_3, and FIELD_4. The field types correspond to dBASE data types. You should refer to the manual to determine the field types for each table type to see how they are defined in SQL. You also can specify a primary key for this table by using the PRIMARY KEY clause. The preceding statement then would read

```
CREATE TABLE "TESTTBL.DB"
(
FIELD_1 CHAR[20],
FIELD_2 NUMERIC(5, 2),
FIELD_3 SMALLINT,
FIELD_4 CHAR(2)
PRIMARY KEY(FIELD_1, FIELD_2)
)
```

To alter an existing table, use the ALTER TABLE SQL clause. An example of an SQL statement using ALTER TABLE follows:

```
ALTER TABLE "TESTTBL.DD" ADD ADDRESS2 CHARACTER(20)
```

Here, ALTER TABLE is used with the ADD clause to add the field ADDRESS2 to the table TESTTBL.DB. Following the field name is the type specifier for the field. To remove a field from a table, use ALTER TABLE with the DROP clause as follows:

```
ALTER TABLE "TESTTBL.DB" DROP ADDRESS2
```

Summary

This chapter introduced you to client/server development. You learned about the Structured Query Language and about record-oriented versus set-oriented databases. You also were introduced to the TQuery component and learned various ways to use SQL with the TQuery component to perform useful database functions. Realize, however, that you've only brushed the surface of client/server development. Client/server is a very new and broad technology that is quickly evolving. You can be certain that the client/server arena will play a major role in software development in the future. In chapters to follow, you use TQuery again to perform even more complex operations. In the next chapter, you learn about an essential element to Windows programming: dynamic link libraries.

18

Dynamic Link Libraries (DLLs)

This chapter discusses Windows dynamic link libraries, otherwise known as DLLs. DLLs are a key component to writing any Windows application. This chapter discusses several aspects of using and creating DLLs, and it provides you with a conceptual overview of how DLLs work. It also discusses when you should and should not use DLLs with your applications. Finally, you learn how to use and create DLLs, and what other considerations you must take into account when using or creating DLLs.

What Exactly Is a DLL?

Dynamic link libraries are program modules that can contain code, data, or resources that can be shared among many Windows applications. Sharing code is the primary use of DLLs. In fact, the files KRNL386.EXE, USER.EXE, and GDI.EXE are three DLLs on which Windows relies heavily. These DLLs are responsible for memory and program management, user interface, and graphics, respectively.

Another advantage to using DLLs is that your applications become modular. This simplifies updating your applications, because you need to replace only DLLs instead of replacing the entire application. The Windows environment presents a typical example of this type of modularity. Each time you install a new device, you also install a device driver DLL for that device to enable it to communicate with Windows. The advantage to modularity becomes obvious when you imagine if you had to reinstall Windows each time you installed a new device to your system.

On disk, a DLL is basically the same as a Window's EXE file. One major difference is that a DLL is not an independently executable file, although it may contain executable code. The most common DLL file extension is DLL. Other file extensions are DRV for device drivers, SYS for system files, and FON for font resources. Be careful not to confuse DLLs with an EXE extension with Windows executable files. This extension is basically a carryover from an older version of Windows before the DLL extension replaced it.

DLLs share their code with other applications through a process called *dynamic linking*, which is discussed later in this chapter. In general, when an application uses a DLL, Windows ensures that only one copy of that DLL resides in memory. Multiple applications or modules share code or resources in a DLL instance. Windows maintains a *usage count* for each DLL that specifies how many modules use it. When applications, or even DLLs, require use of an already loaded DLL, Windows increments the usage count for that DLL. When the application terminates, Windows decrements the usage count and unloads the DLL when the usage count is zero. An application can load and unload a DLL explicitly using the `LoadLibrary()` and `FreeLibrary()` API functions, or implicitly by declaring an external reference to an exported function. Don't worry if you don't understand this quite yet; it is explained in this chapter.

Here are some terms that you will need to know:

Application	A Windows program residing in an EXE file.
Executable	A file containing executable code. Executable files include DLL and EXE files.
Instance	When referring to applications and DLLs, an *instance* is the occurrence of an executable. When an application is run twice, for example, there are two instances of that application. When a DLL is loaded, an instance of that DLL exists. This is not to be confused with an instance of a class. Windows provides a handle for each instance. This handle is referred to as an *instance handle.*
Module	The sharable code and resources associated with an instance. When multiple instances of an application exist, only one module will be shared among them. Windows maintains a database to manage modules and provides a module handle for each module.
Task	Windows is a multitasking, or task-switching, environment. It must be able to allocate system resources and time to the various instances running under it. It does this by maintaining a task database that maintains module handles, instance handles, and other necessary information to enable it to perform its task-switching functions. The task is the element to which Windows grants resources and time blocks.

Figure 18.1 illustrates the relationship between application instances and application modules. Figure 18.2 illustrates the relationship between DLL instances and DLL modules when applications are using them.

FIGURE 18.1.

The application instance and application module relationship.

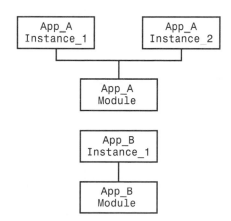

FIGURE 18.2.
The DLL instance/module
relationship.

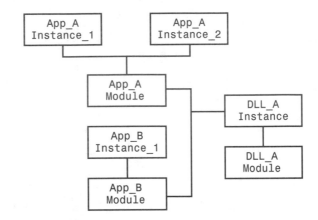

Static Linking Versus Dynamic Linking

Static linking refers to the method by which the Delphi compiler resolves a function or procedure call to its executable code. The function's code can exist in the application module or in
a unit. When linking your applications, these functions and procedures become part of the
final executable file. In other words, on disk, each function will reside at a specific location in
the program's EXE file.

A function's location also is predetermined at a location relative to where the program is loaded
in memory. Any calls to that function cause program execution to jump to where the function
resides, execute the function, and then return to the location from which it was called. The
relative address of the function is resolved during the linking process.

This is a very loose description of a more complex process that the Delphi compiler uses to
perform static linking. However, for the purpose of this book, you don't need to understand
the underlying operations that the compiler performs to effectively use DLLs in your applications.

NOTE

Delphi implements a *smart linker* that automatically removes functions, procedures,
variables, and typed constants that never get referenced in the final project. Therefore,
functions that reside in large units that never get used don't become a part of your
EXE file.

Suppose that you have two applications that use the same function that resides in a unit. Both
applications, of course, would have to include the unit in their uses statement. If you ran both
applications simultaneously in Windows, the function would exist twice in memory. If you

had a third application, there would be a third instance of the function in memory, and you would be using up three times its memory space. This small example illustrates one of the primary reasons for dynamic linking. Through dynamic linking, this function resides in a DLL. Then, when an application loads it into memory, all other applications that need to reference it can share its code. Thus, the function only exists once in memory.

Figure 18.3 illustrates the difference between a statically linked function and a dynamically linked function.

FIGURE 18.3.

Differences between a statically linked function and a dynamically linked function.

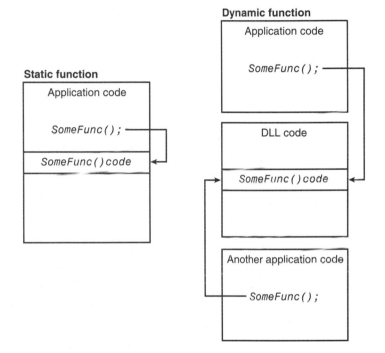

With *dynamic linking*, the link between a function call and its executable code is resolved at runtime by using an external reference to the DLL's function. These references can be declared in the application, but usually are placed in a separate import unit. The import unit declares the imported functions and procedure, as well as defines various types required by DLL functions.

As an example, suppose that you have a DLL named MAXLIB.DLL that contains a function:

```
Function Max(i1, I2: integer): integer;
```

This function returns the higher of the two integers passed to it. A typical import unit would look like this:

```
unit MaxUnit;
interface
  function Max(i1, I2: integer): integer;
implementation
  function Max; external 'MAXLIB' index 1;
end.
```

This looks somewhat like a typical unit, except that you don't define the function Max(). The keyword external simply says that the function resides in the DLL of the name that follows it. Following the DLL name is a unique index that refers to this function in the DLL. This index value is maintained in a table that exists in the DLL itself. To use this unit, an application simply would place MaxUnit in its uses statement. When the application runs, the DLL automatically is loaded into memory, and any calls to Max() are linked to the Max() function in the DLL.

This illustrates one of two ways to load a DLL; it is called *implicitly loading* which causes Windows to automatically load the DLL. Another method is to *explicitly load* the DLL; this is discussed later in this chapter.

Why Use DLLs?

There are several reasons for using DLLs, some of which we mentioned earlier. In general, use DLLs to share code or system resources, to hide your code implementation or low-level system routines, or to design custom controls. We'll discuss these topics in the following sections.

Sharing Code, Resources, and Data

Earlier in this chapter, you learned that the most common reason for creating a DLL is to share code. Unlike units, which enable you to share code with different Delphi applications, DLLs enable you to share code with any Windows application that can call functions from DLLs.

Additionally, DLLs provide a way for you to share resources such as bitmaps, fonts, icons, and so on, that you normally would put into a resource file and link directly into your application. By placing these resources into a DLL, many applications can make use of them without using up the memory required to load them more often than required.

Applications also can store and retrieve data from a DLL. This is one method in which applications can communicate with each other by calling functions and procedures in the DLL that return or set data allocated in its own data segment.

Hiding Implementation

In some cases, you may want to hide the details of the routines that you make available from a DLL. For whatever reason you decide to hide your code's implementation, a DLL provides a way for you to make your functions available to the public and not give away your source code in doing so. All you need to do is provide an interface unit to enable others to access your DLL.

If you take a look at the Window's API, you will see that these functions are provided through DLLs that exist in the \WINDOWS\SYSTEM\ directory. The WINPROCS unit is the interface unit to these DLLs. If you own the VCL runtime library, one of the files you get is WINPROCS.PAS, the source to the WINPROCS unit. In WINPROCS.PAS, you find function definitions like the following in the interface section:

```
procedure ClientToScreen(Wnd: HWnd; var Point: TPoint);
```

The corresponding link to the DLL is in the implementation section as the following:

```
procedure ClientToScreen;        external 'USER' index 28;
```

This basically says that the procedure ClientToScreen() exists in the USER.EXE DLL at index 28.

System-Level Routines

Windows requires some functions to reside in DLL, because Windows guarantees that a DLL's fixed code segment always will be present in memory. These routines follow:

Hook Functions	Functions that intercept Windows messages for special processing, depending on the type of hook function used. Chapter 21, "Hard-Core Windows," shows you how to create two types of hook functions.
Device Drivers	Special DLLs that provide an interface between various devices and Windows. KEYBOARD.DRV is an example of this type of DLL.
ISRs	Interrupt service routines (ISRs) in Windows basically are device drivers driven by DOS interrupts. Such routines should be placed in a DLL, such as serial communications interface routines.
Callback Functions	A function that Windows calls instead of the application that defines it. Windows declares various callback functions that you must define by using the MakeProcInstance() and GetProcAddress() Windows API functions. See the Windows help for *Callback Functions*, *MakeProcInstance*, and *GetProcAddress* topics.

TIP

Microsoft recommends placing routines that call interrupts or extract data from interrupts into DLLs for future portability. If your applications only call functions, they will be easier to port to other platforms.

Custom Controls

Custom controls usually are placed in DLLs. These controls are not the same as Delphi custom components. Custom controls are registered under Windows and can be used by any Windows development environment. These types of custom controls are placed in DLLs to conserve memory by having only one copy of the control's code in memory when multiple copies of the control are being used.

Creating DLLs

The following sections take you through the process of actually creating a DLL with Delphi. You'll see how to create an interface unit so that you can make your DLLs available to other programs. You'll also learn how to incorporate Delphi forms into DLLs before going on to learning to use DLLs in Delphi.

Counting Your Pennies (A Simple DLL)

The following DLL example illustrates placing a routine that is a favorite of many Computer Science professors into a DLL. The routine converts a monetary amount in pennies to the minimum number of nickels, dimes, or quarters needed to add up the total pennies.

Creating the DLL

First, create a new project and remove Form1 by choosing View | Project Manager from the menu and removing the Unit1 from the Project Manager dialog box.

Now choose File | New Unit from the menu. The edit window shows you a unit template. Save this unit as CHANGEU.PAS. Listing 18.1 shows the source code for CHANGEU.PAS.

Listing 18.1. The source code for CHANGEU.PAS.

```
unit Changeu;

interface
type

  TChangeRec = record
    Quarters,
    Dimes,
    Nickels,
    Pennies: word;
  end;

{ Declare function with export keyword }
function PenniesToChange(TotPennies: word; var ChangeRec: TChangeRec):
➥word; export;

implementation
```

```
function PenniesToChange(TotPennies: word; var ChangeRec: TChangeRec): word;
begin
  Result := TotPennies;     { Assign value to Result }
  { Calculate the values for quarters, dimes, nickels, pennies }
  with ChangeRec do begin
    Quarters := TotPennies div 25;
    TotPennies  := TotPennies - Quarters * 25;
    Dimes := TotPennies div 10;
    TotPennies := TotPennies - Dimes * 10;
    Nickels := TotPennies div 5;
    TotPennies := TotPennies - Nickels * 5;
    Pennies := TotPennies;
  end;
end;
end.
```

CHANGEU.PAS contains a simple routine, PenniesToChange(), which replaces pennies with coins of larger denomination. Here, the export keyword specifies that this function will be exported:

```
function PenniesToChange(TotPennies: word; var ChangeRec: TChangeRec):
➥word; export;
```

Now you must create the export clause that actually exports the function. This is done in a DPR file, which is renamed to CHANGE.DPR. Listing 18.2 shows CHANGE.DPR before it was changed; it compiles to a DLL. Listing 18.3 shows CHANGE.DPR after the changes.

Listing 18.2. CHANGE.DPR before modifying.

```
program Change;

uses
  Forms,
  Unit1 in 'UNIT1.PAS';

{$R *.RES}

begin
  Application.Run;
end.
```

Listing 18.3. CHANGE.DPR as a DLL.

```
library Change;

uses
  Changeu in 'CHANGEU.PAS';

exports
  PenniesToChange index 1;
begin
end.
```

First, the keyword program was changed to library. Next, the Forms unit was removed from the uses clause. Also, the code between the begin..end block was removed. The {$R *.RES} statement also was removed. The only statement that was added is an exports clause, which is where exported functions are listed along with their index. After these changes are made, you can compile the DLL, and it will create the file CHANGE.DLL.

Creating an Interface Unit

The interface unit enables users of your DLL to statically import your DLL's routines into their applications by just placing the import unit's name in their module's uses statement. Static importing is explained later in this chapter. For now, just assume that the unit simplifies using your DLL. Listing 18.4 shows the interface unit for CHANGE.DLL.

Listing 18.4. CHANGEI.PAS, the interface unit for CHANGE.DLL.

```
unit Changei;
{ This is the interface unit to the CHANGE.DLL }

interface
type
  { Define  TChangeRec just as it was defined in the DLL }
  TChangeRec = record
    Quarters,
    Dimes,
    Nickels,
    Pennies: word;
  end;

{ Declare the exported function type }
function PenniesToChange(TotPennies: word; var ChangeRec: TChangeRec): word;

implementation
{ Define the imported function }
function PenniesToChange; external 'CHANGE' index 1;

end.
```

CHANGEI.PAS has the same interface section as CHANGEU.PAS. CHANGEI.PAS differs in the implementation section, where it defines the link to CHANGE.DLL's function indexed by the value 1.

NOTE

The following definition shows one of three ways to import a DLL function:

```
function PenniesToChange; external 'CHANGE' index 1;
```

This method is called *importing by ordinal.* Two other methods by which you can import DLL functions are *by name*:

```
function PenniesToChange; external 'CHANGE'
```

or *by new name*:

```
function PenniesToChange; external 'CHANGE' name 'PenniesToCoins'
```

The *by name* method simply uses the same function identifier in the import unit as the function name identifier in the DLL. *By new name* enables you to specify a different name for the imported function by preceding the new name with the name keyword. The *by ordinal* method is preferred—when used, it reduces the DLL's load time, because it doesn't have to look up the function name in the DLL's name table.

If this were an actual DLL that you planned to deploy, you would provide CHANGE.DLL and CHANGEI.PAS to your users. This would enable them to use the DLL by defining the types and functions in CHANGEI.PAS that CHANGE.DLL requires. Additionally, programmers using different languages like C++ could convert CHANGEI.PAS to their language, enabling them to use your DLL in their development environments.

Making Forms Available from DLLs

This section shows you how to make your forms available from a DLL. One of the reasons why placing commonly used forms in a DLL is beneficial is that it enables you to extend your forms for use with any Windows application or development environment like C++, Visual Basic, and Object PAL.

Create a new form as you did before, except this time, don't remove the form from the project. From Options | Project, ensure that Form1 is in the available form's list and not the Auto Create form's list. Place a TCalendar component on Form1 and set the properties as specified in Table 18.1. Form1 is shown in Figure 18.4.

Table 18.1. Form1 and property settings.

Component or Form	Property	Value
Form1	BorderIcons	[]
	BorderStyle	bsNone
Calendar1	Align	alClient

FIGURE 18.4.

Form1 with the calendar component.

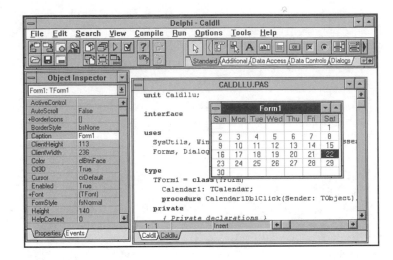

Listings 18.5 and 18.6 show the source code for CALDLL.DPR and CALDLLU.PAS, which shows how to encapsulate the form into a DLL.

Listing 18.5. The source code for CALDLL.DPR.

```
library Caldll;

uses
  Caldllu in 'CALDLLU.PAS' {Form1};

{$R *.RES}

exports
  ShowCalendar index 1;
begin
end.
```

Listing 18.6. The source code for CALDLLU.PAS.

```
unit Caldllu;

interface

uses
  SysUtils, WinTypes, WinProcs, Messages, Classes, Graphics, Controls,
  Forms, Dialogs, Grids, Calendar;

type
  TForm1 = class(TForm)
    Calendar1: TCalendar;
    procedure Calendar1DblClick(Sender: TObject);
```

```
  private
    { Private declarations }
  public
    { Public declarations }
  end;

{ Declare the export function }
function ShowCalendar(X, Y:Integer): TDateTime; export;

implementation
{$R *.DFM}

function ShowCalendar(X, Y:Integer): TDateTime;
var
  Form1: TForm1;
begin
  try                           { wrap this function in a try..except block }
    Form1 := TForm1.Create(nil); { Create the form }
    with Form1 do begin
      Left := X;                { Set Form1's position }
      Top := Y;
      ShowModal;                { Show Form1 one as Model NEVER modeless !}
      Result := Calendar1.CalendarDate;  { Pass the date back in Result }
    end;
    Form1 Free;                 { Free the form }
  except
    on E: Exception do          { Eat up any exceptions to prevent crash in
➥calling app }
      MessageDlg('An '+E.ClassName+' occured. in CALLDLL.DLL', mtWarning,
                 [mbok], 0);
  end;
end;

procedure TForm1.Calendar1DblClick(Sender: TObject);
begin
  Close;  { Close the form }
end;

end.
```

Here, the form is incorporated into the exported function. Notice that Form1's declaration was removed from the interface section and declared Form1 inside the function instead. If ShowCalendar is called more than once, a new instance of Form1 is created. If its declaration had been left in the implementation section, a new instance would have destroyed a previous instance, and probably would cause a calling application to crash.

Next, the function's guts are wrapped in a try..except block. (The reason for this is discussed later in this chapter.) Finally, the form is positioned, and it is displayed as a modal form. When the form closes, the date is passed back that was selected by the user from the Calendar component. The form closes after the user double-clicks the Calendar component.

> **CAUTION**
>
> Never display a form in a DLL as a modeless form (do not display it by calling its
> Show() method). OnActivate and OnDeActivate will not work, and this may cause
> undesirable behavior with your applications.

This is all that is required when encapsulating a form into a DLL. There are other considerations that you should watch for under certain circumstances, which are discussed later in this chapter. The next section explains how to use these DLLs.

Using DLLs in Your Delphi Applications

Earlier in this chapter, you learned that there are two ways to load or import DLLs: implicitly and explicitly. Both techniques are illustrated in this section with the DLLs just created.

Implicitly Loading DLLs

The first DLL created in this chapter included an interface unit. In this section, that unit is used in a sample application to illustrate implicitly linking a DLL. The sample application is very simple. It is basically a form with a TEdit, a TButton, and nine TLabels, as shown in Figure 18.5.

FIGURE 18.5.

Form1.

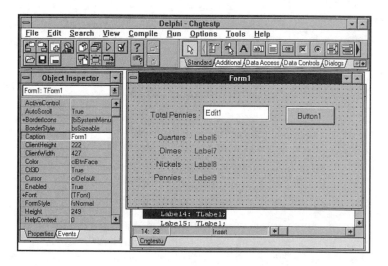

Form1 is defined in the unit CNGTESTU.PAS shown in Listing 18.7. Listing 18.8 shows CNGTESTP.DPR.

Listing 18.7. The source code for CNGTESTU.PAS.

```
unit Cngtestu;

interface

uses
  SysUtils, WinTypes, WinProcs, Messages, Classes, Graphics, Controls,
  Forms, Dialogs, StdCtrls, Mask;

type
  TForm1 = class(TForm)
    Label1: TLabel;
    Label2: TLabel;
    Label3: TLabel;
    Label4: TLabel;
    Label5: TLabel;
    Label6: TLabel;
    Label7: TLabel;
    Label8: TLabel;
    Label9: TLabel;
    Button1: TButton;
    Edit1: TEdit;
    procedure Button1Click(Sender: TObject);
  private
    { Private declarations }
  public
    { Public declarations }
  end;

var
  Form1: TForm1;

implementation
uses Changei;  { Use the interface unit }

{$R *.DFM}

procedure TForm1.Button1Click(Sender: TObject);
var
  ChangeRec: TChangeRec;
  TotPennies: word;
begin
  try
    { Call the DLL function }
    TotPennies := PenniesToChange(StrToInt(Edit1.Text), ChangeRec);
    with ChangeRec do begin
      Label6.Caption := IntToStr(Quarters);
      Label7.Caption := IntToStr(Dimes);
      Label8.Caption := IntToStr(Nickels);
      Label9.Caption := IntToStr(Pennies);
    end
  except
    on EConvertError do
      MessageDlg('Total Pennies must be an integer values', mtError, [mbok], 0);
  end;
end;

end.
```

Listing 18.8. The source code for CNGTESTP.DPR.

```
program Chgtestp;

uses
  Forms,
  Cngtestu in 'CNGTESTU.PAS' {Form1};

{$R *.RES}

begin
  Application.CreateForm(TForm1, Form1);
  Application.Run;
end.
```

Notice that CNGTESTU.PAS includes CHANGEI in its uses statement. Recall that CHANGEI.PAS includes the external declarations to the functions existing in CHANGE.DLL. When this application runs, Windows automatically loads CHANGE.DLL.

Usage of an import unit is optional. You can remove CHANGEI from CNGTESTU.PAS's uses statement, for example, and place the external declaration to PenniesToChange() in CNGTESTU.PAS's implementation section as in the following code:

```
implementation
function PenniesToChange(TotPennies: word; var ChangeRec: TChangeRec): word;
➥far; external 'CHANGE';
```

You also would have to define TChangeRec again in CHGTESTU.PAS. This is fine in the case where you only need access to few routines from a DLL. You'll find that in many cases, you require not only the external declarations to the DLL's routines, but also access to the types defined in the interface unit.

> **NOTE**
>
> Many times, when using another vendor's DLL, you will not have a Pascal interface unit; instead, you will have a C/C++ import library. In this case, you will have to translate the library to a Pascal equivalent interface unit. In Chapter 23, "Testing and Debugging," an entire C import library is converted to a Pascal interface unit. Both files are available on the CD as an example of doing this.

This application's functionality is simple. It asks the user for an amount of pennies and calls the DLL function PenniesToChange(). The labels display the change returned. The try..except block ensures that the user enters a valid number.

Explicitly Loading a DLL

Implicitly loading DLLs is convenient, but it is not always the most desired method. Suppose that you have a DLL that contains a large number of routines. If it is likely that your application will never call any of the DLL's routines, it would be a waste of memory to load the DLL every time your application runs. This is true especially when using multiple DLLs with one application. This is a situation in which it would be beneficial to load the DLL when specifically requested to do so by the application. This is referred to as *explicitly* importing a DLL.

To illustrate explicitly loading a DLL, use the CALDLL example created earlier in this chapter. The calling program is shown in Listings 18.9 and 18.10 as CALTESTP.DPR and CALTESTU.PAS.

Listing 18.9. The source code for CALTESTP.DPR.

```
program Caltestp;

uses
  Forms,
  Caltestu in 'CALTESTU.PAS' {Form1};

{$R *.RES}

begin
  Application.CreateForm(TForm1, Form1);
  Application.Run;
end.
```

Listing 18.10. The source code for CALTESTU.PAS.

```
unit Caltestu;

interface

uses
  SysUtils, WinTypes, WinProcs, Messages, Classes, Graphics, Controls,
  Forms, Dialogs, StdCtrls;

type
  TShowCalendar = function(X, Y: integer): TDateTime;
  EDLLLoadError = class(Exception);

  TForm1 = class(TForm)
    Label1: TLabel;
    Button1: TButton;
    procedure Button1Click(Sender: TObject);
  private
    { Private declarations }
  public
    { Public declarations }
  end;
```

continues

Listing 18.10. continued

```
var
  Form1: TForm1;

implementation

{ function ShowCalendar(X, Y: integer): TDateTime; far; external 'CALDLL'; }

{$R *.DFM}

procedure TForm1.Button1Click(Sender: TObject);
var
  LibHandle: THandle;
  ShowCalendar: TShowCalendar;
begin
  try
    LibHandle := LoadLibrary('CALDLL.DLL');
    if LibHandle < 32 then
      raise EDLLLoadError.Create('Unable to Load DLL');
    @ShowCalendar := GetProcAddress(LibHandle, 'SHOWCALENDAR');
    Label1.Caption := DateToStr(ShowCalendar(Left+30, Top+30));
    FreeLibrary(LibHandle);
  except
    on E: EDLLLoadError do
      MessageDlg(E.Message, mtInformation, [mbok], 0);
  end;
end;

end.
```

The first thing CALTESTU.PAS does is define a procedural data type, TShowCalendar, that describes the function it will be using from CALDLL.DLL. Then it defines a special exception which is raised when there is a problem loading the DLL. In Button1's OnClick event handler, three Windows API functions are introduced: LoadLibrary(), FreeLibrary(), and GetProcAddress().

LoadLibrary() is defined as the following:

```
function LoadLibrary(LibFileName: PChar): THandle;
```

This loads the DLL module specified by LibFileName into memory and returns an instance handle. If the call fails, LoadLibrary() returns a value less than 32 or HINSTANCE_ERROR. You might look up LoadLibrary() in the online help for detailed information on its functionality and return error values.

FreeLibrary() is defined as the following:

```
procedure FreeLibrary(LibModule: THandle);
```

FreeLibrary() decrements the instance count of the library specified by LibModule. It removes the library from memory when the library's instance count is zero. The instance count keeps track of the number of tasks using the DLL.

GetProcAddress() is defined as the following:

```
function GetProcAddress(Module: THandle; ProcName: PChar): TFarProc;
```

GetProcAddress() returns the address of a function within the module specified in its first parameter, Module. Module is the THandle returned from a call to LoadLibrary().

In Button1's OnClick event handler, LoadLibrary() is called, and an EDLLLoadError exception is raised if the call failed. If the call is successful, a call to the window's GetProcAddress() is made to get the address of the function ShowCalendar(). Prepending the procedural data type variable ShowCalendar with the address of operator (@) character prevents the compiler from issuing a type mismatch error due to its strict type-checking. After obtaining the address of ShowCalendar, you can use it as defined by TShowCalendar. Finally, FreeLibrary() is called.

You can see that the library is loaded and freed each time this function is called. If this function was called only once during the run of an application, it becomes apparent how explicit loading can save much needed and often limited memory resources.

Looking at DLL Initialization and Termination Code

You can provide optional entry and exit code for your DLLs when required under various initialization and shutdown operations. This section discusses both of these operations.

DLL Initialization

Typical initialization operations are registering Windows classes, initializing global variables, reading from a file, or even setting up the DLL's exit routine. The DLL's initialization section is in the project file's begin..end block, as shown in the following code:

```
library Dllentry;
uses wintypes, winprocs;
begin
 { Initialization code here }
end.
```

This code is called only once, when the DLL first is loaded into memory. Any subsequent calls to load the DLL don't execute this code; instead, the DLL's usage count is incremented.

DLL Termination

Shutdown operations do the opposite of the initialization routines; here, you perform shutdown operations such as freeing up memory. A little extra work is required in order to create a shutdown procedure.

DLLs in Windows may have a special exported function called *Windows Exit Procedure (WEP)* that Windows calls when it unloads the DLL. The WEP is where any shutdown processing may occur. Object Pascal automatically creates and exports a WEP function in your libraries, which calls the global procedure `ExitProc()`.

`ExitProc()` is a pointer to a `far` procedure. This procedure actually may be part of a chain of more `exit` procedures that you, the programmer, define and install. If these procedures are implemented correctly, they restore the previous instance of `ExitProc()` when they are called so that WEP repeatedly can call `ExitProc()` until it equals nil.

EXIT PROCEDURES

Exit procedures don't apply just to DLLs; they apply to applications and units as well. Each unit in an application can assign its own exit procedure to `ExitProc()`. Before doing so, however, it must save the previous `ExitProc()`'s address. After being called, each exit procedure must replace the `ExitProc` global variable with the address previously saved. The runtime library continues to call `ExitProc()` until it equals nil, so it is imperative that this process is followed. The following code illustrates a standard template for exit procedures:

```
var
  SaveExitProc: pointer;        { declare a pointer to save the exit procedure }
procedure NewExitProc; far;     { declare a far procedure which is the new
exitproc }
begin
  { Do your stuff }             { perform your special exit processing }
  ExitProc := SaveExitProc;     { restore the previous exit procedure THIS IS A
➥MUST! }
end;

initialize                      { Inside the unit's initialization section...}
  SaveExitProc := ExitProc;     { Save the previous exit procedure }
  ExitProc := @NewExitProc;     { Set ExitProc to point to this unit's
➥NewExitProc }
end.
```

Two variables you might find of use in your termination routines are `ExitCode` and `ErrorAddr`. Three situations determine what gets stored in `ExitCode` and `ErrorAddr`:

Normal termination	`ExitCode` equals zero and `ErrorAddr` equals nil.
`Halt()` termination	When `Halt()` is called, `ExitCode` contains the value passed to `Halt()`, and `ErrorAddr` is nil.
Runtime error	`ExitCode` contains the runtime error code, and `ErrorAddr` contains the address at which the error occurred.

Listing 18.11 shows the installation of an exit procedure in the library DLLENTRY.DPR, and Listing 18.12 shows the implementation of that exit procedure in DLLENTRU.PAS.

Listing 18.11. The source code for DLLENTRY.DPR.

```
library Dllentry;

uses
  Wintypes, WinProcs,
  Dllentu in 'DLLENTU.PAS';

exports
  WhoAmI;

begin
  MessageBeep(0);              { Beep When DLL is loaded }
  SaveExitProc := ExitProc;   { Save the ExitProc - WEP }
  ExitProc := @NewExitProc;   { Replace the ExitProc }
end.
```

Listing 18.12. The source code for DLLENTU.PAS.

```
unit Dllentu;

interface
var
  SaveExitProc: pointer;

procedure WhoAmI; export;
procedure NewExitProc; far;

implementation
uses WinTypes, WinProcs, Dialogs;

procedure WhoAmI;
begin
  MessageDlg('DLLENTRY', mtInformation, [mbok], 0);
end;

procedure NewExitProc; {$S-}
begin
  if ExitCode = wep_Free_DLL then  { DLL unloading }
    MessageBeep(0)
  else  { Windows unloading - wep_System_Exit }
    MessageBeep(0);
  ExitProc := SaveExitProc;  { Restore original ExitProc }
end;

end.
```

This simple example illustrates both processes of placing code in the DLL entry section to initialize an exit procedure.

DLL VOODOO

If a DLL is loaded implicitly with the EXE, the DLL is loaded before the EXE starts running. This means that there is no message loop active at the time the DLL initialization code is called. That and the general voodoo surrounding DLL startup means that you cannot do anything visual in the startup code of a DLL.

The same is true of the exit code of a DLL, but for different reasons. The DLL startup code runs on the stack of the host EXE. However, the DLL exit code is run after the host EXE has terminated, and therefore the exit code runs on a system-provided (very small) stack. There is no current task context in the WEP of a DLL—more voodoo.

The startup and exit code of a DLL is more reliable when you explicitly load the DLL with LoadLibrary, because the application context is well defined in both events.

The exit procedure examines the value of ExitCode to determine the type of termination that occurred. This differs from the unit functionality, in that when a DLL terminates, ExitCode contains one of two values:

wep_Free_DLL	The DLL is being unloaded, because the last application using it is shutting down.
wep_System_Exit	Windows is shutting down.

CAUTION

The exit procedure must be compiled with stack checking turned off. Use the compiler directive {S-} to accomplish this.

Examining Special DLL Considerations

There are a few issues you need to concern yourself with when creating or using DLLs with Delphi, which we'll cover in the next section. One issue involves exception occuring inside your DLL. Another involves using the Borland Database Engine in your DLL. Finally, we'll also cover some memory considerations.

Exceptions in Exported Functions

When creating DLLs with Delphi, you also link in Delphi's exception-handling of the runtime library. Although exception-handling is the saving grace for many applications, it can raise havoc with applications using DLLs created with Delphi when an exception is raised inside the DLL.

Exceptions are a compiler/language feature and are not supported by Windows. Therefore, communication of these exceptions between modules is not possible. This presents a problem when an exception is raised in a Delphi DLL. If it is not handled by the DLL, the exception will creep up the calling module's stack, eventually causing it to crash.

To prevent this from happening, you are responsible for wrapping every exported function with a try..except block to ensure that the exception is captured by the DLL. The following template should be used by all exported DLL functions and procedures:

```
procedure SomeDLLFunc;
begin
  try      { wrap this function in a try..except block }
  { Do your stuff! }
  except
   on Exception do
   { Don't let it get away, Handle it! }
  end;
end;
```

Exceptions to Everything!

Although you cannot let exceptions leave DLLs, you still can provide applications with useful information about an exception that occurs from within DLL. This form of communication is performed via a callback function. Inside the DLL, each exported function is wrapped in a try..except construct as previously shown. If an exception occurs, the DLL calls the callback function that the application passed to it. This callback function is the communication link between the DLL and the application. The DLL can pass an error string or an error code to the function. The application then can raise an exception (in its own language-specific context) and do any necessary processing to handle the error.

To illustrate this, Listings 18.13 and 18.14 show CBACK.DPR and CBACKU.PAS, which is a simple DLL that causes an overflow error to occur.

Listing 18.13. The source code for CBACK.DPR.

```
library Cback;
{$Q+}   { Turn overflow checking on }

uses
  Wintypes,
  WinProcs,
  SysUtils,
  Cbacku in 'CBACKU.PAS';

exports
  DoubleIt;
begin

end.
```

Listing 18.14. The source code for CBACKU.PAS.

```pascal
unit Cbacku;

interface
uses WinProcs, WinTypes;
type

  TExceptionProc = procedure(ExceptString: PChar);  { declare the callback
➥function type }

{ declare the DLL's exported  function }
function DoubleIt(Value: Longint; TFP: TFarProc): Longint; export;

implementation
uses SysUtils, Dialogs;

function DoubleIt(Value: Longint; TFP: TFarProc): Longint;
var
  ErrPChar: array[0..50] of char;
begin
  try
    Result := Value * 2;          { Create an obvious overflow error  }
  except
    on E: Exception do begin      { if an exception occurs and a callback
➥function }
      if TFP <> nil then begin    { is present, call it. Typecasting here
➥is necessary }
        { Convert the error string to a PChar, PChars are recognized by other
➥languages }
        StrPCopy(ErrPChar, 'Exception: '+E.Message+' occured in CBACK.DLL');
        TExceptionProc(TFP)(ErrPChar):  { call the callback function }
      end;
    end;
  end; { Exception }
end;

end.
```

Any application can use this DLL and call the `DoubleIt()` function. `DoubleIt()` takes a `longint` and `TFarProc` callback procedure as parameters. It then multiplies the `longint` by two, which may result in a value that exceeds `MaxLongInt`. If so, an exception occurs and the function then calls the `callback` function. The calling application is responsible for defining the callback procedure, which must have the same parameters as `TExceptionProc`. The following line typecasts the procedure as a `TExceptionProc`, which takes a string variable as a parameter:

```pascal
TExceptionProc(TFP)('Exception: '+E.Message+' occured in CBACK.DLL')
```

> **NOTE**
>
> Runtime exceptions occur only when you have enabled runtime error checking such as range checking, {$R+}; stack checking, {$S+}; I/O checking, {$I+}; and overflow checking, {$Q+}.

Listings 18.15 and 18.16 show CBKTESTP.DPR and CBKTESTU.PAS, both of which use CBACK.DLL.

Listing 18.15. The source code for CBKTESTP.DPR.

```
program Cbktestp;

uses
  Forms, classes, sysutils, dialogs,
  Cbktestu in 'CBKTESTU.PAS' {Form1};

{$R *.RES}

begin
  Application.CreateForm(TForm1, Form1);
  Application.Run;
end.
```

Listing 18.16. The source code for CBKTESTU.PAS.

```
unit Cbktestu;

interface

uses
  SysUtils, WinTypes, WinProcs, Messages, Classes, Graphics, Controls,
  Forms, Dialogs, StdCtrls;

type
  TForm1 = class(TForm)
    Button1: TButton;
    procedure Button1Click(Sender: TObject);
  private
    { Private declarations }
  public
    { Public declarations }
  end;

var
  Form1: TForm1;

implementation
{$R *.DFM}

{ Define the DLL's exported procedure }
function DoubleIt(Value: Longint; TFP: TFarProc): Longint;
    far; external 'CBACK';

{ Define the callback procedure which must be an exported procedure }
procedure AppException(ExceptString: PChar); export;
{ This procedure is called by the DLL }
```

continues

Listing 18.16. continued

```
begin
  raise Exception.Create(StrPas(ExceptString));
  { or MessageDlg(StrPas(ExceptString), mtError, [mbok], 0); }
end;

procedure TForm1.Button1Click(Sender: TObject);
var
  l: Longint;
begin
  try
    l := DoubleIt(MaxLongInt, @AppException);    { Call the DoubleIt() function }
  except
    on E:Exception do   { Handle any exceptions that occur }
      MessageDlg(E.Message, mtError, [mbok], 0);
  end;
end;

end.
```

CBKTESTU.PAS defines the callback procedure AppException() using the same parameters as TExceptionProc in CBACKU.PAS. AppException is defined as an exported function with the keyword export. This ensures that the procedure compiles with the far model and that it has the necessary entry and exit code required of an exported procedure. AppException() is passed as the TFarProc parameter to DoubleIt(). Notice that AppException() takes a PChar parameter instead of an Object Pascal string. PChars are recognized by other languages, whereas Pascal strings are not. Using a string would prevent other languages from using this DLL.

When an exception occurs in the DLL, AppException() is called and an exception is raised. This causes the exception to unwind past the DLL's stack into the application where it can be handled accordingly.

This example illustrates Delphi's handling of the DLL exception. Any other language would have to deal with the exception using an error-handling method specific to that language.

> **NOTE**
>
> Some exceptions like EDivByZero are hardware exceptions which are not handled by DLLs, because it is complicated to determine whether the global interrupt occurred in the DLL, and then which client task to notify of the exception.

Using the Borland Database Engine (BDE) in DLLs

The BDE is a service that requires initialization for every task that uses it. Therefore, each application that uses BDE must initialize BDE services for its own task.

The VCL's session variable, which is based on the BDE, is not initialized per task, but rather per module. Recall that a DLL module is only loaded once and shared by multiple tasks. This means that the BDE services cannot be provided through a DLL to multiple application tasks. Because each task must initialize BDE services, this would cause the session variable in the DLL to be destroyed and re-created, which would affect the other tasks using it. Therefore, any DLLs using BDE must ensure that only one application uses that DLL at any time. Borland recommends preventing multiple attempts to use BDE by providing the user with initialization and verification routines. Listings 18.17 and 18.18 show the code for BDEDLL.DPR and BDEDLLU.PAS, which illustrate how to create these routines in a typical DLL using BDE.

Listing 18.17. The source code for BDEDLL.DPR.

```
library Bdedll;

uses
  Bdedllu in 'BDEDLLU.PAS' {Form1};

exports
  IsDLLAvailable,
  ExitDLL,
  ShowForm1;

{$R *.RES}

begin
end.
```

Listing 18.18. The source code for BDEDLLU.PAS.

```
unit Bdedllu;

interface

uses
  SysUtils, WinTypes, WinProcs, Messages, Classes, Graphics, Controls,
  Forms, Dialogs, StdCtrls, Buttons, Grids, DBGrids, DB, DBTables;

const
  DLLAvail         = 0;  { DLL is available for use }
  DLLInUse         = 1;  { DLL is in use by another application }
type

  TForm1 = class(TForm)
    Table1: TTable;
    DataSource1: TDataSource;
    DBGrid1: TDBGrid;
    procedure FormClose(Sender: TObject; var Action: TCloseAction);
    procedure FormActivate(Sender: TObject);
  private
    { Private declarations }
```

continues

Listing 18.18. continued

```
public
  { Public declarations }
end;

var
  Form1: TForm1;

function IsDLLAvailable: integer; export;  { Call to verify that DLL can be used. }
procedure ExitDLL; export;              { Call before application using DLL rerminates }
procedure ShowForm1; export;           { Export function to display form }

implementation

var
  Task: THandle;      { Handle to first task that loads the DLL }

{$R *.DFM}

procedure ShowForm1;
begin
  try
    Form1 := TForm1.Create (nil);  { Create the form instance }
    Form1.ShowModal;               { Show form in modal state }
  except
    on E: Exception do            { Handle exception if one occurs }
      MessageDlg(E.Message, mtError, [mbok], 0);
  end
end;

procedure TForm1.FormClose(Sender: TObject; var Action: TCloseAction);
begin
  Table1.Active := False; { Close table before closing form. }
end;

procedure ExitDLL;
begin
  CallExitProcs;      { Execute all exit procedures }
end;

function IsDLLAvailable: integer;
begin
  if Task <> GetCurrentTask then  { Is task the same that initialized the DLL? }
    Result := DllInUse            { Task is not the same }
  else
   Result := DllAvail            { DLL is available }
end;

procedure TForm1.FormActivate(Sender: TObject);
begin
  Table1.Active := true;  { Activate Table }
end;

begin
  Task := GetCurrentTask; { Initialize Task variable immediately upon
➥loading DLL }
end.
```

This DLL contains a form with `TTable`, `TDataSource`, and `TDBGrid` components. You can connect `Table1` to any table you want. Just be sure to link the `DataSource1` and `DBGrid1` accordingly.

This DLL exports three routines: `IsDLLAvailable()`, `ExitDLL()`, and `ShowForm1()`. Other methods are `FormActivate()`, which opens the table; and `FormClose()`, which closes the table. The following line appears in the `initialization` section of the DLL:

```
Task := GetCurrentTask;
```

This line is executed only once when the DLL first is loaded. `Task` is a global variable that will constantly hold the handle to the first task that loaded the DLL. This variable is used for comparison in the `IsDLLAvailable()` function.

`IsDLLAvailable()` returns the value of one of the two constants, `DLLAvail` and `DLLInUse`. The calling application should call `IsDLLAvailable()` before attempting to call any other DLL functions. If the return value is `DLLInUse`, the calling task should not call other functions until `IsDLLAvailable()` returns `DLLAvail`.

When an application is finished using the DLL, it must call `DLLExit()` to ensure that the BDE is deactivated. BDE cannot be deactivated from within a DLL's `ExitProc` or WEP. Therefore, this should be done through a user-exported function, as shown here.

`ShowForm1()` displays the form with the table data.

Listings 18.19 and 18.20 show TESTBDE.DPR and TESTBDEU.PAS, a project that illustrates using BDEDLL.DLL.

Listing 18.19. The source code for TESTBDE.DPR.

```
program Testbde;

uses
  Forms,
  Testbdeu in 'TESTBDEU.PAS' {Form1};

{$R *.RES}

begin
  Application.CreateForm(TForm1, Form1);
  Application.Run;
end.
```

Listing 18.20. The source code for TESTBDEU.PAS.

```pascal
unit Testbdeu;

interface

uses
  SysUtils, WinTypes, WinProcs, Messages, Classes, Graphics, Controls,
  Forms, Dialogs, StdCtrls;

type
  { Declare the function and procedure types }
  TIsDLLAvailable = function: integer;
  TExitDLL = procedure;
  TShowForm1 = procedure;

  EDLLLoadError = class(Exception);

  TForm1 = class(TForm)
    Button1: TButton;
    procedure Button1Click(Sender: TObject);
  private
    { Private declarations }
  public
    { Public declarations }
  end;

var
  Form1: TForm1;

  implementation

{$R *.DFM}

procedure TForm1.Button1Click(Sender: TObject);
var
  LibHandle: THandle;
  IsDLLAvailable: TIsDLLAvailable;
  ExitDLL: TExitDLL;
  ShowForm1: TShowForm1;
  FuncResult: integer;
begin
  try
    LibHandle := LoadLibrary('BDEDLL.DLL');  { Load the library }
    if LibHandle < 32 then                   { Check for successful load }
      raise EDLLLoadError.Create('Unable to Load DLL'); { raise an exception
➥if not loaded }
    { Retrieve library function/procedure addresses }
    @IsDllAvailable := GetProcAddress(LibHandle, 'ISDLLAVAILABLE');
    @ExitDll := GetProcAddress(LibHandle, 'EXITDLL');
    @ShowForm1 := GetProcAddress(LibHandle, 'SHOWFORM1');
    { Check if DLL is available }
    FuncResult := IsDLLAvailable;
    case FuncResult of
      0: ShowForm1;                                 { Display DLL form }
      1: ShowMessage('DLL In use');               { DLL is currently being used }
      2: ShowMessage('DLL must be unloaded to use');   { DLL is still loaded }
    end; { Case }
```

```
  except
    on E: EDLLLoadError do                    { Handle Load Exception }
      MessageDlg(E.Message, mtInformation, [mbok], 0);
  end;
  FreeLibrary(LibHandle);  { Free library }
end;

end.
```

This project dynamically loads the DLL (BDEDLL.DLL), gets access to its exported functions, and calls IsDLLAvailable() to determine the appropriate action.

Obviously, you can add more robust error handling to prevent ShowForm1() from displaying the form altogether—perhaps by raising an exception instead and passing the error via a callback procedure as previously illustrated. You might experiment a bit here.

> **CAUTION**
>
> Applications that don't use BDE but call DLLs that do must ensure that BDE is loaded before calling the DLL. Not doing so will prevent any other BDE-based applications from initializing BDE. One way to do this is to place a TDataBase onto the calling application and set its Active property to true. This is a quick-and-dirty way to load BDE without placing any requirements on any tables being loaded.

Other Considerations

You should consider a few issues regarding DLL memory: the stack segment and global variables.

A DLL does not own its own stack, and therefore you cannot assume that the stack segment (SS) is the same as the data segment (DS). This is not a problem with Object Pascal, and mainly concerns C programmers or people who want to write assembly routines in your DLLs.

Global variables, file handles, and memory allocated by a calling application belong to the application that loads a DLL. When that application terminates, memory and file handles are freed and the DLL's routines no longer will be working with valid memory (if the DLL retains pointers to the application's memory block) and file handles. It is therefore recommended that you make your DLLs expect the calling application to be responsible for allocating and destroying any memory blocks and to pass them through the DLL routines. The same goes for file handles.

An exception to this is with global allocation from within the DLL itself. DLLs created with Delphi automatically set HeapAllocFlags to include GMEM_SHARE, so these allocations belong to the DLL and not to the calling application.

Calling C and C++ DLLs

Delphi gives you the capability to easily call DLLs written in C, C++, or pretty much anything else that creates Windows DLLs. It is not always straightforward, though, and there are a couple of issues—such as calling convention, name mangling, and type conversion—that you should keep in mind when linking with DLLs written in other languages.

Calling Convention

One thing that is particularly important to keep in mind is the calling convention of the function(s) in the DLL you are trying to use. The *calling convention* defines how the function is named by the compiler, how the parameters are passed to the function, and who is responsible for removing the parameters from the stack after the call. Delphi supports both the Pascal (of course) and the C calling convention, commonly called *Cdecl*.

The Pascal calling convention dictates that all symbol names (functions, variables, and so on) are converted to uppercase (now you know why Object Pascal is case-insensitive!), parameters are pushed on the stack from left to right, and the function being called is responsible for removing the parameters from the stack. This is the default calling convention for Object Pascal. C/C++ functions must use the PASCAL keyword in order to use the Pascal calling convention.

With the Cdecl calling convention, symbol names are kept case-sensitive, and each function name is prepended with an underscore. Parameters are pushed onto the stack from right to left, and the routine calling the function is responsible for cleaning up the stack. You can use the Cdecl directive on your Pascal functions and procedures to cause them to follow the C calling convention. This is, of course, the default for C/C++ functions.

> **NOTE**
>
> When using the Cdecl directive, you should make sure to import the function by ordinal rather than by name.

Name Mangling

C++ compilers, in order to accommodate function overloading, cause the compiled names of functions to be mangled. *Mangled* means that some characters are added to the end of the function name to ensure that each function with a different parameter list has a different name. You will have some trouble linking in DLLs written in C++ because of this, so you should wrap all the functions (including LibMain) in the C++ DLL with extern "C" {}, as shown in this code:

```
// This is a C++ DLL
#include <windows.h>

extern "C" {

// all functions go here

}
```

Doing this ensures that function names will not be mangled, and you will be able to call functions like any other C DLL.

Variable Types

You also want to make sure that the variable types you define in your Object Pascal units match those declared in the DLL. For a complete list of Object Pascal and corresponding C/C++ types, see Table 2.4 in Chapter 2, "Moving to Pascal."

You Make the Call

After you get all the particulars straight, calling a C/C++ DLL is much the same as calling one written in Object Pascal. For practice, though, here are a couple of examples to use as references.

If the function in the C DLL is defined as

```
UINT FAR PASCAL _export foo()
```

the Object Pascal definition is

```
function foo: word; far; export 'DLLNAME';
```

If the function in the C DLL is defined as

```
void FAR _export foo(long l)
```

the Object Pascal definition is

```
procedure foo(l: Longint); cdecl; far; export 'DLLNAME' index 3;
```

Summary

DLLs are an essential part of creating Windows applications while keying in on code reusability. This chapter covered DLLs in depth. Here, you learned the reasons for creating or using DLLs. You learned how to create and use DLLs in your Delphi applications. You learned about

the different methods of loading DLLs, and you also learned about some of the special considerations you must take when using DLLs with Delphi. Now that you have this knowledge of
DLLs under your belt, you should be able to create them with Delphi and use them in your
Delphi applications. This is done in later chapters, so you will have more opportunities to work
with DLLs. It is true that DLLs often are misunderstood. Don't be afraid to use DLLs; they
give you access to a great deal of functionality that you otherwise would have to write yourself.
In the next chapter, you will learn how to port your existing Borland Pascal 7.0 application
over to Delphi.

19

Migrating from Borland Pascal to Delphi

If you are trying to migrate your existing Borland Pascal applications to Delphi, this is the chapter for you. The amount of work involved in porting to Delphi depends on a number of factors, including the amount of code you have to port, whether you are porting from DOS or Windows Pascal, the degree of separation between your application's user interface and engine, and so on. This chapter points out the pitfalls of porting and gives you some advice on how to optimize your code along the way.

Using the *Result* Variable

In Delphi, you return a value from a function by assigning the implicit local variable `Result` to the return value. `Foo`, for example, returns an integer value of `3`:

```
function Foo: integer;
begin
  Result := 3;
end;
```

The implicit `Result` variable, though, did not exist in Borland Pascal (BP). In BP, functions returned values by assigning the function name to the return value. Therefore, the BP version of the `Foo` function looks like this:

```
function Foo: integer;
begin
  Foo := 3;
end;
```

Result: The Codebreaker

It's not crucial that you change all your functions to match Object Pascal's style of returning a value, because Delphi does support the older style. The problem, however, arises when functions in your BP program declare local variables called `Result`. The following function compiles fine under BP, but Delphi's compiler issues a `Duplicate Identifier` error:

```
function Foo: integer;
var
  Result: integer;
begin
  Result := 3;
  Foo := Result;
end;
```

Of course, it's the declaration of the `Result` variable that causes the error. Unfortunately, it is very common to use `Result` as a local variable, so you can expect to have this problem in some of your programs.

Result: Not All Bad

The advantage of the Result variable is that it eliminates the need for local variables in many cases, because it can be used on both the left and right side of equations; the function name cannot be used on both sides, however. The following code, for example, will compile in BP or Delphi, but it will cause the program to call the Foo() function recursively, ad infinitum:

```
function Foo: integer;
begin
  Foo := 1;
  Foo := Foo + 1;
end;
```

However, using the Result variable in Delphi, you easily can access the function result on the left or right side of an equation:

```
function Foo: integer;
begin
  Result := 1;
  Result := Result + 1;
end;
```

The Result variable is a definite improvement over the BP style of function return values. Just keep an eye out for any re-declarations of the Result variable in your old code as you port to Delphi.

case Statements

In Delphi, the values of case statement selectors must not overlap. This means that the following code, which compiles in BP, will not compile in Delphi:

```
var
  i: integer;
begin
  i := 1;
  case i of
    1..2 : DoSomething;
    2..4 : DoAnotherThing;  { selector 2 is duplicated, so this line doesn't
➥compile }
  end;
end;
```

To convert this code to Delphi, you must ensure that selector ranges do not overlap. For example, you could rewrite the preceding code as follows:

```
var
  i: integer;
begin
  i := 1;
  case i of
```

```
    1..2 : DoSomething;
    3..4 : DoAnotherThing;
  end;
end;
```

Working with *PChars*

In BP, the functions and procedures used to manipulate PChar strings were located in the STRINGS unit. In Delphi, you will find these functions in the SYSUTILS unit. These string-handling routines work the same in Delphi as in BP, so the only change your code should require is the units' names in the uses clause.

When you move to SYSUTILS for your string-handling routines, be careful not to mix string allocations using GetMem() with string disposals using StrDispose(). Likewise, take care not to mix allocations made using StrNew() or StrAlloc() and disposals using FreeMem(). GetMem() always should be used with FreeMem(), and StrNew() and StrAlloc() always should be used with StrDispose(). Failure to use the correct function or procedure is likely to result in memory leakage.

Error Handling

Error detection and recovery is another consideration as you migrate to Delphi. In general, you can accomplish error handling to a level of robustness that was not previously available under BP, but it requires a few changes to your code.

As an example, take a standard block of code used to access a file and handle associated errors in BP:

```
var
  F: Text;
  S: String;
begin
  Assign(F, 'SOMEFILE.TXT');
  {$I-}                          { turn off I/O checking }
  Reset(F);                      { try to open file }
  {$I+}                          { turn I/O checking back on }
  if IOResult <> 0 then
    MessageBox(HWindow, 'Could not open file.', 'Error', mb_Ok)
  else  begin
    Readln(F, S);                { will result in Runtime Error on error condition }
    { more file I/O may go here }
    Close(F);                    { close file }
  end;
end;
```

Typically in BP, you turn off error-checking logic during times when you want to handle the errors. While using the built-in error checking, your program terminates rather nastily with a runtime error when some error condition occurs.

Although rewriting old code isn't required, it's a good idea to consider doing so to take advantage of exception handling. For typical file access, you can achieve optimum error control by nesting a `try..finally` block inside a `try..except` block. The outer block will catch any exceptions that occur while the file is being opened. The inner block will ensure that the file is closed if an error occurs during reading or writing. Here is an example:

```
var
  F: TextFile;
  S: String;
begin
  try
    AssignFile(F, 'SOMEFILE.TXT');
    ResetFile(F);                    { will raise exception on error }
    try
      Readln(F, S);                  { will raise exception on error }
      { more file I/O may go here }
    finally
      CloseFile(F);
    end;
  except
    on EInOutError do
      MessageDlg('Big time error accessing file.', mtError, [mbOk], 0);
  end;
```

Not only is the code with exception handling more robust but, by being able to separate the file access from the closure from the error checking, the code is much more readable. Chapter 3, "The Object Pascal Language," gives more information on working with exceptions.

> **NOTE**
>
> Nesting a `try..finally` inside a `try..except` construct is ideal for file access because it enables you to free the allocated file handle (regardless of whether an exception was raised) in the `finally` clause, while still giving you the ability to handle exceptions in the `except` clause.

Accessing Files

The error-handling examples in the preceding section illustrate another important point in porting your BP code to Delphi: Names of a few of the file-related types and procedures have changed. The reason for this is so that the names do not conflict with common properties and events of the same names. Table 19.1 shows new file-related types and procedures and their BP counterparts.

Table 19.1. New names for file-related types and procedures.

Delphi Name	BP Name	Type or Procedure	Function
TextFile	Text	type	Represents a text file
AssignFile	Assign	procedure	Assigns a filename to a file variable
CloseFile	Close	procedure	Closes a file and deallocates the handle

Although Delphi still enables you to use the BP versions of these types and procedures, you usually will need to scope the type or procedure as part of the System unit. For example,

```
Assign(F);
```

becomes

```
System.Assign(F);
```

File I/O errors will raise exceptions only if I/O checking is turned on in the compiler ($I+ in code or Options | Project | Compiler | I/O Checking in IDE) and the SYSUTILS unit is used by some unit in the project. No I/O exceptions will be raised if compiler I/O checking is disabled. Also, when compiling BP code that doesn't use SYSUTILS, runtime errors will not raise exceptions.

Porting DOS Code

Porting your DOS code to Delphi can be a challenging and time-consuming task, and it's a big enough subject for a book to be written on that topic alone. Therefore, this chapter doesn't attempt to give a DOS-to-Windows, step-by-step procedure on porting, but it does raise a couple of important and common issues.

Knowing Where to Begin

Generally, you should start by redesigning your program's front end in Delphi. This should be the easiest part, because Delphi's visual environment enables you to quickly create a user interface (UI) prototype.

Your task should be made considerably easier if you have taken care to separate the back end, or processing part, of your program from the front end. If you used an interface or event-driven library like Turbo Vision as the program font end, that should make the most straightforward port to Delphi.

Differences in Porting from Real Mode and Protected Mode

Was your DOS application designed to run in real mode or protected mode? *Protected mode* means that you used Borland Pascal 7.0 with Objects and set the Protected Mode compiler option so that you can have access to up to 16MB of your PC's memory. If you did compile for protected mode, porting to Delphi will be a bit easier, because Windows is a DOS protected-mode interface (DPMI) environment. If your program runs in real mode, porting might be a bit more difficult—especially if your program's code uses any of the following:

Direct memory access	This is most commonly done by creating pointers from memory addresses with the Ptr() function or by using absolute variables.
An interrupt handler	Windows programs generally do not hook DOS interrupt vectors. As you will learn later in this chapter, you should use Windows messages rather than interrupt handlers when possible.
Interrupt calls	If you use inline, the Built-in Assembler (BASM), or the Intr() or MsDos() procedures to execute interrupts, you may have to modify your code to make the interrupt work in protected mode.
Assembly code modules	You must ensure that the assembly code modules you link into your application are Windows-safe. In particular, use of segment registers as storage for data is not allowed in protected mode. Windows-safe BASM is described in more detail in Chapter 20, "Power Programming: BASM and DPMI."
Overlays or other tricks	Used to eke the most memory out of the lower 640KB.

Using Direct Memory Access

Under Windows, the only areas of memory that you have rights to write to are your own program's auto-data segment and any areas of heap that you have allocated. If you write to any other area of memory, such as to a code segment or to the BIOS memory area, without first taking some very specific steps to tell Windows you're doing so, you're likely to see the ubiquitous General Protection Fault message. Windows runs in protected mode and works with the processor in an attempt to keep applications well-behaved and operating within their own domains.

Sometimes, however, you have a real need to access some area of memory outside of your program. It's common, for example, to access some of the upper regions of memory in order to communicate with the video display adapter or with some other memory-mapped piece of hardware. To do this in real mode DOS, just create a pointer that points to the correct place in

RAM, and access away. The following code, for example, creates a pointer to the region of memory occupied by the monochrome display adapter:

```
var
  P: Pointer;
begin
  P := Ptr($B0000, 0);
```

Real-mode DOS would have no problems with you using this pointer to write directly to the screen. This wouldn't work, however, under Windows because your application doesn't have rights to write to such an area of memory.

Remember that Windows uses a system of memory access in which selectors point to physical addresses in memory; in real mode, segments are used. Because selectors are generated dynamically as memory is allocated, there is no way to know the value of a selector up front to create a pointer. You therefore have to use a few of Windows' memory-management functions to get the job done. The following code shows how to create a pointer to monochrome video memory under Windows:

```
var
  VidSelector: Word;
  P: Pointer;
begin
  { allocate a selector with the same attributes as the data segment... }
  VidSelector := AllocSelector(DSeg);
  { point the selector to the 20-bit linear address of video memory... }
  SetSelectorBase(VidSelector, $B0000);
  { set the limit of the selector to 40K... }
  SetSelectorLimit(VidSelector, 40000);
  { create a pointer using selector and offset... }
  P := Ptr(MySelector, $00);
```

Because selectors are a finite resource, you have to make sure to free them when you're done with them by calling FreeSelector(), as in the following code. Chapter 20 offers further information on memory access and using selectors.

```
FreeSelector(VidSelector);
```

Using Absolute Variables

Absolute variables are those variables declared with the absolute keyword that locates them at an address you specify. It is legal in Windows to use absolute to create variables that occupy the same memory as other variables, as in this example:

```
var
  W: word;
  Also_W: word absolute W;  { this is okay }
```

However, you should not use absolute to locate variables at specific addresses as shown in the following example. To access specific memory regions, you should instead use the technique described earlier for allocating selectors.

```
var
  W: word absolute $10:0000;  { this is not okay }
```

Handling Interrupts

Many DOS programs look for keyboard keystrokes by hooking interrupt 09h, or by polling through interrupts $16 and 21h. Windows, however, grabs keystrokes for you and passes them to your application in the form of wm_KeyDown, wm_KeyUp, and wm_Char messages. Delphi further encapsulates keystrokes into OnKeyDown, OnKeyUp, and OnKeyPress events. You can rewrite your DOS keyboard interrupt-handling code by instead using Delphi's OnKeyDown, OnKeyUp, or OnKeyPress events.

It's very common under DOS to intercept the PC's timer tick interrupt 08h. You shouldn't attempt to do this under Windows; instead, use a TTimer object and set it to notify your application of a timer event at some predetermined interval. Chapter 25, "Creating a Calendar: Scheduler and Alarm Application," shows an example of how to integrate a TTimer into an application.

Another approach to solving this problem is to assign a method to TApplication's OnIdle event. OnIdle is called when there are no messages in your application's queue, and it enters an idle state.

Making Interrupt Calls

Making interrupt calls works differently under Windows than it does under real-mode DOS. Each interrupt must filter through Windows' DPMI server before being passed to DOS, so every interrupt you call must be supported explicitly by Windows' DPMI server. Luckily, Windows supports most of the common interrupt 21h functions directly, so you probably can leave such code that calls interrupt 21h through Intr(), MsDos(), or inline as is.

> **TIP**
>
> If you make an interrupt 21h call through built-in assembler (BASM), you should use the Windows API DOS3Call() procedure instead of directly calling interrupt 21h. DOS3Call() is the preferred way to call the DOS interrupt under Windows, and it executes a bit faster than a regular interrupt call. To use DOS3Call(), just replace your call to interrupt 21h with a call to DOS3Call. For example, replace this:
>
> ```
> int 21h
> ```
>
> with this:
>
> ```
> call DOS3Call
> ```
>
> Note that you should use DOS3Call() only inside an assembly-language block.

If your program makes a call to an interrupt not directly supported by Windows, you must go through a little hocus-pocus known as a *simulate real-mode interrupt* to get the job done. You can simulate a real-mode interrupt through DPMI interrupt 31h, function 0300h. For more information on how to do this, see Chapter 20, "Power Programming: BASM and DPMI."

Linking in Assembly Modules

If your DOS programs link in assembly modules, you will have to make sure that the assembly procedures follow all the rules described in this chapter with regard to memory allocation, segments, and interrupts. Unless you are a developer with a solid knowledge of assembly language, however, you should avoid using large quantities of assembly language in your program.

> **TIP**
>
> We talk to a lot of people in our work at Borland Tech Support that are forced to try to link old assembly code into their applications because "the guy who wrote it left the company, and we're not quite sure what it does." Or worse yet, "we have the object file, but not the source code." Don't fall into this trap. Use assembler wisely and sparingly in your Delphi applications.

Examining Overlays and Memory Issues

Real-mode DOS programmers went to great lengths to squeeze every bit of utility they could out of that 640KB. Some used overlays, some used DOS interrupts 2Fh or 67h to get limited access to extended or expanded memory, and some used techniques to swap areas of RAM to disk. Now that you are in Windows, take this one word of advice: Don't. Under Windows, you have seamless access to multiple megabytes of RAM—a vast empire of memory compared to the real-mode DOS limit of a wimpy 640KB.

Although your Windows programs still must abide by the limitation of a 64KB auto-data segment, the rest of the available memory is yours to use as you want. Think of it as having a really big heap. (If you're not comfortable with terms like *data segment* and *heap*, take a look a the "Thanks for the Memories" sidebar in Chapter 3, "The Object Pascal Language.")

Windows not only makes available practically all of the RAM installed on your computer, but it also can provide a swap file on disk that simulates RAM you don't actually have. When moving your application to Windows, you should remove code that uses any of the techniques just discussed to increase the net available memory. If you are using overlays, for example, remove calls to overlay functions such as OvrInit() or OvrInitEMS(). Now, whenever you allocate a class instance or allocate memory using New(), GetMem(), or GlobalAlloc(), that memory will be allocated from Windows' giant heap, so you won't need to go through convulsions to fit your program in memory.

```
function GetTick:longint;
var
  TI:TTimerInfo;
begin
  TI.dwSize := Sizeof(TI);      { initialize size of TTimerInfo record }
  TimerCount(@TI);
  Result := TI.dwmsThisVM;      { return elaspsed time }
end;

begin
  ET := GetTick;
  Result := False;
  repeat
    { keep processing other messages until delay has been met or app exits }
    Application.ProcessMessages;
  until Application.Terminated or (GetTick-ET > DelayMS);
  Result := Application.Terminated;
end;
```

The GetTick() function in Delay() uses the TimerCount() function located in TOOLHELP.DLL to get the elapsed time in the current Windows session using a high-resolution timer. Delay() stays in a loop processing messages until the application is terminated or until the elapsed time exceeds DelayMS. For more information on TOOLHELP.DLL, see the "TOOLHELP.DLL" sidebar in Chapter 23, "SysWatcher: A System Monitor."

> **NOTE**
>
> The Delay() function shown here will never return *exactly* DelayMS milliseconds after being called. Due to Windows' cooperative multitasking nature, the Delay() function is only guaranteed to return *at least* DelayMS milliseconds after being called.

Using the *Exec()* Procedure

BP provides a procedure under DOS to execute another program called Exec(). The Windows API provides functions called WinExec() and ShellExec() that perform basically the same service, except for one key difference: The Exec() procedure essentially suspends execution of the calling program until the executed program terminates, while WinExec() and ShellExec() execute and run a second program asynchronously.

The preferred method of porting this code to Delphi is to design your application so that it behaves correctly when the second program is executed asynchronously. Sometimes this is not possible, however, and you need a means to simulate the DOS Exec() procedure. The following code shows the WinExecAndWait() function, which executes a second application and waits until that application terminates to continue:

```
uses Wintypes,WinProcs,Toolhelp,Classes,Forms;

Function WinExecAndWait(Path : string; Visibility : word) : word;
```

Using the $M Directive

Under DOS real mode, you can use the $M directive to specify stack size, minimum heap size, and maximum heap size. Under Delphi, you can specify only two parameters with the $M directive: stack size and local heap size. Both these values default to 8KB, which, because Windows expands your local heap dynamically if it has room in the auto-data segment, is sufficient for most applications. The exception is when you use a recursive algorithm in your code, in which case you may want to double the stack size to 16KB.

> **CAUTION**
>
> In the DOS world, your program was allowed up to 64KB of global data *and* up to 64KB of stack. Under Windows, your program's stack, global data, and local heap *all* must fit in 64KB of memory. Keep this detail in mind, and use your limited resources wisely.

Using DOS-Only Functions

There are a few procedures and functions that were very commonly used under DOS, but have no real analogy under Delphi. When faced with this situation, it's generally best to take a step back and determine the right way to solve that particular problem from a Delphi perspective, regardless of your approach in the DOS code.

Using the *Delay* Procedure

Delay() is a procedure that, when called, pauses your program for a specified amount of time. There is no Delay() procedure under Delphi. Our opinion is that Windows is no jackrabbit as it is, so why on earth would you want to *purposefully* make your program go slower? Sometimes the need arises to get this type of functionality, however, and when it does, you can go in one of two directions: a timer or a roll-your-own delay procedure.

Using a timer may require a little redesign on your part, but it is certainly the preferred way to accomplish the task. Just drop a TTimer object on your form and set the Interval property for the length of time you want to delay. Then you can call TTimer.Enabled := True in your code and respond to the OnTimer event appropriately.

If you absolutely have to simulate the DOS delay procedure, the following code shows a home-grown version of a Windows Delay function:

```
uses ToolHelp;

function Delay(DelayMS:longint) : Boolean;
{ Returns false if the application has been asked to QUIT }
var
  Msg : TMsg;
  ET : longint;
```

```
var
  InstanceID : THandle;
  PathLen : integer;
begin
  { inplace conversion of a String to a PChar }
  PathLen := Length(Path);
  Move(Path[1],Path[0],PathLen);
  Path[PathLen] := #00;
  { Try to run the application }
  InstanceID := WinExec(@Path,Visibility);
  if InstanceID < 32 then { a value less than 32 indicates an Exec error }
    WinExecAndWait := InstanceID
  else begin
    Repeat
      Application.ProcessMessages;
    until Application.Terminated or (GetModuleUsage(InstanceID) = 0);
    WinExecAndWait := 32;
  end;
end;
```

NOTE

You should set Enabled equal to False on the current application's active form to prevent reentrancy problems with this function.

You may notice that this procedure works similarly to Delay()—it enters a ProcessMessages loop and does not exit until some condition is met. In this case, WinExecAndWait spawns another application using WinExec(), and then waits until either that or the current application terminates before exiting the loop. The function is able to detect when the executed application terminates by using the GetModuleUsage() function and passing in its instance handle. For more information on instances, see the "TOOLHELP.DLL" sidebar in Chapter 23.

Using *Halt()* and *RunError()*

BP's Halt() and RunError() procedures each cause an application to terminate immediately. These procedures generally are used under DOS to terminate an application when an error condition is encountered—which is all well and fine, and an acceptable thing to do under DOS. Don't, don't, don't use these functions in Delphi. By terminating your application immediately, they don't allow for memory or Windows resources to be deallocated, and they don't allow your message loop to terminate normally. Instead, you should call your main form's Close() method or Application.Terminate to terminate your application.

CAUTION

Don't call Halt() or RunError() from your Delphi application. These functions essentially boil down to crashing your application in one line of code.

Issues Regarding Object Model Versus Class Model

A number of issues arise out of the differences between objects and classes. When you decide to convert your BP objects into classes, you'll need to keep in mind several differences in their implementation and usage—most of these changes are designed to make things easier on you when using classes.

TObject and Object Allocation

Delphi's TObject class is not the same as the BP object of the same name. In particular, the Delphi implementation of TObject has many more methods for you to work with. Also, all Object Pascal classes descend from TObject, whereas the same is not true in BP. This means that Delphi's compiler has an internal awareness of its TObject class. These are some things you should keep in mind as you convert BP objects that descend from TObject or those that have no ancestor.

In BP, objects are allocated using a special form of the New() function that accepts an object pointer and its constructor. Similarly, objects in BP can be destroyed by calling the Dispose() function and passing an object pointer and its destructor. The typical allocation and deallocation of a BP object is as follows:

```
var
  O: PSomeObject; { O is a pointer to some object }
begin
  New(O, Init);
  { use O here }
  Dispose(O, Done);
end;
```

In Delphi, the technique for allocating classes is different. You allocate an object by setting the instance variable equal to the return value of the class constructor. Classes usually are deallocated by calling the Free() method. Here is the Delphi technique:

```
var
  C: SomeClass;  { C is a class instance }
begin
  C := SomeClass.Create;
  { use C here }
  C.Free;
end;
```

The *virtual* Directive

The definition and meaning of BP's virtual directive has changed for Delphi classes. In BP, the virtual directive is used to declare a new virtual method, override an existing virtual method, declare or override a dynamic method, and declare a message-handling method. Delphi uses new directives for many of these tasks, as shown in Table 19.2.

Table 19.2. BP and Delphi method directives.

Task	BP Directive	Delphi Directive
Create a virtual method	`virtual`	`virtual`
Override a virtual method	`virtual`	`override`
Create a dynamic method	`virtual` + index	`dynamic`
Override a dynamic method	`virtual` + index	`override`
Create or override a message	`virtual` +constant + message number	`message` + handler + message number

---

CAUTION

When converting an object to a class, take great care in converting the `virtual` directive to the corresponding Delphi directive as shown in Table 19.2. Failure to do so will have disastrous results.

Streams

Writing objects to streams in BP is not a simple task. You have to create and debug stream registration records, `Load()` constructors, and `Store()` procedures. In Delphi, anything that descends from `TComponent` will have its published properties automatically streamed. You will find this a welcome alternative to the hard work required for BP.

Leaving OWL Behind

Porting your Object Windows Library (OWL) code to Delphi is considerably easier than porting from DOS. After all, it's already Windows code. We were amazed at the fact that we were able to redo an OWL application's entire user interface in Delphi in a fraction of the time it took under BP. After that, you just need to rewire the back end of the application to the new user interface.

As a first step to porting the application to Delphi, you should try to get the OWL code to compile under Delphi. Doing so is surprisingly easy—just follow a few basic steps:

1. Remove the `Win31` unit from the `uses` clauses of your program and associated units. The `Win31` unit has been merged into Delphi `WinTypes` and `WinProcs` units because all Delphi VCL applications require Windows 3.1 to run.

2. Add the Messages unit to the head uses clause (they must be ahead of all OWL units) of any unit that uses Windows message types and constants. This is where all the message-related types and constants are defined.

3. Set the Search Path directory in Options | Project | Directories/Conditionals to point to the Delphi subdirectory containing the BP7 runtime library (C:\DELPHI\SOURCE\RTL70). Your application now will be able to find all the OWL-related units for compiling.

4. All resource (.RES), object (.OBJ), and include (.INC) files that your project includes must reside in the same directory as the .PAS or .DPR source file that references them.

Porting the User Interface

At this point, you should be able to compile and run your application under Delphi with little or no more changes. Once it is running, it's a good idea to print some screen shots of the different dialog boxes and windows your application contains. Then you can have a reference to assist you in redesigning the UI under Delphi.

Go through each of your windows and dialog boxes, and redo them in the Delphi IDE. Again, try not to focus on how your old UI implementation approached design goals; instead, focus on how Delphi can be used to help you better achieve those goals.

> **CAUTION**
>
> Don't mix OWL user-interface objects with VCL. They are mutually exclusive, so don't try to mix TForms, TWindows, and TDialogs in one application, or it probably will crash. Wait until you have ported all the user-interface elements to VCL before trying to run your application.

If your application uses Borland Windows Custom Controls (BWCC), take note that Delphi doesn't have built-in support for BWCC, and you should take that into account as you port your application to Delphi. You can simulate the BWCC look and feel by using TBitBtns as your buttons and using TPanels and TBevels to achieve the three-dimensional look.

> **TIP**
>
> Redoing all of your application's dialog boxes in Delphi rather than in Resource Workshop can be a tedious task. You might want to consider obtaining Borland's Resource Expert, which is available as part of the RAD Pack, to help ease the transition. This expert converts dialogs, menus, and other resources stored in your RC files to Delphi forms and units.

After the application mock-up is complete, you should ensure that the necessary hot keys and shortcut keys are in place for your application. Hot keys are accomplished easily by using the ampersand (&) character to highlight a character on a menu, button, or other interface object. You then can use a combination of Alt and that character as a hot key to that control.

`TMenuItem`'s `ShortCut` property takes the place of the OWL accelerator table. Just assign the shortcut to any item on the list in Object Inspector, or enter your own shortcut.

Porting the Back End

First of all, you can move most of the code from your OWL `TWindow`'s `Init()` and `SetupWindow()` methods to your `TForm`'s `OnCreate` event handler. You can move most of the code from your `TWindow`'s `Done()` method to `TForm`'s `OnDestroy` handler.

The next step in hooking the back end into the new UI is to convert all your message-handling and command-handling methods to Delphi event and message handlers. Start with the Windows message-handling methods; many of these probably can be moved to event-handler methods for `TForm`. Rather than handling `wm_KeyDown`, `wm_KeyUp`, or `wm_Char` messages, for example, create event handlers for `TForm`'s `OnKeyDown`, `OnKeyUp`, and `OnKeyPress` events. For message handlers that do not have a corresponding event, remember to use the Delphi-style message handling. For example, the OWL declaration of

```
procedure WMSize(var Msg: OWindows.TMessage); virtual wm_First + wm_Size;
```

in Delphi becomes

```
procedure WMSize(var Msg: TWMSize); message wm_Size;
```

You should remove the OWL `cm_First` + `cm_SomeID` style of command processing. Instead, use the Delphi IDE to create handlers visually for things such as menu selections and button presses, and copy the code from the OWL handler into the new Delphi handler.

You also must change all the code related to how you interact with Windows controls. The following code, for example, adds a new string to a `PListbox` called `ListBox1` in OWL:

```
Listbox1^.AddString('Hello');
```

The following code does the same for a `TListbox` in Delphi:

```
Listbox1.Items.Add('Hello');
```

> **NOTE**
>
> Remember that OWL deals mostly with `PChar` strings and Delphi deals primarily with `String` types. Unless you need the added capacity of a `PChar`, you should convert your `PChars` to `Strings`.

Most of the non-UI-related, number-crunching code should port to Delphi fairly directly. Just follow the other guidelines outlined in this chapter, and the port should be a smooth ride.

Looking At *TList* Versus *TCollection*

Delphi offers a TList class that is similar in many ways to BP's TCollection object. Each offers a standard object in which you can store many other objects. There are, however, some key differences that you should be aware of when you port from BP to Delphi:

■ A TCollection attempts to dispose of all the objects it contains when it is disposed of, whereas a TList doesn't attempt to free any of the objects it contains when it is disposed of.

■ TList lacks the commonly used methods of ForEach(), FirstThat(), and LastThat() that assist in list manipulation.

These problems take away from what otherwise is an excellent implementation of TList, so we added the functions back in. Listing 19.1 shows the ListColl unit, which contains a TListCollection class—a descendent of TList with all the goodies you have come to appreciate in TCollection.

Listing 19.1. The ListColl unit.

```
unit ListColl;

interface

uses Classes;

type
  TForEachProc = procedure(O: TObject);
  TFirstLastFunc = function(O: TObject): Boolean;

  TListCollection = class(TList)
  public
    destructor Destroy; override;
    procedure ForEach(Proc: TForEachProc);
    function FirstThat(TestFunc: TFirstLastFunc): TObject;
    function LastThat(TestFunc: TFirstLastFunc): TObject;
  end;

implementation

destructor TListCollection.Destroy;
var
  i: integer;
  Temp: TObject;
begin
  repeat
    Temp := Items[0];
    Temp.Free;                    { Delete Item }
```

```
    Delete(0);                  { Free item from list }
  until Count = 0;              { until out of items }
  inherited Destroy;           { call the inherited }
end;

procedure TListCollection.ForEach(Proc: TForEachProc);
{ Proc must be declared far }
var
  i: integer;
begin
  for i := 0 to Count - 1 do          { iterate through the list }
    Proc(Items[i]);                   { call proc and pass each item }
end;

function TListCollection.FirstThat(TestFunc: TFirstLastFunc): TObject;
{ TestFunc must be declared far }
var
  Func: TFirstLastFunc;
  i: integer;
begin
  for i := 0 to Count - 1 do          { iterate through the list }
    if TestFunc(Items[i]) then begin  { call TestFunc and pass each item }
      Result := Items[i];             { return the first match }
      Break;
    end;
end;

function TListCollection.LastThat(TestFunc: TFirstLastFunc): TObject;
{ TestFunc must be declared far }
var
  i: integer;
begin
  for i := Count - 1 downto 0 do      { iterate backward through the list }
    if TestFunc(Items[i]) then begin  { call TestFunc and pass each item }
      Result := Items[i];             { return the first match }
      Break;
    end;
end;

end.
```

Use these new methods exactly as you would their TCollection counterparts, with a few exceptions:

■ The procedure that you pass to ForEach(), FirstThat(), or LastThat() must be declared far, but it cannot be declared local, as with the BP implementation.

■ The signature of the function that you pass to ForEach() must match that of the TForEachProc type. The signature of the function that you pass to FirstThat() or LastThat() must match the TFirstLastFunc type.

■ Pass the actual procedure or function to ForEach(), FirstThat(), or LastThat(). Do not pass the address of the procedure or function.

Summary

Hopefully, this chapter gave you some insight into what it takes to port a Borland or Turbo Pascal program to Delphi. The most important point is to get used to the Delphi style of applications development. Because Delphi applications generally are developed in a manner very different from BP, you will want to do some serious re-thinking of the program's design. Don't keep yourself too tied into the old design just because it's there. Open your mind, and look for a "Delphi way" to solve your problems. Chances are it will be smarter and more elegant than the old way. In the next chapter, "Power Programming: BASM and DPMI," you learn about some of the issues involved in using assembly language and extended DOS techniques in your applications.

20

Power Programming: BASM and DPMI

This chapter gives you an overview of how assembly language programming relates to Delphi and a feel for how DOS Protected Mode Interface (DPMI) relates to Delphi. Because Delphi is based around a true, mature compiler, one of the benefits you receive is the ability to write assembly code right in the middle of your Object Pascal procedures and functions. This capability is facilitated through Delphi's Built-in Assembler, or BASM.

In this chapter, you learn how to use BASM to your advantage. You also learn when using BASM can become a disadvantage and what you need to know about DPMI as a Windows programmer. The end of this chapter ties the two topics together and focuses on how to use BASM to leverage low-level DOS and DPMI operations.

This chapter does not teach you how to program in assembly language. Assembly language programming is a fairly complex topic, and there are a number of good books on the market dedicated to the subject. Assuming you know the basics of assembly language, though, this chapter does teach you how to use your knowledge within the context of BASM.

If you're not familiar with BASM, don't tune out yet. The latter portion of the chapter contains some code for calling powerful DPMI services from your Delphi programs (no assembly required!).

Using BASM with Delphi

Before you learn about BASM, you will learn when to and when not to use assembly language in your Delphi programs. Although it's great to have such a powerful tool at your disposal, like any good thing, BASM can be overdone. If you follow these simple BASM rules, you can help yourself write better, cleaner, more portable code:

- Never use assembly language for something that can be done in Object Pascal. You wouldn't, for example, write assembly-language routines to communicate through the serial ports because Windows provides built-in API functions for serial communications.

- Don't over-optimize your programs with assembly language. Hand-optimized assembly will run much faster than Object Pascal code, but at the price of readability and maintainability. Object Pascal is a language that communicates algorithms so naturally that it's a shame to have that communication muddled by a bunch of low-level register operations.

- Always comment your assembly code thoroughly. Your code will probably be read in the future by another programmer, or even by you, and lack of comments can make it difficult to understand.

- Use extreme care when you use BASM to access the machine hardware. Windows frowns on accessing hardware directly, and, should you port your code to Windows 95 or NT, direct hardware access is even more taboo on those platforms.

■ Where possible, try to wrap your assembly language code in procedures or functions callable from Object Pascal. This will make your code not only easier to maintain, but also easier to port to other platforms when the time comes.

How Does BASM Work?

Using assembly code in your Delphi applications is easier than you might think. In fact, it's so simple it's scary; just use the asm keyword followed by your assembly code, and then an end. The following code fragment demonstrates how to use assembly code inline:

```
var
  i: integer;
begin
  i := 0;
  asm
    mov ax, i
    inc ax
    mov i, ax
  end;
  { i has incremented by one }
```

This snippet declares a variable i and initializes it to 0. It then moves the value of i into the ax register, increments the register by one, and moves the value of the ax register back into i. This illustrates not only how easy it is to use BASM, but, as the usage of the variable i shows, how easily you can access your Pascal variables from BASM.

Easy Parameter Access

Not only is it easy to access variables declared globally or local to a procedure, it's just as easy to access variables passed into procedures, as the following code illustrates:

```
procedure Foo(I: integer);
begin
  { some code }
  asm
    mov ax, I
    inc ax
    mov I, ax
  end;
  { I has incremented by one }
  { some more code }
end;
```

The ability to access parameters by name is important because it means you don't have to reference variables passed into a procedure through the stack base pointer (bp) register as you would in a normal assembly program. In a regular assembly language procedure, you would have to refer to the variable I as [bp+2]—its offset from the stack's base pointer.

> **NOTE**
>
> When you use BASM to reference parameters passed into a procedure, remember that you can access those parameters by name, and you don't have to access them by their offset from the bp register. Accessing by offset from bp makes your code more difficult to maintain.

var Parameters

Remember that when a parameter is declared as var in a function or procedure's parameter list, a pointer to that variable is passed instead of the value. This means that when you reference var parameters within a BASM block, you must take into account that the parameter is a 32-bit pointer to a variable and not a variable instance. To expand on the early sample snippet, the following example shows how you would increment the variable I if it were passed in as a var parameter:

```
procedure Foo(var I: integer);
begin
  { some code }
  asm
    les di, I
    inc word ptr [es:di]
  end;
  { i has now been incremented by one }
  { some more code }
end;
```

Using Extended Registers

BASM does not have built-in support for operating on the 32-bit extended registers of a 386 and higher processor (eax, ebx, ecx, and so on) as would a real assembler such as Borland's Turbo Assembler or Microsoft's Macro Assembler. For example, the following statements will not compile in Delphi:

```
asm
  push eax
  pop  eax
```

You can, however, get around this limitation by defining bytes for instruction opcodes in your assembler statements. You can execute push and pop instructions for the extended registers, for example, by prepending the instruction with a byte containing the value $66, as shown here.

```
asm
  db 66h
  push ax    { push eax }
  db 66h
  pop  ax    { pop eax }
```

> **NOTE**
>
> Every assembly instruction can be represented by a one- or two-byte number called an opcode. *Opcodes* are what your microprocessor digests to perform the actions that make your program run. If you own Turbo Debugger for Windows, you can find the opcode to any instruction in an assembler manual or in the CPU view window of Turbo Debugger, as shown in Figure 20.1. (See Chapter 22, "Testing and Debugging," for more information on the capabilities of Turbo Debugger.)

FIGURE 20.1.

Examining opcodes in Turbo Debugger's CPU view window.

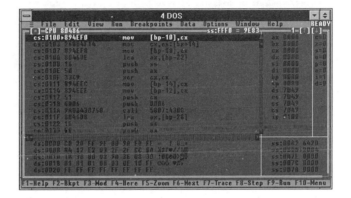

inline

With all this talk about opcodes, now is probably a good time to mention the inline directive. inline enables you to embed instruction opcodes directly into your Object Pascal code. Obviously, a bunch of numbers in the middle of your code can be cryptic and difficult to maintain, but it remains a feature of the language mainly for two reasons: backward compatibility and macros. The syntax of inline is very straightforward—just separate each byte or variable name by a slash. The following line is an example of inline that invokes the DOS print screen interrupt (for illustration purposes only):

```
inline($CD/$05);   { int 05h }
```

Because this is a book for real-world developers, listen to some real-world advice: Don't use inline where you can use BASM. inline code is horribly cryptic, awful to maintain, and a breeding ground for bugs. If you inherit any code that uses inline (such as old Pascal sample code) it might be worth your while to port that code to BASM or to Object Pascal, where possible.

The one case where you should consider using inline is when you need to create macros. A macro is similar to a function, except that it compiles in-line rather than as a function call. The lack of a preprocessor means that Object Pascal is incapable of creating C-like macros, but by using `inline`, you can get the job done. The syntax for a macro looks like a function without a `begin` and `end` pair; it has an `inline` directive instead.

For example, one common macro defined in the WINPROCS unit is `MakeLong()`, which takes two word-sized values and creates a `LongInt`. That macro is defined as follows:

```
function MakeLong(A, B: Word): LongInt;
inline(
  $5A/    { POP DX }
  $58);   { POP AX }
```

Along those lines, a similar macro that is missing from Delphi's runtime library—but still very useful—is one that creates a `word` from two byte-sized values. Here is one called `MakeWord()`:

```
function MakeWord(L, H: Byte): Word;
{ macro creates a word from low and high bytes }
inline(
  $5A/          { pop dx }
  $58/          { pop ax }
  $8A/$E2);     { mov ah, dl }
```

All-Assembly Procedures

Object Pascal enables you to write procedures and functions entirely in assembly language by using the `assembler` directive. Just add the `assembler` directive to the header of your function or procedure and begin the function or procedure with the word `asm` rather than `begin`, as shown here:

```
function IncAnInt(I: Integer): Integer; assembler;
asm
  mov ax, I
  inc ax
end;
```

The preceding procedure accepts an integer variable `I` and increments it. Because the variable value is placed in the `ax` register, that is the value returned by the function. Table 20.1 shows how different types of data are returned from a function in Delphi.

Table 20.1. How values are returned from Delphi functions.

Return Type	Return Method
char, byte	al register
integer, word	ax register
longint, pointer, object	dx:ax register pair
real	dx:bx:ax registers
single, double, extended, comp	ST(0) on 8087's register stack

> **NOTE**
>
> `Strings` are returned as a pointer to a `string` that is temporarily on the stack.

DOS Protected Mode Interface

DOS Protected Mode Interface (DPMI) is a special operating mode under DOS that allows easy access to memory above 640KB and that allows for different portions of memory to varying levels of protection. For example, it enables you full access to a data segment but does not enable you to write to a code segment. The MS Windows operating environment runs in DPMI, so, as a Windows programmer, you must follow the rules established by DPMI with regard to memory access, memory management, and interrupt programming.

DPMI Memory Access

The chief advantage of DPMI is that it makes a great deal of memory available to applications. Not only does DPMI give you seamless access to memory above the 1MB barrier, but it also has the capability to use a swap file on disk and treat it as if it were RAM installed on your PC. On the down side, this introduces a new level of complexity to DPMI applications. Because the amount of physical memory plus virtual memory made available through a swap file can easily exceed the 20-bit limit of a real-mode DOS segment:offset address, DPMI uses a system of allocating handles, called selectors, that point to different areas of memory. Windows' DPMI memory manager keeps a table of selectors and the corresponding physical addresses to which each selector points.

Therefore, whereas a real-mode segment represents the physical address of some area of memory, a selector is just a logical representation of a particular memory address—an index into a table of selectors and memory addresses. That table, called the Local Descriptor Table (LDT), contains not only information about what linear memory address each selector represents, but also information regarding what kind of information is stored at that location. Typically, a given selector represents either a chunk of program code or some type of data. Table 20.2 describes some of the differences between segments and selectors.

Table 20.2. Segments versus selectors.

A Segment...	*A Selector...*
■ is used by real-mode DOS to represent memory addresses.	■ is used by Protected Mode DOS to represent areas of memory.
■ is a physical address.	■ is a logical handle that represents an index into the Local Descriptor Table.

continues

Table 20.2. continued

A Segment...	*A Selector...*
■ as a physical address, has no quali- fiers as to what kind of information is stored in a given segment.	■ as a logical handle, also has information as to what type of information is stored in a given address (that is, code or data).
■ causes memory to overwrite bugs when you accidentally write to the wrong segment.	■ often causes General Protection Faults when you write to the wrong selector.

This brings up another one of DPMI's advantages. Windows' DPMI memory manager keeps track of memory accesses through the LDT, and can tell whether a program is trying to access memory occupied by program code or data. When a program tries to modify memory repre- sented by a code selector (you typically don't want to modify your program's code as it runs), the result is the all-too-familiar General Protection Fault (GP Fault). Two other common causes of GP Faults occur when you try to access data through an invalid selector (that is, the selector does not exist in the LDT) or try to use a selector with the value zero. You will also get a GP Fault if you write beyond the bounds of a given selector. The bottom line is that this feature of DPMI helps ensure that you always write to valid areas of memory and stops memory over- write bugs as they occur rather than as they show up.

> **TIP**
>
> To get a little insight into debugging general protection faults, read Chapter 22, which describes in detail some common causes and resolutions.

DPMI Memory Management

A new selector is created every time you allocate memory through one of the Windows API memory allocation functions: GlobalAlloc(), GlobalAllocPtr(), and GlobalDOSAlloc(). Se- lectors, however, are a limited resource; there is a maximum of about 8000 selectors that can be allocated globally. Because selectors are a finite resource, Delphi has a clever scheme of memory suballocation that allows for multiple memory allocations using New() or GetMem() to share the same GlobalAlloc'd (or global) block.

It works like this: When you initially allocate memory using New() or GetMem() in your pro- gram, Delphi allocates a larger, global block of memory. Subsequent calls to New() or GetMem()

will first check for an available space in a previously allocated global block, and if none is available, another global block is allocated. This suballocation scheme is shown in Figure 20.2.

FIGURE 20.2.

Delphi's memory suballocator.

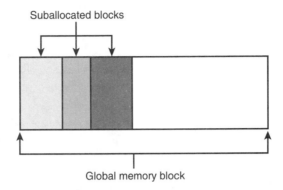

The size of the global blocks and the maximum size of the suballocated blocks are determined by the HeapBlock and HeapLimit global variables. HeapMax defaults to 8KB in size, whereas HeapLimit defaults to 2KB.

Delphi's memory suballocator has the advantage of being easier on selector resources, but it has its disadvantages. Because many allocations share the same global block, DPMI does not have the same full capability to detect when you accidentally overwrite areas of memory. As an example, say you call GetMem() to allocate 1024 bytes, and say you accidentally copy 1025 bytes of data in that area. With suballocation, you would never see the error because your program owns the next 7KB of contiguous memory. Without suballocation, you would probably get a GP Fault because your program would have overwritten the 1024-byte selector it was allocated. This problem is illustrated in Figure 20.3.

FIGURE 20.3.

Memory overwrite bugs caused by suballocation.

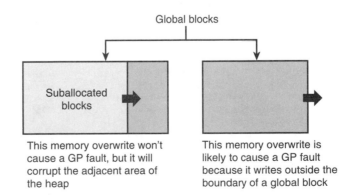

> ### TIP
>
> If you suspect a memory overwrite bug such as the one described here, set the
> HeapLimit global variable to zero with the following line of code:
>
> HeapLimit := 0;
>
> This will cause every allocation you make using New(), GetMem(), or a class constructor
> to receive its own global block instead of being suballocated from a larger global block.

More on Selectors

There are a number of techniques and procedures for you to remember when working with
selectors. Creating your own selectors—or even using existing ones—usually requires some
coding on your part. Even when just using selectors, you have to keep in mind the DOS-
imposed 64KB limit on memory blocks.

Creating Selectors

Under real-mode DOS you could access the text screen directly by reading to or writing from
segment $B800. Or, you could access BIOS information directly with segment $0040. You
could also directly access some memory-mapped piece of hardware at $D000 or $C000, or
wherever it may be. Of course, things aren't that straightforward in a protected-mode environment such as Windows. In order to allocate a selector for a given region of memory under
Windows, you must go through a few gyrations in creating the selector and pointing it to the
right chunk of memory.

To create a new selector that points to a predetermined address requires calls to a few
Windows API functions, as follows:

```
var
  NewSelector: word;
  P: Pointer;
begin
  NewSelector := AllocSelector(DSeg);
  SetSelectorBase(NewSelector, $B8000);
  SetSelectorLimit(NewSelector, $FFFF);
  P := Ptr(NewSelector, 0);
  { use P }
  FreeSelector(NewSelector);
end;
```

The first call is to the AllocSelector() function. AllocSelector() takes an existing selector as
a parameter and returns a new selector with the same attributes as the selector passed in.

DSeg and CSeg are selectors defined by Delphi's runtime library that represent the current data segment and code segment, respectively. When you create new selectors using the AllocSelector() API function, pass DSeg as the parameter if you are creating a data selector, or pass CSeg as a parameter if you are creating a code selector.

After you allocate the new selector you must specify the memory address to which it refers. For this, use the SetSelectorBase() API function. SetSelectorBase() takes two parameters: the selector that has the base address you wish to modify, and the new base address. The catch here is that the new address must be a 20-bit linear address, so if you know the real-mode segment and offset to which you'd like the selector to point, you'll have to convert the *segment:offset* pair into a 20-bit linear address. If you'd rather not go through the mental gymnastics, the following code offers handy functions for converting from *segment:offset* to linear and back again:

```
function GetLinearAddressFromPointer(P: Pointer): Longint;
{ returns a 20-bit linear address given a sement:offset pointer }
begin
  Result := Longint(Seg(P^)) shl 4 + Ofs(P^);
end;

function GetPointerFromLinearAddress(Addr: Longint): Pointer;
{ returns a sement:offset pointer given a 20-bit linear address }
begin
  Result := Ptr((Addr shr 4), (Addr and $0F));
end;
```

The final call you must make before using your new selector is to the SetSelectorLimit() API function. Use this function to set the size of the block of memory you wish your selector to represent. In this example, assume that you want the selector to represent 64KB of data.

Now your selector is ready to use. One of the easiest ways to use the new selector is to create a pointer with it using Delphi's Ptr() function. Ptr() accepts a selector and offset as parameters and returns a selector:offset pointer.

Don't forget to call FreeSelector() when you have finished using a selector you've allocated with AllocSelector(). Remember, selectors are a finite resource.

Using Precreated Selectors

Now that you know how selectors are created behind the scenes it's time you learn a few tricks of the trade. You know that a smart programmer never reinvents the wheel, but takes advantage of advances made by peers, which means you shouldn't have to create a selector if someone has already done it for you. This section will show you some of the preallocated selectors created for you by the Delphi runtime library.

The first important selector is $0040. You may already know that segment $0040 contains information about your PC's BIOS. What you may not know is that Windows always ensures that there is a selector with the value $0040 that represents segment $0040. Feel free to use selector $0040 in your programs to access BIOS data. This gem is not very well documented by the folks at Microsoft.

> **TIP**
>
> Selector $0040 always represents segment $0040, the PC BIOS.

Table 20.3 shows functions that Delphi provides that return some common selectors. These functions all return selectors dealing with where in memory your program is loaded. Each of these functions takes no parameters and returns a word-type variable.

Table 20.3. Delphi's preallocated selectors.

Variable Name	What Is Its Value?
CSeg	Selector representing the current code segment. (The value contained in the cs register.)
DSeg	Selector representing the current data segment. (The value contained in the ds register.)
SSeg	Selector representing the current stack segment. (The value contained in the ss register.)

SelectorInc and Crossing Segment Boundaries

Even though DPMI provides access to large amounts of memory, keep in mind that the dreaded 64KB barrier is still in effect. What this means to you as a developer is that no one structure in your program can exceed 64KB in size.

However, this does not mean that you can't allocate huge blocks of memory; it just means that you don't get to play with more than 64KB of a block of memory at one time. It's important to note that this isn't a Delphi limitation—it's a limitation that is built into the DOS architecture, and because Windows 3.1 runs on top of DOS, you're stuck with this limitation until Windows 95 or NT.

NOTE

In programmer-speak, blocks of memory larger than 64KB are usually referred to as "huge" blocks.

The trick to working with large blocks is to be aware at all times of when you are about to cross a 64KB segment boundary, and, when you do, to adjust the value of the selector you are using to reflect the new segment. When you move from one segment to the next in a huge block of memory, you must increment the selector by the value of a system variable called SelectorInc.

To illustrate how to use SelectorInc to cross segment boundaries, Listing 20.1 contains the TGodzillArray class. This class simulates an array of up to 536,870,911 (MaxLongint div SizeOf(Longint)) Longints.

Listing 20.1. The GZILLA.PAS unit.

```
unit GZilla;

interface

uses WinTypes, WinProcs;

type
  TGodzillArray = class
  private
    FMemBlock: THandle;
    FSize: Longint;
    FLocked: Boolean;
    FPtr: PLongint;
    procedure SetSize(NewSize: Longint);
    function GetItem(Index: Longint): Longint;
    procedure SetItem(Index: Longint; Value: Longint);
    procedure CheckSize(Value: Longint);
  protected
    function GetMaxSize: Longint; virtual;
    procedure GetPointer(Index: Longint); virtual;
    procedure UnlockBlock; virtual;
    procedure SetLock(Value: Boolean); virtual;
  public
    constructor Create(ArraySize: Longint); virtual;
    destructor Destroy; override;
    property Size: Longint read FSize write SetSize;
    property Locked: Boolean read FLocked write SetLock;
    property Items[Index: Longint]: Longint read GetItem write SetItem; default;
  end;

implementation

uses SysUtils;

const
  MemAllocFlags: word = gmem_Moveable or gmem_ZeroInit;
```

continues

Listing 20.1. continued

```pascal
constructor TGodzillArray.Create(ArraySize: Longint);
begin
  if ArraySize > GetMaxSize then
    ArraySize := GetMaxSize;
  FMemBlock := GlobalAlloc(MemAllocFlags, ArraySize * SizeOf(Longint));
  if FMemBlock <> 0 then
    FSize := ArraySize
  else
    raise EOutOfMemory.Create('Couldn''t allocate memory block.');
end;

destructor TGodzillArray.Destroy;
begin
  inherited Destroy;
  UnlockBlock;
  SetLock(False);
  if GlobalFree(FMemBlock) <> 0 then
    raise EInvalidPointer.Create('Couldn''t free memory block');
end;

function TGodzillArray.GetMaxSize: Longint;
begin
  Result := MaxLongint div SizeOf(Longint);
end;

procedure TGodzillArray.SetSize(NewSize: Longint);
begin
  if NewSize <> FSize then begin
    if NewSize > GetMaxSize then
      NewSize := GetMaxSize;
    if GlobalReAlloc(FMemBlock, NewSize * SizeOf(Longint), MemAllocFlags) <> 0
        then
      FSize := NewSize
    else
      raise EOutOfMemory.Create('Couldn''t realloc memory block');
  end;
end;

procedure TGodzillArray.SetLock(Value: Boolean);
begin
  if FLocked <> Value then begin
    if Value then begin
      GlobalLock(FMemBlock);
      FLocked := True;
    end
    else begin
      FLocked := False;
      UnlockBlock;
    end;
  end;
end;

procedure TGodzillArray.GetPointer(Index: Longint);
var
  Selector, OffSet: Word;
```

```
begin
  Index := Index * SizeOf(Longint);
  Selector := (Index div 65536) * SelectorInc + FMemBlock;
  OffSet := Index mod 65536;
  if not FLocked then
    FPtr := GlobalLock(Selector);
  FPtr := Ptr(Selector, Offset);
end;

procedure TGodzillArray.UnlockBlock;
begin
  if not FLocked then GlobalUnlock(FMemBlock);
end;

procedure TGodzillArray.CheckSize(Value: Longint);
begin
  if (Value > FSize) or (Value < 0) then
    raise ERangeError.Create('Index not within established range.');
end;


procedure TGodzillArray.SetItem(Index: Longint; Value: Longint);
begin
  CheckSize(Index);
  GetPointer(Index);
  FPtr^ := Value;
  UnlockBlock;
end;

function TGodzillArray.GetItem(Index: Longint): Longint;
begin
  CheckSize(Index);
  GetPointer(Index);
  Result := FPtr^;
  UnlockBlock;
end;

end.
```

The basic idea of this class is that it allocates a huge block of memory with GlobalAlloc() and uses some selector tricks to index all the way through the block like an array. The heart of this class is the GetPointer() method, which handles the memory block offset manipulation to create valid pointers. Here's a line-at-a-time look at this procedure.

The first line obtains the offset into the huge block of the Longint at the desired index:

```
Index := Index * SizeOf(Longint);
```

The second line figures out how many 64KB segment boundaries there are between the beginning of the block and the desired offset:

```
Selector := (Index div 65536) * SelectorInc + FMemBlock;
```

The number of boundaries is multiplied by `SelectorInc` and added to the selector value for the start of the huge block. The next line finds the offset of the desired index in the current 64KB segment:

```
OffSet := Index mod 65536;
```

The last lines of the procedure lock the global block of memory if it hasn't already been locked, and sets the class's `FPtr` field to point to the selector:offset of the `Longint` at the desired index:

```
if not FLocked then
  FPtr := GlobalLock(Selector);
FPtr := Ptr(Selector, Offset);
```

Using *TGodzillArray*

`TGodzillArray` is designed to be used as much as possible like a normal 0-based array of `Longint`s. In fact, you can use an instance of this class exactly like a real array except for four differences.

- ■ You must call `Create()` to instantiate the class. `Create()` takes one parameter of type `Longint` that represents the desired size of the array.

- ■ You must call `Free()` when you're done with the array to clean up allocated memory.

- ■ You control the size of the array through the `Size` property. If you try to retrieve a value at an index that is greater than `Size`, an exception will be raised.

- ■ You can use the `Locked` property to optimize between memory efficiency and speed. When `Locked` is `false`, the memory block used by the class is movable in memory, so Windows can manage the block when necessary for efficiency. When `Locked` is `true`, the block remains fixed in memory but performs better because it doesn't have to be locked for every read and write. You'll get a good balance if you only set `Locked` to `true` when allocating or reading large amounts of memory in a short period of time— in a loop, for example.

Because `TGodzillArray` holds `Longint` values, you can use it to store pointers to other objects, or even class instances.

The following code demonstrates how to create and use an instance of `TGodzillArray`:

```
var
  G: TGodzillArray;
begin
  G := TGodzillArray.Create(100000);
  G[0] := 1;
  G[5000] := 14;
  G[9999] := 6400;
  Edit1.Text := IntToStr(G[0]);
  Edit1.Text := IntToStr(G[1]);    {note that this value is init'd to zero }
  Edit2.Text := IntToStr(G[5000]);
  Edit3.Text := IntToStr(G[9999]);
end;
```

If you get ambitious, `TGodzillArray` can even be extended to support multiple huge blocks of memory to support arrays of up to 2,147,483,647 (`MaxLongint`) elements. I personally don't have quite that much RAM installed on my computer, but, hey, it is possible!

Interrupts Under DPMI

While Windows runs, its DPMI server takes over all software interrupt traffic, so any interrupt execution or handling you do in your programs must first filter through the DPMI server. It does this in order to manage the processor's switch into real mode for interrupt execution. For this reason, all interrupts that you attempt to execute may need some special treatment before execution. In addition, you need to make special provisions whenever you attempt to directly handle an interrupt. DPMI provides an interface for this special handling under interrupt $31.

Executing Supported Interrupts

The `GetCurrentDir()` example in the following code demonstrates how to call an interrupt that is supported by Windows' DPMI server. This example calls interrupt $21, function $47, which gets the current directory on a specified drive. When calling this interrupt, the `dl` register should contain the drive number, and `ds:si` should contain a pointer to a 65-character buffer that holds the null-terminated string returned by the interrupt.

```
uses SysUtils, WinProcs;

function GetCurrentDir(Drive: byte): String;
{ returns path name of current directory on specified drive.  Returns an
  empty string on error. Drive 0 = default, 1 = a:, 2 = b:, etc. }
var
  P: PChar;
  Error: Boolean;
begin
  Error := False;      { assume success }
  GetMem(P, 65);       { get memory for PChar }
  asm
    mov ax, 4700h    { function 47h = Get Current Directory }
    mov dl, Drive    { low word of dx holds drive. 0 = default, 1 = a:, ... }
    push ds          { preserve ds register }
    push si          { preserve si register }
    lds si, P        { ds:si = pointer to 65-character buffer }
    call DOS3Call    { execute DOS interrupt 21h }
    jnc @@Done       { carry flag set on error.  Jump if not set }
    mov Error, 1     { set error flag }
  @@Done:
    pop si           { restore si }
    pop ds           { restore ds }
  end;
  if not Error then
    Result := '\' + StrPas(P)
  else
    Result := '';
  FreeMem(P, 65);    { free PChar memory }
end;
```

> **NOTE**
>
> In BASM, labels must begin with the @ symbol. The convention, however, is to use a double-at symbol, @@, for clarity.

Let's break this listing down into parts. First, you initialize the error flag, and then allocate memory for the buffer P using GetMem(). Next, you set up the registers for the call to interrupt $21, function $47. Note that the ds and si registers are pushed on the stack to preserve them because the lds si instruction destroys their value. Then comes the call to interrupt $21—it is called through the Windows API DOS3Call procedure. The carry flag is then checked for an error and the ds and si registers are restored. If there was no error, the string held in the buffer P is returned. An empty string is returned on error.

> **TIP**
>
> Use DOS3Call instead of directly calling int 21h to execute a DOS interrupt. It executes faster, and it is the preferred way to execute DOS interrupts under Windows. You should use DOS3Call only from within BASM or an assembly module.

Executing Unsupported Interrupts

If Windows does not directly support the interrupt you wish to execute, then you must execute the interrupt through DPMI interrupt $31, function $300—Simulate Real Mode Interrupt. When executing this interrupt, the registers must be set up as shown in Table 20.4.

Table 20.4. How to set up registers for interrupt $31, function $300.

Register	Value
ax	0300h
bl	Interrupt number you wish to execute.
bh	Flags—must be set to zero.
cx	Number of words to copy from protected-mode to real-mode stack. This value is often zero.
es:di	*Selector:offset* of real-mode register record.

The real-mode register record referenced by es:di is a record that mimics the CPU's registers and flags. You set up the registers in this record exactly the same way you would set up the CPU's registers if you were calling the unsupported interrupt directly. The real-mode register record is defined in the CALLREAL.PAS unit in Listing 20.2.

To make interrupt $31, function $300 more accessible for Delphi programmers, it happens to fit nicely into an Object Pascal wrapper. By passing the interrupt number and register record into this function, you can encapsulate all its functionality into a small package. The CALLREAL.PAS unit shown in Listing 20.2 does this in a function called SimulateRealModeInterrupt().

Listing 20.2. The source code for CALLREAL.PAS.

```
unit CallReal;

interface

type
  PRealModeRegs = ^TRealModeRegs;
  TRealModeRegs = record
    case Integer of
      0: (
        EDI, ESI, EBP, EXX, EBX, EDX, ECX, EAX: Longint;
        Flags, ES, DS, FS, GS, IP, CS, SP, SS: Word);
      1: (
        DI, DIH, SI, SIH, BP, BPH, XX, XXH: Word;
        case Integer of
          0: (
            DX, DXH, DX, DXH, CX, CXH, AX, AXH: Word);
          1: (
            BL, BH, BLH, BHH, DL, DH, DLH, DHH,
            CL, CH, CLH, CHH, AL, AH, ALH, AHH: Byte));
  end;

function SimulateRealModeInterrupt(IntNum: Byte; var Regs: TRealModeRegs):
    word;

implementation

function SimulateRealModeInterrupt(IntNum: Byte; var Regs: TRealModeRegs;
    WordsToCopy: word): word; assembler;
{ This is a wrapper for a call to DPMI int $31, function $300. Returns 0 on
  success, nonzero on failure. }
asm
  push es              { preserve es register }
  push di              { preserve di register }
  mov bl, IntNum       { low byte of bx = real mode interrupt }
  mov bh, 00h          { high byte of bx = 0 }
  mov cx, WordsToCopy  { copy WordsToCopy words from prot. to real stack }
  les di, Regs         { es:di holds pointer to TRealModeRegs structure }
  mov ax, 0300h        { DPMI function 300h }
  int 31h              { execute DPMI interrupt }
  jc @@End             { carry flag set on error, so jump if it's set }
  mov ax, 0000h        { return 0 (in ax) if no error }
@@End:                 { if error, error code will be in ax }
  pop di               { restore di }
  pop es               { restore es }
end;

end.
```

The `SimulateRealModeInterrupt()` function shown in Listing 20.2 sets up the registers as mentioned in Table 20.4, then calls interrupt $31. This interrupt sets the carry flag in the event of an error condition, and the `JC` instruction jumps to the `@@End` label in the event of an error. This leaves the error code in `ax` and causes the function to return a nonzero value.

To put the CALLREAL.PAS unit to good use, rewrite the `GetCurrentDir()` function shown earlier so that the interrupt is called through interrupt $31 instead of directly. Of course, you would be well within your rights to ask, "Why would I want to call interrupt $21, function $47 through DPMI when I already know it is directly supported?" The reason is because showing you how to call the same interrupt both ways will hopefully give you a better perspective on how the entire process works. By seeing the interrupt called both directly and indirectly, you should be better able to pick up on the differences and similarities between the two methods. The following code shows the `GetCurrentDir2()` function, which works through the DPMI interrupt:

```
uses WinProcs, SysUtils, CallReal;

function GetCurrentDir2(Drive: byte): String;
{ returns path name of current directory on specified drive. Returns an
  empty string on error. Drive 0 = default, 1 = a:, 2 = b:, etc. }
var
  P: PChar;
  R: TRealModeRegs;
  M: longint;
begin
  M := GlobalDOSAlloc(65);   { allocate conventional memory for buffer }
  P := Ptr(LoWord(M), 0);    { low word of M contains selector, make pointer }
  with R do begin
    ax := $4700;             { function 47h = Get Current Directory }
    dl := Drive;             { low word of dx holds drive }
    ds := HiWord(M);         { high word of M contains buffer's segment }
    si := 0;                 { ds:si = pointer to 65-character buffer }
  end;
  if SimulateRealModeInterrupt($21, R, 0) = 0 then begin
    Result := '\' + StrPas(P);   { return Pascalized string }
    { carry flag set on error.  Carry flag is least significant bit of flags }
    if (R.Flags and 1) <> 0 then Result := '';
  end
  else
    Result := '';
  GlobalDOSFree(M);          { free buffer memory }
end;
```

You should be able to see the similarity between the `GetCurrentDir2()` function and its cousin, `GetCurrentDir()`. The registers in `R`, the `TRealModeRegs` record, are set up identically to the real registers in the `GetCurrentDir()` function. After setting up the registers in `R`, the `SimulateRealModeInterrupt()` function is called from the CALLREAL.PAS unit, and the interrupt is executed. After execution, notice that the carry flag of `R.Flags` is examined for an error—similar to the `JNC` error check performed in `GetCurrentDir()`.

You also may notice that memory is allocated for the character buffer in this case using the Windows API GlobalDOSAlloc() function. As explained next, GlobalDOSAlloc() allocates a chunk of conventional memory that can be shared between real-mode and protected-mode code. Because the interrupt actually executes in real mode in this case, you must pass the *segment:offset* of the buffer in R.DS and R.SI.

THE GlobalDOSAlloc() FUNCTION

GlobalDOSAlloc() is a Windows API function that enables you to allocate memory that is addressable in both real and protected mode. Just pass it some number representing the amount of bytes you wish to allocate, and it will return a longint value—the high word of which contains a real-mode segment, and the low word contains a protected-mode selector to the same area of memory.

GlobalDOSAlloc() is the ideal function to use when you need to share a block of memory between real and protected mode for a real-mode interrupt or callback.

For the memory block to be addressable in real mode, the memory is allocated from conventional (lower) DOS memory. Because conventional memory is a pretty scarce and limited resource in Windows, you should use the function only when you have to, allocate only as much as you need, and free the memory as soon as possible.

More on DPMI

DPMI does provide for more interrupts that enable you to perform nifty tricks like real-mode callbacks and installing interrupt handlers, but that's about as far as we'll go with DPMI in this chapter. If you're interested in learning more on this topic, we highly recommend you obtain the DPMI Specification document from Intel Corporation.

Summary

This chapter gave you some insight as to how to combine Delphi's Built-in Assembler and a working knowledge of DPMI to solve some pretty low-level problems. The vast majority of the time you won't need to resort to these power programming techniques with Delphi, but it's always good to have the knowledge when the need arises. In the next chapter, "Hard-Core Windows," you learn some advanced Windows and Delphi techniques that you can use in your applications.

21

Hard-Core Windows

This chapter teaches you some advanced techniques that you can use in your Delphi applications. You'll get much closer to the Windows API in this chapter than you did in most of the other chapters, and you'll explore some things that aren't obvious or aren't provided under VCL. You'll learn about concepts such as window procedures, multiple program instances, and Windows hooks.

Understanding the Application Window Procedure

As discussed in Chapter 9, "Understanding Messages," a *window procedure* is a function that Windows calls whenever a particular window receives a message. Because the Application object is a window, it has a window procedure that is called to receive all the messages sent to your application. The TApplication class even comes equipped with an OnMessage event that notifies you whenever one of these messages comes down the pike. Well...not exactly.

TApplication.OnMessage only fires when a message is retrieved from the application's message queue (again, refer to Chapter 9 for a discussion of all this message terminology). Messages found in the application queue are those dealing with window management (wm_Paint and wm_Size, for example) and those sent using the PostMessage() or PostAppMessage() functions. The problem arises when other types of messages are sent directly to the window procedure by Windows or by the SendMessage() function. When this occurs, the TApplication.OnMessage event never happens, and there is no way to know whether the message occurred based on this event.

Subclassing

In order to know when a message is sent to your application, you must replace the Application window's window procedure with your own. In your window procedure, you should do whatever processing or message-handling you need to do before passing the message to the original window procedure. This process is known as *subclassing* a window.

Use the GetWindowLong() function with the gwl_WndProc constant to retrieve the address of a particular window's window procedure. The SetWindowLong() function enables you to set a new function to be the window procedure. A window procedure must have the following signature:

```
function WindowProc(Handle: hWnd; Msg: word; wParam: word; lParam: Longint):
➡Longint; export;
```

The Handle parameter identifies the destination window, the Msg parameter is the window message, and the wParam and lParam parameters contain additional, message-specific information.

As an illustration, create an application that demonstrates subclassing the Application's window procedure and its advantages over Application.OnMessage. First create a new project with a main form containing two TButton components, as shown in Figure 21.1. Call this project WinProc.

FIGURE 21.1.

WinProc's main unit.

Listing 21.1 shows the source code for MAIN.PAS, WinProc's main unit.

Listing 21.1. The source code for MAIN.PAS, WinProc's main unit.

```pascal
unit Main;

interface

uses
  SysUtils, WinTypes, WinProcs, Messages, Classes, Graphics, Controls,
  Forms, Dialogs, StdCtrls;

type
  TForm1 = class(TForm)
    Button1: TButton;
    Button2: TButton;
    procedure Button1Click(Sender: TObject);
    procedure Button2Click(Sender: TObject);
  public
    procedure HandleAppMessage(var Msg: TMsg; var Handled: Boolean);
  end;

var
  Form1: TForm1;

implementation

{$R *.DFM}


procedure TForm1.HandleAppMessage(var Msg: TMsg; var Handled: Boolean);
begin
  if Msg.Message = wm_User then
    ShowMessage('Message seen by OnMessage! Value is: $' +
                IntToHex(Msg.Message, 4));
end;
```

continues

Listing 21.1. continued

```
procedure TForm1.Button1Click(Sender: TObject);
begin
  SendMessage(Application.Handle, wm_User, 0, 0);
end;

procedure TForm1.Button2Click(Sender: TObject);
begin
  PostMessage(Application.Handle, wm_User, 0, 0);
end;

end.
```

When `Button1` is clicked, use the `SendMessage()` API function to send the message `wm_User` to the `Application`'s window handle. When `Button2` is clicked, do the same with `PostMessage()`.

The `HandleAppMessage()` procedure is the procedure that will be assigned to the `Application.OnMessage` event. This procedure simply brings up a ShowMessage dialog box saying that it sees a message. The `OnMessage` event is assigned in the project file, WINPROC.DPR, as shown in Listing 21.2.

Listing 21.2. The source code for WINPROC.DPR.

```
program Winproc;

uses
  Forms,
  Main in 'MAIN.PAS' {Form1},
  Scwndprc in 'SCWNDPRC.PAS';

{$R *.RES}

begin
  MakeNewWndProc;
  Application.CreateForm(TForm1, Form1);
  Application.OnMessage := Form1.HandleAppMessage;
  Application.Run;
end.
```

This module not only sets up `Application.OnMessage`, but it also calls a procedure called `MakeNewWndProc()`. This procedure is located in the SCWNDPRC.PAS unit, and it is in charge of subclassing the `Application` window procedure, as shown in Listing 21.3.

Listing 21.3. The source code for SCWNDPRC.PAS.

```
unit Scwndprc;

interface

uses Forms;

procedure MakeNewWndProc;

implementation

uses WinTypes, WinProcs, Messages, SysUtils, Dialogs;

var
  WProc: TFarProc;

function NewWndProc(Handle: hWnd; Msg: word; wParam: word; lParam: Longint):
➥Longint; export;
begin
  If Msg = wm_User then
    ShowMessage('Message seen by WndProc! Value is: $' + IntToHex(Msg, 4));
  Result := CallWindowProc(WProg, Handle, Msg, wParam, lParam);
end;

procedure MakeNewWndProc;
begin
  WProc := TFarProc(GetWindowLong(Application.Handle, gwl_WndProc));
  SetWindowLong(Application.Handle, gwl_WndProc, Longint(@NewWndProc));
end;

end.
```

MakeNewWndProc() uses GetWindowLong() and SetWindowLong() to subclass the Application window procedure. The NewWndProc() function becomes the new window procedure, and this function merely displays a ShowMessage dialog box when it sees a message with the value wm_User.

CAUTION

Be sure to save the old window procedure returned by GetWindowLong(). If you do not call the old window procedure inside your subclassed window procedure for messages that you don't want to handle, you're likely to crash Windows.

When you run this application, you'll be able to see that the ShowMessage dialog box is shown from the window procedure no matter which button is pushed, but Application.OnMessage sees only the messages that are posted to the window.

Running Multiple Instances

Running *multiple instances* means to run more than one copy of your program simultaneously. The capability to run multiple instances of an application is one of those great features that Windows builds into the operating environment. From a programmer's standpoint, two questions frequently arise when dealing with multiple instances. The first is, "How do I prevent multiple instances?" That is, how do you allow only one copy of your application to run? The second is, "How do I copy data from one instance of an application to another?"

Delphi's runtime library initializes two word-sized global variables called `hInstance` and `hPrevInst` that help you get information about application instances:

- The `hInstance` variable holds the Windows instance handle of the current instance of your application.
- The `hPrevInst` variable contains the instance handle of the previous instance of your application. If the current instance is the first, then `hPrevInst` contains zero.

Preventing Multiple Instances

Sometimes a developer wants to design an application so that only one instance can be run at a time. Usually, in such applications, when you double-click the Program Manager to run a second instance, the previous instance of the application comes into focus. This can happen in one of two ways. First, if an application contains multiple data segments (which Delphi doesn't allow), Windows automatically disallows multiple instances. The second way is to check the value of `hPrevInst` at the beginning of your application. If it is nonzero, focus the previous instance of the application and terminate.

The most elegant approach to focusing the main form of the previous instance is to use a registered window message obtained by the `RegisterWindowMessage()` function to create a message identifier unique to your application. You then can have the initial instance of your application respond to this message by focusing itself. This approach is illustrated in Listings 21.4 and 21.5, which show the complete source code to the OneInst project.

Listing 21.4. The source code for ONEINST.DPR.

```
program OneInst;

uses
  Forms,
  WinTypes,
  WinProcs,
  Main in 'MAIN.PAS' {Form1};

{$R *.RES}

begin
```

```
  { Create a new system-wide Windows message identifier }
  MessageID := RegisterWindowMessage('Check For OneInst Previous Inst');
  if hPrevInst <> 0 then          { if this is not the first instance... }
    { Broadcast the special message }
    PostMessage(hwnd_Broadcast, MessageID, 0, 0)
  else begin
    { otherwise, do the normal stuff }
    Application.CreateForm(TForm1, Form1);
    Application.Run;
  end;
end.
```

Listing 21.5. The source code for MAIN.PAS, OneInst's main unit.

```
unit Main;

interface

uses
  SysUtils, WinTypes, WinProcs, Messages, Classes, Graphics, Controls,
  Forms, Dialogs;

type
  TForm1 = class(TForm)
    procedure FormCreate(Sender: TObject);
  private
    { Private declarations }
    procedure OnAppMessage(var Msg: TMsg; var Handled: Boolean);
  public
    { Public declarations }
  end;

var
  Form1: TForm1;
  MessageID: Word;

implementation

{$R *.DFM}

procedure TForm1.OnAppMessage(var Msg: TMsg; var Handled: Boolean);
begin
  { If it's the special message, then focus this window }
  If Msg.Message = MessageID then
    SetFocus;
end;

procedure TForm1.FormCreate(Sender: TObject);
begin
  { Assign the OnMessage event handler for Application }
  Application.OnMessage := OnAppMessage;
end;

end.
```

Sharing Data Between Instances

Occasionally, people want to share or copy data from one program to another. A variety of approaches to this problem has been suggested: from sharing files to DDE to sharing areas of memory. However, there is a much easier approach if you want to share data from previous instances of the same application: Use the Windows API GetInstanceData() function.

> **CAUTION**
>
> There is a bug in the first release of Delphi in the declaration of GetInstanceData().
> The second parameter to this function is listed as type PByte, but it should be of type
> word. You can get around this by re-declaring GetInstanceData() inside the unit in
> which you plan to use it:
>
> ```
> function GetInstanceData(Instance: THandle; Data: word; Count: Integer):
> ➡Integer; far; external 'KERNEL' index 54;
> ```

The parameter values for this function are

Instance	Defines the instance handle of the previous application instance. In most cases, this is hPrevinst.
Data	The offset of the data buffer you want to share. In most cases, you can obtain this value using the Ofs() function or, in the case of a pointer, by casting the address to a Longint and taking the low word of that value.
Count	Dictates the number of bytes to copy.

To demonstrate this concept, create a new project with a main form containing one TEdit component, as shown in Figure 21.2. This project will be called TstInst.

FIGURE 21.2.

*The main form for the
TstInst project.*

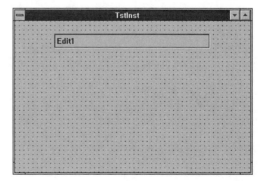

Listing 21.6 shows the complete source code for MAIN.PAS, TstInst's main unit.

Listing 21.6. The source code for MAIN.PAS, TstInst's main unit.

```pascal
unit Main;

interface

uses
  SysUtils, WinTypes, WinProcs, Messages, Classes, Graphics, Controls,
  Forms, Dialogs, StdCtrls;

type
  TForm1 = class(TForm)
    Edit1: TEdit;
    procedure FormCreate(Sender: TObject);
    procedure Edit1Change(Sender: TObject);
  private
    { Private declarations }
  public
    { Public declarations }
  end;

var
  Form1: TForm1;
  DataArray: array[0..255] of char;

implementation

{$R *.DFM}

function GetInstanceData(Instance: THandle; Data: word; Count: Integer): Integer;
    far; external 'KERNEL' index 54;

procedure TForm1.FormCreate(Sender: TObject);
var
  Size: word;
begin
  if hPrevInst<> 0 then begin
    GetInstanceData(hPrevInst, Ofs(DataArray), SizeOf(DataArray));
    Edit1.SetTextBuf(DataArray);
  end;
end;

procedure TForm1.Edit1Change(Sender: TObject);
begin
  Edit1.GetTextBuf(DataArray, Length(Edit1.Text));
end;

end.
```

Whenever the contents of Edit1 are changed, the global buffer called DataArray is updated with the new contents. That way, the global buffer is always in sync with the contents of Edit1.

When the form is created, it checks the value of the hPrevInst variable to see whether it is the first instance. If not, it calls GetInstanceData() to retrieve the value of DataArray for the previous instance of the application and places that value in Edit1.

Try to run more than one instance of this application. You will find that, upon startup, the contents of Edit1 for each new instance always match the contents of Edit1 in the previous instance.

Using Windows Hooks

Windows *hooks* give programmers the means to control the occurrence and handling of system events. A hook offers perhaps the ultimate degree of power for an applications programmer, because a hook enables the programmer to preview and modify system events and messages, and to prevent system events and messages from occurring system-wide.

Setting the Hook

A Windows hook is set using the SetWindowsHookEx() API function:

```
function SetWindowsHookEx(HookID: Integer; Hook: THookProc; Module, Task: THandle):
➥hHook;
```

> **CAUTION**
>
> Use only the SetWindowsHookEx() function, not the SetWindowsHook() function, in your applications. SetWindowsHook() exists only for backward-compatibility with Windows 3.0 applications.

The HookID parameter describes the type of hook to be installed. This can be any one of the predefined hook constants shown in Table 21.1.

Table 21.1. Windows hooks.

Hook Constant	Description
wh_CallWndProc	A Windows procedure filter. The hook procedure is called whenever a message is sent to a window procedure.
wh_CBT	A computer-based training filter. The hook procedure is called before processing most window-management, mouse, and keyboard messages.
wh_Debug	A debugging filter. The hook function is called before any other Windows hook.
wh_GetMessage	A message filter. The hook function is called whenever a message is retrieved from the application queue.

Hook Constant	Description
wh_Hardware	A hardware message filter. The hook function is called whenever a hardware message is retrieved from the application queue.
wh_JournalPlayback	The hook function is called whenever a message is retrieved from the system queue. Typically used to insert system events into the queue.
wh_JournalRecord	The hook function is called whenever an event is requested from the system queue. Typically used to "record" system events.
wh_Keyboard	A keyboard filter. The hook function is called whenever a wm_KeyDown or wm_KeyUp message is retrieved from the application queue.
wh_Mouse	A mouse message filter. The hook function is called whenever a mouse message is retrieved from the application queue.
wh_MsgFilter	A special message filter. The hook function is called whenever an application's dialog box, menu, or message box is about to process a message.
wh_Shell	A shell application filter. The hook function is called when top-level windows are created and destroyed and when the shell application needs to become active.
wh_SysMsgFilter	A system message filter. A MsgFilter that operates system-wide.

The THookProc parameter is the address of the callback function to act as the Windows hook function. This function should look something like the following:

```
function WinHookProc(Code: Integer; wParam: word; lParam: Longint): Longint;
export;
```

The contents of each of the hook function's parameters vary according to the type of hook installed, and are documented in the Windows API help.

The Module parameter should be the value of hInstance in the EXE or DLL containing the hook callback.

The Task parameter identifies the task handle of the task for which the hook should be in effect. If it is zero, the hook is global in scope. You can use the GetCurrentTask() API function to retrieve a handle to the current task.

The return value is a hook handle that you must save in a global variable for later use.

Windows can have multiple hooks installed at one time, and it even can have the same type of hook installed multiple times.

One other important thing to note is that any hook that operates at a system scope must be implemented from a DLL. If you use a hook only within the context of your application, then it's okay to implement it in the EXE.

Using the Hook Function

The values of the hook function's `Code`, `wParam`, and `lParam` parameters vary depending on the type of hook that is installed, and they are documented in the Windows API help. These parameters all have one thing in common: Depending on the value of `Code`, you are responsible for calling the next hook in the chain.

To call the next hook, use the `CallNextHookEx()` API function:

```
Result := CallNextHookEx(HookHandle, Code, wParam, lParam);
```

CAUTION

When calling the next hook in the chain, don't call `DefHookProc()`. This is another Windows 3.0-compatibility holdover.

Using the Unhook Function

When you want to release the Windows hook, you just need to call the `UnhookWindowsHookEx()` API function, passing it the hook handle as a parameter. Again, be careful not to call `UnhookWindowsHook()` here, because it is another old-style function:

```
UnhookWindowsHookEx(HookHandle);
```

Using *SendKeys*: A *JournalPlayback* Hook

If you come to Delphi from environments such as Visual Basic or Paradox for Windows, you might be familiar with a function called `SendKeys()`. `SendKeys()` enables you to pass it a string of characters that it then plays back as if they are typed from the keyboard, and all the keystrokes are sent to the active window. Because Delphi doesn't have a function such as this built in, creating one proves a great opportunity to add a powerful feature to Delphi as well as to demonstrate how to implement a `wh_JournalPlayback` hook from within Delphi.

Deciding Whether To Use a *JournalPlayback* Hook

There are a number of reasons why a hook is the best way to send keystrokes to your application or another application. You might wonder, "Why not just post wm_KeyDown and wm_KeyUp messages?" The primary reason is that the message queue for each application is only eight messages long, so posting any more than four key presses (a wm_KeyUp and a wm_KeyDown for each key press) to any window has the potential to overflow the message queue.

Also, you might not know the window handle of the window to which you want to send keystrokes. And, of course, if you don't know the handle, you can't send a message.

Understanding How *SendKeys* Works

The declaration of the SendKeys() function looks like this:

```
function SendKeys(S: String): TSendKeyError; export;
```

The TSendKeyError return type is an enumerated type that indicates the error condition. It can be any one of the following values:

Value	*Meaning*
sk_None	The function was successful.
sk_FailSetHook	The Windows hook could not be set.
sk_InvalidToken	An invalid token was detected in the string.
sk_UnknownError	Some other unknown but fatal error occurred.

S can include any alphanumeric character or @ for the Alt key, ^ for the Shift key, or ~ for the Shift key. SendKeys() also enables you to specify special keyboard keys in curly braces as depicted in the KEYDEFS.PAS unit in Listing 21.7.

Listing 21.7. KEYDEFS.PAS—special key definitions for SendKeys().

```pascal
unit Keydefs;

interface

uses WinTypes;

const
  MaxKeys = 24;
  ControlKey = '^';
  AltKey = '@';
  ShiftKey = '~';
  KeyGroupOpen = '{';
  KeyGroupClose = '}';

type
  TKeyString = String[7];
```

continues

Listing 21.7. continued

```
TKeyDef = record
  Key: TKeyString;
  vkCode: Byte;
end;

const
  KeyDefArray : array[1..MaxKeys] of TKeyDef = (
    (Key: 'F1';     vkCode: vk_F1),
    (Key: 'F2';     vkCode: vk_F2),
    (Key: 'F3';     vkCode: vk_F3),
    (Key: 'F4';     vkCode: vk_F4),
    (Key: 'F5';     vkCode: vk_F5),
    (Key: 'F6';     vkCode: vk_F6),
    (Key: 'F7';     vkCode: vk_F7),
    (Key: 'F8';     vkCode: vk_F8),
    (Key: 'F9';     vkCode: vk_F9),
    (Key: 'F10';    vkCode: vk_F10),
    (Key: 'F11';    vkCode: vk_F11),
    (Key: 'F12';    vkCode: vk_F12),
    (Key: 'INSERT'; vkCode: vk_Insert),
    (Key: 'DELETE'; vkCode: vk_Delete),
    (Key: 'HOME';   vkCode: vk_Home),
    (Key: 'END';    vkCode: vk_End),
    (Key: 'PGUP';   vkCode: vk_Prior),
    (Key: 'PGDN';   vkCode: vk_Next),
    (Key: 'TAB';    vkCode: vk_Tab),
    (Key: 'ENTER';  vkCode: vk_Return),
    (Key: 'BKSP';   vkCode: vk_Back),
    (Key: 'PRTSC';  vkCode: vk_SnapShot),
    (Key: 'SHIFT';  vkCode: vk_Shift),
    (Key: 'ESCAPE'; vkCode: vk_Escape));


function FindKeyInArray(Key: TKeyString; var Code: Byte): Boolean;

implementation

uses SysUtils;

function FindKeyInArray(Key: TKeyString; var Code: Byte): Boolean;
{ function searches array for token passed in Key, and returns the }
{ virtual key code in Code. }
var
  i: word;
begin
  Result := False;
  for i := Low(KeyDefArray) to High(KeyDefArray) do
    if UpperCase(Key) = KeyDefArray[i].Key then begin
      Code := KeyDefArray[i].vkCode;
      Result := True;
      Break;
    end;
end;

end.
```

After receiving the string, `SendKeys()` parses the individual key presses out of the string, and adds each of the key presses to a list in the form of message records containing `wm_KeyUp` and `wm_KeyDown` messages. These messages then are played back to Windows through a `wh_JournalPlayback` hook.

Creating Key Presses

After each key press is parsed out of the string, the virtual key code and message (the messages can be `wm_KeyUp`, `wm_KeyDown`, `wm_SysKeyUp`, or `wm_SysKeyDown`) are passed to a procedure called `MakeMessage()`. `MakeMessage()` creates a new message record for the key press and adds it to a list of messages called `MessageList`. The message record used here isn't the standard `TMessage` that you are familiar with, or even the `TMsg` record discussed in Chapter 9, "Understanding Messages." This record is called a `TEvent` message, and it represents a system queue message. The definition is

```
type
  PEventMsg = ^TEventMsg;
  TEventMsg = record
    message: Word;
    paramL: Word;
    paramH: Word;
    time: Longint;
  end;
```

The values for a `TEventMsg`'s fields are shown in Table 21.2.

Table 21.2. Values for `TEventMsg` fields.

`TEventMsg` *Field*	*Value*
Message	The message constant. Can be `wm_SysKeyUp` or `wm_SysKeyDown` for a keyboard message. Can be `wm_XButtonUp`, `wm_XButtonDown`, or `wm_MouseMove` for a mouse message.
wParam	If `Message` is a keyboard message, then the high byte contains the scan code, and the low byte contains the virtual key code. If `Message` is a mouse message, then `wParam` contains the X-coordinate of the mouse cursor (in screen units).
lParam	If a keyboard message, bits 0–14 indicate the repeat count, and bit 15 is the extended key flag. If a mouse message, `lParam` contains the Y-coordinate of the mouse cursor.
Time	The time, in system ticks, that the message occurred.

Because the table in the `KeyDefs` unit only maps to virtual key code, you must find a way to determine the scan code of the key given the virtual key code. Luckily, the Windows API provides a function called `MapVirtualKey()` that does just that. Listing 21.8 shows the source for the `MakeMessage()` procedure.

Listing 21.8. The `MakeMessage()` procedure.

```
procedure MakeMessage(vKey: byte; M: word);
{ procedure builds a TEventMsg record that emulates a keystroke and }
{ adds it to message list }
var
  E: PEventMsg;
begin
  New(E);                                { allocate a message record }
  with E^ do begin
    Message := M;                        { set message field }
    { high byte of ParamL is the vk code, low byte is the scan code }
    ParamL := MakeWord(vKey, MapVirtualKey(vKey, 0));
    ParamH := 1;                         { repeat count is 1 }
    Time := GetTickCount;                { set time }
  end;
  MessageList.Add(E);
end;
```

After the entire message list is created, the hook can be set in order to play back the key sequence. You do this through a procedure called `StartPlayback()`. `StartPlayback` primes the pump by placing the first message from the list into a global buffer. It also initializes a global that keeps track of how many messages have been played and flags that indicate the state of the Control, Alt, and Shift keys. This procedure then sets the hook. `StartPlayBack()` is shown in Listing 21.9.

Listing 21.9. The `StartPlayback()` procedure.

```
procedure StartPlayback;
{ Initializes globals and sets the hook }
begin
  { grab first message from list and place in buffer in case we }
  { get a hc_GetNext before and hc_Skip }
  MessageBuffer := TEventMsg(MessageList.Items[0]^);
  { initialize message count and play indicator }
  MsgCount := 0;
  { initialize Alt, Control, and Shift key flags }
  AltPressed := False;
  ControlPressed := False;
  ShiftPressed := False;
  { set the hook! }
  HookHandle := SetWindowsHookEx(wh_JournalPlayback, Play, hInstance, 0);
  if HookHandle = 0 then
    raise ESetHookError.Create('Couldn''t set hook')
  else
    Playing := True;
end;
```

As you might notice from the `SetWindowsHookEx()` call, `Play` is the name of the hook function. The declaration for `Play` follows:

```
function Play(Code: integer; wParam: word; lParam: Longint): Longint; export;
```

Here are its parameters:

Code	A value of hc_GetNext indicates that you should prepare the next message in the list for processing. You do this by copying the next message from the list into your global buffer. A value of hc_Skip means that a pointer to the next message should be placed into the lParam parameter for processing. Any other value means that you should call CallNextHookEx() and pass the parameters on to the next hook in the chain.
wParam	Unused.
lParam	If Code is hc_Skip, you should place a pointer to the next TEventMsg record in the lParam.
Return value	Return zero if Code is hc_GetNext. If Code is hc_Skip, return the amount of time (in ticks) before this message should be processed. If zero is returned, the message is processed. Otherwise, the return value should be the return value of CallNextHookEx().

Listing 21.10 shows the complete source code to the SENDKEY.PAS library.

Listing 21.10. The source code for the SendKey DLL.

```
library SendKey;

uses
 SysUtils, WinTypes, WinProcs, Messages, Classes, KeyDefs;

type
  { Error codes }
  TSendKeyError = (sk_None, sk_FailSetHook, sk_InvalidToken, sk_UnknownError);

  { exceptions }
  ESendKeyError = class(Exception);
  ESetHookError = class(ESendKeyError);
  EInvalidToken = class(ESendKeyError);

  { a TList descendant that knows how to dispose of its contents }
  TMessageList = class(TList)
  public
    destructor Destroy; override;
  end;

destructor TMessageList.Destroy;
var
  i: longint;
begin
  { deallocate all the message records before discarding the list }
  for i := 0 to Count - 1 do
    Dispose(PEventMsg(Items[i]));
  inherited Destroy;
end;
```

continues

Listing 21.10. continued

```
var
  { variables global to the DLL }
  MsgCount: word;
  MessageBuffer: TEventMsg;
  HookHandle: hHook;
  Playing: Boolean;
  MessageList: TMessageList;
  AltPressed, ControlPressed, ShiftPressed: Boolean;
  NextSpecialKey: TKeyString;

function MakeWord(L, H: Byte): Word;
{ macro creates a word from low and high bytes }
inline(
  $5A/            { pop dx }
  $58/            { pop ax }
  $8A/$E2);       { mov ah, dl }

procedure StopPlayback;
{ Unhook the hook, and clean up }
begin
  { if Hook is currently active, then unplug it }
  if Playing then
    UnhookWindowsHookEx(HookHandle);
  MessageList.Free;
  Playing := False;
end;

function Play(Code: integer; wParam: word; lParam: Longint): Longint; export;
{ This is the JournalPlayback callback function.  It is called by Windows }
{ when Windows polls for hardware events.  The code parameter indicates what }
{ to do. }
begin
  case Code of

    hc_Skip: begin
    { hc_Skip means to pull the next message out of our list. If we }
    { are at the end of the list, it's okay to unhook the JournalPlayback }
    { hook from here. }
      { increment message counter }
      inc(MsgCount);
      { check to see if all messages have been played }
      if MsgCount >= MessageList.Count then
        StopPlayback
      else
      { copy next message from list into buffer }
      MessageBuffer := TEventMsg(MessageList.Items[MsgCount]^);
      Result := 0;
    end;

    hc_GetNext: begin
    { hc_GetNext means to fill the wParam and lParam with the proper }
    { values so that the message can be played back.  DO NOT unhook }
    { hook from within here.  Return value indicates how much time until }
    { Windows should play back message.  We'll return 0 so that it's }
    { processed right away. }
      { move message in buffer to message queue }
```

```
      PEventMsg(lParam)^ := MessageBuffer;
      Result := 0  { process immediately }
    end

    else
      { if Code isn't hc_Skip or hc_GetNext, then call next hook in chain }
      Result := CallNextHookEx(HookHandle, Code, wParam, lParam);
  end;
end;

procedure StartPlayback;
{ Initializes globals and sets the hook }
begin
  { grab first message from list and place in buffer in case we }
  { get a hc_GetNext before and hc_Skip }
  MessageBuffer := TEventMsg(MessageList.Items[0]^);
  { initialize message count and play indicator }
  MsgCount := 0;
  { initialize Alt, Control, and Shift key flags }
  AltPressed := False;
  ControlPressed := False;
  ShiftPressed := False;
  { set the hook! }
  HookHandle := SetWindowsHookEx(wh_JournalPlayback, Play, hInstance, 0);
  if HookHandle = 0 then
    raise ESetHookError.Create('Couldn''t set hook')
  else
    Playing := True;
end;

procedure MakeMessage(vKey: byte; M: word);
{ procedure builds a TEventMsg record that emulates a keystroke and }
{ adds it to message list }
var
  E: PEventMsg;
begin
  New(E);                              { allocate a message record }
  with E^ do begin
    Message := M;                      { set message field }
    { high byte of ParamL is the vk code, low byte is the scan code }
    ParamL := MakeWord(vKey, MapVirtualKey(vKey, 0));
    ParamH := 1;                       { repeat count is 1 }
    Time := GetTickCount;              { set time }
  end;
  MessageList.Add(E);
end;

procedure KeyDown(vKey: byte);
{ Generates KeyDownMessage }
begin
  { don't generate a "sys" key if the Control key is pressed (Windows quirk) }
  if (AltPressed and (not ControlPressed) and (vKey in [Ord('A')..Ord('Z')])) or
     (vKey = vk_Menu) then
    MakeMessage(vKey, wm_SysKeyDown)
  else
    MakeMessage(vKey, wm_KeyDown);
end;
```

continues

Listing 21.10. continued

```
procedure KeyUp(vKey: byte);
{ Generates KeyUp message }
begin
  { don't generate a "sys" key if the Control key is pressed (Windows quirk) }
  if AltPressed and (not ControlPressed) and (vKey in [Ord('A')..Ord('Z')]) then
    MakeMessage(vKey, wm_SysKeyUp)
  else
    MakeMessage(vKey, wm_KeyUp);
end;

procedure SimKeyPresses(VKeyCode: Word);
{ This function simulates key presses for the given key, taking into }
{ account the current state of Alt, Control, and Shift keys }
begin
  { press Alt key if flag has been set }
  if AltPressed then
    KeyDown(vk_Menu);
  { press Control key if flag has been set }
  if ControlPressed then
    KeyDown(vk_Control);
  { if Shift is pressed, or shifted key and Control is not pressed... }
  if (((Hi(VKeyCode) and 1) <> 0) and (not ControlPressed)) or ShiftPressed then
    KeyDown(vk_Shift);    { ...press Shift }
  KeyDown(Lo(VKeyCode));  { press key down }
  KeyUp(Lo(VKeyCode));    { release key }
  { if Shift is pressed, or shifted key and Control is not pressed... }
  if (((Hi(VKeyCode) and 1) <> 0) and (not ControlPressed)) or ShiftPressed then
    KeyUp(vk_Shift);      { ...release Shift }
  { if Shift flag is set, reset flag }
  if ShiftPressed then begin
    ShiftPressed := False;
  end;
  { Release Control key if flag has been set, reset flag }
  if ControlPressed then begin
    KeyUp(vk_Control);
    ControlPressed := False;
  end;
  { Release Alt key if flag has been set, reset flag }
  if AltPressed then begin
    KeyUp(vk_Menu);
    AltPressed := False;
  end;
end;

procedure ProcessKey(S: String);
{ This function parses each character in the string to create the message list }
var
  KeyCode: word;
  Key: byte;
  index: integer;
  Token: TKeyString;
begin
  index := 1;
  repeat
    case S[index] of
```

```
      KeyGroupOpen : begin
      { It's the beginning of a special token! }
        Token := '';
        inc(index);
        while S[index] <> KeyGroupClose do begin
          { add to Token until the end token symbol is encountered }
          Token := Token + S[index];
          inc(index);
          { check to make sure the token is not too long }
          if (Length(Token) = 7) and (S[index] <> KeyGroupClose) then
            raise EInvalidToken.Create('No closing brace');
        end;
        { look for token in array, Key parameter will }
        { contain vk code if successful }
        if not FindKeyInArray(Token, Key) then
          raise EInvalidToken.Create('Invalid token');
        { simulate key press sequence }
        SimKeyPresses(MakeWord(Key, 0));
      end;

      AltKey : begin
        { set Alt flag }
        AltPressed := True;
      end;

      ControlKey : begin
        { set Control flag }
        ControlPressed := True;
      end;

      ShiftKey : begin
        { set Shift flag }
        ShiftPressed := True;
      end;

      else begin
      { A normal character was pressed }
        { convert character into a word where the high byte contains }
        { the Shift state and the low byte contains the vk code }
        KeyCode := vkKeyScan(MakeWord(Byte(S[index]), 0));
        { simulate key press sequence }
        SimKeyPresses(KeyCode);
      end;
    end;
    inc(index);
  until index > Length(S);
end;

function SendKeys(S: String): TSendKeyError; export;
{ This is the one entry point.  Based on the string passed in the S  }
{ parameter, this function creates a list of keyup/keydown messages, }
{ sets a JournalPlayback hook, and replays the keystroke messages.   }
var
  i: byte;
begin
  try
    Result := sk_None;                      { assume success }
    MessageList := TMessageList.Create;  { create list of messages }
```

continues

Listing 21.10. continued

```
    ProcessKey(S);                        { create messages from string }
    StartPlayback;                        { set hook and play back messages }
  except
    { if an exception occurs, return an error code, and clean up }
    on E:ESendKeyError do begin
      MessageList.Free;
      if E is ESetHookError then
        Result := sk_FailSetHook
      else if E is EInvalidToken then
        Result := sk_InvalidToken;
    end
    else
      { Catch-all exception handler ensures than an exception }
      { doesn't walk up into application stack }
      Result := sk_UnknownError;
  end;
end;

exports
  SendKeys index 2;

begin
end.
```

Understanding the Interface Unit

Listing 21.11 shows SKEYS.PAS, the small interface unit for SENDKEY.DLL. Place SKeys in the uses clause of units with which you want to use SendKeys().

Listing 21.11. The source code for SKEYS.PAS, the SENDKEY.DLL interface unit.

```
unit SKeys;

interface

type
  { Return values for SendKeys function }
  TSendKeyError = (sk_None, sk_FailSetHook, sk_InvalidToken, sk_UnknownError);

function SendKeys(S: String): TSendKeyError;

implementation

function SendKeys; external 'SendKey' index 2;

end.
```

Using *SendKeys( )*

In this section, you will create a small project that demonstrates the SendKeys() function. Start with a form that contains two TEdit components and one TButton, as shown in Figure 21.3. Call this project TESTSEND.

FIGURE 21.3.
The TESTSEND main form.

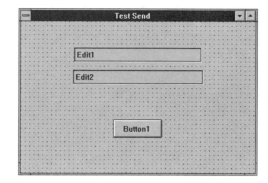

Listing 21.12 shows the source code for TESTSEND's main unit, MAIN.PAS. This unit includes event handlers for the OnDblClick event of Edit1 and the OnClick event of Button1.

Listing 21.12. The source code for MAIN.PAS, TESTSEND's main unit.

```
unit Main;

interface

uses
  SysUtils, WinTypes, WinProcs, Messages, Classes, Graphics, Controls,
  Forms, Dialogs, StdCtrls, Menus;

type
  TForm1 = class(TForm)
    Edit1: TEdit;
    Edit2: TEdit;
    Button1: TButton;
    procedure Edit1DblClick(Sender: TObject);
    procedure Button1Click(Sender: TObject);
  private
    { Private declarations }
  public
    { Public declarations }
  end;

var
  Form1: TForm1;

implementation

{$R *.DFM}
```

continues

Listing 21.12. continued

```
uses SKeys;

procedure TForm1.Edit1DblClick(Sender: TObject);
begin
  if SendKeys('~{DELETE}I Like{TAB}~delphi ~developers ~guide') <> sk_None then
    MessageDlg('Error with SendKeys.', mtError, [mbOk], 0);
end;

procedure TForm1.Button1Click(Sender: TObject);
var
  H: hWnd;
begin
 H := FindWindow('TAppBuilder', Nil);
 Winprocs.SetFocus(H);
 SendKeys('@HA@T@E@A@M');
end;

end.
```

After you double-click in Edit1, SendKeys() is called, and the following key presses are sent: Shift+Delete to delete the contents of Edit1. "I Like" then is typed into Edit1. A Tab character is sent, which moves the focus to Edit2, where Shift+D, "elphi," Shift+D, "elphi," Shift+G, "uide" are sent.

After Button1 is pressed, the FindWindow() API function is called to find the Delphi main window (Delphi must be running). When found, focus is set to the Delphi main window using the API SetFocus() function. At that point, SendKeys() is called, passing the following keystrokes: Alt+H to bring up the Help menu, and A to bring up the About box. Alt+TEAM then is typed to reveal an Easter egg!

Subclassing Forms

Although subclassing TForm descendants isn't strictly a hard-core topic, it's a powerful enough technique to merit a portion of this chapter. Delphi does not support the capability of being able to inherit from non-TForm components in the Form Designer. It is possible to descend from custom forms in source code, however. And it's surprisingly easy to do!

Making Nondirect *TForm* Descendants Child Windows

A good example of inheriting from a TForm is to use forms having a common ancestor as child forms inside a main form. This is a powerful technique that can enable you to create a complete UI in the Form Designer, for example, and then just "drop" it into another form or component in your source code.

Start by designing a main form and several child forms, as shown in Figures 21.4 through 21.8. Notice that the main form contains a TPanel, a TEdit, a TBitBtn, and a TTabSet component.

FIGURE 21.4.
The main form.

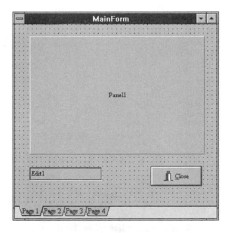

FIGURE 21.5.
Child Form 1.

FIGURE 21.6.
Child Form 2.

FIGURE 21.7.
Child Form 3.

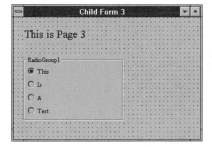

FIGURE 21.8.

Child Form 4.

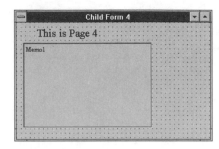

Remove the four child forms from the auto-create list shown in Options | Project | Forms. The child form units do not have any additional source code other than that provided by Delphi's skeleton, except for the fact that you should change the ancestor form in the class definition from TForm to TChildForm. Therefore, for example, the definition for TChildForm1 changes from

```
TChildForm1 = class(TForm);
```

to

```
TChildForm1 = class(TChildForm);
```

TChildForm is created nonvisually and declared in a separate unit called MPGlobal. The source code for MPGLOBAL.PAS is shown in Listing 21.13.

Listing 21.13. The source code for MPGLOBAL.PAS.

```
unit MPGlobal;

interface

uses Controls, Forms;

type
  TChildForm = class(TForm)
  protected
    procedure Loaded; override;
    procedure CreateParams(var Params:TCreateParams); override;
  end;

implementation

uses WinTypes;

procedure TChildForm.Loaded;
begin
  inherited Loaded;
  Visible := False;
  Position := poDefault;
  BorderIcons := [];
  BorderStyle := bsNone;
  HandleNeeded;
  SetBounds(0,0,Width,Height);
end;
```

```
procedure TChildForm.CreateParams(var Params:TCreateParams);
begin
  inherited CreateParams(Params);
  with Params do begin
    WndParent := Application.MainForm.Handle;
    Style := ws_Child or ws_ClipSiblings;
    X := 0;
    Y := 0;
  end;
end;

end.
```

In this unit, you override two of TForm's methods: Loaded() and CreateParams(). In the Loaded() method, you call the inherited and initialize some of the property values necessary to make the form work as desired. You also call the HandleNeeded() method to ensure that a window handle is created. Because you do this in the Loaded() method, this overrides any setting made at design time in the Object Inspector.

> **TIP**
>
> The Loaded() method is called after all of a component's parts have been loaded from the stream. This enables you to initialize stream-dependent parts of components that cannot be initialized in places such as the constructor or OnCreate event handler.

In the CreateParams() method, you assign the Application's main form to the Params.WndParent parameter. You also combine the ws_Child and ws_ClipSiblings styles into the Params.Style parameter using the or operator. This ensures that the TChildForm instance will be a child window and that it will not overlap with its sibling windows.

Listing 21.14 shows the source code for the main form's unit, MAIN.PAS.

Listing 21.14. The source code for MAIN.PAS, the main form's unit.

```
unit Main;

interface

uses
  SysUtils, WinTypes, WinProcs, Messages, Classes, Graphics, Controls,
  Forms, Dialogs, Tabs, ExtCtrls, StdCtrls, Buttons;

type
  TMainForm = class(TForm)
    TabSet1: TTabSet;
    BitBtn1: TBitBtn;
    Edit1: TEdit;
    Panel1: TPanel;
```

continues

Listing 21.14. continued

```
    procedure TabSet1Change(Sender: TObject; NewTab: Integer;
      var AllowChange: Boolean);
    procedure FormShow(Sender: TObject);
  private
    { Private declarations }
  public
    { Public declarations }
    ChildForm : array[0..3] of TForm;
  end;

var
  MainForm: TMainForm;

implementation

{$R *.DFM}

uses MP1,MP2,MP3,MP4;

procedure TMainForm.TabSet1Change(Sender: TObject; NewTab: Integer;
  var AllowChange: Boolean);
begin
  ChildForm[TabSet1.TabIndex].Hide;
  ChildForm[NewTab].Show;
end;

procedure TMainForm.FormShow(Sender: TObject);
var
  i : integer;
begin
  ChildForm[0] := TChildForm1.Create(Application);
  ChildForm[1] := TChildForm2.Create(Application);
  ChildForm[2] := TChildForm3.Create(Application);
  ChildForm[3] := TChildForm4.Create(Application);
  for i := 0 to 3 do begin
    { Set up the Panel parentage and adjust the tab order of the form. }
    ChildForm[i].Parent := Panel1;
    ChildForm[i].TabOrder := Panel1.TabOrder;
    with Panel1 do
      ChildForm[i].SetBounds(Left+2,Top+2,Width-4,Height-4);
  end;
  { Make the initial form visible }
  ChildForm[TabSet1.TabIndex].Show;
end;

end.
```

In the form's OnCreate handler, each of the child forms is created with the Application as the owner. Then Parent, TabOrder, and Size are set up for each of the child forms. The first child form then is made visible.

The TabSet acts as the form selector for the child forms. As the OnChange handler for TabSet1 shows, the current tab corresponds to the current child window being displayed.

The final result of this program shows two things. First, it is possible to descend from nondirect TForm descendants. Second, forms can be placed as children inside other controls, which helps to stimulate code reuse. Views of each of the child forms as a part of the main form are shown in Figures 21.9 through 21.12.

FIGURE 21.9.

Child form 1 as a child of the main form.

FIGURE 21.10.

Child form 2 as a child of the main form.

FIGURE 21.11.

Child form 3 as a child of the main form.

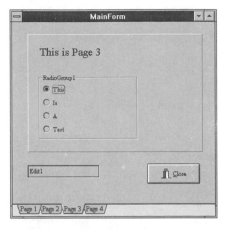

FIGURE 21.12.

Child form 4 as a child of the main form.

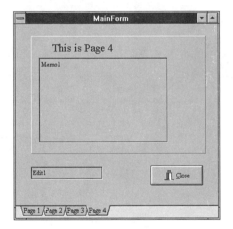

Summary

These "hard-core" topics ought to seem a bit softer and make much more sense to you now than they did when you started this chapter. You covered a pretty wide range of topics in this chapter: from low-level VCL issues such as form inheritance to low-level Windows API operations such as window hooks. As you have the need, you will be able to integrate these techniques into your future Delphi programs. In the next chapter, "Testing and Debugging," you'll learn about the debugging process and discover how to put Delphi's integrated debugger and Turbo Debugger to work for you.

22

Testing and Debugging

There are some programmers in the industry who believe that the knowledge and application of good programming practice makes the need for debugging expertise unnecessary. In reality, however, the two complement each other, and whoever masters both will reap the greatest benefits. This is especially true when there are multiple programmers working on different parts of the same program. It's simply impossible to completely remove the possibility of human error.

A surprising number of people say, "My code compiles okay, so I don't have any bugs, right?" Wrong. There is no correlation between whether a program compiles and whether it has bugs. Also, don't assume that because a particular piece of code worked yesterday or on another system, that it is bug-free. When it comes to hunting software bugs, everything should be suspected until proven innocent.

During the development of any application, you should allow the compiler to help you as much as possible. This can be done in Delphi by enabling all the runtime errors in Options|Project|Compiler (as shown in Fig. 22.1) or by enabling the necessary directives in your code. Many games of "chase the wild goose" have been played needlessly due to failure to use these effective compiler-aided tools. Table 22.1 describes the different runtime error options available through Delphi.

FIGURE 22.1.

The Project Options dialog box.

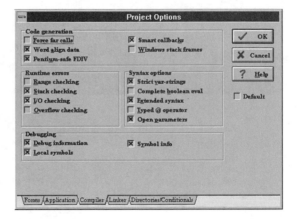

Table 22.1. Delphi runtime errors.

Runtime Error	Directive	Function
Range Checking	{$R+}	Checks to ensure that you don't index an array or string beyond its bounds.
Stack Checking	{$S+}	Checks to ensure that you don't try to use more stack then you have available.
I/O Checking	{$I+}	Checks for Input/Output error after every I/O call (ReadLn() and WriteLn(), for example). This almost always should be enabled.

Runtime Error	Directive	Function
Overflow Checking	{$Q+}	Checks to ensure that you don't overflow the value of an integral variable (try to store more than 64KB in a word, for example).

Keep in mind that each of these runtime errors do exact a performance penalty on your application. Therefore, once you are out of the debugging phase of development and are ready to ship a final product, you can improve performance by disabling some of the runtime errors.

Common Program Bugs

This next section shows you some commonly made mistakes that cause programs to fail or crash. If you know what to look for when you are debugging code, you can lessen the time it takes to find the error.

Using a Class Variable Before It Is Created

One of the most common bugs that creep up when you develop in Delphi occurs because you have used a class variable before it has been created. For example, take a look at the following code:

```
procedure Form1.Button1Click(Sender: TObject);
var
  MyStringList. TStringList;
begin
  MyStringList.Assign(ListBox1.Items);
end;
```

Here, the TEdit class MyEdit has been declared; however, it is used before it is instantiated. This is a sure way to cause a general protection fault. You must be sure to instantiate any class variables before you try to use them. The following code shows the correct way to instantiate and use a class variable. However, it also introduces another bug. Can you see it?

```
procedure Form1.Button1Click(Sender: TObject);
var
  MyStringList: TStringList;
begin
  MyStringList := TStringList.Create;
  MyStringList.Assign(ListBox1.Items);
end;
```

If your answer was, "You didn't free your TStringList class," you're correct. This won't cause your program to fail or crash, but it will eat up memory because every time you call this method, another TStringList is created and the old one is forgotten. The absolute correct version is shown in the following code—minus a necessary enhancement discussed in the following topic:

```
procedure Form1.Button1Click(Sender: TObject);
var
  MyStringList: TStringList;
begin
  MyStringList := TStringList.Create;                { Create it! }
  MyStringList.Assign(ListBox1.Items);               { Use it! }
  { Do your stuff with your TStringList instance }
  MyStringList.Free;                                 { Free it! }
end;
```

Ensuring that Class Instances Are Freed

Suppose that in the previous code example an exception occurs just after TStringList is created. None of the remaining code would be executed, which would cause a memory loss. Make sure that your class instances are freed, even if an exception occurs, by using a try..finally construct, as shown here:

```
procedure Form1.Button1Click(Sender: TObject);
var
  MyStringList: TStringList;
begin
  MyStringList := TStringList.Create;                { Create it! }
  try
    MyStringList.Assign(ListBox1.Items);             { Use it! }
    { Do your stuff with your TStringList instance }
  finally
    MyStringList.Free;                               { Free it! }
  end;
end;
```

After you read the section "Using Breakpoints," later in the chapter, try an experiment and place the following line right after the line where you assign ListBox1's items to the TStringList:

```
Raise Exception.Create('Test Exception');
```

Then place a breakpoint at the beginning of the method's code and step through the code. You'll see that TStringList still gets freed, even after the exception is raised.

Using the Uninitialized Pointer

The uninitialized, or wild, pointer bug is a common error that clobbers some part of memory. This usually happens when you declare some type of pointer a var section, but use the variable before allocating memory. On one machine, the pointer may appear to run just fine until you transfer it to another machine (and maybe make a few code changes in the process), where it begins to malfunction, leading you to believe that the recent changes you made are faulty or the second machine has a hardware problem. All the good programming practice in the world won't save you now. You can start adding WriteLns or MessageDlgs to strategic parts, but this changes your program's memory image and might cause the bug to move around—or worse, disappear! You need to make sure that you always allocate memory for a pointer before attempting to use it.

Using Uninitialized *PChars*

You often will see wild-pointer errors when you use PChar-type variables. Because a PChar is just a pointer to a string, you have to remember to allocate memory for the PChar by using the GetMem(), GlobalAlloc(), StrNew(), or StrAlloc() functions, as well as the FreeMem(), GlobalFree(), or StrDispose() functions to free them.

Dereferencing the Nil Pointer

Besides the wild pointer, another common mistake is dereferencing a Nil, or zero-value, pointer. Dereferencing a Nil pointer always causes a general protection fault. Although this isn't an error you want to have in your application, it isn't fatal. Because it doesn't actually corrupt memory, it's safe to use exception handling to take care of the exception and move along. The sample procedure in Listing 22.1 illustrates this point.

Listing 22.1. A procedure that generates a general protection fault and then recovers.

```
procedure GPFault;
var
  P: PByte;
begin
  P := Nil;
  try
    P^ := 1;
  except
    on EGPFault do
      MessageDlg('You can''t do that!!', mtError, [mbOk], 0);
  end;
end;
```

If you put this procedure in a program, you will see that the Message dialog box appears to inform you of the problem, but your program continues to run.

Using the Integrated Debugger

Delphi provides a pretty feature-rich debugger built right into the Integrated Development Environment (IDE). Most of the facilities of the integrated debugger can be found on the Run menu.

Using Command-Line Parameters

If your program is designed to use command-line parameters, you can specify them in the Run|Parameters dialog box. In this dialog box, simply type the parameters as you would on the DOS command-line or in the Program Manager Run dialog box.

Using Breakpoints

Breakpoints enable you to suspend the execution of your program whenever a certain line of code is reached. You can set a breakpoint by clicking to the far left of a line of code in the Code Editor, or by using the local menu. Whenever you want to see how your program is behaving inside a particular procedure or function, just set a breakpoint on the first line of code in that routine. Figure 22.2 shows a breakpoint set on a line of program code.

FIGURE 22.2.

A breakpoint set in the Code Editor.

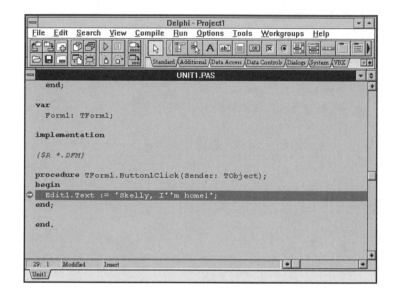

Using Conditional Breakpoints

You also can set a breakpoint to suspend the execution of your program based on some condition rather then when a line of code is reached. A typical example is when you want to examine the code inside of a loop construct. You probably don't want to suspend and resume execution every time your code passes through the loop, especially if the loop occurs hundreds of times. Instead of continually pressing the F9 key, just set a breakpoint to occur whenever a variable reaches a certain value. For example, in a new project, place a TButton on the main form and add the following code to the button's event handler:

```
procedure TForm1.Button1Click(Sender: TObject);
var
   i: integer;
begin
  for i := 1 to 100 do begin
    Caption := IntToStr(i);
    Button1.Caption := Caption;
  end;
end;
```

Now set a breakpoint on the line

```
Caption := IntToStr(i);
```

After you have set a breakpoint, select View|Breakpoints, which will bring up a Breakpoint List dialog box. Your breakpoint should show up in this list. Double-click your breakpoint to invoke the Edit Breakpoint dialog box. In the Condition input line, enter i=50 and select OK. This will cause the breakpoint that you previously set to suspend program execution only when the variable i contains the value 50.

Executing Code Line by Line

You can execute code line by line by using the Step Over (F8) or Trace Into (F7) option. Trace Into steps into your procedures and functions as they are called; Step Over executes the procedure or function immediately without stepping into it. Typically, you use these options after stopping somewhere in your code with a breakpoint. Get to know the F7 and F8 keys; they are your friends.

You also can tell Delphi to run your program up to the line the cursor currently inhabits by using the Run To Cursor (F4) option. This is useful particularly when you want to bypass a loop that is iterated many times, so that F7 or F8 become tedious.

You can breakpoint your code dynamically by using the Program Pause option. This option often helps you determine whether your program is in an infinite loop. Keep in mind that VCL code is being run most of your program's life, so you often will not stop on a line of your program's code with this option.

> **TIP**
>
> If your program is stuck in an infinite loop, pressing Ctrl+Alt+SysRq a few times usually bails you out.

Using the Watch Window

You can use the watch window to track the values of your program's variables as your code executes. Keep in mind that you must be in a code view of your program (a breakpoint should be executed) in order for the watch window to be accurate.

> **TIP**
>
> Don't lament over the integrated debugger's lack of a register window. If you want to view the value of a CPU register, simply insert a watch on the register you want to view (ax or ds, for example) as if it were a variable. This is shown in Figure 22.3.

FIGURE 22.3.

*Using the watch window
to view CPU registers.*

Using the Evaluate and Modify Options

The Evaluate and Modify options enable you to inspect and change the contents of variables, including arrays and records, on-the-fly as your application executes in the integrated debugger. Keep in mind that this feature does not enable you to access functions or variables that are out of scope.

Evaluating and modifying variables is perhaps one of the more powerful features of the integrated debugger, but with that power comes the responsibility of having direct access to memory. You must be careful when changing the values of variables, because it can affect the behavior of your program later.

Accessing the Call Stack

You can access the call stack by choosing View|Call Stack. This enables you to view function and procedure calls along with the parameters passed to them. The call stack is useful for seeing a road map of functions that were called up to the current point in your source code. A typical view of the Call stack window is shown in Figure 22.4.

FIGURE 22.4.

The Call stack window.

TIP

To view any procedure or function listed in the call stack window, simply right-click inside the window. This is a good trick for getting back to a function when you accidentally trace in too far.

Looking at Integrated Debugger Limitations

Arguably, the largest limitation of the integrated debugger is its inability to debug dynamic link libraries. When you need to debug a DLL, you'll need to use a lower-level debugger such as Borland's Turbo Debugger for Windows.

> **NOTE**
>
> Occasionally, while using Delphi's integrated debugger, you may see the message, "Could not stop due to hard mode." Such a message generally prompts the question, "What is hard mode?"
>
> *Hard mode* is a special modal or non-reentrant state of Windows, and in hard mode Windows doesn't allow message processing to take place. Because the integrated debugger is message-based, hard mode prevents debugger breakpoints from executing.
>
> Hard mode occurs when a menu is active, an application is activated, or for any variety of reasons that can crop up in the inner bowels of Windows. You usually can't do much other than continue when this occurs, but at least now you know what's going on.

Looking at the Turbo Debugger Features

Turbo Debugger for Windows (TDW) is a product that is available separately as an add-on to Delphi. Because of the wide selection of features, Borland's Turbo Debugger for Windows is very powerful and makes finding programming bugs easy. Although TDW debugs graphical Windows applications, it interacts with the user in text mode, so that the debugger doesn't get in the way of the program being debugged. This isn't quite as important on more stable platforms like the 32-bit Windows NT and upcoming Windows 95, but on the fragile 16-bit Windows 3.1*x*, it's very important. Turbo Debugger does have a mode that simulates a window on the graphics screen so that the complex action of switching between graphics and text modes need not be used.

All these features are explained in the Turbo Debugger User's Guide that comes with TDW. Although that material is not duplicated here, some of the lesser known but very powerful features that TDW offers are described.

The CPU Window

The CPU window in TDW consists of six panes of information: the CPU pane, the Selector pane, the Dump pane, the Register pane, the Flags pane, and the Stack pane (see Figure 22.5). Each of these panes enables the user to view important aspects of the processor.

FIGURE 22.5.

The Turbo Debugger CPU window.

CPU pane ————

Dump pane ————

Register pane

Flags pane

Stack pane

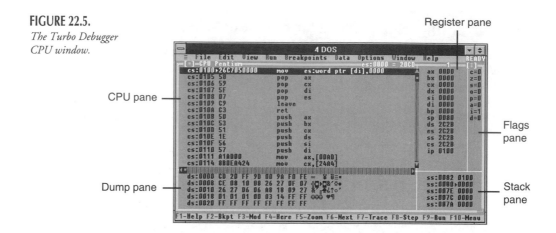

The CPU pane shows the opcodes and pneumonics of the disassembled assembly code that is being executed. You can position the CPU pane at any address anywhere in the machine to view instructions, or you can set the current instruction pointer to any new location, from where execution then continues. It is very helpful to be able to understand the assembly code that the CPU pane displays. Many bugs have been located by simply noticing the assembly code generated for a routine and realizing that it was not performing the desired operation. Someone who doesn't understand assembly language wouldn't be able to find such a bug as quickly.

The Selector pane is useful for determining the attributes of a selector (such as whether it is a valid selector), its limit, whether it is a code or data selector, and whether it currently is in memory. Many general protection faults occur because the selector trying to be used is invalid or out of range.

The Dump pane enables you to view the contents of any range of memory. There are many ways that it can be viewed: as bytes, words, longs, comps, floats, reals, doubles, extended, or in ASCII. Memory can be searched for a sequence of bytes or an ASCII string. The data can be modified directly, copied elsewhere, read in from disk, or written out to disk.

The Register and Flags panes are pretty straightforward. All the CPU registers and flags are displayed here and can be modified.

The Stack pane gives you a stack-based view of the memory that is used for your program stack. Values can be changed and addresses followed.

Breakpoints

Turbo Debugger has a rich set of breakpoints you can set to help you find bugs. Most people think of a breakpoint as an address marker where the debugger stops when the debugged program reaches that location. TDW refers to this as a breakpoint in which the action is to *break* when the condition is met. In addition to this classical type of breakpoint, TDW also offers the capability to log an expression to a log file, to execute another piece of code, or to enable or disable one or more other breakpoints.

Breaking

Breaking is the classic action for a breakpoint. The result of this action is for TDW to stop running the program and give control back to you so that you can look around before continuing.

Logging

Logging is handy if you don't want the program to stop running, but you do want to make a note of some parameters. Here, you can specify any expression to be evaluated and then written to the log window (if you don't expect very many lines) or to an associated disk file (for an unlimited number of lines). After the program runs, you can open the log window or the log file and analyze the data.

Executing

Executing is both powerful and dangerous. The debugger enables you to specify the name of a procedure or function to call when the breakpoint condition is met. Be careful with this, however, because you can cause very bizarre results if executing is used improperly.

Using Group Enable and Disable

Group Enable and Disable is one of the most powerful and time-saving features that TDW offers. Any breakpoint can be set up to enable or disable any other breakpoint, so that a very complex algorithm of breakpoints can be created to find very specific bugs. Suppose that you suspect that a bug occurred in your Paint method only after you choose a particular menu option. You could add a breakpoint to the Paint method, run the program, and constantly tell TDW to continue when you get barraged with hundreds of calls to your Paint method. Or, you could keep that breakpoint on your Paint method, disable it so that it doesn't fire, and add another breakpoint to your menu choice method to enable the Paint method breakpoint. Now you can run full speed in TDW and not break in your Paint handler until after you select the menu choice.

Using Turbo Debugger Advanced User API (*TDUSER*)

If you ever have said to yourself, "If only I could get TDW to do this…," then this feature is for you. The Advanced User API is designed to enable programmers to intercept some of the functionality of the debugger in order to change or enhance it. TDW enables you to do this when it sees a DLL specified in the USERDLL= line of the TDW.INI file. If the DLL has all the right exported functions, it gets loaded and called appropriately. Here are the functions that are provided:

- ■ `function UserAPIInit (var p: TTDUserInfoBlock): Integer;`

    This function is called once, when the debugger starts up, to allow for any initialization work. The parameter is a pointer to a record of various useful things in the debugger. The return value should be zero to signal to TDW that everything is OK, or nonzero for TDW to unload and not use the DLL.

- ■ `procedure UserAPIDone;`

    This procedure is called once, right before the debugger exits, allowing for any cleanup work.

- ■ `procedure UserAPIModuleLoad (ModName: PChar; Handle: longint);`

    This procedure is called once for each module that is loaded in the system. This includes the debugger, the debugee, and this DLL. If you need to know the module handle for something, this will give it to you.

- ■ `function UserAPIPollForKey (BIOSmode: integer): word;`

    This function is called when the debugger wants to check to see whether a key is waiting. Also, it is called to retrieve that key and to check for the "Shift" status. Simply return −1 to let the debugger check for or get the key, or return a scan code that you want to stuff into the debugger. The parameter BIOSmode will be set to the following:

Value	Meaning
0	Is a key waiting
1	Get the key
2	Get the Shift status

- ■ `function UserAPIKeyPressed (BIOSKeyCode: word): word;`

    This function is called for any key that comes in that the debugger wants to process. Return BIOSKeyCode to allow that key to be processed normally, return another scan code, or return −1 to prevent that key from being used.

- ■ `procedure UserAPIChildStart;`

    This procedure is called when the debugger is ready to switch to the debugee and run one or more statements. This could be a full program "run" or a statement step or trace.

- ■ `procedure UserAPIChildStop;`

    This procedure is called any time the debugee stops running and switches back to the debugger. This could be because of a breakpoint, a step, an exception, and so on. (The program state pointer in the record passed into UserAPIInit points to a flag in the debugger containing the reason for the stoppage.)

Looking at the Information in *TTDUserInfoBlock*

The information contained in TTDUserInfoBlock is as follows:

- InfoBlockSize: word;

  This holds the size of the record (in bytes). If the size you calculate differs from this value, then a newer version of the debugger may be using your DLL.

- APIVersion: word;

  This holds the version number of the UserAPI. You can use it to check versions.

- FPEvalFunc: TFarProc;

  This is a pointer to a function in the debugger that evaluates any string as if it were typed in the debugger's Evaluate/Modify window (Ctrl+F4). The result is placed into a string and can be used by the DLL at any time.

- CPUPtr: PCPU;

  This is a pointer to a record that contains a copy of the CPU registers for the debugee.

- p8087: PCoProc;

  This is a pointer to a record that contains a copy of the numeric coprocessor's registers for the debugee.

- PProgState: PByte;

  This is a pointer to a byte in the debugger that contains the state of the debugee. The values are defined in TDTYPES.PAS in the example.

- PScreenSel: PWord;

  This is a pointer to a word in the debugger that is the protected mode selector and can be read from or written to, to provide access to the video screen. Because the debugger is capable of being displayed on the VGA screen in text mode, in a window, or on a mono screen, this selector always points to the proper memory.

Looking at Some Sample Uses for *TDUSER* API

The example program, TDUSER.PAS and TDTYPES.PAS (shown in Listings 22.2 and 22.3, respectively), is a shell that can be used to develop your own custom TDUSER DLL. The example simply writes information about each of the called functions to a log file. Also, if Ctrl+Z is pressed when the debugger is running, the string specified in the TDW.INI file under the [TurboDebugger] section called UserString= is passed to the debugger's evaluate function and then written out to the log file. The log file is specified in that same section of the TDW.INI file called UserLog=. Here a couple of ideas:

- Complex macro recording and playback
- Logging of complex data to a file while the program runs

Listing 22.2. The source code for TDTYPES.PAS.

```pascal
unit TDTypes;
{ This unit contains the types and constants required to interface with TDW }
interface

uses WinTypes;

const
  ep_None          : Byte = 0;
  ep_CtrlBrk       : Byte = 1;
  ep_Trace         : Byte = 2;
  ep_Bkpt          : Byte = 3;
  ep_Term          : Byte = 4;
  ep_Loaded        : Byte = 5;
  ep_Running       : Byte = 6;
  ep_Swapped       : Byte = 7;
  ep_Step          : Byte = 8;
  ep_KeyIntr       : Byte = 10;
  ep_SysBkpt       : Byte = 11;
  ep_Global        : Byte = 12;
  ep_NMI           : Byte = 13;
  ep_HardBkp       : Byte = 14;
  ep_Exception     : Byte = 16;
  ep_FPError       : Byte = 17;
  ep_AllFrozen     : Byte = 18;
  ep_ThreadTerm    : Byte = 19;
  ep_Signal        : Byte = 20;
  ep_NewProcess    : Byte = 21;
  ep_WinBkpt       : Byte = 22;
  ep_ExcepFirstTry : Byte = 23;
  ep_ExcepUnexpected : Byte = 24;
  ep_ExcepTerminate  : Byte = 25;
  ep_SysError      : Byte = 27;

type
  Reg87 = extended;
  ControlFlags = word;
  StatusFlags  = word;
  RegisterTags = word;
  CPUFlags = longint;

  i387 = record
    OffSt: longint;
    Selector: word;
    Opcode: word;
  end;

  PCoProc = ^CoProc;
  CoProc = record
    cn: ControlFlags;
    filler1: word;
    st: StatusFlags;
    filler2: word;
    tg: RegisterTags;
    filler3: word;
    ip: i387;
    op: i387;
```

```
    reg: array[1..8] of Reg87;
  end;

  ProgOffset = longint;

  ProgAddr = record
    offset: ProgOffset;
    segment: word;
  end;

  PCPU = ^CPU;
  CPU = record
    uax, ubx, ucx, udx: longint;
    usp: longint;
    ubp: longint;
    usi: longint;
    udi: longint;
    fl: CPUFlags;
    csip: ProgAddr;
    uds: longint;
    uss: longint;
    ues: longint;
    ufs: longint;
    ugs: longint;
  end;

  PTDUserInfoBlock = ^TTDUserInfoBlock;
  TTDUserInfoBlock = record
    InfoBlockSize: word;
    APIVersion: word;
    fpEvalFunc: TFarProc;
    CPUPtr: PCPU;
    p8087: PCoProc;
    pProgState: PByte;
    pScreenSel: PWord;
  end;

implementation

end.
```

Listing 22.3. The source code for TDUSER.PAS.

```
Library TDUser;
{$S-}
{$R-}
uses TDTypes, WinTypes, WinProcs, SysUtils;
{
 TDUSER.PAS - Example source for TDW User API DLL

 This example will log all the functions and parameters to a log file.
 While the Debugger is running, pressing Ctrl+Z will invoke the
 evaluate function to calculate the value of a string listed in the
 TDW.INI file:
```

continues

Listing 22.3. continued

```
    [TurboDebugger]
    UserDLL=the path and name of this TDUSER.DLL
    UserString=The string that gets evaluated when Ctrl+Z is pressed
    UserLog=the file or device to write logging information to

 Written by Jeffrey J. Peters
}

type
  { function type for calling the Evaluate function in TDW }
  TEvalFunc = function(EvalString: PChar; ResultString: PChar): integer;

  { record for translating the Program State byte into a string }
  TModeBlock = record
    b: byte;
    s: string;
  end;

var
  EvalFunc: TEvalFunc;            { This holds the pointer to function }
  LogF    : TextFile;            { The File variable for writing the log }
  puib    : PTDUserInfoBlock;    { A pointer to the UserBlock record }
  mb: array[0..24] of TModeBlock; { Array to hold the Program State modes }
  TD_DS   : Word;               { A holder for the debugger's data segment }


function EvalExpr (str: string; var answer: string) : integer;
{ This function is a wrapper around the CDecl call to the Debugger's Evaluate }
{ function. }
var
  LocalEvalFunc: TEvalFunc;      { Local copy of pointer to Eval function }
begin
  @LocalEvalFunc := @EvalFunc;   { load up a local copy of this so that }
                                 { we can still access after changing DS }
  str[length (str)+1] := #0;     { prepare the string to make it 'PChar' like }
  asm
    push ds                      { save our DS for later }
    mov ds, [TD_DS]              { load up TDW's debugger }
    les di, [answer]             { get the seg, offset of answer off the stack}
    push es                      { push seg of answer }
    inc di                       { increment past the Pascal length byte... }
    push di                      { and push it }

    lea di, str                  { get the seg, offset of str off the stack}
    push ss                      { push seg of answer }
    inc di                       { increment past the Pascal length byte... }
    push di                      { and push it }

    call dword ptr [LocalEvalFunc]
    add sp, 8                    { clean up the stack after our CDecl call }
    pop ds                       { restore our DS }
    mov [result], ax
  end;
  answer[0] := char (strlen (PChar (@answer[1])));  { Add length byte }
end;
```

```
procedure UserProc;
{ This helper function gets called when the user presses the hot key }
var
  s1,s2 : string[128];
begin
  GetPrivateProfileString('TurboDebugger', 'UserString', 'SelectorInc',
                          PChar(@s1[1]), 80, 'TDW.INI');
  s1[0] := char (strlen (PChar (@s1[1])));  { Add length byte }
  writeln(LogF, '    EvalFunc: S1 called with: ', s1);
  EvalExpr(s1,s2);
  writeln(LogF, '    EvalFunc: ', s1, ' returns: ', s2);
end;

function UserAPIInit(var p: TTDUserInfoBlock): integer; export;
var
  LogName  : array[0..80] of char;
begin
  puib := @p;
  @EvalFunc := p.fpEvalFunc;
  asm mov [TD_DS], ss end;  {save the debugger's data segment for later use}
  GetPrivateProfileString('TurboDebugger', 'UserLog', 'c:\tduser.log',
                          LogName, 80, 'TDW.INI');
  AssignFile(LogF, StrPas (LogName));
  Rewrite(LogF);
  writeln(LogF);
  writeln(LogF, 'UserAPIInit: TDW User API DLL (Delphi 1.0) ');
  writeln(LogF, '  InfoBlockSize: $', IntToHex(p.InfoBlockSize, 4));
  writeln(LogF, '  APIVersion:    $', IntToHex(p.APIVersion, 4));
  writeln(LogF, '  fpEvalFunc:    $', IntToHex(Hiword(longint(p.fpEvalFunc)), 4),
          ':',IntToHex(Loword(longint(p.fpEvalFunc)), 4));
  writeln(LogF, '  CPUPtr:        $', IntToHex(Hiword(longint(p.CPUPtr)), 4),
          ':',IntToHex(Loword(longint(p.CPUPtr)), 4));
  writeln(LogF, '  p8087:         $', IntToHex(Hiword(longint(p.p8087)), 4),
          ':',IntToHex(Loword(longint(p.p8087)), 4));
  writeln(LogF, '  pProgState:    $', IntToHex(Hiword(longint(p.pProgState)), 4),
          ':',IntToHex(Loword(longint(p.pProgState)), 4));
  writeln(LogF, '  pScreenSel:    $', IntToHex(Hiword(longint(p.pScreenSel)), 4),
          ':',IntToHex(Loword(longint(p.pScreenSel)), 4));
  Result := 0;
end;

procedure UserAPIDone; export;
begin
  writeln(LogF, 'UserAPIDone:');
  writeln(LogF);
  CloseFile(LogF);
end;

procedure UserAPIModuleLoad(ModName: PChar; Handle: longint); export;
begin
  writeln(LogF, 'UserAPIModuleLoad: module: ', ModName,
          ' handle: $', IntToHex (Handle, 4));
end;
```

continues

Listing 22.3. continued

```pascal
procedure UserAPIModuleUnload(ModName: PChar; Handle: longint); export;
begin
  writeln (LogF, 'UserAPIModuleUnload: module: ', ModName,
                 ' handle: $', IntToHex (Handle, 4));
end;

function UserAPIKeyPressed(BIOSKeyCode: word): word; export;
begin
  writeln (LogF, 'UserAPIKeyPressed: key: $', IntToHex (BIOSKeyCode, 4));
  if BIOSKeyCode = $001A then begin    { $001A is scan code for Ctrl+Z}
    UserProc;
    Result := $FFFF;
  end
  else
    Result := BIOSKeyCode;
end;

function UserAPIPollForKey(BIOSMode: integer): word; export;
begin
  UserAPIPollForKey := $FFFF;
end;

function GetProgState (b: Byte): String;
{ This helper function translates a Program State into a string }
var
  x: Byte;
begin
  Result := 'Unknown';
  for x := 0 to 24 do
    if (b = mb[x].b) then
      Result := mb[x].s;
end;

procedure UserAPIChildStop; export;
var
  b: Byte;
begin
  b := puib^.pProgState^;
  writeln(LogF, 'UserAPIChildStop: (', GetProgState (b) , ')');
end;

procedure UserAPIChildStart; export;
begin
  writeln(LogF, 'UserAPIChildStart:');
end;

exports
  UserAPIInit,
  UserAPIDone,
  UserAPIModuleLoad,
  UserAPIModuleUnload,
  UserAPIKeyPressed,
  UserAPIPollForKey,
  UserAPIChildStop,
  UserAPIChildStart;
```

```
begin
  { Initialize the array of records that hold the value and string of }
  { each of the Program State values }
  mb[ 0].b:= ep_None        ; mb[ 0].s:='ep_None';
  mb[ 1].b:= ep_CtrlBrk     ; mb[ 1].s:='ep_CtrlBrk';
  mb[ 2].b:= ep_Trace       ; mb[ 2].s:='ep_Trace';
  mb[ 3].b:= ep_Bkpt        ; mb[ 3].s:='ep_Bkpt';
  mb[ 4].b:= ep_Term        ; mb[ 4].s:='ep_Term';
  mb[ 5].b:= ep_Loaded      ; mb[ 5].s:='ep_Loaded';
  mb[ 6].b:= ep_Running     ; mb[ 6].s:='ep_Running';
  mb[ 7].b:= ep_Swapped     ; mb[ 7].s:='ep_Swapped';
  mb[ 8].b:= ep_Step        ; mb[ 8].s:='ep_Step';
  mb[ 9].b:= ep_KeyIntr     ; mb[ 9].s:='ep_KeyIntr';
  mb[10].b:= ep_SysBkpt     ; mb[10].s:='ep_SysBkpt';
  mb[11].b:= ep_Global      ; mb[11].s:='ep_Global';
  mb[12].b:= ep_NMI         ; mb[12].s:='ep_NMI';
  mb[13].b:= ep_HardBkp     ; mb[13].s:='ep_HardBkp';
  mb[14].b:= ep_Exception   ; mb[14].s:='ep_Exception';
  mb[15].b:= ep_FPError     ; mb[15].s:='ep_FPError';
{ mb[16].b:= ep_AllFrozen   ; mb[16].s:='ep_AllFrozen';  } { 32-bit only }
{ mb[17].b:= ep_ThreadTerm  ; mb[17].s:='ep_Threadterm'; } { 32-bit only }
  mb[18].b:= ep_Signal      ; mb[18].s:='ep_Signal';
  mb[19].b:= ep_NewProcess  ; mb[19].s:='ep_NewProcess';
  mb[20].b:= ep_WinBkpt     ; mb[20].s:='ep_WinDkpt';
  mb[21].b:= ep_ExcepFirstTry ; mb[21].s:='ep_ExcepFirstTry';
  mb[22].b:= ep_ExcepUnexpected ; mb[22].s:='ep_ExcepUnexpected';
  mb[23].b:= ep_ExcepTerminate  ; mb[23].s:='ep_ExcepTerminate';
  mb[24].b:= ep_SysError    ; mb[24].s:='ep_SysError';
end.
```

Using Turbo Debugger Video API (*TDVIDEO*)

In order to alleviate the debugger from needing to support all the various video modes that it could be running on and switching between graphics mode and text mode, the TDVIDEO API was developed. This factors out the video-mode switching from TDW and places it in the hands of a separate DLL. Four TDVIDEO DLLs come with TDW:

TDWGUI.DLL   Simulates TDW in a "window" on the desktop. Because everything remains in graphics mode, no video mode switches need to occur and this DLL provides the most compatibility with all the different video cards on the market. This should be the only TDVIDEO DLL you ever need.

SVGA.DLL   Attempts to use some vaguely documented DDK calls inside the current Windows video driver. It tells the driver that a full screen DOS box is about to open and enables it to switch the video modes for it. It works on most video cards. The advantage to using this video DLL is that TDW can display itself much faster in real text mode (although the switch between text and graphics is slow on some video monitors).

DUAL8514.DLL	For special-purpose systems only. You need an 8514 video card and monitor, and a VGA card and monitor. This DLL enables TDW to be displayed in color text mode on the VGA screen, whereas Windows is displayed uninterrupted on the 8514 display.
STB.DLL	Also for special-purpose systems only. You need a multiscreen video card from STB Systems (like the MVP-2 or MVP-4). This card has two or four Tseng ET-4000 video chips on it and the same number of VGA monitor plugs. You can have Windows on one screen and TDW in color text mode on the other.

From time to time, people need custom TDVIDEO DLLs for special video hardware. This API makes it possible to write your own Video DLL, and you can obtain sample source code for custom TDVIDEO DLLs from Borland Technical Support.

Summary

This chapter gave you some insight into the debugging process. It showed you the common problems you might run into while developing applications. It also discussed the useful features of both the integrated and stand-alone debuggers. Finally, you were given a powerful API that enables you to perform complex debugging with the stand-alone debugger. It's important to remember that debugging is as much a part of programming as is writing code. Your debugger can be one of your most powerful allies in writing clean code, so take the time to know it well. In the next part of the book you will develop several real and completely functional applications using many of the techniques covered in this book's first part. The first application is a full-featured utility for viewing your system's vital statistics.

II

Real-World
Building Blocks

23

SysWatcher: A System Monitor

In this chapter, you learn how to create a full-featured utility designed to browse the vital parameters of your system. SysWatcher gives information such as free heap resources, Windows and DOS versions, DOS environment settings, and a list of loaded modules. You learn how to use all the Windows API functions that access these various parameters and how to integrate this information into a functional and aesthetic user interface.

There are a number of reasons why you'd want to get such information from Windows. Perhaps you are writing a program that needs to access DOS environment variables in order to find certain files. Or maybe you need to determine what modules are loaded in order to manually remove modules from memory. Of course, for many of us, learning how and being able to snoop vital system parameters is its own reward.

Prototyping the User Interface

Start by designing the application's user interface. You want to be able to have three pages of data: one for system information, one for the DOS environment, and one for loaded modules. TNotebook and TTabSet components are ideal for this situation—when you need to display different types of data elegantly on one form. You also need something in which to hold all those strings; for that, you place a TListBox on each page.

Drop the TNotebook and TTabSet on a form. They will become Notebook1 and TabSet1. Set the Alignment property of the Notebook1 to alTop. Place TabSet1 at the bottom of the TNotebook component, and set its alignment to alTop as well so that it aligns to the bottom of Notebook1. Edit the Tabs property of TabSet1, and add the following strings: "System", "Environment", and "Modules". Do the same with Notebook1's Pages property. Drop the TListBox component on each of the three pages of Notebook1.

You need to organize the System page (page 0) of Notebook1 into two columns: the first column should contain the item—free heap space, for example; and the second column should contain the value—the number of bytes free. To do this, you use an owner-draw listbox, which is explained in more detail later in this chapter. First, drop a THeader on this page to act as a header for the listbox columns, and set its Alignment property to alTop.

Set the Alignment property of each of the listboxes to alClient, so that they fill up the whole area of NoteBook1. Drop a TBitBtn on the form below TabSet1, and change its Kind property to bkClose. This button closes the application.

Follow the guidelines in Table 23.1 for modifying the properties for each component on the form. Figure 23.1 illustrates what your form should look like when you are done.

> **NOTE**
>
> Table 23.1 contains a Parent property for each component. The *parent* is the component that you should drop each component onto in the form designer.

Table 23.1. The SysWatcher main form.

Component	Parent	Property	Value
TForm1	*(none)*	Name	'TSysWatcherWin'
		Caption	'SysWatcher'
TNotebook	TForm1	Pages	'System'
			'Environment'
			'Modules'
		Alignment	alTop
TTabSet	TForm1	Tabs	'System'
			'Environment'
			'Modules'
		Alignment	alTop
THeader	TNoteBook, page 0	Alignment	alTop
		Sections	'Item'
			'Value'
TListBox	TNoteBook, page 0	Name	'SystemListBox'
		Alignment	alClient
		Style	lbOwnerDrawFixed
TListBox	TNoteBook, page 1	Name	'EnvListBox'
		Alignment	alClient
TListBox	TNoteBook, page 2	Name	'ModListBox'
		Alignment	alClient
TBitBtn	TSysWatcherWin	Kind	bkClose

FIGURE 23.1.

The SysWatcher main window.

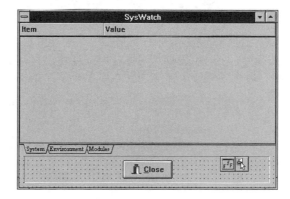

After typing the two strings into Header1's Sections property, you should slide the separator so that each section of the header takes up about half the header.

TIP

You can size the header sections dynamically at design time by placing the mouse cursor over the separator, clicking the right mouse button, and dragging to the desired location.

Formatting Info Strings

This application makes extensive use of the Format() function to format predefined strings with data determined at runtime. The strings that will be used are defined in a const section in the main unit as follows:

```
const
  { Win flags strings }
  CPUString    = 'Processor:' + Spacer + '%s';
  MathCoString = 'Math Coprocessor:' + Spacer + '%s';
  ModeString   = 'Windows Mode:' + Spacer + '%s';
  { Heap info strings }
  UHeapStr     = 'Free User heap:' + Spacer + '%d%% free';
  GDIHeapStr   = 'Free GDI heap:' + Spacer + '%d%% free';
  GlbHeapStr   = 'Free Global heap:' + Spacer + '%d bytes';
  { Version strings }
  WinVerStr    = 'Windows version:' + Spacer + '%d.%d';
  DOSVerStr    = 'DOS version:' + Spacer + '%d.%d';
  { Directory strings }
  WinDirStr    = 'Windows directory:' + Spacer + '%s';
  WinSysDirStr = 'Windows system dir:' + Spacer + '%s';
```

There are two primary reasons for using Format() with predefined strings rather than individually formatting string literals. First, Format() uses much less stack space than handling and combining strings individually. Second, Format() easily handles multiple data types. In this case, we use the %s and %d format strings to format string and numeric data.

NOTE

Use a double percent (%%) to display a single percent symbol in a formatted string.

Spacer is a constant used to separate the two columns of information in SystemListBox. Spacer is a non-printable ASCII character, in this case, #1:

```
const
  Spacer = #1;
```

Getting System Information

You will make use of a variety of API functions to get information about your system. As you will soon see, each function has its own special way of communicating information: through records, flags, numeric return values, or strings.

Determining Free Heap

The first bit of system information that you can put in SystemListBox is the various amounts of free heap space. To get this information, you need to make use of two Windows API functions: SystemHeapInfo() and GetFreeSpace().

SystemHeapInfo() takes by reference a TSysHeapInfo record. The fields of this record that you are concerned with are the wUserFreePercent field, which represents the free USERlocal heap, and the wGDIFreePercent field, which represents the free local GDI heap. Also, before you can call SystemHeapInfo(), you must initialize the dwSize field of the TSysHeapInfo record with the correct size value:

```
var
  Info: TSysHeapInfo;
begin
  Info.dwSize := SizeOf(TSysHeapInfo);
  SystemHeapInfo(@Info);
```

> **TIP**
>
> Don't forget to initialize the dwSize field of a TSysHeapInfo structure before calling SystemHeapInfo. Failure to do so probably will result in the failure of the function.

Now that the Info variable has been filled, you can use the fields to fill SystemListBox:

```
SystemListbox.Items.Add(Format(UHeapStr, [Info.wUserFreePercent]));
SystemListbox.Items.Add(Format(GDIHeapStr, [Info.wGDIFreePercent]));
```

The next call to make is to GetFreeSpace(). This function takes one parameter (which it actually ignores) and returns a longint representing the number of free bytes on the global heap:

```
SystemListbox.Items.Add(Format(GlbHeapStr, [GetFreeSpace(0)]));
```

For more information on the global heap, see the "Thanks for the Memories" sidebar in Chapter 3, "The Object Pascal Language."

Getting the OS Version

You can find out what versions of DOS and Windows you are running under by making a call to the GetVersion() API function. GetVersion() returns a 32-bit value that can be mapped to the following record to easily extract version information:

```
type
  TOSVersion = record
    WinVerMajor: Byte;
    WinVerMinor: Byte;
    DOSVerMinor: Byte;
    DOSVerMajor: Byte;
  end;
```

The following code uses GetVersion() and places the formatted output into SystemListBox:

```
type
  l: longint;
  Version: TOSVersion;
begin
  l := GetVersion;
  Version := TOSVersion(l);
  SystemListbox.Items.Add(Format(WinVerStr, [Version.WinVerMajor,
                          Version.WinVerMinor]));
  SystemListbox.Items.Add(Format(DOSVerStr, [Version.DOSVerMajor,
                          Version.DOSVerMinor]));
```

Getting Processor Information

To get information about the processor and coprocessor, use the GetWinFlags() function. This function returns a longint bitfield value. You can check for the presence of certain flags in this bitfield to determine system parameters:

```
var
  WinFlags: longint;
begin
  WinFlags := GetWinFlags;
  if LongBool(WinFlags and wf_CPU286) then DoSomething
```

This code masks all but the wf_CPU286 bit of WinFlags to determine whether this flag is set. The typecast to LongBool evaluates the expression to true if the flag is contained within WinFlags.

> **NOTE**
>
> Casting an ordinal expression to a LongBool (or to one of its cousins, ByteBool or WordBool), returns True if the expression was non-zero and False if the expression was 0. This makes that typecast a very handy tool for determining whether an expression evaluates to 0, because instead of typing
>
> if *Expression* <> 0 then *DoSomething*
>
> you can cast the expression to one of the *xxxx*Bool types:
>
> if LongBool(*Expression*) then *DoSomething*

Use LongBool on four-byte expressions (longints), WordBool on two-byte expressions (words and integers), and ByteBool on one-byte expressions.

The following code checks for the presence of the other CPU flags to determine the processor type. It sets a local variable called TempStr to the name of the processor:

```
WinFlags := GetWinFlags;
TempStr := '???';
if LongBool(WinFlags and wf_CPU286) then
  TempStr := '80286'
else if LongBool(WinFlags and wf_CPU386) then
  TempStr := '80386'
else if LongBool(WinFlags and wf_CPU486) then
  TempStr := '80486';
```

You then can add the processor name to a constant string using the Format() function and put the resultant string in a listbox, as shown in the following example:

```
SystemListbox.Items.Add(Format(CPUString, [TempStr]));
```

There are also wf_80x87 and wf_Enhanced flags you can use to determine, respectively, the presence of a math coprocessor and whether Windows is currently running in 386 Enhanced mode:

```
if LongBool(WinFlags and wf_80x87) then
  TempStr := 'Present'
else
  TempStr := 'None';
SystemListbox.Items.Add(Format(MathCoString, [TempStr]));

if LongBool(WinFlags and wf_Enhanced) then
  TempStr := 'Enhanced'
else
  TempStr := 'Standard';
SystemListbox.Items.Add(Format(ModeString, [TempStr]));
```

NOTE

For more information on what flags you can check for in GetWinFlags, see the Windows API help file topic "GetWinFlags."

Getting Windows Directory Information

You can learn the location of the Windows and Windows system directories by using the GetWindowsDirectory() and GetSystemDirectory() functions. There's nothing too fancy about these functions; they take a buffer and buffer size as parameters, and return a null-terminated string in the buffer. A non-zero value indicates that the function, for some reason, failed. The following code shows an example of using these functions:

```
const
  PathArraySize = 144;
var
  PathArray: array[0..PathArraySize] of Char;
begin
if GetWindowsDirectory(PathArray, PathArraySize) <> 0 then
    SystemListbox.Items.Add(Format(WinDirStr, [PathArray]));
  if GetSystemDirectory(PathArray, PathArraySize) <> 0 then
    SystemListbox.Items.Add(Format(WinSysDirStr, [PathArray]));
```

Getting the DOS Environment

Obtaining all the DOS environment variables—such as Sets, Path, and Prompt—is easy, thanks to the GetDOSEnvironment() API function. This function takes no parameters and returns a null-separated list of environment strings. The format of this list is a string, followed by a null, followed by a string, followed by a null, and so on, until the entire string is terminated with a double null (#0#0). The following function takes the output from the GetDOSEnvironment() function and places into the EnvListBox:

```
procedure TSysWatchWin.GetEnvStrings;
var
  P: PChar;
begin
  EnvListbox.Items.Clear;
  P := GetDOSEnvironment;
  repeat
    EnvListbox.Items.Add(StrPas(P));   { add string }
    P := P + StrLen(P) + 1;            { increment past string and null }
  until P^ = #0;                       { until double-null is reached }
end;
```

> **NOTE**
>
> The GetEnvStrings() method takes advantage of Object Pascal's capability to do pointer arithmetic on PChar-type strings. PChars are the only type in Object Pascal with which pointer arithmetic is allowed.

Walking the Module List

By using the ModuleFirst() and ModuleNext() functions from the Windows API TOOLHELP.DLL, you can traverse the list of all modules currently loaded in Windows. The following method demonstrates the process of iterating through the module list, and writing the path and name of each module to ModListBox. The pathname of the module is received from the szExePath fields of TModuleEntry record:

```
uses ToolHelp;

procedure TSysWatchWin.GetTheTasks;
var
  Module: TModuleEntry;
begin
  ModListbox.Items.Clear;
  Module.dwSize := SizeOf(Module);
  if ModuleFirst(@Module) then begin
    repeat
      ModListbox.Items.Add(StrPas(Module.szExePath));
    until ModuleNext(@Module) = False;
  end
  else ModListBox.Items.Add('Couldn''t retrieve modules');
end;
```

NOTE

Make certain to initialize the value of the `dwSize` field of the `TModuleEntry` record before passing it to `ModuleFirst()`. Failure to do so results in `ModuleFirst()` returning `False` for an error.

TOOLHELP.DLL

TOOLHELP.DLL is a dynamic link library that is provided as a part of the Windows API. It contains a number of functions designed to help the system-level Windows programmer. You can get a list of all the functions and procedures ToolHelp provides by searching on "ToolHelp Functions (3.1)" in the Windows API portion of the online Delphi Help file.

Many of the functions in ToolHelp refer to three common topics:

Module	A module refers to a dynamic link library, an executable, a driver, or a font that currently is loaded in Windows. Each of these modules is assigned a module-instance handle by Windows.
Instance	Windows creates a unique instance handle for every instance of an executable that is loaded (DLLs and drivers are loaded only once). Therefore, there can be multiple instance handles for any one module. Only one set of code is loaded for any given module, but each instance of each module has its own data. An instance handle also is referred to as a *data-instance handle* because every instance of a module has its own data segment.
Task	Every instance of every currently running executable is assigned a task-instance handle by Windows. Windows uses the task-instance handle to manage scheduling of processing time for different applications.

Using an Owner-Draw Listbox

Recall that you gave SystemListBox the style of lbOwnerDrawFixed. Setting this style means that you have to handle the OnDrawItem event in order to get your listbox to display strings. An OnDrawItem event passes you four parameters, as shown in Table 23.2.

Table 23.2. OnDrawItem parameters.

Parameter	Type	Purpose
Control	TWinControl	This is the instance of the control to be drawn.
Index	integer	This is the index into the component's item list of the item to be drawn.
Rect	TRect	This is the Rect in which the drawing should occur.
State	TOwnerDrawState	Reveals whether the item to be drawn is selected, disabled, or focused.

The idea is that you will divide Rect into two separate rectangles, and draw each half of the system string into each rectangle. The first rectangle will start at the beginning of the listbox, but the second rectangle will start at the x-axis location of Header1's section divider. The following code shows how to use owner-draw to render this application's strings in the listbox:

```
procedure TSysWatchWin.SystemListBoxDrawItem(Control: TWinControl;
   Index: Integer; Rect: TRect; State: TOwnerDrawState);
var
  S1, S2: String;
  A: array[0..255] of Char;
  P: Integer;
begin
  { Get the position of the spacer}
  P := Pos(Spacer, SystemListbox.Items[Index]);
  { S1 := string before spacer }
  S1 := Copy(SystemListbox.Items[Index], 1, P - 1);
  {S2 := string after spacer }
  S2 := Copy(SystemListbox.Items[Index], P + 1,
             Length(SystemListbox.Items[Index]));
  { clear out Rect }
  SystemListbox.Canvas.FillRect(Rect);
  { Draw S1 into the first Rect }
  DrawText(SystemListbox.Canvas.Handle, StrPCopy(A, S1), -1, Rect, dt_SingleLine
           or dt_Left or dt_VCenter);
  { Adjust Rect to start at Header1's section divider }
  Rect.Left := Header1.SectionWidth[0];
  { Draw S2 into the second Rect }
  DrawText(SystemListbox.Canvas.Handle, StrPCopy(A, S2), -1, Rect, dt_SingleLine
           or dt_Left or dt_VCenter);
end;
```

To complete the link between SystemListBox and Header1, make it so that SystemListBox re-draws itself dynamically as you size Header1. Create an event handler for Header1.OnSizing, and cause SystemListBox to repaint inside that handler:

```
procedure TSysWatchWin.Header1Sizing(Sender: TObject; ASection,
    AWidth: Integer);
begin
  SystemListbox.Invalidate;
end;
```

Finishing Touches

You also should hook TabSet1 and Notebook1 together so that Notebook1's page changes as you select a new tab. Do that by using this standard bit of code in TabSet1's OnChange handler:

```
procedure TSysWatchWin.TabSet1Change(Sender: TObject; NewTab: Integer;
  var AllowChange: Boolean);
begin
  if NewTab <> TabSet1.TabIndex then
    Notebook1.PageIndex := NewTab
  else
    AllowChange := False;
end;
```

As a finishing touch, drop a TBevel, a TPopupMenu, and a TFontDialog on the form. Make the TBevel component surround the button on the bottom of the screen to give it the 3D look shown in Figures 23.2 through 23.4. Define the following menu items for PopupMenu1: Font, Reread, and Exit. Select PopupMenu1 into SysWatchWin's PopupMenu property.

When Font is selected on PopupMenu1, bring up FontDialog1 and, if executed properly, assign SysWatchWin.Font to FontDialog.Font as in the following code:

```
procedure TSysWatchWin.Font1Click(Sender: TObject);
begin
  if FontDialog1.Execute then
    Font := FontDialog1.Font;
end;
```

When Exit is selected, cause the application to close; when Reread is selected, cause the application to update the listboxes. The logic for this is shown in Listing 23.2.

By now, you should have a very good idea how the SysWatcher application works. SysWatcher has built on a number of concepts that you learned in Part I, "Getting Started," such as calling API procedures, using the TNotebook and TTabSet components, and using GDI functions. It also gave you a bit more knowledge to build on, such as using the functions in ToolHelp, casting ordinal values to the LongBool family of types, and owner-draw listboxes. Figures 23.2 through 23.4 show each page of the SysWatcher while it is running. Listings 23.1 and 23.2 contain the complete source code for the SysWatcher.

FIGURE 23.2.

The SysWatcher's System page.

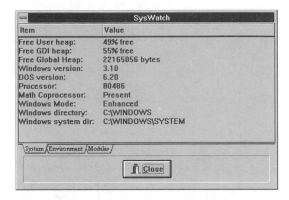

FIGURE 23.3.

The SysWatcher's Environment page.

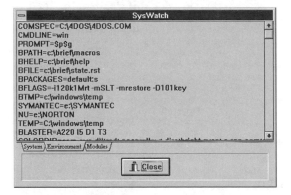

FIGURE 23.4.

The SysWatcher's Modules page.

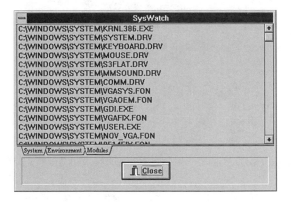

Listing 23.1. The source code for SYSWATCH.DPR.

```
program SysWatch;

uses
  Forms,
  Sysmain in 'SYSMAIN.PAS' {SysWatchWin};

{$R *.RES}

begin
  Application.CreateForm(TSysWatchWin, SysWatchWin);
  Application.Run;
end.
```

Listing 23.2. The source code for SYSMAIN.PAS.

```
unit SysMain;

interface

uses
  SysUtils, WinTypes, WinProcs, Messages, Classes, Graphics, Controls,
  Forms, Dialogs, Menus, ExtCtrls, ToolHelp, StdCtrls, Buttons, Tabs;

type
  TOSVersion = record
     WinVerMajor: Byte;
     WinVerMinor: Byte;
     DOSVerMinor: Byte;
     DOSVerMajor: Byte;
  end;

  TSysWatchWin = class(TForm)
    PopupMenu1: TPopupMenu;
    Font1: TMenuItem;
    N1: TMenuItem;
    Exit1: TMenuItem;
    FontDialog1: TFontDialog;
    BitBtn1: TBitBtn;
    Recheck1: TMenuItem;
    Notebook1: TNotebook;
    SystemListBox: TListBox;
    Header1: THeader;
    TabSet1: TTabSet;
    EnvListBox: TListBox;
    ModListBox: TListBox;
    Bevel1: TBevel;
    procedure Exit1Click(Sender: TObject);
    procedure Font1Click(Sender: TObject);
    procedure SystemListBoxDrawItem(Control: TWinControl; Index: Integer;
      Rect: TRect; State: TOwnerDrawState);
    procedure FormCreate(Sender: TObject);
    procedure Header1Sizing(Sender: TObject; ASection, AWidth: Integer);
    procedure Recheck1Click(Sender: TObject);
```

continues

Listing 23.2. continued

```pascal
    procedure TabSet1Change(Sender: TObject; NewTab: Integer;
      var AllowChange: Boolean);
  private
    procedure ReadAll;
    procedure GetSystemVitals;
    procedure GetEnvStrings;
    procedure GetTheTasks;
  end;

var
  SysWatchWin: TSysWatchWin;

implementation

{$R *.DFM}

const
  PathArraySize = 144;
  Spacer = #1;
  { Win flags strings }
  CPUString    = 'Processor:' + Spacer + '%s';
  MathCoString = 'Math Coprocessor:' + Spacer + '%s';
  ModeString   = 'Windows Mode:' + Spacer + '%s';
  { Heap info strings }
  UHeapStr     = 'Free User heap:' + Spacer + '%d%% free';
  GDIHeapStr   = 'Free GDI heap:' + Spacer + '%d%% free';
  GlbHeapStr   = 'Free Global heap:' + Spacer + '%d bytes';
  { Version strings }
  WinVerStr    = 'Windows version:' + Spacer + '%d.%d';
  DOSVerStr    = 'DOS version:' + Spacer + '%d.%d';
  { Directory strings }
  WinDirStr    = 'Windows directory:' + Spacer + '%s';
  WinSysDirStr = 'Windows system dir:' + Spacer + '%s';

procedure TSysWatchWin.GetSystemVitals;
var
  Info: TSysHeapInfo;
  Version: TOSVersion;
  WinFlags: Longint;
  l: longint;
  TempStr: String[32];
  PathArray: array[0..PathArraySize] of Char;
begin
  SystemListbox.Items.Clear;

  { Get heap information }
  Info.dwSize := SizeOf(TSysHeapInfo);
  SystemHeapInfo(@Info);
  SystemListbox.Items.Add(Format(UHeapStr, [Info.wUserFreePercent]));
  SystemListbox.Items.Add(Format(GDIHeapStr, [Info.wGDIFreePercent]));
  SystemListbox.Items.Add(Format(GlbHeapStr, [GetFreeSpace(0)]));

  { Get Windows and DOS versions }
  l := GetVersion;
  Version := TOSVersion(l);
  SystemListbox.Items.Add(Format(WinVerStr, [Version.WinVerMajor,
                          Version.WinVerMinor]));
```

```
      SystemListbox.Items.Add(Format(DOSVerStr, [Version.DOSVerMajor,
                              Version.DOSVerMinor]));

      { Get CPU and math co info }
      WinFlags := GetWinFlags;
      TempStr := '???';
      if LongBool(WinFlags and wf_CPU286) then
        TempStr := '80286'
      else if LongBool(WinFlags and wf_CPU386) then
        TempStr := '80386'
      else if LongBool(WinFlags and wf_CPU486) then
        TempStr := '80486';
      SystemListbox.Items.Add(Format(CPUString, [TempStr]));

      if LongBool(WinFlags and wf_80x87) then
        TempStr := 'Present'
      else
        TempStr := 'None';
      SystemListbox.Items.Add(Format(MathCoString, [TempStr]));

      if LongBool(WinFlags and wf_Enhanced) then
        TempStr := 'Enhanced'
      else
        TempStr := 'Standard';
      SystemListbox.Items.Add(Format(ModeString, [TempStr]));

      { Get Windows directory info }
      if GetWindowsDirectory(PathArray, PathArraySize) <> 0 then
        SystemListbox.Items.Add(Format(WinDirStr, [PathArray]));
      if GetSystemDirectory(PathArray, PathArraySize) <> 0 then
        SystemListbox.Items.Add(Format(WinSysDirStr, [PathArray]));
    end;

procedure TSysWatchWin.GetEnvStrings;
var
  P: PChar;
begin
  EnvListbox.Items.Clear;
  P := GetDOSEnvironment;
  repeat
    EnvListbox.Items.Add(StrPas(P));
    P := P + StrLen(P) + 1;
  until P^ = #0;
end;

procedure TSysWatchWin.GetTheTasks;
var
  Module: TModuleEntry;
begin
  ModListbox.Items.Clear;
  Module.dwSize := SizeOf(Module);
  if ModuleFirst(@Module) then begin
    repeat
      ModListbox.Items.Add(StrPas(Module.szExePath));
    until ModuleNext(@Module) = False;
  end
  else ModListBox.Items.Add('Couldn''t retrieve modules');
end;
```

continues

Listing 23.2. continued

```
procedure TSysWatchWin.Exit1Click(Sender: TObject);
begin
  Close;
end;

procedure TSysWatchWin.Font1Click(Sender: TObject);
begin
  if FontDialog1.Execute then
    Font := FontDialog1.Font;
end;

procedure TSysWatchWin.SystemListBoxDrawItem(Control: TWinControl;
    Index: Integer; Rect: TRect; State: TOwnerDrawState);
var
  S1, S2: String;
  A: array[0..255] of Char;
  P: Integer;
begin
  { Get the position of the spacer}
  P := Pos(Spacer, SystemListbox.Items[Index]);
  { S1 := string before spacer }
  S1 := Copy(SystemListbox.Items[Index], 1, P - 1);
  { S2 := string after spacer }
  S2 := Copy(SystemListbox.Items[Index], P + 1,
             Length(SystemListbox.Items[Index]));
  { clear out Rect }
  SystemListbox.Canvas.FillRect(Rect);
  { Draw S1 into the first Rect }
  DrawText(SystemListbox.Canvas.Handle, StrPCopy(A, S1), -1, Rect, dt_SingleLine
          or dt_Left or dt_VCenter);
  { Adjust Rect to start at Header1's section divider }
  Rect.Left := Header1.SectionWidth[0];
  { Draw S2 into the second Rect }
  DrawText(SystemListbox.Canvas.Handle, StrPCopy(A, S2), -1, Rect, dt_SingleLine
          or dt_Left or dt_VCenter);
end;

procedure TSysWatchWin.ReadAll;
begin
  GetEnvStrings;
  GetSystemVitals;
  GetTheTasks;
end;

procedure TSysWatchWin.FormCreate(Sender: TObject);
begin
  Notebook1.PageIndex := TabSet1.TabIndex;
  ReadAll;
end;

procedure TSysWatchWin.Header1Sizing(Sender: TObject; ASection,
    AWidth: Integer);
begin
  SystemListbox.Invalidate;
end;
```

```
procedure TSysWatchWin.Recheck1Click(Sender: TObject);
begin
  ReadAll;
end;

procedure TSysWatchWin.TabSet1Change(Sender: TObject; NewTab: Integer;
  var AllowChange: Boolean);
begin
  if NewTab <> TabSet1.TabIndex then
    Notebook1.PageIndex := NewTab
  else
    AllowChange := False;
end;

end.
```

Summary

This chapter demonstrated techniques for accessing system information from within your Delphi programs. You learned a few new API functions along the way, including functions to retrieve heap information and a function to retrieve DOS environment variables. Additionally, you learned some advanced listbox techniques such as dynamically sizable headers and owner-draw. In the next chapter, "Building an Address Book Application," you learn some real-world techniques for writing database applications.

24

Building an Address Book Application

The previous chapters taught you some important techniques for developing robust applications with Delphi. This chapter guides you through developing your first real application that uses and builds on the techniques you already have learned.

The Address Book application uses Delphi's database features and employs the various database components you learned in Chapter 16, "Writing Database Applications." By using these components, you will give the Address Book the capability to browse, add, edit, and delete both business and non-business addresses.

The Address Book uses Paradox tables to store its address data. The address table was created using the Database Desktop. You may do the same, or just use the existing table in the \SOURCE\DATA directory on the CD-ROM accompanying this book. The tables you need for this application are ADDRESS.DB, which stores the actual address information, and STATES.DB, which is a lookup table for state abbreviations. In the sample application, the alias DDGLOCAL, is used which points to the tables on the CD. You'll have to copy the tables to your local drive and modify the alias to point to them using the Borland Database Engine Configuration utility. Refer to your Delphi documentation to see how to use this utility.

The Address Book also uses Clipboard techniques from Chapter 14, "Sharing Information with the Clipboard and DDE," to copy and paste data to and from the Clipboard using custom and text formats.

Defining the Application

The first step in developing an application usually is to define the user needs or requirements for a process the application intends to automate. With larger applications, this can mean doing an entire system analysis before any actual coding even begins. Such a task can last weeks or even months, depending on the complexity of the project. When that information is gathered, a specification is drawn up defining how the application will meet those needs. The Address Book application is fairly straightforward, so you don't require such an analysis—a simple feature list will do. The topic of system analysis is far beyond the scope of this book, and there are many books that are devoted to covering this topic only. Future chapters in this book assume that you know the user requirements, so only feature lists are provided to meet those needs.

Looking at the Feature List

The Address Book application will contain the following features:

- Capability to add, edit, and delete address records
- A TTabSet with the letters A through Z specifying the letter of the last name of records to display
- Capability to store both business and non-business addresses and to differentiate between the two while browsing

■ Capability to copy address information to the Clipboard in both custom and text formats

Defining the Data

Table 24.1 shows the fields and their type, size, and meaning for each record in the ADDRESS.DB table.

Table 24.1. ADDRESS.DB table fields.

Field Name	Type	Size	Meaning
FIRST_NAME	A	30	Addressee's first name
LAST_NAME	A	30	Addressee's last name
MIDDLEINIT	A	1	Addressee's middle initial
ADDR1	A	40	First address entry
ADDR2	A	40	Additional address entry
CITY	A	40	City name
STATE	A	2	State abbreviation
ZIP	A	15	ZIP code
PHONE1	A	20	First phone entry
PHONE2	A	20	Additional phone entry
FAX	A	20	Fax number
BUSINESS	L	1	Business address indicator; True indicates business address, False indicates non-business address
BUSNAME	A	40	Business name (business address only)
BUSCONTACT	A	40	Business contact (business address only)

The fields LAST_NAME and FIRST_NAME are index fields. LAST_NAME is a required field. These fields can be set in the Database Desktop when creating the table. Refer to the Delphi documentation on using the Database Desktop. Chapter 16, "Writing Database Applications," in this book explains indexed fields if you need to freshen your memory.

Table 24.2 shows the fields and their type, size, and meaning for each record in the STATES.DB table. State_Abbr is the indexed field for the STATES.DB table.

Table 24.2. STATES. DB table fields.

Field Name	Type	Size	Meaning
State_Abbr	A	2	Two-character state abbreviation
State_Name	A	30	Proper state name

Creating the Main Form

The main form is fairly straightforward. It contains all the data-aware components to view or edit the various database fields in the ADDRESS.DB table. It also contains some additional components for enhancing the user-interface such as a TTabSet and a few DBLookupCombo components. The main form, which is renamed to AddrForm by changing its Name property, contains a TNoteBook component with two pages. One page contains the address information for a non-business address: first name, last name, and middle initial. The second page contains the address information for a business address: business name and business contact. These pages are named Non_Business and Business accordingly and are created by accessing the NoteBook editor from NoteBook1's Strings property in the Object Inspector.

The two variations of AddrForm are shown in Figures 24.1 and 24.2. Figure 24.1 shows AddrForm's non-business page as the active page, and 24.2 shows AddrForm's business page as the active page.

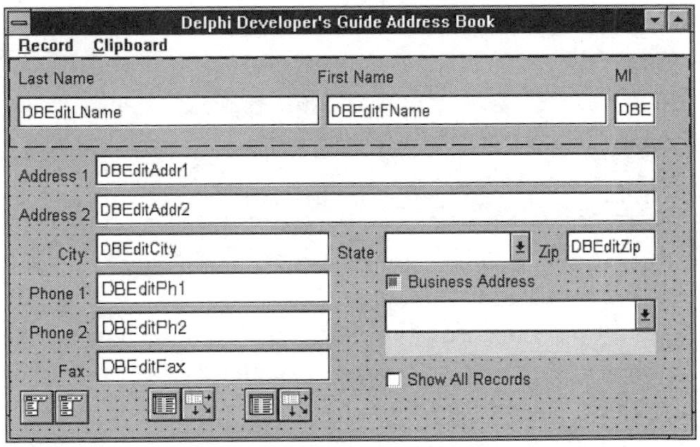

FIGURE 24.1.

AddrForm with the non-business-address page active.

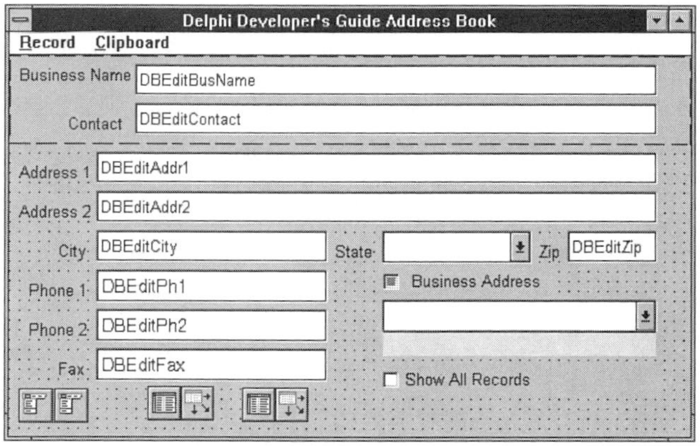

FIGURE 24.2.

AddrForm with the business-address page active.

Connecting the Data-Aware Components

The form contains two TTable components: AddressTable and StatesTable. It also contains two TDataSource components: AddressDS and StatesDS. The TDataSource components are linked to their respective tables accordingly. See Chapter 10, "GDI and Graphics Programming," to review how to connect TTables, TDataSources, and data-aware components. The AutoEdit properties for both TDataSource components is set to false. This prevents the user from accidentally typing in one of the DBEdit components, thus changing the record.

All data-aware controls are linked to AddressDS through their DataSource property. LupStates and LupLastName are TDBLookupCombo components, and they require a bit more explaining.

Using the *TDBLookupCombo* Component

The TDBLookupCombo component is much like the TComboBox component in that it ensures that users enter valid information by providing a list of values from which to choose. Where the TDBLookupCombo differs is that it obtains the values it displays to the user from a second dataset such as a TTable or TQuery. The dataset from which the TDBLookupCombo obtains its values is linked through TDBLookupCombo's LookupSource property.

TDBLookupCombo's DataSource property is linked to the table that gets updated with the value selected by the user. In the Address Book example, LupStates.DataSource is linked to AddressTable. LupStates.DataField is linked to the STATES field in ADDRESS.DB. Therefore, when the user makes a selection, the field STATES in ADDRESS.DB gets modified with the user's selection.

For looking up data, LupStates.LookupSource is linked to StatesTable. LupStates.LookupField is the field from STATES.DB whose value will be used to modify the field specified by LupStates.DataField. LupStates.DisplayField is the field from STATES.DB that has values that are displayed to the user. The Address Book sets this property to the State_Name field in

STATES.DB. This way the user sees the proper state name rather than the state abbreviation. Yet the state abbreviation is what is used to update ADDRESS.DB.

LupLastName is also a TLookupCombo. However, we use this TDBLookupCombo a bit differently as a table lookup. LupLastName.LookupSource is connected to AddressTable. LupLastName.LookupField is set to LAST_NAME. The DataSource and DataField properties aren't set to anything. Code is attached to LupLastName's OnChange event handler to allow it to be used as a navigation control for AddressTable. When the user selects a value from LupLastName, the event handler sets AddressTable's current record to the record specified in the LupLastName's selection. You'll get to the code in another section.

Working with *TField's EditMask* Property

Back in Chapter 10, you were introduced to the TField component. You were shown how to access the TField components at runtime via the Fields array of a TDataSet. You were also shown how to use TDataSet's FieldsByName() method for getting to individual TFields.

We're going to jump ahead a bit to a topic that is covered in more detail in Chapter 28, "Building a Time-Tracker Application," in the section entitled "Working TField and Calculated Fields," which covers creating TField components at design-time. By creating the TField components at design-time, you can modify their properties through the Object Inspector, giving you greater control over the TFields' data type, display format, edit format, and other characteristics.

To create TField instances at design time, you must access the Fields Editor by double-clicking on the AddressTable icon on AddrForm. This invokes the Fields Editor dialog box. From the Fields Editor, select the Add button to display a list of possible database fields for which TField components will be created. By choosing all fields available in the AddressTable, every field name will be added to the Fields Editor, as shown in Figure 24.3.

FIGURE 24.3.
The Fields Editor.

The reasoning for doing all this is to limit, or have control over, the user input to the DBEdit controls for the addressee's last name, phone numbers, and fax number. Because the DBEdit controls are linked to the specific fields of AddressTable, we can use the TField component's EditMask property to specify a mask that limits the data entry to only those characters the mask allows. For detailed information on the various masks you can use for limiting data entry, look up "Edit Mask" in Delphi's online help.

USING EDIT MASKS

Edit masks are an ideal way to validate a user's input or to define how data is to be displayed. They are strings made up of special characters that define what the user can type or how the data is to be displayed.

Edit masks validate user input on a character by character basis. The edit-mask string is made up of three parts separated by semicolons: the actual edit mask, a character to specify whether the literal characters of the mask get saved with the data, and a character used to represent a blank space. The action edit-mask portion may have any number of the 18 characters used for special formatting. These are fully explained in Delphi's online help.

The second portion can contain either a 1 or a 0. A 1 value means that the mask is saved as part of the string. For example, the dash in the string "12345-1234" is saved if the second portion of the edit mask contains a 1. A 0 value does not save the mask's special characters.

The third portion does not require a value. By default, the underscore (_) is used to represent blanks—although you may change this. The following example for a Zip code, uses the special characters 0 and 9. The character 0 requires a numeric value, whereas 9 permits a numeric value but doesn't require it. Notice that the mask character does not get saved, and a blank is used to represent blank spaces:

```
"00000-9999;0; "
```

After adding all the TField instances to the Fields Editor, you can modify various TField properties for that TField instance from the Object Inspector by selecting an individual field. For example, we added the following EditMask to the LAST_NAME and BUSNAME fields:

```
>C<>ccccccccccccccccccccccccccccc;0;
```

This mask forces only the first character of a 30-character string to be uppercase. This way, if the user accidentally types in a last name where the first character is lowercase, it will be set to an uppercase character automatically. The following mask was added to the PHONE1, PHONE2, and FAX fields:

```
!\(999\)000-0000;0;_
```

This mask not only limits the input to numeric characters but also places literal characters in the string so that the number always appears as a valid phone number. You can even invoke an Input Mask Editor dialog box by clicking on the ellipsis button from the EditMask property in the Object Inspector. From the Input Mask Editor, you can select other options and test the edit mask that you've attached to the field. See Figure 24.4. The option to save literal characters is not selected for the PHONE and FAX fields because we only want to save the numbers to the table. You revisit this topic of TFields and EditMasks in Chapter 28.

FIGURE 24.4.

The Input Mask Editor is where you specify edit masks.

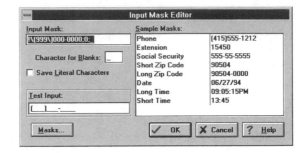

Additional Components

TabSet1 enables the user to specify a range of records for AddressTable to display. It contains a tab for each character in the alphabet that is used to set a range based on the addressee's last name. You see how this works when the code is discussed. CheckBox1 cancels any range set by TabSet1. Figure 24.5 shows how TabSet1 appears when the form is running.

FIGURE 24.5.

AddrForm when running with Tabset's tabs showing.

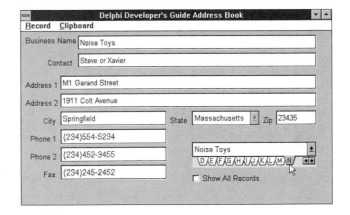

Adding the Menus to the *AddrForm*

The AddressForm contains two menus: MainMenu1 and MainMenu2. Each menu becomes the form's current menu (via AddrForm's Menu property) at different times depending on the form's state. MainMenu1 is the main menu when AddrForm is in browse mode. When in edit mode, MainMenu2 is the form's menu. At runtime, you make these assignments dynamically, which is illustrated in source code momentarily. Tables 24.2 and 24.3 show `MainMenu1` and `MainMenu2` menu items.

Table 24.2. `MainMenu1`'s menu items.

Menubar	Submenu
"&Record"	"&Add"
	"&Delete"
	"&Modify"
"&Clipboard"	"&Copy To"

Table 24.3. MainMenu2's menu items.

Menubar	Submenu
"&Record"	"&Post"
	"&Cancel"
"&Clipboard"	"&Paste From"

Getting to the Source

This section discusses the source code that gives the Address Book its functionality. The source for the Address Book project is shown in Listing 24.1. Listing 24.2 shows the code for `AddrForm`'s unit.

Listing 24.1. The Address Book project file, ADDR.DPR.

```
program Addr;

uses
  Forms,
  Addru in 'ADDRU.PAS' {AddrForm};

{$R *.RES}

begin
  Application.CreateForm(TAddrForm, AddrForm);
  Application.Run;
end.
```

Listing 24.2. AddrForm's unit file, ADDRU.PAS.

```
unit Addru;

interface

uses
  SysUtils, WinTypes, WinProcs, Messages, Classes, Graphics, Controls,
  Forms, Dialogs, DB, DBTables, Grids, DBGrids, TabNotBk, ExtCtrls, Tabs,
  StdCtrls, Mask, DBCtrls, Buttons, Menus, wincrt, DBLookup,
  ddgcbu, ClipBrd;

const
  cEditMode = 1;        { Required for determining state of form .}
  cBrowseMode = 2;

type
  TAddrForm = class(TForm)
    AddressDS: TDataSource;
    MainMenu1: TMainMenu;
    Record1: TMenuItem;
    Add1: TMenuItem;
    Delete1: TMenuItem;
    Modify1: TMenuItem;
    MainMenu2: TMainMenu;
    Record2: TMenuItem;
    Post1: TMenuItem;
    Cancel1: TMenuItem;
    Clipboard1: TMenuItem;
    CopyTo1: TMenuItem;
    Clipboard2: TMenuItem;
    PasteFrom1: TMenuItem;
    Label4: TLabel;
    DBEditAddr1: TDBEdit;
    DBEditAddr2: TDBEdit;
    Label5: TLabel;
    Label6: TLabel;
    DBEditCity: TDBEdit;
    DBEditPh1: TDBEdit;
    Label9: TLabel;
    DBEditPh2: TDBEdit;
    Label7: TLabel;
    DBEditZip: TDBEdit;
    DBEditFax: TDBEdit;
    Label11: TLabel;
    Label8: TLabel;
    NoteBook1: TNotebook;
    Label1: TLabel;
    Label2: TLabel;
    Label3: TLabel;
    DBEditLName: TDBEdit;
    DBEditFName: TDBEdit;
    DBEditMI: TDBEdit;
    Label12: TLabel;
    Label13: TLabel;
    DBEditBusName: TDBEdit;
    DBEditContact: TDBEdit;
    Label10: TLabel;
```

```
      AddressTable: TTable;
      AddressTableFIRST_NAME: TStringField;
      AddressTableLAST_NAME: TStringField;
      AddressTableMIDDLEINIT: TStringField;
      AddressTableADDR1: TStringField;
      AddressTableADDR2: TStringField;
      AddressTableCITY: TStringField;
      AddressTableSTATE: TStringField;
      AddressTableZIP: TStringField;
      AddressTablePHONE1: TStringField;
      AddressTablePHONE2: TStringField;
      AddressTableFAX: TStringField;
      AddressTableBUSNAME: TStringField;
      AddressTableBUSCONTACT: TStringField;
      DBCBBusAddr: TDBCheckBox;
      AddressTableBUSINESS: TBooleanField;
      StatesTable: TTable;
      StatesDS: TDataSource;
      LupStates: TDBLookupCombo;
      LupLastName: TDBLookupCombo;
      TabSet1: TTabSet;
      CheckBox1: TCheckBox;
      procedure FormCreate(Sender: TObject);
      procedure FormActivate(Sender: TObject);
      procedure AddressDSDataChange(Sender: TObject; Field: TField);
      procedure CopyTo1Click(Sender: TObject);
      procedure PasteFrom1Click(Sender: TObject);
      procedure Delete1Click(Sender: TObject);
      procedure Modify1Click(Sender: TObject);
      procedure Post1Click(Sender: TObject);
      procedure Cancel1Click(Sender: TObject);
      procedure DBCBBusAddrClick(Sender: TObject);
      procedure Add1Click(Sender: TObject);
      procedure LupLastNameChange(Sender: TObject);
      procedure TabSet1Change(Sender: TObject; NewTab: Integer;
        var AllowChange: Boolean);
      procedure CheckBox1Click(Sender: TObject);
    private
      { Private declarations }
      Mode: integer;         { Holds the state of the form, cEditMode or
➥cBrowseMode }
      procedure EditMode;        { Places the form in EditMode }
      procedure BrowseMode;      { Places the form in BrowseMode }
      procedure SetNotebookPage; { Sets the notebook page according to record
➥type }
      procedure SetNameRange(NewTab: integer); { Sets a range of addresses
➥based on the }
    public                                     {    last name }
      { Public declarations }
    end;

var
  AddrForm: TAddrForm;

implementation

{$R *.DFM}
```

continues

Listing 24.2. continued

```
procedure TAddrForm.FormCreate(Sender: TObject);
var
  i: integer;
begin
  { Set the tabs in TabSet1 to display letters }
  for i := ord('A') to ord('Z') do
    TabSet1.Tabs.Add(chr(i));
end;

procedure TAddrForm.FormActivate(Sender: TObject);
begin
  { Set the text displayed in the picklist to that of the current
➥AddressTable record }
  LupLastName.Value := AddressTableLAST_NAME.Value;
  BrowseMode;              { Place form into browse mode }
  TabSet1.TabIndex := 0; { Set TabSet to the first tab }
end;

procedure TAddrForm.EditMode;
begin
  { Disable/Enable appropriate controls for this mode }
  DBCBBusAddr.Visible := true;
  LupLastName.Visible := false;
  LupStates.Enabled := true;
  DBCBBusAddr.Checked := false;
  TabSet1.Visible := false;
  CheckBox1.Visible := false;
  Menu := MainMenu2;          { Set Main menu }
  Mode := cEditMode;          { Set Mode }
end;

procedure TAddrForm.BrowseMode;
begin
  { Disable/Enable appropriate controls for this mode }
  LupLastName.Visible := true;
  DBCBBusAddr.Visible := false;
  LupStates.Enabled := false;
  TabSet1.Visible := true;
  CheckBox1.Visible := true;
  Menu := MainMenu1;     { Set main menu }
  Mode := cBrowseMode;   { Set Mode }
end;

procedure TAddrForm.SetNoteBookPage;
begin
  { Set the notebook page according to whether or not the address is a }
  { business address. }
  NoteBook1.PageIndex := ord(AddressTable.FieldByName('BUSINESS').AsBoolean);
end;

procedure TAddrForm.SetNameRange(NewTab: integer);
begin
  LupLastName.OnChange := nil;   { Temporarily set these 2 event handlers }
  AddressDS.OnDataChange := nil; { to nil so that they will not be called }
  with AddressTable do begin      { Then set the AddressTable range to display}
```

```
    if TabSet1.Tabs[NewTab] <> 'Z' then { records according to the selected tab }
      SetRange([TabSet1.Tabs[NewTab]],[TabSet1.Tabs[NewTab+1]]) { in TabSet1 }
    else begin
      SetRangeStart;     { Set the range starting position }
      FieldByName('Last_Name').AsString := TabSet1.Tabs[NewTab];
      SetRangeEnd;
    end;
    ApplyRange;
  end;
  LupLastName.Value := DBEditLName.Text;          { Assign the event handlers back }
  LupLastName.OnChange := LupLastNameChange;     { so that they will be called
➥by user }
  AddressDS.OnDataChange := AddressDSDataChange; { interaction }
  SetNoteBookPage;                                { Call SetNoteBook page }
end;

procedure TAddrForm.AddressDSDataChange(Sender: TObject; Field: TField);
begin
  SetNoteBookPage;  { Any time a record changes call SetNoteBook pages to }
end;                { show proper notebook page. }

procedure TAddrForm.TabSet1Change(Sender: TObject; NewTab: Integer;
  var AllowChange: Boolean);
begin
  SetNameRange(NewTab);  { Set the name range when the tabset control has been }
end;                     { changed }

procedure TAddrForm.LupLastNameChange(Sender: TObject);
begin
  { When the lookuplist changes (the user selected another name ), set
➥AddressTable}
  { to that record. LupLastName is a lookup combo box whose LookupDataSource is }
  { connected to AddressTable, therefore, its normal behavior doesn't affect
➥AddressTable's}
  { Current record. This is one way to have it reposition the current record
➥for AddressTable }
  with AddressTable do begin
    SetKey;
    AddressTable.FieldByName('Last_Name').AsString := LupLastName.Value;
    GoToKey;
  end
end;

procedure TAddrForm.DBCBBusAddrClick(Sender: TObject);
begin
{ Set the notebook page according to the address type, business or non-business }
  NoteBook1.PageIndex := ord(DBCBBusAddr.Checked);
end;

procedure TAddrForm.CheckBox1Click(Sender: TObject);
begin
{ This event handler set the table to either display a range of records or to }
{ display all records in the table }
  AddressTable.First;                    { Go to first record in AddressTable }
  TabSet1.Visible := not TabSet1.Visible; { Reverse Tabset visibility }
  TabSet1.TabIndex := 0;                  { Set to the first tab }
```

continues

Listing 24.2. continued

```
  if CheckBox1.Checked then
    AddressTable.CancelRange              { Cancel or Set a range for
➥AddressTable }
  else                                    { based on Checkbox1's checked state. }
    SetNameRange(0);                      { Set name range as if first tab }
end;                                      { is selected. }

procedure TAddrForm.Add1Click(Sender: TObject);
begin
  AddressTable.Insert; { Set AddressTable into Insert mode }
  EditMode;            { Place the form in cEditMode }
end;

procedure TAddrForm.Delete1Click(Sender: TObject);
begin
  AddressTable.Delete;  { Delete the current record }
end;

procedure TAddrForm.Modify1Click(Sender: TObject);
begin
  EditMode;            { Put the form in edit mode }
  AddressTable.Edit;   { Put the AddressTable into edit mode }
end;

procedure TAddrForm.Post1Click(Sender: TObject);
begin
  { If this is a business address record, copy the contents of the BusinessName}
  { field to the Last_Name field in since the table is keyed on the Last_Name. }
  if DBCBBusAddr.Checked then
    AddressTable.FieldByName('Last_Name').AsString := DBEditBusName.Text;
  AddressTable.Post;  { Post the record to the table }
  BrowseMode;         { Go back to browse mode }
  { Set the picklist's value displayed accordingly }
  LupLastName.Value := AddressTable.FieldByName('Last_Name').AsString;
end;

procedure TAddrForm.Cancel1Click(Sender: TObject);
begin
  AddressTable.Cancel;  { Cancel the edit opertion }
  BrowseMode;           { Go back into cBrowseMode }
end;

procedure TAddrForm.CopyTo1Click(Sender: TObject);
var
  DDGObj: TDDGObject;
begin
  { This method copies the contents of the various controls to the clipboard }
  DDGObj := TDDGObject.Create; { Instanciate a TDDGObj }
  try
    With DDGObj.Rec do
    begin
      FName := AddressTableFIRST_NAME.Value;
      LName := AddressTableLAST_NAME.Value;
      MI := AddressTableMIDDLEINIT.Value;
      Addr1 := AddressTableADDR1.Value;
      Addr2 := AddressTableADDR2.Value;
```

```
        City := AddressTableCITY.Value;
        State := AddressTableSTATE.Value;
        Zip := AddressTableZIP.Value;
        Ph1 := AddressTablePHONE1.Value;
        Ph2 := AddressTablePHONE2.Value;
        Fx := AddressTableFAX.Value;
        BusName := AddressTableBUSNAME.Value;
        BusContact := AddressTableBUSCONTACT.Value;
        Bus := DBCBBusAddr.Checked;
        DDGObj.CopyToClipBoard;              { Copy contents of DDGObj to Clipboard }
      end;
  finally
    DDGObj.Free;                { Free DDGObj }
  end;
end;

procedure TAddrForm.PasteFrom1Click(Sender: TObject);
var
  DDGObj: TDDGObject;
begin
  { This method pastes the data in the clipboard to the various controls on }
  { the form, but only in cEditMode }
  DDGObj := TDDGObject.Create;            { Instanciate a TDDGObj          }
  try
    if ClipBoard.HasFormat(CF_DDGDATA) then begin { Check if format is
➥available }
      DDGObj.GetFromClipBoard;           { Copy contents of clipboard into
➥DDGObj.Rec }
      with DDGObj.Rec do begin
        AddressTableFIRST_NAME.Value := FName;
        AddressTableLAST_NAME.Value := LName;
        AddressTableMIDDLEINIT.Value := MI;
        AddressTableADDR1.Value  := Addr1;
        AddressTableADDR2.Value := Addr2;
        AddressTableCity.Value := City;
        AddressTableState.Value := State;
        AddressTableZip.Value := Zip;
        AddressTablePHONE1.Value := Ph1;
        AddressTablePHONE2.Value := Ph2;
        AddressTableFAX.Value := Fx;
        AddressTableBUSNAME.Value := BusName;
        AddressTableBUSCONTACT.Value := BusContact;
        AddressTableBUSINESS.Value := Bus;
      end;
    end;
  finally
    DDGObj.Free;                { Free DDGObj  }
  end;
end;

end.
```

Much of the project's code is basically just setting up the controls and making sure that they contain the proper data at the right times. AddrForm has two modes: edit mode (the user is editing data) and browse mode (the user is viewing data). Two constants are defined to signify which mode the form is currently in.

```
cEditMode = 1;
cBrowseMode := 2;
```

The FormCreate() event handler makes TabSet1 have a tab for each character in the alphabet. The FormActivate() event handler simply initialized LupLastName with the last name of AddressTable's current record, put the form into browse mode by calling the BrowseMode() method, and set TabSet1's TabIndex property to 0—the first tab in TabSet1's list of tabs.

The BrowseMode() and EditMode() methods simply enable or disable the appropriate components for the specific mode. Each method also set the main menu according to the mode. Finally, AddrForm's Mode variable is set to hold the current mode.

The method SetNoteBookPage() sets Notebook1's page according to the AddressTable's logical field, BUSINESS. If a non-business record is current, the Non_Business page is set to active, otherwise the Business page is made active. This method is called from an event handler when needed.

The SetNameRange() method is an example of using ranges as learned in Chapter 10. Whenever the user selects a new tab, a range is set to display only records from AddressTable that fall within the specified range. In this example, the range is specified by the character contained within the newly selected tab. The range's starting position is the character contained in the selected tab. The range's ending position is the next character unless the character in the selected tab is Z. The code below is the portion of the code from the SetNameRange() method that accomplishes this task.

```
if TabSet1.Tabs[NewTab] <> 'Z' then { records according to the selected tab }
SetRange([TabSet1.Tabs[NewTab]],[TabSet1.Tabs[NewTab+1]]) { in TabSet1 }
else begin
SetRangeStart;    { Set the range starting position }
FieldByName('Last_Name').AsString := TabSet1.Tabs[NewTab];
SetRangeEnd;
end;
```

Notice that in the SetNameRange() method the two event handlers, LupLastName.OnChange and AddressDS.OnDataChange, are temporarily set to nil. The reason for doing this is because events occurring from within the SetNameRange() method would cause those event handlers to be called. The events that cause the event handler to be called are AddressDS's data changing and explicitly changing the value of LupLastName.Value. Both event handlers primarily are for when the user's actions calls them, not when the code does. Therefore, temporarily setting them to nil prevents calling of the methods to which the event handlers point because, as far as the application is concerned, no method exists for those event handlers. When the SetNameRange() is finished, the event handlers are reset to point to their initial methods.

The AddressDS's OnDataChange event handler, AddressDSDataChange(), calls SetNoteBookPage() to ensure that the proper page is displayed for the current record. By the way, had we not set this event handler to nil in SetNameRange(), this method would be called more than once, causing it to flicker, which isn't too appealing.

The TabSet1Change() method is TabSet1's OnChange event handler. This is invoked whenever the user selects a new tab, which means a new range must be set. Therefore, it calls SetNameRange().

Earlier we said that the TDBLookupCombo, LupLastName, wasn't being used as a lookup combo, but rather as a navigational component that sets AddressTable's current record to that specified by LupLastName's Value property. Normally, a TDBLookupCombo doesn't affect the LookupSource from which it populates itself. By adding the code shown below to its OnClick event handler, you cause it to behave as a navigational component for its LookupSource.

```
with AddressTable do begin
  SetKey;
  AddressTable.FieldByName('Last_Name').AsString := LupLastName.Value;
  GoToKey;
end
```

This is another example of setting keys as learned in Chapter 10.

The DBCBCBusAddrClick() method sets the Notebook page accordingly when the form is in edit mode. See Figure 24.6.

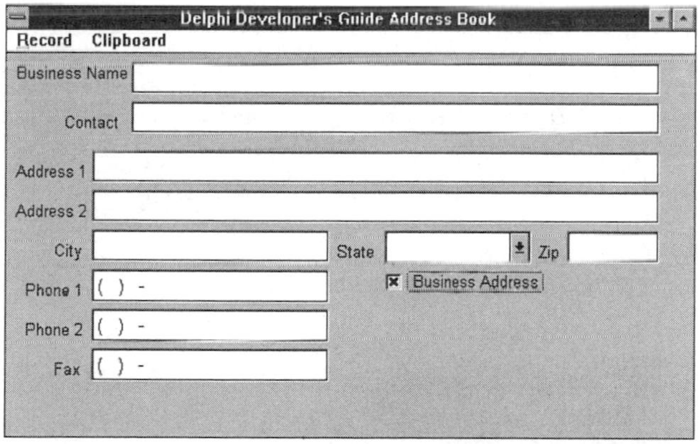

FIGURE 24.6.

AddrForm in EditMode with the Business page active.

CheckBox1's OnClick event handler, CheckBox1Click(), enables or disables the range capability for the project. When Show All Records is checked, TabSet1 is hidden and CancelRange() is called so that AddressTable displays all records, not just those set by a tab's character value.

The remaining event handlers are the event handlers for the two TMainMenus. They call the appropriate TTable methods for AddressTable to perform record adding, modifying, deleting, and posting.

Adding Clipboard Capabilities

In Chapter 14, "Sharing Information with the Clipboard and DDE," you learned how to copy data from your application to the Clipboard in both a custom format and text format so that other applications can use that information. The Address Book is an ideal example of making the address information accessible to other applications. For example, when using a word processor to write a letter, you can use the Address Book not only to look up an address, but to copy the information to the Clipboard so that you can paste it right into your letter. The best part is that you already did the hard part in Chapter 14.

Listing 24.3 shows an updated version of the DDGCBU.PAS unit created in Chapter 14. In this listing you see some minor changes. Basically, it has been made into a self-contained unit. The form from Chapter 14's example project and its methods are removed. The TDDGRec is modified to contain information specific to the Address Book application. Also, the CRLF constant has been moved, and we added a TextString variable and a SetTextData() method to the TDDGObject to format the text of the data that is sent to the Clipboard. Lastly, the CopyToClipBoard() method is changed to use the TextString variable. You might consider creating a more OOP version of the TDDGObject from which you can descend. We didn't for this book because we wanted to focus on the Clipboard routines and not on OOP design.

Listing 24.3. The DDGCBU.PAS Clipboard unit with modifications.

```
unit Ddgcbu;

interface

uses
  SysUtils, WinTypes, WinProcs, Messages, Classes, Graphics, Controls,
  Forms, Dialogs, StdCtrls, clipbrd;
const
  CRLF = #13#10;  { Carriage return line feed }
var
  CF_DDGDATA: word;
type

  PDDGRec = ^TDDGRec;
  TDDGRec = record
    LName, FName: string[30];
    MI: String[1];
    Addr1, Addr2, City: string[40];
    State: string[2];
    Zip: string[15];
    Ph1, Ph2, Fx: string[20];
    BusName, BusContact: string[40];
    Bus: Boolean;
  end;

  TDDGObject = class(TObject)
   protected
     TextString: string;
     procedure SetTextData;
```

```
  public
    Rec: TDDGRec;
    procedure CopyToClipBoard;
    procedure GetFromClipBoard;
  end;

implementation
uses Addru;

procedure TDDGObject.SetTextData;
begin
  { create the text string for clipboard text format }
  with Rec do begin
    if Bus then
      TextString := BusName+CRLF+BusContact+CRLF
    else
      TextString := FName+ ' '+LName+CRLF;
    TextString := TextString+Addr1+CRLF+City+', '+State+' '+Zip;
  end;
end;

procedure TDDGObject.CopyToClipBoard;
var
  Data: THandle;
  DataPtr: Pointer;
  Len: Integer;
begin
  { Add the call to copy the contents from the clipboard }
  SetTextData;
  { Allocate memory from global heap }
  Data := GlobalAlloc(GMEM_MOVEABLE, SizeOf(Rec));
  try
    DataPtr := GlobalLock(Data);        { Get a pointer to the lock memory area }
    try
      Move(Rec, DataPtr^, SizeOf(Rec)); { Move the data in Buffer to DataPtr    }
      ClipBoard.Open; { This is only required if multiple clipboard formats are }
                      { being saved at once. Otherwise, if only one format it }
                      { being sent to the clipboard, don't call it. }
      ClipBoard.SetAsHandle(CF_DDGDATA, Data);
      { Now copy also in the CF_TEXT format }
      ClipBoard.AsText :- TextString;
      Clipboard.Close; { Only call this if you previously called Clipboard.Open() }
    finally
      GlobalUnlock(Data);                { Unlock the globally allocated memory  }
    end;
  except
    GlobalFree(Data);                    { Free the memory allocated, only if    }
    raise;                               { an exception occurs as this memory is }
  end;                                   { managed by the clipboard.             }
end;

procedure TDDGObject.GetFromClipBoard;
var
  Data: THandle;
  DataPtr: Pointer;
  C: Char;
  Size: Integer;
```

continues

Listing 24.3. continued

```
begin
  Data := ClipBoard.GetAsHandle(CF_DDGDATA); { Get the data on the clipboard }
  try
    if Data = 0 then Exit;                    { Exit is unsuccessful }
    DataPtr := GlobalLock(Data);              { Lock the Global memory object }
    try
      if SizeOf(Rec) > GlobalSize(Data) then Size := GlobalSize(Data);
      Move(DataPtr^, Rec, SizeOf(Rec));   { Copy contents of DataPtr to Buffer }
    finally
      GlobalUnlock(Data);                     { Unlock the global memory object }
    end;
  except
    GlobalFree(Data);                    { Free the memory allocated, only if   }
    raise;                               { an exception occurs as this memory is }
  end;
end;

initialization
  CF_DDGDATA := RegisterClipBoardFormat('CF_DDG'); { Register our clipboard }
end.
```

AddrForm's Clipboard methods, CopyTo1Click() and PasteFrom1Click(), are event handlers for the Copy and Paste options. These methods are responsible for assigning the data to and from the DDGObj's record for copying to and pasting from the Clipboard. There's nothing significantly different in this method from the example shown in Chapter 14, other than that you're using different data.

When the application is running, the user can only paste data from the Clipboard to AddrForm's data-aware controls while in edit mode. However, the user can copy data to the Clipboard and paste that data in text format to any Windows application that accepts text-formatted data as shown in Figure 24.7.

Summary

You have completed the Address Book application and your first real, usable application. Consider everything you have done so far; you actually have created a complex database application in a short amount of time. Although you might not realize it, you have gained much knowledge in dealing with Delphi's data-aware components in this chapter alone. You learn even more database techniques in later chapters. In fact, in the next chapter, you will learn how to use more Delphi components, as well as how to add functionality by extending existing components.

FIGURE 24.7.

Clipboard data from the Address Book application in a Word for Windows document.

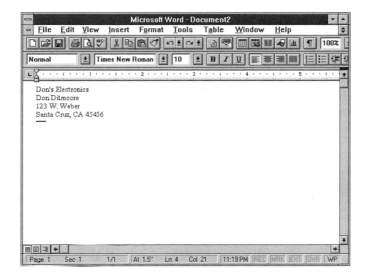

This chapter shows you how to build a complete application that will give you the functionality of a calendar, a daily scheduler, and an alarm. The calendar enables you to view months and years that you select. The scheduler enables you to schedule important dates, and the alarm interacts with the calendar to remind you of important events. In developing this application, you will learn helpful techniques that you'll use often while developing applications in Delphi. First, you'll create another custom component by extending the existing Calendar component that ships with Delphi. You'll learn how to create a special event handler for the new component and how to add custom drawing to the Calendar component. You'll also use Delphi's time and date functions, and perform some simple file I/O operations. Finally, you'll use the TINIFile object, which encapsulates Windows initialization files. When you finish this chapter, you'll have a fully functional calendar/scheduler and alarm.

Examining the Calendar's Functionality

The Calendar program uses four forms: CalendarForm, DayForm, RemAlarmForm, and SetAlarmForm. The figures in this chapter show you what these forms look like.

CalendarForm is the main form. It has the custom Calendar component (DDGCalendar); a main panel; a clock panel; and a few buttons to navigate through the months, days, and years. You access the other forms by double-clicking a day to access the DayForm, or by right-clicking to access a popup menu. A TTimer component on CalendarForm updates the clock panel.

DayForm shows a daily schedule to which you can add or remove reminder messages to the Description column on a TStringGrid component. Schedules are stored in binary files on disk. An s appears in a DDGCalendar component cell in which an event is scheduled.

SetAlarmForm enables you to set an alarm for a specific date and time. When an alarm is set, the DDGCalendar component triggers an OnAlarm event to which you can attach special processing, such as displaying a message or causing a beep to occur. TDDGCalendar stores information about the alarm in a Windows INI file. The TDDGCalendar component displays a red asterisk in the lower-left corner of the day cell for which an alarm is set.

RemAlarmForm enables you to remove all alarms for a specific day.

Looking at the *TDDGCalendar* Class

TDDGCalendar is a TCalendar descendant with added functionality. In addition to the normal TCalendar's behavior, TDDGCalendar provides an alarm that you can make available to users of your applications; it also performs a special drawing of its cells to indicate that an alarm or daily schedule is present for a given day. TDDGCalendar uses a TINIFile class along with a TTimer to detect when an alarm is supposed to fire off. If an alarm is present, an OnAlarm event occurs. TDDGCalendar also looks for the presence of a daily schedule. Daily schedules are stored in binary files.

25

Creating a Calendar/ Scheduler and Alarm Application

Creating the *TDDGCalendar*

The file DDGCAL.PAS, shown in Listing 25.1, defines TDDGCalendar. Here, you see the event-handling mechanism for the alarm behavior and a special drawing required when drawing day cells.

Listing 25.1. The source code for DDGCAL.PAS.

```
unit Ddgcal;

interface

uses
  SysUtils, WinTypes, WinProcs, Messages, Classes, Graphics, Controls,
  Forms, Dialogs, Grids, Calendar, IniFiles, ExtCtrls;

const
  IniFileName = 'DDGCAL.INI';

type

  TOnAlarmEvent = procedure (Sender: TObject; AlarmMessage: string) of object;

  TDDGCalendar = class(TCalendar)
  private
    { Private declarations }
    FIniFile: TIniFile;
    FFileName: string[80];
    FAlarmTimer: TTimer;
    FOnAlarm: TOnAlarmEvent;
    FAlarmMessage: string;
    function GetAlarmEnabled: Boolean;
    procedure SetAlarmEnabled(AAlarmEnabled: Boolean);
    procedure Timer1Timer(Sender: TObject);
  protected
    { Protected declarations }
    function AlarmsExist(AlarmDate: String): Boolean;
    function CheckAlarm(var AlarmMsg: string): boolean;
    procedure DrawCell(ACol, ARow: Longint; ARect: TRect;
             AState: TGridDrawState); override;
  public
    { Public declarations }
    constructor Create(AOwner: TComponent); override;
    destructor Destroy;
    procedure AddAlarm(DateTime: TDateTime; AlMsg: string);
    procedure RemoveAlarms(DateTime: TDateTime);
    procedure GetAlarmsOnDate(DateTime: TDateTime; Sections: TStrings);
  published
    { Published declarations }
    property AlarmEnabled: Boolean read GetAlarmEnabled write SetAlarmEnabled;
    property OnAlarm: TOnAlarmEvent read FOnAlarm write FOnAlarm;
    property Row;
    property Col;
  end;
```

continues

Listing 25.1. continued

```
procedure Register;

implementation
uses DayFormu;

function IsNum(Num: string): boolean;
var
  v: integer;
  code: integer;
begin
  { determine if the value passed in is a number, return true if so }
  val(Num, v, Code);
  Result := (Code = 0)
end;

procedure TDDGCalendar.DrawCell(ACol, ARow: Longint; ARect: TRect;
                                AState: TGridDrawState);
const
  SearchDt = '%d/%d/%2d'; { Format string for a date }
var
  DayText: string;
  TempRect: TRect;
  i: integer;
  SearchDate: String;
  ValidSearch: boolean;
begin
  DayText := CellText[ACol, ARow];  { CellText() returns the text within a cell }
  ValidSearch := IsNum(DayText);    { Determine if the text is a value number }
  if ValidSearch then
    { Create a string from the date returned }
    SearchDate := Format(SearchDt, [Month, StrToInt(DayText), Year-1900]);

  with ARect, Canvas do begin
    TextRect(ARect, Left, Top, DayText);  { Draw the day at the upper left
➡corner }
    { of the cell, then calculate a new rect to draw the remaining items }
    TempRect := Rect(Left, Bottom - TextHeight('W'), Right, Bottom);
    if ValidSearch then
      { If there are alarms then draw a symbol to represent an alarm for this
➡day cell }
      if AlarmsExist(SearchDate) then begin
        Font.Color := clRed;
        TextRect(TempRect, TempRect.Left, TempRect.Top, '*');
      end;
      { If there is a file with the name created below, there is a schedule. }
      { display a symbol to indicate this in the day block }
      FFileName := DayText+IntToStr(Month)+IntToSTr(Year)+'.CAL';
      if FileExists(FFileName) then begin
        Font.Color := clBlue;
        TempRect.Left := TempRect.Left+TextWidth('W');
        TextRect(TempRect, TempRect.Left, TempRect.Top, 's');
      end;
      Font.Color := clBlack;
  end;
end;
```

```
procedure TDDGCalendar.AddAlarm(DateTime: TDateTime; AlMsg: string);
begin
  { Add the alarm data to the INI file }
  FIniFile.WriteString(DateToStr(DateTime), TimeToStr(DateTime), AlMsg);
end;

procedure TDDGCalendar.RemoveAlarms(DateTime: TDateTime);
begin
 { Erase the section }
  FIniFile.EraseSection(DateToStr(DateTime));
end;

function TDDGCalendar.AlarmsExist(AlarmDate: string): boolean;
var
  Sections: TStringList;
begin
  Sections := TStringList.Create;          { Instantiate a TStringList }
  Result := false;                         { default is false }
  FIniFile.ReadSection(AlarmDate, Sections);{ read the sections }
    Result := Sections.Count > 0;          { if there are sections read then }
  Sections.Free;                           { there are alarms. }
end;

function TDDGCalendar.CheckAlarm(var AlarmMsg: string): boolean;
var
    StrMessage: string;
begin
  { Check for alarms }
  StrMessage := FIniFile.ReadString(DateToStr(Date), TimeToStr(Time), 'X');
  if StrMessage <> 'X' then begin
    AlarmMsg := StrMessage;
    Result := true;
  end
  else
    Result := false;
end;

procedure TDDGCalendar.GetAlarmsOnDate(DateTime: TDateTime;
  Sections: TStrings);
begin
  { Get all the alarms for a given date }
  FIniFile.ReadSectionValues(DateToStr(DateTime), Sections);
end;

function TDDGCalendar.GetAlarmEnabled: Boolean;
begin
  { Return if FAlarmTimer is enabled }
  Result := FAlarmTimer.Enabled;
end;

procedure TDDGCalendar.SetAlarmEnabled(AAlarmEnabled: Boolean);
begin
  { Set FAlarmTimer.Enabled accordingly }
  FAlarmTimer.Enabled := AAlarmEnabled;
end;
```

continues

Listing 25.1. continued

```
constructor TDDGCalendar.Create(AOwner: TComponent);
begin
  inherited Create(AOwner);
  FIniFile := TIniFile.Create(IniFileName); { Instantiate a TINIFile class }
  FAlarmTimer := TTimer.Create(self);       { Create a TTimer }
  FAlarmTimer.Interval := 500; ;            { set the TTimer's interval to
➥1/2 second }
  FAlarmTimer.Enabled := false;             { Set TTimer's enabled to false
➥by default }
  FAlarmTimer.OnTimer := Timer1Timer;       { Assign the event handler to
➥the TTimer }
end;

destructor TDDGCalendar.Destroy;
begin
  FIniFile.Free;  { Free the TINIFile instance }
  FAlarmTimer.Free; inherited Destroy;
end;

procedure TDDGCalendar.Timer1Timer(Sender: TObject);
begin
  { On every timer tick, check if an alarm is set for the current time }
  { and if so call the FOnAlarm, an OnAlarm event handler. }
  if CheckAlarm(FAlarmMessage) then
    if Assigned(FOnAlarm) then
      FOnAlarm(self, FAlarmMessage);
end;

procedure Register;
begin
  RegisterComponents('Samples', [TDDGCalendar]);
end;

end.
```

Looking at the Alarm Behavior

TDDGCalendar uses a TTimer and TINIFile to provide the functionality of an alarm. When a user creates an alarm, information about that alarm, date, time, and alarm message are stored in a Windows INI file. Storing this information to an INI file is discussed later in the chapter. TDDGCalendar's TTimer fires every $1/2$ second. Its OnTimer event checks the INI file for the existence of an alarm set for the current date and time. If an alarm exists, TDDGCalendar fires off an OnAlarm event. Developers, using the TDDGCalendar component, can attach any special processing to the OnAlarm event handler, such as sounding a beep.

Creating Alarm Events

Usually, when considering what event you want to make available to users of your component, you can use events already available for all components, such as OnClick, OnDragDrop, OnMouseDown, and so on. In some cases, however, the standard events don't lend themselves to the functionality you require, as is the case with the OnAlarm event. In order to add this functionality, however, you must define a special event-handler type and write the code responsible for triggering the event when it occurs or when an alarm is present.

Defining the *TOnAlarmEvent*

Chapter 3, "The Object Pascal Language," explained that events are merely method pointers that define the method as a procedure and also specify the procedure's parameter list.

When an alarm occurs, the user should be provided with the alarm message associated with that alarm. An event-handler type to provide this information follows (and is defined in Listing 25.1):

```
TOnAlarmEvent = procedure (Sender: TObject; AlarmMessage: string) of Object;
```

> **CAUTION**
>
> Never define an event as a function, because an event-handler variable may not actually point to an event-handler method. In this case, you have an empty function in which the result is undefined. This can result in unexpected behavior in your application. Instead, define events as procedures, and pass back modified data via var parameters.

The preceding event handler is basically a procedure pointer that gets passed a TObject and a string parameter. As standard practice, you always should pass Sender, a TObject type, as a parameter to indicate which object generated the event. AlarmMessage will hold the user-defined message for the alarm.

> **TIP**
>
> Always declare event-handler types as of Object. This declaration tells Delphi that the event is a method and has the implicit self parameter.

The event-handler instance FOnAlarm is a private member of TDDGCalendar. FOnAlarm doesn't point to an actual event handler until the user assigns an event handler to it through the Object Inspector, or at runtime. This assignment is made possible through the property OnAlarm. By making this property published, it will show up in the Object Inspector, and users of the TDDGCalendar component can then assign their own event to it.

A *private implementation* method is where the event really gets triggered. This method should call the event handler, if one exists (or the user-assigned handler), whenever the event occurs. In the case with the OnAlarm event, this implementation method is TDDGCalendar's Timer1Timer()

method:

```
procedure TDDGCalendar.Timer1Timer(Sender: TObject);
begin
   if CheckAlarm(FAlarmMessage) then
     if Assigned(FOnAlarm) then
       FOnAlarm(self, FAlarmMessage);
end;
```

This method first checks to see whether an alarm is present by calling CheckAlarm() and, if so, explicitly calls FOnAlarm and passes the alarm message to the FOnAlarm event handler. The Assigned() function checks to see whether a pointer or procedural pointer is nil. The component's user creates an event handler that FOnAlarm points to through the Object Inspector, which might look like this:

```
procedure TForm1.DDGCalendar1Alarm(Sender: TObject; AlarmMessage: String);
begin
  MessageBeep(0);
end;
```

Notice that the event handler takes on the same form as its type, TOnAlarmEvent.

Working with the *TINIFile* Class

Earlier in this chapter, you learned that the TINIFile class encapsulates the functionality of reading from and writing to Windows INI files. The actual INI files as they exist on your hard drive follow this format:

```
[Section1]
Identifier1=value1
Identifier2=value2

[Section2]
Identifier1=value1
Identifier2=value2
```

Section1 and Section2 define constants under which many different identifiers can exist. Each identifier can have a value associated with it, which can be a number, string, or Boolean value. This structure of INI files makes them commonplace for applications to store configuration information; you'll probably find many files with an INI extension in your Windows directory.

In the example program here, one TINIFile is used to store and retrieve alarm data for a given day. This TINIFile will store the alarm's TDateTime and an alarm message. The TDateTime is used for the INI file's section, the time portion as the identifier, and an alarm message as a value. The TINIFile instance is a private member of TDDGCalendar FINIFile. It is created in TDDGCalendar's Create() method:

```
FIniFile := TIniFile.Create(IniFileName);
```

It is freed in TDDGCalendar's Destroy() method:

```
FIniFile.Free;
```

The `IniFileName` constant defines `TDDGCalendar`'s INI filename.

The `TINIFile` defines several methods to enable you to work with Windows INI files. These are summarized in Table 25.1.

Table 25.1. `TINIFile` methods.

Method	Purpose
EraseSection()	Erases an INI file's entire section.
ReadBool()	Reads a Boolean value from an INI file.
ReadInteger()	Reads an integer value from an INI file.
ReadSection()	Reads all identifiers in a section of an INI file into a `TStringList` object.
ReadSectionValues()	Reads all identifiers and their values into a `TStringList` object.
ReadString()	Reads a string value from an INI file.
WriteBool()	Writes a Boolean value to an INI file.
WriteInteger()	Writes an integer value to an INI file.
WriteString()	Writes a string value to an INI file.

The private method `AlarmsExist()` checks to see whether any alarms exist for an entire day by reading the `TINIFile`'s sections into a `TStringList` and checking the `TStringList`'s `Count` property for a value greater than zero. The `CheckAlarm()` private method checks for the occurrence of a specific alarm. This is the method called by `FAlarmTime`'s `OnTimer` event.

`TDDGCalendar` provides three `public` methods: `AddAlarm()`, `RemoveAlarms()`, and `GetAlarmsOnDate()`. `AddAlarm()` uses the `TINIFile`'s `WriteString()` method to write the `TDateTime`'s date as a section name, its time as an identifier, and the `AlMsg` as the identifier's value. The actual INI file entry would look like this:

```
[3/15/95]
5:00:00 AM=Wake up. It's time to start coding Delphi!
```

`RemoveAlarm()` removes all alarm entries for a given day with `TINIFile`'s `EraseSection()` method. `GetAlarmOnDate()` reads all identifiers and their values into a `TStringList` by calling `TINIFile`'s `ReadSectionValues()` method.

Creating *TDDGCalendar*

TDDGCalendar's Create() method first instantiates a FINIFile. It then creates the TTimer variable and sets its timer interval to $1/2$ second. By default, the timer is disabled; however, the program can enable the timer through the published property AlarmEnabled. AlarmEnabled requires two accessor methods to modify its value: SetAlarmEnabled() and GetAlarmEnabled().

These methods actually set the FAlarmTimers Enabled property. This is one way in which you can publicize the property of a component that is owned by another component. Finally, the FTimer is dynamically assigned the OnTimer event Timer1Timer, which checks for the alarm occurrences.

Drawing *TDDGCalendar*

TDDGCalendar's DrawItem() event handler is called for every cell that must be drawn. This method first extracts the day from the cell being drawn with the following line:

```
DayText := CellText[ACol, ARow];
```

It then determines whether DayText contains a valid number. This test is necessary because some cells don't contain a value number representing a day, so the rest of this method wouldn't execute. If DayText passes, the method calculates values for a TRect variable with which the TextRect() method is called. The following line calculates the TRect values:

```
TempRect := Rect(Left, Bottom - TextHeight('W'), Right, Bottom);
```

TextWidth('W') is used because the letter *W* is normally the widest character in most fonts. Because you're only drawing an asterisk in this example, this will be sufficient. The asterisk is drawn in the event that alarms exist for the day specified by DayText.

The first call to TextRect() is called if there are alarms for the day specified by DayText. The second TextRect() is called when there is a schedule file for the day specified by DayText. This file is discussed later in this chapter in the section titled "Using the Day Scheduler Form." If a schedule file is present, an s appears in the cell. This method also changes the font colors for drawing the alarm and schedule indicators.

This completes the discussion of the TDDGCalendar class. Install it to your samples page in Delphi's Component palette so that you can use it in the Calendar application.

Using the Main Form

CalendarForm has the components and property settings specified in Table 25.2. The components and CalendarForm's popup menu are shown in Figure 25.1.

Table 25.2. `CalendarForm`'s components.

Component	Property	Value
CalendarForm	BorderStyle	bsSingle
	PopupMenu	PopupMenu1
Panel1	Font.Color	clBlue
	Align	alTop
Panel2	Align	alRight
DDGCalendar	Align	alClient
	AlarmEnabled	True
Timer1	Enabled	True
	Interval	1000
Button1	Visible	False

FIGURE 25.1.
CalendarForm's
components.

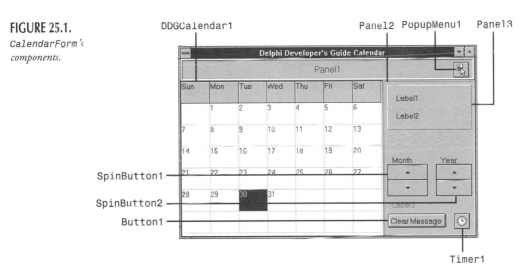

CalendarForm is defined in the unit file CAL.PAS, shown in Listing 25.2. The project file DDGCALP.DPR is shown in Listing 25.3.

Listing 25.2. The source code for CAL.PAS.

```
unit Cal;

interface

uses
  SysUtils, WinTypes, WinProcs, Messages, Classes, Graphics, Controls,
```

continues

Listing 25.2. continued

```pascal
Forms, Dialogs, ExtCtrls, ddgcal, Grids, Calendar, StdCtrls, Buttons,
VBXCtrl, Menus, Spin;

type
  TCalendarForm = class(TForm)
    Panel2: TPanel;
    Panel3: TPanel;
    Label1: TLabel;
    Label2: TLabel;
    Label3: TLabel;
    PopupMenu1: TPopupMenu;
    DayPlanner1: TMenuItem;
    AddAlarm1: TMenuItem;
    RemoveAlarm1: TMenuItem;
    SpinButton1: TSpinButton;
    SpinButton2: TSpinButton;
    Month: TLabel;
    Year: TLabel;
    Panel1: TPanel;
    Timer1: TTimer;
    DDGCalendar1: TDDGCalendar;
    Button1: TButton;
    procedure FormActivate(Sender: TObject);
    procedure Timer1Timer(Sender: TObject);
    procedure SpinButton1UpClick(Sender: TObject);
    procedure SpinButton1DownClick(Sender: TObject);
    procedure SpinButton2DownClick(Sender: TObject);
    procedure SpinButton2UpClick(Sender: TObject);
    procedure AddAlarm1Click(Sender: TObject);
    procedure RemoveAlarm1Click(Sender: TObject);
    procedure DayPlanner1Click(Sender: TObject);
    procedure DDGCalendar1Alarm(Sender: TObject; AlarmMessage: String);
    procedure DDGCalendar1Change(Sender: TObject);
    procedure DDGCalendar1DblClick(Sender: TObject);
    procedure Button1Click(Sender: TObject);
    private
    { Private declarations }
    AlarmMessage: string;
  end;

var
  CalendarForm: TCalendarForm;

implementation
uses DayFormu, SetAlrm, RemAlrm;

{$R *.DFM}

procedure TCalendarForm.FormActivate(Sender: TObject);
begin
  DDGCalendar1.OnChange(Sender); { Call DDGCalendar's OnChange event handler }
end;

procedure TCalendarForm.Timer1Timer(Sender: TObject);
begin
  Label1.Caption := 'Today is: '+DateToStr(Date); { Show today's date in
```

```
➥the label }
  Label2.Caption := 'Time: '+TimeToStr(Time);      { Show current time in
➥the label }
end;

procedure TCalendarForm.SpinButton1UpClick(Sender: TObject);
begin
  DDGCalendar1.PrevMonth; { Go to previous month }
end;

procedure TCalendarForm.SpinButton1DownClick(Sender: TObject);
begin
  DDGCalendar1.NextMonth; { Go to the next month }
end;

procedure TCalendarForm.SpinButton2DownClick(Sender: TObject);
begin
  DDGCalendar1.NextYear; { go to the next year }
end;

procedure TCalendarForm.SpinButton2UpClick(Sender: TObject);
begin
  DDGCalendar1.PrevYear; { go to the previous year }
end;

procedure TCalendarForm.AddAlarm1Click(Sender: TObject);
const
  DTStr = ' %.2d:%.2d:00 %s'; { format string specifier }
var
  DtString,
  AMPMStr: string;
begin
  with SetAlarmForm do begin
    { Use the current date which DDGCalendar is set to }
    Caption := Caption+' for '+DateToStr(DDGCalendar1.CalendarDate);
    if ShowModal  = mrOK then  begin
      if Edit1.Text = '' then
        Edit1.Text := 'Alarm';  { Put a default string there if one wasn't
➥entered }
      if RBAM.Checked then
        AMPMStr := 'AM'          { Specify either A.M. or P.M. according to
➥user's selection }
      else
        AMPMStr := 'PM';
      { Create a string from the calendar's date }
      DtString := DateToStr(DDGCalendar1.CalendarDate)+DtStr;
      { Call the calender's AddAlarm() method to make an entry to an INI file }
      DDGCalendar1.AddAlarm(StrToDateTime(Format(DtString, [SpinEdit1.Value,
          SpinEdit2.Value, AMPMStr])), Edit1.Text);
      DDGCalendar1.Invalidate;  { Redraw the calendar }
    end;
  end;
end;

procedure TCalendarForm.RemoveAlarm1Click(Sender: TObject);
begin
  With RemAlarmForm do begin
    { Set up the form's caption to show the calendar's selected date }
```

continues

Listing 25.2. continued

```
    Caption := 'Remove Alarms For: '+DateToStr(DDGCalendar1.CalendarDate);
    { Retrieve the alarms for the data specified by the cCalendar's data into }
    { the Listbox }
    DDGCalendar1.GetAlarmsOnDate(DDGCalendar1.CalendarDate, ListBox1.Items);
    ShowModal; { Display the form }
  end;
end;

procedure TCalendarForm.DayPlanner1Click(Sender: TObject);
begin
  ShowDayForm(DDGCalendar1.CalendarDate); { Show the DayPlanner form }
end;

procedure TCalendarForm.DDGCalendar1Alarm(Sender: TObject;
  AlarmMessage: String);
begin
  Messagebeep(0);                     { Sound off a message beep }
  Label3.Caption := AlarmMessage;     { Set the label to the alarm's message }
  Label3.Visible := true;             { Make both the label and Button1 }
  Button1.Visible := true;            { visible }
end;

procedure TCalendarForm.DDGCalendar1Change(Sender: TObject);
begin
  { Set Panel1's caption to display the date specified by the calendar }
  Panel1.Caption := FormatDateTime('dddd - mmmm d, yyyy',
                    DDGCalendar1.CalendarDate);
end;

procedure TCalendarForm.DDGCalendar1DblClick(Sender: TObject);
begin
  ShowDayForm(DDGCalendar1.CalendarDate); { Show the day planner form }
end;

procedure TCalendarForm.Button1Click(Sender: TObject);
begin
  Label3.Visible := false;  { Make Label3 and Button1 hidden when alarm
➥is turned }
  Button1.Visible := false; { off. }
end;

end.
```

Listing 25.3. The source code for DDGCALP.DPR.

```
program Ddgcalp;

uses
  Forms,
  Cal in 'CAL.PAS' {CalendarForm},
  Dayformu in 'DAYFORMU.PAS' {DayForm},
  Setalrm in 'SETALRM.PAS' {SetAlarmForm},
```

```
  Remalrm in 'REMALRM.PAS' {RemAlarmForm},
  Ddgcal in 'DDGCAL.PAS';

{$R *.RES}

begin
  Application.CreateForm(TCalendarForm, CalendarForm);
  Application.CreateForm(TSetAlarmForm, SetAlarmForm);
  Application.CreateForm(TRemAlarmForm, RemAlarmForm);
  Application.Run;
end.
```

CalendarForm's OnActivate event handler calls DDGCalendar1's OnChange event, which updates Panel, which updates Panel1's Caption to display the selected date in DDGCalendar1. The selected date is kept in DDGCalendar1.CalendarDate property. Here, you also use the Format() function to format the string accordingly.

The Timer's OnTimer event handler, Timer1Timer(), updates the labels on Panel3 to display the current date and current time. The timer's interval is 1,000 milliseconds (or 1 second).

The spin edits are used to call DDGCalendar's methods (NextMonth, PrevMonth, NextYear, and PrevYear), which advance or move back DDGCalendar's month or year.

The AddAlarm1Click() event handler initializes the Caption for the AddAlarmForm. It then retrieves the information from AlarmForm and uses it to pass to DDGCalendar's AddAlarm() method, which writes the information to an INI file. DDGCalendar.Invalidate is called to show itself with the alarm indicator in the cell for which the alarm was set.

The RemoveAlarm1Click() event handler invokes the RemoveAlarmForm after adding all alarms for the selected day to RemoveAlarmForm's listbox. This is done by using DDGCalendar's GetAlarmsOnDate() event handler.

DayPlanner1Click() invokes the DayForm by calling the ShowDayForm() procedure, which is discussed in the next section.

The DDGCalendar's OnDblClick event handler also invokes the day form.

DDGCalendar's OnAlarm event uses a MessageBeep(0) to sound an alarm, displays the AlarmMessage, and makes Button1.Visible. Button1Click() sets itself and Label3's visible property to false.

Using the Day Scheduler Form

DayForm has the components and property settings specified in Table 25.3. Figure 25.2 shows what DayForm should look like.

Table 25.3. **DayForm's components.**

Component	Property	Value
DayForm	BorderIcons	[bsSystemMenu, bmMinimize]
	BorderStyle	bsSingle
StringGrid1	Align	alLeft
	ColCount	3
	FixedCols	2
	ScrollBars	ssNone
	RowCount	14
	Options	[goFixedVertLine, goFixedHorzLine, goVertLine, goHorzLine, goEditing, goRowSelect]
Panel1	Align	alClient
BitBtn	Kind	OnOk

FIGURE 25.2.

DayForm's components.

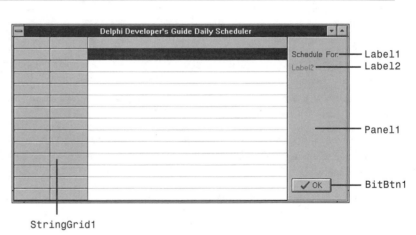

DayForm displays a daily schedule using a TStringGrid component. The data for the schedule is stored in a Pascal-typed file; the filename follows the format DDMMYYYY.CAL. This file is declared as a File of TDayRecord, where TDayRecord is defined as the following:

```
TDayRecord = record
   Hour: integer;
   Reminder: string;
 end;
```

The Hour variable stores the row position for the record. Reminder is a message that is displayed in the Description column of the string grid. The source code for the day scheduler form, DAYFORMU.PAS, is shown in Listing 25.4.

Listing 25.4. The source code for DAYFORMU.PAS.

```
unit Dayformu;

interface

uses
  SysUtils, WinTypes, WinProcs, Messages, Classes, Graphics, Controls,
  Forms, Dialogs, Grids, stdctrls, ExtCtrls, Clkpanl, Buttons;

type
  TDayRecord = record
    Hour: integer;
    Reminder: string;
  end;

  TDayForm = class(TForm)
    StringGrid1: TStringGrid;
    Panel1: TPanel;
    Label1: TLabel;
    Label2: TLabel;
    BitBtn1: TBitBtn;
    procedure FormCreate(Sender: TObject);
    procedure StringGrid1SelectCell(Sender: TObject; Col, Row: Longint;
      var CanSelect: Boolean);
    procedure StringGrid1DblClick(Sender: TObject);
    procedure BitBtn1Click(Sender: TObject);
  private
    { Private declarations }
    FDateTime: TDateTime;
    FFileName: string[80];
  public
    { Public declarations }
  end;

procedure ShowDayForm(DateTime: TDateTime);

implementation
{$R *.DFM}
var
  DayForm: TDayForm;

procedure ShowDayForm(DateTime: TDateTime);
var
  Y, M, D: word;
  f: file of TDayRecord;
  DayRec: TDayRecord;
begin
  DayForm := TDayForm.Create(Application);  { Instantiate the day form }
  with DayForm do begin
    FDateTime := DateTime;                 { Initialize FDateTime to the
➥parameter }
    DecodeDate(FDateTime, Y, M, D);        { value and extract the individual
➥items }
    FFileName := IntToStr(D)+IntToStr(M)+IntToSTr(Y)+'.CAL'; {from it to create
➥a filename }
    Label2.Caption := DateToStr(FDateTime); { Set the caption to display the
➥date passed in }
```

continues

Listing 25.4. continued

```
      if FileExists(FFileName) then begin      { Check if a file exists from the
➥generated file }
        AssignFile(f, FFileName);              { name }
        Reset(f);                              { Open the file for reading }
        while not Eof(f) do begin              { while there's something to read
➥in the file }
          Read(f, DayRec);                     { read a TDayRecord into DayRec }
          StringGrid1.Cols[2][DayRec.Hour] := DayRec.Reminder; { Show the message
➥in the }
        end;                                   { grid column. }
        CloseFile(f);                          { Close the file and delete it. It
➥will be either }
        DeleteFile(FFileName);                 { created or not created }
      end;
      ShowModal;                               { display the form }
  end;
  DayForm.Free;                                { free the form }
end;

procedure TDayForm.FormCreate(Sender: TObject);
var
  i: integer;
begin
  { When the form is created, create all the label columns accordingly }
  with StringGrid1 do begin
    Rows[0][0] := 'From:';
    Rows[0][1] := 'To:';
    Rows[0][2] := 'Description';
    for i := 7 to 12 do
      Cols[0][i-6] := IntToStr(i-1)+':00 am';
    Cols[0][7] := IntToStr(12)+':00 pm';
    for i := 1 to 8 do
      Cols[0][i+7] := IntToStr(i)+':00 pm';
    for i := 1 to 5 do
      Cols[1][i] := IntToStr(i+6)+':00 am';
    Cols[1][6] := IntToStr(12)+':00 pm';
    for i := 7 to 13 do
      Cols[1][i] := IntToStr(i-6)+':00 pm';
  end;
end;

procedure TDayForm.StringGrid1SelectCell(Sender: TObject; Col,
  Row: Longint; var CanSelect: Boolean);
begin
  { Make this particular row editable }
  StringGrid1.Options := StringGrid1.Options - [goEditing]+[goRowSelect];
end;

procedure TDayForm.StringGrid1DblClick(Sender: TObject);
begin
  { Make this row non-editable }
  StringGrid1.Options := StringGrid1.Options + [goEditing]-[goRowSelect];
end;

procedure TDayForm.BitBtn1Click(Sender: TObject);
var
  i: integer;
```

```
    f: File of TDayRecord;
    StufToStore: boolean;
    D,M,Y: word;
    DayRec: TDayRecord;
begin
  { First determine if there are any items in the grid to store }
  StufToStore := false;
  for i := 1 to 13 do
    if StringGrid1.Cols[2][i] <> '' then begin
      StufToStore := true;
      break;
    end;
  { If there are items to store, then create a new data file and store the items }
  { there }
  if StufToStore then begin
    AssignFile(f, FFileName); { Assign and create a new file }
    Rewrite(f);
    for i := 1 to 13 do
      { Now put the data from the string grid into a TDayRecord variable
 ➥and store }
      { the data to the new file }
      if StringGrid1.Cols[2][i] <> '' then begin
        DayRec.Hour := i;
        DayRec.Reminder := StringGrid1.Cols[2][i];
        write(f, DayRec);
      end;
    CloseFile(f); { Close the file }
  end;
end;

end.
```

The ShowDayForm() method instantiates the TDayForm variable and sets up DayForm's various properties which are based on the DateTime parameter. The DecodeDate() procedure separates the month, day, and year from a TDateTime variable and assigns them to word-typed parameters. These values are used to create a filename following the format DDMMYYYY.CAL. The filename then is passed to FileExists(), which returns true if a file is found. If a file exists, each TDayRecord is read from the file in sequential order and is used to initialize the string grid's rows. The Reminder variable is stored in the row specified by the Hour variable in the TDayRecord structure. Finally, the following lines close the file and then delete it:

```
CloseFile(f);
DeleteFile(FFileName);
```

The reason we delete the file is because if the user makes any changes to it, it will be re-created and updated with the recent data. Otherwise, if the user removes all entries, there is no reason to re-create another file. ShowModal() then is called to display the form in its modal state.

TDayForm.FormCreate() initializes fixed titles for the fixed rows and columns in the TStringGrid. The titles are set as shown in Figure 25.3.

Double-clicking a description cell forces it to become editable with the line

```
StringGrid1.Options := StringGrid1.Options + [goEditing] - [goRowSelect];
```

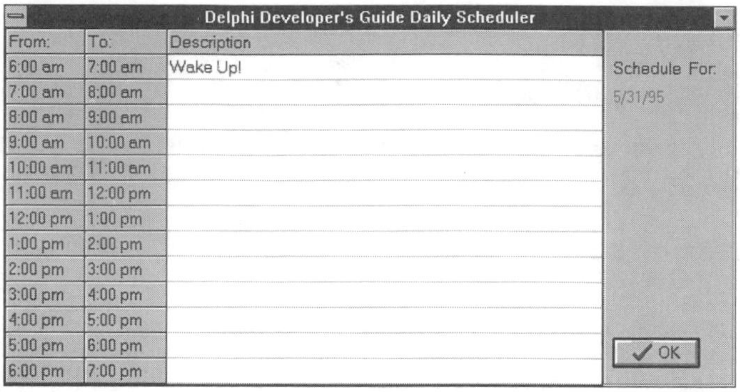

FIGURE 25.3.
Row/Column titles.

After the user leaves the cell, the cell is made read-only again:

```
StringGrid1.Options := StringGrid1.Options - [goEditing] + [goRowSelect];
```

The BitBtn1Click() event handler first checks to see whether there are any reminders in the Descriptions column for the TStringList. If so, it creates a new day schedule file of type TDayRecord, and stores each TDayRecord for those columns that contain data. Finally, the file is closed.

Using the Set Alarm Form

SetAlarmForm has the important components and property settings specified in Table 25.4. Figure 25.4 shows SetAlarmForm.

Table 25.4. SetAlarmForm's components.

Component	Property	Value
SetAlarmForm	BorderStyle	bsSingle
RBAM	Checked	True
RBPM	Checked	False
BitBtn1	Kind	bkOk
BitBtn2	Kind	bkCancel
SpinEdit1	MinValue	1
	MaxValue	13
	Value	0
	Increment	1
SpinEdit2	MinValue	0

Component	Property	Value
	MaxValue	60
	Value	0
	Increment	2
MaskEdit1	ReadOnly	True
MaskEdit2	ReadOnly	True
Edit1	Text	' '

FIGURE 25.4.

*SetAlarmForm's
components.*

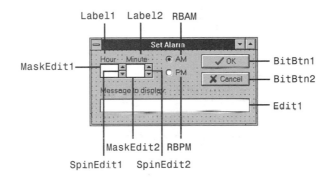

The SetAlarmForm's functionality is somewhat simpler than the previous forms. Listing 25.5 shows the SETALRM.PAS file.

Listing 25.5. The source code for SETALRM.PAS.

```
unit Setalrm;

interface

uses
  SysUtils, WinTypes, WinProcs, Messages, Classes, Graphics, Controls,
  Forms, Dialogs, StdCtrls, Buttons, Spin, Mask;

type
  TSetAlarmForm = class(TForm)
    Label1: TLabel;
    Label2: TLabel;
    RBAM: TRadioButton;
    RMPM: TRadioButton;
    BitBtn1: TBitBtn;
    BitBtn2: TBitBtn;
    Label3: TLabel;
    SpinEdit1: TSpinEdit;
    SpinEdit2: TSpinEdit;
    MaskEdit1: TMaskEdit;
    MaskEdit2: TMaskEdit;
```

continues

Listing 25.5. continued

```
   Edit1: TEdit;
   procedure SpinEdit1Change(Sender: TObject);
   procedure SpinEdit2Change(Sender: TObject);
   procedure FormActivate(Sender: TObject);
 private
   { Private declarations }
 public
   { Public declarations }
 end;

var
  SetAlarmForm: TSetAlarmForm;

implementation

{$R *.DFM}

procedure TSetAlarmForm.SpinEdit1Change(Sender: TObject);
begin
  { This spin edit represents hours }
  SpinEdit1.Value := SpinEdit1.Value mod 13;
  MaskEdit1.Text := Format('%.2d', [SpinEdit1.Value]);
end;

procedure TSetAlarmForm.SpinEdit2Change(Sender: TObject);
begin
  { This spin edit represents seconds, using modulus operator }
  SpinEdit2.Value := SpinEdit2.Value mod 60;
  MaskEdit2.Text := Format('%.2d', [SpinEdit2.Value]);
end;

procedure TSetAlarmForm.FormActivate(Sender: TObject);
begin
  { Set the MaskEdit's accordingly }
  MaskEdit1.Text := Format('%.2d', [SpinEdit1.Value]);
  MaskEdit2.Text := Format('%.2d', [SpinEdit2.Value]);
end;

end.
```

The `TSpinEdit` controls are used to increment values that represent hours and minutes. `TEdit` controls sit directly on top of the `TSpinEdit`'s `TEdit` part, so that they appear as part of the `TSpinEdit`. When the user changes the value of the `SpinEdits`, the `Edit` controls are formatted to contain their value with the `Format()` function. The `Forms OnActive` event handler also formats the `TEdit`'s initial values. Recall that `SetAlarmForm` is invoked from `CalendarForm`'s `AddAlarm1Click()` event handler, where it uses the values obtained from `SetAlarmForm` to pass to `DDGCalendar1`'s `AddAlarm()` method.

Using the Remove Alarm Form

RemAlarmForm has the components and property settings shown in Table 25.5. Figure 25.5 shows RemAlarmForm's components. The RemAlarmForm's unit is shown in Listing 25.6.

Table 25.5. RemAlarmForm's components.

Component	Property	Value
BitBtn1	Kind	bkOk
BitBtn2	Kind	bkCancel

FIGURE 25.5.

RemAlarmForm's components.

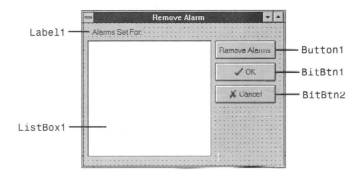

Listing 25.6. The source code for REMALRM.PAS.

```pascal
unit Remalrm;

interface

uses
  SysUtils, WinTypes, WinProcs, Messages, Classes, Graphics, Controls,
  Forms, Dialogs, Buttons, StdCtrls;

type
  TRemAlarmForm = class(TForm)
    ListBox1: TListBox;
    Label1: TLabel;
    BitBtn1: TBitBtn;
    Button2: TButton;
    BitBtn2: TBitBtn;
    procedure BitBtn1Click(Sender: TObject);
    procedure Button2Click(Sender: TObject);
  private
    { Private declarations }
  public
    { Public declarations }
  end;
```

continues

Listing 25.6. continued

```
var
  RemAlarmForm: TRemAlarmForm;

implementation
uses Cal;

{$R *.DFM}

procedure TRemAlarmForm.BitBtn1Click(Sender: TObject);
begin
  ListBox1.Items.Clear;    { Clear the items in the listbox }
end;

procedure TRemAlarmForm.Button2Click(Sender: TObject);
var
  DtStr: string;
begin
  { Create a string out of the calendar's selected date }
  DtStr := DateToStr(CalendarForm.DDGCalendar1.CalendarDate);
  { Remove all the alarms }
  with ListBox1 do begin
   if Items.Count > 0 then
    CalendarForm.DDGCalendar1.RemoveAlarms(StrToDate(DtStr));
    Items.Clear; { Clear the listbox's items. }
  end;
end;

end.
```

RemAlarmForm.BitBtn1Click(), the OK button, clears the listbox's contents to prepare it for the next time it is invoked. The BitBtn2Click() event handler retrieves the selected date from DDGCalendar and passes it to DDGCalendar1's RemoveAlarms() method, which removes all alarms for the date specified by DtStr. Finally, it clears the listbox items. RemAlarmForm is invoked from CalendarForm's RemoveAlarm1Click() event handler, where its listbox is populated with the alarms retrieved from DDGCalendar1's GetAlarmsOnDate() method.

Summary

This chapter showed you how to take existing components and extend upon their functionality. Specifically, you added more features to Delphi's TCalendar component by adding to it a scheduler and an alarm. You also learned how to work with the TINIFile class, as well as got more experience creating Delphi components. You learned how to perform special drawing in a grids cell and made use of some of Delphi's Date/Time functions. This example program not only gives you a usable tool, it serves as a building block for you to extend upon in order to perform whatever suits your needs. Experiment with the components and objects that you have used so far to see how easily you can add powerful functionality to your already existing applications. In the next chapter, you'll see how powerful components can be as we illustrate using a set of third-party components to build a complete phone dialer/terminal application using serial communications.

26

Building a Phone Dialer/ Terminal Application— Serial Communications

This chapter illustrates a serial communications application created with little effort using some powerful serial communications components. Serial communications programming in Windows is one of the more difficult and not well-documented areas of programming in Windows.

This chapter could present you with the details of serial communications and how to use the Window API for developing such applications. Instead, however, you learn how to develop powerful, complex applications in a few hours—if that.

In this chapter, you will look at a completely functional phone dialer/terminal emulation program built using a powerful set of third-party communications components that completely encapsulate the Window's serial communications API. These components are on the accompanying CD in the directory \THRDPRTY\TPOWER\APD and in the CD's \SOURCE\CH26 directory. Before you install and use these components, you need a general understanding of serial communications.

Defining Serial Communications

Generally speaking, *serial communications* is a means by which data is transferred to and from hardware devices via a single wire. This definition can be expanded to mean much more when considering the entire computer industry. For the purposes of this discussion, the definition of serial communications will be limited to developing Windows serial communications applications on the PC.

When people refer to *serial communications*, they typically are referring to information transfer via serial ports that adhere to the RS-232 standard. The RS-232 standard, created by the Electronic Industries Association, defines the protocol for communication through serial ports. The RS-232 specifics are not required for this discussion. The important point to make here is that there is a connection in the back of your computer to which you attach a variety of devices to communicate with your computer. Such devices can be mice, printers, plotters, joysticks, pens, bar-code readers, and many other devices that need to feed or receive data to or from your computer. These connections are called *COM ports*, which are synonymous with *serial ports*.

The chip that controls how COM ports operate is the *UART* or *Universal Asynchronous Receiver/Transmitter*. The details of how this works aren't really applicable to what you do in this chapter. You simply need to know that this UART is the chip that talks to the CPU about incoming and outgoing data via the COM ports. COM ports are discussed in more detail later in this chapter.

Serial Communication Considerations

In the DOS world, developing serial communications required one to have in-depth knowledge of PC hardware and the UART. The PC's BIOS does provide an interface to the serial ports through interrupt 14, but it is limited in its capabilities. Therefore, anybody doing serious development got around interrupt 14 and went directly to the UART. One had to know how to initialize the port, to create an interrupt service routine, and to know how to interface with the UART to read and write data. This process did require one to have a low-level understanding of serial communications overall. Windows made it a bit easier by providing an API that handled the low-level tasks for you through its own communications driver (COMM.DRV).

So now, programmers had the Windows API for developing serial communications. For the experienced programmer, this was a charm. No longer was there a need to interface with the actual hardware. All one had to do was poll the communications driver for incoming data. That was prior to Windows 3.1, which simplified that process further by providing the EnableCommNotification() function. This function causes the Windows communications driver to post a WM_COMMNOTIFY message after an event happens at the COM port.

Windows did ease the process of developing the basic communications programs. Still, there was the issue of what to do with the data, how to display it if required, how to dial and answer via modem, how to send or receive files, and how to deal with the different file-transfer protocols. Then, of course, there was the issue of how to handle the numerous errors that can occur under serial communications. Unless you are a Windows/serial communications programming expert, you were left wishing that you had an easier way of mastering this powerful capability.

A TurboPower-ful Solution to Windows Serial-Communications Programming

Often, developers don't want to concern themselves with the low-level routines to create powerful applications. Instead, they turn to third-party companies that develop tools that suit their needs. One such company excels in the area of serial-communications tools: Turbo Power Software, Inc.

TurboPower initially came out with a communications toolkit: Async Professional for MS-DOS. This toolkit is completely object-oriented, handles all the industry standard file protocols, provides modem support, and offers terminal emulation, just to name a few features. Since then, TurboPower has expanded its product to Windows with Async Professional for Delphi (APD) and soon will be coming out with a Delphi version, Async Professional for Delphi (APD), which probably will be complete by this book's publication date.

We were fortunate that TurboPower allowed us to use a pre-release version of their product in this book. It allowed us to demonstrate how combining Delphi with powerful, well-written components can make the most difficult programming tasks a breeze.

Installing Async Professional for Delphi

Before you can use Async Professional for Delphi, you must install the components to your Components Palette. This section explains how to do that task.

To install the APD components, follow these steps:

1. Create a directory on your hard drive called C:\APD.
2. Change to the C:\APD directory (your DOS prompt should read `C:\APD:>`).
3. Insert the accompanying CD into your CD-ROM drive and copy the Async Professional files and directories from the CD-ROM to your C:\APD directory. For example, if your CD-ROM drive is your D: drive, then from the C:\APD directory, type the following and press Enter:

   XCOPY D:\THRDPRTY\TPOWER\APD*.*

4. While you are at the DOS prompt, you might as well copy the file APDDEMO.INI to your Windows directory. This file needs to exist there in order for you to run the project.

Now you're ready to install the components. Using the method to install components discussed in Chapter 11, "Writing Delphi Custom Components," install APD components by selecting the file APDREG.PAS from the Add Module dialog box, as shown in Figure 26.1. This file exists in the C:\APD\ directory that you just created.

FIGURE 26.1.
*Adding APDREG.PAS to
the Add Module dialog
box.*

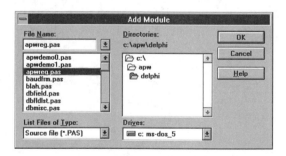

NOTE

The APD shipping with this book is the full-blown, pre-release version of Async Professional for Delphi. Because it is a pre-release, changes probably will be made to the final product. However, the demonstration here was developed with a late enough release that you shouldn't have any problems converting it to the final version. The one catch is that you will not be able to run your projects developed with this version unless you also have Delphi running. This catch was intended so that you could see how to use this powerful tool without giving the product away. Also, you can obtain updated "trial" versions of APD from one of TurboPower's three download sites: the TurboPower BBS, CompuServe, or FTP.

When Delphi completes the installation process, you will see many new components on the APD page of your Component Palette, as shown in Figure 26.2.

FIGURE 26.2.

The APD Component Palette.

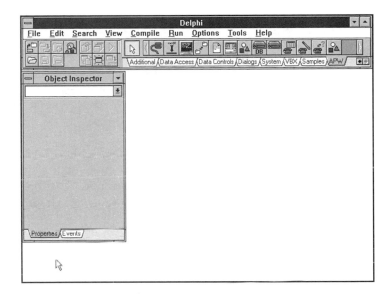

Async Professional for Delphi, Unplugged

This section tells you a bit about the components that are used in the demonstration project before you actually look at the project. There are some extra components on the palette that are part of APD, but those are not discussed here. You are free to use and experiment with them, however.

The *TComPort* Component

TComPort, which is the first from the left on the Component Palette, is the manager of your COM port. It contains the properties for opening, closing, and configuring the port. TComPort also manages sending and receiving data, manages flow control, and provides tracing and logging events to facilitate debugging. Additionally, TComPort provides appropriate event handlers such as OnPortOpen, OnPortClose, and OnTriggerXXXX events that enable you to process certain trigger events (*trigger* simply is another term for events concerning APD).

The *TEmulator* Component

TEmulator interprets the incoming data into something that can be presented meaningfully to the user. As data comes across the COM port, it contains various commands called *escape sequences* that the emulator knows how to handle. Although there are several different standards for commands, the most common among the PC industry is the ANSI standard, which is supported by TEmulator. TEmulator also can perform no interpretation on data, in which case the data will come across in its raw form.

The *TTerminal* Component

TTerminal works with TEmulator to enable the user to see the incoming data through a user interface. When TEmulator is interpreting ANSI data, it interprets the escape sequences and generates the commands telling TTerminal what action to take—for example, to move the cursor up or down, to change colors, to clear the screen, and so on.

The *TProtocol* Component

TProtocol encapsulates a variety of standard protocols for performing file transfer. A *protocol* is simply a set of rules that both the sender and receiver of the communication agree to for performing file transfers. Such rules dictate the handling of transferring file names and sizes, file I/O, how to determine when transmission errors have occurred, and so on. Table 27.1 shows the various protocols that APD supports through TProtocol with general comments about each protocol.

Table 27.1. Protocols supported by Async Professional for Delphi.

Protocol	*Comments*
Xmodem	Uses 128-byte transfer block, uses checksum block checking for data integrity.
XmodemCRC	Uses 128-byte transfer block CRC block checking for data integrity.
Xmodem1K	A derivative of XmodemCRC. Uses 1024-byte transfer block and CRC block checking for data integrity.
Xmodem1KG	Uses 1024-byte transfer blocks with streaming. Streaming means that the receiver does not acknowledge that the blocks received are correct.
Ymodem (batch)	A derivative of Xmodem1K, uses 1024-byte transfer block CRC block checking and facilitates batch transmissions.
YmodemG (batch)	Same as Ymodem but offers streaming capabilities.

Protocol	*Comments*
Zmodem (batch)	Employs headers, data subpackets, and frames instead of simple block transfers. Data subpackets contain 1024-data bytes. Zmodem provides the best option of the protocols listed here.
Kermit (batch)	80-byte transfer block with batch transmission capabilities.
B+ (batch)	File transfer protocol specifically for the CompuServe online service.
ASCII	ASCII character stream transfers.

NOTE

Batch means that the protocol can transmit/receive multiple files in one transfer. When using non-batch protocols, it is up to the user to specify a filename for an incoming file.

TProtocol processes file transfers in the background. This means that your application can transmit or receive data while it continues on its way doing other tasks. TProtocol traps any messages that occur as a result of the transfer and translates them into events for which your application can provide an event handler. TProtocol provides other event handlers, as described in the following list:

OnProtocolAccept	Occurs before receiving a file, giving you the opportunity to accept or reject the file transfer. You also can rename the file in this event handler.
OnProtocolLog	Occurs at the start and end of each file transfer, enabling the user and/or the TProtocolLog component to log that status of the transfer.
OnProtocolStatus	Occurs approximately once per second, enabling the user to display protocol status such as elapsed time, bytes transferred, and so on. The TProtocolStatus component can be used for this purpose.
OnProtocolError	Occurs whenever a fatal error occurs during a file transfer. The transfer terminates soon after this messages is sent.
OnProtocolFinish	Occurs when the protocol is finished with the transfer, either normally or as a result of an error.

The *TProtocolLog* Component

TProtocol looks for a TProtocolLog component, and if it finds one, it routes its OnProtocolLog events to the TProtocolLog component and calls the user's OnProtocolLog event if one occurs. The TProtocolLog component then gets to add that information to a log file specified by one of its properties.

The *TProtocolStatus* Component

TProtocol looks for a TProtocolStatus component and, if it finds one, it routes the OnProtocolStatus events to the TProtocolStatus component to display progress information. Like the TProtocolLog component, TProtocolStatus also calls the user's OnProtocolStatus event handler if one exists.

The *TModem* Component

The TModem component encapsulates the routines needed for handling modem functions like answering, dialing, and configuring. TModem works with any Hayes-compatible modem. TModem requires a TComPort component and, therefore, automatically searches the form for one.

The *TModemDialer* Component

TModemDialer works like any other common dialog box. You drop it on the form and set its properties accordingly to customize it. When TModemDialer is running, you call its Execute() method to dial the specified number. TModemDialer searches for a TModem component on your form and hooks to it automatically.

The APD Demonstration Project

The APD demo is located in the \APD directory and is named APDDEMO.DPR. Before you loaded it, however, remember to place the APDDEMO.INI file, located in the same directory, into your Windows directory. There are really only two entries in this file that you should concern yourself with:

```
[ComPort]
Port=1
Baud=9600
```

If you don't place this file in the Windows directory, TComPort will set its properties to some default values that might fail when attempting to connect to a COM port. Therefore, ensure that you have the correct COM port specified for the entry Port and that Baud is set according to your modem's capability.

> **NOTE**
>
> You need a modem to run this project. If you don't have one, don't worry—this chapter still will get you geared for when you do want to get into serial communications programming.

After you have APD loaded, the APD Demo main form appears, as shown in Figure 26.3.

FIGURE 26.3.

The APD Demo main form.

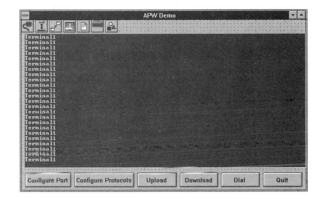

The main form is the starting point for the Phone Dialer/Terminal program. From the main form, you can call the methods to read/write INI file settings, and write data to or get data from other forms for setting the various APD component properties. The main form is also from where you invoke dialing and/or the displaying status information.

The project uses five other forms named `ComPortOptions`, `DialDialog`, `DownloadDialog`, `ProtocolOptions`, and `UploadDialog`. These forms enable you to configure the various properties for the AWD components at runtime or to get necessary information when uploading or downloading files. All the forms, other than the main form, really only exist to enable the user to set up various options for the APD components.

The Com Port Options Form

The Com Port Options form enables you to specify various properties for `TComPort`. This form is shown in Figure 26.4.

You will see six groups in this form: Com Ports, Baud Rates, Parity, Data Bits, Stop Bits, and Flow Control.

FIGURE 26.4.

The Com Port Options form.

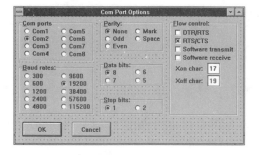

The Com Port Options enable you to specify through which COM port the application will be communicating or transferring data or files. On IBM PC computers, there are, at most, four available COM ports (1 through 4). On PS/2 machines, there are, at most, eight COM ports. COM ports are signified by their base address and by an IRQ number. *IRQ numbers* refer to hardware-interrupt lines that are set up to handle interrupts by priority. Table 26.1 lists the base address and IRQ numbers for COM ports on the IBM PC.

Table 26.1. COM port base addresses and IRQ settings for PCs.

Port Name	Base Address	IRQ
COM1	03F8	4
COM2	02F8	3
COM3	03E8	4
COM4	02E8	3

This chapter is concerned only with the IBM PC COM ports, because these are the most common. Notice how COM1 and COM3 share the same IRQ line and use them at the same time. The same goes for COM2 and COM4.

CAUTION

Unless you have special hardware enabling you to share IRQs, you cannot connect two different devices to the same IRQ. This may cause a conflict and also will cause your application to fail. An example here would be to connect your mouse to COM3 and your modem to COM1.

The Baud Rates group offers you measurements that determine the speed of data transfer. With APD, this is measured as bits per second. Your selection here depends on the capability of your modem and the device sending you data.

The Data Bits options enable you to select how many bits make up a data byte. This can be 5, 6, 7, or 8 bits—usually, it is 7 or 8 bits.

The Stop Bits options follow the data bits in a transfer and mark the end of the data byte.

> **TIP**
>
> Unless connecting to a device that specifically requests two data bits, always use only one stop bit.

The Parity group refers to how the integrity of the data transfer is checked—all the bits in a byte that has been transferred are added. The sum then is added with an additional bit, which may or may not be set. The result will be even or odd, depending on the type of parity checking you specify.

The Flow Control group refers to how your application stops the sending or receiving of data. The first four options are hardware based, and the Xon Char and Xoff Char options are software based. When transferring files to or from BBSs or other host systems you will usually select RTS/CTS.

The Protocol Options Form

The Protocol Options form enables you to specify certain options for specific protocols. There are some general options that you can specify, as well as options specific to Zmodem, Kermit, or ASCII protocol.

The *DownLoadDialog* Form

The DownLoadDialog form enables you to specify the protocol to use to perform file downloads. You also can specify the directory on which the file will be placed on your system. For non-batch protocols, you must also specify the name to give to the incoming file.

The *UploadDialog* Form

The UploadDialog form is much like the DownloadDialog form, except that you specify a filename, or for batch protocols, a file mask such as *.pas, to upload to another system. In the UploadDialog you also choose the protocol to use for the transfer.

The *DialDialog* Form

The DialDialog form is a simple form that prompts you for a phone number to dial.

The Main Form

The main form contains all the necessary AWD components required to run the project, and this is where most of the grunt work is done. You can select the TComPort component and specify the COM port by changing the ComNumber property as well as modifying the Baud property.

As mentioned earlier, some of these components automatically look for components that they require in order for them to work. If you remove the TProtocolLog component from the form and look at the ProtocolLog property for TProtocol, for example, you will see that it is blank. Now, place a TProtocolLog component back on the form, and TProtocol's ProtocolLog property will contain the name of the added component.

No changes were made to the default property settings to make this application work. You shouldn't have to change anything other than TComPort's ComNumber property or its Baud, if these already are set to how you have your system is configured. Otherwise, change these properties in the Object Inspector.

Listing 26.1 shows the source code for the main form.

Listing 26.1. The main form's source file.

```
unit APDMain;

interface

uses
  SysUtils, WinTypes, WinProcs, Messages, Classes, Graphics, Controls,
  Forms, Dialogs, IniFiles, AdMisc, AdExcept, AdTerm, AdProtcl, AdPStat,
  AdPort, ExtCtrls, StdCtrls, AdXPort, AdXProt, AdXUp, AdXDown, AdDial,
  AdModem, AdXDial, AdIni;

const
  APDIniFileName = 'APDEMO.INI';

type
  TMain = class(TForm)
    ComPort1: TComPort;
    Protocol1: TProtocol;
    ProtocolStatus1: TProtocolStatus;
    ProtocolLog1: TProtocolLog;
    Terminal1: TTerminal;
    Upload: TButton;
    Download: TButton;
    Quit: TButton;
    PortConfig: TButton;
    ProtConfig: TButton;
    Emulator1: TEmulator;
    Modem1: TModem;
    ModemDialer1: TModemDialer;
    Dial: TButton;
    procedure FormActivate(Sender: TObject);
    procedure UploadClick(Sender: TObject);
    procedure DownloadClick(Sender: TObject);
    procedure Protocol1ProtocolFinish(CP: TObject; ErrorCode: Integer);
```

```
    procedure QuitClick(Sender: TObject);
    procedure PortConfigClick(Sender: TObject);
    procedure ProtConfigClick(Sender: TObject);
    procedure DialClick(Sender: TObject);
    procedure FormCreate(Sender: TObject);
    procedure FormDestroy(Sender: TObject);
  private
    { Private declarations }
    APDIni: TAPDIni;
  public
    { Public declarations }
  end;

var
  Main: TMain;

implementation

{$R *.DFM}

procedure TMain.FormActivate(Sender: TObject);
const
  Loaded : Boolean = False;
begin
  Terminal1.Active := True;      { Set the terminal to active }
   if not Loaded then begin      { Execute code in this block once }
    Loaded := True;
    APDIni.GetComPort(ComPort1);  { Get the ComPort options from the Ini file }
    APDIni.GetProtocol(Protocol1);{ Get the Protocol options from the Ini file }
  end;
end;

procedure TMain.UploadClick(Sender: TObject);
begin
  {Stuff current options into dialog}
  UploadDialog.Mask := Protocol1.FileMask;        { Specify a filename }
  UploadDialog.Protocol := Protocol1.ProtocolType; { Specify the protocol type }

  {Process the dialog and upload the file(s)}
  if UploadDialog.ShowModal = idOK then begin      { If user chose to upload...}
    Protocol1.FileMask := UploadDialog.Mask;       { Set the mask specified by
➥user }
    Protocol1.ProtocolType := UploadDialog.Protocol;{ Set the protocol type
➥specified by user }
    Protocol1.StartTransmit;                       { Upload the file }
  end
  else
    Terminal1.SetFocus;                            { Set the focus back to the
➥Terminal }
end;

procedure TMain.DownloadClick(Sender: TObject);
begin
  {Stuff the current option into the dialog}
  DownloadDialog.Protocol := Protocol1.ProtocolType;  { Set a default
➥ProtocolType }
  DownloadDialog.DestDirectory :=                      { Set to a default
➥directory }
        Protocol1.DestinationDirectory;
```

continues

Listing 26.1. continued

```
{Process the dialog and download the files}
if DownloadDialog.ShowModal = idOk then begin        { If user chose to
➥download ... }
   Protocol1.ProtocolType := DownloadDialog.Protocol; { Set to protocol
➥type specified by user }
   { Set to destination directory specified by user }
   Protocol1.DestinationDirectory := DownloadDialog.DestDirectory;
   case Protocol1.ProtocolType of { If the protocol type is
➥ptXModem..ptXmodem1K the user }
      ptXmodem..ptXmodem1KG,        { Must specify a name to which the file
➥will be download }
      ptASCII : Protocol1.FileName := DownloadDialog.ReceiveName;
   end;
   Protocol1.StartReceive;          { Begin to download the file }
 end else
   Terminal1.SetFocus;              { Set focus back to the terminal }
end;

procedure TMain.Protocol1ProtocolFinish(CP: TObject; ErrorCode: Integer);
begin
  if ErrorCode = 0 then  { If no error, tell user that file transfer completed }
    MessageDlg('Transfer complete', mtInformation, [mbok], 0)
  else
    MessageDlg(ErrorMsg(ErrorCode), mtInformation, [mbok], 0);
  Terminal1.SetFocus;                        { Set focus back to the terminal }
end;

procedure TMain.QuitClick(Sender: TObject);
begin
  Close;  { Close the main form }
end;

procedure TMain.PortConfigClick(Sender: TObject);
begin
  ComPortOptions.ComPort := ComPort1;   { Initialize the dialogs CompPort
➥property }
  if ComPortOptions.Execute then begin  { Show the dialog }
    {Close current port, if open}
    if Assigned(ComPort1) then
      ComPort1.Open := False;

    {Assign new comport values and open the port}
    ComPort1.Assign(ComPortOptions.ComPort);
    ComPort1.Open := True;
    APDIni.WriteComPort(ComPort1);       { Write the new options to an INI file }
  end;
  Terminal1.SetFocus;                    {Give focus back to terminal window}
end;

procedure TMain.ProtConfigClick(Sender: TObject);
  {-Get new protocol options}
begin
  if Assigned(Protocol1) then                  { Initialize the ProtocolOptions }
    ProtocolOptions.Protocol := Protocol1;     { Dialog }
```

```
   if ProtocolOptions.Execute then begin      { If new options were set, set }
     Protocol1.Assign(ProtocolOptions.Protocol);{ Protocol1's options and then }
     APDIni.WriteProtocol(Protocol1);          { save the options to an INI file }
   end;

   Terminal1.SetFocus;                        { Set focus back to Terminal window}
end;
procedure TMain.DialClick(Sender: TObject);
begin
   DialDialog.Number.Text := '1-719-260-9726'; { Specify a default number to dial }
   if DialDialog.ShowModal = idOK then begin   { If user selected to dial ... }
     ModemDialer1.PhoneNumber := DialDialog.Number.Text; { Set the number to that
➥in the dialog }
     ModemDialer1.Execute;                    { Dial away! }
   end;
   Terminal1.SetFocus;                        { Set focus back to the terminal }
end;

procedure TMain.FormCreate(Sender: TObject);
begin
   APDIni := TAPDIni.Create(APDIniFileName); { Create an APDIni class which is a
➥smart }
end;                                         { Inifile that knows about APD's
➥properties }
procedure TMain.FormDestroy(Sender: TObject);
begin
   APDIni.Free;                              { Close the APDIni class }
end;
end.
```

The main form's OnCreate event handler instantiates a TAPDIni class. This is just a class wrapper for a TINIFile which knows about TComPort and TProtocol configuration settings. The main form's OnDestroy event handler frees the TAPDIni class instance.

The main form's OnActive handler initializes it's ComPort1 and Protocol1 variables with the settings in the INI file. This is done by calling APDIni.GetComport() and APDIni.GetProtocol(). These are just utility methods to read in the TComport and TProtocol settings from an INI file.

The form contains a method for configuring ComPort1 PortConfigClick() and another method for configuring Protocol1, ProtConfigClick().

PortConfigClick() uses the ComPortOptions dialog to retrieve TComPort configuration settings. If these settings have been modified by the user, then they are saved to the INI file with the call to APDIni.WriteComPort().

PortConfigClick() does the same except that it uses the ProtocolOptions dialog to retrieve TProtocol configuration settings. Again, the settings get saved to the INI file with a call to APDIniWriteProtocol().

Pressing the Dial button on the main form invokes the `DialClick()` method. This method initializes the `DialDialog` with the number to TurboPower's BBS. It then invokes the dialog and if the user presses the OK button, it calls `DialClick.Execute`, which dials the number specified by `DialDialog.Number.Text` through your modem.

The Upload button invokes the `UploadClick()` method. This method uses `UploadDialog` to retrieve information and obtain a protocol for the transfer. It then calls the `TProtocol` component's `StartTransmit()` method to start the upload process. The Download button invokes the `DownLoadClick()` method which does pretty much the same as the Upload button's event handler, but it invokes the `StartReceive()` method to receive a file rather than to send it. Also, notice the following lines:

```
case Protocol1.ProtocolType of
  ptXmodem..ptXmodem1KG,
  ptASCII : Protocol1.FileName := DownloadDialog.ReceiveName;
end;
```

The XModem and ASCII protocols don't know the filename or file size, as do the other protocols. Therefore, the receiver must give this information to the `TProtocol` component.

Running Through the Demo

At this point, go ahead and compile the project. You should know about your modem configuration, and you should set up the APDDEMO.INI file accordingly. Once compiled, run the project so that the main form comes up. In the terminal, type **at** and press Enter to see if you get a modem response. You should see `OK` if the modem responded, as shown in Figure 26.5.

FIGURE 26.5.

APDDemo's main form.

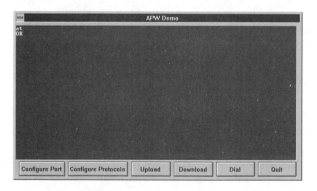

Now go ahead and bring up some of the other forms you like. Make sure that you keep the settings for your specific modem's capabilities. When you're satisfied, click the Dial button to bring up the Dial dialog box, as shown in Figure 26.6.

FIGURE 26.6.

The Dial dialog box with a default number.

With the default number, click the Dial button again. Your modem should start dialing the number. If nothing happens, or if you get an error, make sure to check your hardware and double check the settings for your configuration. The number you're dialing is to TurboPower's BBS. Download a file from TurboPower about Async Professional for Delphi. You should see the Dial progress dialog box as the modem dials. Follow the prompts to log onto the BBS until you get to the screen shown in Figure 26.7. You will have to join the BBS and create a password to get onto the BBS.

FIGURE 26.7.

TurboPower's bulletin board screen.

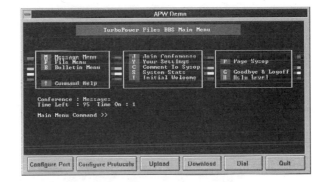

Press F for the File menu and then press D for Download at the next screen.

You will be asked for File # 1?. Type **apd.bro** and press Enter. When asked for File # 2, just press Enter. Figure 26.8 shows what your screen should look like at this point.

FIGURE 26.8.

The screen after typing the file name to download.

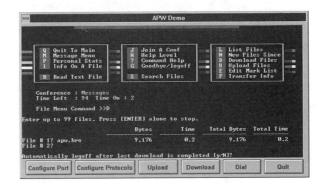

Press Y and press Enter to log off. When asked to begin the download, click the Download button. You then are asked to supply a directory name. Type the directory name, as shown in Figure 26.9.

FIGURE 26.9.

Typing a directory name.

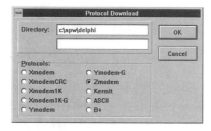

After you click OK, the Protocol Status dialog box appears, as shown in Figure 26.10. When the download is complete, you automatically are logged off the BBS. The file you downloaded contains the most recent information on APD. You might take a moment to read it if you're interested in serial communications development.

FIGURE 26.10.

The Protocol Status dialog box.

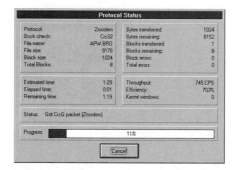

> **NOTE**
>
> You may also retrieve the most up-to-date trial versions of the APD components by downloading APDTR.EXE, a self-extracting zipped file.

Summary

In this chapter, you learned about a powerful set of serial communications components. It wouldn't be possible to go over the full capabilities of these components in one chapter. TurboPower alone provides a 662-page reference on Async Professional for Delphi. It might be a good idea to download the latest version of this demo from TurboPower's BBS. The next chapter will show you how easy it is to build your own File Manager application in Delphi.

27

Building a File Manager Application

This chapter illustrates how to build a File Manager application. Here, you will learn how to perform various file operations in Delphi, as well as how to take advantage of Delphi's ease of development to incorporate such operations into an advanced user interface. You will use techniques covered in previous chapters such as drag and drop, BASM programming, and exception handling. You also will learn new techniques, such as object arrays and owner-draw controls. Additionally, you will expand your knowledge in component design as you create a TStatusBar component that you can add to a component bar. When you complete this chapter, you will have a fully functional File manager application.

Examining the Feature List

The File Manager will contain the following features:

- A multiple document interface (MDI), where child forms show the directory structure of a given drive.
- The capability to run, copy, move, delete, and rename files.
- The capability to use the drag and drop technique to copy selected files from one location to another.
- A display showing drive and file information on a status bar custom component TStatusBar.
- The capability to display file attributes, size, modification date, and version information if available.
- The capability to create and remove directories.
- The capability to search through directories and subdirectories for a specified file that contains wildcard characters.

Creating the Necessary Forms

In the following sections, you'll create the necessary form for the File Manager. You'll then add functionality to each form later on in the chapter. Of course, you always can load the projects from the accompanying CD and read the chapter to see what the project actually does.

The Main Form

Create a new project, save the project as DDGFILE.DPR, and save the main form's unit as DDGFILEU.PAS. Rename Form1's Name property to DDGFileForm. DDGFileForm is an MDIForm, so change its FormStyle property to fsMDIForm. Also, change the Caption property to Delphi Developer's Guide File Manager. Add the components shown in Table 27.1 to the form and set their properties accordingly.

Table 27.1. DDGFileForm components.

Component	Parent	Property	Value
Panel1	DDGFileForm	Align	alTop
ComboBox1	Panel1	Style	csOwnerDrawFixed
MainMenu1	DDGFileForm		

Notice the Parent column in the table. This column is included because some components have a different parent, or container, than the form itself. Figure 27.1 shows DDGFileForm. Table 27.2 shows the menu items for the main form. This completes the main form's creation.

FIGURE 27.1.

DDGFileForm's components.

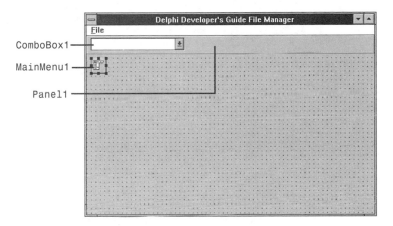

Table 27.2. DDGFileForm's main menu.

Menubar	Submenu
"&File"	"&Run"
	"-"
	"E&xit"
"&Window"	"&Cascade"
	"&Tile"
	"&Arrange Icons"
	"&Close All"

The Child Forms

The child forms display information pertaining to a disk drive, directories, and files; for that purpose, they contain a TDirectoryListBox and TFileListBox component. Choose File | New Form from Delphi's main menu and save the new form as DDGCHLD.PAS. Change its Name property to DriveForm and its Caption to a blank string. Because this is an MDIChild form, change its FormStyle property to fsMDIChild. Add the components shown in Table 27.3 to DriveForm, and set their properties accordingly.

Table 27.3. DriveForm's components.

Component	Property	Value
FileListBox1	Align	alRight
	DragMode	dmAutomatic
	FileType	[ftReadOnly, ftHidden, ftSystem, ftVolumeID, ftDirectory, ftArchive, ftNormal]
	MultiSelect	True
	ParentColor	True
DirectoryListBox1	Align	alClient
	DragMode	dmAutomatic
	FileList	FileListBox1
	ParentColor	True
MainMenu1		

Figure 27.2 shows what TDriveForm looks like.

FIGURE 27.2.

DriveForm's components.

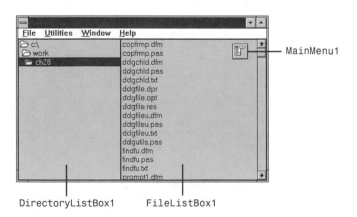

DirectoryListBox1   FileListBox1

Now add the menu items shown in Table 27.4 to `DriveForm`'s main menu, and you'll be done creating the `DriveForm`.

Table 27.4. `DriveForm`'s main menu.

Menubar	Submenu
"&File"	"&Run"
	"&Copy"
	"&Move"
	"&Delete"
	"&Rename"
	"-"
	"Properties"
	"&Options"
	"-"
	"&Create Directory"
	"&Remove Directory"
	"&Prune"
"&Utilities"	"&File Find"
"&Window"	"&Cascade"
	"&Tile"
	"&Arrange Icons"
	"&Close All"
"&Help"	"&About"

Prompt Forms

The File Manager uses two additional forms to prompt the user for information. One form prompts the user for one data string, and the other form prompts the user for two strings. These forms differ from the `InputQuery()` function, which also queries the user for information, because they contain a Browse button for which the event handler invokes a `TFileOpen` dialog box. These forms are generic because they are used for different purposes; therefore, their labels (or *prompts*) change, depending where they are used in the application. The forms are named `Prompt1Form` and `Prompt2Form`.

Prompt1Form

Create a new form by choosing File | New Form from Delphi's main menu. Save this form as PROMPT1.PAS and change its Name property to Prompt1Form. Add the components listed in Table 27.5 and change their properties accordingly. Figure 27.3 shows what Prompt1Form should look like.

Table 27.5. Prompt1Form's properties and components.

Component	Property	Value
Prompt1Form	ActiveControl	Edit1
	BorderStyle	bsDialog
Label1	Caption	"Prompt"
Edit1		
BitBtn1	Kind	bkOk
BitBtn2	Kind	bkCancel
BitBtn3	Caption	"Browse..."
OpenDialog1	Title	"Select File"

FIGURE 27.3.
Prompt1Form's components.

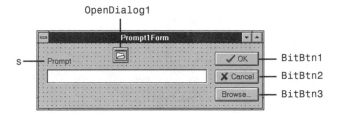

Prompt2Form

Create a new form and save it as PROMPT2.PAS. Change its Name property to Prompt2Form. Add the components and properties specified in Table 27.6. Figure 27.4 shows what Prompt2Form should look like.

Table 27.6. Prompt2Form's properties and components.

Component	Property	Value
Prompt2Form	ActiveControl	Edit1
	BorderStyle	bsDialog
Label1	Caption	"Prompt1"
Label2	Caption	"Prompt2"

Component	Property	Value
Edit1		
Edit2		
BitBtn1	Kind	bkOk
BitBtn2	Kind	bkCancel
BitBtn3	Caption	"Browse..."
OpenDialog1	Title	"Select File"

FIGURE 27.4.
Prompt2Form's
components.

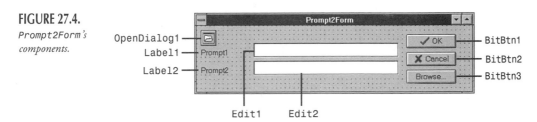

The Find File Form

The FileFindForm displays a list of files found during a file-search operation. Create a new form and save it as FINDFU.PAS. Change its Caption to Find File and its Name property to FileFindForm. This form contains only a TListBox component with its Align Property set to alClient. Figure 27.5 shows how FileFindForm should appear.

FIGURE 27.5.
FileFindForm's
components.

The Properties Form

The last form you'll create is the PropertiesForm, which displays various file properties. Create the form, save it as PROPRTY.PAS, and change its name to PropertiesForm. Change its Caption property to File Properties, and its Style property to bsDialog. Add the components and properties shown in Table 27.7. Figure 27.6 shows the PropertiesForm.

Table 27.7. `PropertiesForm`'s properties and components.

Component	Property	Value
BitBtn1	Kind	bkOk
Label1	Caption	"File:"
Label2	Caption	"File Size:"
Label3	Caption	"Last Modified:"
Label4	Caption	"Version Information:"
Label4	Font.Color	clNavy
Label6	Font.Color	clNavy
Label7	Font.Color	clNavy
GroupBox1		
CheckBox1	Caption	"Archive"
CheckBox2	Caption	"Read Only"
CheckBox3	Caption	"System File"
CheckBox4	Caption	"Hidden"
CheckBox5	Caption	"Volume ID"
CheckBox6	Caption	"Directory"
Panel1	Align	alBottom
Memo1	Align	alRight
	Font.Color	clNavy
ListBox1	Align	alClient

FIGURE 27.6.

PropertiesForm's components.

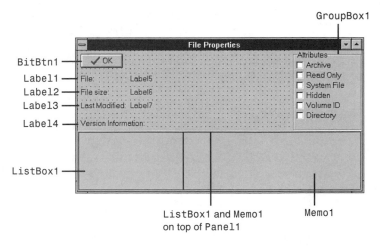

Adding Functionality to the Forms

The File Manager's forms, other than TDDGFileForm and TDriveForm, are completely self-contained—that is, you can use the form in any other application by just adding its unit's name to your application's uses clause and calling an interface function that displays the form.

Other than the DDGFileForm, none of the other forms are created automatically. To prevent a form from being created automatically, choose Options | Project and move the form from the Auto-Create Forms list to the Available Forms list. Additionally, move the declaration of the form's variable from its unit's interface section to its implementation section. This action prevents the form's variable instance from being accessed outside of the unit's scope. Finally, you must create an interface function that is responsible for creating and displaying the form. Depending on the situation, you might have to pass information to and receive information from the interface function. A typical form's unit looks like the one shown in Listing 27.1.

Listing 27.1. A typical form's unit.

```
unit somefrm;
interface
type
  TSomeForm = class(TForm)
  { ... }
  end;
var
  SomeForm: TSomeForm
implementation
{ ... }
end.
```

Using the technique described here, this unit would appear as shown in Listing 27.2.

Listing 27.2. A self-contained form.

```
unit somefrm;
interface
type
  TSomeForm = class(TForm)
  { ... }
  end;
function ShowForm(InData: SomeType): OutData: SomeType;

implementation
var
  SomeForm: TSomeForm;  { moved to implementation section to hide from
➥outside apps }

function ShowForm(InData: SomeType): OutData: SomeType;
begin
  Application.CreateForm(SomeForm, TSomeForm);
```

continues

Listing 27.2. continued

```
try
  with SomeForm do
    { ...}
    ShowModal;
  end;
finally
  SomeForm.Free;
end;
end;
end.
```

TIP

Maximize on code reuse by making your forms self-contained and adding an interface function to display them. One advantage to doing this is that it simplifies placing your form into a DLL (as explained in Chapter 18, "Dynamic Link Libraries (DLLs)") It also furthers reusability because you can execute your forms from other Delphi or non-Delphi applications. Overall, it lessens the time you spend recoding something you already have created.

Creating *TStatusBar*—A Custom Component

The File Manager's specification calls for a status bar custom control. Before creating the main form's functionality, you must create the TStatusBar custom component. Create the unit for TStatusBar by choosing File | New Component from Delphi's menu. After the Component Expert dialog box appears, enter TStatusBar as the ClassName and TWinControl as the Ancestor type. Delphi creates a new unit, as shown in Listing 27.3.

Listing 27.3. The source code for STATUS.PAS.

```
unit Status;

interface

uses
  SysUtils, WinTypes, WinProcs, Messages, Classes, Graphics, Controls,
  Forms, Dialogs;

type

  TStatusBar = class(TWinControl)
  private
    { Private declarations }
  protected
    { Protected declarations }
```

```
public
  { Public declarations }
published
  { Published declarations }
end;

procedure Register;

implementation

procedure Register;
begin
  RegisterComponents('Samples', [TStatusBar]);
end;

end.
```

Listing 27.4 shows the final version of STATUS.PAS.

Listing 27.4. The finalized version of STATUS.PAS.

```
unit Status;

interface

uses
  SysUtils, WinTypes, WinProcs, Messages, Classes, Graphics, Controls,
  Forms, Dialogs, ExtCtrls;

type

  TStatusPanel = class(TPanel)        { Container object for two panels }
  private
    { Private declarations }
    FLeftPanel: TPanel;               { The left panel }
    FRightPanel: TPanel;              { The right panel }
  public
    { Public declarations }
    constructor Create(AOwner: TComponent); override;
  end;

  TStatusBar = Class(TWinControl)
      StatusPanel: TStatusPanel;      { TStatusPanel instance variable }
  private
    function GetCaption(Index: Integer): string;        { Get a caption }
    procedure SetCaption(Index: Integer; Cap: string);  { Set a caption }
    procedure SetCenterBar(Value: Integer);             { Reposition center bar }
    function GetCenterBar: Integer;                      { Get center bar pos }
  public
    constructor Create(AOwner: TComponent); override;
    destructor Destroy; override;
    property Captions[Index: Integer]: string read GetCaption write SetCaption;
  published
    property CenterBar: Integer read GetCenterBar write SetCenterBar;
    property Font;         { Publish this property }
```

continues

Listing 27.4. continued

```
    property ParentFont; { Publish this property }
    property Align;      { Publish this property }
  end;

procedure Register;

implementation

constructor TStatusPanel.Create(AOwner: TComponent);
begin
  inherited Create(AOwner);
  Align := alBottom;        { Set Align to bottom of form }

  { Creat the right panel }
  FRightPanel := TPanel.Create(self);
  with FRightPanel do
  begin
    Parent := self;                { Set parent to self }
    Align := alRight;              { Set alignment to right }
    BevelOuter := bvLowered;       { Set bevel appearances }
    BevelInner := bvLowered;
    Caption := 'Right Panel';      { Set caption text }
    Alignment := taLeftJustify;    { Left-justify caption }
    ParentFont := true;            { Assume the parent's font }
  end;

  FLeftPanel := TPanel.Create(self);
  with FLeftPanel do
  begin
    Parent := self;                { Set parent to self }
    Align := alClient;             { Set alignment to client }
    BevelOuter := bvLowered;       { Set bevel appearances }
    BevelInner := bvLowered;
    Caption := 'Left Panel';       { Set caption text }
    Alignment := taLeftJustify;    { Left-justify caption }
    ParentFont := true;            { Assume the parent's font }
  end;
end;

constructor TStatusBar.Create(AOwner: TComponent);
begin
  inherited Create(AOwner);
  Align := alBottom;                        { Default to alBottom }
  StatusPanel := TStatusPanel.Create(self); { Create a TStatusPanel instance }
  with StatusPanel do
  begin
    Parent := self;                         { Set parent to self }
    Align := alClient;                      { Set alignment to client }
  end;
  Height := StatusPanel.Height + 1;         { Set height to StatusPanel's height }
end;

destructor TStatusBar.Destroy;
begin
  inherited Destroy;
end;
```

```
function TStatusBar.GetCaption(Index: Integer): string;
begin
  case Index of
    0: Result := StatusPanel.FLeftPanel.Caption;  { Return Left caption }
    1: Result := StatusPanel.FRightPanel.Caption; { Return Right caption }
    { Show error if any other Index was entered }
    else MessageDlg('Invalid Index Value', mtWarning, [mbok], 0);
  end;
end;

procedure TStatusBar.SetCaption(Index: Integer; Cap: string);
begin
  case Index of
    0: StatusPanel.FLeftPanel.Caption := Cap;  { Set Left Caption }
    1: StatusPanel.FRightPanel.Caption := Cap; { Set Right Caption }
    { Show an error if any other Index was entered }
    else MessageDlg('Invalid Index Value', mtWarning, [mbok], 0);
  end;
end;

procedure TStatusBar.SetCenterBar(Value: Integer);
begin
  if (Value < Width - 50 ) and (Value > 50 )then       { Keep each panel within }
    StatusPanel.FRightPanel.Width := Width - (Value+1){ 50 pixels of the client}
  else                                                 { area }
    MessageDlg('Invalid Value', mtWarning, [mbok], 0);
end;

function TStatusBar.GetCenterBar: Integer;
begin
  Result := StatusPanel.FRightPanel.Left;     { Return value of center bar }
end;

procedure Register;
begin
  RegisterComponents('Samples', [TStatusBar]); { Register the component }
end;

end.
```

STATUS.PAS now declares a new class type: TStatusPanel. TStatusPanel is a TPanel descendant that encapsulates two TPanels: FLeftPanel and FRightPanel. TStatusPanel serves as a container for these two TPanels. To create the status bar appearance, TStatusPanel's BevelInner and BevelOuter properties keep their default values, while the FLeftPanel and FRightPanel, TPanel's BevelInner and BevelOuter properties are set to bvLowered. TStatusPanel.Create() creates the two TPanel classes and assigns the necessary values to their properties.

TStatusBar is the wrapper class for TStatusPanel. You could leave the wrapper class at the TStatusPanel level. However, all of TStatusPanel's inherited published properties would show up in the Object Inspector, and you might not want this. Creating a wrapper class enables you to publish only those properties you want. You create new properties to modify properties of the owned components, such as you have done here with CenterBar and Captions.

`CenterBar` is a published property that uses the assessor methods `GetCenterBar()`, which returns a value, and `SetCenterBar()`, which assigns a value. The `Captions` property demonstrates how to create an array-based property to make assignments to `FLeftPanel`'s and `FRightPanel`'s `Caption` property. This is not a published property and is accessible only at runtime. To change `FLeftPanel`'s caption, you would make the following assignment:

```
StatusBar1.Caption[0] := 'Ta da....';
```

This actually resolves to the following:

```
StatusBar1.SetCaption(0, 'Ta da....');
```

You never see this, however. The `SetCaption()` method handles making the assignment. Notice that the `TStatusBar`'s properties—`Font`, `ParentFont`, and `Align`—have been publicized so that they will show up in the Object Inspector when you install the component into Delphi's Component Palette.

`TStatusBar.Create()` creates an instance of `TStatusPanel` and makes the necessary assignment to its properties. Install the `TStatusBar` onto Delphi's Component palette. Review Chapter 11, "Writing Delphi Custom Components," if you are unsure how to install components. When done, add a `TStatusBar` to the `MainForm`. Figure 27.7 shows what `TDDGFileForm` now looks like.

Using the Main Form—*TDDGFileForm*

The main form, `TDDGFileForm`, performs a few special operations that you will need to store away for later use. First, you will learn how to find all valid drives on your system. Then you will learn how to determine whether a drive is a network drive or a CD-ROM drive by using a simple `BASM` function. You also will learn how to store `TObject` descendants into an object array and how to work with owner-draw comboboxes. Listing 27.5 shows the source code for DDGFILEU.PAS.

Listing 27.5. The source code for DDGFILEU.PAS.

```
unit Ddgfileu;

interface

uses
  SysUtils, WinTypes, WinProcs, Messages, Classes, Graphics, Controls,
  Forms, Dialogs, Menus, StdCtrls, ExtCtrls, Buttons, Status;

type
  TDriveObject = class
    DriveLetter: string[1];
    DriveType:   string[20];
  end;

  TDDGFileForm = class(TForm)
    MainMenu1: TMainMenu;
```

```
    File1: TMenuItem;
    Exit1: TMenuItem;
    Panel1: TPanel;
    ComboBox1: TComboBox;
    Help1: TMenuItem;
    About1: TMenuItem;
    StatusBar1: TStatusBar;
    procedure FormCreate(Sender: TObject);
    procedure ComboBox1DrawItem(Control: TWinControl; Index: Integer;
      Rect: TRect; State: TOwnerDrawState);
    procedure ComboBox1Change(Sender: TObject);
    procedure Exit1Click(Sender: TObject);
    procedure FormDestroy(Sender: TObject);
  private
    procedure CreateDriveForm(Drive: string);
  public
  end;

var
  DDGFileForm: TDDGFileForm;

implementation
uses ddgchld, DDGUtils, prompt1;

function IsCDDrive(Drive: byte): Boolean;
var
  MyAX, MyBX: word;
begin
  asm
  mov AX, $150b    { function $15 CD-ROM MSCDEX Installation check }
  xor BX, BX       { Zero BX }
  mov BX, $0000    { Move $0000 to BX }
  mov CL, Drive    { Place drive number in CL register }
  mov CH, 0        { Place 0 in CH register }
  int $2f          { Call interrupt $2f }
  mov MyAX, AX     { Move value of AX to MYAX variable }
  mov MyBX, BX     { Move value of BX to MyBX variable }
  end;
  { }
  result := (MyAX <> $0000) and (MyBX = $adad);
end;

{$R *.DFM}

procedure TDDGFileForm.CreateDriveForm(Drive: String);
begin
    with TDriveForm.Create(self) do           { Create a TDriveForm }
    begin
      DirectoryListBox1.Drive := Drive[1];    { Set to Drive selected }
      Caption := DirectoryListBox1.Directory; { Set caption to directory }
      GetDiskData;                            { Get disk information }
      GetSelectedFileSize;                    { Get Selected File Size }
    end;
end;

procedure TDDGFileForm.FormCreate(Sender: TObject);
var
  i: integer;
```

continues

Listing 27.5. continued

```pascal
  w: byte;
  DriveObj: TDriveObject;
  DType: string[20];
  DriveStr: array[0..5] of char;
  TempStr: array[0..20] of char;
  retval: word;
begin
  for i := 0 to 25 do                         { Loop from A to Z }
  begin
    w := GetDriveType(i);                      { Removable, Fixed, Remote? }
    case w of
      DRIVE_REMOVABLE: DType := 'Floppy Drive'; { Drive is Floppy Drive }
      DRIVE_FIXED: DType := 'Hard Disk';       { Drive is Hard disk }
      DRIVE_REMOTE:                            { Drive is remote drive }
        if IsCDDrive(i) then                   { Test for CD-ROM }
          DType := ' CD-ROM Drive'             { Drive is CD-ROM }
        else
        begin
          StrPCopy(DriveStr, chr(i+65));       { Convert letter to PChar }
          DType := ' Network Drive';           { Drive is network drive }
        end;
    end; { Case }
    if w <> 0 then                             { A valid drive was found }
    begin
      DriveObj := TDriveObject.Create;         { Create a TDriveObject }
      DriveObj.DriveLetter := chr(i+65);       { Assign drive letter }
      DriveObj.DriveType := DType;             { Assign Drive type string }
      ComboBox1.Items.AddObject(IntToStr(i), DriveObj); { Add to objects array }
    end;
  end;
  StatusBar1.Captions[0] := '';                { Set Captions to Empty string }
  StatusBar1.Captions[1] := '';
end;

procedure TDDGFileForm.ComboBox1DrawItem(Control: TWinControl;
  Index: Integer; Rect: TRect; State: TOwnerDrawState);
var
  DriveObj: TDriveObject;
  A: array[0..255] of char;
begin
  DriveObj := ComboBox1.Items.Objects[Index] as TDriveObject; { Get Object }
  ComboBox1.Canvas.FillRect(Rect);   { Clear the drawing rect }
  StrPCopy(A, DriveObj.DriveLetter); { Copy the drive letter to A }
                                     { Draw A to the drawing rect }
  DrawText(ComboBox1.Canvas.Handle, A, StrLen(A), Rect, dt_Left or dt_VCenter);
  Rect.Left := Rect.Left + 20;       { Increment the drawing rect by 20 pixels }
  StrPCopy(A, DriveObj.DriveType);   { Copy the DriveType string to A }
                                     { Draw the DriveType to drawing rect }
  DrawText(ComboBox1.Canvas.Handle, A, StrLen(A), Rect, dt_Left or dt_VCenter);
end;

procedure TDDGFileForm.ComboBox1Change(Sender: TObject);
begin
  with ComboBox1 do { Create a TDriveForm MDIChild }
    CreateDriveForm(TDriveObject(Items.Objects[ItemIndex]).DriveLetter);
end;
```

```
procedure TDDGFileForm.Exit1Click(Sender: TObject);
begin
  Close; { Close the application }
end;

procedure TDDGFileForm.FormDestroy(Sender: TObject);
var
 i: integer;
begin
  with ComboBox1 do
  for i := 0 to Items.Count - 1 do
    TDriveObject(Items.Objects[i]).Free; { Free the TDriveObjects previously }
                                    { Created in FormCreate() }
end;

end.
```

FIGURE 27.7.

TDDGFileForm with a
TStatusBar component.

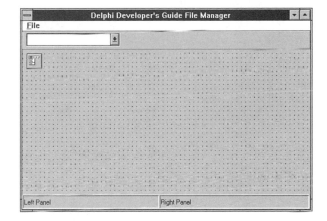

Searching for Valid Drives

Finding valid drives and determining their types is rather simple. TDDGForm.FormCreate() contains a for loop that increments i from 0 to 25, where i represents a drive number (0–A, 1–B, and so on). It then calls the Window's API function GetDriveType, which determines whether a disk is removable, fixed, or remote. It returns a word value corresponding to one of the constants DRIVE_REMOVABLE, DRIVE_FIXED, or DRIVE_REMOVE; or a zero value if the drive is not valid.

If the drive is DRIVE_REMOTE, the drive can be a networked drive or a CD-ROM drive, so the function IsCDDrive() is called, which contains BASM code to determine whether the drive number passed to is a CD-ROM.

Given a valid drive, FormCreate() then creates a TDriveObject instance, initializes it with the drive information, and adds it to ComboBox1.Items's Objects array through its AddObjects() method. AddObjects takes two parameters: a string to identify the object and the object itself. This object is retrieved when ComboBox1 draws its items in its OnDrawItems() event handler.

Using Owner-Draw Comboboxes

The `ComboBox1DrawItem()` event handler is called whenever an item in an owner-draw control—in this case, `ComboBox1`—needs to be displayed. The first step is to retrieve the information to draw, which you previously stored in the `ComboBox1.Item`'s `Objects` array. The following line serves this purpose:

```
DriveObj := ComboBox1.Items.Objects[Index] as TDriveObject; { Get Object }
```

The event handler then clears the drawing area specified by `Rect` and uses the `Canvas` method, `DrawText()`, to draw the strings at locations within the rectangle. Notice that the rectangle is repositioned to the left to create a tabbed effect.

Exiting the Application

`TDDGFileForm.Exit1Click()` exits the application by calling the `Close()` method.

Adding Functionality to *TPrompt1Form*

`TPrompt1Form` enables you to prompt the user for a filename. The prompts that the form displays are different, depending on the purpose for which the user invokes the form: to run a file, to delete a file, or to ask the user for a filename. Figure 27.8 shows each variation of this form.

FIGURE 27.8.

Three variations of
Prompt1Form.

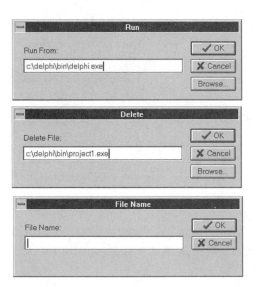

Move `TPrompt1Form`'s variable instance to its unit's implementation section. `TPrompt1Form` requires the following constants and enumerated type in its interface section:

```
const
  RunFilter = 'Executables|*.exe;*.pif;*.bat;*.com';
  AllFilter = 'All Files|*.*';

type
  TPrompt1Mode = (pmRunMode, pmDeleteMode, pmFileNameMode);
```

`TPrompt1Form` uses `TPromptMode` to determine which prompts to display. The interface function
is passed one of these values by the calling application, and it sets up the appropriate prompts
based on that value.

`TPrompt1Form` requires an array constant that contains the strings used to set up the prompts.
This constant is defined as the following:

```
type

  TPromptRec = record
    Caption: string[10];    { Form's Caption         }
    Prompt: string[15];     { Form's Prompt          }
    Filter: string[40];     { OpenDialog1's Filter   }
  end;

const

PromptArray: array[1..3] of TPromptRec = (
    (Caption:'Run'; Prompt:'Run From: ';Filter:RunFilter),
    (Caption:'Delete'; Prompt:'Delete File: ';Filter:AllFilter),
    (Caption:'File Name'; Prompt:'File Name: ';Filter:AllFilter));
```

Here, a record is defined that has three strings to represent the form's caption, prompt, and
filter for the `OpenDialog1`. The `PromptArray`-typed constant's index corresponds to one of the
three `TPromptMode` values. This prevents you from having to use a `case` statement to set the
prompts on the form in the interface function. For example, instead of using the following
code:

```
case Mode of
  pmRunMode: begin
    Caption := 'Run';
    Label1.Caption := 'Run From';
    OpenDialog1.Filter := 'Run Filter'
  end;
  pmDeleteMode: { assign Delete prompts }
  pmFileNameMode: { assign FileName prompts }
end; { case }
```

you could use this code:

```
Caption := PromptArray[Mode].Caption;
Label1.Caption := PromptArray[Mode].Prompt;
OpenDialog1.Filter := PromptArray[Mode].Filter;
```

The interface function is defined in the interface section as the following:

```
function ShowPrompt1Form(Mode: TPrompt1Mode; FileName: string): string;
```

It is declared in the implementation section, as shown in this code:

```
function ShowPrompt1Form(Mode: TPrompt1Mode; FileName: string): string;
var
  Prompt1Form: TPrompt1Form;
begin
 Result := '';                      { NULL String by default }
 Prompt1Form := TPrompt1Form.Create(Application); { Intanciate the form }
 try
   with Prompt1Form do
     begin
       Edit1.Text := FileName;              { Initialize the file name }
       if Mode = pmFileNameMode then        { Browse button does not display when }
         BitBtn3.Visible := false;          { for is used for the FileNameMode }
       Caption := PromptArray[Mode].Caption; { Assign the appropriate captions }
       Label1.Caption := PromptArray[Mode].Prompt; { to form's caption, label, }
       OpenDialog1.Filter := PromptArray[Mode].Filter;   { and OpenDialog1.Filter }
     end;
     if Prompt1Form.ShowModal = mrOk then { Display the form as a modal form }
       result := Prompt1Form.Edit1.Text;  { Set result to Edit1.Text's contents }
 finally
   Prompt1Form.Free;                        { Free the form }
 end;
end;
```

This function creates a `TPrompt1Form` instance, sets up the form's prompts based on the mode value, and calls `ShowModal`. If the modal result is `mrOk`, it passes back the string contained in `Edit1.Text` to the calling application. Finally, it frees the form instance. `BitBtn2Click()` sets `Edit1`'s `Text` property to an empty string, because it cancels the operation. `BitBtn2Click()` extracts a filename from `OpenDialog1`. PROMPT1.PAS is shown in Listing 27.6.

Listing 27.6. The source code for PROMPT1.PAS.

```
unit Prompt1;

interface

uses
  SysUtils, WinTypes, WinProcs, Messages, Classes, Graphics, Controls,
  Forms, Dialogs, StdCtrls, Buttons;
const
  RunFilter = 'Executables¦*.exe;*.pif;*.bat;*.com';
  AllFilter = 'All Files¦*.*';

type
  TPrompt1Mode = (pmRunMode, pmDeleteMode, pmFileNameMode);

  TPromptRec = record
    Caption: string[10];    { Form's Caption            }
    Prompt: string[15];     { Form's Prompt             }
    Filter: string[40];     { OpenDialog1's Filter      }
  end;

const
  { Array constant of prompts }
```

```
  PromptArray: array[TPrompt1Mode] of TPromptRec = (
     (Caption:'Run'; Prompt:'Run From: ';Filter:RunFilter),
     (Caption:'Delete'; Prompt:'Delete File: ';Filter:AllFilter),
     (Caption:'File Name'; Prompt:'File Name: ';Filter:AllFilter));
type

  TPrompt1Form = class(TForm)
    BitBtn1: TBitBtn;
    BitBtn2: TBitBtn;
    BitBtn3: TBitBtn;
    Label1: TLabel;
    Edit1: TEdit;
    OpenDialog1: TOpenDialog;
    procedure BitBtn2Click(Sender: TObject);
    procedure BitBtn3Click(Sender: TObject);
  private
    { Private declarations }
  public
    { Public declarations }
  end;


function ShowPrompt1Form(Mode: TPrompt1Mode; FileName: string): string;

implementation

{$R *.DFM}


function ShowPrompt1Form(Mode: TPrompt1Mode; FileName: string): string;
var
  Prompt1Form: TPrompt1Form;
begin
  Result := '';                    { NULL String by default }
  Prompt1Form := TPrompt1Form.Create(Application); { Intanciate the form }
  try
    with Prompt1Form do
      begin
        Edit1.Text := FileName;          { Initialize the file name }
        if Mode = pmFileNameMode then    { Browse button does not display when }
          BitBtn3.Visible := false;      { for is used for the FileNameMode }
        Caption := PromptArray[Mode].Caption; { Assign the appropriate captions }
        Label1.Caption := PromptArray[Mode].Prompt;  { to form's caption, label, }
        OpenDialog1.Filter := PromptArray[Mode].Filter;   { and OpenDialog1.Filter }
      end;
      if Prompt1Form.ShowModal = mrOk then  { Display the form as a modal form }
        result := Prompt1Form.Edit1.Text;   { Set result to Edit1.Text's contents }
  finally
    Prompt1Form.Free;                      { Free the form }
  end;
end;

procedure TPrompt1Form.BitBtn2Click(Sender: TObject);
begin
  Edit1.Text := ''; { Set to NULL string }
end;
```

continues

Listing 27.6. continued

```
procedure TPrompt1Form.BitBtn3Click(Sender: TObject);
begin
  if OpenDialog1.Execute then                      { Execute OpenDialog1 and
➥if mrok then }
    Edit1.Text := LowerCase(OpenDialog1.FileName);  { Assign its filename to
➥Edit1.Text }
end;
end.
```

Adding Functionality to *Prompt2Form*

TPrompt2Form is much like TPrompt1Form because it enables you to prompt the user for information. TPrompt2Form differs, in that it asks for two filenames as opposed to one. Like TPrompt1Form, its prompts differ depending on the purpose for which the user invokes the form: to copy a file, move a file, or rename a file. Figure 27.9 shows each variation of this form.

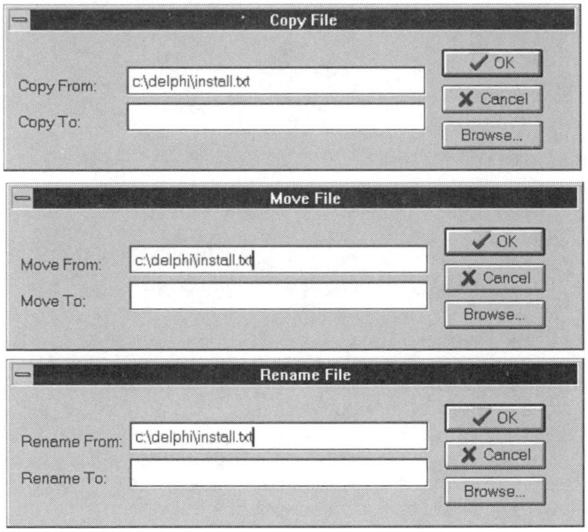

FIGURE 27.9.

Three variations of TPrompt2Form.

TPrompt2Form's variable instance declaration also must be moved from the unit's interface section to the implementation section. TPrompt2Form requires the following enumerated type in its interface section:

```
type
  TPrompt2Mode = (pmCopyMode, pmMoveMode, pmRenameMode);
```

TPrompt2Form uses TPrompt2Mode to determine which prompts to display.

Like TPrompt1Form, TPrompt2Form requires an array constant that contains the strings used to set up the prompts. This constant is defined as the following:

```
type

  TPromptRec = record
    Caption: string[12];     { Form's Caption }
    Label1: string[15];      { Form's Prompt1 }
    Label2: string[15];      { Form's Prompt2 }
  end;

const

PromptArray: array[1..3] of TPromptRec = (
    (Caption:'Run'; Prompt:'Run From: ';Filter:RunFilter),
    (Caption:'Delete'; Prompt:'Delete File: ';Filter:AllFilter),
    (Caption:'File Name'; Prompt:'File Name: ';Filter:AllFilter));
```

Like the preceding example, the array index corresponds to one of the three mode values. The interface function is defined in the unit's interface section as

```
function ShowPrompt2Form(Mode: TPrompt2Mode; FromF: string): string;
```

It is declared in the implementation section, as shown in the following code:

```
function ShowPrompt2Form(Mode: TPrompt2Mode; FromF: string): string;
begin
  Result := ''; { Null string by default }
  Prompt2Form := TPrompt2Form.Create(Application);
  try
    with Prompt2Form do
    begin
      Edit1.Text := FromF;  { Initialize Edit controls }
      Edit2.Text := '';
      Caption := PromptArray[Mode].Caption;       { Initialize Prompts and }
      Label1.Caption := PromptArray[Mode].Label1; { Captions with data based }
      Label2.Caption := PromptArray[Mode].Label2; { On the mode value }
    end;
    if Prompt2Form.ShowModal = mrOk then   { Show the form as modal and if }
    { modal result is mrOk pass back the concatanation of both Edit.Text }
      Result := Prompt2Form.Edit1.Text+DefaultDelim+Prompt2Form.Edit2.Text;
  finally
    Prompt2form.Free;      { Free Prompt2Form }
  end;
end;
```

ShowPrompt2Form() creates a TPrompt2Form instance, sets up the prompts based on the mode value, and calls ShowModal. If the modal result is mrOk, it passes back to the calling application Edit1's and Edit2's concatenated Text properties separated by a space delimiter. Finally, it frees the form instance.

BitBtn2Click() is the event handler for the Cancel button's OnClick event. It sets Edit1's and Edit2's Text properties to some arbitrary value, as in this code:

```
Edit1.Text := 'X' ;   { Just set temporary fake data in both edit controls }
Edit2.Text := 'X' ;    { To allow OnCloseQuery to pass }
```

This ensures that the `FormCloseQuery()` event handler will not keep the form from closing, because `FormCloseQuery()` prevents the form from closing when one of the edit controls contains an empty string, as shown in the following code. In this case, a `Cancel` operation should cause the form to close, and placing a temporary value in the `TEdit`'s Text properties enables it to do so.

```
procedure TPrompt2Form.FormCloseQuery(Sender: TObject; var CanClose: Boolean);
begin
  CanClose := false;            { Set to false by default }
  if Edit1.Text = '' then       { Test the value of each Edit1.Text and if any are }
    ActiveControl := Edit1      { nil, do not allow the form to close. Set the }
  else if Edit2.Text = ''then   { Active control to that with the nil string }
    ActiveControl := Edit2
  else
    CanClose := true;           { Let form close after Exec Call }
  if not CanClose then          { Display the error }
    MessageDlg('Entry Required', mtWarning, [mbok], 0);
end;
```

When invoking the `Open1Dialog` from the Browse button, the Browse button gains focus. Because Browse is used to get a file pathname, you need to know which edit control last had focus before invoking it. `Edit1`'s `OnEnter` event handler does this with the following line:

```
LastActive := Sender as TEdit; { Assign to LastActive the component loosing focus }
```

You then can link `Edit2`'s `OnEnter` event handler to this event handler. `LastActive` then will point to the last edit control having focus, as shown in this code:

```
procedure TPrompt2Form.BitBtn3Click(Sender: TObject);
begin
  if OpenDialog1.Execute then
    LastActive.Text := LowerCase(OpenDialog1.FileName);
  ActiveControl := LastActive;
end;
```

The source code to PROMPT2.PAS is shown in Listing 27.7.

Listing 27.7. The source code for PROMPT2.PAS.

```
unit Prompt2;

interface

uses
  SysUtils, WinTypes, WinProcs, Messages, Classes, Graphics, Controls,
  Forms, Dialogs, StdCtrls, Buttons;

type
  TPrompt2Mode = (pmCopyMode, pmMoveMode, pmRenameMode);

  TPromptRec = record
    Caption: string[12];    { Form's Caption }
    Label1: string[15];     { Form's Prompt1 }
    Label2: string[15];     { Form's Prompt2 }
  end;
```

```
const
  DefaultDelim = ' '; { Space serves as a delimiter }
  { Array constant of prompts }
  PromptArray: array[TPrompt2Mode] of TPromptRec = (
    (Caption:'Copy File'; Label1:'Copy From: ';Label2:'Copy To: '),
    (Caption:'Move File'; Label1:'Move From: ';Label2:'Move To: '),
    (Caption:'Rename File'; Label1:'Rename From: ';Label2:'Rename To: '));
type

  TPrompt2Form = class(TForm)
    Label1: TLabel;
    Label2: TLabel;
    Edit1: TEdit;
    Edit2: TEdit;
    BitBtn1: TBitBtn;
    BitBtn2: TBitBtn;
    BitBtn3: TBitBtn;
    OpenDialog1: TOpenDialog;
    procedure BitBtn2Click(Sender: TObject);
    procedure BitBtn3Click(Sender: TObject);
    procedure FormCloseQuery(Sender: TObject; var CanClose: Boolean);
    procedure Edit1Enter(Sender: TObject);
  private
    LastActive: TEdit;
    { Private declarations }
  public
    { Public declarations }
  end;

function ShowPrompt2Form(Mode: TPrompt2Mode; FromF: string): string;

implementation
{$R *.DFM}

var
  Prompt2Form: TPrompt2Form;

function ShowPrompt2Form(Mode: TPrompt2Mode; FromF: string): string;
begin
  Result := ''; { Null string by default }
  Prompt2Form := TPrompt2Form.Create(Application);
  try
    with Prompt2Form do
    begin
      Edit1.Text := FromF;  { Initialize Edit controls }
      Edit2.Text := '';
      Caption := PromptArray[Mode].Caption;          { Initialize Prompts and }
      Label1.Caption := PromptArray[Mode].Label1; { Captions with data based }
      Label2.Caption := PromptArray[Mode].Label2; { On the mode value }
    end;
    if Prompt2Form.ShowModal = mrOk then   { Show the form as modal and if }
    { modal result is mrOk pass back the concatanation of both Edit.Text }
      Result := Prompt2Form.Edit1.Text+DefaultDelim+Prompt2Form.Edit2.Text;
  finally
    Prompt2form.Free;     { Free Prompt2Form }
  end;
end;
```

continues

Listing 27.7. continued

```
procedure TPrompt2Form.BitBtn2Click(Sender: TObject);
begin
  Edit1.Text := 'X' ;   { Just set temporary fake data in both edit controls }
  Edit2.Text := 'X' ;   { To allow OnCloseQuery to pass }
end;

procedure TPrompt2Form.BitBtn3Click(Sender: TObject);
begin
  if OpenDialog1.Execute then  { Invoke the OpenDialog1 and assign the text }
    LastActive.Text := LowerCase(OpenDialog1.FileName); { to the control that }
  ActiveControl := LastActive; { Lost focus when the dialog was invoked }
end;

procedure TPrompt2Form.FormCloseQuery(Sender: TObject; var CanClose: Boolean);
begin
  CanClose := false;         { Set to false by default }
  if Edit1.Text = '' then    { Test the value of each Edit1.Text and if any are }
    ActiveControl := Edit1   { nil, do not allow the form to close. Set the }
  else if Edit2.Text = ''then { Active control to that with the nil string }
    ActiveControl := Edit2
  else
    CanClose := true;        { Let form close after Exec Call }
  if not CanClose then        { Display the error }
    MessageDlg('Entry Required', mtWarning, [mbok], 0);
end;

procedure TPrompt2Form.Edit1Enter(Sender: TObject);
begin
  LastActive := Sender as TEdit; { Assign to LastActive the component loosing }
                                 { focus }
end;

end.
```

OnCloseQuery() and BitBtn3Click() are event handlers. BitBtn2Click() sets Edit1's Text property to an empty string because it cancels the operation. BitBtn2Click() extracts a filename from OpenDialog1.

Searching for Files Using Recursion

The TFileFindForm, like the previous forms, is encapsulated in its unit and is accessible through an interface function. This function takes a path and filename as arguments and searches the directory and subdirectories of the given path for the filename to display in the form's TListBox component. To search through directories, you use a recursive algorithm.

RECURSION

Recursion is when a procedure or function calls itself. Recursive algorithms are often very clean to implement but can have some nasty side effects. Traversing a directory tree is one of those few cases where a recursive algorithm is the best choice. In general, you should try to avoid recursion because it can eat stack space very quickly (see the "Thanks for the Memories" sidebar in Chapter 3, "The Object Pascal Language," for a discussion on stack space). Each time a function recurses, it pushes more information on the stack. The more parameters and local variables your function contains, the more stack it eats through each iteration. Because your stack is a limited resource, things can go bad in a hurry. Recursion is great for computer science professors and programmers using 32-bit operating systems, but you should use it with care when developing real-world applications for 16-bit Windows 3.1.

Move the TFileFindForm's variable instance to the implementation section and declare an interface function:

```
function FindFile(DirPath, FName: string): string;
```

This function's code is shown in Listing 27.8.

Listing 27.8. The source code for FindFile.

```
function FindFile(DirPath, FName: string): string;
begin
  Result := '';                                 { Empty string by default }
  FileFindForm := TFileFindForm.Create(Application); { Create the FileFindForm }
  try
    with FileFindForm do begin
      MainPath := DirPath;               { Assign DirPath to MainPath variable }
      FileName := FName;                 { Assign FName to FileName variable }
      Screen.Cursor := crHourGlass;      { Set Screen cursor to hour glass }
      FindFiles(MainPath);               { Call the find files function }
      if ListBox1.Items.Count <> 0 then begin
        ShowModal;                       { Show it, and if an item was selected }
        if ListBox1.ItemIndex >= 0 then  { pass it back to the calling app. }
          Result := Listbox1.Items[ListBox1.ItemIndex];
      end
      else
        MessageDlg('No Files Found', mtInformation, [mbok], 0); { None found }
    end;
  finally
    FileFindForm.Free;                   { Free the Form }
    Screen.Cursor := crDefault;     { Reset screen cursor back to normal }
  end;
end;
```

FindFile() creates a TFileFindForm instance, initializes its variables, and calls FindFiles(), which is responsible for searching through the directories passed as a parameter for the file. FindFiles() makes use of the function defined in a unit called DDGUTILS.PAS. This unit defines various functions and structures used by other units, so it makes sense to have them in their own unit. DDGUTILS.PAS is shown in Listing 27.9.

Listing 27.9. The source code for DDGUTILS.PAS.

```
unit Ddgutils;

interface
uses SysUtils, Dialogs, Forms, controls, LZExpand, WinProcs, WinTypes;

type
  ELZCopyError = class(Exception);  { Create an LZCopy error exception class }
  EWinExecError = class(Exception); { Create a WinExec error exception class }

procedure CopyFile(FromFileName, ToFileName: string);
procedure MoveFile(FromFileName, ToFileName: string);
function GetDirectoryName(Dir: string): string;
function DDGExec(RunFile: string): word;

implementation

procedure CopyFile(FromFileName, ToFileName: string);
var
  FromFile, ToFile: File;
begin
  AssignFile(FromFile, FromFileName); { Assign FromFile to FromFileName }
  AssignFile(ToFile, ToFileName);     { Assign ToFile to ToFileName }
  Reset(FromFile);                    { Open file for input }
  try
    Rewrite(ToFile);                  { Create file for output }
    try
      { copy the file an if a negative value is returned raise an exception }
      if LZCopy(TFileRec(FromFile).Handle, TFileRec(ToFile).Handle) < 0 then
        raise ELZCopyError.Create('Error using LZCopy')
    finally
      CloseFile(ToFile);  { Close ToFile }
    end;
  finally
    CloseFile(FromFile);  { Close FromFile }
  end;
end;

procedure MoveFile(FromFileName, ToFileName: string);
begin
  RenameFile(FromFileName, ToFileName);   { Rename the file }
end;

function GetDirectoryName(Dir: string): string;
begin
  if Dir[length(Dir)] <> '\' then { If the directory doesn't contain a '\' }
    Result := Dir+'\'             { character add one. }
```

```
   else
      Result := Dir;                    { Result is the Dir }
end;

function DDGExec(RunFile: string): Word;
var
   RunFilePC: PChar;
begin
   GetMem(RunFilePC, length(RunFile)+1);              { Allocate memory
➥for RunFilePC }
   try
      Result := WinExec(StrPCopy(RunFilePC, RunFile),    { Run the program
➥pass back }
         sw_ShowNormal);                              { the returned result }
      if Result < 32 then                             { An error was returned }
         raise EWinExecError.Create('Error using WinExec');{ Raise an exception }
   finally
      Freemem(RunFilePC, length(RunFile)+1);             { Free RunFilePC's
➥memory }
   end;
end;
end.
```

In DDGUTILS.PAS, `CopyFile()`, `MoveFile()`, and `DDGExec()` are used by different units, and are discussed in later sections of this chapter. The function of interest here is `GetDirectoryName()`, which adds the backslash (\) as the last character to a directory name passed to it if it does not already contain one. This is just a utility function that prevents you from having to recode it whenever you require such a directory name, as is the case in the `FindFiles()` method shown in Listing 27.10.

Listing 27.10. The `TFileFindForm.FindFiles()` method.

```
procedure TFileFindForm.FindFiles(APath: TDirStr);
var
   FSearchRec,
   DSearchRec: TSearchRec;
   FindResult: integer;
begin
   APath := GetDirectoryName(APath); { Set up a valid directory name }
   { Find the first occurance of the specified file name }
   FindResult := FindFirst(APath+FileName,faAnyFile+faHidden+
                           faSysFile+faReadOnly,FSearchRec);
   try
      { Continue to search for the specified filename and if found add its path }
      while (FindResult = 0) do begin    { To the listbox }
         ListBox1.Items.Add(LowerCase(APath+FSearchRec.Name));
         FindResult := FindNext(FSearchRec);
      end;

      { Search the Subdirectories. This calls FindFiles() again recursively }
      FindResult := FindFirst(APath+'*.*', faDirectory, DSearchRec);
      while (FindResult = 0) do begin
```

continues

Listing 27.10. continued

```
      if ((DSearchRec.Attr and faDirectory) = faDirectory) and
         (pos('.', DSearchRec.Name) = 0) then
        FindFiles(APath+DSearchRec.Name); { Recursion here }
      FindResult := FindNext(DSearchRec);
    end;
  finally
    FindClose(FSearchRec);  { Call for portability to 32-bit Windows }
  end;
end;
```

One Object Pascal structure and two functions merit mention here. The `TSearchRec` record defines data returned by the `FindFirst()` and `FindNext()` functions. Object Pascal defines this record as the following:

```
TSearchRec = record
  Fill: array[1..21] of Byte;
  Attr: Byte;
  Time: Longint;
  Size: Longint;
  Name: string[12];
end;
```

`TSearchRec`'s fields are modified by the aforementioned functions when a file is found. The `Attr` field contains one or more of the attributes shown in Table 27.8.

Table 27.8. File attributes.

Attribute	Value	Description
faReadOnly	$01	Read-only file
faHidden	$02	Hidden file
faSysFile	$04	System file
faVolumeID	$08	Volume ID file
faDirectory	$10	Directory
faArchive	$20	Archive file
faAnyFile	$3F	Any file

TIP

Test to see if a file contains a specific attribute by performing an AND operation with the file's `Attr` field and one of the attribute constants for which you are testing. For example, to test for a system file, use this code:

```
if (SearchRec.Attr and faSysFile) then
```

The Time field contains the DOS file time in longint format, the Size field contains the file's size in bytes, and the Name field contains the file's name.

Both FindFirst() and FindNext() take a path as a parameter that can contain wildcard characters—for example, C:\DELPHI\BIN*.EXE means all files with an EXE extension in the C:\DELPHI\BIN directory. The Attr parameter specifies the file attributes on which to search. Suppose that you want to search on system files only; you would invoke FindFirst() and/or FindNext(), as in this code:

```
FindFirst(Path, faSysFile, SearchRec);
```

In the FindFiles() method, the first while .. do construct searches for files in the directory specified by the Path parameter and adds them to ListBox1. The second while..do construct finds subdirectories and adds them to the Path variable. It then passes Path, now with a subdirectory name, to itself, resulting in a recursive call. This process continues until no subdirectories exist.

> **CAUTION**
>
> Be sure to match a FindClose() method for every occurrence of FindFirst()..FindNext(). It does nothing in the current version of Windows; however, in Windows 95 it will be a required call.

Figure 27.10 shows the result of a search where the path is C:\DELPHI and the filename is *.PAS. Here, all files in this directory and its subdirectories will be found.

FIGURE 27.10.

File Find results.

The event handler TFileFindForm.ListBoxDblClick() causes TFileFindForm to close by assigning mrOk to the ModalResult property. TFileFindForm.ListBox1KeyDown() also closes the form with an mrCancel or mrOk ModalResult based on the key pressed:

```
case Key of
    vk_Return: ModalResult := mrOk;
    vk_Escape: ModalResult := mrCancel;
  end;
```

The source to FINDFU.PAS is shown in Listing 27.11.

Listing 27.11. The source code for FINDFU.PAS.

```pascal
unit Findfu;

interface

uses
  SysUtils, WinTypes, WinProcs, Messages, Classes, Graphics, Controls,
  Forms, Dialogs, StdCtrls;
type

  TDirStr = string[80];  { Save stack space }

type
  TFileFindForm = class(TForm)
    ListBox1: TListBox;
    procedure ListBox1DblClick(Sender: TObject);
    procedure ListBox1KeyDown(Sender: TObject; var Key: Word;
      Shift: TShiftState);
  private
    { Private declarations }
    MainPath: TDirStr;
    FileName: string;
    procedure FindFiles(APath: TDirStr);
  public
    { Public declarations }
  end;

function FindFile(DirPath, FName: string): string;

implementation
{ Remember to add the units to the uses clause }
uses DDGUtils;
{$R *.DFM}

var
  FileFindForm: TFileFindForm; { Move this instance to implementation section }

function FindFile(DirPath, FName: string): string;
begin
  Result := '';                                   { Empty string by default }
  FileFindForm := TFileFindForm.Create(Application); { Create the FileFindForm }
  try
    with FileFindForm do begin
      MainPath := DirPath;            { Assign DirPath to MainPath variable }
      FileName := FName;              { Assign FName to FileName variable }
      Screen.Cursor := crHourGlass;   { Set Screen cursor to hour glass }
      FindFiles(MainPath);            { Call the find files function }
      if ListBox1.Items.Count <> 0 then begin
        ShowModal;                    { Show it, and if an item was selected }
        if ListBox1.ItemIndex >= 0 then { pass it back to the calling app. }
          Result := Listbox1.Items[ListBox1.ItemIndex];
      end
      else
        MessageDlg('No Files Found', mtInformation, [mbok], 0); { None found }
    end;
  finally
    FileFindForm.Free;                    { Free the Form }
    Screen.Cursor := crDefault;     { Reset screen cursor back to normal }
```

```
    end;
end;

procedure TFileFindForm.FindFiles(APath: TDirStr);
var
  FSearchRec,
  DSearchRec: TSearchRec;
  FindResult: integer;
begin
  APath := GetDirectoryName(APath); { Set up a valid directory name }
  { Find the first occurance of the specified file name }
  FindResult := FindFirst(APath+FileName,faAnyFile+faHidden+
                          faSysFile+faReadOnly,FSearchRec);
  try
    { Continue to search for the specified filename and if found add its path }
    while (FindResult = 0) do begin    { To the listbox }
      ListBox1.Items.Add(LowerCase(APath+FSearchRec.Name));
      FindResult := FindNext(FSearchRec);
    end;

    { Search the Subdirectories. This calls FindFiles() again recursively }
    FindResult := FindFirst(APath+'*.*', faDirectory, DSearchRec);
    while (FindResult = 0) do begin
      if ((DSearchRec.Attr and faDirectory) = faDirectory) and
         (pos('.', DSearchRec.Name) = 0) then
        FindFiles(APath+DSearchRec.Name); { Recursion here }
      FindResult := FindNext(DSearchRec);
    end;
  finally
    FindClose(FSearchRec);  { Call for portability to 32-bit Windows }
  end;
end;

procedure TFileFindForm.ListBox1DblClick(Sender: TObject);
begin
  ModalResult := mrOk; { Close the form with a mrOK modal result }
end;

procedure TFileFindForm.ListBox1KeyDown(Sender: TObject; var Key: Word;
  Shift: TShiftState);
begin
  case Key of
    vk_Return: ModalResult := mrOk;    { Enter key causes a mrOk modal result }
    vk_Escape: ModalResult := mrCancel;{ Cancel key causes a mrCancel result }
  end;
end;

end.
```

Displaying File Properties and Version Information

The TPropertiesForm enables the user to view information about a file—such as its properties, size, modification date, and version information. This form also is contained inside of its unit, and is accessed through an interface procedure. To add this functionality to the form, you first must move the `TPropertiesForm` variable instance to the `implementation` section, remove it from the auto-create list in Options | Project, and add `VERINFO` to the unit's uses clause, as shown in the following code:

```
implementation
uses VerInfo;
```

The `VerInfo` unit defines the `TVerInfoRes` class, which you can use to obtain version information on a given file. This unit is discussed later in the section entitled "Defining the `TVerInfoClass`."

You also must declare a private variable `FileName` to the form and add two methods: `DDGGetVersionInfo()` and `DDGGetAttrSize()`, as shown in the following code:

```
TPropertiesForm = class(TForm)
  {...}
  private
    FileName: String;
    procedure DDGGetVersionInfo;
    procedure DDGGetAttrSize;
  {...}
end;
```

Define a class of `TVerInfoData`, as shown in this code:

```
TVerInfoData = class
  Data: String;
end;
```

The interface procedure is declared in the `interface` section of the unit as

```
procedure ShowPropertyForm(FName: string);
```

It takes `FName`, a string, as a parameter that specifies the filename on which to display the information. `ShowPropertyForm()`'s code is shown in the following code:

```
procedure ShowPropertyForm(FName: string);
begin
  PropertiesForm := TPropertiesForm.Create(Application); { Create the form }
  try
    with PropertiesForm do
    begin
      FileName := FName;             { Assign FName to the FileName property }
      Label5.Caption := FileName;    { Assign FileName to the Caption }
      DDGGetVersionInfo;             { Get the version information }
      DDGGetAttrSize;                { Get the size information }
    end;
    PropertiesForm.ShowModal;        { Show the form }
  finally
    Propertiesform.Free;             { Free the form }
  end;
end;
```

`ShowPropertyForm()` is rather straightforward. It creates a form instance, initializes its properties, and calls `DDGGetVersionInfo()` and `DDGGetAttrSize()` before showing the form. When the user closes the form, it frees the form's instance. Listing 27.12 shows the complete source code for PROPRTY.PAS.

Listing 27.12. The source code for PROPRTY.PAS.

```
unit Proprty;
interface

uses
  SysUtils, WinTypes, WinProcs, Messages, Classes, Graphics, Controls,
  Forms, Dialogs, ExtCtrls, StdCtrls, Buttons, VerInfo;

type
  TPropertiesForm = class(TForm)
    Label1: TLabel;
    Label2: TLabel;
    Label3: TLabel;
    Panel1: TPanel;
    Label4: TLabel;
    BitBtn1: TBitBtn;
    Label5: TLabel;
    Label6: TLabel;
    Label7: TLabel;
    Memo1: TMemo;
    GroupBox1: TGroupBox;
    CheckBox2: TCheckBox;
    CheckBox4: TCheckBox;
    CheckBox3: TCheckBox;
    CheckBox5: TCheckBox;
    CheckBox1: TCheckBox;
    CheckBox6: TCheckBox;
    ListBox1: TListBox;
    procedure ListBox1Click(Sender: TObject);
    procedure FormDestroy(Sender: TObject);
  private
    { Private declarations }
    FileName: String;
    VerInfoRes: TVerInfoRes;          { Declare a TVerInfoRes data variable }
    procedure DDGGetVersionInfo;
    procedure DDGGetAttrSize;
  public
    { Public declarations }
  end;

procedure ShowPropertyForm(FName: string);

implementation

{ Move variable instance to the implementation section }
var
  PropertiesForm: TPropertiesForm;

const
  VerNameArray: array[1..8] of PChar =
  ('Company Name', 'Comments', 'File Description', 'File Version',
   'Internal Name', 'Legal Copyright', 'Legal Trademarks',
   'Original Filename');
```

continues

Listing 27.12. continued

```
{$R *.DFM}

procedure ShowPropertyForm(FName: string);
begin
  PropertiesForm := TPropertiesForm.Create(Application); { Create the form }
  try
    with PropertiesForm do
    begin
      FileName := FName;          { Assign FName to the FileName property }
      Label5.Caption := FileName; { Assign FileName to the Caption }
      DDGGetVersionInfo;          { Get the version information }
      DDGGetAttrSize;             { Get the size information }
    end;
    PropertiesForm.ShowModal;     { Show the form }
  finally
    Propertiesform.Free;          { Free the form }
  end;
end;

procedure TPropertiesForm.DDGGetVersionInfo;
var
  VerString: string;
  i: integer;
begin
  VerInfoRes := TVerInfoRes.Create(FileName);  { Create a TVerInfoRes instance }
  try
    for i := 1 to 8 do
    begin
      VerString := VerInfoRes.GetVerNameString(TVerInfoType(i)); { Get the
➥VerInfo String }
      if VerString <> '' then
        ListBox1.Items.AddObject(StrPas(VerNameArray[i]),{ Add a pointer to a }
                    pointer(NewStr(VerString)));     { string to objects }
    end;                                             { array }
  finally
    VerInfoRes.Free;  { Free the TVerInfoRes instance }
  end;
end;

procedure TPropertiesForm.DDGGetAttrSize;
var
  SearchRec: TSearchRec;
  FloatSize: double;
  FileDate: TDateTime;
begin
  FindFirst(FileName, faAnyFile, SearchRec); { Find the FileName }
  try
    { Have CheckBoxes indicate attribute results }
    CheckBox1.Checked := Boolean(SearchRec.Attr and faArchive);
    CheckBox2.Checked := Boolean(SearchRec.Attr and faReadOnly);
    CheckBox3.Checked := Boolean(SearchRec.Attr and faSysFile);
    CheckBox4.Checked := Boolean(SearchRec.Attr and faHidden);
    CheckBox5.Checked := Boolean(SearchRec.Attr and faVolumeID);
    CheckBox6.Checked := Boolean(SearchRec.Attr and faDirectory);
```

```
      FloatSize := SearchRec.Size; { Get the file size and format it }
      Label6.Caption := FormatFloat('#,###,###,##0', FloatSize)+' bytes';
      { Convert from DOS DateTime format to a TDataTime record. }
      Label7.Caption := DateTimeToStr(FileDateToDateTime(SearchRec.Time));
    finally
      FindClose(SearchRec); { Use for 32-bit Windows portability }
    end;
end;

procedure TPropertiesForm.ListBox1Click(Sender: TObject);
begin
  with ListBox1 do
    Memo1.Text := PString(Items.Objects[ItemIndex])^;  { Typecast as a PString }
end;

procedure TPropertiesForm.FormDestroy(Sender: TObject);
var
  i: integer;
begin
  With ListBox1 do
    for i := 0 to Items.Count - 1 do            { Free the PStrings previously }
      DisposeStr(pointer(Items.Objects[i]));    { allocated }
end;

end
```

Defining the *TVerInfoRes* Class

The TVerInfoRes class encapsulates some of the Windows API functions for extracting version information from files that contain such information. Version information on a file may include data such as company name, file description, version, and comments, just to name a few. Here is the data that TVerInfoRes retrieves:

Company Name	This refers to the company that created the file.
Comments	Any additional comments that may be attached to the file.
File Description	A description about the file.
File Version	A version number.
Internal Name	An internal name as defined by the company generating the file.
Legal Copyright	All copyright notices that apply to the file.
Legal Trademarks	Legal trademarks that apply to the file.
Original File name	If any, the original filename.

The unit that defines the TVerInfoRes class, VERINFO.PAS, is shown in Listing 27.13.

Listing 27.13. The source code for VERINFO.PAS.

```pascal
unit VerInfo;

interface

uses SysUtils, WinTypes, Dialogs;

type
  { define an exception class for version info }
  EVerInfoError = class(Exception);

  { define enum type representing different types of version info }
  TVerInfoType = (viCompanyName, viComments, viFileDescription, viFileVersion,
                  viInternalName, viLegalCopyright, viLegalTrademarks,
                  viOriginalFilename);

  { the version info class }
  TVerInfoRes = class
  private
    Handle: Longint;
    Size: Integer;
    RezBuffer: PChar;
    TransTable: PLongint;
  public
    constructor Create(const FileName: String);
    destructor Destroy; override;
    function GetVerNameString(VerKind: TVerInfoType): String;
  end;

implementation

uses WinProcs, Ver;

const
  { strings that must be fed to VerQueryValue() function }
  SFInfo = '\StringFileInfo\';

  VerNameArray: array[viCompanyName..viOriginalFilename] of String[20] =
  ('\CompanyName', '\Comments', '\FileDescription', '\FileVersion',
   '\InternalName', '\LegalCopyright', '\LegalTrademarks',
   '\OriginalFilename');


constructor TVerInfoRes.Create(const FileName: String);
var
  PFileName: PChar;
  SBSize: word;
begin
  { copy FileName String into PChar }
  PFileName := StrPCopy(StrAlloc(Length(FileName) + 1), FileName);
  try
    { Determine size of version information }
    Size := GetFileVersionInfoSize(PFileName, Handle);
    if Size <= 0 then          { raise exception if size <= 0 }
      raise EVerInfoError.Create('File not found or unaccessable.');
    GetMem(RezBuffer, Size);  { allocate memory buffer for resource info }
    { Fill the buffer with version information, raise exception on error }
```

```
    if not GetFileVersionInfo(PFileName, Handle, Size, RezBuffer) then
      raise EVerInfoError.Create('Cannot obtain version info.');
    { Get translation info, raise exception on error }
    if not VerQueryValue(RezBuffer, '\VarFileInfo\Translation',
                        Pointer(TransTable), SBSize) then
      raise EVerInfoError.Create('No language info.');
  finally
    StrDispose(PFileName);    { Get ride of file name PChar }
  end;
end;

destructor TVerInfoRes.Destroy;
begin
  FreeMem(RezBuffer, Size);
end;

function TVerInfoRes.GetVerNameString(VerKind: TVerInfoType): String;
const
  FormatStr = '%s%.4x%.4x%s%s';
var
  P: PChar;
  S: Word;
begin
  Result := Format(FormatStr, [SfInfo, LoWord(TransTable^), HiWord(TransTable^),
                            VerNameArray[VerKind], #0]);
  { get and return version query info, return empty string on error }
  if VerQueryValue(RezBuffer, @Result[1], Pointer(P), S) then
    Result := StrPas(P)
  else
    Result := '';
end;

end.
```

First, we define an enumerated type to represent the version-specific information that the TVerInfoRes class obtains. The TVerInfoRes contains the various variables that it requires and defines the method GetVerNameString().

The string constants that are defined in the implementation section as SFInfo and VerNameArray and required to build appropriate parameters for the VerQueryValue() Windows API function.

The TVerInfoRes.Create() takes a string holding a filename as a parameter. Because Windows API functions require a PChar type, we must convert the FileName string type to a PChar. The Windows API function GetFileVersionInfoSize() returns the size of a buffer that would be required to hold the version information for the file, if any. In our method, we raise an exception if the filename passed to Create() contains no version information. Otherwise, we allocate the memory required and call GetFileVersionInfo(), another Windows API function which fills the allocated buffer with the file's version information. Specific version information data is contained in sub-blocks within the buffer retrieved from GetFileVersionInfo(). The specific version information is retrieved by calling VerQueryValue() and passing to it a string specifying which version information to retrieve. This is the purpose of the VerNameArray. If the call to

`GetFileVersionInfo()` is successful, we call `VerQueryValue()` to return a pointer to the translation information required to translate the specific version information items in the buffer to an appropriate language when retrieved from the buffer.

`GetVerNameString()` is where the specific version information item is obtained. We first construct the appropriate string to pass to `VerQueryValue()` from the predefined constants. If the call to `VerQueryValue()` is successful, we return the requested data to the caller of the method as a string.

Getting File Attribute and Size Information

The `DDGGetAttrSize()` method uses the `FindFirst()` function to retrieve information about the file. It sets each `TCheckBox` instance by examining the value of the `Attr` field of the `TSearchRec` record ANDed with the corresponding attribute constant. It then uses the `FormatFloat()` function to format the `Size` field with thousandths separators and converts the `TSearchRec`'s DOS file date/time field `Time` to a `TDateTime` value. These values are added to the appropriate `Label` captions.

`TPropertyForm.ListBox1Click()` shows the version information in `Memo1` for the item clicked by retrieving that information from `ListBox1`'s `Objects` list. Recall that it was stored there from `DDGGetVersionInfo()`.

Figure 27.11 shows how this form appears when viewing the file WINHELP.EXE.

FIGURE 27.11.

Version information for
WINHELP.EXE.

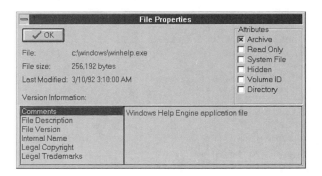

Setting Up *TDriveForm*

`TDriveForm` is the `MDIChild` form where the bulk of the file operations exist. Most operations are invoked from the menu. Unlike the other forms you have created, `TDriveForm` is not a self-contained form. It will need to access the main form, as well as other `MDIChild` forms' properties and components. Add the following units to `TDriveForm`'s unit's uses clause:

```
implementation
uses DDGFileu, prompt2, prompt1, Proprty, findfu, DDGUtils;
```

Listing 27.14 shows DDGCHLD.PAS.

Listing 27.14. The source code for DDGCHLD.PAS.

```
unit Ddgchld;
interface

uses
  SysUtils, WinTypes, WinProcs, Messages, Classes, Graphics, Controls,
  Forms, Dialogs, FileCtrl, StdCtrls, ExtCtrls, Menus;

type
  TDriveForm = class(TForm)
    MainMenu1: TMainMenu;
    File1: TMenuItem;
    Exit1: TMenuItem;
    N1: TMenuItem;
    RemoveDirectory1: TMenuItem;
    CreateDirectory1: TMenuItem;
    N2: TMenuItem;
    Properties1: TMenuItem;
    N3: TMenuItem;
    Rename1: TMenuItem;
    Delete1: TMenuItem;
    Move1: TMenuItem;
    Copy1: TMenuItem;
    Run1: TMenuItem;
    Utiliies1: TMenuItem;
    FileFind1: TMenuItem;
    Grep1: TMenuItem;
    Window1: TMenuItem;
    ArrangeIcons1: TMenuItem;
    Tile1: TMenuItem;
    Cascade1: TMenuItem;
    Help1: TMenuItem;
    About1: TMenuItem;
    FileListBox1: TFileListBox;
    DirectoryListBox1: TDirectoryListBox;
    CloseAll1: TMenuItem;
    procedure FormClose(Sender: TObject; var Action: TCloseAction);
    procedure DirectoryListBox1DragOver(Sender, Source: TObject; X,
      Y: Integer; State: TDragState; var Accept: Boolean);
    procedure DirectoryListBox1DragDrop(Sender, Source: TObject; X,
      Y: Integer);
    procedure DirectoryListBox1Change(Sender: TObject);
    procedure CreateDirectory1Click(Sender: TObject);
    procedure RemoveDirectory1Click(Sender: TObject);
    procedure Run1Click(Sender: TObject);
    procedure FormCreate(Sender: TObject);
    procedure Copy1Click(Sender: TObject);
    procedure Move1Click(Sender: TObject);
    procedure Delete1Click(Sender: TObject);
    procedure Rename1Click(Sender: TObject);
    procedure FileListBox1Change(Sender: TObject);
    procedure FormDeactivate(Sender: TObject);
    procedure FormActivate(Sender: TObject);
    procedure Properties1Click(Sender: TObject);
    procedure FileFind1Click(Sender: TObject);
    procedure Cascade1Click(Sender: TObject);
    procedure Tile1Click(Sender: TObject);
```

continues

Listing 27.14. continued

```
    procedure ArrangeIcons1Click(Sender: TObject);
    procedure CloseAll1Click(Sender: TObject);
    procedure Exit1Click(Sender: TObject);
  private
    { Private declarations }
    function GetFileName: String;
  public
    { Public declarations }
    procedure GetDiskData;
    procedure GetSelectedFileSize;
  end;

var
  DriveForm: TDriveForm;

implementation
uses DDGFileu, prompt2, prompt1, Proprty, findfu, DDGUtils;

{$R *.DFM}
procedure TDriveForm.GetDiskData;
const
  FormatStr = '%s: Size: %d Free: %d';
var
  Drive: string[1];
  DriveNum: Byte;
  DSize,
  DFree: LongInt;
begin
  Drive := UpperCase(DirectoryListBox1.Drive);        { Get Drive Letter }
  DriveNum := ord(Drive[1])-65+1;                      { Determine Drive Number }
  DSize := DiskSize(DriveNum);                         { Get Disk Size }
  DFree := DiskFree(DriveNum);                         { Get Free Space }
{ Update the status bar with the drives information }
  DDGFileForm.StatusBar1.Captions[0] := Format(FormatStr, [Drive, DSize, DFree]);
end;

procedure TDriveForm.GetSelectedFileSize;
var
  TotalSize: double;
  Path: string;
  SearchRec: TSearchRec;
  i: integer;
begin
 { show total size and date of all files selected}
  Path := GetDirectoryName(DirectoryListBox1.Directory); { Get Path }
  TotalSize := 0;                                     { Set Totalsize to
➥zero initially }
  with FileListBox1 do
  begin
    for i := 0 to Items.Count - 1 do                  { Interate through
➥listbox items }
      if Selected[i] then                             { Check if item is
➥selected }
      begin
        Path := Path + Items[i];                      { Get full path }
        try
          FindFirst(Path, faAnyFile, SearchRec);       { Get file data }
```

```
      finally
        FindClose(SearchRec);
      end;
      TotalSize := TotalSize + SearchRec.Size;          { Calculate Total Size }
    end;
  end;
  { Put data in Panel3's Caption }
  DDGFileForm.StatusBar1.Captions[1] := 'Selected Files Size: '+
    FormatFloat('#,###,###,##0', TotalSize)+' Bytes';
end;

function TDriveForm.GetFileName: string;
begin
  if (FileListBox1.Items.Count = 0) then   { FileListBox empty }
    Result := ''                           { Set to an empty string }
  else
  begin                                    { Otherwise return a valid filename }
    Result := GetDirectoryName(DirectoryListBox1.Directory)+
              FileListBox1.Items[FileListBox1.ItemIndex];
  end;
end;

procedure TDriveForm.FormClose(Sender: TObject;
  var Action: TCloseAction);
begin
  Action := caFree;                        { Allow form to close }
  DDGFileForm.StatusBar1.Captions[0] := ''; { Clear the Disk data }
end;
procedure TDriveForm.DirectoryListBox1DragOver(Sender, Source: TObject; X,
  Y: Integer; State: TDragState; var Accept: Boolean);
begin
  { Accept only if the source is a TFileListbox and it's not from the
    same form }
  Accept := (Source is TFileListBox) and (Sender <> Source) and
    (TDriveForm(TFileListBox(Source).Owner).Caption <> Caption);
end;

procedure TDriveForm.DirectoryListBox1DragDrop(Sender, Source: TObject; X,
  Y: Integer);
var
  i: integer;
  FromFName, ToFName: string;
  CopyAll: boolean;
  MsgVal: word;
  Callingform: TDriveForm;
begin
  CopyAll := false;                                      { Default to false }
  CallingForm := TDriveForm(DDGFileForm.ActiveMDIChild);  { Temp Pointer to
➥the calling form. }
  for i := 0 to Callingform.FileListBox1.Items.Count - 1 do  { Increment through
➥each selected items }

    if CallingForm.FileListBox1.Selected[i] then
    begin
      with CallingForm do                          { Create the From File name }
        FromFName := GetDirectoryName(Caption)+
          FileListBox1.Items[i];
                                                   { Create the To File name }
```

continues

Listing 27.14. continued

```pascal
    ToFName := GetDirectoryName(Caption)+
      FileListBox1.Items[i];

    if not CopyAll then
      MsgVal := MessageDlg('Copy '+FromFName+      { Display message box in not
➥copying all files }
          ' to '+ToFName+'?', mtConfirmation,[mbYes, mbNo, mbAll, mbCancel],0);

    if MsgVal = mrAll then CopyAll := true;         { Set CopyAll to true. }

    if (MsgVal = mrYes) or (MsgVal = mrAll) then
      begin                                          { copy file, call the
➥CopyFile() function }
      try
        CopyFile(FromFName, ToFName);
      except
        on E: ELZCopyError do MessageDlg(E.Message, mtError, [mbok], 0);
        on E: EInOutError do MessageDlg(E.Message, mtError, [mbok], 0);
      end;
      FileListBox1.Update; { Redisplay the listbox to show new data }
    end;
    if MsgVal = mrCancel then
      Exit;                     { Abort operation if user cancels. }
  end;
 end;

procedure TDriveForm.DirectoryListBox1Change(Sender: TObject);
begin
  Caption := DirectoryListBox1.Directory; { Set Caption to current directory }
end;

procedure TDriveForm.CreateDirectory1Click(Sender: TObject);
var
 DirName: string;
begin
  DirName := GetDirectoryName(DirectoryListBox1.Directory); { get directory }
  { Ask the user for a directory name }
  If InputQuery('Make Directory', 'Enter New Directory Name', DirName) then
  begin
    MkDir(DirName);               { Make the directory }
    DirectoryListBox1.Update;  { Update the DirectoryListBox to show change }
  end;
end;

procedure TDriveForm.RemoveDirectory1Click(Sender: TObject);
var
  DirName: string;
begin
  DirName := DirectoryListBox1.GetItemPath(DirectoryListBox1.ItemIndex);
  { Verify directory removal }
  If (MessageDlg('Remove Directory '+DirName+'? ', mtConfirmation,
                       [mbYes, mbNo], 0) = mrYes) then
  begin
    DirectoryListBox1.ItemIndex := DirectoryListbox1.ItemIndex - 1;
    RmDir(DirName);             { Remove the directory }
    DirectoryListBox1.Update; { Redisplay the direcotory }
```

```pascal
    end;
end;

procedure TDriveForm.FormCreate(Sender: TObject);
begin
  Caption := DirectoryListBox1.Directory;
  GetDiskData;  { Update DDGFileForm's Panel with Data }
end;

procedure TDriveForm.Run1Click(Sender: TObject);
var
  RunFile: string;
begin
  RunFile := GetFileName;
  RunFile := ShowPrompt1Form(pmRunMode, RunFile); { return value from Prompt1 }
  if RunFile <> '' then
    DDGExec(RunFile); { Run the program }
end;

procedure TDriveForm.Copy1Click(Sender: TObject);
var
  FromF, ToF: String;
  Files: string;
  SpPos: integer;
begin
  FromF := GetFileName;
  Files := ShowPrompt2Form(pmCopyMode, FromF);
  if Files <> '' then
  begin
    SpPos := Pos(' ', Files);           { Find the position of the space }
    FromF := copy(Files , 1, SpPos-1);  { Copy over the From file name }
    ToF := copy(Files, SpPos+1,
           length(Files)-SpPos+1);      { Copy over the To file name }
    CopyFile(FromF, ToF);               { Copy the file }
  end;
end;

procedure TDriveForm.Move1Click(Sender: TObject);
var
  FromF, ToF: String;
  Files: string;
  SpPos: integer;
begin
  FromF := GetFileName;                        { Get the file name }
  Files := ShowPrompt2Form(pmMoveMode, FromF); { Get file names from user }
  if Files <> '' then
  begin                                        { Find first filename's pos }
    SpPos := Pos(' ', Files);
    FromF := copy(Files , 1, SpPos-1);         { Copy over FromF from
➡Files string }
    ToF := copy(Files, SpPos+1,
        length(Files)-SpPos+1);                { Copy over ToF from
➡Files string }
    MoveFile(FromF, ToF);                      { Move the file }
  end;
end;

procedure TDriveForm.Delete1Click(Sender: TObject);
var
```

continues

Listing 27.14. continued

```
  DelFile: string;
begin
  DelFile := GetFileName;                              { Get the delete file name }
  DelFile := ShowPrompt1Form(pmDeleteMode, DelFile); { return value from Prompt1 }
  if DelFile <> '' then
    DeleteFile(DelFile);                              { Delete the file }
end;

procedure TDriveForm.Rename1Click(Sender: TObject);
var
  FromF, ToF: String;
  Files: string;
  SpPos: integer;
begin
  FromF := GetFileName;                            { Get the FromF file name }
  Files := ShowPrompt2Form(pmRenameMode, FromF); { Get file names from the user }
  if Files <> '' then
  begin
    SpPos := Pos(' ', Files);                      { Find the first file name }
    FromF := copy(Files , 1, SpPos-1);             { Copy over FromF }
    ToF := copy(Files, SpPos+1,
        length(Files)-SpPos+1);                    { Copy over ToF }
    MoveFile(FromF, ToF);                          { Move FromF to ToF }
  end;
end;

procedure TDriveForm.FileListBox1Change(Sender: TObject);
begin
  GetSelectedFileSize;    { Call to get file size of selected files }
end;

procedure TDriveForm.FormDeactivate(Sender: TObject);
begin
  DDGFileForm.StatusBar1.Captions[0] := ''; { Set caption to blank }
end;

procedure TDriveForm.FormActivate(Sender: TObject);
begin
  GetDiskData;             { Get information on the disk }
end;

procedure TDriveForm.Properties1Click(Sender: TObject);
var
  Path: string;
begin
  { Get a valid directory name }
  Path := GetDirectoryName(DirectoryListBox1.Directory)+
          FileListBox1.Items[FileListBox1.ItemIndex];
  ShowPropertyForm(Path); { Display the properties form }
end;

procedure TDriveForm.FileFind1Click(Sender: TObject);
var
  FileName: string;
begin
  FileName := ShowPrompt1Form(pmFileNameMode, ''); { Get Filename to search on }
```

```
  if FileName <> '' then
  begin
    { Look for the file }
    FileName := FindFile(DirectoryListBox1.Directory, FileName);
    if FileName <> '' then
      MessageDlg('File Selected: '+FileName, mtInformation, [mbok], 0);
  end;
end;

procedure TDriveForm.Cascade1Click(Sender: TObject);
begin
  DDGFileForm.Cascade;                    { Cascade all Windows }
end;

procedure TDriveForm.Tile1Click(Sender: TObject);
begin
  DDGFileForm.Tile;                       { Tile all Windows }
end;

procedure TDriveForm.ArrangeIcons1Click(Sender: TObject);
begin
  DDGFileForm.ArrangeIcons;               { Arrange form's icons }
end;

procedure TDriveForm.CloseAll1Click(Sender: TObject);
var
  i: integer;
begin
  for i := 0 to DDGFileForm.MDIChildCount - 1 do { Increement through MDI
➥Children }
    DDGFileForm.MDIChildren[i].Close;          { and close them }
end;

procedure TDriveForm.Exit1Click(Sender: TObject);
begin
  DDGFileForm.Close;                      { Exit the DDGFileForm }
end;

end.
```

DirectoryListBox1's OnChange event handler sets the form's caption to its current directory. TFileListBox1's OnChange event handler calls the GetSelectedFileSize() method, which updates DDGFileForm's StatusBar1 with the total size of all selected files. This event handler uses the FindFirst() function to read the file information into a TSearchRec record variable, from which the file size information is received. TFileListBox1's OnClick event handler also is linked to the OnChange event handler from the Object Inspector.

Executing Other Programs

The TDriveForm.Run1Click() event handler invokes the Prompt1Form and acquires a filename from the user. It then calls DDGExec(), which was defined in the DDGUTILS.PAS unit shown in Listing 27.12. Because WinExec() requires PChar types instead of a string, DDGExec() takes care of performing the String-to-PChar conversion and also raises a special exception EWinExecError, if WinExec() returns an error.

Copying Files Using Drag and Drop Capabilities

When the user drags selected files from TDriveForm's FileListBox1 to another TDriveForm child form, those selected items are copied from the source form's directory to the target form's directory. This requires enabling drag and drop options for TDriveForm's DirectoryListBox1 and FileListBox1.

You already set the Dragmode property to dmAutomatic for both components when you created the forms. The statement in DirectoryListBox1's OnDragOver event handler that follows basically says to *accept the drag operation if the source is a TFileListbox, the source isn't itself, and the destination directory is not the same as the source directory:*

```
Accept := (Source is TFileListBox) and (Sender <> Source) and
    (TDriveForm(TFileListBox(Source).Owner).Caption <> Caption);
```

The FileListBox1's OnDragOver event is hooked to TDirectoryListBox's OnDragOver event handler through the Object Inspector. TDriveForm.DirectoryListBox1DragDrop() is a bit more detailed, with logic to copy all selected files from one TDriveForm MDIChild to another TDriveForm.

The variable CopyAll is set to False by default, which causes the user to verify each file copy. CallingForm is a temporary pointer to the form invoking the dragging operation—in this case, ActiveMDIChild. The following for loop iterates through each selected item in CallingForm's FileListBox1, creates its path as the source, and also creates a destination path:

```
for i := 0 to Callingform.FileListBox1.Items.Count - 1 do
    if CallingForm.FileListBox1.Selected[i] then
```

The event handler then verifies the copy operation from the user and calls the CopyFile() procedure.

The user is presented with a verification dialog box; he or she then can choose to copy the file, cancel the operation, or copy all files without being asked to verify each copy.

The CopyFile() procedure is defined in DDGUTILS.PAS, shown in Listing 27.12. CopyFile() uses the AssignFile() procedure to associate an external filename with a file variable. FromFile and ToFile are declared as binary file variables. The Reset() procedure opens FromFile for input. Rewrite() creates a new file. If a file already exists under the name associated with ToFile, it is erased and re-created. CopyFile() then uses the WindowsAPI LZCopy() function defined in the LZEXPAND unit to copy FromFile to ToFile. To use this function, you must include LZEXPAND in DDGUTILS.PAS's uses clause.

The LZCopy() function takes two parameters: a source file handle and a destination file handle. It copies the source file associated with FromFile's handle to the destination file associated with ToFile's handle.

FILE HANDLES

Most file-management functions are really operating system functions or interrupts that have been wrapped up in Object Pascal routines. The Reset() function, for example, is really a Pascal wrapper to interrupt $21 function $3D (Open file using handle). The operating system maintains the handles to files that have been open and performs the necessary cleanup when the file is closed. By wrapping up these interrupts into Object Pascal functions, you do not have to worry about the implementation details of these file operations, which are written mostly in assembly language for efficiency. However, it also obscures how to access certain file details when needed (like the file handle) because these are hidden for Object Pascal's usage.

When using non-native Object Pascal functions that require a file handle, such as LZCopy(), you can get the file handle by typecasting your text file and binary file variables as TTextRec or TFileRec, respectively. These record types contain the file handle as well as other file details. Other than the file handle, you rarely will (and probably shouldn't) access the other data fields. The correct procedure for getting to the handle follows:

```
TFileRec(MyFileVar).Handle
```

The definition of the TFileRec and TTextRec data fields follows:

```
TFileRec = record
  Handle: Word;              { File Handle }
  Mode: Word;                { File Mode }
  RecSize: Word;             { Size of each file record }
  Private: array[1..26] of Byte;   { Used internally by Object Pascal }
  UserData: array[1..16] of Byte;  { Not used, you may use this for something }
  Name: array[0..79] of Char;      { Pathname as used with the assign()
➥procedure }
end;
PTextBuf = ^TTextBuf;
TTextBuf = array[0..127] of Char;  { Text buffer for first 127 characters in
➥the text file }
TTextRec = record
  Handle: Word;              { File Handle }
  Mode: Word;                { File Mode }
  BufSize: Word;             { These fields are used for a memory
buffering
➥scheme }
  Private: Word;             { and usually shouldn't be tinkered with. }
  BufPos: Word;
  BufEnd: Word;
  BufPtr: PTextBuf;
  OpenFunc: Pointer;         { The func pointers are pointers to file
➥access functions }
  InOutFunc: Pointer;        { and they can be modified in order to
➥write ext-file }
  FlushFunc: Pointer;        { device drivers. }
  CloseFunc: Pointer;
  UserData: array[1..16] of Byte;  { Not used, you may use this for
➥something }
```

```
   Name: array[0..79] of Char;        { Pathname as used with the assign()
➥procedure }
   Buffer: TTextBuf;                   { Buffer containing first 127 characters
➥of file }
end;
```

Lastly, both files are closed. The ELZCopyError exception is raised if a negative value is returned from the LZCopy() function. Otherwise, LZCopy() returns the destination file's size in bytes. The online help shows to what errors the different negative values from LZCopy() refers. You might consider creating more detailed exceptions to cover each error.

Copying Files Through the Menu

TDriveForm.Copy1Click() also performs the copy operation, except that it is not quite so elaborate as the drag and drop copy operation. It retrieves the source and destination file paths and invokes the CopyFile() function in the same manner.

Moving and Renaming Files

The TDriveForm.Move1Click() and TDriveFormRename1Click() event handlers are virtually the same, except that they each pass a different mode to ShowPrompt2Form(), causing it to display different prompts. Both event handlers also use the MoveFile() function defined in DDGUTILS.PAS (Listing 27.12), which invokes the Object Pascal Rename() procedure. Rename() changes the name of an external file, including the pathname, if requested to do so.

Deleting a File

The TDriveForm.Delete1Click() event handler prompts the user for a filename to delete and erases the external file using the Object Pascal DeleteFile() procedure.

Creating and Removing Directories

TDriveForm's CreateDirectory1Click() and RemoveDirectory1Click() event handlers use the Object Pascal MkDir() and RmDir() procedures to create and remove a directory, respectively. Both event handlers prompt the user for verification before performing their operation.

Searching for Files

The TDriveForm.FileFind1Click() event handler asks the user for a file on which to search. It then invokes the FindFile() function to search for the file entered.

Exiting the Application

Finally, the File | Exit menu calls TDDGFileForm.Close, which closes the application.

Performing the Final Touches

An MDI application wouldn't be an MDI application without the standard Windows commands to cascade, tile, arrange icons, or close all windows.

Summary

This chapter taught you how to combine Delphi's powerful visual development capabilities with regular file-operation functions to build a totally useable File manager application. Additionally, you created another reusable component, TStatusBar, and you learned how to work with owner-draw components. You will use this knowledge to create even more powerful applications as well. In fact, with the knowledge you already have, you might even consider extending the functionality of the File Manager. The next chapter teaches you how to create yet another useful tool for keeping track of the time you spend on various projects.

28

Building a Time-Tracker Application

This chapter demonstrates how to build a time-tracker program that enables you to track the time spent on user-definable tasks. This chapter puts to use what you learned in Chapter 16, "Writing Database Applications," and teaches you some additional tricks in working with master-detail tables and calculated fields. You also will learn how to safely and accurately work with currency values. Additionally, you will do some more work with the TDataTime data type.

Examining the Feature List

The time-tracker program will contain the following features:

- The capability to calculate time spent on task/subtasks.
- A feature that enables users to define their own task/subtasks.
- A feature that enables users to track time spent on a task/subtask against a client with whom they want to associate the task/subtask.
- An automatic calculation of a total amount for the time spent on a task based on a per-hour rate.

Creating the Tables

The Task Manager uses five tables. These tables already are created and exist on the accompanying CD in the directory \SOURCE\DATA\. Copy all files contained in that directory to a local directory on your hard drive, and then use the use the BDE configuration utility to set up an alias to point to these tables. We named our alias DDGLOCAL. Tables 28.1 through 28.5 show the table structures and purpose for each of their fields. Table 28.1 shows the Task table.

Table 28.1. The Task table (TASK.DB).

Field	Type Size	Purpose
Task*	A 20	Stores a task as defined by the user.
*This field is keyed.		

The task table contains all the main tasks that are defined by the user. Each task record in TASK.DB has subtask records that exist in SUBTASKS.DB. The records in SUBTASKS.DB are linked to the task table by the Task field, as shown in Table 28.2. The word *linked* is used here to describe how TASK.DB and SUBTASKS.DB form a *master-detail* relationship, which is explained later in this section.

Table 28.2. The Subtask table (SUBTASKS.DB).

Field	Type Size	Purpose
Task*	A 20	Linked to the Task field in TASK.DB.
SubTask*	A 20	A subtask name enabling the user to define more specific tasks for each task in TASK.DB.
RatePrHr	N	Rate per hour in pennies.
*This field is keyed.		

The Task field, an Alpha field, serves a link to another table. Such links are explained momentarily in this section. The Field SubTask, also an Alpha field, represents a subtask name. The Numeric field RatePrHr stores a monetary amount in cents to represent a chargeable rate per hour.

The Task Manager enables you to associate a client, person, or business with each task that you are tracking. The entries for this information are stored in the TSKCLNT.DB shown in Table 28.3.

Table 28.3. The Task Client table (TSKCLNT.DB).

Field	Type Size	Purpose
ClientNo*	N	Unique identifier for this record. This value is received from the CLIENTNO.DB table.
Name	A 30	Name of client.
Street	A 40	Street address.
City	A 20	City name.
State	A 2	State abbreviation.
ZIP	A 10	ZIP code.
*This field is keyed.		

TSKCLNT.DB's records store address information about a client. The field CLIENTNO is a Numeric field; its value is received from the CLIENTNO.DB table shown in Table 28.4. This table contains only one record, which is a Numeric field used to retrieve unique identifiers for each client record.

Table 28.4. The Client Number table (CLIENTNO.DB).

Field	Type Size	Purpose
ClientNo*	N	Used for generating a unique identifier for the TSKCLNT.DB table.

*This field is keyed.   ❦

The last table is the task-tracker table TASKTRKR.DB, which stores tracking information about each task. TASKTRKR.DB is shown in Table 28.5.

Table 28.5. The Task-Tracker table (TASKTRKR.DB).

Field	Type Size	Purpose
ClientNo*	N	Link to the CLIENTNO.DB table.
SubTask*	A 20	Subtask to which entry applies.
StartTime	@ (TimeStamp)	Date/Time that the task started.
EndTime	@ (TimeStamp)	Date/Time that the task ended.
TotalInCents	N	Total amount charged for task.
AtRate	N	Rate per hour for task received from RatePrHr in the SUBTASKS.DB table.

*This field is keyed.

Here you see two fields, ClientNo and SubTask, which also appear in previous tables. These fields are present to allow the record entries in TASKTRKR.DB to link to TSKCLNT.DB and SUBTASKS.DB, forming a master-detail relationship.

MASTER-DETAIL RELATIONSHIPS

A *master-detail table relationship* is also known as a *one-to-many relationship*. This relationship basically links two tables together by common values existing in a specific field in both tables. In the master table, one record refers to one or more records in the detail table where the value in the linked field is the same for both tables. For example, suppose that you have two entries in the TASK.DB table: School Work and Exercise. Now suppose that you have the following three subtasks in the SUBTASKS.DB table that apply to the School Work task: Studying, Homework, and Researching. The subtasks that apply to Exercise are Jogging, Weight Lifting, and Swimming. To establish this master-detail relationship, both tables require a field with which to link their records. The following illustrates how the one-to-many relationship is used:

TASK.DB

KEYFIELD	*Task*
1001	School Work
1002	Excercise

SUBTASKS.DB

KEYFIELD	*Task*
1001	Studying
1001	Homework
1001	Researching
1002	Jogging
1002	Weight Lifting
1002	Swimming

Notice how the link is established by KEYFIELD. When looking at the TASK.DB record for School Work, all records in SUBTASKS.DB that apply to School Work in TASK.DB must have the value 1001 in their KEYFIELD fields. The same goes for the Exercise task except the value is different.

Looking at the Required Forms

The Task Manager uses six forms:

MainForm	The main form for the project. From the main form, you can select a task or subtask; select a client; keep track of time spent on a task; and see a report displaying the time spent and amount due, if applicable, for tasks that have been tracked.
TaskManageForm	This is where you can add and remove tasks and subtasks. From TaskManageForm, you can invoke the AddTaskForm or the SubTaskDataForm.
AddTaskForm	This is where you enter specific data for the task.
SubTaskDataForm	This is where you enter specific data for the subtask.
ClientManForm	This is where you can add and remove clients.
ReportForm	This is where you can see a report of the tasks that have been tracked.

The entire project is called DDGTT.DPR. Its forms are stored in the units MAINFRM.PAS, TASKMAN.PAS, CLNTMAN.PAS, ADDTASK.PAS, SUBDATA.PAS, and REPORT.PAS (each of these is discussed later in this chapter).

Creating *MainForm*

MainForm has the important components and properties shown in Table 28.6. MainForm is shown in Figure 28.1. MainForm's menus are shown in Table 28.7.

Table 28.6. MainForm's components.

Component	Property	Value
MainForm	BorderStyle	bsSingle
Panel1	Align	alClient
SpeedButton1	Glyph	GO.BMP
	Layout	blGlyphTop
Panel2	Align	alRight
BevelInner	bvLowered	
	BevelOuter	bvLowered
Timer1	Enabled	False
	Interval	1000
TimeTrkrTable (TTable)	DataBaseName	DDGLOCAL
	TableName	TASKTKRK.DB

FIGURE 28.1.

MainForm's components.

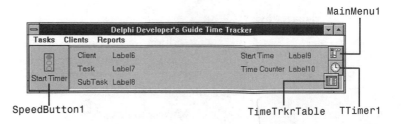

Table 28.7. MainForm's menus.

Menubar	Submenus
"Tasks"	"Task Management"
	"-"
	"Choose Task"
"Clients"	"Client Management"
	"-"
	"Choose Client"

Menubar	*Submenus*
"Reports"	"Show Report"
	"Print Report"

Creating *TaskManageForm*

TaskManageForm's components and their property settings are shown in Table 28.8 and Figure 28.2.

Table 28.8. TaskManageForm's components.

Component	*Property*	*Value*
TaskManageForm	BorderStyle	bsSingle
TaskTable (TTable)	DataBaseName	DDGLOCAL
	TableName	TASK.DB
DataSource1	DataSet	TaskTable
SubTaskTable	DataBaseName	DDGLOCAL
	TableName	SUBTASKS.DB
	MasterSource	DataSource1
	MasterFields	Task
DateSource2	DataSet	SubTaskTable
Query1	DataBaseName	DDGLOCAL

FIGURE 28.2.

TaskManageForm's components.

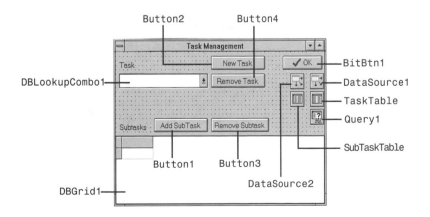

`Query1`'s `SQL` property contains the following SQL statement to delete all records in SUBTASKS.DB:

```
delete  from subtasks where task = :task
```

The `task` fields contain the value specified by the parameter. Additionally, you must define the calculated fields for `SubTaskTable`.

Working *TField* and Calculated Fields

Normally, to access field values for a table, you simply use `TTable`'s `Fields` property or the `FieldByName()` method. Using this method, you access dynamically created `TField` components at runtime. Delphi, however, provides a way for you to have more control over specific `TField` components by enabling you to create an instance variable for each `TField` over which you want control. This is done by invoking the Fields Editor, shown in Figure 28.3, by double-clicking the `TTable` component on your form. From the Fields Editor, you can add, remove, and clear `TField` variables for your form.

FIGURE 28.3.

The Fields Editor.

NOTE

Delphi initially creates hidden `TField` components that data-aware controls access for displaying data. After you explicitly add `TFields` using the Fields Editor, only those fields that you have made available are accessible by data-aware controls. A `TDBGrid`, by default, shows all fields (columns) in a table, for example, but it will show only those fields specified in the Fields Editor when used. Therefore, make sure to add all fields that you want accessible.

The Define Button enables you to create calculated fields. Clicking the Add button from the Fields Editor brings up the Add Fields dialog box, from which you can select the fields in the table that you want to make available. Figure 28.4 shows the `SubTaskTable` component fields.

After you select the fields, they appear in the listbox in the Fields Editor. This causes Delphi to create a `TField` component for each field selected. The component's type will correspond to the field's type as it exists in its table unless otherwise defined in the Fields Editor. Delphi's online help nicely describes each TField descendant type.

FIGURE 28.4.

The Add Fields dialog box.

After you place fields into the Fields Editor's listbox, you can modify their various properties for each field in the Object Inspector as you would any other component. Refer to Delphi's online help for the meaning of each of these properties.

All fields for the SubTaskTable were added to the TaskManagerForm. Additionally, a calculated field was defined, called CalcRatePerHr. This was done by invoking the Define Field dialog box, shown in Figure 28.5, by clicking the Define button in the Fields Editor.

FIGURE 28.5.

The Define Field dialog box.

RatePerHr was entered in the Field name box. Then, the Component name box was changed to CalcRatePerHr to shorten it, because Delphi prepends the table name to the component name, which makes it rather long. The Field type was set to Currency, and the Calculated checkbox was enabled.

Setting Field type to Currency causes its Currency property to be set to true. This makes the field's type a TCurrencyField, which sets its range of values and accuracy to that of a TFloatField. It also forces Delphi to control the formatting for the field when DisplayFormat and EditFormat are not assigned. In this case, data-aware controls linked to this field allow only numeric entry and display the value with a currency format.

NOTE

`DisplayFormat` and `EditFormat` take the same arguments as the `EditMask` for a `MaskEdit` control. `DisplayFormat` controls how the data in a data-aware control is displayed, whereas the `EditFormat` controls what the user can enter into the data-aware control linked to the specific field. See Delphi's online help for further information on these and other `TField` properties.

Enabling the Calculated checkbox sets the field's `Calculated` property to `true`. Values in Calculated fields are not received from or stored in the actual table. Instead, they are calculated and assigned values in the table's `OnCalcField`'s event handler. Here, the calculated field's values can be derived from another lookup table, an expression involving other field values, or any other expression used in calculating a valid return value. You learn how to derive a value for your calculated field when the functionality of `TaskManageForm` is discussed later in this chapter in the section entitled "Examining `TaskManageForm`'s Functionality."

CAUTION

A table goes into a special state, or mode, while executing its `OnCalcFields` event handler. In the `OnCalcFields` event handler, an application cannot assign any values to noncalculated fields; if it tries to, an exception is raised. Only assignments to calculated fields are allowed while in this state.

Creating *AddTaskForm* and *SubTaskDataForm*

`AddTaskForm` is fairly simple. Its components are shown in Figure 28.6. Be sure to change `AddTaskForm`'s `Borderstyle` to `bsSingle` (this is not illustrated in the figure).

FIGURE 28.6.

AddTaskForm's components.

`SubTaskDataForm` also is simple. It is shown in Figure 28.7, and its `Borderstyle` property is set to `bsSingle`.

FIGURE 28.7.

*SubTaskDataForm's
components.*

Creating *ClientManForm*

ClientManForm's components and their property settings are shown in Table 28.9 and Figure 28.8.

Table 28.9. TaskManageForm's components.

Component	Property	Value
ClientManForm	BorderStyle	bsSingle
ClientTable (TTable)	DataBaseName	DDGLOCAL
	TableName	TSKCLNT.DB
DataSource1	DataSet	ClientTable
ClientNoTable	DataBaseName	DDGLOCAL
	TableName	CLIENTNO.DB

FIGURE 28.8.

*ClientManForm's
components.*

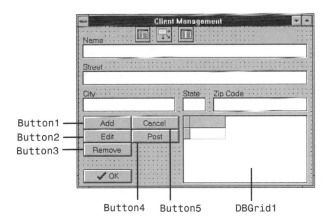

The TDBEdit components' DataSource property is set to DataSource1, and each component's Field property is set to the table's corresponding field, as indicated by the TLabel captions. The TDBGrid component also is set to DataSource1.

Creating *ReportForm*

ReportForm's components and their property settings are shown in Table 28.10 and Figure 28.9.

Table 28.10. ReportForm's components.

Component	Property	Value
ReportForm	BorderStyle	bsSingle
ReportTable (TTable)	DataBaseName	DDGLOCAL
	TableName	TASKTRKR.DB
DataSource1	DataSet	ReportTable
	AutoEdit	False
DBGrid1	DataSource	DataSource1
	Align	alBottom

FIGURE 28.9.
ReportForm's components.

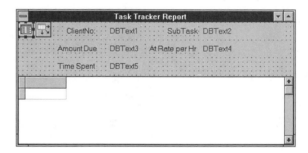

Here, ReportTable's fields have been added from the Field Editor, and three additional calculated fields have been defined. The calculated field properties are shown in Table 28.11.

Table 28.11. ReportForm's calculated fields.

Field Name	Property	Value
TotalDue(TCurrencyField)	Name	ReportTableTotalDue
	Calculated	True
	Currency	True
RateInDollars(TCurrencyField)	Name	ReportTableRateInDollars
	Calculated	True
	Currency	True
TimeSpent(TStringField)	Name	ReportTableTimeSpent
	Calculated	True

Examining *MainForm*'s Functionality

The MainForm's unit is MAINFRM.PAS. This unit is shown in Listing 28.1.

Listing 28.1. The source code for MAINFRM.PAS.

```
unit Mainfrm;

interface

uses
  SysUtils, WinTypes, WinProcs, Messages, Classes, Graphics, Controls,
  Forms, Dialogs, Menus, ExtCtrls, DBTables, DB, Buttons, StdCtrls,
  Taskman, ClntMan, Report;

type

  TTimeRecord = record
    Hrs,
    Mins,
    Secs: word;
  end;

  TMainForm = class(TForm)
    Panel1: TPanel;
    MainMenu1: TMainMenu;
    Tasks1: TMenuItem;
    TaskMan1: TMenuItem;
    ChooseTask1: TMenuItem;
    Clients1: TMenuItem;
    ClientMan1: TMenuItem;
    N1: TMenuItem;
    Panel2: TPanel;
    Label1: TLabel;
    Label2: TLabel;
    Label3: TLabel;
    Label4: TLabel;
    Label5: TLabel;
    Label6: TLabel;
    Label7: TLabel;
    Label8: TLabel;
    Label9: TLabel;
    Label10: TLabel;
    SpeedButton1: TSpeedButton;
    Reports1: TMenuItem;
    ShowReport1: TMenuItem;
    N2: TMenuItem;
    ChooseClient1: TMenuItem;
    Timer1: TTimer;
    TimeTrkrTable: TTable;
    procedure FormCreate(Sender: TObject);
    procedure TaskMan1Click(Sender: TObject);
    procedure ChooseTask1Click(Sender: TObject);
    procedure ClientMan1Click(Sender: TObject);
    procedure ChooseClient1Click(Sender: TObject);
    procedure ShowReport1Click(Sender: TObject);
```

continues

Listing 28.1. continued

```
    procedure SpeedButton1Click(Sender: TObject);
    procedure Timer1Timer(Sender: TObject);
  private
    { Private declarations }
    TaskRec: TTaskRecord;
    ClientRec: TClientRecord;
    StartTime, EndTime: TDateTime;
    procedure StartTiming;
    procedure EndTiming;
    function GetTimeRecord(StartTime, EndTime: double): TTimeRecord;
    function CalcChargeForTime(TimeRec: TTimeRecord; Rate: double): double;
  public
    { Public declarations }
  end;

var
  MainForm: TMainForm;

implementation

{$R *.DFM}

procedure TMainForm.FormCreate(Sender: TObject);
var
  i: integer;
begin
  for i := 0 to ComponentCount -1 do        { All TLabels have a tag set to 1 }
    if Components[i].Tag = 1 then            { so we iterate through them and }
      TLabel(Components[i]).Caption := '';   { assign an empty string to them }
  TaskRec.Task := '';                        { Clear the TaskRec record }
  TaskRec.SubTask := '';
  ClientRec.Name := '';                      { Clear the ClientRec record }
  ClientRec.ClientNo := -1;
end;

procedure TMainForm.TaskMan1Click(Sender: TObject);
begin
  DoTaskManage;                              { Invoke the TaskManageForm }
end;

procedure TMainForm.ChooseTask1Click(Sender: TObject);
begin
  TaskRec := GetTaskRecord;                  { Call the GetTaskRecord function }
  if TaskRec.Task <> '' then begin           { Set the captions accordingly with }
    Label7.Caption := TaskRec.Task;          { data received in the TaskRec }
    Label8.Caption := TaskRec.SubTask;
  end;
end;

procedure TMainForm.ClientMan1Click(Sender: TObject);
begin
  DoClientManagement;
end;

procedure TMainForm.ChooseClient1Click(Sender: TObject);
begin
  ClientRec := GetClientRecord;              { Call the GetClientRecord function }
```

```
    if ClientRec.ClientNo <> -1 then          { Set label caption accordingly  }
      Label6.Caption := ClientRec.Name;
end;

procedure TMainForm.ShowReport1Click(Sender: TObject);
begin
  DoReport;          { Call DoReport to display report data }
end;

procedure TMainForm.SpeedButton1Click(Sender: TObject);
begin
  if ClientRec.ClientNo = -1 then       { If a client record is not loaded }
    MessageDlg('Client Required!', mtWarning, [mbok], 0)
  else if TaskRec.Task = '' then        { If a task record is not loaded }
    MessageDlg('Task Required!', mtWarning, [mbok], 0)
  else
    with SpeedButton1 do
      if Caption = 'Start Timer' then begin
        Glyph.LoadFromFile('Stop.bmp'); { Load the Stop bitmap }
        Caption := 'Stop Timer';        { Change the caption }
        StartTiming;                    { Call the StartTiming method }
      end
      else begin
        Glyph.LoadFromFile('go.bmp');   { Load the Go bitmap }
        Caption := 'Start Timer';       { Change the caption }
        EndTiming;                      { Call the EndTiming method }
      end;
end;

procedure TMainForm.StartTiming;
begin
  StartTime := Now;            { Get the current date/time & store in StartTime }
  Timer1.Enabled := true;      { Start the timer }
  Label9.Caption := TimeToStr(StartTime);   { Set the labels caption to show time }
end;

procedure TMainForm.EndTiming;
var
  TimeRec: TTimeRecord;
begin
  EndTime := Now;             { Get the current date/time and store in EndTime }
  Timer1.Enabled := false;    { Stop the timer }
  Label10.Caption := '';      { Set Label caption to empty string }
  with TimeTrkrTable do  begin
    Active := true;                 { Open the TimeTrkrTable }
    Append;                         { Append mode }
    { Set the fields in TimeTrkrTable with data in ClientRec, TaskRec, and
      the EndTime and StartTime variables. Also store Rate and Total values }
    FieldByName('ClientNo').AsInteger := ClientRec.ClientNo;
    FieldByName('SubTask').AsString := TaskRec.SubTask;
    FieldByName('StartTime').AsDateTime := StartTime;
    FieldByName('EndTime').AsDateTime := EndTime;
    TimeRec := GetTimeRecord(StartTime, EndTime);
    FieldByName('TotalInCents').AsFloat := CalcChargeForTime(TimeRec,
➡TaskRec.Rate);
    FieldByName('AtRate').AsFloat := TaskRec.Rate;
```

continues

Listing 28.1. continued

```
    Post;  { Post the values to the table }
    Active := false;  { Close the table }
  end;
end;

procedure TMainForm.Timer1Timer(Sender: TObject);
const
  TimeDisplay = '%.2d:%.2d:%.2d';          { Constant string to use with format() }
var
  DiffTime: TDateTime;
  hrs, mins, secs, ms: word;
begin
  DiffTime := Now - StartTime;                      { Calculate a time difference }
  DecodeTime(DiffTime, Hrs, Mins, Secs, Ms);        { Extract time data }
  Label10.Caption := Format(TimeDisplay, [Hrs, Mins, Secs]); { Format the string }
end;

function TMainForm.GetTimeRecord(StartTime, EndTime: double): TTimeRecord;
var
  DateTimeDiff: double;
  Yrs,Mos,Days,
  Hrs, Mins, Secs, Ms: word;
begin
  DateTimeDiff := EndTime - StartTime;             { Calculate date difference }
  DecodeDate(DateTimeDiff, Yrs, Mos, Days);        { Get the date information }
  DecodeTime(DateTimeDiff, Hrs, Mins, Secs, Ms);   { Get time data }
  Result.Hrs := (Days*60)+Hrs;                     { Calculate total hours }
  Result.Mins := Mins;                             { Assign minutes to result }
  Result.Secs := Secs;                             { Assign seconds to result }
end;

function TMainForm.CalcChargeForTime(TimeRec: TTimeRecord; Rate: double): double;
begin
{ Remember that rate is really in pennies per hour }
  Result := 0.0;
  with TimeRec do begin
    Result := (Hrs*Rate)+           { Calculate pennies per hours }
              round((Mins / 60)*Rate); { Calculate pennies per minutes }
    if Secs >= 30 then    { Larger than 1/2 of a second count up one }
      Result := Result + round((1 / 60)*Rate); { Calculate rate for 1 minute }
  end;
end;

end.
```

The FormCreate() event handler just sets all the labels to an empty string and initializes its ClientRec and TaskRec variables, also with empty strings.

TaskMan1Click() calls the procedure DoTaskManage, which is defined in TASKMAN.PAS, and invokes the TaskManageForm which we'll discuss later in this chapter in the section "Examining TaskMananageForm's Functionality."

Choosing Task1Click() calls the GetTaskRecord() function, which retrieves a TaskRec record. This function also is defined in TASKMAN.PAS.

ClientMan1Click() calls the procedure DoClientManagement(), which invokes the ClientManForm. This procedure is defined in CLNTMAN.PAS.

Choosing Client1Click() retrieves a ClientRec record. This function also is defined in CLNTMAN.PAS.

ShowReport1Click() calls DoReport, which invokes the ReportForm. This is defined in REPORT.PAS.

SpeedButton1Click() starts or stops a timing process, depending on its current state as indicated by its caption. Both a ClientRec and a TaskRec must be present in order for the timing process to begin. After loading the appropriate bitmap, this function calls the StartTiming() or EndTiming() method.

StartTiming() simply stores the current TDateTime value in the StartTime variable by invoking the Now() function, which returns a TDateTime value. It then sets a caption to display it and enables Timer1.

EndTiming() is more detailed. It first stores the time the process was ended in the EndTime variable by invoking the Now() function. It stops Timer1 and creates a new record for TimeTrkrTable. All the fields are set with information contained in the ClientRec, TaskRec, EndTime, and StartTime variables—with the exception of the TotalInCents field, which gets the return value of the function CalcChargeForTime(). Finally, the record is posted and the table is closed.

Timer1Timer() displays a counter of the elapsed time since StartTimer() was called by calculating a difference from StartTime and the current time, extracting the specific values from the difference, and using those values in a format string. GetTimeRecord() takes StartTime and EndTime as parameters and uses their values to fill a TTimeRecord defined as the following:

```
TTimeRecord = record
    Hrs,
    Mins,
    Secs: word;
  end;
```

This record is used by EndTimer() and is passed to CalcChargeForTime(). Its purpose is basically to simplify the code in CalcChargeForTime(); it isn't necessary other than to make the code clearer. CalcChargeForTime() uses the values in the TTimeRecord to calculate a total amount based on the parameter rate.

The Rate variable is of a Double type, but it is used a bit differently here. Instead of storing the dollar amount in the integer portion and the cents amount in the fractional portion, the entire amount is converted to cents, and the total cents amount is stored in Rate's integer portion. Thus, the fractional part of Rate is never used. In fact, this is done for all currency values, and is stored in the table in that manner.

FLOATING-POINT ACCURACY

In an ideal system, floating-point values are represented by an infinite range of real numbers that may fall anywhere between two other numbers. For example, between 3.5 and 4.5 are the values 3.50086, 4.0, and 4.203949993902. In computers, however, floating-point numbers must succumb to the limitation imposed by the computer's register and memory sizes. This, in effect, limits the precision of numbers that a computer can accommodate and deems it representative of only a finite and discrete subset of the whole real-number system.

The IEEE floating-point specification allows a coprocessor to represent a useful approximation of the real-number system. When the result of a calculation falls within the gap of numbers not representable by the coprocessor, it rounds that result to a number that it can represent, which may result in some loss of accuracy.

With floating-point variables, the decimal point must float around. The value 2.5, for example, is actually 25×10 to the −1 power. Likewise, 34.56 is really 3,456×10 to the −2 power. A floating-point variable needs to store two values. In the latter example, the value 3,456 is stored in the integral portion, whereas its mantissa (10 to the −2 power) is stored in the floating point's fractional portion. You can see that the decimal point must "float" between different locations to represent different decimal values. As the space required to store the mantissa increases, less significant digits may get dropped from the integral part, causing a loss of accuracy.

When reliable decimal numbers are required, such as when working with large amounts of currency, use fixed-point variables. Unlike floating points, the decimal doesn't "float" around. Just assume that the decimal is fixed at a location (10 to the −2 power, for example). You then no longer need to encode its location; 2.5 can be stored as 25, and 34.56 can be stored as 3,456. These two fixed values can be stored in fast integer variables. When they are printed for the user to interact with, you can multiply them by 10 to the power of −2 (or divide them by 100) to retrieve their integral part and perform a mod-by-100 operation to retrieve their fractional part. Even on the fastest Intel Pentium-based machines, integers are faster to add, subtract, multiply, and divide than are real numbers.

Another benefit to using fixed-point variables is that they always are exact up to their fixed precision, unlike real numbers, which may not be exact.

One disadvantage to using a longint type in Object Pascal, however, is that its range is limited to plus or minus two billion. If larger values are required, you can use real-type variables to store only the integer values, because a double has a range of 10 to the power of 308 and an extended has a range of 10 to the power of 4,932. Using these types to store integer values is safe and accurate but slower than the main processor's built-in integer types. The comp type is a special form of the coprocessor integer type. This means that it can hold only integer values, it has a range of 10 to the power of 18, and it is manipulated only by the coprocessor and is therefore somewhat slower.

Examining *TaskManageForm*'s Functionality

The TaskManageForm's unit is TASKMAN.PAS. This unit is shown in Listing 28.2.

Listing 28.2. The source code for TASKMAN.PAS.

```
unit Taskman;

interface

uses
  SysUtils, WinTypes, WinProcs, Messages, Classes, Graphics, Controls,
  Forms, Dialogs, Buttons, StdCtrls, DBCtrls, DBTables, DB, Grids, DBGrids,
  DBLookup, Mask;

type

  TTaskRecord = record
    Task: string[20];
    SubTask: String[20];
    Rate: Double;
  end;

  TTaskManageForm = class(TForm)
    Label1: TLabel;
    Label2: TLabel;
    DBGrid1: TDBGrid;
    TaskTable: TTable;
    DataSource1: TDataSource;
    SubTaskTable: TTable;
    SubTaskTableTask: TStringField;
    SubTaskTableSubtask: TStringField;
    CalcRatePerHr: TCurrencyField;
    SubTaskTableRatePrHr: TFloatField;
    DataSource2: TDataSource;
    Button1: TButton;
    BitBtn1: TBitBtn;
    DBLookupCombo1: TDBLookupCombo;
    Button2: TButton;
    Button3: TButton;
    Button4: TButton;
    Query1: TQuery;
    procedure FormActivate(Sender: TObject);
    procedure DBLookupCombo1Change(Sender: TObject);
    procedure Button1Click(Sender: TObject);
    procedure Button2Click(Sender: TObject);
    procedure Button4Click(Sender: TObject);
    procedure Button3Click(Sender: TObject);
    procedure SubTaskTableBeforePost(DataSet: TDataset);
    procedure SubTaskTableCalcFields(DataSet: TDataset);
  private
    { Private declarations }
  public
    { Public declarations }
  end;
```

continues

Listing 28.2. continued

```pascal
procedure DoTaskManage;
function GetTaskRecord: TTaskRecord;

 var
  TaskManageForm: TTaskManageForm;

implementation
uses SubData, AddTask;
{$R *.DFM}

procedure DoTaskManage;
begin
  { Instanciate the form }
  Application.CreateForm(TTaskManageForm, TaskManageForm);
  try
    with TaskManageForm do begin
      TaskTable.Active := true;        { Open TaskTable }
      SubTaskTable.Active := true;     { Open SubTaskTable }
      ShowModal;                       { Display the form }
    end;
  finally
    TaskManageForm.Free;               { Free the form }
  end;
end;

function GetTaskRecord: TTaskRecord;
begin
  Result.Task := '';                 { Initialize the result to empty strings }
  Result.SubTask := '';
  Application.CreateForm(TTaskManageForm, TaskManageForm); { Instantiate the form }
  try
    with TaskManageForm do begin
      TaskTable.Active := true;                            { Open TaskTable }
      SubTaskTable.Active := true;                         { Open SubTaskTable }
      DBLookupCombo1.Value := TaskTable.Fields[0].AsString;   { Initialize
➡DBLookupCombo1 }
      Button1.Visible := false;                            { Hide all buttons
➡as they're }
      Button2.Visible := false;                            { not needed }
      Button3.Visible := false;
      Button4.Visible := false;
      if ShowModal = mrOk then begin                       { Show the form }
        Result.Task := TaskTable.Fields[0].AsString;       { Set result field
➡to the }
        Result.SubTask := SubTaskTable.Fields[1].AsString;    { propery values }
        Result.Rate := SubTaskTable.FieldByName('RatePrHr').AsFloat;
      end;
    end;
  finally
    TaskManageForm.Free;             { Free the form }
  end;
end;

procedure TTaskManageForm.FormActivate(Sender: TObject);
begin
```

```
  { Initialize the DbLookUpCombo1 }
  DBLookupCombo1.Value := TaskTable.Fields[0].AsString;
end;

procedure TTaskManageForm.DBLookupCombo1Change(Sender: TObject);
begin
  TaskTable.SetKey;          { Put the table in the SetKey state }
  { Set the first field to the value contained in DBLookupCombo1 }
  TaskTable.Fields[0].AsString := DBLookupCombo1.Value;
  TaskTable.GoToKey;   { Move the record specified by the keyed field }
end;

procedure TTaskManageForm.Button1Click(Sender: TObject);
begin
  SubTaskTable.Append;  { Append a new record }
  if SubTaskDataForm.ShowModal = mrOk then begin { display the SubTaskDataForm }
    SubTaskTable.Fields[0].AsString := DBLookupCombo1.Value;   { Set the fields
➥values }
    SubTaskTable.Post;     { Post the recored }
  end
  else
    SubTaskTable.Cancel; { Cancel the append operation }
end;

procedure TTaskManageForm.Button2Click(Sender: TObject);
begin
  TaskTable.Append;         { Append a new record }
  if AddTaskForm.ShowModal = mrOk then { Invoke the addtask form }
    TaskTable.Post          { Post the date to the TaskTable }
  else
    TaskTable.Cancel;       { Cancel the append operation. }
end;

procedure TTaskManageForm.Button3Click(Sender: TObject);
begin
  { Confirm the delete operation }
  if MessageDlg('Delete Subtask '+SubTaskTable.Fields[0].AsString+'?',
                mtConfirmation, mbYesNoCancel, 0) = mrYes then
    SubTaskTable.Delete; { Delete the record }
end;

procedure TTaskManageForm.Button4Click(Sender: TObject);
begin
  { Confirm delete operation }
  if MessageDlg('Delete task '+TaskTable.Fields[0].AsString+'?',
                mtConfirmation, mbYesNoCancel, 0) = mrYes then
  begin
    Query1.Close; { Close the query  and set up the params}
    Query1.Params[0].AsString := TaskTable.Fields[0].AsString;
    Query1.ExecSQL;  { Execute the deletion query on SubTaskTable }
    TaskTable.Delete;{ Delete the task from TaskTable }
  end;
end;

procedure TTaskManageForm.SubTaskTableBeforePost(DataSet: TDataset);
begin
  { Make sure that the value stored in RatePrHr is stored as the dollar }
  { amount in pennies }
```

continues

Listing 28.2. continued

```
  SubTaskTable.FieldByName('RatePrHr').AsFloat :=
    Round(SubTaskTable.FieldByName('RatePrHr').AsFloat * 100);
end;

procedure TTaskManageForm.SubTaskTableCalcFields(DataSet: TDataset);
begin
  { Since this value is in pennies, show it as dollars }
  CalcRatePerHr.Value :=  SubTaskTableRatePrHr.Value * 0.01;
end;

end.
```

The unit declares the procedure `DoTaskManage()` and the function `GetTaskRecord()`. Both invoke the `TaskManageForm` but use it differently. `DoTaskManage()` is used to perform task management such as adding and deleting tasks and subtasks. `GetTaskRecord()` is used to retrieve information about a task and a specific subtask. The `TTaskRecord` is the record type returned by `GetTaskRecord()`. You will notice that `DoTaskManage()` simply invokes the `TaskManageForm`, whereas `GetTaskRecord()` hides the controls, preventing you from performing task management and just enabling you to select a specific task.

The `FormActive()` method simply initializes the `DBLookupComboBox` with a value from the first record in the table. Take special notice as to how the `DBLookupCombo1` is used in much the same way that a `TDBGrid` is used. A `TDBLookupCombo1`'s intended use is to set a field in its dataset specified by `DataSource1` and `DataField` properties, with values from a lookup dataset specified with its `LookupSource` and `LookupField` properties. The `LookupSource` property is not affected at all by the `DBLookupCombo`—it just populates it with values from a specific column in that dataset.

The `LookupSource` property is used to populate `LookupCombo1`'s data with `TaskTable`'s Task field. `LookupCombo1` then is used to force `TaskTable` to go to the field indicated by `DBLookupCombo`'s value in `DBLookupCombo`'s `OnChange` event handler. The following lines put `TaskTable` in a setkey state:

```
TaskTable.SetKey;
TaskTable.Fields[0].AsString := DBLookupCombo1.Value;
TaskTable.GoToKey;
```

The value from `DBLookupCombo` then is added to `TaskTable`'s keyed field. `GoToKey()` then is called to make `TaskTable1` search for the record containing the value specified in `Field[0]`.

`Button1Click()` appends a new record to `SubTaskTable`. It uses the data received from the `SubTaskDataForm` to populate the record for the `SubTaskTable`. `SubTaskTable`'s unit is SUBDATA.PAS and is shown in Listing 28.3.

Listing 28.3. The source code for SUBDATA.PAS.

```
unit Subdata;

interface

uses
  SysUtils, WinTypes, WinProcs, Messages, Classes, Graphics, Controls,
  Forms, Dialogs, StdCtrls, Buttons, Mask, DBCtrls;

type
  TSubTaskDataForm = class(TForm)
    Label1: TLabel;
    Label2: TLabel;
    BitBtn1: TBitBtn;
    DBEdit1: TDBEdit;
    DBEdit2: TDBEdit;
    BitBtn2: TBitBtn;
    procedure FormActivate(Sender: TObject);
  private
    { Private declarations }
  public
    { Public declarations }
  end;

var
  SubTaskDataForm: TSubTaskDataForm;

implementation
uses TaskMan;

{$R *.DFM}

procedure TSubTaskDataForm.FormActivate(Sender: TObject);
begin
  with TaskManageForm do begin
    DBEdit1.DataSource := DataSource2;
    DBEdit1.DataField := 'SubTask';
    DBEdit2.DataSource := DataSource2;
    DBEdit2.DataField := 'RatePrHr';
  end;
end;

end.
```

SubTaskDataForm's only method is an OnActivate method, which links its data-aware controls to SubTaskTable from TaskManageForm.

Button2Click() appends a new record to the TaskTable. It gets the data for the TaskTable from the AddTaskForm. AddTaskForm's unit is ADDTASK.PAS, and is shown in Listing 28.4.

Listing 28.4. The source code for ADDTASK.PAS.

```
unit Addtask;

interface

uses
  SysUtils, WinTypes, WinProcs, Messages, Classes, Graphics, Controls,
  Forms, Dialogs, StdCtrls, Mask, DBCtrls, DB, DBTables, Buttons;

type
  TAddTaskForm = class(TForm)
    DBEdit1: TDBEdit;
    Label1: TLabel;
    BitBtn1: TBitBtn;
    BitBtn2: TBitBtn;
    procedure FormActivate(Sender: TObject);
  private
    { Private declarations }
  public
    { Public declarations }
  end;

var
  AddTaskForm: TAddTaskForm;

implementation
uses TaskMan;

{$R *.DFM}

procedure TAddTaskForm.FormActivate(Sender: TObject);
begin
  DBEdit1.DataSource := TaskManageForm.DataSource1;
  DBEdit1.DataField := 'Task';
end;

end.
```

AddTaskForm's OnActivate event handler links its data-aware controls to TaskTable from TaskManageForm.

Button3Click() deletes a subtask from the SubTaskTable. Button4Click() deletes a task from TaskTable and all of its corresponding subtasks in SubTaskTable. The event handler uses a TQuery component to delete the subtasks from SubTaskTable, because it simplifies deleting all records on the condition specified in the query statement:

```
delete  from subtasks where task = :task
```

Earlier in this chapter, you learned that all currency values were stored as cents. In the OnBeforePost event handler for SubTaskTable, the value in the RatePrHr field is converted to cents before posting the record.

In SubTaskTableCalcFields(), the calculated field, CalcRatePerHr, is set to normal currency format.

Examining *ClientManForm's* Functionality

The ClientManForm's unit is CLNTMAN.PAS. This unit is shown in Listing 28.5.

Listing 28.5. The source code for CLNTMAN.PAS.

```
unit Clntman;

interface

uses
  SysUtils, WinTypes, WinProcs, Messages, Classes, Graphics, Controls,
  Forms, Dialogs, DB, DBTables, StdCtrls, Buttons, Mask, DBCtrls, Grids,
  DBGrids;

type

  TClientRecord = record
    Name: string[40];
    ClientNo: integer;
  end;

  TClientManForm = class(TForm)
    ClientTable: TTable;
    DataSource1: TDataSource;
    DBEdit1: TDBEdit;
    DBEdit2: TDBEdit;
    DBEdit3: TDBEdit;
    DBEdit4: TDBEdit;
    DBEdit5: TDBEdit;
    Label1: TLabel;
    Label2: TLabel;
    Label3: TLabel;
    Label4: TLabel;
    Label5: TLabel;
    ClientTableClientNo: TFloatField;
    ClientTableName: TStringField;
    ClientTableStreet: TStringField;
    ClientTableCity: TStringField;
    ClientTableState: TStringField;
    ClientTableZip: TStringField;
    BitBtn1: TBitBtn;
    ClientNoTable: TTable;
    DBText1: TDBText;
    DBGrid1: TDBGrid;
    Button1: TButton;
    Button2: TButton;
    Button3: TButton;
    Button4: TButton;
    Button5: TButton;
    procedure FormActivate(Sender: TObject);
    procedure Button1Click(Sender: TObject);
    procedure Button2Click(Sender: TObject);
    procedure Button3Click(Sender: TObject);
    procedure Button4Click(Sender: TObject);
```

continues

Listing 28.5. continued

```
    procedure Button5Click(Sender: TObject);
  private
    { Private declarations }
    NewRecord: boolean;
    procedure EditMode;
    procedure BrowseMode;
  public
    { Public declarations }
  end;

procedure DoClientManagement;
function GetClientRecord: TClientRecord;

implementation

{$R *.DFM}
var
  ClientManForm: TClientManForm;

procedure DoClientManagement;
begin
  Application.CreateForm(TClientManForm, ClientManForm); { Instantiate the form }
  try
    with ClientManForm do begin
      ClientTable.Active := true;             { Open ClientTable }
      ShowModal;                              { Display the form }
    end;
  finally
    ClientManForm.Free;                       { Free the form }
  end;
end;

function GetClientRecord: TClientRecord;
var
 i: integer;
begin
  Result.Name := '';       { Initialize values with empty strings }
  Result.ClientNo := -1;
  Application.CreateForm(TClientManForm, ClientManForm); { Instantiate the form }
  try
    with ClientManForm do begin
      ClientTable.Active := true;             { Open Client Table }
      Button1.Visible := false;               { Hide controls not }
      Button2.Visible := false;               { needed.           }
      Button3.Visible := false;
      Button4.Visible := false;
      Button5.Visible := false;
      if ShowModal = mrOk then begin          { Display the form }
        Result.Name := ClientTable.Fields[1].AsString;    { Set Result to values
➥gotten }
        Result.ClientNo := ClientTable.Fields[0].AsInteger;
      end;
    end;
  finally
    ClientManForm.Free;                       { Free the form }
  end;
end;
```

```pascal
procedure TClientManForm.FormActivate(Sender: TObject);
begin
  BrowseMode;  { Initially go to browse mode }
end;

procedure TClientManForm.Button1Click(Sender: TObject);
begin
  NewRecord := true;          { adding a record, not editing one }
  EditMode;                   { Go into edit mode }
  ClientTable.Append;         { Append a new record }
end;

procedure TClientManForm.Button2Click(Sender: TObject);
begin
  { Confirm delete }
  if MessageDlg('Remove Client '+ClientTable.FieldByName('Name').AsString,
      mtConfirmation, mbYesNoCancel, 0) = mrYes then
    ClientTable.Delete;  { Delete record }
end;

procedure TClientManForm.Button3Click(Sender: TObject);
begin
  NewRecord := false; { Editing a record, not adding one }
  EditMode;              { Go into Edit mode }
  ClientTable.Edit;   { Edit current record }
end;

procedure TClientManForm.Button4Click(Sender: TObject);
begin
  ClientTable.Cancel;  { Cancel Edit or Append operation }
  BrowseMode;             { Go into Browse mode }
end;

procedure TClientManForm.Button5Click(Sender: TObject);
var
  ClientNo: integer;
begin
  if NewRecord then begin                     { if appending a record }
    ClientNoTable.Active := true;
    with ClientNoTable do begin               { Open clientno table }
      ClientNo := Fields[0].AsInteger;        { Open clientno table }
      Edit;                                   { Set to edit mode }
      Fields[0].AsInteger := ClientNo + 1;    { increment client no }
      Post;                                   { Post the new value }
      Active := false;                        { close the table }
    end;
    ClientTable.FieldByName('ClientNo').AsInteger := ClientNo - 1; { Assign
➥unique number }
  end;
  ClientTable.Post;                { Post the new client information }
  BrowseMode;                      { Go into browse mode }
end;

procedure TClientManForm.EditMode;
begin
  { Enable and disable appropriate buttons }
  Button1.Enabled := false;
```

continues

Listing 28.5. continued

```
  Button2.Enabled := false;
  Button3.Enabled := false;
  Button4.Enabled := true;
  Button5.Enabled := true;
  DBGrid1.Enabled := false;
end;

procedure TClientManForm.BrowseMode;
begin
  { Enable and disable appropriate buttons }
  Button1.Enabled := true;
  Button2.Enabled := true;
  Button3.Enabled := true;
  Button4.Enabled := false;
  Button5.Enabled := false;
  DBGrid1.Enabled := true;
end;

end.
```

CLNTMAN.PAS defines the procedure `DoClientManagement()` and the function `GetClientRecord()`. `DoClientManagement()` enables you to add, edit, and delete clients from the `ClientTable`. `GetTaskRecord()` is used to retrieve client information. `TClientRecord` is the record type returned by `GetClientRecord()`. `DoClientManagement()` simply invokes the `ClientManForm`, whereas `GetClientRecord()` hides the controls to prevent you from modifying the `ClientTable`—it just enables you to select a client.

`FormActivate()` puts `ClientManForm` in Browse mode initially. `ClientManForm` can be in two modes: Browse mode and Edit mode. When in Browse mode, you can browse through records in `ClientTable`, but you cannot edit them. When in Edit mode, you are editing a record or adding a new record to `ClientTable`. `ClientManForm` is placed into either one of those modes by calling the `BrowseMode()` or `EditMode()` method.

`Button1Click()` puts `ClientManForm` into Edit mode and puts `ClientTable` into the state to append a new record.

`Button2Click()` is responsible for deleting a client from `ClientTable`, but first it confirms the request.

`Button3Click()` puts `ClientTable` into Edit mode and also places the form into `EditMode`.

`Button4Click()` cancels any append or edit operation and places the form back into `BrowseMode`.

`Button5Click()` is responsible for posting a new or edited record to `ClientTable`. Before it posts the record, it checks to see whether the record is a new record as specified by the `NewRecord` variable. If so, it retrieves a number from the `ClientNoTable`, which maintains the next unique identifier for the `ClientTable`. One way to generate unique identifiers for your tables is to create a smaller table to maintain them.

Examining *ReportForm*'s Functionality

The ReportForm's unit is REPORT.PAS. This unit is shown in Listing 28.6.

Listing 28.6. The source code for REPORT.PAS.

```
unit Report;

interface

uses
  SysUtils, WinTypes, WinProcs, Messages, Classes, Graphics, Controls,
  Forms, Dialogs, DBTables, StdCtrls, DBCtrls, DB, Grids, DBGrids;

type
  TReportForm = class(TForm)
    ReportTable: TTable;
    DataSource1: TDataSource;
    DBGrid1: TDBGrid;
    ReportTableClientNo: TFloatField;
    ReportTableSubTask: TStringField;
    ReportTableStartTime: TDateTimeField;
    ReportTableEndTime: TDateTimeField;
    ReportTableTotalInCents: TFloatField;
    ReportTableAtRate: TFloatField;
    DBText1: TDBText;
    Label1: TLabel;
    Label2: TLabel;
    DBText2: TDBText;
    DBText3: TDBText;
    Label3: TLabel;
    Label4: TLabel;
    DBText4: TDBText;
    ReportTableTotalDue: TCurrencyField;
    ReportTableRateInDollars: TCurrencyField;
    Label5: TLabel;
    ReportTableTimeSpent: TStringField;
    DBText5: TDBText;
    procedure ReportTableCalcFields(DataSet: TDataset);
  private
    { Private declarations }
  public
    { Public declarations }
  end;

procedure DoReport;

var
  ReportForm: TReportForm;

implementation

{$R *.DFM}

procedure DoReport;
```

continues

Listing 28.6. continued

```
begin
  Application.CreateForm(TReportForm, ReportForm); { Instanciate the form }
  try
    with ReportForm do begin
      ReportTable.Active := true;        { Open ReportTable }
      ShowModal;                         { Display the form }
    end;
  finally
    ReportForm.Free;                     { Free the form }
  end;
end;

procedure TReportForm.ReportTableCalcFields(DataSet: TDataset);
const
  TimeDisplay = '%.2d:%.2d:%.2d'; { Time display format string }
var
  DiffTime: TDateTime;
  hrs, mins, secs, ms: word;
begin
  { Convert penny values to display as dollars and cents }
  ReportTableRateInDollars.Value := ReportTable.FieldByName('AtRate')
➥.AsFloat * 0.01;
  ReportTableTotalDue.Value := ReportTable.FieldByName('TotalInCents')
➥.AsFloat * 0.01;
  { Calculate the time difference }
  DiffTime := ReportTable.FieldByName('EndTime').AsFloat -
              ReportTable.FieldByName('StartTime').AsFloat;
  { Decode the time }
  DecodeTime(DiffTime, Hrs, Mins, Secs, Ms);
  { Display time spent using TimeDisplay format string }
  ReportTableTimeSpent.Value := Format(TimeDisplay, [Hrs, Mins, Secs]);
end;

end.
```

The `DoReport()` procedure simply displays the form after activating the `ReportTable`, which actually is linked to TASKTRKR.DB.

`ReportTableCalcFields()` is where the calculated fields are assigned their values. Notice that the fields `AtRate` and `TotalInCents` are converted from cents decimal values so that they appear as dollars to the user. The time difference and time spent also is displayed. Figure 28.10 shows what `ReportForm` looks like when running. Listing 28.7 shows DDGTT.DPR.

Listing 28.7. The source code for DDGTT.DPR.

```
program Ddgtt;

uses
  Forms,
  Mainfrm in 'MAINFRM.PAS' {MainForm},
  Addtask in 'ADDTASK.PAS' {AddTaskForm},
  Taskman in 'TASKMAN.PAS' {TaskManageForm},
```

```
  Clntman in 'CLNTMAN.PAS' {ClientManForm},
  Subdata in 'SUBDATA.PAS' {SubTaskDataForm},
  Report in 'REPORT.PAS' {ReportForm};

{$R *.RES}

begin
  Application.CreateForm(TMainForm, MainForm);
  Application.CreateForm(TSubTaskDataForm, SubTaskDataForm);
  Application.CreateForm(TAddTaskForm, AddTaskForm);
  Application.Run;
end.
```

FIGURE 28.10.

Running the ReportForm.

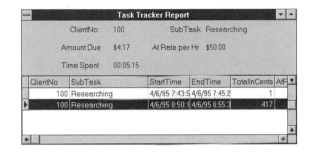

Summary

In this chapter, you exercised your knowledge in building a database application. You learned useful techniques such as working with master-detail tables and calculated fields. You also learned how to safely work with currency or, rather, floating-point values.

At this point, you're ready to go on to the third part of the book where you will see how to build two larger applications: an Inventory Manager and a Personal Information Manager. The first application presents, in greater depth, the use of the TQuery component. You will learn some powerful techniques in using SQL-based databases. The second application illustrates many useful techniques, including how to maximize code reusability.

III

Real-World Applications

29

Inventory Manager—
Preliminary Design Issues

In the next three chapters, you will build an Inventory Manager application from concept to deployment. In this chapter, you'll set the ball rolling by designing a data model and database and creating a specification for the application.

This chapter assumes that you are familiar with general database concepts like columns, rows, tables, and databases. If these words sound a bit foreign to you, you might want to revisit their introduction in Chapters 16, "Writing Database Applications," and 17, "Working with SQL and the *TQuery* Component."

The Concept

The business model you'll use for the Inventory Manager program is an auto parts shop. Such a shop would need an Inventory Manager application to keep track of three primary sets of data:

- Product inventory. This includes the quantities of each item in the inventory and how much an item is worth.
- Sales. You need a system by which to sell the inventory and collect money.
- Customer information and what products those customers buy.

You will need to tie all this data together into one user interface that is designed for the use of the auto parts shop employees.

The Data Model

The next step in the database application development process is to design a data model for the data that you need to manage. This data model first should be developed independent of physical data or tables, and should instead focus on data objects, relationships between objects, and data integrity.

Each one of the three data sets represents a data object. Each data object contains multiple items of data that describe each object's specific attributes.

There is a data object that represents the parts inventory; each item in this inventory is made up of a part number, description, quantity on hand, and various prices.

The customer data object encapsulates all the vital data points of the customer. A customer object consists of a unique customer identification number, customer name, address, phone number, credit line, and some additional free-form comments.

The sales data object is made up of the ID of the customer making the purchase, part number, quantity purchased, purchase price, and unique sales number ID.

You probably already can see how each of these objects relates to one another. One customer object can relate to many sales objects, and those sales can, in turn, relate to multiple parts in the inventory. This means that to maintain integrity, there could never be a sales object containing a part or customer not already found in its respective object set.

> **NOTE**
>
> Keep in mind while designing the database that the logical and physical layout of the data does not necessarily dictate the look and feel of the application that manipulates the data. First, concentrate on designing a good data model and database, and then worry about the user interface.

The Database

After you have a well thought-out data model, you can extend the model into an actual database. Rather than thinking conceptually, as with the model, you now should concern yourself with the specifics of databases, tables, and physical storage.

With this application, you will use Local InterBase Server (LIBS) as the database back end. This gives you the capability to design the database entirely through SQL. It also offers the flexibility of being able to move some of the data processing to the server side of the equation through the use of triggers, generators, and stored procedures—which also helps to ensure better data integrity. Another more tangible benefit of the LIBS back end is that it is easily scaleable to a true client/server environment.

In this section, you'll learn about the step-by-step creation of the database. Because this database encapsulates the overall sales/inventory model of the auto parts business, call this database SALES.GDB.

> **NOTE**
>
> The SQL used in this section should be entered through the WISQL tool that comes as a part of the Local InterBase Server. That is the tool provided to use for the job of creating LIBS databases.

Creating Domains

Before defining any tables, triggers, or any of the other fancy stuff, you should think about defining new domains for use throughout the rest of your SQL. Think of a *domain* as an entity similar to a user-defined type in Object Pascal. Domains enable you to define special data types with more structure than the built-in data types.

Domains help simplify data and constraint declarations by enabling you to create shorthand names for types that are common throughout your database. Note that you cannot alter a domain once table columns have used them.

You will use the following domains in the SALES database:

■   `CREATE DOMAIN DCUSTOMERID AS INTEGER;`

This is a straightforward domain. It defines a new domain called DCUSTOMERID as a type identical to that of your standard, run-of-the-mill integer.

■   `CREATE DOMAIN DCREDITLINE AS SMALLINT`
      `default 0 CHECK (VALUE BETWEEN 0 AND 3000);`

This defines a new smallint-type domain, but it applies the additional constraint that the value must lie between 0 and 3000.

■   `CREATE DOMAIN DNAME AS CHAR(20);`

This defines a domain called DNAME that is a fixed-length string of exactly 20 characters.

■   `CREATE DOMAIN DADDRESS AS VARCHAR(50);`
`CREATE DOMAIN DCITY AS VARCHAR(20);`
`CREATE DOMAIN DSTATE AS VARCHAR(20);`
`CREATE DOMAIN DZIP AS VARCHAR(10);`
`CREATE DOMAIN DPHONE AS VARCHAR(20);`

This defines several domains as variable-length strings of up to 50, 20, 20, 10, and 20 characters, respectively.

NOTE

The CHAR(*n*) data type always stores *n* characters to the database. If the string contained in a particular field is less than *n* characters, then unused characters will be padded with spaces.

The VARCHAR(*n*) data type stores the exact size of the string, up to a maximum of *n*. Its advantage over CHAR is that it is more space-efficient, but operations on VARCHARs tend to be slightly slower.

■   `CREATE DOMAIN DPRICE AS NUMERIC(15, 2)`
      `default 0.00;`

This creates a domain representing a decimal number. The first number, 15, specifies the digits of precision to store. The second number, 2, specifies the number of decimal places to store. The default value for columns of this domain is 0.00.

Creating Tables

Using these domains, you now can create new tables that mimic the relationship of the conceptual data objects you developed earlier. Each table is created using the CREATE TABLE SQL statement, followed by the enumeration of table fields and data types or domains.

The CUSTOMER Table

The CUSTOMER table represents the customer data object, and it is defined as the following:

```
CREATE TABLE CUSTOMER (CUSTOMER_ID INTEGER NOT NULL,
        FNAME DNAME NOT NULL,
        LNAME DNAME NOT NULL,
        CREDIT_LINE DCREDITLINE NOT NULL,
        WORK_ADDRESS DADDRESS,
        ALT_ADDRESS DADDRESS,
        CITY DCITY,
        STATE DSTATE,
        ZIP DZIP,
        WORK_PHONE DPHONE,
        ALT_PHONE DPHONE,
        COMMENTS BLOB SUB_TYPE TEXT SEGMENT SIZE 80,
        COMPANY VARCHAR(40),
CONSTRAINT PCUSTOMER_ID PRIMARY KEY (CUSTOMER_ID));
```

The fields that are defined with the NOT NULL specifier mean that the user must enter a value for those fields before a record can be posted to the table. In other words, those fields cannot be left blank.

The COMMENTS field requires a bit of explanation. This field is of type BLOB (Binary Large Object), which means that any type of free-form data can be stored there. The SUB TYPE of TEXT, however, means that the data contained within the BLOB is ASCII text, and therefore compatible with the Delphi TDBMemo component.

The CONSTRAINT statement creates a primary key on the CUSTOMER_ID field, which ensures that each record's value for this field will be unique. This also is the first step to ensuring referential integrity throughout the database; the PRIMARY KEY field acts as a lookup field for the FOREIGN KEY field defined in another table.

The PART Table

The PART table is the abstraction of the shop inventory. This table's definition is fairly straightforward and it is defined as the following:

```
CREATE TABLE PART (PART_NUMBER VARCHAR(10) NOT NULL,
        DESCRIPTION VARCHAR(18),
        QUANTITY SMALLINT NOT NULL,
        LIST_PRICE DPRICE NOT NULL,
        RETAIL_PRICE DPRICE NOT NULL,
        DEALER_PRICE DPRICE NOT NULL,
        JOBBER_PRICE DPRICE NOT NULL,
CONSTRAINT PPART_NUMBER PRIMARY KEY (PART_NUMBER));
```

Each record represents the inventory of one unique part, holding description, quantity, and pricing information. Notice that this table also has a primary key—this time, on the PART_NUMBER field.

The SALE Table

The SALE table is the table that contains records for every sale to a customer of some inventory item. This table is defined as the following:

```
CREATE TABLE SALE (SALE_NUMBER INTEGER NOT NULL,
        CUSTOMER_ID INTEGER NOT NULL,
        PART_NUMBER VARCHAR(10) NOT NULL,
        QUANTITY_SOLD SMALLINT NOT NULL,
        SALE_DATE DATE NOT NULL,
        PRICE DPRICE NOT NULL);
ALTER TABLE SALE ADD FOREIGN KEY (CUSTOMER_ID) REFERENCES CUSTOMER(CUSTOMER_ID);
ALTER TABLE SALE ADD FOREIGN KEY (PART_NUMBER) REFERENCES PART(PART_NUMBER);
```

Take note of the two FOREIGN KEYs defined at the end of the table. A *foreign key* is a column or set of columns in one table that correspond in exact order to a column or set of columns defined as the primary key in another table. The foreign keys complete the referential integrity with the CUSTOMER and PART tables. They ensure that no entries for the CUSTOMER_ID or PART_NUMBER will be posted to this table unless they first exist in the CUSTOMER and PART tables.

Using Generators

Think of a generator as a mechanism that automatically generates sequential numbers to be inserted into a table. Generators often are used to create unique numbers to be inserted into a table's keyed field. The SALES database will use generators to automatically generate new customer IDs for the CUSTOMER table. This generator is defined as the following:

```
CREATE GENERATOR GEN_CUSTID;
```

> **NOTE**
>
> After you add a generator to a database, it cannot be easily removed. The simplest technique is to remove or modify the trigger or stored procedure so that GEN ID() is not called. You also can remove your generator from the RDB$GENERATORS systems table.

Using Triggers

A *trigger* is a routine that is automatically to perform some action whenever a record in a table is inserted, updated, or deleted. Triggers enable you to let the database perform repetitive tasks as records are committed to tables, thereby freeing the application(s) used to access and modify the data from doing so.

For starters, you need triggers that add new customer and sales numbers to their respective tables using the generators created earlier. The trigger to insert a new unique customer ID would appear as the following:

```
CREATE TRIGGER TCUSTOMER_ID FOR CUSTOMER
ACTIVE BEFORE INSERT POSITION 0
as begin
  new.customer_id = gen_id(gen_custid, 1);
end
```

The following trigger also works on the SALE table. Every time a new record is inserted, this trigger updates the SALE_DATE field with the current date and time, and it computes the PRICE by multiplying the PRICE by QUANTITY_SOLD:

```
CREATE TRIGGER TSALES_NO FOR SALE
ACTIVE BEFORE INSERT POSITION 0
as begin
  new.SALE_DATE = "now";
  new.PRICE = new.PRICE * new.QUANTITY_SOLD;
end
```

This trigger works very much the same as the preceding trigger, except this trigger fires on update, rather than insert:

```
CREATE TRIGGER TSALES_UPDATE FOR SALE
ACTIVE BEFORE UPDATE POSITION 0
as begin
  new.PRICE = new.PRICE * new.QUANTITY_SOLD;
end
```

NOTE

The are a couple of additional triggers in this database that convert a two-letter state abbreviation to a full state name. You can find these triggers in SALES.DDL, shown in Listing 29.2.

Using Stored Procedures

A *stored procedure* is a stand-alone routine that is located on the server as part of a database's metadata. *Metadata* is all of the objects (tables, indexes, and so on) contained as part of a database definition. You can invoke a stored procedure and have it return a dataset just like a normal query. The advantages of stored procedures are that they cut down, again, on the amount of processing required at the client end, they reduce the network traffic, and they centralize some particular functionality. Stored procedures also can improve performance, because all of the work is done on the server instead of across a network.

The SALES database employs one stored procedure that generates a report of sales between two particular dates. The code for this stored procedure is shown in Listing 29.1.

NOTE

If you are using the ISQL tool to enter database metadata, you need to change the terminating character. Because all statements within a procedure must be terminated by a semicolon (;)—which is also the SQL terminating character—you must set the SQL terminating character to some other symbol to avoid conflicts. Do this by using the SET TERM command.

In SALES, you will use the caret symbol as the terminating character. This line of SQL code will invoke the change:

```
SET TERM ^ ;
```

Listing 29.1. The SALES_REPORT stored procedure.

```
CREATE PROCEDURE SALES_REPORT AS BEGIN EXIT; END ^
ALTER PROCEDURE SALES_REPORT (START_DATE DATE,
END_DATE DATE)
RETURNS (PART CHAR(10),
QUANTITY INTEGER)
AS

 BEGIN
  FOR SELECT PART_NUMBER, QUANTITY_SOLD
  FROM SALE
  WHERE ((SALE_DATE >= :START_DATE) AND
                 (SALE_DATE <= :END_DATE))
  INTO :PART, QUANTITY
 DO
  SUSPEND;
END
  ^
```

The SALES_REPORT stored procedure accepts the start and end date as parameters, and then performs a SQL query based on those parameters to retrieve part numbers and quantities sold within the given dates.

Granting Permissions

The final step in defining a database is granting permission to the tables to particular users. For simplicity, you can grant all users SELECT and UPDATE rights on the CUSTOMER table with the following statement:

```
GRANT SELECT, UPDATE ON CUSTOMER TO PUBLIC WITH GRANT OPTION;
```

Or, you can grant all rights to the SALE table with the following statement:

```
GRANT ALL ON SALE TO PUBLIC WITH GRANT OPTION;
```

The GRANT OPTION clause means that those who are granted access to tables also are allowed to grant others access to the data.

Using the Data-Definition File

Listing 29.2 shows the entire data-definition file, SALES.DDF, which describes the sales database.

Listing 29.2. The source code for SALES.DDF.

```
CONNECT "sales.gdb";

/* Domain definitions */
/* Domains act as templates for defining columns in   */
/* subsequent CREATE TABLE or ALTER TABLE statements.  */
/* See page 67 of the Borland InterBase Data          */
/* Definition Guide, and page 38 of the Borland       */
/* InterBase Language Reference.                       */
CREATE DOMAIN DCUSTOMERID AS INTEGER;
CREATE DOMAIN DCREDITLINE AS SMALLINT
  default 0 CHECK (VALUE BETWEEN 0 AND 3000);
/* The preceding line defaults the column to 0 if no */
/* data is put into the field;  It also checks the    */
/* data value to be between 0 and 3000.                        */
CREATE DOMAIN DNAME AS CHAR(20);
CREATE DOMAIN DADDRESS AS VARCHAR(50);
/* NOTE: VARCHAR is a variable character field.  it    */
/* does not pad the entire field length with spaces.  */
/* Bottom Line: A VARCHAR field takes up less space   */
/* but is slightly slower to do operations upon.      */
CREATE DOMAIN DCITY AS VARCHAR(20);
CREATE DOMAIN DSTATE AS VARCHAR(20);
CREATE DOMAIN DZIP AS VARCHAR(10);
```

continues

Listing 29.2. continued

```
CREATE DOMAIN DPHONE AS VARCHAR(20);
CREATE DOMAIN DPRICE AS NUMERIC(15, 2)
  default 0.00;

/* Create the Customer table.  NOTE: Many fields are   */
/* using domain declarations rather than datatypes.    */
/* Table: CUSTOMER */
CREATE TABLE CUSTOMER (CUSTOMER_ID INTEGER NOT NULL,
        FNAME DNAME NOT NULL,
        LNAME DNAME NOT NULL,
        CREDIT_LINE DCREDITLINE NOT NULL,
        WORK_ADDRESS DADDRESS,
        ALT_ADDRESS DADDRESS,
        CITY DCITY,
        STATE DSTATE,
        ZIP DZIP,
        WORK_PHONE DPHONE,
        ALT_PHONE DPHONE,
        COMMENTS BLOB SUB_TYPE TEXT SEGMENT SIZE 80,
/* A Binary Large OBject(BLOB) holds large amounts of */
/* information.  A SUB_TYPE of TEXT creates a BLOB    */
/* that is compatible with Delphi's TDBMemo Object.   */
        COMPANY VARCHAR(40),
CONSTRAINT PCUSTOMER_ID PRIMARY KEY (CUSTOMER_ID));
/* A field which is a primary key is one part in the  */
/* enforcement of referential integrity.  The primary */
/* key field is basically a lookup field for the      */
/* foreign key field which is in another table.  See  */
/* pages 20-22 and 86-90 in the Borland InterBase     */
/* Data Definition Guide.                             */

/* Table: PART */
CREATE TABLE PART (PART_NUMBER VARCHAR(10) NOT NULL,
        DESCRIPTION VARCHAR(18),
        QUANTITY SMALLINT NOT NULL,
        LIST_PRICE DPRICE NOT NULL,
        RETAIL_PRICE DPRICE NOT NULL,
        DEALER_PRICE DPRICE NOT NULL,
        JOBBER_PRICE DPRICE NOT NULL,
CONSTRAINT PPART_NUMBER PRIMARY KEY (PART_NUMBER));

/* Table: SALE */
CREATE TABLE SALE (SALE_NUMBER INTEGER NOT NULL,
        CUSTOMER_ID INTEGER NOT NULL,
        PART_NUMBER VARCHAR(10) NOT NULL,
        QUANTITY_SOLD SMALLINT NOT NULL,
        SALE_DATE DATE NOT NULL,
        PRICE DPRICE NOT NULL);
ALTER TABLE SALE ADD FOREIGN KEY (CUSTOMER_ID) REFERENCES CUSTOMER(CUSTOMER_ID);
ALTER TABLE SALE ADD FOREIGN KEY (PART_NUMBER) REFERENCES PART(PART_NUMBER);
/* A field which is a foreign key is the second part  */
/* in the enforcement of referential integrity.  A    */
/* foreign key is a column or a set of columns in one */
/* table that correspond in exact order to a column   */
/* or a set of columns defined as a primary key in    */
/* another table.                                     */
```

```
/* A generator is used to create a unique, sequential */
/* number that is automatically inserted into a column*/
/* by the database.  It is most commonly used as a    */
/* unique field identifier in a primary key.  See     */
/* pages 175-177 in the Borland InterBase Data        */
/* Definition Guide.                                  */
CREATE GENERATOR GEN_CUSTID;
CREATE GENERATOR SALES_NO;

COMMIT WORK;
SET AUTODDL OFF;
SET TERM ^ ;
/* This sets the SQL terminating character to a '^'   */
/* not the usual ';'.  This is done because each      */
/* statement in a procedure body MUST be terminated by */
/* a semicolon.                                       */

/* Stored procedures */
/* This stored procedure takes in two dates and       */
/* returns the parts and quantities that match the    */
/* SELECT statement.  See pages 117-152 in the Borland */
/* InterBase Data Definition Guide.                   */
CREATE PROCEDURE SALES_REPORT AS BEGIN EXIT; END ^
ALTER PROCEDURE SALES_REPORT (START_DATE DATE,
END_DATE DATE)
RETURNS (PART CHAR(10),
QUANTITY INTEGER)
AS

 BEGIN
  FOR SELECT PART_NUMBER, QUANTITY_SOLD
  FROM SALE
  WHERE ((SALE_DATE >= :START_DATE) AND
                 (SALE_DATE <= :END_DATE))
  INTO :PART, QUANTITY
 DO
  SUSPEND;
END
 ^
SET TERM ; ^
COMMIT WORK ;
SET AUTODDL ON;
SET TERM ^ ;

/* A trigger is a self-contained routine associated   */
/* with a table that automatically performs an action */
/* when a row in the table is inserted, updated or    */
/* deleted.  See pages 153-169 in the Borland         */
/* InterBase Data Definition Guide.                   */

/* This trigger changes the corresponding state       */
/* abbreviation code into the full state name.  This  */
/* trigger is "fired" when an update has occurred.    */
CREATE TRIGGER CHECK_STATE_UPDATE FOR CUSTOMER
ACTIVE BEFORE UPDATE POSITION 0
AS BEGIN
```

continues

Listing 29.2. continued

```
IF (UPPER(NEW.STATE) = "WA") THEN BEGIN
  NEW.STATE = "Washington"; END
IF (UPPER(NEW.STATE) = "OR") THEN BEGIN
  NEW.STATE = "Oregon"; END
IF (UPPER(NEW.STATE) = "CA") THEN BEGIN
  NEW.STATE = "California"; END
IF (UPPER(NEW.STATE) = "ID") THEN BEGIN
  NEW.STATE = "Idaho"; END
IF (UPPER(NEW.STATE) = "NV") THEN BEGIN
  NEW.STATE = "Nevada"; END
IF (UPPER(NEW.STATE) = "AZ") THEN BEGIN
  NEW.STATE = "Arizona"; END
IF (UPPER(NEW.STATE) = "UT") THEN BEGIN
  NEW.STATE = "Utah"; END
IF (UPPER(NEW.STATE) = "WY") THEN BEGIN
  NEW.STATE = "Wyoming"; END
IF (UPPER(NEW.STATE) = "MT") THEN BEGIN
  NEW.STATE = "Montana"; END
IF (UPPER(NEW.STATE) = "ND") THEN BEGIN
  NEW.STATE = "North Dakota"; END
IF (UPPER(NEW.STATE) = "SD") THEN BEGIN
  NEW.STATE = "South Dakota"; END
IF (UPPER(NEW.STATE) = "CO") THEN BEGIN
  NEW.STATE = "Colorado"; END
IF (UPPER(NEW.STATE) = "NM") THEN BEGIN
  NEW.STATE = "New Mexico"; END
IF (UPPER(NEW.STATE) = "NE") THEN BEGIN
  NEW.STATE = "Nebraska"; END
IF (UPPER(NEW.STATE) = "KS") THEN BEGIN
  NEW.STATE = "Kansas"; END
IF (UPPER(NEW.STATE) = "OK") THEN BEGIN
  NEW.STATE = "Oklahoma"; END
IF (UPPER(NEW.STATE) = "TX") THEN BEGIN
  NEW.STATE = "Texas"; END
IF (UPPER(NEW.STATE) = "LA") THEN BEGIN
  NEW.STATE = "Louisiana"; END
IF (UPPER(NEW.STATE) = "AR") THEN BEGIN
  NEW.STATE = "Arkansas"; END
IF (UPPER(NEW.STATE) = "MO") THEN BEGIN
  NEW.STATE = "Missouri"; END
IF (UPPER(NEW.STATE) = "IO") THEN BEGIN
  NEW.STATE = "Iowa"; END
IF (UPPER(NEW.STATE) = "MN") THEN BEGIN
  NEW.STATE = "Minnesota"; END
IF (UPPER(NEW.STATE) = "IL") THEN BEGIN
  NEW.STATE = "Illinois"; END
IF (UPPER(NEW.STATE) = "WI") THEN BEGIN
  NEW.STATE = "Wisconsin"; END
IF (UPPER(NEW.STATE) = "MI") THEN BEGIN
  NEW.STATE = "Michigan"; END
IF (UPPER(NEW.STATE) = "IN") THEN BEGIN
  NEW.STATE = "Indiana"; END
IF (UPPER(NEW.STATE) = "KY") THEN BEGIN
  NEW.STATE = "Kentucky"; END
IF (UPPER(NEW.STATE) = "TN") THEN BEGIN
  NEW.STATE = "Tennessee"; END
```

```
  IF (UPPER(NEW.STATE) = "MS") THEN BEGIN
    NEW.STATE = "Mississippi"; END
  IF (UPPER(NEW.STATE) = "AL") THEN BEGIN
    NEW.STATE = "Alabama"; END
  IF (UPPER(NEW.STATE) = "GA") THEN BEGIN
    NEW.STATE = "Georgia"; END
  IF (UPPER(NEW.STATE) = "FL") THEN BEGIN
    NEW.STATE = "Florida"; END
  IF (UPPER(NEW.STATE) = "SC") THEN BEGIN
    NEW.STATE = "South Carolina"; END
  IF (UPPER(NEW.STATE) = "NC") THEN BEGIN
    NEW.STATE = "North Carolina"; END
  IF (UPPER(NEW.STATE) = "VA") THEN BEGIN
    NEW.STATE = "Virginia"; END
  IF (UPPER(NEW.STATE) = "WV") THEN BEGIN
    NEW.STATE = "West Virginia"; END
  IF (UPPER(NEW.STATE) = "OH") THEN BEGIN
    NEW.STATE = "Ohio"; END
  IF (UPPER(NEW.STATE) = "NY") THEN BEGIN
    NEW.STATE = "New York"; END
  IF (UPPER(NEW.STATE) = "DE") THEN BEGIN
    NEW.STATE = "Delaware"; END
  IF (UPPER(NEW.STATE) = "MD") THEN BEGIN
    NEW.STATE = "Maryland"; END
  IF (UPPER(NEW.STATE) = "PA") THEN BEGIN
    NEW.STATE = "Pennsylvania"; END
  IF (UPPER(NEW.STATE) = "NJ") THEN BEGIN
    NEW.STATE = "New Jersey"; END
  IF (UPPER(NEW.STATE) = "CT") THEN BEGIN
    NEW.STATE = "Connecticut"; END
  IF (UPPER(NEW.STATE) = "RI") THEN BEGIN
    NEW.STATE = "Rhode Island"; END
  IF (UPPER(NEW.STATE) = "MA") THEN BEGIN
    NEW.STATE = "Massachusetts"; END
  IF (UPPER(NEW.STATE) = "VT") THEN BEGIN
    NEW.STATE = "Vermont"; END
  IF (UPPER(NEW.STATE) = "NH") THEN BEGIN
    NEW.STATE = "New Hampshire"; END
  IF (UPPER(NEW.STATE) = "ME") THEN BEGIN
    NEW.STATE = "Maine"; END
  IF (UPPER(NEW.STATE) = "HI") THEN BEGIN
    NEW.STATE = "Hawaii"; END
  IF (UPPER(NEW.STATE) = "AK") THEN BEGIN
    NEW.STATE = "Alaska"; END
END
  ^


/* This trigger changes the corresponding state      */
/* abbreviation code into the full state name.  This  */
/* trigger is "fired" when an insert has occurred.     */
CREATE TRIGGER CHECK_STATE FOR CUSTOMER
ACTIVE BEFORE INSERT POSITION 1
AS BEGIN
  IF (UPPER(NEW.STATE) = "WA") THEN BEGIN
    NEW.STATE = "Washington"; END
  IF (UPPER(NEW.STATE) = "OR") THEN BEGIN
    NEW.STATE = "Oregon"; END
```

continues

Listing 29.2. continued

```
IF (UPPER(NEW.STATE) = "CA") THEN BEGIN
  NEW.STATE = "California"; END
IF (UPPER(NEW.STATE) = "ID") THEN BEGIN
  NEW.STATE = "Idaho"; END
IF (UPPER(NEW.STATE) = "NV") THEN BEGIN
  NEW.STATE = "Nevada"; END
IF (UPPER(NEW.STATE) = "AZ") THEN BEGIN
  NEW.STATE = "Arizona"; END
IF (UPPER(NEW.STATE) = "UT") THEN BEGIN
  NEW.STATE = "Utah"; END
IF (UPPER(NEW.STATE) = "WY") THEN BEGIN
  NEW.STATE = "Wyoming"; END
IF (UPPER(NEW.STATE) = "MT") THEN BEGIN
  NEW.STATE = "Montana"; END
IF (UPPER(NEW.STATE) = "ND") THEN BEGIN
  NEW.STATE = "North Dakota"; END
IF (UPPER(NEW.STATE) = "SD") THEN BEGIN
  NEW.STATE = "South Dakota"; END
IF (UPPER(NEW.STATE) = "CO") THEN BEGIN
  NEW.STATE = "Colorado"; END
IF (UPPER(NEW.STATE) = "NM") THEN BEGIN
  NEW.STATE = "New Mexico"; END
IF (UPPER(NEW.STATE) = "NE") THEN BEGIN
  NEW.STATE = "Nebraska"; END
IF (UPPER(NEW.STATE) = "KS") THEN BEGIN
  NEW.STATE = "Kansas"; END
IF (UPPER(NEW.STATE) = "OK") THEN BEGIN
  NEW.STATE = "Oklahoma"; END
IF (UPPER(NEW.STATE) = "TX") THEN BEGIN
  NEW.STATE = "Texas"; END
IF (UPPER(NEW.STATE) = "LA") THEN BEGIN
  NEW.STATE = "Louisiana"; END
IF (UPPER(NEW.STATE) = "AR") THEN BEGIN
  NEW.STATE = "Arkansas"; END
IF (UPPER(NEW.STATE) = "MO") THEN BEGIN
  NEW.STATE = "Missouri"; END
IF (UPPER(NEW.STATE) = "IO") THEN BEGIN
  NEW.STATE = "Iowa"; END
IF (UPPER(NEW.STATE) = "MN") THEN BEGIN
  NEW.STATE = "Minnesota"; END
IF (UPPER(NEW.STATE) = "IL") THEN BEGIN
  NEW.STATE = "Illinois"; END
IF (UPPER(NEW.STATE) = "WI") THEN BEGIN
  NEW.STATE = "Wisconsin"; END
IF (UPPER(NEW.STATE) = "MI") THEN BEGIN
  NEW.STATE = "Michigan"; END
IF (UPPER(NEW.STATE) = "IN") THEN BEGIN
  NEW.STATE = "Indiana"; END
IF (UPPER(NEW.STATE) = "KY") THEN BEGIN
  NEW.STATE = "Kentucky"; END
IF (UPPER(NEW.STATE) = "TN") THEN BEGIN
  NEW.STATE = "Tennessee"; END
IF (UPPER(NEW.STATE) = "MS") THEN BEGIN
  NEW.STATE = "Mississippi"; END
IF (UPPER(NEW.STATE) = "AL") THEN BEGIN
  NEW.STATE = "Alabama"; END
```

```
    IF (UPPER(NEW.STATE) = "GA") THEN BEGIN
      NEW.STATE = "Georgia"; END
    IF (UPPER(NEW.STATE) = "FL") THEN BEGIN
      NEW.STATE = "Florida"; END
    IF (UPPER(NEW.STATE) = "SC") THEN BEGIN
      NEW.STATE = "South Carolina"; END
    IF (UPPER(NEW.STATE) = "NC") THEN BEGIN
      NEW.STATE = "North Carolina"; END
    IF (UPPER(NEW.STATE) = "VA") THEN BEGIN
      NEW.STATE = "Virginia"; END
    IF (UPPER(NEW.STATE) = "WV") THEN BEGIN
      NEW.STATE = "West Virginia"; END
    IF (UPPER(NEW.STATE) = "OH") THEN BEGIN
      NEW.STATE = "Ohio"; END
    IF (UPPER(NEW.STATE) = "NY") THEN BEGIN
      NEW.STATE = "New York"; END
    IF (UPPER(NEW.STATE) = "DE") THEN BEGIN
      NEW.STATE = "Delaware"; END
    IF (UPPER(NEW.STATE) = "MD") THEN BEGIN
      NEW.STATE = "Maryland"; END
    IF (UPPER(NEW.STATE) = "PA") THEN BEGIN
      NEW.STATE = "Pennsylvania"; END
    IF (UPPER(NEW.STATE) = "NJ") THEN BEGIN
      NEW.STATE = "New Jersey"; END
    IF (UPPER(NEW.STATE) = "CT") THEN BEGIN
      NEW.STATE = "Connecticut"; END
    IF (UPPER(NEW.STATE) = "RI") THEN BEGIN
      NEW.STATE = "Rhode Island"; END
    IF (UPPER(NEW.STATE) = "MA") THEN BEGIN
      NEW.STATE = "Massachusetts"; END
    IF (UPPER(NEW.STATE) = "VT") THEN BEGIN
      NEW.STATE = "Vermont"; END
    IF (UPPER(NEW.STATE) = "NH") THEN BEGIN
      NEW.STATE = "New Hampshire"; END
    IF (UPPER(NEW.STATE) = "ME") THEN BEGIN
      NEW.STATE = "Maine"; END
    IF (UPPER(NEW.STATE) = "HI") THEN BEGIN
      NEW.STATE = "Hawaii"; END
    IF (UPPER(NEW.STATE) = "AK") THEN BEGIN
      NEW.STATE = "Alaska"; END
END
^

/* This trigger generates a new customer number and  */
/* places the value into the CUSTOMER_ID field of    */
/* new record.                                       */
CREATE TRIGGER TCUSTOMER_ID FOR CUSTOMER
ACTIVE BEFORE INSERT POSITION 0
as begin
  new.customer_id = gen_id(gen_custid, 1);
end
^
/* This trigger inserts the current time into the    */
/* SALE_DATE field along with computing the total    */
/* price of the part sold.                           */
CREATE TRIGGER TSALES_NO FOR SALE
ACTIVE BEFORE INSERT POSITION 0
```

continues

Listing 29.2. continued

```
as begin
  new.SALE_DATE = "now";
  new.PRICE = new.PRICE * new.QUANTITY_SOLD;
end
  ^

/* This trigger computes the total price of the part  */
/* sold when an update hes occurred to the record.    */
CREATE TRIGGER TSALES_UPDATE FOR SALE
ACTIVE BEFORE UPDATE POSITION 0
as begin
  new.PRICE = new.PRICE * new.QUANTITY_SOLD;
end
  ^

COMMIT WORK ^
SET TERM ; ^

/* Grant permissions for this database */
/* This grants SELECT and UPDATE rights to anyone    */
/* with a valid user account.  See pages 179-191 of  */
/* the Borland InterBase Data Definition Guide.      */
GRANT SELECT, UPDATE ON CUSTOMER TO PUBLIC WITH GRANT OPTION;
GRANT ALL ON SALE TO PUBLIC WITH GRANT OPTION;
GRANT SELECT ON CUSTOMER TO PUBLIC WITH GRANT OPTION;
```

Application Specification

The application for this database should be a customer-focused interface that incorporates the following design goals:

- Capability to view, add, edit, and remove customers
- Capability to view, add, edit, and remove auto parts
- Interface for selling parts to a particular customer, and collecting the right amount of money
- Option to print sales receipt
- Provision by which to execute the sales report stored procedure

Summary

That concludes the definition for the database you'll use with the Inventory Manager program. This chapter gave you a flavor for working in SQL with the WISQL tool, as well as some theoretical background on client/server databases. Now that the database has been created, you can move on to creating the application. In the next chapter, you once again break out Delphi to build the user-interface application to the SALES database.

30

Inventory Manager—User Interface Development

In this chapter, you will develop the user interface for the Inventory Manager application. The last chapter got you rolling with creating the database and application specification, so now it's time to get down to brass tacks and write some Delphi code.

This chapter shows you how to take advantage of some of the client/server features you build into the SALES database. Also, you will get a feel for working inside a larger application than you might be used to.

> **NOTE**
>
> The complete source code for the Inventory Manager application is included on the CD-ROM provided with this book.

The User Interface

Begin the application by creating the user interface (UI) prototype. The UI will consist of a main form that can support many different data views—for example, different views for browsing customer, sales, or parts information. To transparently accommodate multiple views on one form, use a TNotebook component aligned to alClient, and place the various views on the different pages of the Notebook. Also use three panels aligned to the bottom of the form to display status information.

The Customer Information Page

The Customer Information page of the Notebook will be used to browse, edit, and insert data into the CUSTOMER table. This page should contain several TDBEdit components and a TDBMemo component that will hook to the fields of the CUSTOMER table. This page also contains a TDBNavigator, and Save and Cancel buttons to be used while inserting. This page is shown in Figure 30.1.

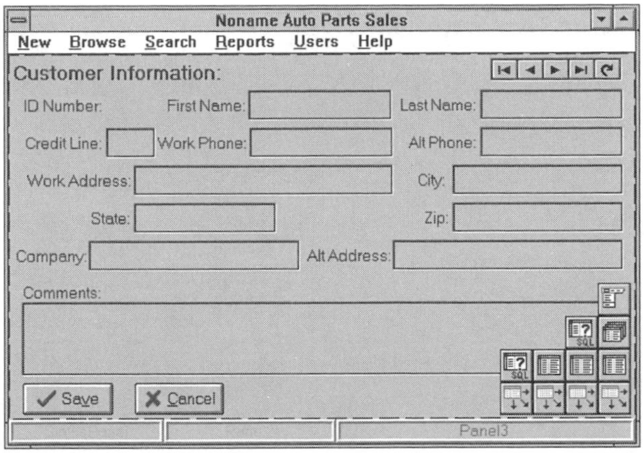

FIGURE 30.1.

The Customer Information page of the main form.

The Parts Information Page

The Parts Information page will be used to browse, edit, and insert data into the PARTS table. This page contains several TDBEdit components that hook to the different fields of the PARTS table and one TDBNavigator to navigate through the fields. This page also contains Save and Cancel buttons. The Parts Information page is shown in Figure 30.2.

FIGURE 30.2.

The Parts Information page of the main form.

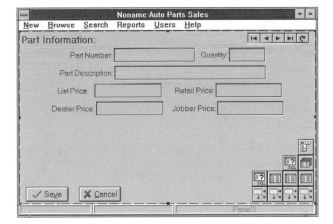

The Sales Information Page

The Sales Information page will be used similarly for the SALES table. Because the SALES table relates to both CUSTOMER and PARTS, this page is a bit more complex than the other (see Figure 30.3).

FIGURE 30.3.

The Sales Information page of the main form.

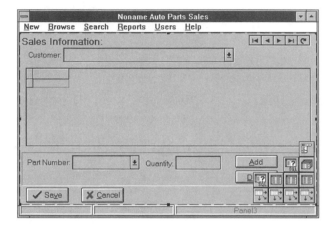

The DBLookupCombo labeled Customer contains the customer's first and last name from the CUSTOMER table so that the user can choose a customer from the table to make a sales transaction. This page also contains a TDBGrid component that lists the different sales by parts for the current transaction. The Parts Number list, Quantity edit control, and Add and Delete buttons are used to manage the parts and quantities involved in the current sale.

Linking to Data

Now that the basic user interface is in place, you can hook up the database functionality by adding the different data-access components, as shown in Table 30.1.

Table 30.1. Data-access components for the Inventory Manager.

Type	*Name*	*Purpose*
TTable	CustomerTable	Links to CUSTOMER table.
	SaleTable	Links to SALES table.
	PartTable	Links to PARTS table.
TQuery	CustQuery	Queries on CUSTOMER data.
	RptQuery	Queries used for reporting stored procedures.
TDatabase	AutoPartsDatabase	Creates a persistent link to SALES database.

Type	*Name*	*Purpose*
TDataSource	DataSource1 – DataSource4	Links TTables and RptQuery to data-aware controls.

The AutoPartsDatabase's AliasName property is Sales. This is the alias you established for SALES.GDB. The DatabaseName of AutoPartsDatabase is SalesDB. Each of the TTables and TQueries have their DatabaseName property also set to SalesDB. This means that all the connections are going through AutoPartsDatabase, rather than directly to an alias.

Connecting

Each of the data-aware controls is initially in an unconnected state. The reason for this is so that, for security, the user must log into the database every time the program is run. To log the user into the database, a method called LoginUser() is called from the main form's OnCreate handler. This method opens the database and all the associated tables, and then initializes the user-interface, as follows:

```
procedure TMainForm.LoginUser;
begin
  try
    AutoPartsDatabase.Open;
    CustomerTable.Open;
    PartTable.Open;
    SaleTable.Open;
    Notebook1.ActivePage := 'Customer';
    Panel2.Caption := IntToStr(CustomerTable.RecordCount) + ' Records';
    EnableMenuItems(True);
  except
    { If user not able to login, display the reason and show logged out page }
    on E:EDBEngineError do begin
      MessageDlg(E.Message, mtError, [mbOK], 0);
      Notebook1.ActivePage := 'Logged Out';
      EnableMenuItems(False);
      StatusPanel.Caption := '';
      Panel2.Caption := '';
      Panel3.Caption := '';
    end;
  end;
end;
```

To allow a custom login form, a handler is created for AutoPartsDatabase's OnLogin event. This event is called every time the database is opened. This event is shown in the following code. It invokes PasswordDlg, the custom password-entry form shown in Figure 30.4, and then assigns the user name and password from that form to the LoginParams parameter. The Supervisor flag is activated if the user name is SYSDBA.

```
procedure TMainForm.AutoPartsDatabaseLogin(Database: TDatabase;
  LoginParams: TStrings);
{ Receives a user name and password to log into the Sales database.  If user }
{  name or password are incorrect, display the logged out user screen. }
begin
  if PasswordDlg.GetPassword then begin
    { Set login params from PasswordDlg }
    LoginParams.Values['USER NAME'] := PasswordDlg.UName.Text;
    LoginParams.Values['PASSWORD'] := PasswordDlg.PWord.Text;
    { If the user is SYSDBA show supervisor information. }
  end;
  if UpperCase(PasswordDlg.UName.Text) = 'SYSDBA' then begin
    Supervisor := True;
    Panel3.Caption := 'User: SYSDBA   Supervisor';
  end
  else begin
    { If user is not SYSDBA show user information. }
    Supervisor := False;
    Panel3.Caption := 'User: ' + PasswordDlg.UName.Text + '   Employee';
  end;
end;
```

FIGURE 30.4.

PasswordDlg, the database login form.

> **TIP**
>
> Remember that the default database administrator login for Local InterBase is the user SYSDBA and the password MASTERKEY.

Switching Views

At this point, each of the data-aware controls should be live and contain data. In order to help facilitate switching through the different views of data, create a TMainMenu component with an organization similar to that shown in Table 30.2.

Table 30.2. MainForm's main menu.

Main Menu	Submenu
&New	&Customer
	&Part
	&Sale
	&Exit

Main Menu	Submenu
&Browse	&Customer
	&Part
	&Sale
&Search	&Customer
	&Part
	&Sale
&Reports	&Accounting
&Users	Lo&gin
	Log&out
	&Close Application
&Help	&About

The Browse buttons are the most straightforward, because they just set the Notebook to the proper page and cancel any range applied to the corresponding table. The following code shows the event handlers for each of the three options on the Browse menu.

```
procedure TMainForm.BrowsePartClick(Sender: TObject);
{ Changes focus to the "Part" page and cancels any range settings on the part }
{ table. }
begin
  NoteBook1.ActivePage := 'Parts';
  PartTable.CancelRange;
end;

procedure TMainForm.BrowseCustomerClick(Sender: TObject);
{ Changes focus to the "Customer" page and cancels any range settings on the }
{ customer table. }
begin
  NoteBook1.ActivePage := 'Customer';
  CustomerTable.CancelRange;
end;

procedure TMainForm.BrowseSaleClick(Sender: TObject);
{ Changes focus to the "Sales" page and cancels any range settings on the }
{ sale table. }
begin
  NoteBook1.ActivePage := 'Sales';
  SaleTable.CancelRange;
end;
```

Adding New Data

The items found on the New menu enable users to enter new customers, parts, or sales into their respective tables. Each of these items operates slightly differently, so each is examined in the following sections, from least to most complex.

New Part

The New|Part menu selection is the most straightforward, and its handler is shown in the following code. It disables some of the menu items using EnableMenuItems(), activates the proper Notebook page, and put the PARTS table into Insert mode.

```
procedure TMainForm.NewPartClick(Sender: TObject);
{ Adds a new part to the part table. }
begin
  EnableMenuItems(False);
  NoteBook1.ActivePage := 'Parts';
  { Place a new record into the table. }
  PartTable.Insert;
end;

procedure TMainForm.EnableMenuItems(EnableThem: Boolean);
{ Receives a Boolean value which determines enable / disable of menu items. }
begin
  New1.Enabled := EnableThem;
  Browse1.Enabled := EnableThem;
  Search1.Enabled := EnableThem;
  Accounting1.Enabled := EnableThem;
end;
```

After the user clicks the Save button to post the new record to the PARTS table, the PartSaveBtnClick() method shown in the following code is executed. This method first calls the TableState() method to determine the current state of the dataset. The record is then posted to the table. The Refresh() method is called because the trigger on this table modifies data, and the BDE needs to be manually re-synced with the information provided to the table by the trigger. Some user-interface elements are then updated to reflect the changed state.

> **NOTE**
>
> Because of the trigger set up for the JOBBER_PRICE field in the database, set the Required property of this field to False so that the information can be posted to the table without this record. You can do this by double-clicking on the table object to reveal the Fields Editor, selecting this record from the list, and modifying the Required property in the Object Inspector.

```
procedure TMainForm.PartSaveBtnClick(Sender: TObject);
{ Saves a newly added or updated part. }
var
  Mode: String;
begin
  Mode := TableState(PartTable);
  PartTable.Post;
  PartTable.Refresh;        { must Refresh because trigger modifies data }
  PartSaveBtn.Visible := False;
  PartCancelBtn.Visible := False;
  EnableMenuItems(True);
  StatusPanel.Caption := Format('%s Saved', [Mode]);
  PartNavigator.Enabled := True;
end;
```

```
function TMainForm.TableState(CurrentTable: TTable): String;
{ Determine what the state of a table is and return a string describing the }
{  state. }
begin
  { Determine what state the table is in. }
  case CurrentTable.State of
    dsInactive: TableState := 'Inactive';
    dsBrowse: TableState := 'Browse';
    dsEdit: TableState := 'Edit';
    dsInsert: TableState := 'Insert';
    dsSetKey: TableState := 'Set Key';
    dsCalcFields: TableState := 'Calc Fields';
  end;
end;
```

New Customer

The New | Customer menu choice adds a new customer record to the CUSTOMER table. The event handler for this menu is shown in the following code. It sets the active page to Customer, calls EnableMenuItems to disable some of the menus, and then attempts to put the table into Insert mode. The CustCreditLine DBEdit then is enabled, and focus is set to the CustFName DBEdit.

```
procedure TMainForm.NewCustomerClick(Sender: TObject);
{ Adds a new customer to the customer table. }
begin
  Notebook1.ActivePage := 'Customer';
  EnableMenuItems(False);
  { Place table into insert mode. }
  CustomerTable.Insert;
  CustCreditLine.Enabled := True;
  CustFName.SetFocus;
end;
```

After the record is inserted and the Save button is clicked, the new customer record is posted to the table. The OnClick event handler for the Save button is shown in the following code. Notice in this event that the Required property of the CUSTOMER_ID field is set to zero because that field is being filled by the generator and trigger in the database:

```
procedure TMainForm.CustSaveBtnClick(Sender: TObject);
{ Saves a new or existing customer's information. }
var
  Mode: string;
begin
  Mode := TableState(CustomerTable);
  CustSaveBtn.Visible := False;
  CustCancelBtn.Visible := False;
  CustomerTable.Post;
  CustomerTable.Refresh;
  CustCreditLine.Enabled := False;
  StatusPanel.Caption := Format('%s Saved', [Mode]);
  CustNavigator.Enabled := True;
  EnableMenuItems(True);
end;
```

New Sale

The logic to generate a new sale is slightly more complex than that of the new customer or part, as the code for the New | Sale event handler shows in the following code. As with the other listings, the Notebook is set to the proper page—in this case, Sales. The method then uses CustQuery to perform a query to determine the highest sales ID number used so far. Once determined, that number is incremented and stored in a variable called SalesNumber. A range is set on the SaleTable that filters all but the records in which the SALE_NUMBER field match SalesNumber, and the table is placed in Insert mode.

```
procedure TMainForm.NewSaleClick(Sender: TObject);
begin
  NoteBook1.ActivePage := 'Sales';
  SalePrice := 0.0;
  with CustQuery do begin
    Close;
    SQL.Clear;
    SQL.Add('SELECT MAX(SALE_NUMBER) FROM SALE;');
    Open;
    SalesNumber := Fields[0].AsInteger + 1;
    Close;
  end;
  with SaleTable do begin
    SetRangeStart;
    FieldByName('SALE_NUMBER').AsInteger := SalesNumber;
    SetRangeEnd;
    FieldByName('SALE_NUMBER').AsInteger := SalesNumber;
    ApplyRange;
    Insert;
  end;
end;
```

Figure 30.5 shows a new sales record being entered into the Inventory Manager.

FIGURE 30.5.

Entering a new sale.

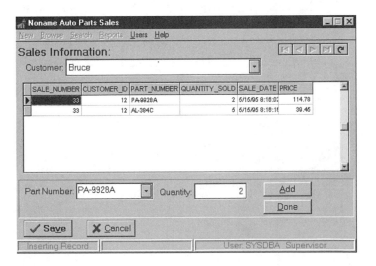

When the sales information is saved by using the Save or Add button, the SavePartSale() method is called to verify the sale and, if valid, create a new record in the SALES table. The following code shows the SavePartSale() method. This method first determines whether the stock on hand is enough to satisfy the current sales request. If so, it sets the SALE_NUMBER field to that previously calculated, sets the Required property of the SALE_DATE field to False (because this field will be filled in by a trigger), and sets the PRICE field equal to the RETAIL_PRICE field of the PARTS table. The user interface then is updated.

```
procedure TMainForm.SavePartSale;
begin
  if PartTable.FieldByName('QUANTITY').AsInteger <
               SaleTable.FieldByName('QUANTITY_SOLD').AsInteger then begin
    MessageDlg('Cannot sell quantity requested.  Not enough in stock',
               mtInformation, [mbOk], 0);
    SaleTable.Cancel;
    Exit;
  end;
  with SaleTable do begin
    FieldByName('SALE_NUMBER').AsInteger := SalesNumber;
    FieldByName('SALE_DATE').Required := False;
    FieldByName('PRICE').AsFloat :=
                      PartTable.FieldByName('RETAIL_PRICE').AsFloat;
    Post;
  end;
  with PartTable do begin
    Edit;
    FieldByName('QUANTITY').AsInteger := FieldByName('QUANTITY').AsInteger -
                        SaleTable.FieldByName('QUANTITY_SOLD').AsInteger;
    Post;
  end;
  SaleTable.Refresh;
  SaleSaveBtn.Visible := False;
  SaleCancelBtn.Visible := False;
end;
```

Searching

The Search menu offers a means for searching through customers, sales, or parts. Once again, each of these routines varies in individual complexity, so this section starts with the simpler routines.

Part Search

The Search | Part menu options enable users to search for a particular auto part based on part number. The listing for this event handler, `SearchPartClick()`, is shown in the following code. This method sets the Parts page to be active, displays an `InputQuery` form asking for the part number to be searched on, and attempts to jump to that part number in the table using the `FindKey()` function.

```
procedure TMainForm.SearchPartClick(Sender: TObject);
{ Search for a specific part and display part information. }
var
  PartNumber: string;
begin
  NoteBook1.ActivePage := 'Parts';
  PartNumber := '';
  { Get the part number to be searched on. }
  if InputQuery('Part Search', 'Please Enter a Part Number', PartNumber) then
    if not PartTable.FindKey([PartNumber]) then      { Try to find the part. }
        MessageDlg('Part number not found', mtInformation, [mbOk], 0);
end;
```

> **TIP**
>
> Delphi's `InputQuery()` function is an excellent way to query the user for a one-string response.

Sale Search

As the following code shows, the mechanism for Search | Sale is nearly identical to that of Search | Part. `InputQuery` is used to determine the sales number on which to search, and `FindKey()` takes you there.

```
procedure TMainForm.SearchSaleClick(Sender: TObject);
var
  SalesNumber: string;
begin
  NoteBook1.ActivePage := 'Sales';
  SalesNumber := '';
  if InputQuery('Sales Search', 'Please Enter a Sales Number', SalesNumber) then
  begin
    SaleTable.CancelRange;
    if not SaleTable.FindKey([SalesNumber]) then
      MessageDlg('Sale not found', mtInformation, [mbOk], 0);
  end;
end;
```

Customer Search

The customer search engine, found at Search | Customer, works differently than its cousins. This option displays a form that enables you to search for a customer based on any one or a combination of values for the CUSTOMER table's fields.

The customer search form is shown in Figure 30.6. Note that it provides a means for the user to search on name, address, phone, or any field in the CUSTOMER table.

FIGURE 30.6.

CustomerSearch: the
Customer Search form.

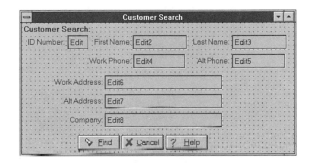

A search is performed by clicking one or more of the TLabels representing a table column and entering the value to search for in the corresponding TEdit component. After the user clicks a TLabel, the label turns red, thanks to the following OnClick handler, to which each label is hooked:

```
procedure TCustomerSearch.IDNumberClick(Sender: TObject);
begin
  with (Sender as TLabel) do
    if Font.Color = clNavy then
      Font.Color := clRed
    else
      Font.Color := clNavy;
end;
```

After the user clicks the Find button, a SQL query is constructed on the fly, based on which labels are read and which are not. This on-the-fly SQL generation is shown in the following code:

```
function TCustomerSearch.BuildSQLStatement: string;
var
  Sep: String[3];
begin
  Sep := '';
  Result := '';
  if IDNumber.Font.Color = clRed then begin
    Result := Format('(CUSTOMER_ID = %s)', [Edit1.Text]);
    Sep := 'AND';
  end;
```

```
  if LastName.Font.Color = clRed then begin
    Result := Format('%s %s (UPPER(LNAME) = "%s")',
                     [Result, Sep, UpperCase(Edit3.Text)]);
    Sep := 'AND';
  end;

  if FirstName.Font.Color = clRed then begin
    Result := Format('%s %s (UPPER(FNAME) = "%s")',
                     [Result, Sep, UpperCase(Edit2.Text)]);
    Sep := 'AND';
  end;

  if WorkPhone.Font.Color = clRed then begin
    Result := Format('%s %s (UPPER(WORK_PHONE) = "%s")',
                     [Result, Sep, UpperCase(Edit4.Text)]);
    Sep := 'AND';
  end;

  if AltPhone.Font.Color = clRed then begin
    Result := Format('%s %s (UPPER(ALT_PHONE) = "%s")',
                     [Result, Sep, UpperCase(Edit5.Text)]);
    Sep := 'AND';
  end;

  if WorkAddress.Font.Color = clRed then begin
    Result := Format('%s %s (UPPER(WORK_ADDRESS) = "%s")',
                     [Result, Sep, UpperCase(Edit6.Text)]);
    Sep := 'AND';
  end;

  if AltAddress.Font.Color = clRed then begin
    Result := Format('%s %s (UPPER(ALT_ADDRESS) = "%s")',
                     [Result, Sep, UpperCase(Edit7.Text)]);
    Sep := 'AND';
  end;

  if Company.Font.Color = clRed then begin
    Result := Format('%s %s (UPPER(COMPANY) = "%s")',
                     [Result, Sep, UpperCase(Edit8.Text)]);
  end;

  if Length(Result) > 0 then
    Result := Format('SELECT CUSTOMER_ID FROM CUSTOMER WHERE (%s)',[Result]);
end;
```

This procedure is definitely not subtle; it plows through all the labels in the form and checks to see whether they are red. If a label is red, the corresponding TEdit's Text property is folded into the SQL query. After a SQL statement is returned from the CustomerSearch form, the remainder of the SearchCustomerClick() handler, shown in the following code, continues to execute.

This method adds the query returned by CustomerSearch to the CustQuery component. If the customer is found in the given search, the CUSTOMER table is positioned to that customer's record.

```
procedure TMainForm.SearchCustomerClick(Sender: TObject);
{ Runs a SQL query and looks for the customer number that is returned. }
var
  CustomerId: Word;
begin
  StatusPanel.Caption := 'Customer Search';
  if CustomerSearch.ShowModal = mrOk then begin
    Screen.Cursor := crSQLWait;
    try
      with CustQuery do begin
        Close;
        SQL.Clear;
        SQL.Add(CustomerSearch.QueryString);
        Open;
      end;
      try
        { Check to see if a customer was found at all. }
        if CustQuery.FieldByName('CUSTOMER_ID').IsNull then begin
          Screen.Cursor := crDefault;
          MessageDlg('Customer not found', mtInformation, [mbOk], 0);
          Exit;
        end;
        { If the customer was found, show the customer, else display error. }
        if not CustomerTable.FindKey([CustQuery.Fields[0].AsInteger]) then
          MessageDlg('Inconsistancy in database.', mtError, [mbOk], 0)
        else
          Notebook1.ActivePage := 'Customer';
      finally
        CustQuery.Close;
      end;
    finally
      Screen.Cursor := crDefault;
    end;
  end
  else
    StatusPanel.Caption := 'Search Cancelled';
end;
```

Generating Reports

The Inventory Manager application has the capability to generate reports based on stored procedures contained in the database. These reports can be generated by using the Reports | Generate menu choice. Choosing this option causes the Reports page of the Notebook to be displayed, as shown in Figure 30.7.

FIGURE 30.7.

*The Accounting
Reports page.*

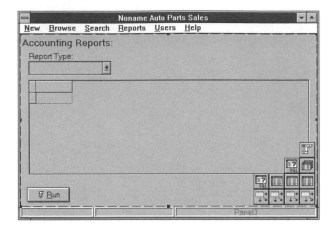

Choose a report type from the drop-down list on the Reports page. Currently, only the Sales report has been implemented. Click the Run button; this invokes its OnClick handler, RunRptBtnClick() (shown in the following code):

```
procedure TMainForm.RunRptBtnClick(Sender: TObject);
var
  StartDate, EndDate: String;
begin
  StatusPanel.Caption := 'Running Report';
  if ComboBox1.Items.Strings[ComboBox1.ItemIndex] = 'Past Due' then begin
    StartDate := '';
    EndDate := '';
    if InputQuery('Start Date', 'Enter beginning sales date', StartDate) and
       InputQuery('End Date', 'Enter ending sales date', EndDate) then begin
      with RptQuery do begin
        Close;
        SQL.Clear;
        SQL.Add('Select * from SALES_REPORT(:START, :END);');
        Prepare;
        Params[0].AsDate := StrToDate(StartDate);
        Params[1].AsDate := StrToDate(EndDate);
        Open;
      end;
    end;
  end
  else
    MessageDlg(Format('%s Report has not been implemented',
               [ComboBox1.Items.Strings[ComboBox1.ItemIndex]]),
               mtInformation, [mbOk], 0);
  StatusPanel.Caption := 'Report Done';
end;
```

This handler prompts you for starting and ending dates of the sales report. Your input to these queries is then passed on to the RptQuery component, which invokes the SALES_REPORT stored procedure. The output of the report is shown in the grid on the form. Figure 30.8 shows a sample of this report.

FIGURE 30.8.

A report in action.

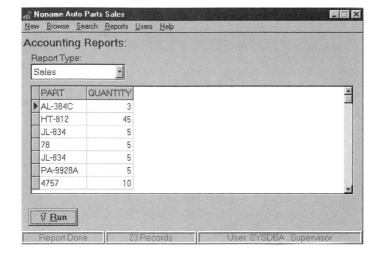

Summary

That concludes this overview of the Inventory Manager application. By now, you should have a better understanding of how to incorporate some of the niceties of client/server programming into your applications. You also should be more familiar in general with creating and managing Delphi applications that manipulate databases. In the next chapter, you'll learn how to take the Inventory Manager to the next level: deployment.

31

Inventory Manager— Finishing Touches

Now that you have completed the Inventory Manager program, the next step is to get the product installed. Because Delphi doesn't come with a utility that helps you install your Delphi applications, it's up to you to purchase a third-party installation utility or to create your own install program. Being the out-of-control developer that you are, you choose your own program. Good choice, because that's what this chapter is all about.

Now that you have decided to write your own installation utility, you have another choice to make. Should you write a quick-and-dirty program that is designed specifically for the Inventory Manager application, or should you go the whole nine yards and write a general-purpose utility that can be used for many applications? The answer to a question of this type is almost always to go the extra mile and write a generic and reusable piece of code. You will thank yourself later.

The first part of this chapter focuses on writing and documenting the installation utility. Later in the chapter, you will put your installation utility to work in the real world by using it to install the Inventory Manager.

Writing an Installation Program

Step number one in development, as with any application, is to write a specification: What is the software going to do, and how will it do it? As an install program, of course, it should have the capability to copy files from a source disk to a destination disk. As a Windows install program, it probably should have the capability to create Program Manager groups and items. And, as a Delphi install program, it should be able to install Delphi's Borland Database Engine (BDE) and SQL Links redistributable drivers.

Writing Utility Routines

Before writing the main parts of the install program, you need to write a few utility functions and procedures to help you handle some of the common situations and some of the unique situations. This section shows you how to write these gems, and you'll learn about a unit called UTILS.PAS, which is presented later in this chapter.

Of *Strings* and *PChars*

You probably have noticed by now that the String/PChar dilemma is a recurring theme throughout Delphi. Most of Delphi and VCL uses Strings, which are user friendly and easy to work with, but the Windows API prefers null-terminated PChar-type strings. Although you can't have it both ways, there is a shortcut you can use to make life a bit easier.

Because a String is nothing more that an array of characters preceded by a length byte, and a PChar is just a pointer to an array of characters terminated by a #0 character, you can pass Strings to functions and procedures that expect PChars by adding a #0 character to the end of a string and passing the address of the first element of the string. The "gotcha" here is that a string can hold a maximum of 255 characters, so you have to be careful when adding the null character not to exceed the 255th character.

The following code shows the `StringAsPChar()` function, which performs a length check and null-terminates a `String`. Note that if the string is already 255 characters, it will be truncated by one.

```
function StringAsPChar(var S: OpenString): PChar;
{ This function null-terminates a string so that it can be passed to functions }
{ that require PChar types. If string is longer than 254 chars, then it will   }
{ be truncated to 254. }
begin
  if Length(S) = High(S) then Dec(S[0]); { Truncate S if it's too long }
  S[Ord(Length(S)) + 1] := #0;           { Place null at end of string }
  Result := @S[1];                       { Return "PChar'd" string }
end;
```

> **TIP**
>
> Notice the use of the `OpenString` type parameter in the `StringAsPChar()` function. This allows `Strings` of any declared size to be passed to the function. The size of the `String` is then determined using the `High()` function.

You now can pass the return value of this function or the address of the first element of the string array to a function or procedure requiring a `PChar`. Here is an example:

```
var
  S: String;
begin
  S := 'Praise the Lord and pass the ammunition';
  NeedsAPCharProc(StringAsPChar(S));
end;
```

The Famous Backslash

Invariably, when working with routines that handle DOS pathnames, you will find that you constantly need to add or remove a trailing backlash from a pathname, depending on the situation. Luckily, you can help yourself by writing functions that handle this task in just a few lines of efficient code. The following code shows two such functions:

```
function AddBackSlash(const S: String): String;
{ Adds a backslash to string S.  If S is already 255 chars or already has }
{ trailing backslash, then function returns S. }
begin
  if (S[0] < #255) and (S[Ord(S[0])] <> '\') then
    Result := S + '\'
  else
    Result := S;
end;
```

```
function StripBackSlash(const S: String): String;
{ Removes trailing backslash from S, if one exists }
begin
  if S[Ord(S[0])] = '\' then
    Dec(S[0]);
  Result :=  S;
end;
```

> **NOTE**
>
> Notice that, as in StringAsPChar(), you directly address the 0th element of the string to assign a length value.

Waiting for Execution of Another Program

In order to deploy programs that use the BDE, SQL Links, or ReportSmith, the install program must have the capability to invoke their respective installation programs. To give the program the capability to invoke the installation program and wait for it to terminate, use a variation of the WinExecAndWait() function from Chapter 19, "Migrating from Borland Pascal to Delphi." The function, which calls WinExec() to execute another program, then sits in an Application.ProcessMessages() loop until the other program terminates, is shown in the following code:

```
function WinExecAndWait(Path: String; Visibility: word): word;
var
  InstanceID : THandle;
begin
  { Convert String to PChar, and try to run the application }
  InstanceID := WinExec(StringAsPChar(Path),Visibility);
  if InstanceID < 32 then { a value less than 32 indicates an Exec error }
    WinExecAndWait := InstanceID
  else begin
    repeat
      Application.ProcessMessages;
    until Application.Terminated or (GetModuleUsage(InstanceID) = 0);
    WinExecAndWait := 32;
  end;
end;
```

Reading Environment Variables

The installation program will need to copy some files to the user's temporary directory, so you need to determine the value of the TEMP environment variable. Windows doesn't provide a function to do this directly, but the API does offer a function called GetDOSEnvironment(), which returns a pointer to the entire environment string. In this string, each environment variable is separated by a null character, and the list is terminated by a double null. For example, the list looks like this in memory:

```
EnvVar1=Value1(null)EnvVar2=Value2(null)...EnvVarX=ValueX(null)(null)
```

It's up to you, the programmer, to parse this list looking for the environment variable in question. Of course, it would be a serious bummer to parse this string every time you need to get at an environment variable, so the answer to the problem is to write a generic function that you can call whenever you need to get the value of an environment variable. The GetEnvVar() function in this code is such a function:

```
function GetEnvVar(EnvVar: String): String;
var
  P: PChar;
begin
  Result := '';                               { return empty string on fail }
  P := GetDOSEnvironment;                      { retrieve pointer to env vars }
  if EnvVar[0] > #253 then EnvVar[0] := #253;  { truncate if too long }
  EnvVar := EnvVar + '=';                      { append "=" sign to string }
  PCharAString(EnvVar);                        { add null-terminator }
  while P^ <> #0 do
    { does first environment variable match EnvVar? }
    if StrLIComp(P, @EnvVar[1], Length(EnvVar)) <> 0 then
      inc(P, StrLen(P) + 1)                    { if not, then go to next }
    else begin
      inc(P, Length(EnvVar));                  { if so, the get value }
      Result := StrPas(P);                     { return a string }
      Break;                                   { get out of loop }
    end;
end;
```

This function first assigns P to the environment string returned by GetDOSEnvironment(). It then appends an equal sign and a null terminator to the string passed in by the user; that way, you can use the StrLIComp() to perform a case-insensitive search between the environment variable you are searching for and the environment variable pointed to by P. If the strings do not match, P is incremented by the length of the current string in P plus one (for the null terminator), which causes P to point to the next environment string. This process is repeated until P points to a null character (meaning that the end of the environment string has been reached) or the first part of P matches EnvVar, in which case the value of P as a string is returned.

Copying a File

Because Object Pascal also lacks a procedure to copy a file to another directory, you again must improvise. Again, you will drop down to the Windows API to get the functionality that you need. The Windows API has a collection of file-management functions in a DLL called LZEXPAND, which you will use.

To open the source and destination files, use the LZOpenFile() function. Copy the file using the LZCopy() function, and close the files using the LZClose() function. The following code shows the source for the CopyFile() function:

```
procedure CopyFile(Source, Dest: String);
var
  SourceHand, DestHand: Integer;
  OpenBuf: TOFStruct;
begin
```

```
    { Open source file, and pass our psuedo-PChar as the filename }
    SourceHand := LZOpenFile(@Source[1], OpenBuf, of_Share_Deny_Write or of_Read);
    { raise an exception on error }
    if SourceHand = -1 then
      raise EInOutError.CreateFmt('Error opening source file "%s",[Source]);
    try
      { Open destination file, and pass our psuedo-PChar as the filename }
      DestHand := LZOpenFile(StringAsPChar(Dest), OpenBuf, of_Share_Exclusive or
  ➥of_Write
                            or of_Create);
      { Check for error and raise exception }
      if DestHand = -1 then
        raise EInOutError.CreateFmt('Error opening destination file "%s"',[Dest]);
      try
        { copy source to dest, raise exception on error }
        if LZCopy(SourceHand, DestHand) < 0 then
          raise EInOutError.CreateFmt('Error copying file "%s"', [Source]);
      finally
        { whether or not an exception occurs, we need to close the files }
        LZClose(DestHand);
      end;
    finally
      LZClose(SourceHand);
    end;
end;
```

Notice the extensive error checking built into this function. This error checking causes an EInOutError exception to be raised in the event of an error, such as failure to open a file or failure to copy the file. By using the LZEXPAND functions, you put the burden of low-level error checking on the Windows API and concern yourself only with whether the open or copy is successful.

Listing 31.1 shows the complete source code for the UTILS.PAS unit.

Listing 31.1. The source code for UTILS.PAS.

```
unit Utils;

interface

function StringAsPChar(var S: OpenString): PChar;
function AddBackSlash(const S: String): String;
function StripBackSlash(const S: String): String;
function WinExecAndWait(Path: String; Visibility: word): word;
function GetEnvVar(EnvVar: String): String;
procedure CopyFile(Source, Dest: String);

implementation

uses SysUtils, LZExpand, WinTypes, WinProcs, Forms;

function StringAsPChar(var S: OpenString): PChar;
{ This function null-terminates a string so that it can be passed to functions }
{ that require PChar types. If string is longer than 254 chars, then it will   }
{ be truncated to 254. }
```

```
begin
  if Length(S) = High(S) then Dec(S[0]); { Truncate S if it's too long }
  S[Ord(Length(S)) + 1] := #0;            { Place null at end of string }
  Result := @S[1];                        { Return "PChar'd" string }
end;

function AddBackSlash(const S: String): String;
{ Adds a backslash to string S.  If S is already 255 chars or already has }
{ trailing backslash, then function returns S. }
begin
  if (Length(S) < 255) and (S[Length(S)] <> '\') then
    Result := S + '\'
  else
    Result := S;
end;

function StripBackSlash(const S: String): String;
{ Removes trailing backslash from S, if one exists }
begin
  Result := S;
  if Result[Length(Result)] = '\' then
    Dec(Result[0]);
end;

function WinExecAndWait(Path: String; Visibility: word): word;
var
  InstanceID : THandle;
begin
  { Convert String to PChar, and try to run the application }
  InstanceID := WinExec(StringAsPChar(Path),Visibility);
  if InstanceID < 32 then { a value less than 32 indicates an Exec error }
    WinExecAndWait := InstanceID
  else begin
    repeat
      Application.ProcessMessages;
    until Application.Terminated or (GetModuleUsage(InstanceID) = 0);
    WinExecAndWait := 32;
  end;
end;

function GetEnvVar(EnvVar: String): String;
{ Returns the value of the DOS environment variable passed in EnvVar.      }
{ Note: EnvVar must be 253 chars or less, or it will be truncated to 253.  }
{ Note2: Under Win32, the GetEnvironmentVariable() function should be used. }
var
  P: PChar;
begin
  Result := '';                           { return empty string on fail }
  P := GetDOSEnvironment;                 { retrieve pointer to env vars }
  if EnvVar[0] > #253 then EnvVar[0] := #253; { truncate if too long }
  EnvVar := EnvVar + '=';                 { append "=" sign to string }
  StringAsPChar(EnvVar);                  { add null-terminator }
  while P^ <> #0 do
    { does first environment variable match EnvVar? }
    if StrLIComp(P, @EnvVar[1], Length(EnvVar)) <> 0 then
      inc(P, StrLen(P) + 1)               { if not, then go to next }
    else begin
      inc(P, Length(EnvVar));             { if so, the get value }
```

continues

Listing 31.1. continued

```
        Result := StrPas(P);                    { return a string }
        Break;                                  { get out of loop }
      end;
end;

procedure CopyFile(Source, Dest: String);
var
  SourceHand, DestHand: Integer;
  OpenBuf: TOFStruct;
begin
  { Open source file, and pass our psuedo-PChar as the filename }
  SourceHand := LZOpenFile(StringAsPChar(Source), OpenBuf, of_Share_Deny_Write
➥or of_Read);
  { raise an exception on error }
  if SourceHand = -1 then
    raise EInOutError.Create('Error opening source file "' + Source + '"');
  try
    { Open destination file, and pass our psuedo-PChar as the filename }
    DestHand := LZOpenFile(@Dest[1], OpenBuf, of_Share_Exclusive or of_Write
                           or of_Create);
    { Check for error and raise exception }
    if DestHand = -1 then
      raise EInOutError.CreateFmt('Error opening destination file "%s"',[Dest]);
    try
      { copy source to dest, raise exception on error }
      if LZCopy(SourceHand, DestHand) < 0 then
        raise EInOutError.CreateFmt('Error copying file "%s"', [Source]);
    finally
      { whether or not an exception occurs, we need to close the files }
      LZClose(DestHand);
    end;
  finally
    LZClose(SourceHand);
  end;
end;

end.
```

Conversing with Program Manager

The proper way to create and delete program groups and items in Program Manager is through dynamic data exchange. Although Delphi's WINAPI.HLP file, under the "Shell Dynamic Data Exchange" topic, gives complete details on the implementation of this, you will create a simplified version of the ProgMan DDE implementation and encapsulate it into a Delphi component.

The TProgMan component's interface is shown in this code:

```
type
  TProgMan = class(TComponent)
  private
```

```
    FDdeClientConv: TDdeClientConv;
    procedure InitDDEConversation;
    function ExecMacroString(Macro: String): Boolean;
  public
    { Public declarations }
    constructor Create(AOwner: TComponent); override;
    destructor Destroy; override;
    procedure CreateGroup(GroupName: String);
    procedure DeleteGroup(GroupName: String);
    procedure DeleteItem(ItemName: String);
    procedure AddItem(CmdLine, ItemName: String);
  end;
```

As you can see, the interface to this object is fairly straightforward. You can create or delete a new group based on a group name, delete an item based on its name, or create an item based on the filename and item name. In the `private` section, `FDdeClientConv` is the component that maintains the DDE conversation with Program Manager, the `InitDDEConversation()` procedure is responsible for creating the `FDdeClientConv` instance and establishing the initial connection, and the `ExecMacroString()` function is used by the `public` procedures to send DDE macro strings to Program Manager.

The macro strings sent to Program Manager follow:

```
const
  SDDECreateGroup        = '[CreateGroup(%s)]';
  SDDEShowGroup          = '[ShowGroup(%s, 1)]';
  SDDEDeleteGroup        = '[DeleteGroup(%s)]';
  SDDEDeleteItem         = '[DeleteItem(%s)]';
  SDDEAddItem : PChar    = '[AddItem(%s, "%s", %s)]';
```

In each case, the file or item name is substituted for `%s` using the `Format()` or `StrFmt()` function. The `SDDEAddItem` string is defined as a `PChar` because it is possible that that string could exceed the 255-character limit of a `String`. Listing 31.2 shows the complete source for the PM.PAS unit in which the `TProgMan` component is defined.

Listing 31.2. The source code for PM.PAS.

```
unit Pm;

interface

uses
  SysUtils, Classes, DdeMan;

type
  EProgManError = class(Exception);

  TProgMan = class(TComponent)
  private
    FDdeClientConv: TDdeClientConv;
    procedure InitDDEConversation;
    function ExecMacroString(Macro: String): Boolean;
```

continues

Listing 31.2. continued

```
public
  { Public declarations }
  constructor Create(AOwner: TComponent); override;
  destructor Destroy; override;
  procedure CreateGroup(GroupName: String);
  procedure DeleteGroup(GroupName: String);
  procedure DeleteItem(ItemName: String);
  procedure AddItem(CmdLine, ItemName: String);
end;

implementation

uses Utils;

const
  { Program Manager DDE macro strings }
  SDDECreateGroup    = '[CreateGroup(%s)]';
  SDDEShowGroup      = '[ShowGroup(%s, 1)]';
  SDDEDeleteGroup    = '[DeleteGroup(%s)]';
  SDDEDeleteItem     = '[DeleteItem(%s)]';
  SDDEAddItem : PChar = '[AddItem(%s, "%s", %s)]';  { likely to be > 255 chars }

constructor TProgMan.Create(AOwner: TComponent);
begin
  inherited Create(AOwner);
  InitDDEConversation;          { establish DDE link with ProgMan }
end;

destructor TProgMan.Destroy;
begin
  if Assigned(FDDEClientConv) then
    FDdeClientConv.CloseLink;     { terminate DDE link to ProgMan }
  inherited Destroy;              { inherited clean up }
end;

function TProgMan.ExecMacroString(Macro: String): Boolean;
begin
  PCharAString(Macro);
  Result := FDdeClientConv.ExecuteMacro(@Macro[1], False);
end;

procedure TProgMan.InitDDEConversation;
{ Establishes a DDE link with Program Manager }
begin
  { create DDE component }
  FDdeClientConv := TDdeClientConv.Create(Self);
  { attempt to establish DDE link with ProgMan }
  if not FDdeClientConv.SetLink('PROGMAN', 'PROGMAN') then
    raise EProgManError.Create('Failed to establish DDE Link');
end;

procedure TProgMan.CreateGroup(GroupName: String);
{ Creates a Program Manager group with name given by GroupName }
begin
  { attempt to create group }
  if not ExecMacroString(Format(SDDECreateGroup, [GroupName])) then
    raise EProgManError.Create('Could not create group. Group name: ' +
                               GroupName);
```

```
  { attempt to show group }
  if not ExecMacroString(Format(SDDEShowGroup, [GroupName])) then
    raise EProgManError.Create('Could not show group. Group name: ' +
                                GroupName);
end;

procedure TProgMan.DeleteGroup(GroupName: String);
begin
  if not ExecMacroString(Format(SDDEDeleteGroup, [GroupName])) then
    raise EProgManError.Create('Could not delete group. Group name: ' +
                                GroupName);
end;

procedure TProgMan.DeleteItem(ItemName: String);
begin
  if not ExecMacroString(Format(SDDEDeleteItem, [ItemName])) then
    raise EProgManError.Create('Could not delete item. Item name: ' +
                                ItemName);
end;

procedure TProgMan.AddItem(CmdLine, ItemName: String);
{ Adds an item to the active Program Manager group.  CmdLine is the path name }
{ of the item, and ItemName is the name as it will appear in Program Manager. }
var
  P: PChar;
  PSize: Word;
begin
  { determine amount of memory needed for AddItem DDE string }
  PSize := StrLen(SDDEAddItem) + (Length(CmdLine) * 2) + Length(ItemName) + 1;
  GetMem(P, PSize);                   { allocate memory }
  try
    { format AddItem DDE macro string }
    StrFmt(P, SDDEAddItem, [CmdLine, ItemName, CmdLine]);
    { attempt to add item to group }
    if not FDdeClientConv.ExecuteMacro(P, False) then
      raise EProgManError.Create('Could not add item. Item: ' + ItemName);
  finally
    FreeMem(P, PSize);               { clean up }
  end;
end;

end.
```

Note the EProgManError exception object that is defined at the top of the unit. This exception is raised if any of the ExecuteMacro commands fail.

Understanding the INI File

Now that the preliminaries are out of the way, you can focus on the implementation of the installation program proper. Before you get to the code, though, take a look at how the application will work.

In order to facilitate maximum reusability, the installation program will be configured entirely from an INI file. In the INI file, there should be options for things like number of disks, files on each disk, Program Manager groups and items to create, and directories in which to install. The following section enumerates all the possible INI file sections, items, and settings.

[General]

The `[General]` section will hold all the general information about the program being installed. Items for this section include the following:

`Program=`	The value for this item should be a string indicating the name of the product being installed. Here's an example:
	`Program=Fast Eddy's Database Program`
`Version=`	The value of this item is a string indicating the version number. Here's an example:
	`Version=Version 1.0`
`Copyright=`	The value of this item is a copyright string. Here's an example:
	`Copyright=Copyright (c) 1995 - Large Canine Productions`
`NumDisks=`	This item's value should indicate the number of installation disks. Here's an example:
	`NumDisks=1`
`InstallBDE=`	A Boolean (0 or 1) flag that indicates whether to invoke the Borland Database Engine installation. Here's an example:
	`InstallBDE=1`
`InstallSQL=`	A Boolean (0 or 1) flag that indicates whether to invoke the Borland SQL Links installation. Here's an example:
	`InstallSQL=1`
`InstallRpt=`	A Boolean (0 or 1) flag that indicates whether to invoke the Borland ReportSmith Runtime installation. Here's an example:
	`InstallRpt=0`
`DefaultDir=`	This item's value should be a string representing the default installation path. The user will have the capability to modify this default at runtime from a form in the install program. Here's an example:
	`DefaultDir=C:\BIGDOG\`
`PMGroup=`	The value for this item is a string that indicates the name of the Program Manager group to create. If this item is absent, then a Program Manager group will not be created. Here's an example:
	`PMGroup=My New Group`

[SubDirs]

In the `[SubDirs]` section, you enumerate the subdirectories to be installed off the main directory (in which the default value is obtained from the `DefaultDir` item in `[General]`). The items in this section will be sequential numbers (starting with zero), and the value for each item will be a subdirectory name. As an example, the following lines create two subdirectories off the main directory called SIMBA and DAKOTA:

```
[SubDirs]
0=SIMBA
1=DAKOTA
```

[DiskX]

You should have a [DiskX] section—where X is the disk number, starting from one—for each of the disks (not including the BDE and SQL Links redistributables) in your installation. The number of disks will match the value of the NumDisks item in the [General] section.

Each item in a [DiskX] section should be a filename located on that disk. The value for each item should be a code representing the destination of the file. Table 31.2 shows valid code values.

Table 31.2. File destination codes for [DiskX] items.

Code	Destination	Typically Used For
i	Installation directory	Files that you want to install into the installation directory chosen by the user.
w	Windows directory	Files, such as VBXs, that must reside in the Windows directory.
s	Windows System directory	Shared DLLs like CTL3DV2.DLL that need to be accessed from multiple applications.
0, 1, ..., X	A subdirectory of the installation directory	Files that you want to be in a subdirectory of the main install directory. The number here should coincide with a number from the [SubDirs] section.

The following example installs three files from disk one to the INSTALL, WINDOWS, and Windows SYSTEM directory, and one file to a custom subdirectory called ASUBDIR:

```
[SubDirs]
0=ASUBDIR

[Disk1]
FILEONE.EXE=i
FILETWO.VBX=w
FILE3.DLL=s

[Disk2]
ANOTHER.FIL=0
```

[PMGroup]

Each item in the [PMGroup] section indicates files for which you want to create Program Manager group icons. The files listed already must exist in one of the [FilesX] sections, and the value of these items should be the same directory code as listed in the [FilesX] section. The icons will be installed in the group indicated by the PMGroup item in the [General] section. To install an icon for the FILEONE.EXE file, for example, the INI file section should look like this:

```
[PMGroup]
FILEONE.EXE=i
```

Creating the Install User Interface

The general usage of the install program should be pretty clear by now, so it's time to discuss creating the user interface and writing the code. Start a new project and call it INST.DPR. Figure 31.1 shows the main form for the Inst project, called SetupForm. This form contains a number of TLabel components, a TGauge, three TBitBtns, and several panels.

FIGURE 31.1.

Inst's main form,
SetupForm.

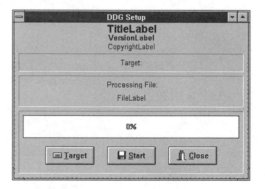

You also need a second form, which will be used to query the user for a pathname. This form is called DirectoryForm, and it contains a TPanel, TLabel, TEdit, and two TBitBtns. DirectoryForm is shown in Figure 31.2.

FIGURE 31.2.

DirectoryForm.

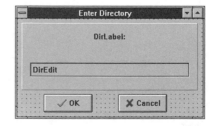

DirectoryForm

The DirectoryForm form is a simple form that enables the user to enter a pathname in the edit control, and dismiss the form using the OK or Cancel button. For the sake of reusability, you will add one new function to the TDirectoryForm class definition that initializes the label's contents and displays the form. The complete source for TARGET.PAS, DirectoryForm's unit, is shown in Listing 31.3.

Listing 31.3. The source code for TARGET.PAS.

```
unit Target;

interface

uses
  SysUtils, WinTypes, WinProcs, Messages, Classes, Graphics, Controls,
  Forms, Dialogs, StdCtrls, Buttons, ExtCtrls;

type
  TDirectoryForm = class(TForm)
    Panel1: TPanel;
    DirEdit: TEdit;
    DirLabel: TLabel;
    BitBtn1: TBitBtn;
    BitBtn2: TBitBtn;
  public
    function ShowForm(const LabelCap, DefaultDir: String): integer;
  end;

var
  DirectoryForm: TDirectoryForm;

implementation

{$R *.DFM}

function TDirectoryForm.ShowForm(const LabelCap, DefaultDir: String): integer;
{ this is the interface function for DirectoryForm. It allows the controls }
{ to be initialized before showing form. }
begin
  DirLabel.Caption := LabelCap;
  DirEdit.Text := DefaultDir;
  Result := ShowModal;
end;

end.
```

OnCreate: Windows and System Directories

In the OnCreate handler for SetupForm, you read INI file values from the [General] section described earlier. Because the Install Program needs to have the capability to install to the WINDOWS and Windows SYSTEM directories, you need to determine the locations of the directories. You do this by using the `GetWindowsDirectory()` and `GetSystemDirectory()` API functions. The following code shows these values being read into `String` variables called `WindowsDir` and `SystemDir`:

```
GetWindowsDirectory(@WindowsDir[1], SizeOf(WindowsDir) - 1);
WindowsDir[0] := Chr(StrLen(@WindowsDir[1])); { Set length byte of string }
WindowsDir := AddBackSlash(WindowsDir);       { Make sure path ends in '\' }

GetSystemDirectory(@SystemDir[1], SizeOf(SystemDir) - 1);
SystemDir[0] := Chr(StrLen(@SystemDir[1]));   { Set length byte of string }
SystemDir := AddBackSlash(SystemDir);         { Make sure path ends in '\' }
```

Note that a little bit of trickery is used in reading these values into `String`, rather than `PChar` or array buffers. Because you're treating the string like an array, though, it's important to set the length byte of the string to the size that you determine with the `StrLen` function. Make sure the pathname ends in a backslash by using the `AddBackSlash()` function from the `utils` unit.

Count the Files

In order to allow the gauge to count properly from 0 percent to 100 percent of files installed, you must determine exactly how many files will be installed. This is done by iterating through each `[DiskX]` section in the INI file, and counting the number of items in each section. The total number of files is saved in a variable called `TotalFiles`. The following code shows the `GetNumFiles()` procedure, in which this process takes place:

```
procedure TSetupForm.GetNumFiles;
{ This procedure iterates over the INI file and counts the number of files to }
{ be installed.  It then initializes the TotalFiles variable. }
var
  i: integer;
  S: TStringList;
begin
  TotalFiles := 0;
  S := TStringList.Create;
  try
    { count number of files in each Disk group }
    for i := 1 to NumDisks do begin
      IniFile.ReadSectionValues('Disk' + IntToStr(i), S);
      inc(TotalFiles, S.Count);
      S.Clear;
    end;
  finally
    S.Free;
  end;
end;
```

Check Your Paths

When someone uses the install program, he or she first must select the Target button to determine in which directory the software should be installed. The event handler for this button press is responsible for determining whether the target directories exist, and creating them if necessary.

You can use the DirExists() function from the utils unit to determine whether a directory exists. If a specified directory doesn't exist, Delphi offers two procedures to create new directories, MkDir() and ForceDirectories():

```
procedure MkDir(S: String);
procedure ForceDirectories(S: String);
```

MkDir() creates a new subdirectory provided each higher level directory specific already exists. For example, to create a subdirectory called C:\ONE\TWO\THREE, the ONE and TWO directories must already exist.

ForceDirectories(), found in the FILECTRL unit, creates all directories along a path if they don't already exist. To create a subdirectory called C:\ONE\TWO\THREE using ForceDirectories(), it isn't necessary that any of the directories exist prior to the call.

To provide for maximum flexibility, the install program uses the ForceDirectories() function to create installation directories. The following code shows TargetBtn's OnClick event handler, which validates and creates the target directories:

```
procedure TSetupForm.TargetBtnClick(Sender: TObject);
var
  S: TStringList;
  i: word;
begin
  { get directory from dialog }
  if DirectoryForm.ShowForm('Enter target directory:',
                  IniFile.ReadString('General', 'DefaultDir', '')) = mrOk then
    { if it's not there, prompt for permission to create the directory }
    if not DirExists(DirectoryForm.DirEdit.Text) then begin
      if MessageDlg(Format(SDirNotFound, [DirectoryForm.DirEdit.Text]),
                  mtConfirmation, [mbYes, mbNo], 0) = mrYes then begin
        { make the directory }
        ForceDirectories(StripBackSlash(DirectoryForm.DirEdit.Text));
        { update InstallDir variable }
        InstallDir := AddBackSlash(DirectoryForm.DirEdit.Text);
        { update panel }
        TargetPanel.Caption := 'Target: ' +
                              AddBackSlash(DirectoryForm.DirEdit.Text);
      end;
    end
    else begin
      { if directory exists, then update InstallDir and panel }
      InstallDir := AddBackSlash(DirectoryForm.DirEdit.Text);
      TargetPanel.Caption := 'Target: ' +
                            AddBackSlash(DirectoryForm.DirEdit.Text);
    end;
    { Create subdirectories }
    S := TStringList.Create;
    try
      IniFile.ReadSectionValues('SubDirs', S);
      for i := 0 to S.Count - 1 do
        if not DirExists(InstallDir + S.Values[IntToStr(i)]) then
          ForceDirectories(InstallDir + S.Values[IntToStr(i)]);
    finally
      S.Free;
    end;
end;
```

Commence Copying

After all the paths have been determined and target directories have been created, you can get down to the whole point of the exercise: actually copying files from point A to point B. You do this with a method called `StartInstall()`.

`StartInstall()` iterates over each file in each `[DiskX]` section in the INI file, calling the `CopyFile()` procedure (from the UTILS unit) to copy each file from its source to its intended destination. It also is responsible for updating the gauge and `FileLabel` with the new progress and file name as each file is copied.

When finished copying files, `StartInstall()` also calls the `CreateGroup()` procedure to create the Program Manager group and items and calls the `NextInst()` procedure to install the Borland Database Engine, SQL Links, or ReportSmith Runtime as required.

> **NOTE**
>
> At the time of this writing, the Borland Database Engine, Borland SQL Links, and ReportSmith Runtime redistributable licenses require that you install each of these products only with the SETUP program provided in each product's REDIST subdirectory. Also, only owners of Delphi Client/Server have license to redistribute SQL Links.

The following shows the source code for the `StartInstall()` function:

```
procedure TSetupForm.StartInstall;
{ This is the meat of the installation.  It copies files from source to }
{ destination. It also invokes the BDE install if necessary. }
var
  Disk, Curr: word;
  S: TStringList;
  FName: String[13];
begin
  Gauge1.Progress := 0;                    { reset gauge }
  S := TStringList.Create;
  try
    for Disk := 1 to NumDisks do begin     { iterate for each disk }
      { read files and destination codes from INI file }
      IniFile.ReadSectionValues('Disk' + IntToStr(Disk), S);
      if CheckDisk(Disk, S) then           { make sure we're on the right disk }
        for Curr := 0 to S.Count - 1 do begin  {iterate for each file }
          { get file name from stringlist }
          FName := Copy(S.Strings[Curr], 1, Pos('=', S.Strings[Curr]) - 1);
          FileLabel.Caption := FName;
          { copy file from source to target directory given by code }
          try
            CopyFile(SourceDir + FName, GetTarget(S.Values[FName][1]) + FName);
          except
            on E:EInOutError do
              if MessageDlg(E.Message + '. Continue?', mtError, [mbYes, mbNo],
                            0) = mrNo then
                Raise;
```

```
          end;
        Gauge1.Progress := Gauge1.Progress + 1;
        Application.ProcessMessages;    { allow controls to update }
      end;
    end;
  finally
    S.Free;
  end;
  MessageDlg(SSetupDone, mtInformation, [mbOk], 0);
  CreateGroup;                               { create ProgMan group }
  if InstallBDE then NextInst(itBDE);   { execute BDE install if necessary }
  if InstallSQL then NextInst(itSQL);   { execute SQL install if necessary }
  StartBtn.Enabled := True;
end;
```

You might notice that a function called CheckDisk() is called, which determines whether the disk in the current source directory is the right one. You can see the full source to this, and the rest of the functions in this unit, by looking at the complete source to MAIN.PAS in Listing 31.4. The MAIN unit is associated with the main window of the installation program, and this is where all the code we've discussed to this point comes together in a working unit.

Listing 31.4. The source code for MAIN.PAS.

```pascal
unit Main;

{$C Moveable Preload Permanent}

interface

uses
  SysUtils, WinTypes, WinProcs, Messages, Classes, Graphics, Controls,
  Forms, Dialogs, StdCtrls, IniFiles, ExtCtrls, Buttons, Gauges;

type
  { used to invoke BDE, SQL Links, and ReportSmith setup }
  TInstType = (itBDE, itSQL, itRpt);

  TSetupForm = class(TForm)
    TitleLabel: TLabel;
    CopyrightLabel: TLabel;
    VersionLabel: TLabel;
    Panel1: TPanel;
    Label1: TLabel;
    FileLabel: TLabel;
    Panel2: TPanel;
    Gauge1: TGauge;
    StartBtn: TBitBtn;
    CloseBtn: TBitBtn;
    TargetPanel: TPanel;
    TargetBtn: TBitBtn;
    procedure FormCreate(Sender: TObject);
    procedure FormDestroy(Sender: TObject);
    procedure CloseBtnClick(Sender: TObject);
    procedure StartBtnClick(Sender: TObject);
    procedure TargetBtnClick(Sender: TObject);
```

continues

Listing 31.4. continued

```
  private
    IniFile: TIniFile;
    NumDisks: integer;
    InstallBDE: Boolean;
    InstallSQL: Boolean;
    InstallRpt: Boolean;
    TotalFiles: Word;
    procedure GetNumFiles;
    function CheckDisk(DiskNum: word; S: TStringList): Boolean;
    function GetTarget(Code: Char): String;
    procedure StartInstall;
    procedure NextInst(InstType: TInstType);
    procedure CreateGroup;
  public
    SourceDir: String;
    InstallDir: String;
    WindowsDir: String;
    SystemDir: String;
  end;

var
  SetupForm: TSetupForm;

implementation

{$R *.DFM}

uses FileCtrl, Utils, Target, PM;

const
  { Informational strings }
  SNeedDisk     = 'Insert disk %d into drive %s.';
  SDirNotFound  = 'Directory "%s" does not exist. Okay to create?';
  SSetupDone    = 'Setup Complete! Select "Ok" to create Program Manager group';
  SInstNotFound = '%s setup not found at "%s". Press "Ok" to try again.';
  SNoTargetPath = 'You must first specify a target path.';
  SNextInst     = 'Setup will now execute the %s installation. ';
  SPressIfDone  = 'Press "Ok" after the %s installation has COMPLETED.';
  SEnterPath    = 'Enter source path for %s install';

procedure TSetupForm.GetNumFiles;
{ This procedure iterates over the INI file and counts the number of files to }
{ be installed.  It then initializes the TotalFiles variable. }
var
  i: integer;
  S: TStringList;
begin
  TotalFiles := 0;
  S := TStringList.Create;
  try
    { count number of files in each Disk group }
    for i := 1 to NumDisks do begin
      IniFile.ReadSectionValues('Disk' + IntToStr(i), S);
      inc(TotalFiles, S.Count);
      S.Clear;
    end;
```

```pascal
  finally
    S.Free;
  end;
end;

procedure TSetupForm.FormCreate(Sender: TObject);
{ The OnCreate handler }
begin
  { source path is passed as second parameter to INST.EXE }
  SourceDir := ParamStr(2);
  FileLabel.Caption := '(none)';
  IniFile := TIniFile.Create(ExtractFilePath(ParamStr(0)) + 'DDGSETUP.INI');
  { read values from INI file }
  with IniFile do begin
    TitleLabel.Caption := ReadString('General', 'Program', 'DDG Setup');
    VersionLabel.Caption := ReadString('General', 'Version', '');
    CopyrightLabel.Caption := ReadString('General', 'Copyright', '');
    NumDisks := ReadInteger('General', 'NumDisks', 1);
    InstallBDE := ReadBool('General', 'InstallBDE', False);
    InstallSQL := ReadBool('General', 'InstallSQL', False);
    InstallRpt := ReadBool('General', 'InstallRpt', False);
  end;
  GetNumFiles;
  Gauge1.MaxValue := TotalFiles;                 { initialize gauge }
  { Find the Windows directory, and Pass "PChar-String" to API }
  GetWindowsDirectory(@WindowsDir[1], SizeOf(WindowsDir) - 1);
  WindowsDir[0] := Chr(StrLen(@WindowsDir[1])); { Set length byte of string }
  WindowsDir := AddBackSlash(WindowsDir);        { Make sure path ends in '\' }
  { Find the Windows System directory, and Pass "PChar-String" to API }
  GetSystemDirectory(@SystemDir[1], SizeOf(SystemDir) - 1);
  SystemDir[0] := Chr(StrLen(@SystemDir[1]));    { Set length byte of string }
  SystemDir := AddBackSlash(SystemDir);          { Make sure path ends in '\' }
end;

procedure TSetupForm.FormDestroy(Sender: TObject);
{ The OnDestroy handler }
begin
  IniFile.Free;
end;

procedure TSetupForm.CloseBtnClick(Sender: TObject);
begin
  Release;
end;

procedure TSetupForm.StartBtnClick(Sender: TObject);
{ This procedure invokes the install in response to the button press }
begin
  if InstallDir <> '' then begin
    StartBtn.Enabled := False;
    StartInstall;
  end
  else
    MessageDlg(SNoTargetPath, mtError, [mbOk], 0);
end;
```

continues

Listing 31.4. continued

```
function TSetupForm.CheckDisk(DiskNum: word; S: TStringList): Boolean;
{ Returns False if Cancel button is pushed, True if correct disk found. }
var
  FName: String[13];
begin
  Result := True;
  { get first filename from string list }
  FName :=Copy(S.Strings[1], 1, Pos('=', S.Strings[1]) - 1);
  { keep iterating until file exists or cancel is pressed }
  while not FileExists(SourceDir + FName) do
    if MessageDlg(Format(SNeedDisk, [DiskNum, SourceDir[1]]), mtInformation,
              mbOkCancel, 0) = mrCancel then begin
      Result := False;
      Break;
    end;
end;

function TSetupForm.GetTarget(Code: Char): String;
{ This procedure returns the target directory based on the INI file setting }
begin
  case code of
    'i' : Result := InstallDir;
    'w' : Result := WindowsDir;
    's' : Result := SystemDir;
  else
    Result := AddBackSlash(AddBackSlash(InstallDir) +
              IniFile.ReadString('SubDirs', Code, ''));
  end;
end;

procedure TSetupForm.StartInstall;
{ This is the meat of the installation.  It copies files from source to }
{ destination. It also invokes the BDE install if necessary. }
var
  Disk, Curr: word;
  S: TStringList;
  FName: String[13];
begin
  Gauge1.Progress := 0;                      { reset gauge }
  S := TStringList.Create;
  try
    for Disk := 1 to NumDisks do begin    { iterate for each disk }
      { read files and destination codes from INI file }
      IniFile.ReadSectionValues('Disk' + IntToStr(Disk), S);
      if CheckDisk(Disk, S) then          { make sure we're on the right disk }
        for Curr := 0 to S.Count - 1 do begin  {iterate for each file }
          { get filename from stringlist }
          FName := Copy(S.Strings[Curr], 1, Pos('=', S.Strings[Curr]) - 1);
          FileLabel.Caption := FName;
          { copy file from source to target directory given by code }
          try
            CopyFile(SourceDir + FName, GetTarget(S.Values[FName][1]) + FName);
          except
            on E:EInOutError do
              if MessageDlg(E.Message + '. Continue?', mtError, [mbYes, mbNo],
                      0) = mrNo then
                Raise;
          end;
```

```
            Gauge1.Progress := Gauge1.Progress + 1;
            Application.ProcessMessages;   { allow controls to update }
        end;
    end;
  finally
    S.Free;
  end;
  MessageDlg(SSetupDone, mtInformation, [mbOk], 0);
  CreateGroup;                           { create ProgMan group }
  if InstallBDE then NextInst(itBDE);    { execute BDE install if necessary }
  if InstallSQL then NextInst(itSQL);    { execute SQL install if necessary }
  If InstallRpt then NextInst(itRpt);    { execute Rpt install if necessary }
  StartBtn.Enabled := True;
end;

procedure TSetupForm.CreateGroup;
{ Uses the TProgMan component to install Program Manager group }
var
  ItemList: TStringList;
  GroupName: String;
  ItemName: String;
  i: word;
begin
  { Get the GroupName string from the INI file }
  GroupName := IniFile.ReadString('General', 'PMGroup', '');
  { If there is one, then install group }
  if GroupName <> '' then begin
    ItemList := TStringList.Create;
    try
      { read items to be installed }
      IniFile.ReadSectionValues('PMGroup', ItemList);
      with TProgMan.Create(Self) do
      try
        CreateGroup(GroupName);
        for i := 0 to ItemList.Count - 1 do begin
          { get file name }
          ItemName := Copy(ItemList.Strings[i], 1, Pos('=',
                      ItemList.Strings[i]) - 1);
          { append file name to path and add the item }
          AddItem(GetTarget(ItemList.Values[ItemName][1]) + ItemName, ItemName);
        end;
      finally
        Free;
      end;
    finally
      ItemList.Free;
    end;
  end;
end;

procedure TSetupForm.NextInst(InstType: TInstType);
{ Installs the BDE by WinExec'ing the BDE setup program }
var
  InstallProg: String[32];
  UniqueFile: String[13];
  InstallEXE: String[13];
  NextSetup: String;
```

continues

Listing 31.4. continued

```
begin
  { figure out type of install and set string accordingly }
  case InstType of
    itBDE : begin
      InstallProg := 'Borland Database Engine';
      UniqueFile := 'idapicfg.pak';              { unique file on BDE disk #1 }
      InstallEXE := 'setup.exe';
    end;
    itSQL : begin
      InstallProg := 'Borland SQL Links';
      UniqueFile := 'mnovlwp.pak';               { unique file on SQL disk #1 }
      InstallEXE := 'setup.exe';
    end;
    itRpt : begin
      InstallProg := 'Borland ReportSmith Runtime';
      UniqueFile := 'instxtra.pak';              { unique file on Rpt disk #1 }
      InstallEXE := 'install.exe';
    end;
  end;
  MessageDlg(Format(SNextInst, [InstallProg]), mtInformation, [mbOk], 0);
  if DirectoryForm.ShowForm(Format(SEnterPath, [InstallProg]),
                            SourceDir) = mrOk then begin
    { make sure current disk is the install disk, and keep iterating until }
    { correct disk/path or cancel is pressed }
    while not ((FileExists(AddBackSlash(DirectoryForm.DirEdit.Text) +
               InstallEXE)) and
              (FileExists(AddBackSlash(DirectoryForm.DirEdit.Text) +
               UniqueFile))) do begin
      MessageDlg(Format(SInstNotFound, [InstallProg,
                        DirectoryForm.DirEdit.Text]), mtError, [mbOk], 0);
      if DirectoryForm.ShowForm(Format(SNextInst, [InstallProg]),
                                SourceDir) <> mrOk then break;
    end;
    { when the path is correct, execute the setup }
    if DirectoryForm.ModalResult = mrOk then begin
      NextSetup := AddBackSlash(DirectoryForm.DirEdit.Text) + InstallEXE;
      Enabled := False;                    { disable main window }
      WinExecAndWait(NextSetup, sw_ShowNormal);
      Enabled := True;                     { re-enable the main window }
    end;
  end;
end;

procedure TSetupForm.TargetBtnClick(Sender: TObject);
var
  S: TStringList;
  i: word;
begin
  { get directory from dialog }
  if DirectoryForm.ShowForm('Enter target directory:',
                   IniFile.ReadString('General', 'DefaultDir', '')) = mrOk
➡then begin
    { if it's not there, prompt for permission to create the directory }
    if not DirectoryExists(DirectoryForm.DirEdit.Text) then begin
      if MessageDlg(Format(SDirNotFound, [DirectoryForm.DirEdit.Text]),
                    mtConfirmation, [mbYes, mbNo], 0) = mrYes then begin
```

```
          { make the directory }
          ForceDirectories(StripBackSlash(DirectoryForm.DirEdit.Text));
          { update InstallDir variable }
          InstallDir := AddBackSlash(DirectoryForm.DirEdit.Text);
          { update panel }
          TargetPanel.Caption := 'Target: ' + AddBackSlash(DirectoryForm.
➡DirEdit.Text);
        end;
      end
      else begin
        { if directory exists, then update InstallDir and panel }
        InstallDir := AddBackSlash(DirectoryForm.DirEdit.Text);
        TargetPanel.Caption := 'Target: ' + AddBackSlash(DirectoryForm.
➡DirEdit.Text);
      end;
      { Create subdirectories }
      S := TStringList.Create;
      try
        IniFile.ReadSectionValues('SubDirs', S);
        for i := 0 to S.Count - 1 do
          if not DirectoryExists(InstallDir + S.Values[IntToStr(i)]) then
            ForceDirectories(InstallDir + S.Values[IntToStr(i)]);
      finally
        S.Free;
      end;
    end;
  end;
end;

end.
```

Creating the SETUP Stub

One problem inherent in installation programs that run off a floppy disk is this: It's possible (likely, in fact) that Windows may attempt to look for the code to the executable on disk as the program runs. When you change to another floppy disk, this means that the code to the install program in no longer accessible to Windows when it is required. The result is that Windows does not enable you to change disks.

To circumvent this problem, the best course of action is first to copy the installation program to a TEMP directory on the hard disk, and then to execute the installation from the hard disk. The little program that copies the installation to the hard disk sometimes is referred to as a *stub* program.

Because this installation program supports copying over multiple floppy disks, you will need to implement such a stub. This program is shown in Listing 31.5.

Listing 31.5. The SETUP program.

```
program Setup;
{ This is a stub program designed to copy the "real" install program to }
{ the hard disk, run the install, then terminate itself. }
uses SysUtils, Utils, WinTypes, WinProcs;

const
  SFailSpawn : PChar = 'Fatal Error: Failed to spawn INST.EXE. Error code: %d';
  SFailCopy : PChar  = 'Fatal Error: Failed to copy files to temp directory';

var
  S: String;
  a: array[0..255] of char;
  ErrString: array[0..127] of char;
  WEReturn: word;
begin
  S := GetEnvVar('temp');                            { find temp directory }
  if S = '' then S := 'c:\';                          { use root if none exists }
  S := AddBackSlash(S);
  try
    { copy install program }
    CopyFile(ExtractFilePath(ParamStr(0)) + 'inst.exe', S + 'inst.exe');
    { copy ini file }
    CopyFile(ExtractFilePath(ParamStr(0)) + 'ddgsetup.ini', S + 'ddgsetup.ini');
  except
    on EInOutError do begin                           { if error copying files, }
      MessageBox(0, SFailCopy, 'Error', mb_Ok);       { show message }
      Raise;                                          { reraise exception to exit }
    end;
  end;
  StrPCopy(a, S + 'inst.exe foobar ' + ExtractFilePath(ParamStr(0)));
  WEReturn := WinExec(a, sw_ShowNormal);              { execute install from HD }
  if WEReturn < 32 then                               { show error if exec fails }
    MessageBox(0, StrFmt(ErrString, SFailSpawn, [WEReturn]), 'Error', mb_Ok);
end.
```

The first thing this program does is determine the value of the TEMP environment variable, because that will be the destination for the install program. It does this using the GetEnvVar function from the utils unit. Next, utils' CopyFile() function again is called to copy the install program, INST.EXE, and the INI file to the TEMP directory. Finally, the WinExec() API function is called to invoke the installation.

> **NOTE**
>
> The SETUP stub program does not use any VCL units. Doing this will help ensure that the stub footprint is as small as possible.

Notice the special foobar parameter that is passed to INST.EXE. This parameter is passed as a safeguard to ensure that INST.EXE is executed only via this install program. A check is built in for this parameter in the INST.DPR file shown in Listing 31.6.

Listing 31.6. The source code for INST.DPR.

```
program Inst;

uses
  Forms,
  SysUtils,
  Dialogs,
  Main in 'MAIN.PAS' {SetupForm},
  Utils in 'UTILS.PAS',
  Target in 'TARGET.PAS' {DirectoryForm};

{$R *.RES}

const
  ErrBadParam = 'You must run SETUP.EXE to invoke the installation.';
  ErrNoIni    = 'Failed to find Initialization file';

begin
  if ParamStr(1) <> 'foobar' then
    MessageDlg(ErrBadParam, mtError, [mbOk], 0)
  else if not FileExists(ExtractFilePath(ParamStr(0)) + 'DDGSETUP.INI') then
    MessageDlg(ErrNoIni, mtError, [mbOk], 0)
  else begin
    Application.CreateForm(TSetupForm, SetupForm);
    Application.CreateForm(TDirectoryForm, DirectoryForm);
    Application.Run;
  end;
end.
```

With that, the installation program is complete, and you now have a utility capable of installing almost any basic application.

Looking at Other Ideas

There certainly are many ways to expand the installation program. Some examples are the capability to modify INI files, to modify AUTOEXEC.BAT and CONFIG.SYS, or even to manipulate the IDAPI.CFG file. Another great feature would be the capability to determine the file version by using Version Info resources. This install is intended as a starting point—where you go from here is limited only by your imagination.

Creating the Inventory Manager Install

You may think that you took the long way around the barn in creating an installation utility for the Inventory Manager program. Once again though, after a little foresight and coding up front, you now have an installer that applies to practically anything.

Determining Which Files You Need

The Inventory Manager program comes as a mere two files: SALES.EXE, the executable file, and SALES.GDB, the InterBase database file. Because the application uses CTL3D, you also need to redistribute CTL3DV2.DLL. Because the application uses an InterBase database, you need to deploy the BDE, SQL Links, and Local InterBase Server itself.

Using the INI File

After you know what files you need to install, it's just a matter of plugging the correct values in the installation INI file. Listing 31.7 shows the DDGSETUP.INI file used to install the Inventory Manager program.

Listing 31.7. The source code for DDGSETUP.INI.

```
[General]
Program=Auto Inventory Manager
Version=Version 1.0
Copyright=Copyright (c) 1995 - Steve Teixeira and Xavier Pacheco
NumDisks=4
InstallBDE=1
InstallSQL=1
DefaultDir=c:\sales\
PMGroup=Auto Inventory Manager

[SubDirs]
0=iblocal

[Disk1]
sales.exe=i
sales.gdb=i
ctl3dv2.dll=s
interbas.log=0
interbas.msg=0
isc4.gdb=0
isc_lic.dat=0

[Disk2]
ibmgr.exe=0
blint04.hlp=0
comdiag.hlp=0
comdiag.ini=0
comdiag.exe=0
dsql.dll=0
fileio.dll=0

[Disk3]
gback.dll=0
gds.dll=0
intl.dll=0
iutls.dll=0
remote.dll=0
stack.dll=0
sqlref.hlp=0
```

```
[Disk4]
jrd.dll=0
svrmgr.hlp=0
wisql.exe=0
wisql.hlp=0

[PMGroup]
sales.exe=i
```

NOTE

This installation program presumes that you have license to redistribute the Local InterBase Server and SQL Links. See the DEPLOY.TXT file that comes with Delphi for licensing issues for all redistributable files.

Summary

Now that the INI file is set up, that's all there is to it! Just pair the DDGSETUP.INI file along with the INST and SETUP program that you created in this chapter in order to install the Inventory Manager program. This chapter helped to hone your skills in a few Delphi programming topics such as INI file access, working with DOS paths, and invoking external programs. In Chapter 32 you will begin work on your next application, a Personal Information Manager.

32

Personal Information Manager—Preliminary Design Issues

Because Part III, "Real-World Applications," is the final part of the book, you might expect it to be the most difficult. The truth is, it's probably one of the easiest. The Personal Information Manager (PIM), unlike the other programs described in this book, illustrates the advantages of code reuse. In this chapter and Chapter 33, "Personal Information Manager—User Interface Development," you will use projects from other chapters to create the PIM and expand some of their functionality. You'll learn how to print a calendar from the TDDGCalendar component, for example. You'll also learn how to add a note-taking feature to the PIM. You'll even add a trash can that enables you to throw away notes without actually deleting them. Finally, Chapter 34, "Personal Information Manager—Finishing Touches," teaches you how to add online help to your applications.

A *Personal Information Manager* should be just as the name implies—a tool that enables you to manage your personal affairs. Although it would be nice to give you a full-blown PIM that not only lets you track time but also does your checkbook and makes your dinner, there just isn't enough time or space for such elaborate features. Instead, you'll get a usable tool that you can easily expand with the knowledge you already have about Delphi development.

Before you get started with the PIM, take a look at its feature list.

Examining the PIM Feature List

In general, the PIM will have three parts: a calendar/scheduler, a note taker, and a user-definable program launcher. Other features will be added as specified in this list:

Calendar/scheduler	Enables the user to schedule events. The user also can set an alarm when the calendar/scheduler is activated. The calendar displays to the user indicators that events are scheduled, and an alarm is set for a particular day. Additionally, the user can print a copy of a calendar.
Note taker	Enables the user to enter notes to which a date is attached. The user can add, delete, or modify notes.
Trash can component	Works with the note taker. The user can drag a note to the trash which serves as a temporary storage bin for notes to be deleted.
Program launcher	Enables the user to add SpeedButtons to a form from which other Windows applications can be launched. The speedbutton will extract the icon for the application to which it is linked.
Online help	The PIM will contain online help that explains the functionality of its features. The online help can be invoked from the menu or by pressing F1 from a particular page of the PIM.

As you know, most of the PIM already is written from previous chapters. Of course, this doesn't mean that you don't have to write any code at all. Instead, you'll just add the missing features and enhance the already existing ones. In this chapter, you'll create the user interface. In the next chapter, you'll add functionality to the user interface created here. Finally, in Chapter 34, you'll add the finishing touches—specifically, the help file. Remember, you'll find this project on the CD included with this book. Here, you'll learn how to create the project.

Creating the Main Form

The main form is easy. It's nothing more than a form with a TNotebook and TTabSet component. The TNoteBook and the TTabSet have their Align properties set to AlTop.

Make sure to set Notebook1's Align property to AlTop first. Otherwise, TabSet1 will awkwardly position itself on top of Notebook1.

Activate the Notebook Editor dialog box from NoteBook1's Pages property in the Object Inspector. Then add the strings "Calendar/Scheduler", "Note Taker", and "Launch Pad" which creates three pages of the same names.

In the PIMMainForm's OnCreate event handler, add the following line of code:

```
TabSet1.Tabs := NoteBook1.Pages;
```

This code creates tabs for the tab sets that match the notebook's pages when the form is created. You will not synchronize TabSet1 and Notebook1 yet, because you must add more code to TabSet1's OnChange event handler later.

Creating the Calendar/Scheduler Page

The Calendar/Scheduler page has exactly the same functionality as the DDGCalendar that you created in Chapter 25, "Creating a Calendar/Scheduler and Alarm Application." There two ways to approach this page. You can launch the calendar as a separate program, or you can use a much more intuitive approach and add the Calendar form created in Chapter 26, "Building a Phone Dialer/Terminal Application—Serial Communications," as a child control to the panel on NoteBook1's Calendar/Scheduler page. You'll use the intuitive approach and put to work a technique you learned in Chapter 21, "Hard-Core Windows." First add a TPanel to NoteBook1's Calendar/Scheduler page, as shown in Figure 32.1.

You will need to make some minor changes to the calendar's unit. For the most part, the changes are very simple. First, you need to copy the following files to the directory in which you are creating the PIM:

    CAL.DFM
    CAL.PAS
    CLKPANL.PAS

DAYFORMU.DFM
DAYFORMU.PAS
REMALARM.DFM
REMALRM.PAS
SETALARM.DFM
SETALRM.PAS

FIGURE 32.1.

The Calendar/Scheduler page for the PIM.

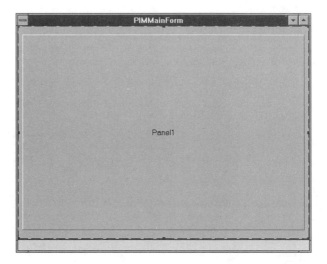

Also, copy the file MPGLOBAL.PAS from Chapter 21's example code directory. Remember, you always can just copy the files from the \SOURCE\ directory.

Now, add the unit MPGLOBAL to CAL.PAS's uses clause:

```
{ Add child form unit }
  MPGlobal;
...
```

Next, change the declaration of `TCalendarForm` from this:

```
TCalendarForm = class(TForm)
```

to this:

```
TCalendarForm = class(TChildForm)
```

`TChildForm` is defined in MPGLOBAL.PAS. (Refer to Chapter 21 to see what `TChildForm` does.)

Now add the following lines of code to `PIMMainForm`'s `OnShow` event handler:

```
CalendarForm := TCalendarForm.Create(Application);
CalendarForm.Parent := Panel1;
CalendarForm.TabOrder := Panel1.TabOrder;
With Panel1 do
```

```
CalendarForm.SetBounds(NoteBook1.Left+Panel1.Left+2, NoteBook1.Top+Top+2,
➥Width-4,Height-4);
CalendarForm.Show;
```

As shown in Chapter 21, this code creates the form and sets its parent to Panel1. It then gives the form Panel1's TabOrder, resizes it to fit within the panel, and displays it. Later, you will add code to TabSet1's OnChange event handler to hide or redisplay the form accordingly.

The last thing you have to do for this page is to ensure that DayForm, RemAlarmForm, and SetAlarmForm are part of the application. If you try to activate these forms by clicking the right mouse button when you run the application now, you will get a general protection fault. To make these forms auto-created, choose View | Project Manager to access the Project Manager dialog box. From that, you can add DAYFORMU.PAS, REMALRM.PAS, and SETALRM.PAS, which add the forms to your projects and make them auto-create forms.

Now add the following to TabSet1's OnChange event handler:

```
if Assigned(CalendarForm) then
  if NewTab = 0 then
     CalendarForm.Show
  else
    CalendarForm.Hide;
NoteBook1.PageIndex := NewTab;
```

This code displays the calendar when the page selected is page 0. Otherwise, the calendar is hidden.

At this point, this is all you have to do to set up the Calendar/Scheduler page. You can run the application, and the Calendar/Scheduler page will function just as the DDGCalendar form in Chapter 25. Figure 32.2 shows what the form looks like while running as a child to the Panel component.

FIGURE 32.2.

The Calendar form as a child component.

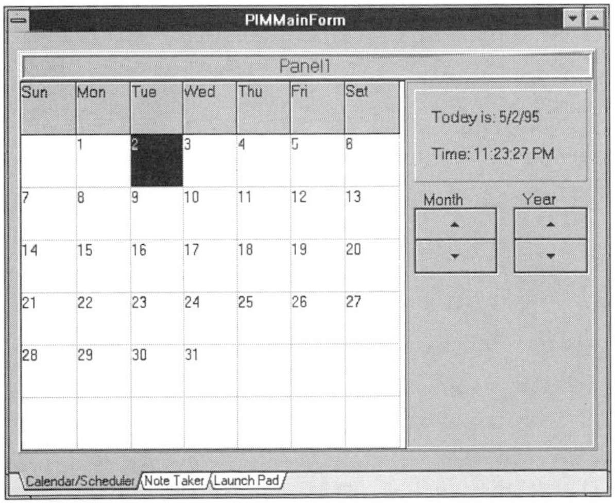

Creating the Note Taker Page

The Note Taker page is shown in Figure 32.3. This page has three TButtons, and two TBitBtn's of the types bkOK and bkCancel. The TBitBtns' Visible property is initially set to false in the Object Inspector. The page also has a THeader, TListBox, TMemo, and TEdit control. Figure 32.3 shows a picture of a trash can. This is just a TImage picture containing the TRASH.BMP bitmap file that is in the SOURCE directory on the accompanying CD. Also, add the strings "Date" and "Title" to the THeader component as shown in the figure.

FIGURE 32.3.

The Note Taker page.

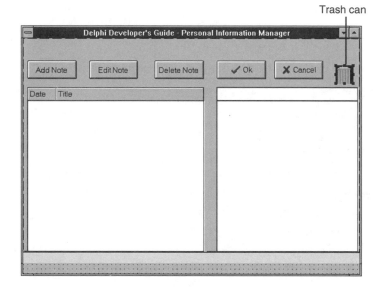

You can load this bitmap by invoking the Picture Editor dialog box from the Picture property in the Object Inspector. Also, set the TImage's Stretch property to true.

Because you are just creating the user interface, you will not add the full functionality to the Note Taker page yet. You are just adding the components for now. Later, in Chapter 33, we'll attach event handlers to these components.

Creating the Launch Pad Page

The launch pad, shown in Figure 32.4, is nothing more than a TScrollBox and a TButton on the Launch Pad page. On this page, you will dynamically create the TRunButton component that you learned about in Chapter 11, "Writing Delphi Custom Components." You will en-hance the TRunButton a bit to extract the icon from the application that is set up to launch. If an application does not contain an icon, you will just set it to the PIM's application icon as a default. Also, add a TOpenDialog component and a TButton component to the form as shown in Figure 32.4.

FIGURE 32.4.
The Launch Pad page.

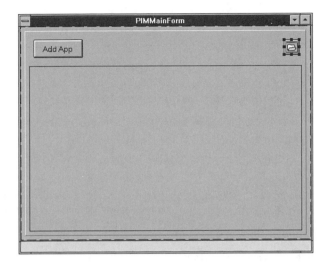

Defining a *TRunButton*

Listing 32.1 shows the source code for the TRunButton component with the added enhancements for this chapter.

Listing 32.1. The source code for RUNBUTN.PAS.

```pascal
unit Runbutn;

interface

uses
  SysUtils, WinTypes, WinProcs, Messages, Classes, Graphics, Controls,
  Forms, Dialogs, Buttons, extctrls;

type
  ERunError = class(Exception);

  TRunImage = class(TImage)
    procedure cmHitTest(var Msg: TCMHitTest);
            message cm_HitTest;
  end;

  TRunButton = class(TSpeedButton)
  private
    FCommandLine: String;
    FIconImage: TRunImage;
  public
    procedure Click; override;
    procedure GetIcon;
    constructor Create(AOwner: TComponent);
  published
    property CommandLine: String read FCommandLine write FCommandLine;
    property IconImage: TRunImage read FIconImage;
  end;
```

continues

Listing 32.1. continued

```
procedure Register;

implementation
uses ShellAPI;

procedure TRunImage.cmHitTest(var Msg: TCMHitTest);
begin
  Msg.Result := 0; { Force mouse down even to go to control under the TRunImage }
end;

constructor TRunButton.Create(AOwner: TComponent);
begin
  inherited Create(AOwner);
  FIconImage := TRunImage.Create(self);  { Create the TImage Component }
  width := 32;                { Added to increase the icon size }
  Height := 32;              { Added to increase the icon size }
end;

procedure TRunButton.GetIcon;
var
  IC: HIcon;
  pCommandLine: array[0..255] of char;
begin
  with FIconImage do begin
    Parent := self.parent;                 { same as the TRunButton's }
    if FCommandLine = '' then
      exit;
    StrPCopy(pCommandLine, FCommandLine); { You may pass in a different number }
    IC := ExtractIcon(hInstance, pCommandLine, 0);
    if IC <= 1 then
      Picture.Icon.Assign(Application.Icon) { Assign the application icon by
➨default }
    else
      Picture.Icon.Handle := IC;
    Left := self.Left;       { superImpose TRunImage over TRunButton }
    Top := self.Top;
    Visible := true;
  end;
end;

procedure TRunButton.Click;
var
  WERetVal: word;
begin
  { do the default behavior }
  inherited Click;
  { if string is at maximum, then reduce size by one.  This shouldn't hurt }
  { anything, since 255 is larger than the maximum DOS command line.  This }
  { is mainly a safety precaution. }
  if FCommandLine[0] = #255 then
    FCommandLine[0] := #254;
  { Add a null terminater to the end of the string so we can emulate a PChar }
  FCommandLine[Ord(FCommandLine[0]) + 1] := #0;
  { Call the WinExec() API function. Passing the address of element 1 makes }
```

```
{ this string look like a PChar }
WERetVal := WinExec(@FCommandLine[1], sw_ShowNormal);
{ a return value of less than 32 indicates error.  Raise exception on error }
if WERetVal < 32 then
  raise ERunError.Create('Error executing program.  Code: ' +
                        IntToStr(WERetVal));  inherited Click;
end;

procedure Register;
begin
  RegisterComponents('DDG', [TRunButton]);
end;

end.
```

Now what wasn't explained in Chapter 11 will be explained here. First, a descendant to TImage is created called TRunImage. TRunImage holds a Windows application's icon. You cannot put an icon in a SpeedButton without jumping through hoops, so you use the TRunImage to display the icon by superimposing the TRunImage over the TRunButton. To enable the mouse clicks to pass through the TRunImage to the component it covers, the TRunButton, you create a message handler for the cm_HitTest message. The cm_HitTest response method normally determines whether a mouse click fell on top of a component. If true, the value 1 is assigned to Msg.Result. Otherwise, Msg.Result gets 0 as a value. In your response method, you pass 0 to Msg.Result, forcing the mouse click to travel to the component underneath the TRunButton. Therefore, the TRunButton can respond to the Click event.

In the TRunButton's Create() method, it first creates a TRunImage instance and then sizes itself to 32×32 pixels, the standard size for an application's icon.

In the TRunButton's Click() method you'll see the lines:

```
IC := ExtractIcon(hInstance, pCommandLine, 0);
 if IC <= 1 then
   Picture.Icon.Assign(Application.Icon) { Assign the application icon by default }
 else
   Picture.Icon.Handle := IC;
```

These lines extract an icon from the executable file that the TRunButton is intended to launch. The ExtractIcon() method is a Windows API function that retrieves a Windows executable file's icon handle. The if statement then tests to see if a valid icon was retrieved. A value less then or equal to one means that an icon was not retrieved, in which case the PIM's icon is attached to the TRunButton. Otherwise the executables file's icon is attached by assigning the icon handle to FIconImage.Picture.Icon.

The TOpenDialog contains the filter EXE File | *.EXE, which you must add from the Object Inspector. Also, the TScrollBox component has its ShowHint property set to true.

The button's OnClick event handler does the following:

```
if OpenDialog1.Execute then
    if Uppercase(ExtractFileExt(OpenDialog1.FileName)) = '.EXE' then
      with TRunButton.Create(ScrollBox1) do begin
        CommandLine := OpenDialog1.FileName;
        Parent := ScrollBox1;
        GetIcon;
        Visible := true;
        Hint := ExtractFileName(OpenDialog1.FileName);
      end;
```

Here, you first execute the TOpenDialog. If an executable file was selected, you create a TRunButton, set its CommandLine property to OpenDialog.FileName, and set its parent to the TScrollBox. You call the GetIcon() procedure, which creates the TRunImage component. You then set the hint to the FileName. When you have this compiled, run that application and select a file to add to the launch pad. Then select it and watch it go. Don't try this more than once in one running, however; you haven't added logic to deal with more than one TRunButton on the launch pad (you do that in the next chapter).

Finally, add a TMainMenu to the form and to it, add only one item "E&xit" whose event handler calls the form's Close() method. Listings 32.2 and 32.3 show the source code so far for PIM.DPR, the project file, and PIMU.PAS, the main forms unit. You'll add much more to this code in the following chapter.

Listing 32.2. The source code for PIM.DPR.

```
program Pim;

uses
  Forms,
  Pimu in 'PIMU.PAS' {PIMMainForm},
  Dayformu in 'DAYFORMU.PAS' {DayForm},
  Remalrm in 'REMALRM.PAS' {RemAlarmForm},
  Setalrm in 'SETALRM.PAS' {SetAlarmForm};

{$R *.RES}

begin
  Application.CreateForm(TPIMMainForm, PIMMainForm);
  Application.CreateForm(TRemAlarmForm, RemAlarmForm);
  Application.CreateForm(TSetAlarmForm, SetAlarmForm);
  Application.Run;
end.
```

Listing 32.3. The source code for PIMU.PAS.

```
unit Pimu;

interface
```

```
uses
  SysUtils, WinTypes, WinProcs, Messages, Classes, Graphics, Controls,
  Forms, Dialogs, StdCtrls, Menus, ExtCtrls, TabNotBk, Buttons, Grids,
  Calendar, cal, Tabs, Notes;
type
  TPIMMainForm = class(TForm)
    Notebook1: TNotebook;
    AddBtn: TButton;
    EditBtn: TButton;
    DeleteBtn: TButton;
    OkBtn: TBitBtn;
    CancelBtn: TBitBtn;
    Memo1: TMemo;
    ListBox1: TListBox;
    Panel1: TPanel;
    TabSet1: TTabSet;
    Panel2: TPanel;
    ScrollBox1: TScrollBox;
    Image2: TImage;
    Edit1: TEdit;
    Button1: TButton;
    Header1: THeader;
    OpenDialog1: TOpenDialog;
    procedure FormCreate(Sender: TObject);
    procedure FormShow(Sender: TObject);
    procedure TabSet1Change(Sender: TObject; NewTab: Integer;
      var AllowChange: Boolean);
    { Launch Pad Methods }
    procedure Button1Click(Sender: TObject);
    procedure Exit1Click(Sender: TObject);
  private
    { Private declarations }
  public
    { Public declarations }
  end;

var
  PIMMainForm: TPIMMainForm;

implementation
uses runbutn;
{$R *.DFM}

procedure TPIMMainForm.FormCreate(Sender: TObject);
begin
  TabSet1.Tabs := NoteBook1.Pages;    { Add TabSet Pages to correspond to the  }
                                      { Notebook's Pages. }
end;

{ Methods for the Calendar/Schedular Page }
procedure TPIMMainForm.FormShow(Sender: TObject);
var
  i: integer;
begin
  CalendarForm := TCalendarForm.Create(Application);  { Create a CalendarForm }
  CalendarForm.Parent := Panel1;                      { Set CalendarForm's
➥parent }
```

continues

Listing 32.3. continued

```
  CalendarForm.TabOrder := Panel1.TabOrder;          { To Panel1. Then set its }
  With Panel1 do                                     { TabOrder to Panel1's
➥TabOrder }
    CalendarForm.SetBounds(NoteBook1.Left+Panel1.Left+2, { Adjust CalendarForm's
➥sizes }
      NoteBook1.Top+Top+2,Width-4,Height-4);         { to fit within the
➥Notebook }
  CalendarForm.Show;     { Display CalendarForm }
end;

procedure TPIMMainForm.Exit1Click(Sender: TObject);
begin
  Close;  { Close the main form }
end;

procedure TPIMMainForm.TabSet1Change(Sender: TObject; NewTab: Integer;
  var AllowChange: Boolean);
begin
  if Assigned(CalendarForm) then   { Display the CalendarForm when the Calendar/ }
    if NewTab = 0 then             { Scheduler page is selected. otherwise hide it }
        CalendarForm.Show
    else
      CalendarForm.Hide;
  NoteBook1.PageIndex := NewTab;   { Syncronize the NoteBook to the TabSet }
end;

{ Methods for the Launch Pad Page }
procedure TPIMMainForm.Button1Click(Sender: TObject);
begin
  { Execute the OpenDialog }
  if OpenDialog1.Execute then
    { check if this is an executable file }
    if Uppercase(ExtractFileExt(OpenDialog1.FileName)) = '.EXE' then
      with TRunButton.Create(ScrollBox1) do begin  { Create a TRunButton }
      { Set the TRunButton.CommandLine to the Filename in OpenDialog }
        CommandLine := OpenDialog1.FileName;
        Parent := ScrollBox1; { Set parent to the scrollBox }
        GetIcon;               { Get the icon for the application }
        Hint := ExtractFileName(OpenDialog1.FileName); { Add a hint for the button }
        Visible := true;       { Make the TRunButton visible }
      end;
end;

end.
```

Summary

You now are ready to start writing the code that will add full functionality to your PIM. This chapter showed you how you might approach creating something that will become much larger as you go along in your development process. However, you can see that by reusing existing code, you have come quite a way. You already have a fully functional Calendar Scheduler program as one part of this overall application. In the next chapter, you will see how to perform tasks like file-streaming and more on printing!

33

Personal Information Manager—User Interface Development

In the last chapter, you set up a prototype for a Personal Information Manager (PIM) application. In this chapter, you will add the functionality to the PIM based on the feature list from the last chapter. The work to do here is simplified because the user interface (UI) is, for the most part, already created. This approach is typical: Create the UI before adding any real functionality, and then add the guts. After you have the insides working correctly with the user interface, you can add the bells and whistles. Here, you will add one enhancement to the Calendar Scheduler page by enabling it to print a calendar for a given month. Then, you will make the Note Taker complete by providing a means to create, save, and remove notes. You'll use Delphi's TFileStream for this purpose. Finally, you'll set up the Launch Pad to work as it is intended—to add applications to its page from which they can be launched.

Printing a Calendar

By now, printing shouldn't be too complicated. You pretty much know what needs to be done to get your output to the printer.

A calendar monthly printout is nothing more than a rectangle with horizontal and vertical lines drawn inside it. Of, course, you probably should put the month's name and day titles in the appropriate columns and the day numbers inside the boxes created by the lines. Figure 33.1 shows what the calendar printout will look like.

FIGURE 33.1.

Calendar printout.

May 1995

Sunday	Monday	Tuesday	Wednesday	Thursday	Friday	Saturday
	1	2	3	4	5	6
7	8	9	10	11	12	13
14	15	16	17	18	19	20
21	22	23	24	25	26	27
28	29	30	31			

To lessen the modification that has to be made to the CAL.PAS unit, the printing functionality is provided in a separate unit, PRNTCAL.PAS, shown in Listing 33.1.

Listing 33.1. The source code for PRNTCAL.PAS.

```pascal
unit Prntcal;

interface
uses Printers, wintypes, winprocs, classes, sysutils, Dialogs;

const
  UIn = 100; { In the MM_LOENGLISH mapping mode each unit is 1/100th of an }
             { inch. Therefore this multiplier is required for calculations }
  Days: array[1..7] of string[10] = ('Sunday', 'Monday', 'Tuesday', 'Wednesday',
    'Thursday', 'Friday', 'Saturday');
  Months: array[1..12] of string[10] = ('January', 'February', 'March', 'April',
    'May', 'June', 'July', 'August', 'September', 'October', 'November',
    'December');

procedure PrintCalendar;

implementation
uses Cal;

procedure RotatePrintFont;
var
  LogFont: TLogFont;
begin
  with Printer.Canvas do begin
    with LogFont do begin
      lfHeight := Font.Height;                   { Set to Printer.Canvas.font.height }
      lfWidth := 0;                              { let font mapper choose width}
      lfEscapement := 900;                       { tenths of degrees so 900 = 90
degrees }
      lfOrientation := 0;                        { ignored by Windows }
      lfWeight := FW_NORMAL;                     { default }
      lfItalic := 0;                             { no italics }
      lfUnderline := 0;                          { no underline }
      lfStrikeOut := 0;                          { no strikeout }.
      lfCharSet := ANSI_CHARSET;                 { default }
      StrPCopy(lfFaceName, 'Helvetica');         { Printer.Canvas's font's name }
      lfQuality := PROOF_QUALITY;                { Windows gets a better one if avail}
      lfOutPrecision := OUT_TT_ONLY_PRECIS;      { force True type fonts }
      lfClipPrecision := CLIP_DEFAULT_PRECIS;    { default }
      lfPitchAndFamily := Variable_Pitch;        { default }
    end;
  end;
  Printer.Canvas.Font.Handle := CreateFontIndirect(LogFont);
end;

procedure PrintCalendar;
var
  R: TRect;
  i: integer;
  LinePos: double;
  DayStr: string;
  PixInInchX, PixInInchY: integer;
  TwnthOfInchX, TwnthOfInchY: integer;
  StrHeight: integer;
  Col, Row: integer;
  ColPos, RowPos: integer;
```

continues

Listing 33.1. continued

```
begin

  R := Rect(1*UIn, 1*UIn, round(6.5*UIn), 8*UIn);      { Calculate the Rect points }
  with Printer do begin
    BeginDoc;                                          { Start the print job }
    SetMapMode(Printer.Canvas.Handle, MM_LOENGLISH);   { Change the mapping mode }
                                                       { to MM_LOENGLISH }
    { Draw a rectangle to the printer }
    Canvas.Rectangle(R.Left, -R.Top, R.Right, -R.Bottom);
    for i := 1 to 5 do begin                           { Draw horizontal and vertical }
      LinePos := 0.5 + i;                              { lines to create the matrix to }
      Canvas.MoveTo(Round(LinePos*UIn), -1*UIn);       { represent a month }
      Canvas.LineTo(Round(LinePos*UIn), -8*UIn);
    end;
    for i := 2 to 7 do
    begin
      Canvas.MoveTo(1*UIn, -i*UIn);
      Canvas.LineTo(round(6.5*UIn), -i*UIn);
    end;

    SetMapMode(Canvas.Handle, MM_TEXT);  { Set the mapping mode back to MM_TEXT }
    RotatePrintFont;                     { Rotate the font 90 degrees }
    { Calculate the Pixels per inch along the horizontal and vertical axis }
    { For the printer's canvas }
    PixInInchX := GetDeviceCaps(Printer.Canvas.Handle, LOGPIXELSX);
    PixInInchY := GetDeviceCaps(Printer.Canvas.Handle, LOGPIXELSY);
    TwnthOfInchX := PixInInchX div 20;   { Calculate 1/20th of a inch along }
    TwnthOfInchY := PixInInchY div 20;   { the X and Y axis }

    { Draw the day titles in their appropriate block }
    for i := 1 to 7 do begin
      StrHeight := Canvas.TextHeight(Days[i]);
      Canvas.TextOut(round(1.5*PixInInchX)-(StrHeight+TwnthOfInchX),
            ((9-i)*PixInInchY)-TwnthOfInchY, Days[i]);
    end;

    { Now draw the day numbers where the block in which they belong }
    for Row := 1 to 5 do begin
      ColPos := Round((Row+0.5)*PixInInchX)+TwnthOfInchX;
      for Col := 0 to 6 do
        Canvas.TextOut(ColPos, ((8-Col)*PixInInchY)-TwnthOfInchY,
          CalendarForm.DDGCalendar1.CellText[Col, Row]);
    end;

    { Draw the month/year string on the upper left side of the calendar }
    StrHeight := Canvas.TextHeight(Months[CalendarForm.DDGCalendar1.Month]);
    Canvas.TextOut(1*PixInInchX-StrHeight, 8*PixInInchY,
      Months[CalendarForm.DDGCalendar1.Month]+
      ' '+IntToStr(CalendarForm.DDGCalendar1.Year));

    EndDoc;    { Finish the print job }
  end;
end;

end.
```

This unit provides the function `PrintCalendar()`, which performs the printing operations. The month printed is the month the Calendar Scheduler page is displaying.

The first thing you do is set the constants that you need. The constant `UIn` stands for *Units In Inches*. You will change the mapping mode to `MM_LOENGLISH` to perform the drawing routines and therefore require a multiplier of 100, because in this mapping mode, each unit represents only 1/100 inch. See Chapter 10, "GDI and Graphics Programming," for information on mapping modes if you need to review this topic. Then you declare array constants to hold your day and month strings.

Be sure to include the CAL.PAS unit in the `uses` statement to access the `DDGCalendar` component from this unit.

The procedure `RotatePrintFont()` is the same procedure used in Chapter 12, "Printing in Delphi," for printing an envelope. It is used here because you will be printing the calendar vertically on the printed page.

TIP

You can also print vertically by setting the Printer's `Landscape` property to `poPortrait`. Look up `TPrinter` in Delphi's online help for further information.

Finally, `PrintCalendar()` is where all the printing is performed. There really isn't much code here. First, you calculate a rectangle's position to create a 6½×8-inch rectangle. Notice that you multiply these values by the multiplier `UIn`:

```
R := Rect(1*UIn, 1*UIn, round(6.5*UIn), 8*UIn);     { Calculate the Rect points }
```

Immediately after calling the `BeginDoc()` method, you change the mapping mode to `MM_LOENGLISH` by calling `SetMapMode()`. You then perform the code to draw the rectangle and the horizontal and vertical lines to create a matrix of boxes to represent a month's days. Recall that in the `MM_LOENGLISH` mapping mode, the orientation is such that as values along the Y-axis increase, the position moves upward. With the origin at (0,0), this would draw any lines or shapes above the printed page unless you negate the value, as was done in the following line:

```
Canvas.LineTo(Round(LinePos*UIn), -8*UIn);
```

By negating the Y value, the line is drawn downward—inside the printed area.

After the matrix is drawn, the mapping mode is set back to `MM_TEXT` because only text is being drawn at this point. Then the printer canvas's font is rotated 90 degrees because you are printing vertically. The following lines set up two variables to specify the number of pixels per inch along the horizontal and vertical axis:

```
PixInInchX := GetDeviceCaps(Printer.Canvas.Handle,  LOGPIXELSX);
PixInInchY := GetDeviceCaps(Printer.Canvas.Handle,  LOGPIXELSY);
```

The following lines set up the two other variables for positioning the text as it is drawn:

```
TwnthOfInchX := PixInInchX div 20;   { Calculate 1/20th of a inch along }
TwnthOfInchY := PixInInchY div 20;   { the X and Y axis }
```

These values are used to move the text strings away from the block lines so that the text doesn't clip what already has been drawn. After the day titles and day numbers are drawn, you print the month name and year, and finish the print job by calling `Printer`'s `EndDoc()` method.

That is it in a nutshell—simple, but effective.

Now all you have to do is make the `DDGCalendar` aware of the `PrintCalendar()` function, which you do by adding PRNTCAL.PAS to CAL.PAS's `uses` statement. Additionally, add another menu option to `CalendarForm`'s popup menu, Print Calendar, to call `PrintCalendar()`. You might have to choose File | Open File to open the file CAL.PAS, which will bring up the form and enable you to add the new item to the calendar.

That completes adding functionality to the Calendar Scheduler page of your PIM. Now, onward to your Note Taker.

Adding the Note Taker Functionality with *TFileStream*

In this section, you will add the complete functionality for the Note Taker page of your PIM. Really, all that's required is the capability to create, destroy, load, and save the notes that the user enters. This is a great opportunity to introduce the `TFileStream` object to you. By using the `TFileStream` object, you can see how to make the object that you create streamable, so that it knows how to store itself.

Going Gently Down the Stream

Streams provide a means for reading and writing information to and from a sequential and linear storage medium. Like their real-life counterparts, streams have a concept of a beginning and an end. Streams also have a concept of your current position within the stream. A stream's storage medium can be a disk file, RAM, or some other device such as a serial port. The goal is that all streams work similarly, and the storage medium is as transparent as possible to the user of the stream. Streams are represented easily by some object-oriented abstraction; in Delphi, this abstraction is called the `TStream` class.

`TStream` is an abstract class that lays down the basic rules for how streams work in Delphi. Three more specific stream types are derived from `TStream`: `THandleStream`, `TFileStream`, and `TMemoryStream`. An additional `TBlobStream` class also is provided for use with VCL's database framework.

TStream

TStream is the base class from which TMemoryStream and THandleStream descend. TFileStream is a descendant of THandleStream. Because TStream is an abstract class, you wouldn't instantiate a TStream object; instead, you would use one of its existing descendants or create another descendant.

TStream's Size and Position properties specify the size of the stream and the position to or from which the stream will be written or read.

TStream provides two methods to read or write data from or to a given buffer: ReadBuffer() and WriteBuffer(). When used, the TStream's Position property is advanced by the number of bytes read or written. It's important to note that both ReadBuffer() and WriteBuffer() call TStream's abstract methods Read() and Write(). Therefore, TStream itself serves no purpose other than being the base class for its descendants. A CopyFrom() method enables the stream to read data from another stream. You will find additional information on TStream in the Component Writer's Guide online help file (CWG.HLP) which you'll find in the \DELPHI\BIN directory.

THandleStream

THandleStream enables objects to store and retrieve information from a medium requiring some type of handle—a file-handle, for example. In fact, TFileStream descends from THandleStream for this reason. The storage medium's handle is kept in THandleStream's Handle property. THandleStream overrides TStream's abstract methods Read(), Write(), and Seek(). Read() and Write() enable you to read or write information to or from the stream using a given buffer. Seek() enables you to go to a specific position in the stream.

TFileStream

TFileStream, as the name implies, enables you to store object information in a disk file. TFileStream overrides THandleStream's Create() constructor and its Destroy() destructor. You pass a filename to the Create() constructor and the TFileStream handles any continuing I/O. You use the TFileStream's Read(), Write(), and Seek() methods to retrieve from, write to, or position the stream.

TMemoryStream

TMemoryStream can be used much like TFileStream, except that instead of a Handle property, it has a Memory property that is a pointer to memory. Additionally, TMemoryStream has the methods LoadFromStream(), which enables it to copy data from another stream; and SaveToStream(), which enables it to copy its contents to another stream. There is also a LoadFromFile() and SaveToFile() method for retrieving and saving data from and to a disk file. The SetSize() method enables you to change the size of the TMemoryStream's memory pool.

Using Streams

Classes derived from the TPersistent class typically have their own LoadFromStream() and SaveToStream() methods. These methods take a TStream descendant as a parameter and use its methods to save their data to the stream. You can create objects that have similar methods that save and retrieve their data. For example, a typical SaveToStream definition might look like this:

```
procedure TMyObject.SaveToStream(Stream: TStream);
begin
  Stream.Write(FSomeInteger, SizeOf(Integer)); { Writes an integer }
  Stream.Write(FSomeString, length(FTitle)+1); { Writes a string   }
end;
```

Because the Write() method is virtual, the appropriate stream descendant's method will be called. Therefore, if a TMemory stream was passed to the SaveToStream method, that data will go to a memory block. Likewise, if a TFileStream was passed, the data will go to the file. The reverse of the preceding example follows:

```
procedure TNote.LoadFromStream(Stream: TStream);
begin
  Stream.Read(FSomeInteger, SizeOfInteger));          { Read an integer }
  Stream.Read(FSomeString[0], 1);                     { Read a string's length
➥byte }
  Stream.Read(FSomeString[1], Ord(FSomeString[0]));   { Now read the string based
➥on the length read }
end;
```

Typically, you would use one of the existing TStream descendants unless you needed to create a special type of stream or if you needed to stream a nonobject such as a record. In this case, a record does not know how to store itself, and therefore the stream must handle this. See the sidebar "Streaming Records" later in the chapter.

Creating the Note Taker Classes

In order for the note taker to manage notes, it must store note information in a structure that can be read from and saved to a file. Additionally, it must be able to transfer this data from the list of notes onto the trash can, using the drag-drop features. Given this, it makes sense to wrap this data in a class that can be dragged and a class that also is streamable. The note taker also needs to be able to maintain these notes in a list of notes. Listing 33.2 shows the NOTES.PAS unit, which defines the classes TNote and TNoteList.

Listing 33.2. The source code for NOTES.PAS.

```
unit Notes;

interface
uses
  SysUtils, WinTypes, WinProcs, Messages, Classes, Graphics, Controls,
  Forms, Dialogs, StdCtrls;
```

```
const
  NoteFileName = 'NOTES.STM';
  TrashFileName = 'TRASH.STM'; { Added the Trash file name }
type

  { TNote is the class that maintains an individual note, it contains }
  { a title, TimeDate stamp and the note text - a TStringList from a }
  { TMemo or some other TStringList container. This object has the }
  { capablity to read itself from a TFileStream }
  TNote = class
  private
    FTitle: string;              { A Note title }
    FNoteText: TStringList;      { This received from a TMemo }
    FDateTime: TDateTime;        { This stores the Date and Time of the Note }
    procedure SetNoteText(ANoteText: TStringList);
    procedure SaveToStream(Stream: TStream);
    procedure LoadFromStream(Stream: TStream);
  public
    constructor Create;
    destructor Destroy; override;
    procedure CopyNote(SrcNote: TNote);
    property Title: string read FTitle write FTitle;
    property NoteText: TStringList read FNoteText write SetNoteText;
    property DateTime: TDateTime read FDateTime write FDateTime;
  end;

  { TNoteList is a class that maintains a list of TNotes. It has its own
    SaveToStream() and LoadFromStream() INTERNAL methods. These are invoked by
    Calling SaveToFile or LoadFromFile() therefore the streaming is hidden }
  TNoteList = class(TList)
  private
    procedure SaveToStream(Stream: TStream);
    procedure LoadFromStream(Stream: TStream);
  public
    destructor Destroy; override;
    procedure LoadFromFile(const FileName: string);
    procedure SaveToFile(const FileName: string);
    function AddNote(ANote: TNote): integer;
    procedure RemoveNote(Index: integer);
    function GetNote(Index: integer): TNote;
  end;

implementation
{ TNote }

constructor TNote.Create;
begin
  inherited Create;              { Call inherited create method }
  FDateTime := now;              { Set the notes date/time stamp to now }
  FNoteText := TStringList.Create;  { Initializes the TString List }
end;

destructor TNote.Destroy;
begin
  FNoteText.Free;                { Frees the TStringList }
  inherited Destroy;
end;
```

continues

Listing 33.2. continued

```pascal
procedure TNote.SetNoteText(ANoteText: TStringList);
begin
  FNoteText.Assign(ANoteText);
end;

procedure TNote.CopyNote(SrcNote: TNote);
begin
  FTitle := SrcNote.Title;        { Copy the Title }
  SetNoteText(SrcNote.NoteText); { Copy the NoteText }
  FDateTime := SrcNote.DateTime; { Copy the DateTime stamp }
end;

procedure TNote.SaveToStream(Stream: TStream);
var
  NumLines, i: integer;
  Line: string;
begin
  with Stream do begin
    Write(FTitle, length(FTitle)+1); { Write the title (string) }
    Write(FDateTime, sizeof(TDateTime)); { Write the date and the time }
    { Now write the TStringList contents but first write the number of strings }
    NumLines := FNoteText.Count;        { Get the number of lines }
    Write(NumLines, sizeof(Integer));   { Write the number of lines to the stream }
    for i := 0 to NumLines - 1 do begin { Write each line separately }
      Line := FNoteText[i];             { Get the line }
      Write(Line, length(Line) + 1);    { Write the line to the stream }
    end;
  end;
end;

procedure TNote.LoadFromStream(Stream: TStream);
var
  NumLines, i: integer;
  Line: string;
begin
  with Stream do begin
    Read(FTitle[0], 1);                 { First read the string length }
    Read(FTitle[1], Ord(FTitle[0]));    { Now read the string based on the length
➡read }
    Read(FDateTime, SizeOf(TDateTime)); { Read the Date and Time for the note }
    Read(NumLines, SizeOf(Integer));    { Read how many lines are in the stream }
    for i := 0 to NumLines - 1 do begin { Read NumLines lines }
      Read(Line[0], 1);                 { Read the string length }
      Read(Line[1], Ord(Line[0]));      { Read the string based on string length }
      FNoteText.Add(Line);              { Add the string to the FNoteText
➡StringList }
    end;
  end;
end;

{ TNoteList }

destructor TNoteList.Destroy;
var
  i: integer;
```

```
begin
  for i := 0 to Count - 1 do   { Destroy each TNote in the list }
    TNote(Items[i]).Free;      { By calling its Free() method }
  inherited Destroy;           { Call in inherited destroy }
end;

procedure TNoteList.SaveToStream(Stream: TStream);
var
  NumNotes, i: integer;
begin
  NumNotes := Count;                      { Store Note count in an integer
➥variable }
  Stream.Write(NumNotes, sizeof(Integer)); { Write the count to the stream }
  for i := 0 to Count - 1 do               { Make each TNote in the TNoteList
➥write }
    TNote(Items[i]).SaveToStream(Stream);  { itself to the stream }
end;

procedure TNoteList.LoadFromStream(Stream: TStream);
var
  NoteCount, i: integer;
  ANote: TNote;
begin
  { This must be called so that the TNote object instance can free itself and  }
  { its data members from memory, otherwise, the TNote's TStringList wouldn't }
  { get freed  and a memory loss would occur, the reason for this is that }
  { TNoteList.Destroy is not virtual. If it were, we would have taken care of }
  { this there. }
  for i := 0 to Count - 1 do
    TNote(Items[i]).Free;

  Clear;                                    { Free Notes already in list }
  Stream.Read(NoteCount, sizeof(Integer)); { Read the number of notes in the }
  for i := 0 to NoteCount - 1 do           { stream }
  begin
    ANote := TNote.Create;                 { Instantiate a note }
    ANote.LoadFromStream(Stream);          { Have the note read its contents }
    Add(ANote);                            { From the stream and add it to the }
  end;                                     { list }
end;

procedure TNoteList.LoadFromFile(const FileName: string);
var
  Stream: TFileStream;
begin
  { Instantiate a TStream }
  Stream := TFileStream.Create(FileName, fmOpenRead);
  try
    LoadFromStream(Stream);        { Load the list of TNotes }
  finally
    Stream.Free;                   { Free the TFileStream }
  end;
end;

procedure TNoteList.SaveToFile(const FileName: string);
var
  Stream: TFileStream;
```

continues

Listing 33.2. continued

```
begin
  { Instantiate a TNote stream but create the new file }
  Stream := TFileStream.Create(FileName, fmCreate);
  try
    SaveToStream(Stream);        { Save the notes to the stream }
  finally
    Stream.Free;                 { Free the stream }
  end;
end;

function TNoteList.AddNote(ANote: TNote): integer;
var
  Note: TNote;
begin
  Note := TNote.Create;            { Instantiate a TNote class }
  Note.CopyNote(ANote);            { Copy A note to the new note }
  Result := Add(Note);             { Return the position of the note added }
end;

procedure TNoteList.RemoveNote(Index: integer);
begin
  TNote(Items[Index]).Free; { First Free the object Instance }
  Delete(Index);            { Then set the pointer to nil }
end;

function TNoteList.GetNote(Index: integer): TNote;
begin
  Result := Items[Index];    { Return the note specified by index }
end;

end.
```

The TNote's class has three storage variables: FTitle, FNoteText, and FDateTime. TNote contains three private methods: SetNoteText(), SaveToStream(), and LoadFromStream(). It has the public method CopyNote() and overrides the Create() constructor and Destroy() destructor. SetNoteText() is the accessor method for the FNoteText variable. SaveToStream() and LoadFromStream() are where the TNote object saves itself to a stream.

TNote's Create() constructor initializes the FDateTime variable with the current date and instantiates the FNoteText TStringList variable. TNote's Destroy() destructor frees FNoteText. SetNoteText() copies the TStringList that it was passed to the FNoteText TStringList.

SaveToStream() and LoadFromStream() both take a TStream object as a parameter. The SaveToStream() method calls the stream's Write() method to store each of its variables to the stream. Notice that SaveToStream() writes the number of lines in FNoteText before writing the lines. This is necessary because each TNote written to the stream can contain a different number of lines. Doing this enables the TNote to read back only the number of lines that it had written, as shown in the TNote's ReadFromStream() method.

`TNote.LoadFromStream()` first reads the first byte of the `FTitle` variable. Recall that the first byte of a string is the length byte that determines the length of the string. `LoadFromStream` uses that value to read only the amount of bytes necessary to retrieve the rest of the string. After reading `FDateTime`, it reads the number of lines that were written in the `SaveToStream()` method, telling it how many lines to read into `TNoteText`. Each line then is read using the same technique used to read `FTitle` and added to `FNoteText`.

`CopyNote()` copies the contents from `SrcNote` to its own private data members.

`TNoteText` is a descendant of `TList` and doesn't need to override the `Create()` constructor, because it has no variables to initialize. Like `TNote`, it has the private methods `SaveToStream()` and `LoadFromStream()`.

`TNoteList.SaveToStream()` first writes the number of `TNotes` that it has and then calls each `TNote`'s own `SaveToStream()` method, enabling it to write itself to the stream.

`TNoteList.LoadFromStream()` reads the number of notes previously written to the stream telling it how many `TNotes` it must read. It then instantiates a `TNote` class and calls the `TNote`'s own `LoadFromStream()` method, enabling it to read its data. It does this for the total amount of `TNotes` indicated by `NoteCount - 1`.

`TNoteList`'s `Destroy()` destructor ensures that any `TNotes` in its list of items are properly freed before calling its inherited `Destroy()` method.

`TNoteList`'s `SaveToFile()` and `LoadFromFile()` are where it instantiates a `TFileStream` object and passes it to its `SaveToStream()` and `LoadFromStream()` methods.

The `LoadFromFile()` method creates the stream for read-only access by passing the `fmOpenRead` constant to its `Create()` constructor. The `FileName` parameter contains the path and filename for the stream. This constant correlates to the DOS file-mode constants, and can be masked with other modes such as `fmShareDenyRead` to prevent other applications from reading the file for that stream. The `SaveToFile()` method passes `fmCreate` to the stream's `Create()` constructor, causing it to destroy any existing file and create a new one.

`TNoteList`'s `AddNote()` method adds a `TNote` to `TNoteList`, and `RemoveNote()` removes a `TNote` from `TNoteList`. `GetNote()` returns a pointer to the `TNote` at the position specified by `Index`.

With the `TNote` and `TNoteList` classes defined, you can move along and apply them to the note taker in your PIM application.

Adding the Note Taker Classes to the PIM

With the classes for the `TNoteList` and `TNote` fully defined, you now can add them to your project for the Note Taker page. Add the three private variables, `NoteList`, `TrashList`, and `Mode` to the main form:

```
private
   { Private declarations }
   Mode;
   NoteList, TrashList: TNoteList;
```

Also, define three constants cAddMode, cEditMode, and cReadMode:

```
const
  cAddMode  = 1;
  cEditMode = 2;
  cReadMode = 3;
```

NoteList will hold the notes that the user enters. It is also the class that is streamed to an external file along with all the TNotes that it has. TrashList is a list of notes that the user has deleted or dragged to the trash can image. Mode keeps track of the note taker's state.

You will have to initialize these TNoteList variables in the form's OnCreate event handler, as shown in the following code:

```
NoteList  := TNoteList.Create;
if fileexists(ExtractFilePath(Application.ExeName)+NoteFileName)then
  NoteList.LoadFromFile(ExtractFilePath(Application.ExeName)+NoteFileName);
TrashList := TNoteList.Create;
if FileExists(ExtractFilePath(Application.ExeName)+TrashFileName) then
  TrashList.LoadFromFile(ExtractFilePath(Application.ExeName)+TrashFileName);
```

NoteFileName and TrashFileName were declared in NOTES.PAS. Here, you use the method ExtractFilePath() on the application's ExeName property to ensure that the stream files exist in the same directory as the application. The files don't have to exist when the application first runs. They will be created the first time the applications shuts down in the form's OnDestroy event handler's code:

```
NoteList.SaveToFile(ExtractFilePath(Application.ExeName)+NoteFileName);
NoteList.Free;
TrashList.SaveToFile(ExtractFilePath(Application.ExeName)+TrashFileName);
TrashList.Free;
```

Here, you call the TNoteList's SaveToFile() method to save the file to the directory where the application's EXE file is located. You then free both lists. You added code to the form's OnShow event handler:

```
for i := 0 to NoteList.Count - 1 do
  ListBox1.Items.Add(TNote(NoteList.Items[i]).Title);
ReadMode;
```

This code simply populates ListBox1 with the value of each TNote's Title property. More code also was added to the AddMode(), EditMode(), and ReadMode() methods that enable and disable various controls accordingly.

The EditMode() method, in addition to setting the controls, populates the TMemo and TEdit components with the value of the currently selected item in the listbox so that the user can edit that item:

```
Memo1.Lines.Assign(NoteList.GetNote(ListBox1.ItemIndex).NoteText);
Edit1.Text := NoteList.GetNote(ListBox1.ItemIndex).Title;
```

Listing 33.3 shows the AddMode(), EditMode(), and ReadMode() event handlers.

Listing 33.3. Mode event handlers.

```
procedure TPIMMainForm.AddMode;
begin
  { Disable and Enable buttons accordingly }
  AddBtn.Enabled := false;
  EditBtn.Enabled := false;
  DeleteBtn.Enabled := false;
  OKBtn.Visible := true;
  CancelBtn.Visible := true;
  { Note Enable the Editable controls }
  Edit1.Text := '';
  Memo1.Lines.Clear;
  Edit1.Enabled := true;
  Memo1.Enabled := true;
  Edit1.SetFocus;
  Mode := cAddMode;
end;

procedure TPIMMainForm.EditMode;
begin
  If ListBox1.ItemIndex >= 0 then begin
    { Disable and Enable buttons accordingly }
    AddBtn.Enabled := false;
    EditBtn.Enabled := false;
    DeleteBtn.Enabled := false;
    OKBtn.Visible := true;
    CancelBtn.Visible := true;
    ListBox1.Enabled := false;
    Memo1.Lines.Assign(NoteList.GetNote(ListBox1.ItemIndex).NoteText);
    Edit1.Text := NoteList.GetNote(ListBox1.ItemIndex).Title;
    Edit1.Enabled := true;
    Memo1.Enabled := true;
    Mode := cEditMode;
    Edit1.SetFocus;
  end;
end;

procedure TPIMMainForm.ReadMode;
begin
  { Disable and Enable buttons accordingly }
  AddBtn.Enabled := true;
  EditBtn.Enabled := true;
  DeleteBtn.Enabled := true;
  ListBox1.Enabled := true;
  Edit1.Enabled := false;
  Memo1.Enabled := false;
  OKBtn.Visible := false;
  CancelBtn.Visible := false;
  Mode := cReadMode;
end;
```

When the form is in Edit mode, the Cancel and OK buttons are the only buttons that are active, as shown in Figure 33.2.

FIGURE 33.2.

The Note Taker page in Edit mode.

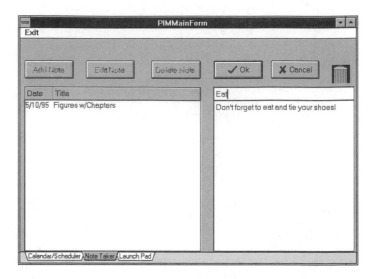

After the user clicks the Cancel button, the form goes back into Read mode. However, after the user clicks the OK button, that button's event handler first calls the AddEditNote() method, which contains the logic for updating or adding another note to the list, depending on the mode that the form is in, as shown in Listing 33.4.

Listing 33.4. The AddEditNote() event handler.

```
procedure TPIMMainForm.AddEditNote;
var
  SrcNote: TNote;
  SL: TStringList;
begin
  SL := TStringList.Create;    { Instantiate a temporary TStringList }
  try
    SL.Assign(Memo1.Lines);       { Assign the TMemo's contents to SL }
    SrcNote := TNote.Create;            { Instantiate  a TNote }
    try
      SrcNote.Title := Edit1.Text;       { Init its title with Edit1 }
      SrcNote.NoteText := SL;            { Init its NoteText with SL which }
      case Mode of
        cAddMode: begin                         { When adding a note, call the }
          NoteList.AddNote(SrcNote);         { AddNote() method here. Then add the }
          ListBox1.Items.Add(Edit1.Text);  { Notes title to the listbox }
          Edit1.Text := '';                      { Clear the contents Edit1's contents }
          Memo1.Clear;                          { Clear the contents Memo1's contents }
        end;
        cEditMode: begin
          { Copy the same Date as the previous note }
          SrcNote.DateTime := NoteList.GetNote(ListBox1.ItemIndex).DateTime;
          { Now copy the temporary TNote }
          NoteList.GetNote(ListBox1.ItemIndex).CopyNote(SrcNote);
```

```
      end;
    end;
  finally
    SrcNote.Free;          { Free the temporary TNote }
  end;
finally
  SL.Free;                 { Free the temporary TStringList }
end;
end;
```

The first thing this method does is create a temporary TStringList. Then, it creates a new TNote object, assigns the value of Edit1.Text to its Title property, and assigns the temporary TStringList, SL, to its NoteText property. If the form is in Add mode, the new TNote object is added to the NoteList's list. Otherwise, its values are used to update the Note in NoteList, based on the currently selected item in ListBox1.

Image2's OnDragOver and OnDragDrop event handlers contain the logic for adding the TNote based on the currently selected item in ListBox1 to TrashList's list of TNotes. OnDragDrop first adds the note to TrashList and then calls NoteList's Remove() method to remove that same note. You can look at these methods in Listing 33.5, which contains the complete code to PIMU.PAS.

> **TIP**
>
> Nothing special is done with the TrashList notes other than to save them to the stream. You have been given the knowledge here to decide what you want to do with that data. You later might add code to allow the user to view the items in the trash, for example, and then purge them or restore them to the list of notes.

You can verify that the item in the TrashList was saved by renaming TRASH.STM in the application's directory to NOTES.STM. Then, the notes that were stored in the trash list will show up in the notes listbox the next time you run the application.

ListBox1's OnClick event handler gets the TNote's Title and NoteText property values and supplies both Edit1 and Memo1 with those values. This way, whenever the user clicks on a new item, Memo1 and Edit1 are updated with the new data (see Figure 33.3).

Finally, ListBox1's OnDrawItem and Header1's OnSizing event handlers take care of drawing the TNote's Date and Title in the listbox. Remember, you set up ListBox1 as an lbOwnerDraw listbox from the previous chapter to facilitate this special drawing.

That takes care of adding the Note Taker page's functionality. The complete listing of the project is shown in Listing 33.5, including the code for the next part of this chapter, where you will add TRunButtons to the Launch Pad page.

FIGURE 33.3.

Edit1 and Memo1 getting
new data from NoteList.

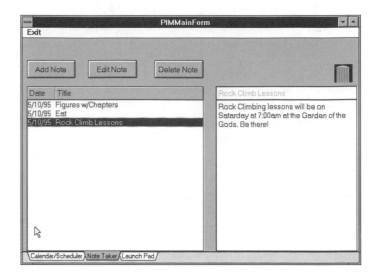

Listing 33.5. The complete code for PIMU.PAS.

```pascal
unit Pimu;

interface

uses
  SysUtils, WinTypes, WinProcs, Messages, Classes, Graphics, Controls,
  Forms, Dialogs, StdCtrls, Menus, ExtCtrls, TabNotBk, Buttons, Grids,
  Calendar, cal, Tabs, Notes;
const
  cAddMode  = 1;
  cEditMode = 2;
  cReadMode = 3;

  MaxIconsAcross = 2;                { Max runbuttons across. }
  RunFileName = 'RunFiles.stm';     { Saves TRunButton classes }

type
  TPIMMainForm = class(TForm)
    NoteBook1: TNoteBook;
    AddBtn: TButton;
    EditBtn: TButton;
    DeleteBtn: TButton;
    OkBtn: TBitBtn;
    CancelBtn: TBitBtn;
    Memo1: TMemo;
    ListBox1: TListBox;
    Panel1: TPanel;
    TabSet1: TTabSet;
    Panel2: TPanel;
    ScrollBox1: TScrollBox;
    Image2: TImage;
    Edit1: TEdit;
    Button1: TButton;
```

```
    OpenDialog1: TOpenDialog;
    Header1: THeader;
    MainMenu1: TMainMenu;
    Exit1: TMenuItem;
    procedure FormCreate(Sender: TObject);
    procedure FormDestroy(Sender: TObject);
    procedure FormShow(Sender: TObject);
    procedure TabSet1Change(Sender: TObject; NewTab: Integer;
      var AllowChange: Boolean);
    { NoteBook Methods }
    procedure AddBtnClick(Sender: TObject);
    procedure EditBtnClick(Sender: TObject);
    procedure OkBtnClick(Sender: TObject);
    procedure CancelBtnClick(Sender: TObject);
    procedure DeleteBtnClick(Sender: TObject);
    procedure Image2DragOver(Sender, Source: TObject; X, Y: Integer;
      State: TDragState; var Accept: Boolean);
    procedure Image2DragDrop(Sender, Source: TObject; X, Y: Integer);
    procedure ListBox1Click(Sender: TObject);
    procedure ListBox1DrawItem(Control: TWinControl; Index: Integer;
      Rect: TRect; State: TOwnerDrawState);
    procedure Header1Sizing(Sender: TObject; ASection, AWidth: Integer);
    { Launch Pad Methods }
    procedure Button1Click(Sender: TObject);
    procedure Exit1Click(Sender: TObject);
  private
    { Private declarations }
    NoteList, TrashList: TNoteList;
    Mode: integer;
    IconsAcross: integer;
    IconsTop: integer;
    procedure AddMode;
    procedure EditMode;
    procedure ReadMode;
    procedure AddEditNote;
    procedure ReadRunFiles;
    procedure SaveRunFiles;
  public
    { Public declarations }
  end;

var
  PIMMainForm: TPIMMainForm;

implementation
uses runbutn, prntcal;
{$R *.DFM}

{ TRunImages's definition }

procedure TPIMMainForm.FormCreate(Sender: TObject);
begin
  TabSet1.Tabs := NoteBook1.Pages;    { Add TabSet Pages to correspond to the  }
                                      { Notebook's Pages. }
  IconsAcross := 0;                   { Initialize IconsAcross/IconsTop to 0 }
  IconsTop := 0;
```

continues

Listing 33.5. continued

```
  { Create the TNoteList variables and read in their data from the stream file }
  { if it is present }
  NoteList := TNoteList.Create;
  if FileExists(ExtractFilePath(Application.ExeName)+NoteFileName)then
    NoteList.LoadFromFile(ExtractFilePath(Application.ExeName)+NoteFileName);
  TrashList := TNoteList.Create;
  if FileExists(ExtractFilePath(Application.ExeName)+TrashFileName) then
    TrashList.LoadFromFile(ExtractFilePath(Application.ExeName)+TrashFileName);
  { Read in the TRunButton components if there are any to read }
  if FileExists(ExtractFilePath(Application.ExeName)+RunFileName) then
    ReadRunFiles;
 end;

procedure TPIMMainForm.FormDestroy(Sender: TObject);
{ Code added here to delete notes that have been created }
begin
  { Save the NoteList and the TrashList before closing the form. }
  NoteList.SaveToFile(ExtractFilePath(Application.ExeName)+NoteFileName);
  NoteList.Free;
  TrashList.SaveToFile(ExtractFilePath(Application.ExeName)+TrashFileName);
  TrashList.Free;
end;

{ Methods for the Calendar/Scheduler Page }
procedure TPIMMainForm.FormShow(Sender: TObject);
var
  i: integer;
begin
  CalendarForm := TCalendarForm.Create(Application);  { Create a CalendarForm }
  CalendarForm.Parent := Panel1;                      { Set CalendarForm's
➥parent }
  CalendarForm.TabOrder := Panel1.TabOrder;           { To Panel1. Then set
➥its }
  With Panel1 do                                      { TabOrder to Panel1's
➥TabOrder }
    CalendarForm.SetBounds(NoteBook1.Left+Panel1.Left+2, { Adjust CalendarForm's
➥sizes }
      NoteBook1.Top+Top+2,Width-4,Height-4);          { to fit within the
➥Notebook }
  CalendarForm.Show;     { Display CalendarForm }

  for i := 0 to NoteList.Count - 1 do
    ListBox1.Items.Add(TNote(NoteList.Items[i]).Title);
  ReadMode;
end;

procedure TPIMMainForm.Exit1Click(Sender: TObject);
begin
  Close;  { Close the main form }
end;

procedure TPIMMainForm.TabSet1Change(Sender: TObject; NewTab: Integer;
  var AllowChange: Boolean);
begin
  if Assigned(CalendarForm) then  { Display the CalendarForm when the Calendar/ }
    if NewTab = 0 then             { Scheduler page is selected. Otherwise hide it }
```

```
        CalendarForm.Show
    else
      CalendarForm.Hide;
  NoteBook1.PageIndex := NewTab;  { Syncronize the NoteBook to the TabSet }
end;

{ Methods for the NoteBook page }
procedure TPIMMainForm.AddBtnClick(Sender: TObject);
begin
  AddMode;   { Go into Add Mode }
end;

procedure TPIMMainForm.EditBtnClick(Sender: TObject);
begin
  EditMode;  { Go into Edit Mode }
end;

procedure TPIMMainForm.OkBtnClick(Sender: TObject);
begin
  AddEditNote;  { Add or Edit a TNote }
  ReadMode;     { Go into Read Mode }
end;

procedure TPIMMainForm.CancelBtnClick(Sender: TObject);
begin
  ReadMode;
end;
procedure TPIMMainForm.DeleteBtnClick(Sender: TObject);
begin
  If ListBox1.ItemIndex >= 0 then begin        { If an item is actually
➥selected }
    NoteList.RemoveNote(ListBox1.ItemIndex);   { First remove it from the
➥TNoteList }
    ListBox1.Items.Delete(ListBox1.ItemIndex); { And then the list box }
    Edit1.Text := '';                          { Clear both Edit1 and Memo1 }
    Memo1.Lines.Clear;
  end;
end;

procedure TPIMMainForm.Image2DragOver(Sender, Source: TObject; X,
  Y: Integer; State: TDragState; var Accept: Boolean);
begin
  Accept := Source is TListBox; { Accept the drag operation only if Source is
➥a TListBox }
end;

procedure TPIMMainForm.Image2DragDrop(Sender, Source: TObject; X,
  Y: Integer);
begin
  with TListBox(Source) do begin
    TrashList.AddNote(NoteList.GetNote(ItemIndex)); { Add the note to the Trash }
    NoteList.RemoveNote(ItemIndex);                 { list of notes and remove }
    Items.Delete(ItemIndex);                        { it from the NoteList }
  end;
  Edit1.Text := '';                                 { Clear both Edit1 and Memo1 }
  Memo1.Lines.Clear;
end;
```

continues

Listing 33.5. continued

```
procedure TPIMMainForm.ListBox1Click(Sender: TObject);
begin
  with ListBox1, Memo1 do begin
    Lines.Assign(NoteList.GetNote(ItemIndex).NoteText);
    Edit1.Text := NoteList.GetNote(ItemIndex).Title;
  end;
end;

procedure TPIMMainForm.ListBox1DrawItem(Control: TWinControl;
  Index: Integer; Rect: TRect; State: TOwnerDrawState);
var
  A: array[0..50] of char;
begin
  ListBox1.Canvas.FillRect(Rect);
  StrPCopy(A, DateToStr(NoteList.GetNote(Index).DateTime));
  DrawText(ListBox1.Canvas.Handle, A, StrLen(A), Rect, dt_Left or dt_VCenter);

  StrPCopy(A, NoteList.GetNote(Index).Title);
  Rect.Left := Rect.Left + Header1.SectionWidth[0];
  DrawText(ListBox1.Canvas.Handle, A, StrLen(A), Rect, dt_Left or dt_VCenter);
end;

procedure TPIMMainForm.Header1Sizing(Sender: TObject; ASection,
  AWidth: Integer);
begin
  ListBox1.Invalidate;
end;

procedure TPIMMainForm.AddMode;
begin
  { Disable and Enable buttons accordingly }
  AddBtn.Enabled := false;
  EditBtn.Enabled := false;
  DeleteBtn.Enabled := false;
  OKBtn.Visible := true;
  CancelBtn.Visible := true;
  { Note Enable the Editable controls }
  Edit1.Text := '';
  Memo1.Lines.Clear;
  Edit1.Enabled := true;
  Memo1.Enabled := true;
  Edit1.SetFocus;
  Mode := cAddMode;
end;

procedure TPIMMainForm.EditMode;
begin
  If ListBox1.ItemIndex >= 0 then begin
    { Disable and Enable buttons accordingly }
    AddBtn.Enabled := false;
    EditBtn.Enabled := false;
    DeleteBtn.Enabled := false;
    OKBtn.Visible := true;
    CancelBtn.Visible := true;
    ListBox1.Enabled := false;
```

```pascal
    Memo1.Lines.Assign(NoteList.GetNote(ListBox1.ItemIndex).NoteText);
    Edit1.Text := NoteList.GetNote(ListBox1.ItemIndex).Title;
    Edit1.Enabled := true;
    Memo1.Enabled := true;
    Mode := cEditMode;
    Edit1.SetFocus;
  end;
end;

procedure TPIMMainForm.ReadMode;
begin
  { Disable and Enable buttons accordingly }
  AddBtn.Enabled := true;
  EditBtn.Enabled := true;
  DeleteBtn.Enabled := true;
  ListBox1.Enabled := true;
  Edit1.Enabled := false;
  Memo1.Enabled := false;
  OKBtn.Visible := false;
  CancelBtn.Visible := false;
  Mode := cReadMode;
end;

procedure TPIMMainForm.AddEditNote;
var
  SrcNote: TNote;
  SL: TStringList;
begin
  SL := TStringList.Create;    { Instantiate a temporary TStringList }
  try
    SL.Assign(Memo1.Lines);        { Assign the TMemo's contents to SL }
    SrcNote := TNote.Create;                { Instantiate  a TNote }
    try
      SrcNote.Title := Edit1.Text;       { Init its title with Edit1 }
      SrcNote.NoteText := SL;          { Init its NoteText with SL }
      case Mode of
        cAddMode: begin                    { When adding a note, call the }
          NoteList.AddNote(SrcNote);       { AddNote() method here. Then add }
          ListBox1.Items.Add(Edit1.Text); { the Notes title to the listbox }
          Edit1.Text := '';               { Clear Edit1's contents }
          Memo1.Clear;                     { Clear Memo1's contents }
        end;
        cEditMode: begin
          { Copy the same Date as the previous note }
          SrcNote.DateTime := NoteList.GetNote(ListBox1.ItemIndex).DateTime;
          { Now copy the temporary TNote }
          NoteList.GetNote(ListBox1.ItemIndex).CopyNote(SrcNote);
        end;
      end;
    finally
      SrcNote.Free;          { Free the temporary TNote }
    end;
  finally
    SL.Free;                 { Free the temporary TStringList }
  end;
end;
```

continues

Listing 33.5. continued

```
{ Methods for the Launch Pad Page }
procedure TPIMMainForm.Button1Click(Sender: TObject);
begin
  { Execute the OpenDialog }
  if OpenDialog1.Execute then
    { check if this is an executable file }
    if Uppercase(ExtractFileExt(OpenDialog1.FileName)) = '.EXE' then
      with TRunButton.Create(ScrollBox1) do begin  { Create a TRunButton }
        { Set the TRunButton.ComandLine to the Filename in OpenDialog }
        Parent := ScrollBox1; { Set parent to the scrollBox }
        CommandLine := OpenDialog1.FileName;
        if IconsAcross < MaxIconsAcross then  begin
          Left := (Width+5)  * IconsAcross;
          Inc(IconsAcross);
        end
        else begin
          IconsAcross := 1;
          IconsTop := IconsTop + Height + 5
        end;
        Top := IconsTop;
        GetIcon;                { Get the icon for the application }
        Hint := ExtractFileName(OpenDialog1.FileName); { Add a hint for the
➥button }
        Visible := true;        { Make the TRunButton visible }
      end;
  SaveRunFiles;
end;

procedure TPIMMainForm.SaveRunFiles;
var
  s: TFileStream;
  i: integer;
begin
  { Instantiate a TFileStream  and create a new stream file. }
  S := TFileStream.Create(ExtractFilePath(Application.ExeName)+RunFileName,
                          fmCreate);
  try
    i := ScrollBox1.ComponentCount; { Get ScrollBox1's component count }
    S.Write(i, sizeof(i));          { Write this count to the stream }
    { Now write each TRunButton and each TRunImage to the stream }
    for i := 0 to ScrollBox1.ComponentCount - 1 do begin
      S.WriteComponent(ScrollBox1.Components[i]);
      S.WriteComponent(TRunButton(ScrollBox1.Components[i]).IconImage);
    end;
  finally
    S.Free; { Free the TFileStream }
  end;
end;

procedure TPIMMainForm.ReadRunFiles;
var
  Count: integer;
  RunBtn: TRunButton;
  S: TFileStream;
  i: integer;
  Image: TRunImage;
```

```
begin
 { Instantiate a TFileStream for read access }
 S := TFileStream.Create(ExtractFilePath(Application.ExeName)+RunFileName,
       fmOpenRead);
 try
   { Read the number of components stored there }
   S.Read(Count, sizeof(Integer));

   for i := 0 to Count  - 1 do begin
     RunBtn := TRunButton.Create(ScrollBox1);     { Create a TRunButton }
     S.ReadComponent(RunBtn);                      { Read it from the stream }
     RunBtn.Parent := ScrollBox1;                  { Assign its parent as
➡ScrollBox1 }

     Image := TRunImage.Create(RunBtn);            { Create a TRunImage }
     S.ReadComponent(Image);                       { Read it from the stream }
     Image.Parent := ScrollBox1;                   { Set its parent to ScrollBox1 }

     if IconsAcross < MaxIconsAcross then          { Position the TRunButton's }
       Inc(IconsAcross)                            { accordingly. }
     else begin
       IconsAcross := 1;
       IconsTop := IconsTop + RunBtn.Height + 5
     end;
     Top :- IconsTop;
   end;
 finally
   S.Free;                                         { Free the stream }
 end;
end;

end.
```

STREAMING RECORDS

Streams are a handy way for classes to store themselves to disk for later retrieval. However, what if the item you want to store isn't a class, but rather a record? A record can't have methods, so it can't know how to save itself. There are several solutions to this. One solution is to use standard I/O to save your data. Another is to to wrap your data with an class that can know how to store your records data as was done in this example. A third approach is to derive a descendant of TFileStream and have it know about your record data. The following code illustrates this type of streaming. Take a close look at the streams methods. They're really just doing simple file I/O in a fancier way. Simple, yes, but certainly in the spirit of OOP.

```
unit Recstrm;

interface

uses
  SysUtils, Classes;
```

```
type
  { Define the record }
  TDataRecord = record
    S: String;
    i: integer;
  end;

  { Create a descendant of TFileStream }
  TRecordStream = class(TFileStream)
  private
    function GetNumRecs: Longint;
    function GetCurRec: Longint;
    procedure SetCurRec(RecNo: Longint);
  protected
    function GetRecSize: Longint; virtual;
  public
    function SeekRec(RecNo: Longint; Origin: Word): Longint;
    function WriteRec(const Rec): Longint;
    function ReadRec(var Rec): Longint;
    procedure First;
    procedure Last;
    procedure NextRec;
    procedure PreviousRec;
    property NumRecs: Longint read GetNumRecs;
    property CurRec: Longint read GetCurRec write SetCurRec;
  end;

implementation

function TRecordStream.GetRecSize: Longint;
begin
  { This function returns the size of the record that this stream knows about }
  Result := Sizeof(TDataRecord);
end;

function TRecordStream.GetNumRecs: Longint;
begin
  { This function returns the number of records in the stream }
  Result := Size div GetRecSize;
end;

function TRecordStream.GetCurRec: Longint;
begin
  { This function returns the position of the current record }
  Result := Position div GetRecSize;
end;

procedure TRecordStream.SetCurRec(RecNo: Longint);
begin
  { This function set the positon to the record in the stream specified by
➥RecNo }
  Position := RecNo * GetRecSize;
end;

function TRecordStream.SeekRec(RecNo: Longint; Origin: Word): Longint;
```

```
begin
  { This function positions the file pointer to a location specified by RecNo }
  Result := Seek(RecNo * GetRecSize, Origin);
end;

function TRecordStream.WriteRec(const Rec): Longint;
begin
  { This function writes the record Rec to the stream }
  Result := Write(Rec, GetRecSize);
end;

function TRecordStream.ReadRec(var Rec): Longint;
begin
  { This function read the record Rec from the stream }
  Result := Read(Rec, GetRecSize);
end;

procedure TRecordStream.First;
begin
  { This function positions the file pointer to the beginning of the stream }
  Seek(0, 0);
end;

procedure TRecordStream.Last;
begin
  { This function positions the file pointer to the end of the stream }
  Seek(0, 2);
end;

procedure TRecordStream.NextRec;
begin
  { This function positions the file pointer at the next record location }
  Seek(GetRecSize, 1);
end;

procedure TRecordStream.PreviousRec;
begin
  { This function positions the file pointer at the previous record location }
  Seek(-GetRecSize, 1);
end;

end.
```

Adding Applications to the Launch Pad

You can see in Listing 33.5 that two more constants have been added: MaxIconsAcross and RunFileName. MaxIconsAcross specifies the maximum number of icons that can be placed horizontally across ScrollBox1. You can change this if you like. RunFileName is a file to which you are going to stream the new TRunButtons that you place on ScrollBox1. Streaming the TRunButtons is a way to save the state of the launch pad. Otherwise, you wouldn't have a way of making your application remember the applications that you have added there. You could save this information to an INI file, but you would have to save the icon's position, and the application's name, the image properties yourself. It just wouldn't be worth the effort because saving this information already is built into VCL's streaming system.

The main form requires two additional variables, IconsAcross and IconsTop, to store temporarily the current icon's across position and the last icon's top position. There also are two additional methods, ReadRunFiles() and SaveRunFiles(), which read and write the TRunButtons from and to the file stream.

First, examine the OnClick event handler for Button1 in the Launch Pad page. This method invokes OpenDialog1 to get a filename and checks to see whether the returned filename is a valid EXE file. It then creates a TRunButton, passing ScrollBox1 as the owner, and assigns ScrollBox1 as its parent. TRunButton's CommandLine property is assigned the OpenDialog1's FileName property. The code that follows determines the position of the TRunButton on ScrollBox1. The call to the TRunButton's GetIcon attempts to get the icon from the application that it is representing; if it is not successful, it uses Application.Icon. The filename is assigned as the TRunButton's hint. Finally, the SaveRunFiles() method is called to save ScrollBox1's current state.

The SaveRunFiles() method first creates a TFileStream. Then, it saves the number of components that ScrollBox1 contains to the stream. Finally, it increments through ScrollBox1's components list and saves both the TRunImages and TRunButton by passing them to the stream's WriteComponent() method. WriteComponent() is used by Delphi to stream components for your forms when you leave Delphi's development environment. You also have the functionality at your disposal using the method described here. The other side of WriteComponent() is ReadComponent().

ReadRunFiles() makes use of the ReadComponent() method. It first creates a TFileStream for read access and reads the number of components that have been saved to it. It then reads both the TRunButton and TRunImage components from the stream and arranges them accordingly on ScrollBox1. Finally, the TFileStream is freed.

When you run the application, try adding various applications to your launch pad. A few already have been added, as shown in Figure 33.4. Figure 33.5 shows what happens after you click one of the buttons you have added.

FIGURE 33.4.
A launch pad with application icons.

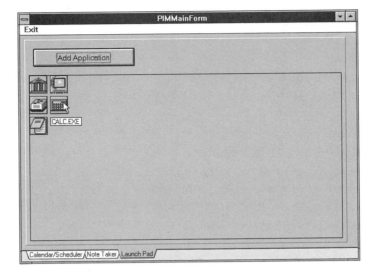

FIGURE 33.5.
Windows' Calculator, launched from the launch pad.

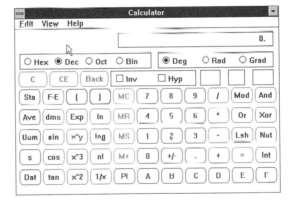

Summary

You actually have provided quite a bit of functionality to the PIM without doing much coding at all—not in the last two chapters, at least. This chapter revisited the topic of printing and showed you how to print out a calendar. It also demonstrated streaming, a technique you'll need if you're going to become a component writer. The next chapter shows you how to add online help to your application, including context-sensitive help.

34

Personal Information Manager—Finishing Touches

In this chapter, you will learn how to add online help to your applications through the Personal Information Manager. This chapter discusses the elements that make up a help system, defines terminology that you'll see when building help, and shows you how easily you can hook help into your Delphi applications. This chapter does not teach you how to create the help system itself, although it does define many of the terms used in just about any help-authoring tool. You will find that there are many help-authoring tools available that simplify building help to a great extent. If you are interested in doing it the hard way, however, Borland conveniently provides you with extensive information on building help files in the help file CWH.HLP, which is in the \DELPHI\BIN directory.

Adding Help to Your Application

In many cases, the developers of an application aren't the help authors who build the help system. The help authors and the developers work together to ensure that the help system and the application correlate with each other. For larger applications, such as Delphi, the help system and application are built concurrently. For smaller or less complex applications, however, help may be part of the final process. In other situations, the developer is also the help author. Whatever the situation, it's absolutely essential that the help author and developer work together to define what goes into the help system and how the help system is structured.

One of the considerations when building a help system is what the target audience for the help system is going to expect out of that help system. Look at Delphi developers, for example. Typically, they want quick access to some bit of information, such as a function or property. Given this scenario, the help authors would want to capitalize on the use of topic searches and context-sensitive help.

Topic searches are invoked by placing the cursor on a symbol in the Delphi Editor and then pressing Ctrl+F1, which takes you directly to the help topic screen for that particular function.

Context-sensitive help is help on any user-input element, such as a dialog box or even an edit control. Go to any one of the Delphi dialog boxes such as Options | Project and press F1, for example. You then are taken to the help screen for that dialog box.

In other situations, help might need to be more extensive and explanatory. A program that helps you fill out your tax forms, for example, probably should provide detailed information on each item explaining the various rules and regulations that might apply to the user. In this case, the user probably is going to spend quite a bit more time in help.

Writing an effective help system requires more than just sitting down and writing. It requires careful planning as to the structure and content of what goes into the system. It also requires that you have a few tools.

Obtaining the Necessary Tools

At a minimum, you will require all of the following files:

- The Microsoft Windows Help Compiler HC31.EXE, located in your \DELPHI\BIN directory.
- The help error message resource file HC31.ERR, also located in your \DELPHI\BIN directory.
- A word processor or editor that can save both Rich Text Format (RTF) files and text files. Microsoft Word for Windows 6.0 is an example of an RTF-capable word processor that commonly is used for creating help files when not using another help-authoring toolkit.

TIP

You might consider purchasing a help-authoring tool such as Forehelp or many others that are on the market. These tools can save you hours of time when creating your help files.

Looking at the Elements of a Help System

There are several elements to a help system that you should be familiar with if you're going to be designing help. These next sections go on to explain many of those elements.

Help Topics

The main element of a help system is the help topic. A *topic* is basically a section of the help system that provides help on a particular item. This item can be a function, operation, term definition, illustration, or just about anything with which you think your users might need help. In the actual online help, a topic is simply one screen of information, as shown in Figure 34.1.

When you go to a new screen, you are viewing another topic. There are certain elements associated with a topic, as shown in Table 34.1.

FIGURE 34.1.
A help topic.

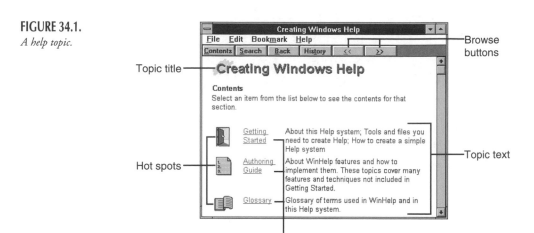

Topic title — Creating Windows Help

Hot spots — (Getting Started, Authoring Guide, Glossary)

Browse buttons

Topic text

Contents topics, also hot spots

Table 34.1. Topic elements.

Element	Definition
Browse sequence	This number signifies in which order the topics will be displayed when the user browses topics in the help file by using the Browse buttons.
Contents topics	Appear in the section in a help topic. Tell the user to what other topics they can jump. Contents topics also are hot spots (refer to Figure 34.1).
Context number	A unique identifier associated with a context string. Applications link elements to the user interface to context numbers. In Delphi, this is referred to as the HelpContext property.
Context string	A unique string identifier for a given topic. Applications can link elements of the user interface to a context string in a help file for context-sensitive help.
Footnotes	Control codes that enable you to define various properties for a topic. The topic title, context string, and browse sequence all are designated by a footnote.
Hot spots	Graphics or text in the topic that, after clicked by the user, jump to another topic, display a window, or execute a macro (refer to Figure 34.1).
Keywords	Words associated with a given topic that are used when the user clicks the Search button from the help.

Element	Definition
Topic text	Actual information about the topic. The topic text is not limited to text only. It can contain links to other topics (known as *jumps*), pictures, or embedded code (to invoke a macro that is capable of performing tasks such as calling functions in DLL).
Topic title	The name of the topic, which typically appears as the first line of the topic.

TIP

Look up each of the terms described in Table 34.1 in the *Creating Windows Help* online help file that ships with Delphi. This file, CWH.HLP, contains extensive information to familiarize yourself with building Windows help files using the RTF codes for specifying topic footnotes.

Looking at the Help System Structure

Although there are no set rules as to how a help system is structured, many help systems follow a hierarchical layout. The system has a main topic—usually in the form of an index. Under the main topic are various categories, each having their own subtopics and so on until the help contents are complete. By using the various hot spots, keywords, and browse sequences, your users don't have to follow the hierarchy to get to a specific topic. They simply can jump across to other topics.

Using the PIM's Help System

A help system for the Personal Information Manager is provided for you in the directory \SOURCE\CH34 as DDGPIM.HLP on the CD-ROM at the back of this book.

If you're interested in seeing the RTF-formatted version of this file, it also is included as DDGPIM.RTF, and the help file's project file is included as DDGPIM.HPR. A project file has the information that the help compiler needs to compile the help file. See the online help CWH.HLP for detailed information on the help project files.

The Hierarchy

The Personal Information Manager's help file has 13 topics arranged in a hierarchical manner based on the functionality of the PIM itself. The top level items in this hierarchy are Note Taker, Launch Pad, and Calendar Scheduler. This hierarchy is shown in Figure 34.2.

The hierarchy also shows the various jumps that you can perform in each topic level. If it isn't clear from the hierarchy, Table 34.2 should clarify this for you.

FIGURE 34.2.

*The Personal Information
Manager's help file
hierarchy.*

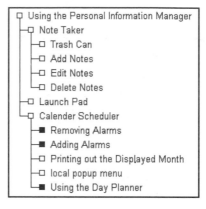

Table 34.2. Jumps made from PIM help file topics.

Title	*Jumps To*
Calendar Scheduler	Removing Alarms
	Adding_Alarms
	Printing_out_the_Displayed_Month
	Using_the_Day_Planner
NoteTaker	Add_Notes
	Edit_Notes
	Delete_Notes
Using the Day Planner	Calendar_Scheduler
Using the Personal Information Manager	Note_Taker
	Launch_Pad
	Calendar_Scheduler

Table 34.3 displays the context strings and context numbers for each of the topics for the PIM's help file.

Table 34.3. Context strings/context numbers for PIM help.

Context Strings	*Context Numbers*
Add_Notes	8
Adding_Alarms	11
Calendar_Scheduler	2
Delete_Notes	10
Edit_Notes	9
Launch_Pad	4
local_popup_menu	5
Note_Taker	3
Printing_out_the_Displayed_Month	13
Removing_Alarms	12
Trash_Can	7
Using_the_Day_Planner	6
Using_the_Personal_Information_Manager	1

Making Help Part of the Application

There are two primary methods for making help available to users of your applications. One is to let them invoke help from the menu. From there, they can navigate through your help system. Another way is to provide context-sensitive help. We'll illustrate both techniques here.

Adding the Help File

Making help part of your applications is really quite simple. Just choose Project | Options from within Delphi and select the Application page. From there, enter the name of the help file where specified on the dialog box as shown in Figure 34.3, or select it by clicking the Browse button to invoke a file selection dialog box.

This filename entered also is the HelpFile property for TApplication. With help now as part of the application, whenever your application requests help, this file will be used. This doesn't automatically invoke help for you, however. Still, the process is a simple one-liner.

FIGURE 34.3.

The Project Options dialog box to add a help file.

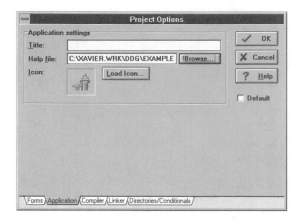

Invoking Help

You must provide a way for your users to invoke help from your application. A typical way to do this is from a menu, as shown in Figure 34.4.

FIGURE 34.4.

The PIM Help menu.

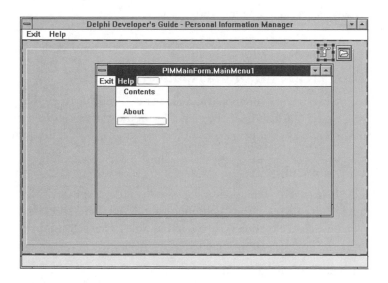

TApplication has three methods that you can call to invoke help: HelpCommand(), HelpContext(), and HelpJump(). All three functions call the Windows API function, WinHelp(), which invokes WINHELP.EXE. WINHELP.EXE reads the HLP files and enables you to navigate through the help system. This program installs with Windows and should be in your Windows directory.

Use `HelpCommand()` when you want to perform any of the help commands available from the `WinHelp()` Windows API function. You can look up these commands in the Windows API help, where they are described in detail. Mostly, however, you will just use `HelpContext()` or `HelpJump()`.

`HelpContext()` calls `WinHelp()` and enables you to pass the context number for a particular topic. The following line, for example, invokes the first page of the Personal Information Manager's help:

```
Application.HelpContext(1);
```

In fact, this is exactly what you want to do in the event handler for the Help | Contents menu option.

`HelpJump()`, like `HelpContext()`, also calls `WinHelp()`. The difference is that you pass the context string instead of the context number. Therefore, the equivalent to the preceding example follows:

```
Application.HelpJump('Using_the_Personal_Information_Manager');
```

Adding Context-Sensitive Help

You can add context-sensitive help for specific controls into your applications. To demonstrate this, context-sensitive help has been added to each page of the Personal Information Manager. This was done by setting all the controls that can have input focus on each page to the value for help on that particular page. Therefore, for the Calendar Scheduler page, the `HelpContext` property for `Panel1` was set to 2, which is the value for the `Calendar Scheduler` topic in the help file. On the Note Taker page, each control's `HelpContext` property was set to 3; and on the Launch Pad, each control's `HelpContext` was set to 4. The latter two values correspond to the `Note Taker` and `Launch Pad` help topics in the help file.

Additionally, when you first change pages, it's possible that no control will have input focus. Therefore, only `PIMMainForm`'s `HelpContext` property will be evaluated. To handle this situation, the following code was added to `TabSet1`'s `OnChange` event handler:

```
case NewTab of
    0 : HelpContext := 2;
    1 : HelpContext := 3;
    2 : HelpContext := 4;
  end; { case }
```

This effectively sets `PIMMainForm`'s `HelpContext` property to correspond to the context number for the page that is active. Now the appropriate help page will be displayed to the users when they press F1 on any given page.

Summary

Adding help to applications often is overlooked or not given enough effort to design an adequate help system. Nonetheless, the help you provide in your applications, or lack thereof, may be the deciding factor over how users accept or reject your application. It's definitely worth the extra effort to see that you have not just a sufficient help system for your applications, but one that goes beyond your users' expectations.

A

Error Messages and Exceptions (Common Causes and Resolutions)

One difference between good software and great software is that although good software runs well, great software runs well and *fails* well. In Delphi programs, errors that are detected at runtime usually are reported and handled as exceptions. This allows your code the opportunity to respond to problems and recover (by backing up and trying another approach) or at least to "degrade gracefully" (free allocated resources, close files, and display an error message) instead of just crashing and making a mess of your system. Most exceptions in Delphi programs are raised and handled completely within the program—very few runtime errors actually will bring a Delphi program to a screeching halt.

This appendix lists the most common error messages that can be reported by a Delphi application and provides field notes to help you find the cause of the error condition. Because each component you add to your Delphi environment often has its own set of error messages, this list can never be complete, so we'll focus on the most common or most insidious error messages you're likely to face while developing and debugging your Delphi applications.

Layers of Handlers, Layers of Severity

Every Delphi program has two default exception handlers, one below the other. The default exception handler you'll see most of the time is provided by VCL. VCL wraps an exception handler around the window procedure entry points of every VCL object. If an exception occurs while your program is responding to a Windows message (which is what your program spends 99 percent of its lifetime doing), and the exception is not handled by your code or a VCL component, the exception eventually will wind up stopping at the VCL default exception handler in the window procedure. That exception handler calls `Application.HandleException`, which will show the exception instance's text message to the user in a popup message box. After that, your program continues running and processing additional window messages.

The lowest-level exception handler lives at the heart of the Delphi RTL, several sub-basements below the default VCL exception handler. If an exception occurs outside the context of message processing—such as during program startup or shutdown, or during the execution of the VCL default exception handler—and the exception goes unhandled, it eventually will wind up stopping at the RTL default exception handler. At this level, there is no recourse for recovery—no message loop to keep things going. When activated, the RTL default exception handler displays a detailed error message to the user and then terminates the application.

In addition to the exception message text, the RTL default exception handler also reports the address of the code that raised the exception, in the form of hexadecimal *segment:offset*. Use the Search|Find Error option in the Delphi IDE, and enter this address in the dialog. Delphi will move the cursor to the place in your source code that corresponds to this address, if it can locate the address and the source code.

If Delphi responds with `Address not Found`, that could mean that the error occurred in another module (for example, a "wild" pointer overwrote memory in use by some other application). More often, however, `Address not Found` indicates that you have disabled line-number information in the unit that the address corresponds to (`{$D-}`), or that you don't have source code for that unit. Double-check that you are compiling your project with compiler debug info enabled, in the Options: Project dialog, Compiler page, Debugging section. While you've got the Options: Project dialog open, check to see that the Search Path on the Directories/Conditionals page contains all the source code directories you want to use during debugging—if the Delphi IDE can't find a source file, it can't show you the source code line that corresponds to the exception error address. Use Compile: Build All to force all your units to be recompiled with the new compiler settings.

Runtime Errors

In previous versions of Borland's Pascal compiler products (before exceptions were introduced into the language), runtime errors were fatal conditions that halted the execution of the program. In Delphi, runtime errors are just a subset of the exception system—nearly all the dreaded, fatal runtime errors of yore have been domesticated to the level of the common house cat. They still may occasionally hiss and scratch, but you no longer have to worry about them eating you alive.

DOS Errors

This is a listing of the error codes returned by DOS and their corresponding messages. The error messages common to Delphi are marked with an asterisk (*) and contain some additional information on the nature of the error. The errors not marked with an asterisk are less common but are listed anyway because you might run into them if you write low-level code that talks directly to DOS interrupts using the Built-in Assembler. The ultimate source of information about DOS error codes is, of course, the *MS-DOS Technical Reference* manual. If your program runs into one of the nonasterisked DOS error codes listed in this section, you're going to need that manual (and a lot of coffee).

The exception class used to report all of these DOS error codes is `EInOutError`. In your own exception handler, you can retrieve the DOS error code from the exception instance's `ErrorCode` field.

1. `Invalid function number`—You attempted to call a DOS function that does not exist.

*2. `File not found`—Reported by `Reset()`, `Append()`, `Rename()`, `Rewrite()`, or `Erase()` if an invalid or nonexistent filename is specified.

*3. `Path not found`—Reported by `Reset()`, `Rewrite()`, `Append()`, `Rename()`, `Erase()`, `ChDir()`, `MkDir()`, or `RmDir()` if an invalid or nonexistent pathname is specified.

*4. `Too many open files`—Reported by `Reset()`, `Rewrite()`, or `Append()` when the operating system has run out of file handle space. Because Windows virtualizes the file handle space for each Windows application, increasing your `FILES=` value in CONFIG.SYS won't help. Calling the `SetFileHandles()` Windows API function won't help either because VCL has already done that for you (requesting the maximum number of file handles—255). More often than not, this error indicates that you have exceeded the file handle space not of DOS, but of a DOS device driver such as a network redirector. If you're using Netware NETX, you may need to increase the `FILEHANDLES=` value in your NET.CFG file. If your application uses the Borland Database Engine, you also can decrease the size of the file handle pool used by BDE. Run `BDECFG`, select the System page, and edit the `MaxFileHandles` value. The BDE default for `MaxFileHandles` is 48. NETX defaults to providing 40 file handles.

*5. `File access denied`—Most commonly, this error occurs when you attempt to open a file on a network that is already opened by another user. You can get around this by first opening the file in one of the share modes shown in Table A.1. Reported by `Reset()`, `Rewrite()`, `Append()`, `Erase()`, or `Rename()` if the file is read-only. Reported by `Read()`/`BlockRead()` and `Write()`/`BlockWrite()` if the file is not open for reading/ writing. Reported by `MkDir()` if the directory already exists. Reported by `RmDir()` if the directory is the root or is not empty.

*6. `Invalid file handle`—Reported when a bogus file handle is passed to a DOS function. This is usually an indication that you are using an uninitialized variable, or the variable has become corrupted.

7. `Memory control blocks destroyed`—The DOS memory manager has been corrupted, probably by a memory overwrite bug in your program.

8. `Insufficient memory`

9. `Invalid memory block address`

10. `Invalid environment`

11. `Invalid format`

*12. `Invalid file access code`—Reported by `Reset()`, `Rewrite()`, and `Append()` when `FileMode` has been set to an invalid value. See Table A.1 for valid `FileMode` settings.

13. `Invalid data`

14. `Reserved`

*15. `Invalid drive number`—Reported by `GetDir()` or `ChDir()` when the drive number or letter is invalid.

*16. `Cannot remove current directory`—Reported by `RmDir()` when the path parameter specifies the current directory.

*17. `Cannot rename across drives`—Reported by `Rename()` when the `NewName` parameter is on a different drive than the source file.

*18. `No more files`—Reported by `FindFirst()` and `FindNext()` when there are no more files matching the file specification.

19. `Disk write-protected`

20. `Unknown unit`—This does not refer to Delphi units, but to some internal DOS memory structure.

21. `Drive not ready`—There is no diskette in the drive, the drive door is open, or the device is offline.

22. `Unknown command`

23. `CRC error`

24. `Bad request structure length`

25. `Seek Error`

26. `Unknown media type`—The media byte signature in the boot sector of the drive does not contain a media type number recognized by DOS. The disk might be formatted for a non-IBM compatible computer system, or the disk might not be formatted at all. Usually, formatting the disk in question will resolve this error.

27. `Sector not found`—Usually the result of a disk read error or corrupted File Allocation Table. Back up what files you can, then run a disk analysis program or reformat the drive.

28. `Out of paper`—The printer being written to via a DOS file handle cannot accept any more data because it has run out of paper.

29. `Write fault`

30. `Read fault`

31. `General failure`

32. `Sharing violation`—Two programs are trying to access the same file using incompatible file sharing modes. If one program has opened the file in exclusive mode, a second program attempting to open the same file in any mode will receive a sharing violation error from DOS.

33. `Lock violation`—Two programs have the same file open using compatible share modes, but they are trying to lock the same region of the file.

34. `Invalid disk change`

35. `FCB Unavailable`

36. `Sharing buffer overflow`

37. `Code page mismatch`

38. `Error handling EOF`

39. `Handle disk full`

40–49. Reserved

50. Network request not supported

51. Remote computer not listening

52. Duplicate name on network

53. Network name not found

54. Network busy

55. Network device no longer exists

56. NetBIOS command limit exceeded

57. Network adapter error

58. Incorrect network response

59. Unexpected network error

60. Incompatible remote adapter

61. Print queue full

62. Not enough space for print file

63. Print file deleted

64. Network name deleted

65. Access denied

66. Network device type incorrect

67. Network name not found

68. Network name limit exceeded

69. NetBIOS session limit exceeded

70. Temporarily paused

71. Network request not accepted

72. Print or disk redirection is paused

73–79. Reserved

80. File already exists

81. Reserved

82. Cannot make directory entry

83. Fail on Interrupt 24

84. Too many redirections

85. Duplicate redirection

86. Invalid password

87. Invalid parameter

88. Network data fault

I/O Errors

Input/Output errors are caused while reading from and writing to files and devices. These errors are only reported when I/O Checking is enabled using `{$I+}` in code or Options|Project|Compiler|I/O Checking in IDE. These errors all are reported using the `EInOutError` exception class.

100. `Disk read error`—Reported when you attempt to use `Read()` to read beyond the end of a typed file.

101. `Disk write error`—Reported by `CloseFile()`, `Write()`, `Writeln()`, and `Flush()` when the disk on which the file is located becomes full.

102. `File not assigned`—Reported when you attempt to use a `File` or `TextFile` type variable without first calling `Assign()`.

103. `File not open`—Reported by `CloseFile()`, `Read()`, `Write()`, `Seek()`, `EOF()`, `FilePos()`, `FileSize()`, `Flush()`, `BlockRead()`, and `BlockWrite()` if the file has not been opened using `Reset()`, `Rewrite()`, or `Append()`.

104. `File not open for input`—Reported by `Read()`, `Readln()`, `EOF()`, `EOLn()`, `SeekEOF()`, and `SeekEOLn()` when a file of type `TextFile` is not open for input. Be sure to open the text file with `Reset()` if you intend to read from it.

105. `File not open for output`—Reported by `Write()` and `Writeln()` when writing to a text file which was not opened using `Rewrite()` or `Append()`. Note that the standard output file (Output) is not open by default in Windows programs. If you want to use `Write()` or `Writeln()` to display text on the screen, you will have to include the `WinCRT` unit in your uses clause.

106. `Invalid numeric format`—Reported by `Read()` or `Readln()` when you attempt to read a nonnumeric value from a text file into a numeric variable.

Nonfatal Errors

These exceptions generally indicate an error in your program logic, that is, when the logic fails to take into account the full range of data values that can be encountered at runtime, which can lead to memory overwrites and/or incorrect calculations. Because these errors are raised as exceptions, they technically are not fatal conditions, but you should still consider these serious flaws in your program.

Each of these errors has its own exception class, listed in the next section.

200. `Division by zero`—This error means that your program attempted to divide some number by zero. This error will occur when using the `div`, `/`, or `mod` operators.

201. `Range check error`—This error indicates either that you have attempted to address an array beyond its declared size or that you are trying to store a number into a variable, but the value of the number is not between the minimum and maximum values of the

variable type. Range checking must be enabled with {$R+} in code or Options|Project|Compiler|Range Checking in the IDE for this error to occur.

203. `Heap overflow error`—This error occurs when there is not enough global heap for `New()` or `GetMem()` to fulfill an allocation request.

204. `Invalid pointer operation`—This error occurs when you attempt to use `Dispose()` or `FreeMem()` with an unitialized or garbage pointer. This error usually means that your code is trying to dispose the same pointer twice, or that a memory overwrite bug has corrupted your pointer variable.

205. `Floating point overflow`—Occurs when the result of a floating-point calculation is too large to be represented in a floating-point type variable.

206. `Floating point underflow`—Occurs when the result of a floating-point calculation is too small (diminishing to zero) to be represented a floating-point type variable. Floating-point underflow checking is not performed by default: it must be enabled explicitly using `BASM` instructions to set the numeric coprocessor's control word flags to unmask underflow exceptions. With underflow checking disabled (the default), underflows are rounded to zero.

207. `Invalid floating point operation`—This error occurs when `Trunc()` or `Round()` cannot convert the floating point value to a number within the range of a `Longint`, the argument passed to `Sqrt()` is negative, the argument passed to `Ln()` is less than one, or a numeric coprocessor stack overflow occurred.

215. `Arithmetic overflow error`—This error means than an operation on an integral value produced a result value which was too large to be stored in the available data type. This error will only occur if overflow checking is enabled using {$Q+} in code or Options|Project|Compiler|Overflow Checking in the IDE.

216. `General protection fault`—This error indicates a general protection fault. See Chapter 22, "Testing and Debugging" for a discussion on causes for GP Faults.

217. `Unhandled exception`—Usually indicates that a processor exception other than a GP Fault occurred, and a handler could not be located.

219. `Invalid typecast`—You attempted to use the as operator to typecast a class to an incompatible class.

Fatal Errors

Fatal errors indicate that a disaster already has occurred in your program that is so severe that you have no recourse but to terminate the program. These errors do not raise exceptions; they simply halt the program immediately, pausing only long enough to display an error message on the way out.

202. `Stack overflow`—A stack overflow occurs when the combined size of all the stack-based variables exceeds the stack size allocated with the $M directive. This usually is

caused either by infinite recursion or by failing to maintain the stack properly when using the Built-in Assembler.

210. `Call to an abstract method`—You are attempting to execute a method of an object that is defined as abstract. This can happen if you mistakenly instantiate an abstract class, or if you forget to override an abstract method that your descendent class inherits from an abstract class.

File Modes

The value of the `FileMode` variable dictates what mode the file is opened with when using the `Reset()` and `Append()` procedures. The default is mode 2, which prevents other processes from accessing the same file—across a network, for example. To avoid this problem, you should set the `FileMode` variable to one of the share modes described in Table A.1.

Table A.1. Values for the `FileMode` variable.

Access Method	Compatibility Mode	Share Deny Both	Share Deny Write	Share Deny Read	Share Deny None
Read Only	0	16	32	48	64
Write Only	1	17	33	49	65
Read/Write	2	18	34	50	66

Other Exceptions

This section describes additional exceptions that can be raised by Delphi's VCL components. Keep in mind that custom components and your own code can (and often should) define additional exception classes specific to the task at hand.

Several of the exception classes listed here describe related error conditions—families of errors. The relationship of the exception classes to one another is captured by creating a general-purpose exception class to represent the entire family, and specific exception classes that inherit from the general-purpose class. When you want to handle all errors in that family the same way, use the general-purpose exception class in the on clause of your except block. When you want to handle only certain specific errors from that family, use the specific exception classes in on clauses in your except block.

In the following list, indentation is used to group related exception classes together beneath their common generic ancestor class.

Exception—This is the ancestor of all exception classes. There is nothing wrong with using this class to raise exceptions in quick-and-dirty code, but in production code you'll want to be able to distinguish between the multitude of families of errors that your application can encounter. The best way to distinguish a family of related error conditions from the rest of the pack is to use a custom exception class to report those related errors.

EAbort—Referred to as Delphi's "silent" exception, this exception is trapped by the VCL default exception handler, but VCL does not inform the user that the exception occurred. Use EAbort when you want to take advantage of the exception's ability to abort and unwind out of a complicated process but you don't want the user to see an error message. Remember, the terms *exception* and *error* are **not** equivalent: Exceptions are a means of changing program flow to facilitate error handling... among other things.

EComponentError—This exception is raised in two situations: (1) When you use RegisterClasses() to attempt to register a component outside the Register() procedure. (2) When the name of your component is invalid or not unique.

EInOutError—This exception is raised when any I/O error occurs in your program. This exception will only occur when I/O checking is enabled using {$I+} in code or Options|Project|Compiler|I/O Checking in IDE.

EIntError—This is the ancestor of all integer math exceptions. The descendants of this class are:

EDivByZero—Raised when you divide an integral number by zero. This exception is raised as a result of Runtime error 200. This code sample will cause an EDivByZero exception:

```
var
  I: integer;
begin
  I := 0;
  I := 10 div I;   { exception raised here }
end;
```

EIntOverflow—Raised when you attempt to perform an operation that overflows an integral variable beyond that variable type's capacity. This exception is raised as a result of Runtime error 215. This exception will be raised only if overflow checking is enabled using {$Q+} in code or Options|Project|Compiler|Overflow Checking in the IDE. The following code will cause this exception to be raised:

```
var
  l: longint;
begin
  l := MaxLongint;
  l := l * l;   { exception raised here }
end;
```

ERangeError—Raised when you attempt to index an array beyond its declared bounds or when you attempt to store a too-large value in an integral type variable. This exception is raised as a result of Runtime error 201. Range checking must be enabled with {$R+} in code or Options|Project|Compiler| Range Checking in the IDE for this error to occur. The following sample will cause Delphi to raise this exception:

```
var
  a: array[1..16] of integer;
  i: integer;
begin
  i := 17;
  a[i] := 1;  { exception raised here }
end;
```

EInvalidCast—This exception is raised when you attempt to use the as operator to typecast a class as an incompatible class. This exception is raised as a result of Runtime error 219. The following code will cause this exception to be raised:

```
var
  B: TObject;
begin
  B := TButton.Create(nil);
  with B as TMemo do    { exception raised here - TMemo is not an ancestor of
➥TButton }
  ...
end;
```

EInvalidGraphic—This exception is raised when you attempt to LoadFromFile() a file that is not a compatible graphics format into a class expecting a graphics file.

EInvalidGraphicOperation—This exception is raised when you attempt to perform an illegal operation on a graphic object. For example, resizing a TIcon is illegal.

EInvalidOperation—This exception occurs when you try to display or perform any other operation that requires a window handle on a control without a Parent. For example,

```
var
  b: TBitBtn;
begin
  b := TBitBtn.Create(Self);
  b.SetFocus;    { exception raised here }
end;
```

EInvalidPointer—This exception is raised usually when you attempt to free an invalid or already-freed portion of memory in a call to Dispose(), FreeMem(), or a class destructor. This example causes an EInvalidPointer exception to be raised:

```
var
  p: pointer;
begin
  GetMem(p, 8);
  FreeMem(p, 8);
  FreeMem(p, 8);   { exception raised here }
end;
```

`EListError`—This exception will be raised if you try to index past the end of a `TList` descendant. For example,

```
var
  S: TStringList;
  Strng: String;
begin
  S := TStringList.Create;
  S.Add('One String');
  Strng := S.Strings[2]; { exception raised here }
end;
```

`EMathError`—This is the ancestor object from which the floating-point exceptions are derived.

> `EInvalidOp`—This exception is raised when an invalid instruction is sent to the numeric coprocessor. This exception is uncommon unless you control the coprocessor directly with BASM code.

> `EOverflow`—Raised as a result of floating-point overflow—that is, when a value becomes too large to hold in a floating-point variable. This exception corresponds to Runtime error 205.

> `EUnderflow`—Raised as a result of floating-point underflow—that is, when a value becomes too small to hold in a floating-point variable. This exception corresponds to Runtime error 206.

> `EZeroDivide`—Raised when a floating point number is divided by zero.

`EMenuError`—This is a generic exception that occurs in almost any error condition involving a `TMenu`, `TMenuItem`, or `TPopupMenu` component.

`EOutlineError`—This is a generic exception that is raised when an error occurs while working with a `TOutline` component.

`EOutOfMemory`—This exception is raised when you call `New()`, `GetMem()`, or a class constructor and there is not enough memory available on the heap for the allocation. This exception corresponds to Runtime error 203.

`EOutOfResources`—This exception occurs when Windows cannot fill an allocation request for a Windows resource, such as a Window handle. This exception often reflects bugs in your video driver, especially if you're running in a high-color (32KB or 64KB colors) mode. If this error goes away when you switch to using the standard Windows VGA driver, or to a lesser mode of your normal video driver, it's very likely that you've found a bug in your video driver. Contact your video card manufacturer for a driver update.

`EParserError`—Raised when Delphi is unable to parse your text form file back to the binary .DFM format. Generally, this is the result of a syntax error while editing the form in the IDE.

`EPrinter`—This is a generic exception that will be raised when an error occurs while you are trying to use the printer.

EProcessorException—This is the base class for exceptions that are raised as a result of some processor exception.

> EBreakpoint—This exception occurs when your application generates a breakpoint interrupt. Generally, you will not use this exception in your applications. If you have trouble using the Delphi integrated debugger, or encounter EBreakpoint exceptions when your program is running stand-alone, you probably have a prerelease version video driver that contains embedded breakpoint interrupt instructions. This can interfere with debuggers and your program, so you should contact your video card manufacturer for a driver update. (It's possible for other drivers in your system to contain embedded breakpoints, but this problem has been observed in widely distributed beta versions of video drivers from certain manufacturers.)

> EFault—The base class for processor fault exceptions.

>> EGPFault—A General Protection Fault. Corresponds to Runtime error 216.

>> EInvalidOpCode—Raised when the processor encounters an invalid instruction. This exception is generally indicative of memory corruption.

>> EPageFault—This exception is normally raised as a result of an error in Windows' memory management rather than as a result of some error in your code. It's a good idea to restart Windows after this exception occurs.

>> EStackFault—Represents a serious operating environment-level error in management of the stack. Compiling your program with stack checking enabled (({$S+} in code or Options|Project|Compiler|Stack Checking in the IDE) will help spot low stack conditions before a processor stack fault occurs. Even with stack checking enabled, a processor stack fault still can occur if you call a stack-intensive Windows API function (such as DrawText or FloodFill) when your available stack space is very low. In Windows 3.*x*, processor stack faults are absolutely the worst kind of application-induced error. If your machine is still operational after this fault occurs, you should restart Windows immediately.

> ESingleStep—Like EBreakpoint, this exception is triggered by a debugger interrupt which you should never see in your application.

EReportError—A generic exception for an error that occurs while working with a Report component.

EResNotFound—This exception is raised when there are problems loading a form from a .DFM file. This exception usually indicates that you have edited the .DFM file to make it invalid, the .DFM or .EXE file has become corrupted, or the .DFM file was not linked into the .EXE. Make sure you haven't deleted or altered the {$R *.DFM} directive in your form unit.

EStreamError—This exception is the base class of all stream exceptions. This exception usually indicates a problem loading a TStrings from a stream or setting the capacity of a memory stream. The following descendent exception classes signal other specific error conditions:

EFCreateError—Raised when an error occurs while creating a stream file. This exception often indicates that a file can't be created because the filename is invalid or in use by another process.

EFilerError—This exception is raised when you attempted to register the same class twice using the RegisterClasses() procedure. This class also serves as the base for other filer-related exceptions:

EClassNotFound—This exception is raised when Delphi reads a component class name from a stream but cannot find a declaration for the component in its corresponding unit. Remember that code and declarations that are not used by a program will not be copied into the .EXE file by Delphi's smart linker.

EInvalidImage—Raised when you attempt to read components from an invalid resource file.

EMethodNotFound—Raised when a method specified in the .DFM file or resource does not exist in the corresponding unit. This can happen if you have deleted code from the unit, recompiled the .EXE, ignored the many warnings about the .DFM file containing references to deleted code, and run the .EXE anyway.

EReadError—Occurs when your application doesn't read the number of bytes from a stream that it is supposed to (for example, unexpected end-of-file) or when Delphi cannot read a property.

EFOpenError—Raised when the specified stream file cannot be opened. Usually occurs when the file does not exist.

EStringListError—A generic exception that is raised when an error condition results while working with a TStringList object.

I

Index

Add to Your Sams Library Today with the Best Books for Programming, Operating Systems, and New Technologies

The easiest way to order is to pick up the phone and call

1-800-428-5331

between 9:00 a.m. and 5:00 p.m. EST.

For faster service please have your credit card available.

ISBN	Quantity	Description of Item	Unit Cost	Total Cost
0-672-30499-6		Delphi Programming Unleashed (Book/CD-ROM)	$45.00	
0-672-30600-X		Teach Yourself OWL Programming in 21 Days (Book/Disk)	$39.99	
0-672-30568-2		Teach Yourself OLE Programming in 21 Days (Book/CD-ROM)	$39.99	
0-672-30226-8		Windows Programmer's Guide to OLE/DDE	$34.95	
0-672-30736-7		Teach Yourself C Programming in 21 Days, Premier Edition	$35.00	
0-672-30546-1		Tom Swan's Mastering Borland C++ 4.5, Second Edition	$49.99	
0-672-30667-0		Teach Yourself Web Publishing with HTML in a Week	$25.00	
0-672-30519-4		Teach Yourself the Internet: Around the World in 21 Days	$25.00	
0-672-30562-3		Teach Yourself Game Programming in 21 Days (Book/CD-ROM)	$39.99	
0-672-30520-8		Your Internet Consultant: The FAQs of Online Life	$25.00	
0-672-30612-3		The Magic of Computer Graphics (Book/CD-ROM)	$45.00	
0-672-30638-7		Super CD-ROM Madness (Book/CD-ROMs)	$39.99	
❏ 3 ½" Disk		Shipping and Handling: See information below.		
❏ 5 ¼" Disk		TOTAL		

Shipping and Handling: $4.00 for the first book, and $1.75 for each additional book. Floppy disk: add $1.75 for shipping and handling. If you need to have it NOW, we can ship product to you in 24 hours for an additional charge of approximately $18.00, and you will receive your item overnight or in two days. Overseas shipping and handling adds $2.00 per book and $8.00 for up to three disks. Prices subject to change. Call for availability and pricing information on latest editions.

201 W. 103rd Street, Indianapolis, Indiana 46290

1-800-428-5331 — Orders   1-800-835-3202 — FAX   1-800-858-7674 — Customer Service

Book ISBN 0-672-30704-9

Installing Your Disk

What's on the CD-ROM

The included disc contains code examples from the book, sample applications, new Delphi Components, and more. To examine the contents of the CD-ROM, run the install program as instructed in the following section, and then run the CD Guide application. The CD Guide application enables you to install any of the software from the CD-ROM to your hard drive.

Installing the CD-ROM

Insert the disc in your CD-ROM drive, and follow these steps to install the software:

1. From Windows File Manager or Program Manager, choose **F**ile | **R**un from the menu.
2. Type **x:\INSTALL** and press Enter, where **x** is the letter of your CD-ROM drive.

Follow the on-screen instructions provided by the installation program. The CD Guide application will be installed to a directory named C:\DDG unless you change the default directory name or drive letter provided by the install program.

When the installation is complete, a Program Manager group named "Delphi Developer's Guide" will be created by the installation program. It contains icons for the CD Guide application, the Third-Party Software document, and the Read Me document. The CD Guide application then starts up automatically. After using the application the first time, you can start it up again by double-clicking the CD Guide icon.